E. M. BOUNDS
ON
PRAYER

E. M. BOUNDS
ON
PRAYER

E. M. BOUNDS

Whitaker House

E. M. BOUNDS ON PRAYER

ISBN: 0-88368-416-0
Printed in the United States of America
Copyright © 1997 by Whitaker House

Whitaker House
30 Hunt Valley Circle
New Kensington, PA 15068

Library of Congress Cataloging-in-Publication Data

Bounds, Edward M. (Edward McKendree), 1835–1913.
    [Selections. 1997]
    E. M. Bounds on prayer / E. M. Bounds.
        p.   cm.
    ISBN 0-88368-416-0 (pbk. : alk. paper)
    1. Prayer—Christianity.   I. Title.
BV215.B6182   1997
248.3'2—dc21   97-3207

3 4 5 6 7 8 9 10 11 12 / 07 06 05 04 03 02 01 00 99 98

Contents

Introduction

EDWARD McKendree Bounds was born on August 15, 1835, in a small, northeastern Missouri town. He attended a one-room school in Shelbyville, where his father served as a county clerk, and he was admitted to the bar shortly before he reached the age of nineteen. An avid reader of the Scriptures and an ardent admirer of John Wesley's sermons, Bounds practiced law until the age of twenty-four, when he suddenly felt called to preach the Gospel.

His first pastorate was in the nearby town of Monticello, Missouri. Yet in 1861, while he was pastor of a Methodist Episcopal church in Brunswick, the Civil War began, and Bounds was arrested by Union troops and charged for sympathizing with the Confederacy. He was made a prisoner of war and was held for a year and a half before being transferred to Memphis, Tennessee, and finally securing his release.

Armed only with an unquenchable desire to serve God, Bounds traveled nearly one hundred miles on foot to join General Pierce's command in Mississippi. Soon afterward he was made chaplain to the Confederate troops in Missouri. After the defeat of General John Hood's troops at Nashville, Tennessee, Bounds was again among those who were captured and held until swearing loyalty to the United States.

After the war, Bounds pastored churches in Nashville, Tennessee; Selma, Alabama; and St. Louis, Missouri. It was in Selma that he met Emma Barnett, whom he later married in 1876, and with whom he had three children, one of whom died at the age of six. After Emma's death, in 1887, Bounds married Emma's cousin, Harriet Barnett, who survived him. The family included their five children, as well as two daughters from his first marriage.

While he was in St. Louis, Bounds accepted a position as associate editor for the regional Methodist journal, the *St. Louis Advocate*. Then, after only nineteen months, he moved to Nashville to become the editor of the *Christian Advocate,* the weekly paper for the entire Methodist Episcopal denomination in the South.

The final seventeen years of his life were spent with his family in Washington, Georgia, where both Emma and Harriet had grown up. Most of the time he spent reading, writing, and praying, but he often took an active part in revival ministry. Bounds was also in the habit of rising at four o'clock each morning in order to pray to God, for the great cares of the world were always upon his heart. He died on August 24, 1913, still relatively unknown to most of the Christian sphere.

Since the time of the apostles, no man besides Edward McKendree Bounds has left such a rich inheritance of research into the life of prayer. Prayer was as natural to him as breathing the air. He made prayer first and foremost in his life because he knew it as the strongest link between man and God. In the time of E. M. Bounds, human weakness, through prayer, could access the power of the overcoming Son of God, Jesus Christ. The same is true to this day.

Book
One

Purpose in Prayer

1

The Force That Shapes the World

My creed leads me to think that prayer is efficacious, and surely a day's asking God to overrule all events for good is not lost.   *—James Gilmour*

THE prayers of God's saints are the capital stock in heaven by which Christ carries on His great work upon the earth. Great throes and mighty convulsions in the world have come about as a result of these prayers. The earth is changed, revolutionized; angels move on more powerful, more rapid wings; and God's policy is shaped when the prayers of His people are more numerous and more efficient.

The most important lesson we can learn is how to pray. Indeed, we must pray so that our prayers take hold of God. The man who has done the most and the best praying is the most immortal, because prayers do not die. Perhaps the lips that uttered them are closed in death, or the heart that felt them may have ceased to beat, but the prayers live before God, and God's heart is set on them. Prayers outlive the lives of those who uttered them—outlive a generation, outlive an age, outlive a world.

Prayer is no fitful, short-lived thing. It is no voice crying unheard and unheeded in the silence. It is a voice that goes into God's ear, and it lives as long as God's ear is open to holy pleas, as long as God's heart is alive to holy things.

The mightiest successes that come to God's cause are created and carried on by prayer in God's day of power. When God's church comes into its mightiest inheritance of the mightiest faith and

11

mightiest prayer, the angelic days of powerful activity occur. God's conquering days are when the saints have given themselves to mightiest prayer.

The life of the church is the highest life, and its office is to pray. Its prayer life is the highest life, the most fragrant, the most conspicuous. When God's house on the earth is a house of prayer, then God's house in heaven is busy and powerful in its plans and movements. *"For mine house shall be called an house of prayer for all people"* (Isa. 56:7), says our God. Then, His earthly armies are clothed with the triumphs and spoils of victory, and His enemies are defeated on every hand.

God shapes the world by prayer. The more praying there is in the world, the better the world will be and the mightier the forces against evil everywhere. Prayer, in one phase of its operation, is a disinfectant and a preventive. It purifies the air; it destroys the contagion of evil.

The very life and prosperity of God's cause—even its very existence—depend on prayer. And the advance and triumph of His cause depend on one thing: that we ask of Him.

The Lord has issued His decree, immutable and eternal, in which we find the great condition of prayer:

> *I will declare the decree:...**Ask of me**, and I shall give thee the heathen for thine inheritance, and the uttermost parts of the earth for thy possession. Thou shalt break them with a rod of iron; thou shalt dash them in pieces like a potter's vessel.*
> *(Ps. 2:7–9, emphasis added)*

Ask of Me. That is the condition—God desires a praying people, willing and obedient. Under this universal and simple promise, men and women of old laid themselves out before God. They prayed, and God answered their prayers. Thus, the cause of God was kept alive in the world by the flame of their praying.

The second Psalm contains the divine description of the establishment of God's cause through Jesus Christ. All inferior dispensations have merged in the enthronement of Jesus Christ. In the following passage, God declares the enthronement of His Son:

> *Yet have I set my king upon my holy hill of Zion. I will declare the decree: the LORD hath said unto me, Thou art my Son; this day have I begotten thee.*
> *(Ps. 2:6–7)*

All the nations are incensed with bitter hatred against His cause, but God is described as laughing at their enfeebled hate:

Why do the heathen rage, and the people imagine a vain thing?...He that sitteth in the heavens shall laugh: the Lord shall have them in derision.   *(Ps. 2:1, 4)*

Prayer puts God in full force in the world. To a prayerful man, God is present in realized force. The man who has prayed many acceptable prayers has done the truest and greatest service to the incoming generation. To a prayerful church, God is present in glorious power. The prayers of God's saints strengthen the unborn generation against the desolating waves of sin and evil. Woe to the generation of sons who find their own censers empty of the rich incense of prayer, whose fathers have been too busy or too unbelieving to pray, and who have inexpressible perils and untold consequences for their heritage! They whose fathers and mothers have left them a wealthy legacy of prayer are very fortunate, indeed.

Prayer is God's settled and singular condition to move ahead His Son's kingdom. Therefore, the believer who is the most highly skilled in prayer will do the most for God. Men are to pray—to pray for the advance of God's cause. The one who can wield the power of prayer is the strong one, the holy one, in Christ's kingdom. He is one of God's heroes, God's saints, God's servants, God's agents. *"Ask, and it shall be given you; seek, and ye shall find; knock, and it shall be opened unto you"* (Matt. 7:7). The strongest one in Christ's kingdom is he who can knock the best, and the secret of success in Christ's kingdom is the ability to pray.

2

The Fire That Consumes

The prayers of holy men appease God's wrath, drive away temptations, resist and overcome the Devil, procure the ministry and service of angels, rescind the decrees of God. Prayer cures sickness and obtains pardon; it arrests the sun in its course and stays the wheels of the chariot of the moon; it rules over all gods and opens and shuts the storehouses of rain; it unlocks the cabinet of the womb and quenches the violence of fire; it stops the mouths of lions and reconciles our suffering and weak faculties with the violence of torment and violence of persecution; it pleases God and supplies all our need. —Jeremy Taylor

PRAYER has an incredible power to arrest and change the purposes of God. The stroke of His power is relieved by the prayers of righteous men. We can witness both the possibilities and the necessity of prayer when we see how, in the following examples from the Scriptures, the prayers of God's saints brought about a change in God's plans. Our first example of this is found in Genesis, when Abimelech had been smitten by God:

So Abraham prayed unto God: and God healed Abimelech, and his wife, and his maidservants; and they bare children. For the LORD had fast closed up all the wombs of the house of Abimelech, because of Sarah Abraham's wife. (Gen. 20:17–18)

In another example, Job's miserable, mistaken comforters had so behaved themselves in their controversy with Job that God's wrath was kindled against them:

> *My servant Job shall pray for you: for him will I accept: lest I*
> *deal with you after your folly, in that ye have not spoken of me*
> *the thing which is right, like my servant Job....And the LORD*
> *turned the captivity of Job, when he prayed for his friends.*
>
> *(Job 42:8, 10)*

When Jonah tried to run from the Lord, he was in a dire condition. *"The LORD sent out a great wind into the sea, and there was a mighty tempest"* (Jonah 1:4). When lots were cast among those aboard the ship, *"the lot fell upon Jonah"* (v. 7). He was cast overboard into the sea, but,

> the LORD had prepared a great fish to swallow up Jonah....Then Jonah prayed unto the LORD his God out of the fish's belly, and said, I cried by reason of mine affliction unto the LORD, and he heard me; out of the belly of hell cried I, and thou heardest my voice....And the LORD spake unto the fish, and it vomited out Jonah upon the dry land.
>
> *(Jonah 1:17–2:2, 10)*

Jonah prayed while imprisoned in the great fish; and when the disobedient prophet lifted up his voice in prayer, God heard him and sent deliverance. Thus Jonah came to dry land, saved from storm and sea and monsters of the deep, by the mighty energy of his praying.

It was the purpose of God to destroy the great and wicked city of Nineveh. *"Yet forty days, and Nineveh shall be overthrown"* (Jonah 3:4) was God's decree against the city. However, Nineveh prayed. Covered with sackcloth and sitting in ashes, she cried *"mightily unto God"* (v. 8). *"And God repented of the evil, that he had said that he would do unto them; and he did it not"* (v. 10).

Pharaoh was a firm believer in the possibilities of prayer and its ability to relieve. While staggering under the woeful curses of God, he pleaded with Moses to intercede for him. "Entreat the Lord for me" was his pathetic appeal, which he repeated four times (see Exodus 8:8, 28; 9:28; 10:17) when the plagues were scourging Egypt. Four times were these urgent appeals made to Moses, and four times did prayer lift the awful curse from the hard ruler and his doomed land.

The blasphemy and idolatry of Israel, in making the golden calf and declaring their devotion to it, were fearful crimes. The anger of

God waxed hot, and He declared that He would destroy the offending people. The Lord was also extremely angry with Aaron. He said to Moses, *"Let me alone, that I may destroy them"* (Deut. 9:14). Undaunted, Moses prayed, and he kept on praying for forty days and nights. He recorded his prayer struggle in the ninth chapter of Deuteronomy:

> *And I fell down before the LORD, as at the first, forty days and forty nights: I did neither eat bread, nor drink water, because of all your sins which ye sinned, in doing wickedly in the sight of the LORD, to provoke him to anger. For I was afraid of the anger and hot displeasure, wherewith the LORD was wroth against you to destroy you. But the LORD hearkened unto me at that time also. And the LORD was very angry with Aaron to have destroyed him: and I prayed for Aaron also the same time.* (Deut. 9:18–20)

The message of God to Hezekiah was a warning of death, as can be seen in this passage from Isaiah:

> *Thus saith the LORD, Set thine house in order: for thou shalt die, and not live. Then Hezekiah turned his face toward the wall, and prayed unto the LORD, and said, Remember now, O LORD, I beseech thee, how I have walked before thee in truth and with a perfect heart, and have done that which is good in thy sight. And Hezekiah wept sore. Then came the word of the LORD to Isaiah, saying, Go, and say to Hezekiah, Thus saith the LORD, the God of David thy father, I have heard thy prayer, I have seen thy tears: behold, I will add unto thy days fifteen years.* (Isa. 38:1–5)

Hezekiah's prayer changed God's purpose, and fifteen years were added to his life.

The Syrophenician woman (see Mark 7:24–30), the importunate[1] widow (see Luke 18:1–7), and the friend at midnight (see Luke 11:5–10) are wonderful lessons of what dauntless prayer can do in mastering or defying conditions, in changing defeat into victory and triumphing in the regions of despair.

All these people of God knew how to pray and how to prevail in prayer. Their faith in prayer was no passing attitude that changed

---

[1] Importunate: persistent in request or demand, to the point of being troublesome.

with the wind or with their own feelings and circumstances; they were confident that God always heard and answered, that His ear was always open to the cry of His children, and that the power to do what was asked of Him was equal to His willingness. Thus, strong in faith and in prayer, they

> *subdued kingdoms, wrought righteousness, obtained promises, stopped the mouths of lions, quenched the violence of fire, escaped the edge of the sword, out of weakness were made strong, waxed valiant in fight, turned to flight the armies of the aliens.* (Heb. 11:33–34)

Everything was possible to the men and women who knew how to pray, and it is still possible today. Prayer, indeed, opened a limitless storehouse, and God's hand withheld nothing. Prayer introduced those who practiced it into a world of privilege, and brought the strength and wealth of heaven down to the aid of finite man. What rich and wonderful power they had who had learned the secret of victorious approach to God! With Moses it saved a nation; with Ezra it saved a church. (See Ezra 1:1–4 and Ezra 7–9.)

And yet, strange as it seems when we contemplate the wonders of which God's people had been witnesses, they became slack in prayer. The mighty hold upon God, which had so often struck awe and terror into the hearts of their enemies, lost its grip. The people, backslidden and apostate, had gone off from their praying— if the bulk of them had ever truly prayed. The Pharisee's cold and lifeless praying was substituted for any genuine approach to God, and because of that formal method of praying, the whole of their worship became a parody of its real purpose. The dispensation was glorious, and gloriously executed, by Moses, by Ezra, by Daniel and Elijah, by Hannah and Samuel; but the circle seemed limited and short-lived; the praying ones were few and far between. They had no survivors, none to imitate their devotion to God, none to preserve the roll of the elect.

In vain had the decree established the divine order, the divine call, *Ask of Me.* From their earnest and fruitful crying to God, the Israelites turned their faces to pagan gods and cried in vain for the answers that could never come. Thus, they sank into that godless and pitiful state in which they lost their purpose in life, because the link with the Eternal had been broken. Their favored dispensation of prayer was forgotten; they no longer knew how to pray.

What a contrast to the achievements that brighten up other pages of the Holy Scriptures! The power that worked through Elijah and Elisha, in answer to prayer, reached down even to the grave. Through both men, a child was raised from the dead (see 1 Kings 17:17–24; 2 Kings 4:18–37), and the powers of famine were broken. (See 1 Kings 18:1–2, 41–45; 2 Kings 4:38–44.) Note what James wrote about Elijah:

> *The effectual fervent prayer of a righteous man availeth much. Elias was a man subject to like passions as we are, and he prayed earnestly that it might not rain: and it rained not on the earth by the space of three years and six months. And he prayed again, and the heaven gave rain, and the earth brought forth her fruit.*   *(James 5:16–18)*

How wide is the provision of the grace of praying, as administered in that marvelous dispensation! The saints of old prayed wondrously. Why could their praying not save the era from decay and death? Was it not because they had lost the fire without which all praying degenerates into a lifeless form? It takes effort and toil and care to prepare the incense. Prayer is no laggard's work. When all the rich, spiced graces from the body of prayer have been blended and refined and intermixed by labor and beating, the fire is needed to unloose the incense and make its fragrance rise to the throne of God. The spirit and life of the incense is created by the fire that consumes. Without this fire, prayer has no spirit. Like dead spices, it is for corruption and worms.

The casual, intermittent prayer is never bathed in this divine fire. This haphazard way of praying lacks the earnestness that lays hold of God and is determined not to let Him go until the blessing comes. (See Genesis 32:26.) *"Pray without ceasing"* (1 Thess. 5:17), counseled the great apostle. That is the habit that drives prayer right into the mortar that holds the building stones together. "You can do more than pray after you have prayed," said the godly Dr. A. J. Gordon, "but you cannot do more than pray until you have prayed." The story of every great Christian achievement is the history of answered prayer.

Alexander Whyte wrote,

> The greatest and the best talent that God gives to any man or woman in this world is the talent of prayer. And the

best payment of interest that any man or woman brings back to God when He comes to reckon with them at the end of this world, is a life of prayer. And those servants best put their Lord's money *"to the exchangers"* (Matt. 25:27) who rise early and sit late, as long as they are in this world, ever finding out and ever following after better and better methods of prayer, and ever forming more secret, more steadfast, and more spiritually fruitful habits of prayer, until they literally *"pray without ceasing"* (1 Thess. 5:17); and until they continually strike out into new enterprises in prayer, and new achievements, and new enrichments.

When once asked what his plans for the following day were, Martin Luther answered, "Work, work, from early until late. In fact, I have so much to do that I shall spend the first three hours in prayer." Cromwell, too, believed in being much upon his knees. On one occasion, while looking at some statues of famous men, he turned to a friend and said, "Make mine kneeling, for thus I came to glory."

It is only when the whole heart is gripped with the passion of prayer that the life-giving fire descends, for none but the earnest man gets access to the ear of God; and that is the purpose of prayer.

3

"Ask of Me"

We must remember that the goal of prayer is the ear of God. Unless that is gained, the prayer has utterly failed. The uttering of it may have kindled devotional feeling in our minds, the hearing of it may have comforted and strengthened the hearts of those with whom we have prayed, but if the prayer has not gained the heart of God, it has failed in its essential purpose. —Charles Spurgeon

IN prayer, man's access to God opens everything, and makes his impoverishment his wealth. We have seen how prayer changes the purposes of God, and stays or moves His mighty hand. All things are available to man through prayer. Man is given the privilege to command God, who has all this authority and power, in accordance with the demands of God's earthly kingdom. Look again at the passage in Psalm 2, beginning with verse eight:

Ask of me, and I shall give thee the heathen for thine inheritance, and the uttermost parts of the earth for thy possession. Thou shalt break them with a rod of iron; thou shalt dash them in pieces like a potter's vessel. (Ps. 2:8–9)

Heaven, with all that it has, is under obligation to carry out the ultimate, final, and glorious purposes of God. Why, then, is the time so long in carrying out these wise benedictions for man? Why, then, does sin reign so long? Why are the oath-bound covenant promises so long in coming to their gracious end? Sin reigns, Satan reigns, sighing marks the lives of many; all tears are fresh and full.

Why is all this so? Because we have not prayed to bring the evil to an end; we have not prayed as we must pray. We have not met the conditions of prayer.

More praying, and better praying, is the key to the whole matter. The more time we spend in prayer, and the more preparations we make to meet God, the more we will commune with God through Christ. But our manner of praying, and the things about which we pray, are not entirely pleasing to God. Baptist philosopher John Foster has said, "More and better praying will bring the surest and readiest triumph to God's cause; feeble, formal, listless praying brings decay and death."

What, then, are we to do? We must prepare ourselves to pray, to be like Christ, and to pray like Christ. We must meet the conditions of prayer. We can begin to examine the conditions of prayer by reading these verses from Isaiah:

> *Thus saith the LORD, the Holy One of Israel, and his Maker,*
> *Ask me of things to come concerning my sons, and concerning*
> *the work of my hands command ye me. I have made the earth,*
> *and created man upon it: I, even my hands, have stretched out*
> *the heavens, and all their host have I commanded.*
>
> *(Isa. 45:11–12)*

Ask of Me. Ask of God. We have not rested on prayer. We have not made prayer the sole condition. There has been a violation of the primary condition of prayer. We have not prayed correctly. We have not prayed at all. God is willing to give, but we are slow to ask. The Son, through His saints, is ever praying (see Hebrews 7:25), and God the Father is ever answering.

Ask of Me. In the invitation is conveyed the assurance of an answer; the shout of victory is there and may be heard by the listening ear. The Father holds the authority and power in His hands. How easy is the condition, and yet how slow we are in fulfilling the condition! Nations are in bondage; the uttermost parts of the earth are still not possessed. The earth groans (see Romans 8:22); the world is still in bondage; and Satan and evil hold sway.

Ask of Me. The Father holds Himself in the attitude of Giver, and a petition to God the Father empowers all agencies, inspires all movements. The Gospel is divinely inspired, and behind all its inspirations is prayer. Standing as the endowment of the enthroned Christ is the oath-bound covenant of the Father: *"Ask of me, and I shall give thee the heathen for thine inheritance, and the uttermost parts of the earth for thy possession"* (Ps. 2:8). And men shall pray to Him continually. (See Psalm 72:15.)

The prayers of holy men are ever streaming up to God, as fragrant as the richest incense. And God, in many ways, is speaking to us, declaring His wealth and our impoverishment: "I am the Maker of all things; the wealth and glory are Mine. *Command ye Me."* (See Isaiah 45:11–12.) Nevertheless, we can have all that God has for us. *Command ye Me.* We can do all things by God's aid, and we can have the whole of His aid by asking. This is no figment of the imagination, no idle dream, no vain fancy.

The Gospel, in its success and power, depends on our ability to pray. The dispensations of God depend on man's ability to pray. And yet, conscious as we are of the importance of prayer, of its vital importance, we let the hours pass away as a blank. Fénelon, a French prelate and writer of the late 1600s and early 1700s, has said,

> Of all the duties enjoined by Christianity, none is more essential and yet more neglected than prayer. Most people consider the exercise a fatiguing ceremony, which they are justified in abridging as much as possible. Even those whose profession or fears lead them to pray, pray with such languor and wanderings of mind that their prayers, far from drawing down blessings, only increase their condemnation.

This is the way in which many, if not all, of us act about prayer; yet, in the end, we will only lament in death the irreparable loss that we have laid upon ourselves. The true Christian does not pray to stir himself up, but his prayer is the stirring up of himself to take hold of God.

When we calmly reflect upon the fact that the progress of our Lord's kingdom is dependent upon prayer, it is sad to think that we give so little time to the holy exercise. Everything depends on prayer, and yet we neglect it—not only to our own spiritual hurt, but also to the delay and injury of our Lord's cause upon earth. The forces of good and evil are contending for the world. If we would pray, we could add to the conquering power of the army of righteousness; and yet our lips are sealed, our hands hang listlessly by our sides, and by holding back from the prayer chamber we jeopardize the very cause in which we profess to be deeply interested.

Prayer is the one prime, eternal condition by which the Father is pledged to put the Son in possession of the world. Christ prays through His people. If there had been importunate, universal, and continuous prayer by God's people, the earth would have been possessed for Christ long before this. The delay is not to be accounted for by the inveterate obstacles, but by the lack of the right asking.

God has no force and demands no conditions but prayer. John Foster made this statement about the need for prayer in our lives:

> I am convinced that every man who, amidst his serious projects, is apprised of his dependence on God as completely as that dependence is a fact, will be impelled to pray and anxious to induce his serious friends to pray almost every hour. He will not without it promise himself any noble success any more than a mariner would expect to reach a distant coast by having his sails spread in a stagnation of air....The individual who should determine to try the last possible efficacy of prayer might probably find himself becoming a much more prevailing agent in his little sphere.

And, continued Foster, if more or all of the disciples of Christianity were to pray, with an earnest and unalterable resolution, in order that heaven should not withhold anything that the most persistent prayer could obtain, "it would be a sign that a revolution of the world was at hand."

Edward Payson said of Foster's statement, "Probably very few missionaries, since the apostles, have tried the experiment. He who shall make the first trial will, I believe, effect wonders." Payson went on to say,

> Religion consists very much in giving God the place in our views and feelings that He actually fills in the universe. We know that in the universe He is all in all. Therefore, so far as He is constantly all in all to us, so far as we comply with the psalmist's charge to his soul, *"My soul, wait thou only upon God"* (Ps. 62:5), so far, I understand, have we advanced toward perfection.
>
> It is comparatively easy to wait upon God; but to wait upon Him only—to feel, so far as our strength, happiness, and usefulness are concerned, as if all creatures and second causes were annihilated, and we were alone in the universe with God—is, I suspect, a difficult and rare attainment. At

23

least, I am sure it is one that I am very far from having made. In proportion as we make this attainment, we will find everything easy; for we will become, emphatically, men of prayer; and we may say of prayer as Solomon says of money, that it *"answereth all things"* (Eccl. 10:19).

Again, John Foster, when approaching death, said,

> I never prayed more earnestly nor probably with such faithful frequency. *"Pray without ceasing"* (1 Thess. 5:17) has been the sentence repeating itself in my thoughts, and I am sure it must be my practice until the last conscious hour of life. Oh, why has it not been so throughout that long, indolent, inanimate half-century past?

We do more of everything else than of praying. As poor as our giving is, our contributions of money exceed our offerings of prayer. Perhaps, in the average congregation, fifty people aid in paying, while one saintly, ardent soul shuts himself up with God and wrestles for the deliverance of the heathen world. Official praying on set or state occasions counts for nothing in this estimate. We emphasize other things more than we do the necessity of prayer.

We often say prayers according to a certain prescription, but we do not have the world in the grasp of our faith. We are not praying in a way that moves God and brings all divine influences to help us. The world needs more true praying to save it from the reign and ruin of Satan.

We do not pray as Elijah prayed. John Foster put the whole matter very practically: "When the church of God is aroused to its obligation and duties and right faith to claim what Christ has promised—*'all things whatsoever'* (Matt. 21:22)—a revolution will take place."

But not all praying is true praying. The driving power, the conquering force in God's cause, must be God Himself. *"Call unto me, and I will answer thee, and show thee great and mighty things, which thou knowest not"* (Jer. 33:3), is God's challenge to pray. Prayer puts God in full force into His own work. *"Ask me of things to come concerning my sons, and concerning the work of my hands command ye me"* (Isa. 45:11), is God's carte blanche to prayer. Faith is only omnipotent when on its knees; and when its outstretched hands take hold of God, then it draws upon the utmost of

God's capacity, for only a praying faith can get God's *"all things whatsoever."*

A marvelous prayer of the Old Testament—a prayer that I have already cited in an earlier chapter—is related again in the New Testament in order to provoke and stimulate our praying. This prayer of Elijah is preceded with a declaration, the dynamic energy of which we can scarcely translate:

> *The effectual fervent prayer of a righteous man availeth much. Elias was a man subject to like passions as we are, and he prayed earnestly that it might not rain: and it rained not on the earth by the space of three years and six months. And he prayed again, and the heaven gave rain, and the earth brought forth her fruit.*   *(James 5:16–18)*

But why do we not obtain results by our praying? Why are our prayers not answered? Our lack of results, and the cause of all our feebleness in faith, was explained by the apostle James in these words: *"Ye have not, because ye ask not. Ye ask, and receive not, because ye ask amiss, that ye may consume it upon your lusts"* (James 4:2–3).

Oneness with Christ is the glorious climax of spiritual attainment, because we can then *"ask what* [we] *will, and it shall be done unto* [us]" (John 15:7). Therefore, we must be one with Him. We must pray in His name, for prayer in Jesus' name puts the crowning crown on God; it glorifies Him through the Son and pledges the Son to give to men *"whatsoever"* and anything they ask. That is the whole truth, in a nutshell.

4

Living in an Attitude of Prayer

In God's name, I beseech you, let prayer nourish your soul as your meals nourish your body. Let your fixed seasons of prayer keep you in God's presence through the day, and may His presence frequently remembered through it be an ever fresh spring of prayer. Such a brief, loving recollection of God renews a man's whole being, quiets his passions, supplies light and counsel in difficulty, gradually subdues the temper, and causes him to possess his soul in patience, or rather gives it up to the possession of God.　　　　　　　*—Fénelon*

IT was said of the late Charles Spurgeon that he glided from laughter to prayer with the naturalness of one who lived in both elements. With him, the habit of prayer was free and unfettered. His life was not divided into compartments, the one shut off from the other with a rigid exclusiveness that barred all intercommunication. He lived in constant fellowship with his Father in heaven. He was ever in touch with God, and thus it was as natural for him to pray as it was for him to breathe.

"What a fine time we have had; let us thank God for it," he said to a friend on one occasion, when, out under the blue sky and wrapped in glorious sunshine, they had enjoyed a holiday with the unfettered enthusiasm of schoolboys. Prayer sprang as spontaneously to his lips as ordinary speech did, and there was never the slightest incongruity in his approach to the divine throne after any of his activities.

That is the attitude with regard to prayer that ought to mark every child of God. There are, and there ought to be, set seasons of

26

communion with God, when everything else is shut out and we come into His presence to talk to Him and to let Him speak to us. And out of such seasons will spring that beautiful habit of prayer that weaves a golden bond between earth and heaven. Without these seasons of prayer, set as a pattern in our lives, the habit of prayer can never be formed; without them, there is no nourishment for the spiritual life. By means of them, the soul is lifted into a new atmosphere—the atmosphere of the heavenly city, in which it is easy to open the heart to God and to speak with Him as friend speaks with friend.

Thus, in every circumstance of life, prayer is the most natural outpouring of the soul, the unhindered turning to God for communion and direction. Whether in sorrow or in joy, in defeat or in victory, in weakness or in health, in calamity or in success, the heart leaps to meet with God, just as a child runs to his mother's arms, ever sure that her sympathy will meet every need.

Dr. Adam Clarke, in his autobiography, recorded that, when Mr. Wesley was returning to England by ship, considerable delay was caused by contrary winds. Wesley was reading, when he became aware of some confusion on board; and asking what was the matter, he was informed that the wind was contrary. "Then," was his reply, "let us go to prayer."

After Dr. Clarke had prayed, Wesley broke out into fervent supplication that seemed to be more the offering of faith than of mere desire. "Almighty and everlasting God," he prayed, "You have sway everywhere, and all things serve the purpose of Your will. You hold the winds in Your fists and sit upon the floods of water, and You reign as King forever. Command these winds and these waves, that they may obey You, and take us speedily and safely to the haven where we wish to go."

The power of this petition was felt by all. Wesley rose from his knees, made no remark, but took up his book and continued reading. Dr. Clarke went on deck, and to his surprise found the vessel under sail, standing on her right course. Nor did she change until she was safely at anchor. On the sudden and favorable change of wind, Wesley made no remark; he so fully expected to be heard that he took it for granted that he was heard.

That was prayer with a purpose—the definite and direct utterance of one who knew that he had the ear of God, and that God had the willingness as well as the power to grant the petition that he asked of Him.

Major D. W. Whittle, in an introduction to writings on the wonders of prayer, told this story about George Müller:

> I met Mr. Müller in the express, the morning of our sailing from Quebec to Liverpool. About half an hour before the tender[2] was to take the passengers to the ship, he asked of the agent if a deck chair had arrived for him from New York. He was answered, "No," and told that it could not possibly come in time for the steamer. I had with me a chair I had just purchased, and told Mr. Müller of the place nearby, and suggested, as but a few moments remained, that he had better buy one at once.
>
> His reply was, "No, my brother. Our heavenly Father will send the chair from New York. It is one used by Mrs. Müller. I wrote ten days ago to a brother, who promised to see it forwarded here last week. He has not been prompt, as I would have desired, but I am sure our heavenly Father will send the chair. Mrs. Müller is very sick on the sea, and has particularly desired to have this chair; and not finding it here yesterday, we have made a special prayer that our heavenly Father would provide it for us, and we will trust Him to do so."
>
> As this dear man of God went peacefully on board, running the risk of Mrs. Müller making the trip without a chair, when, for a couple of dollars, she could have been provided for, I confess I feared Mr. Müller was carrying his faith principles too far and not acting wisely. I was kept at the express office ten minutes after Mr. Müller left. Just as I started to hurry to the wharf, a team of horses drove up the street, and on top of a load just arrived from New York was Mr. Müller's chair.
>
> It was sent at once to the tender and placed in my hands to take to Mr. Müller, just as the boat was leaving the dock (the Lord having a lesson for me). Mr. Müller took it with the happy, pleased expression of a child who has just received a kindness deeply appreciated, and reverently removing his hat and folding his hands over it, he thanked the heavenly Father for sending the chair.

One of Melancthon's correspondents wrote of Luther's praying,

---

[2] Tender: a ship that attends other ships, or a boat that communicates between shore and a larger ship.

I cannot enough admire the extraordinary cheerfulness, constancy, faith, and hope of the man in these trying and vexatious times. He constantly feeds these gracious affections by a very diligent study of the Word of God. Not a day passes in which he does not employ in prayer at least three of his very best hours. Once I happened to hear him at prayer. Gracious God! What spirit and what faith is there in his expressions! He petitions God with as much reverence as if he were in the divine presence, and yet with as firm a hope and confidence as he would address a father or a friend.

"I know," he would say in his prayers, "You are our Father and our God; and, therefore, I am sure You will bring to naught the persecutors of Your children. For if You fail to do this, Your own cause, being connected with ours, would be endangered. It is entirely Your own concern. We, by Your providence, have been compelled to take a part. You, therefore, will be our defense."

While I was listening to Luther praying in this manner, at a distance, my soul seemed on fire within me, to hear the man address God so like a friend, yet with so much gravity and reverence; and also to hear him, in the course of his prayer, insisting on the promises contained in the Psalms, as if he were sure his petitions would be granted.

Of William Bramwell, a Methodist preacher from England, noted for his zeal and prayer, the following has been related by a sergeant major:

In July 1811, our regiment was ordered for Spain, then the seat of a prolonged and bloody war. My mind was painfully exercised with the thoughts of leaving my dear wife and four helpless children in a strange country, unprotected and unprovided for. Mr. Bramwell felt a lively interest in our situation, and his sympathizing spirit seemed to drink in all the agonized feelings of my tender wife. He supplicated the throne of grace day and night on our behalf.

My wife and I spent the evening previous to our march at a friend's house, in company with Mr. Bramwell, who sat in a very pensive mood and appeared to be in a spiritual struggle the entire time. After supper, he suddenly took his hand from his chest, laid it on my knee, and said, "Brother Riley, mark what I am about to say! You are not to go to Spain. Remember, I tell you, you are not; for I have been wrestling with God on your behalf, and when my heavenly Father condescends in mercy to bless me with power to lay hold on Himself, I do not easily let Him go; no, not until I am favored with an answer. Therefore, you may depend on it, that the next time I hear from you, you will be settled in quarters." This came to pass exactly as he said. The next day the order for going to Spain was countermanded.

These men prayed with a purpose. To them, God was not far away, in some inaccessible region, but near at hand, ever ready to listen to the call of His children. There was no barrier between. They were on terms of perfect intimacy, if one may use such a phrase in relation to man and his Maker. No cloud obscured the face of the Father from His trusting child, who could look up into the divine countenance and pour out the longings of his heart. And that is the type of prayer that God never fails to hear. He knows that it comes from a heart at one with His own, from one who is entirely yielded to the heavenly plan, and so He bends His ear and gives to the pleading child the assurance that his petition has been heard and answered.

Have we not all had some such experience when we have approached the face of our Father with set and undeviating purpose? In an agony of soul, we have sought refuge from the oppression of the world in the anteroom of heaven; the waves of despair seemed to threaten destruction, and as no way of escape was visible anywhere, we fell back, like the disciples of old, upon the power of our Lord, crying to Him to save us lest we perish. (See Luke 8:24.) And then, in the twinkling of an eye, the thing was done. The billows sank into a calm; the howling wind died down at the divine command; the agony of the soul passed into a restful peace as over the whole being there crept the consciousness of the divine presence, bringing with it the assurance of answered prayer and sweet deliverance.

"I tell the Lord my troubles and difficulties, and wait for Him to give me the answers to them," said one man of God. Then he continued:

And it is wonderful how a matter that looked very dark will in prayer become crystal clear by the help of God's Spirit. I think Christians fail so often to get answers to their prayers because they do not wait long enough on God. They just drop down and say a few words, and then jump up and forget it and expect God to answer them. Such praying always reminds me of the small boy ringing his neighbor's doorbell, and then running away as fast as he can go.

When we acquire the habit of prayer, we enter into a new atmosphere. "Do you expect to go to heaven?" asked someone of a devout Scotsman. "Why, sir, I live there," was the quaint and unexpected reply. It was an elegant yet compelling statement of great truth, for the entire way to heaven is already the beginning of heaven to the Christian who walks near enough to God to hear the secrets He has to impart.

This attitude is beautifully illustrated in a story of Horace Bushnell, told by Dr. Parkes Cadman. Bushnell was found to be suffering from an incurable disease. One evening, the Rev. Joseph Twichell visited him, and, as they sat together under the starry sky, Bushnell said, "One of us ought to pray." Twichell asked Bushnell to do so, and Bushnell began his prayer. Burying his face in the earth, he poured out his heart until, said Twichell, in recalling the incident, "I was afraid to stretch out my hand in the darkness lest I should touch God."

To have God thus near is to enter the Holy of Holies—to breathe the fragrance of the heavenly air, to walk in Eden's delightful gardens. Nothing but prayer can bring God and man into this happy communion. That was the experience of Samuel Rutherford, just as it is the experience of everyone who passes through the same gateway. When this saint of God was at one time confined in jail because he refused to act against his convictions, he enjoyed, in a rare degree, the divine companionship, recording in his diary that Jesus entered his cell, and that at His coming "every stone flashed like a ruby."

Many others have borne witness to the same sweet fellowship, when prayer had become the one habit of life that meant more than anything else to them. David Livingstone lived in the realm of prayer and knew its gracious influence. It was his habit every birthday to write a prayer; and on the next to the last birthday of all, this was his prayer: "O Divine One, I have not loved You earnestly, deeply, sincerely enough. Grant, I pray You, that before this year is ended I may have finished my task." It was just on the threshold of the year that followed that his faithful men, as they looked into the hut of Ilala, while the rain dripped from the eaves, saw their master on his knees beside his bed in an attitude of prayer. He had died on his knees in prayer.

Stonewall Jackson was a man of prayer. He said, "I have so fixed the habit in my mind that I never raise a glass of water to my lips without asking God's blessing, never seal a letter without putting a word of prayer under the seal, never take a letter from the mailbox without a brief sending of my thoughts heavenward, never change my classes in the lecture room without a minute's petition for the cadets who go out and for those who come in."

James Gilmour, the pioneer missionary to Mongolia, was a man of prayer. He had a habit in his writing of never using a blotter. He made a rule that when he got to the bottom of any page he would wait until the ink dried and spend the time in prayer.

In this way, the whole beings of these men were saturated with the divine, and they became the reflectors of the heavenly fragrance and glory. Walking with God down the avenues of prayer, we acquire something of His likeness, and unconsciously we become witnesses to others of His beauty and His grace. Professor James, in his famous work, *Varieties of Religious Experience,* told of a man of forty-nine who said,

> God is more real to me than any thought or thing or person. I feel His presence positively, and even more as I live in closer harmony with His laws, as they are written in my body and mind. I feel Him in the sunshine or rain; my feelings are most nearly described by saying that everything is mingled with a delicious restfulness. I talk to Him as to a companion in prayer and praise, and our communion is delightful. He answers me again and again, often in words so clearly spoken that it seems my outer ear must have carried the tone, but generally in strong mental impressions. Usually a text of Scripture will unfold to me some new view of Him and His love for me, and His care for my safety. The knowledge that He is mine and I am His never leaves me; it is an abiding joy. Without it, life would be a blank, a desert, a shoreless, trackless waste.

Equally notable is the testimony of Sir Thomas Browne, the beloved physician who lived in Norwich, England, in 1605, and was the author of a very remarkable book of wide circulation, *Religio Medici.* In spite of the fact that England was passing through a period of national convulsion and political excitement, he found comfort and strength in prayer. "I have resolved," he wrote in a journal found among his private papers after his death, "to pray more and pray always, to pray in all places where quietness invites me to pray: in the house, on the highway, and on the street. And I have resolved to know no street or passage in this city that may not witness that I have not forgotten God." And he added,

> I purpose to take occasion of praying upon the sight of any church that I may pass, that God may be worshipped there in spirit, and that souls may be saved there. I purpose to pray daily for my sick patients and for the patients of other physicians; to say at my entrance into any home, "May the peace of God abide here"; to pray, after hearing a sermon, for a blessing on God's truth and upon the messenger; to bless God, upon the sight of a beautiful person, for His creatures, and to pray for the beauty of such a soul, that God may enrich her with inward graces, and that the outward and inward may correspond; to pray God, upon the sight of a deformed person, to give them wholeness of soul, and by and by to give them the beauty of the resurrection.

What an illustration of the praying spirit! Such an attitude represents prayer without ceasing; it reveals the habit of prayer in its unceasing supplication, in its uninterrupted communion, in its constant intercession. What an illustration, too, of purpose in prayer! Of how many of us can it be said that as we pass people in the street we pray for them, or that as we enter a home or a church we remember the residents or the congregation in prayer to God?

The explanation of our thoughtlessness or forgetfulness lies in the fact that prayer, with so many of us, is simply a form of selfishness; it means asking for something for ourselves—that and nothing more.

And from such an attitude we need to pray to be delivered.

5

The Energy of Prayer

The potency of prayer has subdued the strength of fire; it has bridled the rage of lions, hushed anarchy to rest, extinguished wars, appeased the elements, expelled demons, burst the chains of death, expanded the gates of heaven, assuaged diseases, repelled frauds, rescued cities from destruction, stayed the sun in its course, and arrested the progress of the thunderbolt. Prayer is an all-efficient panoply, a treasure undiminished, a mine that is never exhausted, a sky unobscured by clouds, a heaven unruffled by the storm. It is the root, the fountain, the mother of a thousand blessings.

—St. Chrysostom

ARE we praying as Christ did? Do we abide in Him? Are our pleas and spirit the overflow of His pleas and Spirit? Does love rule the spirit—perfect love? These questions must be considered as proper and highly appropriate at a time like the present. We have every reason to fear that we are doing more of other things than prayer. This is not a praying age; it is an age of great activity, of great movements, but one in which the tendency is very strong to stress the seen and the material, and to neglect and discount the unseen and the spiritual. Prayer is the greatest of all forces because it honors God and brings Him into active aid.

There can be no substitute, no rival for prayer; it stands alone as the great spiritual force, and this force must be imminent and acting. It cannot be dispensed with during one generation, nor can it be held in abeyance if any great movement is to be advanced.

Rather, it must be continuous and particular, always, everywhere, and in everything. The book of Revelation says nothing about prayer as a great duty or a hallowed service, but much about prayer in its aggregated force and energies. It is the prayer force, ever living and ever praying; it is all saints' prayers going out as a mighty, living energy, while the lips that uttered the words may be stilled and sealed in death. The living church has an energy of faith to inherit the forces of all the past praying and to make it deathless.

But we cannot run our spiritual operations on the prayers of the past generations. Many people believe in the efficacy of prayer, but not many people pray. Prayer is the easiest and hardest of all things. It is the simplest and the most sublime, the weakest and the most powerful. Its results lie outside the range of human possibilities; they are limited only by the omnipotence of God.

Few Christians have anything but a vague idea of the power of prayer; fewer still have any experience of that power. The church seems almost wholly unaware of the power God puts into her hand. This spiritual carte blanche on the infinite resources of God's wisdom and power is rarely, if ever, used—never used to the full measure of honoring God. It is astounding how little we use it, and how little we reap its benefits. Prayer is our most formidable weapon, but the one in which we are the least skilled and the most averse to using. We do everything else for the heathen, except the thing God wants us to do. Prayer is the only thing that does any good, the only thing that makes effective everything else that we do.

Yet, in spite of the benefits and blessings that flow from communion with God, the sad confession must be made that we are not praying much. A comparatively very small number lead in prayer at the meetings. Fewer still pray with their families. Fewer still are in the habit of praying regularly in their prayer closets. Meetings specially for prayer are as rare as frost in June. In many churches there is neither the name nor the semblance of a prayer meeting. In the town and city churches, the prayer meeting in name is not a prayer meeting in fact. A sermon or a lecture is the main feature. Prayer is only the nominal attachment.

Our people are not essentially a praying people. That is evident by their lives.

Prayer is a trade to be learned, and it is a life trade. We must be apprentices and serve our time at it. Painstaking care, much thought, practice, and labor are required to be a skillful tradesman in praying. Practice in this, as well as in all other trades, makes perfect. One who is clumsy in the trade of praying will also mishandle the trade of salvation. Only toiling hands and hearts will make the workers proficient in this heavenly trade.

Prayer and a holy life are one. They mutually act and react. Neither can survive alone, for the absence of the one is the absence of the other. The hindrances of prayer are the hindrances in a holy life; and the conditions of praying are the conditions of righteousness, holiness, and salvation. The piety of saints is made, refined, and perfected by prayer. The first and last stages of holy living are crowned with praying.

A bird's-eye view of what has been accomplished by prayer shows what we lost when the dispensation of real prayer was substituted with pharisaical pretense and sham. It shows, too, how imperative is the need for holy men and women who will give themselves to earnest, Christlike praying. Monks, in general, have spoken ill of prayer; and they have substituted superstition for praying, and hypocritical ceremonies and routines for a holy life. And so, those who have been thought to live holy and pious lives, have turned out to be poor examples to the rest of believers.

We are all in danger of substituting church work and a ceaseless round of showy activities for prayer and holy living. A holy life does not live in the closet, but it cannot live without the prayer closet. If, by any chance, a person should establish a prayer chamber but not have an accompanying holy life, it would be a chamber without the presence of God in it.

The burden of the apostolic effort and the keynote of apostolic success is this: Put the saints everywhere to the task of praying. The Gospel moves with slow and timid pace when the saints are not at their prayers early and late and long. Jesus Christ strove to put the saints to this task in the days of His personal ministry. He was moved with infinite compassion at seeing the ripened fields of earth perishing for lack of laborers (see Matthew 9:37–38); and, pausing in His own praying, He tried to awaken the sleeping sensibilities of His disciples to the duty of prayer, as He charged them: *"Pray ye therefore the Lord of the harvest, that he will send forth labourers into his harvest"* (v. 38). *"And he spake a parable unto them to this end, that men ought always to pray"* (Luke 18:1).

Before Pentecost, the apostles could get only glimpses of this great importance of prayer. But, when the Spirit came and filled them on Pentecost, prayer was elevated to its vital and all-commanding position in the Gospel of Christ. Now the call of prayer to every saint is the Spirit's loudest and most urgent call.

Where are the Christlike leaders who can teach the modern saints how to pray? Where are the leaders who will put them to the task? Do our leaders know we are raising up a prayerless set of saints? Where are the apostolic leaders who can put God's people to praying? Let them come to the front and do the work, and it will be the greatest work that can be done.

An increase of educational facilities and a great increase of financial support will be the most disastrous curse to religion, if these things are not sanctified by more and better praying than we are doing. And more praying will not just happen. We are a generation of non-praying saints who, like beggars, have neither the ardor nor the beauty nor the power of saints. Who will restore this branch? (See John 15:2–5.) We greatly need someone who can set the saints to this business of praying; and the one who can set the church to praying will be the greatest of reformers and apostles.

The campaign for the twentieth or thirtieth century will not help our praying, but it will hinder it if we are not careful. Nothing but a specific effort from a praying leadership will avail. None but praying leaders can have praying followers. Praying apostles will beget praying saints. A praying pulpit will beget praying pews.

Holy men have, in the past, changed the whole force of affairs; they have revolutionized character and country by prayer. And such achievements are still possible for us. The power is only waiting to be used. Prayer is simply the expression of faith.

I do not have enough time to tell of the mighty things effected by prayer, for by it holy ones have

> *subdued kingdoms, wrought righteousness, obtained promises, stopped the mouths of lions, quenched the violence of fire, escaped the edge of the sword, out of weakness were made strong, waxed valiant in fight, turned to flight the armies of the aliens.* (Heb. 11:33–34)

Prayer honors God; it dishonors self. It is man's plea of weakness, ignorance, need—a plea that heaven cannot disregard. God delights to have us pray.

Prayer is not the opposite of work; it does not paralyze activity. Rather, prayer itself is the greatest work; it works mightily. It springs activity, stimulates desire and effort. Prayer is not an opiate, but a tonic; it does not lull to sleep, but arouses anew for action. The lazy man does not, cannot pray, for prayer demands energy. Paul calls it a striving, an agony. (See Romans 15:30.) With Jacob it was a wrestling; with the Syrophenician woman it was a struggle that called into play all the higher qualities of the soul, and that demanded great force to meet it.

The prayer closet is not an asylum for the indolent and worthless Christian. It is not a nursery where none but babes belong. It is the battlefield of the church, its citadel, the scene of heroic and unearthly conflicts. The closet is the base of supplies for the Christian and the church. Cut off from it, there is nothing left but retreat and disaster. The energy for work, the mastery over self, the deliverance from fear, and all spiritual results and graces, are much advanced by prayer.

The differences in the strength, experience, and holiness of one Christian compared with another, are found in the contrast in their praying. A man whose prayers are few, short, and feeble is surely a man of low spiritual condition; whereas the eminent Christian is the man who has been eminent in prayer. Men ought to pray much and ought to apply themselves to prayer. The deep things of God are learned only in prayer. Great things for God are done by great prayers. He who prays much, studies much, loves much, and works much, does much for God and humanity. The execution of the Gospel, the vigor of faith, the maturity and excellence of spiritual graces wait on prayer. Therefore, we ought to pray often, with both energy and perseverance.

6

Persistence in Prayer

"Nothing is impossible to industry," said one of the seven sages of Greece. Let us change the word "industry" to "persevering prayer," and the motto will be more Christian and more worthy of universal adoption. I am persuaded that we are all more deficient in a spirit of prayer than in any other grace. God loves importunate prayer so much that He will not give us much blessing without it. And the reason that He loves such prayer is that He loves us and knows that it is a necessary preparation for our receiving the richest blessings that He is waiting and longing to bestow. —Adoniram Judson

THROUGHOUT His ministry, Christ made it clear that importunity is a distinguishing characteristic of true praying. We must not only pray, but we must also pray with great urgency, with intensity, and with repetition. We must not only pray, but we must also pray again and again. We must not get tired of praying. We must be thoroughly in earnest, deeply concerned about the things for which we ask, for Jesus Christ made it very plain that the secret of prayer and its success lie in its urgency. We must press our prayers upon God.

Adoniram Judson said, "I never prayed sincerely and earnestly for anything but it came at some time. No matter at how distant a day, somehow, in some shape, probably the last I would have devised, it came." Oh, that we could all know this and know it well!

In a parable of exquisite pathos and simplicity, our Lord taught not simply that men ought to pray, but that men ought to pray with full heartiness, and press the matter with vigorous energy and courage.

> *And he spake a parable unto them to this end, that men ought always to pray, and not to faint; saying, There was in a city a judge, which feared not God, neither regarded man: and there was a widow in that city; and she came unto him, saying, Avenge me of mine adversary. And he would not for a while: but afterward he said within himself, Though I fear not God, nor regard man; yet because this widow troubleth me, I will avenge her, lest by her continual coming she weary me. And the Lord said, Hear what the unjust judge saith. And shall not God avenge his own elect, which cry day and night unto him, though he bear long with them? I tell you that he will avenge them speedily. Nevertheless when the Son of man cometh, shall he find faith on the earth?* (Luke 18:1–8)

This poor woman's case was a most hopeless one, but importunity brought hope from the realms of despair and created success where neither success nor its conditions existed. There is no stronger case to show how our unwearied and dauntless prayer gains its ends where everything else fails. The preface to this parable says, *"He spake a parable unto them to this end, that men ought always to pray, and not to faint"* (v. 1). He knew that men would soon grow fainthearted in praying; so, to encourage us, He gives this picture of the marvelous power of persistence in prayer.

The widow, weak and helpless, is helplessness personified; bereft of every hope and influence that could move an unjust judge, she yet wins her case solely by her tireless and offensive requests. Could the necessity of importunity, its power and tremendous importance in prayer, be pictured in deeper or more impressive coloring? Importunate prayer surmounts or removes all obstacles, overcomes every resisting force, and gains its ends in the face of invincible hindrances. We can do nothing without prayer, but all things can be done by importunate prayer. That is the teaching of Jesus Christ.

Another parable spoken by Jesus enforces the same great truth. A man at midnight goes to his friend for a loan of a few loaves of bread. (See Luke 11:5–10.) His pleas are strong, based on friendship and the embarrassing and exacting demands of necessity, but these all fail. He gets no bread at first, so he stays and presses, and he waits and gains. Sheer importunity succeeded where all other pleas and influences had failed.

The case of the Syrophenician woman is a parable in action. (See Mark 7:24–30.) She was stopped in her approaches to Christ by the information that He would not see anyone. She was denied His presence, and then in His presence was treated with seeming indifference, with the chill of silence and unconcern. Yet she pressed and approached, and the pressure and approach were repulsed by the stern and crushing statement that He was not sent to her kith[3] or kind, that she was reprobated from His mission and power.

She was humiliated by being called a dog; yet she accepted all, overcame all, and won all by her humble, dauntless, invincible importunity. The Son of God, pleased, surprised, overpowered by her unconquerable persistence, said to her, *"O woman, great is thy faith: be it unto thee even as thou wilt"* (Matt. 15:28). Jesus Christ surrendered Himself to the importunity of a great faith. *"And shall not God avenge his own elect, which cry day and night unto him, though he bear long with them?"* (Luke 18:7).

Jesus Christ presents the ability to importune as one of the elements of prayer, one of the main conditions of prayer. The prayer of the Syrophenician woman is an example of the matchless power of persistence in prayer, of a conflict more real and involving more vital energy, endurance, and all the higher elements than was ever illustrated in the conflicts of Isthmia or Olympia.[4]

The first lessons of persistence are taught in the Sermon on the Mount: *"Ask, and it shall be given you; seek, and ye shall find; knock, and it shall be opened unto you"* (Matt. 7:7). These are steps of advance, *"for every one that asketh, receiveth; and he that seeketh, findeth; and to him that knocketh it shall be opened"* (v. 8).

Without persistence, prayers may go unanswered. Importunity is made up of the ability to hold on, to continue, to wait with unrelaxed and unrelaxable grasp, restless desire, and restful patience. Importunate prayer is not an incidental occurrence, but the main thing; not a performance, but a passion; not an option, but a necessity.

---

[3] Kith: familiar friends, neighbors, or relatives.

[4] Isthmia: the Isthmus of Corinth, where, in ancient times, biennial pan-Hellenic games were held. Similar festivals of athletic contests were held in ancient Greece on the plan of Olympia; these have been revived and are now known as the international Olympic Games.

Prayer, in its highest form and its grandest success, assumes the attitude of a wrestler with God. Prayer is the contest, trial, and victory of faith—a victory not secured from an enemy, but from Him who tries our faith that He may enlarge it. He tests our strength to make us stronger. Few things give such quickened and permanent vigor to the soul as a long, exhaustive season of importunate prayer. It provides an experience, an epoch, a new calendar for the spirit; it gives a new life, a soldierly training, to religion.

The Bible never wearies in its illustration of the fact that the highest spiritual good is secured as the return of the highest form of spiritual effort. John Wesley put it in these words: "Bear up the hands that hang down, by faith and prayer; support the tottering knees. (See Hebrews 12:12.) Have you any days of fasting and prayer? Storm the throne of grace and persevere therein, and mercy will come down." There is neither encouragement nor room in the religion of the Scriptures for feeble desires, listless efforts, lazy attitudes. All must be strenuous, urgent, ardent. Inflamed desires and impassioned, unwearied insistence are the things that delight heaven.

God would have His children unalterably in earnest and persistently bold in their efforts. Heaven is too busy to listen to half-hearted prayers or to respond to hasty, thoughtless calls to God.

Our whole being must be in our praying; like John Knox, we must say and feel, "Give me Scotland, or may I die." Our experience and revelations of God are born of our costly sacrifice, our costly conflicts, our costly praying. The wrestling, the all-night praying of Jacob (see Genesis 32:24–28), began an era never to be forgotten by him; it brought God to the rescue, changed Esau's attitude and conduct, changed Jacob's character, saved and affected his life, and entered into the habits of a nation.

Our seasons of importunate prayer cut themselves, like the print of a diamond, into our hardest places, and mark our characters with ineffaceable traces. They are the salient periods of our lives, the memorial stones that endure and to which we turn. (See 1 Samuel 7:12.)

Importunity, it may be repeated, is a condition of prayer. We are to press the matter, not with vain repetitions, but with urgent repetitions. We repeat, not to count the times, but to gain the answer to our prayer. We cannot quit praying, because heart and soul are in our prayers. We pray *"with all perseverance"* (Eph. 6:18); we hang on to our prayers because we live by them. We press our pleas because we must have them or die.

I have already shown that Christ gave us two most expressive parables to emphasize the necessity of importunity in praying. Perhaps Abraham lost Sodom by failing to press, to the utmost, his privilege of praying. (See Genesis 18:16–33.) We know that Joash lost because he held off his smiting to appease an enemy king. (See 2 Kings 11:1–12:21.)

Perseverance counts much with God, just as it does with man. If Elijah had ceased at his first petition, the heavens would scarcely have yielded their rain to his feeble praying. (See James 5:17–18.) If Jacob had quit praying at decent bedtime, he would hardly have survived the next day's meeting with Esau. If the Syrophenician woman had allowed her faith to faint by silence, humiliation, or rejection, or to stop midway in its struggles, her grief-stricken home would never have been brightened by the healing of her daughter.

Pray and never faint, is the motto Christ gives us for praying. It is the test of our faith, and the more severe the trial and the longer the waiting, the more glorious the results.

The benefits and necessity of importunity are taught by the lives of the Old Testament saints. Praying men must be strong in hope and faith and prayer. They must know how to wait and to press, to wait on God and be in earnest in their approaches to Him.

Abraham left us an example of importunate intercession in his passionate pleading with God on behalf of Sodom and Gomorrah. If, as already indicated, he had not ceased in his asking, perhaps God would not have ceased in His giving. "Abraham left off asking before God left off granting," is how the saying goes. Moses taught the power of importunity when he interceded for Israel forty days and forty nights, by fasting and prayer. And he succeeded in his importunity.

Jesus, in His teaching and example, illustrated and perfected this principle of Old Testament pleading and waiting. What a mystery that the only Son of God should be under the law of prayer— He who came on a mission direct from His Father, He whose only heaven on earth, whose only life and law, were to do His Father's will in that mission. How strange that the blessings that came to Him were impregnated and purchased by prayer. It is stranger still that importunity in prayer was the process by which His wealthiest supplies from God were gained.

Had He not prayed with importunity, no transfiguration would have been in His history, no mighty works would have rendered His career divine. His all-night praying was that which filled His all-day work with compassion and power. The importunate praying of His life crowned His death with triumph. He learned the high lesson of submission to God's will in the struggles of importunate prayer, before He illustrated that submission so sublimely on the cross.

Charles Spurgeon has said:

> Whether we like it or not, asking is the rule of the kingdom. *"Ask, and ye shall receive"* (John 16:24). It is a rule that never will be altered in anybody's case. Our Lord Jesus Christ is the elder brother of the family, but God has not relaxed the rule even for Him. Remember this text: Jehovah says to His own Son, *"Ask of me, and I shall give thee the heathen for thine inheritance, and the uttermost parts of the earth for thy possession"* (Ps. 2:8). If the royal and divine Son of God cannot be exempted from the rule of asking that He may have, you and I cannot expect the rule to be relaxed in our favor. Why should it be?
>
> What reason can be given why we should be exempted from prayer? What argument can there be why we should be deprived of the privilege and delivered from the necessity of supplication? I can see none; can you? God will bless Elijah and send rain on Israel, but Elijah must pray for it. If the chosen nation is to prosper, Samuel must plead for it. If the Jews are to be delivered, Daniel must intercede. God will bless Paul, and the nations will be converted through him, but Paul must pray. Indeed, he did pray without ceasing; his epistles show that he expected nothing except by asking for it. If you may have everything by asking, and nothing without asking, I beg you to see how absolutely vital prayer is, and I beseech you to abound in it.

I have no doubt that much of our praying fails for lack of persistence. So many of our prayers are said without the fire and strength of perseverance. Persistence is the essence of true praying. It may not be always called into exercise, but it must be there as the reserve force. Jesus taught that perseverance is the essential element of prayer. Therefore, men must be in earnest when they kneel at God's footstool.

Too often we get fainthearted and quit praying at the point where we ought to begin. We let go at the very point where we should most strongly hold on. Consequently, our prayers are weak because they are not impassioned by an unfailing and resistless will.

God loves the importunate pleader, and sends him answers that would never have been granted but for the persistence that refuses to let go until the petition craved for is granted.

7

Secret Prayer

Be sure you look to your secret duty; keep that up whatever you do. The soul cannot prosper in the neglect of it. Apostasy generally begins at the closet door. Be much in secret fellowship with God. It is secret trading that enriches the Christian. Let prayer be the key of the morning and the bolt at night. The best way to fight against sin is to fight it on our knees.   *—Philip Henry*

"MEN *ought **always** to pray, and not to faint"* (Luke 18:1, emphasis added). These words are the words of our Lord, who not only always sought to impress upon His followers the urgency and the importance of prayer, but also set them an example that they, unfortunately, have been far too slow to copy.

The *always* speaks for itself. Prayer is not a meaningless function or duty to be crowded into the busy or weary activities of the day; and we are not obeying our Lord's command when we content ourselves with a few minutes on our knees in the morning rush or late at night, when the faculties, tired with the tasks of the day, call out for rest. God is always ready to hear our call, it is true; His ear is ever attentive to the cry of His child, but we can never get to know Him if we use the vehicle of prayer as we use the telephone—for a few words of hurried conversation. Intimacy requires development. We can never know Him by brief and fragmentary and thoughtless repetitions of intercessions that are requests for personal favors and nothing more.

That is not the way in which we can come into communication with heaven's King. "The goal of prayer is the ear of God," said Spurgeon; and this is a goal that can only be reached by patient and continuous waiting upon Him, by pouring out our hearts to Him, and permitting Him to speak to us. Only by so doing can we expect to know Him; and as we come to know Him better, we will spend more time in His presence and find that presence a constant and ever increasing delight.

Always does not mean that we are to neglect the ordinary duties of life; what it means is that the soul that has come into intimate contact with God in the silence of the prayer chamber is never out of conscious touch with the Father; that the heart is always going out to Him in loving communion; and that the moment the mind is released from the task upon which it is engaged, it returns as naturally to God as the bird does to its nest. What a beautiful conception of prayer we get if we regard it in this light, if we view it as a constant fellowship, an unbroken audience with the King! Prayer then loses every vestige of dread that it may once have possessed; we regard it no longer as a duty that must be performed, but rather as a privilege that is to be enjoyed, a rare delight that is always revealing some new beauty.

Thus, when we open our eyes in the morning, our thoughts instantly turn heavenward. To many Christians, the morning hours are the most precious portion of the day, because they provide the opportunity for the hallowed fellowship that gives the keynote to the day's program. And what better introduction can there be to the never ceasing glory and wonder of a new day than to spend it alone with God? It is said that D. L. Moody, at a time when no other place was available, kept his morning watch in the coal shed, pouring out his heart to God, and finding in his precious Bible a true *"feast of fat things"* (Isa. 25:6).

George Müller also combined Bible study with prayer in the quiet morning hours. At one time, his practice was to give himself to prayer in the morning, after having dressed. Then his plan underwent a change. As he himself put it,

> I saw the most important thing I had to do was to give myself to the reading of the Word of God, and to meditation on it, that thus my heart might be comforted, encouraged, warned, reproved, instructed; and that, by means of the Word of God, while meditating on it, my heart might be brought into communion with the Lord. I began, therefore, to meditate on the New Testament early in the morning.
>
> The first thing I did, after having asked in a few words for the Lord's blessing upon His precious Word, was to begin

to meditate on the Word of God, searching, as it were, into every verse to get blessing out of it. I did this not for the sake of the public ministry of the Word, nor for the sake of preaching on what I had meditated on, but for the sake of obtaining food for my own soul. Almost invariably, I have found the result to be that, after a very few minutes, my soul has been led to confession, or to thanksgiving, or to intercession, or to supplication; so that, though I did not, as it were, give myself to prayer, but to meditation, yet it turned almost immediately more or less into prayer.

The study of the Word and prayer go together, and we find that when the one is truly practiced, the other is sure to be seen in close alliance.

But we do not pray *always*. That is the trouble with so many of us. We need to pray much more than we do and much longer than we do.

It has been said of the gifted and saintly Robert Murray McCheyne: "Whether viewed as a son, a brother, a friend, or a pastor, he was the most faultless and attractive exhibition of the true Christian they had ever seen embodied in a living form." He knew what it was to spend much time upon his knees, and he never wearied in urging upon others the joy and the value of holy intercession. "God's children should pray," he said. "They should cry day and night unto Him. God hears every one of your cries in the busy hours of the daytime and in the lonely watches of the night." In every way, by preaching, by exhortation when present, and by letters when absent, McCheyne emphasized the vital duty of prayer, importunate and unceasing prayer.

In his diary we find this: "In the morning I was engaged in preparing the head, then the heart. This has been frequently my error, and I have always felt the evil of it, especially in prayer. Reform it then, O Lord."

While on his trip to the Holy Land, McCheyne wrote, "For much of our safety I feel indebted to the prayers of my people. If the veil of the world's machinery were lifted off, how much we would find done in answer to the prayers of God's children!"

In an ordination sermon he said to the preacher,

Give yourself to prayers and the ministry of the Word. (See Acts 6:3–4.) If you do not pray, God will probably lay you aside from your ministry, as He did me, to teach you to pray. Remember Luther's maxim: "To have prayed well is to have studied well." Get your texts, your thoughts, your words from God. Carry the names of the little flock upon your breast like the high priest. (See Exodus 28:1–2, 15–21, 29.) Wrestle for the unconverted.

Luther spent his last three hours in prayer; John Welch prayed seven or eight hours a day. He used to keep a blanket on his bed that he might wrap himself in when he rose during the night. Sometimes his wife found him lying on the ground, weeping. When she complained, he would say, "O woman, I have the souls of three thousand to answer for, and I know not how it is with many of them."

McCheyne exhorted and charged the people,

> Pray for your pastor. Pray for his body, that he may be kept strong and spared many years. Pray for his soul, that he may be kept humble and holy, a burning and shining light. Pray for his ministry, that it may be abundantly blessed, that he may be anointed to preach good tidings. Let there be no secret prayer without naming him before your God, no family prayer without carrying your pastor in your hearts to God.

Even McCheyne's biographer said of him, "Two things he seems never to have ceased from—the cultivation of personal holiness and the most anxious efforts to win souls." These two things are the inseparable attendants to the ministry of prayer. Prayer fails when the desire and effort for personal holiness fail.

No person is a soulwinner who is not an expert in the ministry of prayer. "It is the duty of ministers," said McCheyne, "to begin the reformation of religion and manner with themselves, their families, etc., with confession of past sin, and with earnest prayer for direction, grace, and full purpose of heart." He began with himself, with the following resolution, under the heading of "Reformation in Secret Prayer":

> I ought not to omit any of the parts of prayer—confession, adoration, thanksgiving, petition, and intercession. Proceeding from low views of God and His law, slight views of my heart, and the sin of my past life, there is a fearful tendency to omit *confession*. This must be resisted. There is a constant tendency to omit *adoration* when I forget to

whom I am speaking, when I rush heedlessly into the presence of Jehovah without thought of His awe-inspiring name and character. When I have little eyesight for His glory, and little admiration of His wonders, my heart has a native tendency to omit giving *thanks*, and yet it is specially commanded. Often when the heart is dead to the salvation of others, I omit *intercession*, and yet it especially is the spirit of the great Advocate who has the name of Israel on His heart.

I ought to pray before seeing anyone. Often when I sleep long or meet with others early, and then have family prayer and breakfast and forenoon callers, it is eleven or twelve o'clock before I begin secret prayer. This is a wretched system; it is unscriptural. Christ rose before day and went into a solitary place. David said, *"Early will I seek thee"* (Ps. 63:1), and, *"My voice shalt thou hear in the morning"* (Ps. 5:3). Mary Magdalene came to the sepulchre while it was yet dark.

Family prayer loses much of the power and sweetness of prayer; and I can do no good to those who come to seek from me if I have forgotten my time alone with God in the early morning. The conscience feels guilty, the soul unfed, the lamp not trimmed. (See Matthew 25:1–13.) I feel it is far better to begin with God, to see His face first, to get my soul near Him before it is near another. *"When I awake, I am still with thee"* (Ps. 139:18). If I have slept too long, or if I am going on an early journey, or if my time is in any way shortened, it is best to dress hurriedly and have a few minutes alone with God than to give up all for lost. But, in general, it is best to have at least one hour alone with God before engaging in anything else. I ought to spend the best hours of the day in communion with God. When I awake in the night, I ought to rise and pray as John Welch and David did.

McCheyne believed in being always in prayer; and his fruitful life, short though that life was, affords an illustration of the power that comes from long and frequent visits to the secret place where we keep tryst with our Lord.

Secret praying is the test, the gauge, the preserver of man's relation to God. The prayer chamber, while it is the test of the sincerity of our devotion to God, becomes also the measure of the devotion. The self-denial, the sacrifices that we make for our prayer chambers, the frequency of our visits to that hallowed place of meeting with the Lord, the lingering to stay, the loathsomeness to leave, are values that we put on communion alone with God; they are the price we pay for the Spirit's hours of heavenly love.

When the prayer chambers of saints are closed or are entered casually or coldly, then church rulers are secular, fleshly, materialistic; spiritual character sinks to a low level, and the ministry becomes restrained and enfeebled.

William Wilberforce was high in social position, a member of Parliament, and the friend of the famous statesman William Pitt. His conversion was announced to his friends—to Pitt and others—by letter. He was not called by God to forsake his high social position or to quit Parliament, but he was called to order his life according to the pattern set by Jesus Christ and to give himself to prayer. To read the story of his life is to be impressed with his holiness and his devotion to the claims of the quiet hours alone with God.

In the beginning of his religious career he recorded,

> My chief reasons for a day of secret prayer are that (1) the state of public affairs is very critical and calls for earnest deprecation of the divine displeasure; (2) my station in life is a very difficult one, wherein I am at a loss to know how to act; direction, therefore, should be specially sought from time to time; and (3) I have been graciously supported in difficult situations of a public nature. I have gone out and returned home in safety, and a kind reception has attended me. I would humbly hope, too, that what I am now doing is a proof that God has not withdrawn His Holy Spirit from me. I am covered with mercies.

The recurrence of his birthday led Wilberforce again to review his situation and employment. He wrote,

> I find that books alienate my heart from God as much as anything. I have been framing a plan of study for myself; but let me remember but one thing is needful, that if my heart cannot be kept in a spiritual state without so much prayer, meditation, Scripture reading, etc., as are incompatible with study, I must *seek first* the righteousness of God.

Everything was to be surrendered for spiritual advance.

We also find him saying,

> I fear that I have not studied the Scriptures enough. Surely, in the summer recess, I ought to read the Scriptures

an hour or two every day, besides prayer, devotional reading, and meditation. God will prosper me better if I wait on Him. The experience of all good men shows that, without constant prayer and watchfulness, the life of God in the soul stagnates.

Doddridge's morning and evening devotions were serious matters. Colonel Gardiner always spent hours in prayer in the morning before he went forth. Bonnell practiced private devotions largely morning and evening, and repeated Psalms while both dressing and undressing, in order to raise his mind to heavenly things. I must look to God to make the means effectual. I fear that my devotions are too hurried, that I do not read the Scriptures enough. I must grow in grace; I must love God more; I must feel the power of divine things more. Whether I am more or less learned signifies nothing. Whether even I execute the work that I deem useful is comparatively unimportant. But beware, my soul, of lukewarmness.

The New Year began with Holy Communion and new vows. "I will press forward," wrote Wilberforce,

and labor to know God better and love Him more. Assuredly I may, because God will give His Holy Spirit to them that ask Him (see Luke 11:13), and the Holy Spirit will shed abroad the love of God in the heart. (See Romans 5:5.) Oh, then, pray, pray; be earnest, press forward (see Philippians 3:14) and follow on to know the Lord. (See Hosea 6:3.) Without watchfulness, humiliation, and prayer, the sense of divine things must languish.

To prepare for the future, he said he found nothing more effectual than private prayer and the serious perusal of the New Testament.

And again he wrote.

I must put down that I have lately too little time for private devotions. I can sadly confirm Doddridge's remark that when we go on ill in the prayer closet, we commonly do so everywhere else. I must mend here. I am afraid of getting into what Owen calls the trade of sinning and repenting. Lord, help me; the shortening of private devotions starves the soul; it grows lean and faint. This must not be. I must redeem more time. I see how lean in spirit I become without full allowance of time for private devotions; I must be careful to be watching unto prayer.

At another time Wilberforce put on record,

> I must try what I long ago heard was the rule of E———
> the great upholsterer, who, when he came from Bond Street
> to his little villa, always first retired to his closet. I have been
> keeping too late hours, and hence have had but a hurried half
> hour to myself. Surely the experience of all good men con-
> firms the proposition, that without due measure of private
> devotions, the soul will grow lean.

To his son he wrote,

> Let me implore you not to be seduced into neglecting,
> curtailing, or hurrying over your morning prayers. Of all
> things, guard against neglecting God in the prayer closet.
> There is nothing more fatal to the life and power of religion.
> More solitude and earlier hours—prayer three times a day, at
> least. How much better might I serve if I cultivated a closer
> communion with God!

Wilberforce knew the secret of a holy life. Is that not where
most of us fail? We are so busy with other things, so immersed
even in doing good and in carrying out the Lord's work, that we
neglect the quiet seasons of prayer with God; and before we are
aware of it, our souls are lean and impoverished.

The prayer chamber conserves our relation to God. It hems
every raw edge; it tucks up every flowing and entangling garment
(see 2 Timothy 2:4); it girds up every fainting loin. (See 1 Peter
1:13.) The sheet anchor[5] does not hold the ship more surely and
safely than the prayer chamber holds us to God. Satan has to break
our hold on, and close up our way to, the prayer chambers, before
he can break our hold on God or close up our way to heaven.

"One night alone in prayer," said Spurgeon,

> might make us new men, changed from poverty of soul to spiri-
> tual wealth, from trembling to triumphing. We have an exam-
> ple of it in the life of Jacob. He was once the crafty shuffler,
> always bargaining and calculating, unlovely in almost every re-
> spect. Yet, one night in prayer turned the supplanter into a
> prevailing prince, and robed him with celestial grandeur. From

---

[5] Sheet anchor: a large, strong anchor formerly carried in a ship and used as a spare in
emergencies.

that night, he lived on the sacred page as one of the nobility of heaven. Could we not, at least now and then, in these weary earthbound years, hedge about a single night for such enriching traffic with the skies?

What, have we no sacred ambition? Are we deaf to the yearnings of divine love? Yet, my fellow believers, men will cheerfully quit their warm couches for wealth and for science. Can we not do it now and again for the love of God and the good of souls? Where is our zeal, our gratitude, our sincerity? I am ashamed while I thus upbraid both myself and you. May we often tarry at Jabbok,[6] and cry with Jacob, as he grasped the angel—

> With thee all night I mean to stay,
> And wrestle till the break of day.

Surely, brethren, if we have given whole days to folly, we can afford a space for heavenly wisdom.

There was a time when we gave whole nights to chambering[7] and wantonness, to dancing and the world's revelry; we did not tire then; we were chiding the sun that he rose so soon, and wishing the hours would lag awhile that we might delight in wilder merriment and perhaps deeper sin. Oh, why then do we weary in heavenly employments? Why do we grow weary when asked to watch with our Lord? Up, sluggish heart, Jesus calls you! Rise and go forth to meet the heavenly Friend in the place where He manifests Himself.

We can never expect to grow in the likeness of our Lord unless we follow His example and give more time to communion with the Father. A revival of real praying would produce a spiritual revolution.

> Be not afraid to pray; to pray is right;
>   Pray if thou canst with hope, but ever pray,
> Though hope be weak or sick with long delay;
>   Pray in the darkness if there be no light;
> And if for any wish thou dare not pray
>   Then pray to God to cast that wish away.

---

[6] Jabbok: the river near which Jacob wrestled through the night with God; a tributary of the Jordan River.

[7] Chambering: lewd and immodest behavior.

8

Praying Men and Personal Purity

Let me burn out for God. After all, whatever God may appoint, prayer is the great thing. Oh, that I may be a man of prayer!
—Henry Martyn

MEN of Wilberforce's character are needed today—praying men, who know how to give themselves to the greatest task demanding their time and their attention, men who can give their whole heart to the holy task of intercession, men who can pray through. God's cause is committed to men; indeed, God commits Himself to men. Praying men are the vicegerents[8] of God; they do His work and carry out His plans.

Yet men, in general, have quit praying. They are too busy to pray. Time and strength and every faculty are given over to money, to business, to the affairs of the world. Few men expend themselves in great praying. The great business of praying is a hurried, petty, starved, beggarly business with most men.

Better praying and more of it—that is what we need. We need holier men, and more of them, holier women, and more of them to pray—women like Hannah, who, out of their greatest griefs and temptations brew their greatest prayers. (See 1 Samuel 1.) We are obliged to pray if we are citizens of God's kingdom. Prayerlessness is banishment, or worse, from God's kingdom. It is outlawry, a high crime, a constitutional breach. The Christian who relegates prayer to a subordinate place in his life soon loses whatever spiritual zeal

---

[8] Vicegerent: an administrative deputy of a king or magistrate.

he may once have possessed; and the church that makes little of prayer cannot maintain vital piety, and is powerless to advance the Gospel. The Gospel cannot live, fight, or conquer without prayer— prayer that is unceasing, instant, and ardent.

That the men in Paul's time had quit praying we cannot certainly affirm. Yet Paul called a halt, and laid a levy on men for prayer. "Put the men to praying" was Paul's unfailing remedy for great evils in the church, in the state, in business, and in the home. Put the men to praying, then politics will be cleansed, business will be thriftier, the church will be holier, the home will be sweeter.

> *I exhort therefore, that, first of all, supplications, prayers, intercessions, and giving of thanks, be made for all men; for kings, and for all that are in authority; that we may lead a quiet and peaceable life in all godliness and honesty. For this is good and acceptable in the sight of God our Saviour....I will* [or, desire] *therefore that men pray every where, lifting up holy hands, without wrath and doubting.* (1 Tim. 2:1-3, 8)

Praying women and children are invaluable to God, but if their praying is not supplemented by praying men, there will be a great loss in the power of prayer—a great breach and depreciation in the value of prayer, a great paralysis in the energy of the Gospel. As we have noted, Jesus Christ spoke a parable to the people, telling them that men ought always to pray and not faint (Luke 18:1). Men who are strong in everything else ought to be strong in prayer, and never yield to discouragement, weakness, or depression. Men who are brave, persistent, and respectable in other pursuits ought to be full of courage, unfainting, and strong-hearted in prayer.

Men are to pray; *all men* are to pray. Men, as distinguished from women, men in their strength, in their wisdom. Jesus presented an absolute, specific command that men should pray; it is an absolute, imperative necessity that men pray. The first of beings, man, should also be first in prayer.

The *men* are to pray for men. The direction in 1 Timothy is specific and classified. Just underneath it, however, we have a specific direction with regard to women. (See 1 Timothy 2:9–12.) The Bible here deals with the men in contrast to, and distinct from, the women, in relation to prayer, its importance, its wideness, and its practice. The men are definitely commanded, seriously charged, and strongly exhorted to pray. Perhaps it was that men were averse to prayer, or indifferent to it; it may be that they deemed it a small thing, and gave to it neither time nor value nor significance. But God would have all men pray, and so the great apostle lifted the subject into prominence and emphasized its importance.

Prayer is of transcendent importance, for it is the mightiest agent to advance God's work. The cause of God has no commercial age, no cultured age, no age of education, no age of money. But it has one golden age, and that is the age of prayer. Only praying hearts and hands can do God's work. When its leaders are men of prayer, when prayer is the prevailing element of worship, like incense that gives continual fragrance to its service, then the cause of God will be triumphant.

Prayer succeeds when all else fails. Prayer has won great victories and has rescued, with notable triumph, God's saints when every other hope was gone. Men who know how to pray are the greatest boon God can give to earth—they are the richest gift earth can offer heaven. Men who know how to use this weapon of prayer are God's best soldiers, His mightiest leaders.

Praying men are also God's chosen leaders. The distinction between the leaders that God brings to the front to lead and bless His people, and those leaders who owe their position of leadership to a worldly, selfish, unsanctified selection, is this: God's leaders are preeminently men of prayer. This distinguishes them as the simple, divine affirmation of their call, the seal of their separation by God. Whatever other graces or gifts they may have, the grace and gift of prayer towers above them all. In whatever else they may share or differ, in the gift of prayer they are one.

What would God's leaders be without prayer? Strip Moses of his power in prayer, a gift that made him eminent in the eyes of the heathen, and the crown is taken from his head, the food and fire of his faith are gone. Elijah, without his praying, would have neither record nor place in the divine legacy—his life would have been insipid and cowardly; its energy, defiance, and fire would have disappeared. Without Elijah's praying, the Jordan would never have yielded to the stroke of his mantle (see 2 Kings 2:6–8), nor would the stern angel of death have honored him with the chariot and horses of fire. (See verses 9–11.) The argument that God used to quiet the fears of Ananias and convince him of Paul's condition and sincerity (see Acts 9:10–15) is the epitome of Paul's history, the answer to his life and work: *"Behold, he prayeth"* (v. 11).

Paul, Luther, Wesley—what would these chosen ones of God be without the distinguishing and controlling element of prayer? They were leaders for God because they were mighty in prayer. They were not leaders because of brilliancy in thought, nor because of their exhaustless resources, their magnificent culture, or their natural endowment; but they were leaders because, by the power of prayer, they could command the power of God. *Praying men* means much more than "men who pray by habit." It means "men with whom prayer is a mighty force," an energy that moves heaven and pours untold treasures of good on earth.

Praying men are the men who have done so much for God in the past. They are the ones who have won the victories for God, and spoiled His foes. They are the ones who have set up His kingdom in the very camps of His enemies. It is no different today; there are no other conditions of success for our times. This century has no law that will suspend the necessity or force of prayer—no substitute by which its gracious ends can be secured.

Praying men keep the church safe from the materialism that is affecting all its plans and policies, and that is hardening its life-blood. By this I mean that the secret and poisonous insinuation circulates, that the church is not so dependent on purely spiritual forces as it used to be—that changed times and changed conditions have brought it out of its spiritual straits and dependencies and put it where other forces can bear it to its climax.

A fatal snare of this kind has allured the church into worldly embraces, dazzled her leaders, weakened her foundations, and deprived her of much of her beauty and strength. Praying men are the saviors of the church from this material tendency. They pour into it the original spiritual forces, lift it off the sandbars of materialism, and press it out into the ocean depths of spiritual power. Praying men keep God in the church in full force, keep His hand on the helm, and train the church in strength and trust.

The world is coming into the church at many points and in many ways. It oozes in; it pours in; it comes in with brazen front or soft, insinuating disguise; it comes in at the top and comes in at the bottom; and it percolates through many a hidden way. The only protection or rescue that we have from worldliness lies in our intense and radical spirituality; and our only hope for the existence and maintenance of this high, saving spirituality, under God, is in the purest and most aggressive leadership—a leadership that knows the secret power of prayer, the sign by which the church has conquered; and a leadership that has conscience, conviction, and courage to hold true to its symbols, true to its traditions, and true to the hidden resources of its power.

We need this prayerful leadership; we must have it, so that, by the perfection and beauty of its holiness, by the strength and elevation of its faith, by the potency and pressure of its prayers, by the authority and spotlessness of its example, by the fire and contagion of its zeal, by the singularity, sublimity, and unworldliness of its piety, it may influence God, and hold and mold the church to its heavenly pattern.

How mightily such leaders are felt! How their flame arouses the church! How they stir it by the force of their Pentecostal presence! How they embattle and give victory by the conflicts and triumphs of their own faith! How they fashion it by the impress and importunity of their prayers! How they inoculate it by the contagion and fire of their holiness! How they lead the march in great spiritual revolutions! How the church is raised from the dead by the resurrection call of their sermons! Holiness emerges in their wake as flowers at the voice of spring; and where they tread, the desert blooms as the garden of the Lord. (See Isaiah 35:1.) God's cause demands such leaders along the whole line of official position, from subordinate to superior. How feeble, aimless, or worldly are our efforts; how demoralized and worthless for God's work are we without them!

These leaders are not given as a result of any power on the part of the church. They are God's gifts. Their being, their presence, their number, and their ability are the tokens of His favor; their lack the sure sign of His disfavor, the indication of His withdrawal. Let the church of God be on her knees before the Lord of Hosts, that He may more mightily endow the leaders we already have, and put others in rank, and lead all along the line of our embattled front.

We are left with this: only praying hands can build for God. They are God's mighty ones on earth, His master builders. They may be destitute of all else, but with the wrestlings and prevailings of a simple-hearted faith, they are mighty—the mightiest for God. Church leaders may be gifted in all else, but without this greatest of gifts, they are as Samson shorn of his locks, or as the temple without the divine presence or the divine glory and on whose altars the heavenly flame has died.

Praying men are needed in all fields of spiritual labor. There is no position in the church of God, high or low, that can be well filled without earnest prayer. There is no position where Christians are found that does not demand the full play of a faith that always prays and never faints. Praying men are needed in the house of business, as well as in the house of God, that they may order and direct trade, not according to the maxims of this world, but according to Bible precepts and the maxims of the heavenly life.

The number and efficiency of God's laborers in all lands is dependent on the men of prayer. By a divinely arranged process, the mightiness of these men of prayer increases the number and success of their consecrated labors. Prayer opens wide their doors of access, gives holy aptness to enter, and leads to holy boldness, firmness, and fruit.

Men of prayer are needed especially in the positions of church influence, honor, and power. These leaders of church thought, of church work, and of church life should be men of demonstrated power in prayer. It is the praying heart that sanctifies the toil and skill of the hands, and the toil and wisdom of the mind. Prayer keeps work in the line of God's will, and keeps thought in the line of God's Word. The solemn responsibilities of leadership in God's church, in a large or limited sphere, should be so hedged about with prayer that between it and the world there should be an impassable gulf; they should be so elevated and purified by prayer that neither cloud nor night can stain the radiance or dim the sight of a constant, elevated view of God.

Many church leaders seem to think that if they can be prominent as men of business, of money or influence, of thought, of plans, of scholarly attainments, of eloquent gifts, of conspicuous activities, that these are enough, and will atone for the absence of the higher spiritual power that only much praying can give. But how vain and paltry are these achievements in the serious work of bringing glory to God, controlling the church for Him, and bringing it into full accord with its divine mission!

We are looking for praying men and holy men—men of purity, whose presence in the church will make it like a censer of holiest incense flaming up to God. With God, the man counts for everything. Rites, forms, and organizations have little meaning; unless they are backed by the holiness of the man, they are offensive in God's sight.

*Incense is an abomination unto me; the new moons and sab-
baths, the calling of assemblies, I cannot away with; it is iniquity, even the solemn meeting.* (Isa. 1:13)

Why has God spoken so strongly against His own ordinances?
Because personal purity has failed. The impure man has tainted all
the sacred institutions of God and defiled them. Men have built
Him glorious temples and have striven and exhausted themselves
to please God by all manner of gifts; but in lofty strains He has rebuked these proud worshippers and rejected their princely gifts:

*Heaven is my throne, and the earth is my footstool: where is
the house that ye build unto me? and where is the place of my
rest? For all those things hath mine hand made, and all those
things have been, saith the LORD....He that killeth an ox is as
if he slew a man; he that sacrificeth a lamb, as if he cut off a
dog's neck; he that offereth an oblation, as if he offered
swine's blood; he that burneth incense, as if he blessed an idol.*
(Isa. 66:1–3)

Turning away in disgust from these costly and profane offerings,
He declares, *"But to this man will I look, even to him that is poor
and of a contrite spirit, and trembleth at my word"* (v. 2).

This truth is fundamental, that God regards the personal purity of the man more than He regards any sacrifice or any ceremony. In fact, God has given so much regard to men that He has
put a kind of discount on all else. This truth suffers when ordinances are made much of and forms of worship multiply. The man
and his spiritual character depreciate as church ceremonies increase. The simplicity of worship is lost in religious aesthetics, or in
the gaudiness of religious forms.

This truth that the personal purity of the individual is the only
thing for which God cares, is lost sight of when the church begins
to value men for what they have. When the church in any way eyes
a man's money, social standing, or belongings, then spiritual values
are at a fearful discount; and the tears of penitence, the heaviness
of guilt, are never seen at her portals. Worldly bribes have opened
and stained the pearly gates of the church by the entrance of the
impure.

This truth that God is looking for personal purity is swallowed
up when the church has a greed for numbers. "Not numbers, but

61

personal purity is our aim," said the fathers of Methodism. The parading of church statistics runs strongly against the grain of spiritual religion. Eyeing numbers greatly hinders the looking after personal purity. The increase of quantity is generally at a loss of quality. Bulk lessens preciousness.

The age of church organization and church machinery is not an age noted for elevated and strong personal piety. Machinery looks for engineers, and organizations look for managers or generals; but neither looks for saints to run its affairs. The simplest organization may aid purity as well as strength; but beyond that narrow limit, organizations swallow up the individual, and they are careless of personal purity. Activity, enthusiasm, and zeal for the organization of the church, come in as the vicious substitutes for spiritual character. Holiness and spiritual graces are discarded as too slow and too costly for the progress and rush of the age. Because of machinery, new organizations, and spiritual weakness, results are vainly expected to be secured that can only be secured by faith, prayer, and waiting on God.

The man and his spiritual character are what God is looking after. If men, holy men, can be turned out readier and better by the easy processes of church machinery than by the old-time processes, we would gladly invest in every new and improved patent; but we do not believe it. We adhere to the old way, the way the holy prophets went, the King's highway of holiness. (See Isaiah 35:8.)

So, once more, let us apply the emphasis and repeat that the great need of the church in this and all ages is for men of such commanding faith, of such unsullied holiness, of such marked spiritual vigor and consuming zeal, that they will work spiritual revolutions through their mighty praying. As someone has said,

> Natural ability and educational advantages do not figure as factors in this matter; but a capacity for faith, the ability to pray, the power of a thorough consecration, the ability of self-littleness, an absolute losing of oneself in God's glory, and an ever present and insatiable yearning and seeking after all the fullness of God. Our need is for men who can set the church ablaze for God, not in a noisy, showy way, but with an intense and quiet heat that melts and moves everything for God.

9

The Possibilities
of Prayer

More things are wrought by prayer
Than this world dreams of. Wherefore, let thy voice
Rise like a fountain for me night and day.
For what are men better than sheep or goats,
That nourish a blind life within the brain,
If, knowing God, they lift not hands of prayer
Both for themselves and those who call them friend?
For so the whole round earth is every way
Bound by gold chains about the feet of God.
                              —Alfred, Lord Tennyson

IT may be said with emphasis that no lazy saint prays. Can there be a lazy saint? Can there be a prayerless saint? Does not slack praying cut short sainthood's crown and kingdom? Can there be a cowardly soldier? Can there be a saintly hypocrite? Can there be virtuous vice? It is only when these impossibilities are brought into being that we then can find a prayerless saint.

To go through the motion of praying is a dull business, though not a difficult one. To say prayers in a decent, delicate way is not heavy work. But to really pray, to pray until hell feels the ponderous stroke, to pray until the iron gates of difficulty are opened, to pray until the mountains of obstacles are removed, or until the mists are exhaled and the clouds are lifted, and the sunshine of a cloudless day brightens—this is hard work, but it is God's work and man's best labor. Never was the toil of hand, head, and heart less spent in vain than when praying.

It may be difficult to wait and press and pray, and hear no voice, but you must stay until God answers. The joy of answered prayer is the joy of a travailing mother when a son is born into the world, the joy of a slave whose chains have been burst asunder and to whom new life and liberty have just come.

It is not an easy thing to pray. Behind the praying, all the conditions of prayer must be met. These conditions are possible, but they are not to be seized in a moment by the prayerless. Of course, they may exist in the faithful and holy, but they cannot exist in or be met by a frivolous, negligent, laggard spirit.

Prayer does not stand alone. It is not an isolated performance. Prayer stands in closest connection with all the duties of an ardent piety. It comes as a result of a vigorous and commanding faith. Prayer honors God, acknowledges His being, exalts His power, adores His providence, secures His aid. But to pray well is to do all things well. A sneering half-rationalism cries out against devotion, that it does nothing but pray. If it is true that devotion does nothing but pray, then it does nothing at all. To do nothing but pray fails to do the praying, for the antecedent, coincident, and subsequent conditions of prayer are but the sum of all the energized forces of a practical, working piety.

Prayer, like faith, obtains promises, enlarges their operation, and adds to the measure of their results. The possibilities of prayer run parallel with the promises of God. Prayer opens an outlet for the promises, removes the hindrances in the way of their execution, puts them into working order, and secures their gracious ends. God's promises were to Abraham and to his seed, but a barren womb and many obstacles stood in the way of the fulfillment of these promises; nevertheless, prayer removed them all, made a highway for the promises, added to the facility and speediness of their realization; and by prayer the promise shone bright and perfect in its execution.

The possibilities of prayer are found in its alliance with the purposes of God, for God's purposes and man's praying are the combination of all potent and omnipotent forces. More than this, the possibilities of prayer are seen in the fact that prayer changes the purposes of God. It is in the very nature of prayer to plead and give directions. Prayer is not a negation; it is a positive force. It never rebels against the will of God, never comes into conflict with that will, but it is evident that it does seek to change God's purposes.

Christ said, *"The cup which my Father hath given me, shall I not drink it?"* (John 18:11), and yet He had prayed that very night, *"If it be possible, let this cup pass from me"* (Matt. 26:39). Paul sought to change the purposes of God about the thorn in his flesh. (See 2 Corinthians 12:7–9.) God was set on destroying Israel, and the prayer of Moses changed the purposes of God and saved the nation. (See Deuteronomy 9:12–21.) In the time of the judges, the people of Israel were apostate and greatly oppressed. They repented and cried unto God, and He said, *"Ye have forsaken me, and served other gods: wherefore I will deliver you no more"* (Judg. 10:13). But they humbled themselves and put away their strange gods, and God's *"soul was grieved for the misery of Israel"* (v. 16). In His mercy, He sent them deliverance by Jephthah.

God sent Isaiah to say to Hezekiah, *"Set thine house in order; for thou shalt die, and not live"* (2 Kings 20:1). So Hezekiah prayed, and God sent Isaiah back to say, *"I have heard thy prayer, I have seen thy tears: behold…I will add unto thy days fifteen years"* (vv. 5–6).

"Yet forty days, and Nineveh shall be overthrown" (Jonah 3:4) was God's message by Jonah. But Nineveh cried mightily to God, and *"God repented of the evil, that he had said that he would do unto them; and he did it not"* (v. 10).

The possibilities of prayer may be seen from the various conditions it reaches and the diverse ends it secures. Elijah prayed over a dead child, and he came to life; Elisha did the same thing. Christ prayed at Lazarus' grave, and Lazarus came forth. Peter kneeled down and prayed beside dead Dorcas, and she opened her eyes and sat up; and Peter presented her alive to the distressed company. Paul prayed for Publius' father and he was healed. Jacob's praying changed Esau's murderous hate into the kisses of the tenderest brotherly embrace.

God gave Jacob and Esau to Rebecca because Isaac prayed for her. Joseph was the child of Rachel's prayers. Hannah's praying gave Samuel to Israel. John the Baptist was given to Elizabeth, barren and past the age of childbearing, in answer to the prayer of Zacharias. Elisha's praying brought famine or harvest to Israel; as he prayed, so it was. Ezra's praying carried the Spirit of God in heartbreaking conviction to the entire city of Jerusalem, and brought them, in tears of repentance, back to God. Isaiah's praying carried the shadow of the sun back ten degrees on the dial of Ahaz.

In answer to Hezekiah's praying, an angel slew one hundred and eighty-five thousand of Sennacherib's army in one night. Daniel's praying opened to him the vision of prophecy, helped him to administer the affairs of a mighty kingdom, and sent an angel to shut the lions' mouths. The angel was sent to Cornelius, and the Gospel was opened through Cornelius to the Gentile world, because his *"prayers and...alms* [had become] *a memorial before God"* (Acts 10:4).

"And what shall I more say? for the time would fail me to tell of Gedeon, and of Barak, and of Samson, and of Jephthae; of David also, and Samuel, and of the prophets" (Heb. 11:32); of Paul and Peter, and John and the apostles, and the holy company of saints, reformers, and martyrs, who, through praying,

> *subdued kingdoms, wrought righteousness, obtained promises, stopped the mouths of lions, quenched the violence of fire, escaped the edge of the sword, out of weakness were made strong, waxed valiant in fight, turned to flight the armies of the aliens.*   *(Heb. 11:33–34)*

Prayer puts God in the matter with commanding force: *"Ask me of things to come concerning my sons,"* says God, *"and concerning the work of my hands command ye me"* (Isa. 45:11). We are charged in God's Word *"always to pray"* (Luke 18:1), *"in every thing by prayer"* (Phil. 4:6), *"continuing instant in prayer"* (Rom. 12:12), to *"pray every where"* (1 Tim. 2:8), *"praying always"* (Eph. 6:18). And the promise is as immeasurable as the command is comprehensive: *"All things, whatsoever ye shall ask in prayer, believing, ye shall receive"* (Matt. 21:22); *"whatsoever ye shall ask in my name, that will I do"* (John 14:13); *"if ye shall ask any thing"* (v. 14); *"ye shall ask what ye will, and it shall be done unto you"* (John 15:7); *"whatsoever ye shall ask the Father...he will give it you"* (John 16:23).

If there is anything not involved in the words *all things whatsoever,* or not found in the phrase *ask anything,* then these things may be left out of prayer. Language could not cover a wider range, nor involve more fully all of the smallest details. These statements are only samples of the all-comprehending possibilities of prayer under the promises of God to those who meet the conditions of right praying.

These passages, though, give only a general outline of the immense regions over which prayer extends its influence. Beyond these, the effects of prayer reach and secure good from regions that cannot be traversed by language or thought.

Paul exhausted both language and thought in praying; but, being conscious of necessities not covered and realms of good not reached, he covered these impenetrable and undiscovered regions by this general plea: *"Unto him that is able to do exceeding abundantly above all that we ask or think, according to the power that worketh in us"* (Eph. 3:20). The promise is, *"Call unto me, and I will answer thee, and show thee great and mighty things, which thou knowest not"* (Jer. 33:3).

James declared that *"the effectual fervent prayer of a righteous man availeth much"* (James 5:16). There was much that he could not put into words, but he illustrated the idea by the power of Old Testament praying. In this way, he stirred up New Testament saints to imitate, by the fervor and influence of their praying, the holy men of old, and to duplicate and surpass the power of their praying. Elijah, said James,

> was a man subject to like passions as we are, and he prayed
> earnestly that it might not rain: and it rained not on the earth
> by the space of three years and six months. And he prayed
> again, and the heaven gave rain, and the earth brought forth
> her fruit.   (James 5:17–18)

In the Revelation of John, the whole lower order of God's creation and His providential government, the church and the angelic world, are in an attitude of waiting. They are waiting for the efficiency of the prayers of the saints on earth to carry out the various interests of earth and heaven. The angel takes the fire kindled by prayer and casts it earthward, *"and there were voices, and thunderings, and lightings, and an earthquake"* (Rev. 8:5). Prayer is the force that creates all these alarms, disturbances, and struggles. *"Ask of me,"* says God to His Son, and to the church of His Son, *"and I shall give thee the heathen for thine inheritance, and the uttermost parts of the earth for thy possession"* (Ps. 2:8).

The men who have done mighty things for God have always been mighty in prayer, have well understood the possibilities of prayer, and have made the most of these possibilities. The Son of God, the first of all and the mightiest of all, has shown us the all-powerful and far-reaching possibilities of prayer. Paul was mighty for God because he knew how to use, and how to get others to use, the mighty spiritual forces of prayer.

The seraphim, burning, sleepless, adoring, is the emblem of prayer. (See Isaiah 6:1–7.) It is resistless in its ardor, devoted and tireless. There are hindrances to prayer that nothing but pure, intense flame can surmount. There are toils and outlays and endurance that nothing but the strongest, most ardent flame can withstand. Prayer may be low-tongued, but it cannot be cold-tongued. Its words may be few, but they must be on fire. Its feelings may not be impetuous, but they must be white with heat. It is the *"effectual fervent prayer"* (James 5:16) that influences God.

When prayer fails, the world prevails. When prayer fails, the church loses its divine characteristics, its divine power; the church is swallowed up by a proud ecclesiasticism, and the world scoffs at its obvious impotence.

God's house is the house of prayer (see Isaiah 56:7); God's work is the work of prayer. It is the zeal for God's house (see Psalm 69:9) and the zeal for God's work that make God's house glorious and His work abide.

10

Prayerless Praying

We ought to give ourselves to God with regard to things both temporal and spiritual, and seek our satisfaction only in the fulfilling of His will, whether He leads us by suffering, or by consolation, for all would be equal to a soul truly resigned. Prayer is nothing else but a sense of God's presence.
—*Brother Lawrence*

WHY do we not pray? What are the hindrances to prayer? These are not curious or trivial questions. They reach not only to the whole matter of our praying, but also to the whole matter of our religion. Religion is bound to decline when praying is hindered. That which hinders praying, hinders religion. He who is too busy to pray will be too busy to live a holy life.

Other duties often become pressing and absorbing and crowd out prayer. If an inquest could be secured on this dire, spiritual calamity, the coroner's verdict, in many cases of dead praying, would be, "Choked to death." This way of hindering prayer has become so natural, so easy, so innocent, that it comes on us without warning. If we will once allow our praying to be crowded out, it will always be crowded out.

More than anything else, Satan wants us to let the grass grow on the path to our prayer chamber. A vacant chamber of prayer means that a believer has gone out of business religiously, or, what is worse, has made a change and is carrying out our religion in some other name than God's and to somebody else's glory. In the business of religion, God's glory is only secured when we practice that religion with a large capital of prayer.

The apostles understood this when they declared that their time must not be employed in even the sacred duties of almsgiving; they must give themselves, they said, *"continually to prayer, and to the ministry of the word"* (Acts 6:4); prayer was put first with them, and the ministry of the Word derived its efficiency and life from prayer.

The process of hindering prayer by crowding it out is simple and goes in stages, one after the other. First, one hurries through prayer. Unrest and agitation, which are fatal to all devout exercises, come in. Then the time one spends at prayer is shortened, while one's inclination for the exercise dwindles. Then prayer is crowded into a corner and depends on fragments of time for its exercise. Its value depreciates. By this point, the duty has lost its importance. It no longer commands respect or brings any benefit. It has fallen out of esteem, out of the heart, out of the habits, out of the life. When one ceases to pray, he ceases to live spiritually.

There is no defense against the desolating floods of worldliness and business and cares, except prayer. Christ meant this when He charged us to *"watch and pray"* (Matt. 26:41). There is no pioneering corps for the Gospel except prayer. Paul knew this when he declared that *"night and day* [we pray] *exceedingly that we might see your face, and might perfect that which is lacking in your faith"* (1 Thess. 3:10). There is no arriving at a high state of grace without much praying, and there is no staying in those high altitudes without great praying. Epaphras knew this when he labored *"fervently...in prayers"* for the Colossian church, *"that* [they might] *stand perfect and complete in all the will of God"* (Col. 4:12).

The only way to preserve our praying from being hindered is to regard prayer at its true and high value. We must esteem it as Daniel did, who,

> *when* [he] *knew that the writing was signed, he went into his house; and his windows being opened in his chamber toward Jerusalem, he kneeled upon his knees three times a day, and prayed, and gave thanks before his God, as he did aforetime.*
>
> *(Dan. 6:10)*

Set a high value on praying, as Daniel did, above prestige, honor, leisure, wealth, or life. Make praying one of your habits, as Daniel did. The phrase *as he did aforetime* has much in it to give firmness and fidelity in the hour of trial, much in it to remove hindrances and to master opposing circumstances.

One of Satan's wiliest tricks is to destroy the best by the good. Business and other duties are good, but we are so filled with these that they crowd out and destroy the best. Prayer holds the citadel for God; and if Satan can by any means weaken prayer, he has succeeded so far. When prayer is dead, the citadel is taken. We must keep prayer in the same way that the faithful sentinel keeps guard—with sleepless vigilance. We must not keep it half-starved and feeble as a baby, but we must keep it in giant strength. Our prayer chamber should have our freshest strength, our calmest time; its hours should be unfettered, without intrusion, without haste.

Having a private place and plenty of time in which to pray, is the life of prayer. To kneel upon our knees three times a day and pray and give thanks before God as we did aforetime (see Daniel 6:10), is the very heart and soul of religion, and makes men, like Daniel, of *"an excellent spirit"* (Dan. 5:12; 6:3), *"greatly beloved"* (Dan. 10:11) in heaven.

The greatness of prayer, in the most intense form, is not realized without spiritual discipline, because it involves the whole man. Richard Cecil has said, "Prayer is faith passing into act—a union of the will and intellect being realized in an intellectual act. It is the whole man that prays. Less than this is wishing or lip service, a sham or a mummery." This makes prayer hard work; and before this exacting and consuming effort, our spiritual sloth or feebleness stands abashed.

The simplicity of prayer and its childlike elements also form a great obstacle to true praying. Intellect gets in the way of the heart. Only the childlike spirit is the spirit of prayer, and it is no easy task to make the man a child again. In song, in poetry, in memory he may wish himself a child again, but in prayer he must be a child again in reality—just as he was at his mother's knee: artless, sweet, intense, direct, trustful; with no shade of doubt, no temper to be denied. He must have a desire that burns and consumes, that can only be voiced by a cry. It is not easy work to have this childlike spirit of prayer.

If praying meant spending only one hour in prayer each day, difficulties would confront and hinder even that hour; but praying is keeping one's whole life in preparation for the prayer closet. How difficult it is to cover home and business, all the sweets and all the bitters of life, with the holy atmosphere of the prayer closet! A holy life is the only preparation for prayer. It is just as difficult to pray as it is to live a holy life.

In this fact we find the reason why a wall of exclusion is built around our prayer closets: men do not love holy praying because they do not love and because they do not determine to live holy lives. Montgomery set forth the difficulties of true praying when he declared the sublimity and simplicity of prayer:

> Prayer is the simplest form of speech
>   That infant lips can try.
> Prayer is the sublimest strains that reach
>   The Majesty on high.

This is not only good poetry, but a profound truth as to the loftiness and simplicity of prayer. There are great difficulties in reaching the exalted, angelic strains of prayer. The difficulty of coming down to the simplicity of infant lips is not much less.

Prayer in the Old Testament is called wrestling. Conflict and skill and strenuous, exhaustive effort are involved. In the New Testament we have the terms *striving, laboring fervently, fervent, effectual, agony,* all indicating that when intense effort is put forth, difficulties are overcome. We, in our praises, sing out—

> What various hindrances we meet
> In coming to a mercy seat.

We have also learned that the gracious results secured by prayer are generally proportional to the effort we put forth in removing the hindrances that obstruct our soul's high communion with God.

Christ said, *"Men ought always to pray, and not to faint"* (Luke 18:1), and He gave us a parable to illustrate this. The parable of the importunate widow teaches the difficulties in praying, how they are to be surmounted, and the happy results that follow from valorous praying. Difficulties will always obstruct the way to the prayer closet as long as it remains true

> That Satan trembles when he sees
> The weakest saint upon his knees.

Courageous faith is made stronger and purer when it masters difficulties. These difficulties simply focus the eye of faith on the glorious prize that is to be won by the successful wrestler in prayer. (See 1 Corinthians 9:24.) Men must not faint in the contest of prayer, but to this high and holy work they must give themselves, defying the difficulties in the way, and thereby experiencing more than an angel's happiness in the results. Luther said, "To have prayed well is to have studied well." More than that, to have prayed well is to have fought well; to have prayed well is to have lived well; to pray well is to die well.

Prayer is a rare gift, not a popular, ready gift. Prayer is not the fruit of natural talents; rather, it is the product of faith, of holiness, of deeply spiritual character. Men learn to pray as they learn to love, for, as Fénelon said, "Perfect prayer is only another name for love." Perfection in simplicity, in humility, in faith—these form its chief ingredients. Novices in these graces cannot be experts in prayer. It cannot be seized upon by untrained hands; only graduates in heaven's highest school of art can touch its finest keys, raise its sweetest, highest notes. For to graduate from the school of prayer is to master the whole course of a religious life. Fine material, fine finish are requisite. Master workmen are required, for mere journeymen cannot execute the work of prayer.

The spirit of prayer should rule our spirits and our conduct. The spirit of the prayer chamber must control our lives, or the hour in the prayer closet will be dull and sapless. Always praying in our spirits, always acting in the spirit of praying—these make our praying strong. The spirit of every moment is that which imparts strength to the communion of the prayer closet. It is what we are outside of the prayer closet that gives victory or brings defeat to the prayer closet. If the spirit of the world prevails in our non-closet hours, the spirit of the world will prevail in our closet hours, and that will be a vain and idle farce.

We must live for God out of the prayer closet if we want to meet God in the prayer closet. We must bless God with praying lives if we want to have God's blessing in the prayer closet. We must do God's will in our lives if we want to have God's ear in the prayer closet. We must listen to God's voice in public if we want God to listen to our voice in private. God must have our hearts out of the prayer closet if we want to have God's presence in the prayer closet. If we want to have God in the prayer closet, God must have us out of the prayer closet. There is no way of praying to God, except by living to God. The prayer closet is not a confessional, simply, but the hour of holy communion, of high and sweet communication, and of intense intercession.

Men would pray better if they lived better. They would get more from God if they lived more obediently and with the intention to please God. We would have more strength and time for the divine work of intercession if we did not have to expend so much strength and time settling old scores and paying our delinquent taxes. Our spiritual liabilities are so greatly in excess of our spiritual assets that our time in the prayer chamber is spent in filing claims for bankruptcy instead of being a time of great spiritual wealth for us and for others. Our prayer closets are too much like the sign that says, "Closed for Repairs."

John said, regarding the praying of the first Christians, *"Whatsoever we ask, we receive of him, because we keep his commandments, and do those things that are pleasing in his sight"* (1 John 3:22). We should note what measureless grounds were covered, what measureless gifts were received, by their strong praying. *"Whatsoever"*—how comprehensive is the range and reception of mighty praying, how suggestive of the reasons for the ability to pray and to have prayers answered! Theirs was obedience, but more than mere obedience; they were doing the things that please God well.

They went to their prayer closets, having been made strong by strict obedience and loving fidelity to God in their conduct. Their lives were not only true and obedient, but they were thinking about things above obedience, searching for and doing things to make God glad. This sort of Christian can come with eager step and radiant countenance to meet his Father in the prayer chamber, not simply to be forgiven, but to be approved and to receive.

It makes much difference whether we come to God as a criminal or a child; to be pardoned or to be approved; to settle scores or to be embraced; for punishment or for favor. Our praying, to be strong, must be buttressed by holy living. The name of Christ must be honored by our lives before it will honor our intercessions. The life of faith perfects the prayer of faith.

Our lives not only give color to our praying, but they give body to it as well. Bad living leads inevitably to bad praying, and we pray feebly because we live feebly. The stream of praying cannot rise higher than the fountain of living. The force of the prayer closet is made up of the energy that flows from the confluent streams of living. Therefore, any feebleness of living will throw its faintness into our prayer chambers. We cannot talk to God strongly when we have not lived for God strongly. The prayer closet cannot be made holy to God when the life has not been holy to God. Note that the Word of God emphasizes how our conduct affects the value of our praying:

> *Then shalt thou call, and the LORD shall answer; thou shalt cry, and he shall say, Here I am. If thou take away from the midst of thee the yoke, the putting forth of the finger, and speaking vanity.* (Isa. 58:9)

Men are to pray, *"lifting up holy hands, without wrath and doubting"* (1 Tim. 2:8). We are to pass the time of our sojourning here in the fear of the Lord if we wish to call on the Father. We cannot divorce praying from conduct. *"Whatsoever we ask, we receive of him, because we keep his commandments, and do those things that are pleasing in his sight"* (1 John 3:22). *"Ye ask, and receive not, because ye ask amiss, that ye may consume it upon your lusts"* (James 4:3). The injunction of Christ, *"Watch and pray"* (Matt. 26:41), is to cover and guard our conduct, that we may come to our prayer closets with all the force secured by a vigilant guard over our lives.

Our religion breaks down most often and most sadly in our conduct. Beautiful theories are marred by ugly lives. The most difficult, as well as the most impressive, point in piety is to live it. Our praying suffers from bad living as much as our religion does. Preachers were charged in earlier times to preach by their lives or to not preach at all. So Christians everywhere ought to be charged to pray by their lives or to not pray at all.

Of course, the prayer of repentance is acceptable; but repentance means to quit doing wrong and learn to do well. A repentance that does not produce a change in conduct is a sham. Praying that does not result in pure conduct is a delusion; it is prayerless.

We have missed the whole office and virtue of praying if it does not rectify our conduct. The very nature of things is that we must either quit praying or quit bad conduct. Cold, dead praying may exist with bad conduct, but cold, dead praying is no praying in God's eyes. Our praying advances in power as it rectifies our lives. A life growing in its purity and devotion will be a more prayerful life.

The pity is that so much of our praying is without an objective or aim. It is without purpose. How much praying there is by men and women who never abide in Christ—hasty praying, sweet praying full of sentiment, pleasing praying, but not backed by a life wedded to Christ! Popular praying! How much of this praying is from unsanctified hearts and unhallowed lips!

For many people, prayers spring into life under the influence of some great excitement, by some pressing emergency, through some popular clamor, or because of some great peril. However, the conditions of prayer are not there. We rush into God's presence and try to link Him to our cause, inflame Him with our passions, move Him by our peril; but all things are to be prayed for with clean hands, with absolute deference to God's will, and by abiding in Christ. Otherwise, our prayers are prayerless.

Prayerless praying by lips and hearts untrained in prayer, by lives out of harmony with Jesus Christ; prayerless praying, which has the form and motion of prayer but is without the true heart of prayer, never moves God to an answer. It is of such praying that James said, *"Ye have not, because ye ask not. Ye ask, and receive not, because ye ask amiss"* (James 4:2–3).

The two great evils—not asking, and asking in a wrong way. Perhaps the greater evil is wrong asking, for it has in it the show of duty done, of praying when there has been no praying—a deceit, a fraud, a sham. The times of the most praying are not really the times of the best praying. The Pharisees prayed much, but they were actuated by vanity; their praying was the symbol of their hypocrisy, by which they made God's house of prayer a den of robbers. (See Matthew 21:13.) Theirs were the prayers of state occasions—mechanical, perfunctory, professional, beautiful in words, fragrant in sentiment, well ordered, well received by the ears that heard, but utterly devoid of every element of real prayer. They acted as formalists, described in the following words from Charles Spurgeon:

> A mere formalist can always pray so as to please himself. What has he to do but to open his book and read the prescribed words, or bow his knee and repeat such phrases as suggest themselves to his memory or his fancy? Like the Tartarian Praying Machine, give but the wind and the wheel, and the business is fully arranged. So much knee-bending and talking, and the prayer is done. The formalist's prayers are always good, or, rather, always bad, alike.

76

"But the living child of God never offers a prayer that pleases himself," continued Spurgeon. "His standard is above his attainments; he wonders that God listens to him, and though he knows he will be heard for Christ's sake, yet he accounts it a wonderful instance of condescending mercy that such poor prayers as his should ever reach the ears of the Lord God of Sabaoth."[9]

The conditions of prayer are well ordered and clear: one of the first necessities, if we are to grasp the infinite possibilities of prayer, is to get rid of prayerless praying. Prayerless praying is often beautiful in words and in execution; it has the drapery of prayer in rich and costly form, but it lacks the soul of praying. It has been said that

> there are no possibilities, no necessity for prayerless praying. A heartless performance, a senseless routine, a dead habit, a hasty, careless performance, it justifies nothing. Prayerless praying has no life, gives no life, is dead, breathes out death. Not a battle-ax, but a child's toy—for play, not for service. Prayerless praying does not come up to the importance and aims of a recreation. Prayerless praying is only a weight, an impediment in the hour of struggle, of intense conflict, a call to retreat in the moment of battle and victory.

We must pray, but we fall so easily into the habit of prayerless service, of merely filling a program. As Richard Cecil put it, "A man may pray night and day and deceive himself."

If only men prayed on all occasions and in every place where they go through the motion! If only there were holy, inflamed hearts behind all these beautiful words and gracious forms! If only there were always uplifted hearts in these "upstanding" men, who are uttering flawless but vain words before God! If only there were always reverent hearts when men on bended knees are uttering words before God to please men's ears!

There is nothing that will preserve the life of prayer—its vigor, sweetness, obligations, seriousness, and value—so much as a deep conviction that prayer is an approach to God, a pleading with God, an asking of God. Reality will then be in it; reverence will then be in the attitude, in the place, and in the air. Faith will draw, kindle, and open. Formality and deadness cannot live in this high and all-serious home of the soul.

---

[9] Sabaoth: armies, as in Romans 9:29 and James 5:4.

Prayerless praying lacks the essential element of true praying; it is not based on desire, and it is devoid of earnestness and faith. Desire burdens the chariot of prayer, and faith drives its wheels. Prayerless praying has no burden, because it has no sense of need; no ardency, because it has none of the vision, strength, or glow of faith. It has no mighty pressure, no holding on to God with the deathless, despairing grasp, *"I will not let thee go, except thou bless me"* (Gen. 32:26). It has no utter self-abandonment, lost in the throes of a desperate, pertinacious, and consuming plea: *"Yet now, if thou wilt forgive their sin—; and if not, blot me, I pray thee, out of thy book"* (Exod. 32:32); or, "Give me Scotland, or may I die."

Prayerless praying stakes nothing on the issue, for it has nothing to stake. It comes with empty hands, indeed, but they are listless hands, as well as empty. They have never learned the lesson of empty hands clinging to the Cross; this lesson, to them, has no form or comeliness. (See Isaiah 53:2.)

Prayerless praying has no heart in its praying. The lack of heart deprives praying of its reality, and makes it an empty and unfit vessel. Heart, soul, life must be in our praying; the heavens must feel the force of our crying, and must be brought into oppressed sympathy for our bitter and needy state. A need that oppresses us, and has no relief but in our crying to God, must voice our praying.

Prayerless praying is insincere. It has no honesty at heart. We name in words what we do not want in heart. Our prayers give formal utterance to the things for which our hearts are not only not hungry, but for which they really have no taste.

I once heard an eminent and saintly preacher, now in heaven, speak abruptly and sharply to a congregation that had just risen from prayer, with the question and statement, "What did you pray for? If God should take hold of you and shake you, and demand what you prayed for, you could not tell Him to save your life what the prayer was that has just died from your lips." So it always is, that prayerless praying has neither memory nor heart. A mere form, a heterogeneous mass, an insipid compound, a mixture thrown together for sound and to fill up time, but with neither heart nor aim, is prayerless praying. A dry routine, a dreary drudge, a dull and heavy task, is this prayerless praying.

But prayerless praying is much worse than either task or drudgery. Indeed, it divorces praying from living; it utters its words against the world, but with heart and life runs into the world; it prays for humility, but nurtures pride; prays for self-denial, while indulging the flesh. Nothing exceeds true praying in its gracious results; but it is better not to pray at all than to pray prayerless prayers, for they are but sinning, and the worst of sinning is to sin on our knees.

The prayer habit is a good habit, but prayer done only by force of habit is a very bad habit. This kind of praying is not conditioned after God's order, nor is it generated by God's power. It is not only a waste, a perversion, and a delusion, but it is also a prolific source of unbelief. Prayerless praying gets no results. God is not reached, self is not helped. It is better not to pray at all than to secure no results from praying—better for the one who prays, better for others.

Men hear of the prodigious results that are to be secured by prayer: the matchless good promised in God's Word to prayer. These keen-eyed worldlings, or timid ones of little faith, mark the great discrepancy between the results promised and results realized, and they are led necessarily to doubt the truth and worth of that which is so big in promise and so beggarly in results. Religion and God are dishonored, doubt and unbelief are strengthened, by much asking and no getting.

In contrast to this, what a mighty force prayerful praying is! Real prayer helps God and man. God's kingdom is advanced by it. The greatest good comes to man by it. Prayer can do anything that God can do. The pity is that we do not believe this as we ought, and we do not put it to the test.

11

Wonderful Results of Prayer

Do not we rest in our day too much on the arm of flesh? Cannot the same wonders be done now as of old? Do not the eyes of the Lord run to and fro throughout the whole earth still to show Himself strong on behalf of those who put their trust in Him? Oh, that God would give me more practical faith in Him! Where is now the Lord God of Elijah? He is waiting for Elijah to call on Him. —James Gilmour

THE preceding chapter closed with the statement that prayer can do anything that God can do. It is a tremendous statement to make, but it is a statement borne out by history and experience. If we are abiding in Christ (and if we abide in Him we are living in obedience to His holy will and can approach God in His name; see John 15:4-11, 16), then there lie open before us the infinite resources of the divine treasure-house.

The man who truly prays gets from God many things denied to the prayerless man. The aim of all real praying is to get the thing prayed for, as the child's cry for bread has for its end the getting of bread. This view removes prayer clean out of the sphere of religious performances. Prayer is not acting a part or going through religious motions. Prayer is neither official nor formal nor ceremonial, but direct, hearty, intense. Prayer is not religious work that must be gone through, and that avails because it is well done. Rather, prayer is the helpless and needy child crying to the compassion of the Father's heart and the bounty and power of the Father's hand. The answer is as sure to come as the Father's heart can be touched and the Father's hand be moved.

The purpose of asking is to receive. The aim of seeking is to find. The goal of knocking is to arouse attention and get in. This is Christ's iterated and reiterated affirmation: the prayer will be answered, without a doubt, and its end will undoubtedly be secured, not by some roundabout way, but by getting the very thing asked for.

The value of prayer does not lie in the number of prayers or the length of prayers; rather, its value is found in the great truth that we are privileged, by our relationship to God, to unburden our desires and to make our requests known to Him (see Philippians 4:6), and that He will relieve by granting our petitions. The child asks because the parent is in the habit of granting the child's requests. Likewise, we, as the children of God, need something, and we need it badly; and so we go to God for it.

Neither the Bible nor the child of God knows anything of that half-infidel declaration that we are to answer our own prayers. God answers prayer. And the heart of faith knows nothing of that specious skepticism that holds back the steps of prayer and chills its ardor by whispering that prayer does not affect God.

D. L. Moody used to tell a story of a little child whose father and mother had died, and who was taken into another family. The first night she asked whether she could pray as she used to do. They said, "Oh, yes!" So she knelt down and prayed as her mother had taught her; and when that was ended, she added a little prayer of her own: "O God, make these people as kind to me as Father and Mother were." Then she paused and looked up, as if expecting the answer, and then added, "Of course you will." How sweetly simple was that little one's faith! She expected God to answer, and, "of course," she got her request. That is the spirit in which God invites us to approach Him.

In contrast to that incident is the story told of the quaint Yorkshire class leader, Daniel Quorm, who was visiting a friend. One morning he came to his friend and said, "I am sorry you have met with such a great disappointment." "Why, no," said the man, "I have not met with any disappointment." "Yes," said Daniel, "you were expecting something remarkable today." "What do you mean?" asked the friend. "Why, you prayed that you might be kept sweet and gentle all day long. And, by the way things have been going, I see you have been greatly disappointed." "Oh," said the man, "I thought you meant something particular." Obviously, this man never expected his prayer to be answered, whereas Daniel fully expected God to hear his friend's prayer.

Prayer is mighty in its operations, and God never disappoints those who put their trust and confidence in Him. They may have to wait long for the answer, and they may not live to see it, but the prayer of faith never misses its objective.

Dr. J. Wilbur Chapman told this story:

> A friend of mine in Cincinnati had preached his sermon and sank back in his chair, when he felt impelled to make another appeal. A boy at the back of the church lifted his hand. My friend left the pulpit and went down to him, and said, "Tell me about yourself." The boy said, "I live in New York. I am a prodigal. I have disgraced my father's name and broken my mother's heart. I ran away and told them I would never come back until I became a Christian or they brought me home dead." That night there went from Cincinnati a letter telling his father and mother that their boy had turned to God.
>
> Seven days later, in a black-bordered envelope, a reply came, and it read, "My dear boy, when I got the news that you had received Jesus Christ, the sky was overcast; your father was dead." Then the letter went on to tell how the father had prayed for his prodigal boy with his last breath, and concluded, "You are a Christian tonight because your old father would not let you go."

A fourteen-year-old boy was given a task by his father. It so happened that a group of boys came along just then and enticed the boy away with them, and so the work went undone. But the father came home that evening and said, "Frank, did you do the work that I gave you?"

"Yes, sir," said Frank. He told a lie, and his father knew it, but said nothing. It troubled the boy, but he went to bed as usual. Next morning his mother said to him, "Your father did not sleep all last night." "Why didn't he sleep?" asked Frank. His mother said, "He spent the whole night praying for you."

This sent the arrow into his heart. He was deeply convicted of his sin, and knew no rest until he got right with God. Long afterward, when the boy became Bishop Warne, he said that his decision for Christ came from his father's prayer that night. He saw his father keeping his lonely and sorrowful vigil praying for his boy, and it broke his heart. He said, "I can never be sufficiently grateful to him for that prayer."

A certain evangelist once began a series of meetings in a little church of about twenty members who were very cold and dead, and much divided. A little prayer meeting was kept up there by two or three women. This man, who was much used of God, said,

> I preached, and closed at eight o'clock. There was no one to speak or pray. The next evening one man spoke. The next morning, I rode six miles to a minister's study, and kneeled in prayer. I went back, and said to the little church, "If you can come up with enough money to board me, I will stay until God opens the windows of heaven. God has promised to bless these means, and I believe He will."
>
> Within ten days there were so many anxious souls that I met one hundred and fifty of them at a time in an inquiry meeting, while Christians were praying in another house of worship. Several hundred, I think, were converted. It is safe to believe God.

A mother asked the late John B. Gough to visit her son, in order to win him to Christ. Gough found the young man's mind full of skeptical notions, and impervious to argument. Finally, the young man was asked to pray, just once, for light. He replied, "I do not know anything perfect to whom or to which I could pray."

"How about your mother's love?" said the orator. "Isn't that perfect? Hasn't she always stood by you, and been ready to take you in and care for you, when even your father had really kicked you out?" The young man, choked with emotion, said, "Yes, sir; that is so." "Then pray to Love—it will help you. Will you promise?" He promised.

That night the young man prayed in the privacy of his room. He kneeled down, closed his eyes, and, struggling a moment, uttered the words, "O Love." Instantly, as if by a flash of lightning, the old Bible text came to him: *"God is love"* (1 John 4:8); and he said, brokenly, "O God!" Then came another flash of divine truth, and a voice said, *"God so loved the world, that he gave his only begotten Son"* (John 3:16)—and there, instantly, he exclaimed, "O Christ, incarnation of most divine love, show me light and truth." It was all over; he was in the light of the most perfect peace. He ran downstairs and told his mother that he was saved. That young man is today an eloquent minister of Jesus Christ.

A water famine was threatened in Hakodate, Japan. Miss Dickerson, of the Methodist Episcopal Girls' School, saw the water supply getting smaller daily, and, in one of the fall months, appealed to the Board in New York for help. There was no money on hand, and nothing was done. Miss Dickerson inquired the cost of putting down an artesian well, but found the expense too great to be undertaken.

On the evening of December 31, when the water was almost exhausted, the teachers and the older pupils met to pray for water, though they had no idea how their prayer was to be answered. A couple of days later, a letter was received in the New York office, and it went something like this: "Philadelphia, January 1. It is six o'clock in the morning of New Year's Day. All the other members of the family are asleep, but I was awakened with a strange impression that someone, somewhere, is in need of money, which the Lord wants me to supply." Enclosed was a check for an amount that just covered the cost of the artesian well and the piping of the water into the school buildings.

A well-known minister once said to me,

> I have seen God's hand stretched out to heal among the heathen in as mighty wonder-working power as in apostolic times. I was preaching to two thousand starving orphan girls at Kedgaum, India, at Ramabai's Mukti (salvation) Mission. A swarm of serpents, as venomous and deadly as the reptile that smote Paul, suddenly raided the walled grounds. They were "sent of Satan," said Ramabai, and several of her most beautiful and faithful Christian girls were smitten by them, two of them bitten twice. I saw four of the very flower of her flock in convulsions at once, unconscious and apparently in the agonies of death.
>
> Ramabai believed the Bible with an implicit and obedient faith. There were three of us missionaries there. She said, "We will do just what the Bible says. I want you to minister for their healing according to James 5:14–18." She led the way into the dormitory where her girls were lying in spasms, and we laid our hands upon their heads and prayed, and anointed them with oil in the name of the Lord. Each of them was healed as soon as anointed, and they all sat up and sang with their faces shining. That miracle and marvel among the heathen mightily confirmed the word of the Lord, and was a profound and overpowering proclamation of God.

Some years ago, the record of a wonderful work of grace in connection with one of the stations of the China Inland Mission attracted a good deal of attention. Both the number and spiritual character of the converts had been far greater than at other stations, where the consecration of the missionaries had been just as great as at the more fruitful place.

This rich harvest of souls remained a mystery until Hudson Taylor, on a visit to England, discovered the secret. At the close of one of Mr. Taylor's addresses, a gentleman came forward to make his acquaintance. In the conversation that followed, Mr. Taylor was surprised at the accurate knowledge the man possessed concerning this inland China station. "But how is it," Mr. Taylor asked, "that you are so conversant with the conditions of that work?"

"Oh!" he replied, "the missionary there and I are old college mates. For years we have regularly corresponded; he has sent me names of inquirers and converts, and these I have daily taken to God in prayer."

At last the secret was found! A praying man at home, praying definitely, praying daily, for specific cases among the heathen— that is the real intercessory missionary.

Hudson Taylor himself, as all the world knows, was a man who knew how to pray and whose praying was blessed with fruitful answers. In the story of his life, told by Dr. and Mrs. Howard Taylor, we find page after page aglow with answered prayer. On his way out to China for the first time, in 1853, when he was only twenty-one years of age, Hudson Taylor had a definite answer to prayer that was a great encouragement to his faith. The biographers set the scene:

They had just come through the Dampier Strait, but were not yet out of sight of the islands. Usually a breeze would spring up after sunset and last until about dawn. The utmost use was made of it, but during the day they lay still with flapping sails, often drifting back and losing a good deal of the advantage gained at night.

The story continues in Hudson Taylor's own words:

This happened notably on one occasion when we were in dangerous proximity to the north of New Guinea. Saturday night had brought us to a point some thirty miles off the land,

and during the Sunday morning service, which was held on deck, I could not fail to see that the captain looked troubled and frequently went over to the side of the ship. When the service had ended, I learned from him the cause. A four-knot current was carrying us toward some sunken reefs, and we were already so near that it seemed improbable that we should get through the afternoon in safety. After dinner, the longboat was put out, and all hands endeavored, without success, to turn the ship's head from the shore.

After standing together on the deck for some time in silence, the captain said to me, "Well, we have done everything that can be done. We can only await the result."

A thought occurred to me, and I replied, "No, there is one thing we have not done yet."

"What is that?" he queried.

"Four of us on board are Christians. Let us each retire to his own cabin, and in agreed prayer ask the Lord to immediately give us a breeze. He can as easily send it now as at sunset."

The captain complied with this proposal. I went and spoke to two of the other men, and after prayer with the carpenter, we all four retired to wait upon God. I had a good but very brief season in prayer, and then felt so satisfied that our request was granted that I could not continue asking, and very soon went up again on deck. The first officer, a godless man, was in charge. I went over and asked him to let down the clews or corners of the mainsail, which had been drawn up in order to lessen the useless flapping of the sail against the rigging.

"What would be the good of that?" he answered roughly.

I told him we had been asking for a wind from God; that it was coming immediately; and we were so near the reef by this time that there was not a minute to lose.

With an oath and a look of contempt, he said he would rather see a wind than hear of it. But while he was speaking, I watched his eye, following it up to the royal, and there, sure enough, the corner of the topmost sail was beginning to tremble in the breeze.

"Don't you see the wind is coming? Look at the royal!" I exclaimed.

"No, it is only a cat's paw," he rejoined, describing a mere puff of wind.

"Cat's paw or not," I cried, "please let down the mainsail and give us the benefit."

This he was not slow to do. In another minute the heavy tread of the men on deck brought up the captain from his cabin to see what was the matter. The breeze had indeed come! In a few minutes we were plowing our way at six or seven knots an hour through the water...and though the wind was sometimes unsteady, we did not altogether lose it until after passing the Pelew Islands.

Thus God encouraged me, before landing on China's shores, to bring every variety of need to Him in prayer, and to expect that He would honor the name of the Lord Jesus and give the help each emergency required.

In an address at Cambridge some time ago, S. D. Gordon told in his own inimitable way the story of a man in his own country, the United States, to illustrate the reality of prayer, and that it is not mere talking. Said Mr. Gordon,

This man came from an old New England family, a bit farther back an English family. He was a giant in size, and a keen man mentally, and a university-trained man. He had gone out West to live, and represented a prominent district in our House of Congress, answering to your House of Commons. He was a prominent leader there. He was reared in a Christian family; but he was a skeptic, and he used to lecture against Christianity. He told me he was fond, in his lectures, of proving, as he thought, conclusively, that there was no God. That was the type of his unbelief.

One day, he told me, he was sitting in the Lower House of Congress. It was at the time of a presidential election, when party feelings ran high. One would have thought that was the last place where a man would be likely to think about spiritual things. He said, "I was sitting in my seat in that crowded House and that heated atmosphere, when a feeling came to me that the God whose existence I thought I could successfully disprove, was right above me, looking down on me, and that He was displeased with me, and with the things I was doing. I said to myself, 'This is ridiculous, I guess I've been working too hard. I'll go and get a good meal and take a long walk and shake myself, and see if that will take this feeling away.'"

He got his extra meal, took a walk, and came back to his seat, but he could not shake the impression that God was there and was displeased with him. He went for a walk, day after day, but could never shake off the feeling. Then he went back to his constituency in his state, he said, to arrange matters there. He had an ambition to be the governor of his state, and his party was the dominant party in the state; and, as far as such things could be judged, he was in the line to become governor there, in one of the most dominant states of our Central West.

But then, he said, "I went home to fix that thing up as far as I could, and to get ready for it. But I had hardly reached home and exchanged greetings, when my wife, who was an earnest Christian woman, said to me that a few of them had made a little covenant of prayer that I might become a Christian." He did not want her to know the experience that he had just been going through, and so he said as carelessly as he could, "When did this thing begin, this praying of yours?" She named the date. Then he did some very quick thinking, and he knew, as he thought back, that it was the same day when that strange impression came to him for the first time.

This man said to me, "I was tremendously shaken. I wanted to be honest. I was perfectly honest in not believing in God, and I thought I was right. But if what she said was true, then merely as a lawyer sifting his evidence in a case, it would be good evidence that there was really something in their prayer. I was terrifically shaken, and wanted to be honest, and did not know what to do. That same night I went to a little Methodist chapel, and if somebody had known how to talk with me, I think I should have accepted Christ that night."

Then he said that the next night he went back again to that chapel, where meetings were being held each night, and there he knelt at the altar, and yielded his great strong will to the will of God. Then he said, "I knew I was to preach," and he is still preaching in a Western state at the time of this writing.

That is half of the story. I also talked with his wife, because I wanted to put the two halves together, and she told me the following. She had been a Christian—what you might call a nominal Christian—which is a strange confusion of terms. Then there came a time when she was led into a full surrender of her life to the Lord Jesus Christ.

Then she said to me, "At once there came a great intensifying of desire that my husband might be a Christian, and we made that little compact to pray for him each day until he became a Christian. That night I was kneeling at my bedside before going to sleep, praying for my husband, praying very earnestly; and then a voice said to me, 'Are you praying for the results that will come if your husband is converted?'"

The little message was so very distinct that she said she was frightened; she had never had such an experience. But she went on praying still more earnestly, and again there came the quiet voice, "Are you praying for the consequences?" And again there was a sense of being startled, frightened. But she still went on praying and wondering what this meant; and a third time the quiet voice came more quietly than ever, as she described it, "Are you praying for the consequences?"

Then she told me that she said with great earnestness, "O God, I am praying for anything You think is good, if only my husband may know You, and become a true Christian man." She told me that when that prayer came from her lips, there instantly came into her heart a wonderful sense of peace, a great peace that she could not explain, a *"peace...*[that] *passeth all understanding"* (Phil. 4:7); and from that moment—it was the very night of the covenant, the night when her husband had that first strange experience—the assurance never left her that he would accept Christ.

But all those weeks she prayed with the firm assurance that the result was coming. What were the consequences? They were of a kind that I think no one would think small. She was the wife of a man in a very prominent political position; she was the wife of a man who was in the line of becoming the first official of his state, and she officially the first lady socially of that state, with all the honor that that social standing would imply. Now she is the wife of a Methodist preacher, with her home changed every two or three years, she going from this place to that—a very different social position—and having a very different income than she would otherwise have had. Yet I never met a woman who had more of the wonderful peace of God in her heart, and of the light of God in her face, than that woman.

And Mr. Gordon's comment on that incident is this:

Now, you can see at once that there was no change in the purpose of God through that prayer. The prayer worked out

His purpose; it did not change it. But the woman's surrender gave the opportunity of working out the will that God wanted to work out. If we would give ourselves to Him and learn His will, and use all our strength in learning His will and bending to His will, then we would begin to pray, and there is simply nothing that can resist the tremendous power of the prayer. Oh, for more men who will be simple enough to get in touch with God, and give Him the mastery of their whole lives, and learn His will, and then give themselves, as Jesus gave Himself, to the sacred service of intercession!

To the man or woman who is acquainted with God and who knows how to pray, there is nothing remarkable in the answers that come. They are sure of being heard, since they ask in accordance with what they know to be the mind and the will of God. Dr. William Burt, Bishop of Europe in the Methodist Episcopal Church, when he visited their Boys' School in Vienna, found that, although the year was not up, all available funds had been spent. He hesitated to make a special appeal to his friends in America. He counseled with the teachers. They took the matter to God in earnest and continued prayer, believing that He would grant their request.

Ten days later, Bishop Burt was in Rome, and there came to him a letter from a friend in New York, which read substantially thus: "As I went to my office on Broadway one morning [and the date was the very one on which the teachers were praying], a voice seemed to tell me that you were in need of funds for the Boys' School in Vienna. I very gladly enclose a check for the work." The check was for the amount needed. There had been no human communication between Vienna and New York. But while they were yet speaking, God answered them.

Some time ago there appeared in an English religious weekly the report of an incident narrated by a well-known preacher in the course of an address to children. This preacher was able to vouch for the truth of the story. A child lay sick in a country cottage, and her younger sister heard the doctor say, as he left the house, "Nothing but a miracle can save her." The little girl went to her money box, took out the few coins it contained, and in perfect simplicity of heart went to shop after shop in the village street, asking, "Please, I want to buy a miracle." From each she came away disappointed. Even the local chemist had to say, "My dear, we don't sell miracles here."

But outside his door two men were talking, and had overheard the child's request. One was a great doctor from a London hospital, and he asked her to explain what she wanted. When he understood the need, he hurried with her to the cottage, examined the sick girl, and said to the mother, "It is true—only a miracle can save her, and it must be performed at once." He got his instruments, performed the operation, and the patient's life was saved.

D. L. Moody gave this illustration of the wonderful results of prayer:

> While I was in Edinburgh, a man was pointed out to me by a friend, who said, "That man is chairman of the Edinburgh Infidel Club." I went and sat beside him and said, "My friend, I am glad to see you in our meeting. Are you concerned about your welfare?"
>
> "I do not believe in any hereafter," he replied.
>
> "Well, just get down on your knees and let me pray for you."
>
> "No, I do not believe in prayer."
>
> So I knelt beside him as he sat, and I prayed for him. He made a great deal of sport of it. A year later, I met him again. I took him by the hand and said, "Hasn't God answered my prayer yet?"
>
> "There is no God," he said. "If you believe in one who answers prayer, try your hand on me."
>
> "Well, a great many people are now praying for you, and God's time will come, and I believe you will be saved yet."
>
> Some time afterwards, I got a letter from a leading barrister in Edinburgh telling me that my infidel friend had come to Christ, and that seventeen of his club men had followed his example. I did not know *how* God would answer prayer, but I knew He would answer. Let us come boldly to God.

Robert Louis Stevenson told a vivid story of a storm at sea. The passengers below were greatly alarmed, as the waves dashed over the vessel. At last, one of them, against orders, crept to the deck, and came to the pilot, who was tied with rope to the wheel, which he was turning without flinching. The pilot caught sight of the terror-stricken man, and gave him a reassuring smile. Below went the passenger, and comforted the others by saying, "I have seen the face of the pilot, and he smiled. All is well."

That is how we feel when, through the gateway of prayer, we find our way into the Father's presence. We see His face, and we know that all is well, since His hand is on the helm of events, and *"even the winds and the sea obey him"* (Matt. 8:27). When we live in fellowship with Him, we come with confidence into His presence, asking in the full confidence of receiving and meeting with the justification of our faith. (See Hebrews 4:16.)

12

The Birthplace
of Revival

Let your hearts be much set on revivals of religion. Never forget that the churches have hitherto existed and prospered by revivals; and that if they are to exist and prosper in time to come, it must be by the same cause which has from the first been their glory and defense. —*Joel Hawks*

IT has been said that the history of revivals is the history of religion, and no one can study their history without being impressed with their mighty influence upon the destiny of the race. To look back over the progress of the divine kingdom upon earth is to review revival periods that have come like refreshing showers upon dry and thirsty ground, making the desert to blossom as the rose (see Isaiah 35:1), and bringing new eras of spiritual life and activity just when the church had fallen under the influence of the apathy of the times, and needed to be aroused to a new sense of her duty and responsibility.

"From one point of view, and that not the least important," wrote Principal Lindsay, in *The Church and the Ministry in the Early Centuries,*

> the history of the church flows on from one time of revival to another; and whether we take the awakenings in the old Catholic, the medieval, or the modern church, these have always been the work of men specially gifted with the power of seeing and declaring the secrets of the deepest Christian life; and the effect of their work has always been proportional to the spiritual receptivity of the generation they have spoken to.

As God, from the beginning, has worked prominently through revivals, there can be no denial of the fact that revivals are a part of the divine plan. The kingdom of our Lord has been advanced in large measure by special seasons of gracious and rapid accomplishment of the work of conversion; and it may be inferred, therefore, that the means through which God has worked in other times will be employed in our time to produce similar results.

"The quiet conversion of one sinner after another, under the ordinary ministry of the Gospel," according to one writer on the subject,

> must always be regarded with feelings of satisfaction and gratitude by the ministers and disciples of Christ; but a periodical manifestation of the simultaneous conversion of thousands is also to be desired, because it affords a visible and impressive demonstration that God has made Jesus, who was rejected and crucified, both Lord and Christ. (See Acts 2:36.) The conversion of many also demonstrates that, in virtue of His divine mediatorship, He has assumed the royal scepter of universal supremacy, and *"must reign, till he hath put all enemies under his feet"* (1 Cor. 15:25). It is therefore reasonable to expect that, from time to time, He will repeat that which, on the day of Pentecost, formed the conclusive and crowning evidence of His messiahship and sovereignty.
>
> By so doing, He will startle the slumbering souls of careless worldlings, gain the attentive ear of the unconverted, and, in a remarkable way, break in upon those brilliant dreams of earthly glory, grandeur, wealth, power, and happiness, which the rebellious and God-forgetting multitudes so fondly cherish. Such an outpouring of the Holy Spirit will form at once a demonstrative proof of the completeness and acceptance of His once offering of Himself as a sacrifice for sin (see Hebrews 10:10), and a prophetic pledge of the certainty that He *"shall...appear the second time without sin unto salvation"* (Heb. 9:28), to *"judge the world with righteousness"* (Ps. 96:13).

That revivals are to be expected, proceeding as they do from the right use of the appropriate means, is a fact that needs not a little emphasis in these days, when the material is exalted at the expense of the spiritual, and when ethical standards are supposed to be supreme. But a revival is not a miracle. This was powerfully taught by Charles Finney. There might, he said, be a miracle among its antecedent causes, or there might not. The apostles employed miracles simply as a means by which they arrested attention to their message, and established its divine authority.

> But the miracle was not the revival. The miracle was one thing; the revival that followed it was quite another thing. The revivals in the apostles' days were connected with miracles, but they were not miracles.

All revivals are dependent upon God; but, in revivals, as in other things, He invites and requires the assistance of man, and the full result is obtained when there is cooperation between the divine and the human. In other words, to employ a familiar phrase, "God alone can save the world, but God cannot save the world alone." God and man unite for the task; the response of the Divine Being is invariably in proportion to human effort and desire. Edward Payson has said of this needed desire,

> I do not believe that my desires for a revival were ever half so strong as they ought to be; nor do I see how a minister can help being in a "constant fever" when his Master is dishonored and souls are destroyed in so many ways.

This cooperation, then, being necessary, what is the duty that we, as coworkers with God, are required to undertake? First of all, and most important of all—the point that I particularly desire to emphasize—we must give ourselves to prayer. "Revivals," as Dr. J. Wilbur Chapman has reminded us,

> are born in prayer. When Wesley prayed, England was revived; when Knox prayed, Scotland was refreshed; when the Sunday school teachers of Tannybrook prayed, eleven thousand young people were added to the church in a year. Whole nights of prayer have always been succeeded by whole days of soulwinning.

When D. L. Moody's church in Chicago lay in ashes, he went over to England, in 1872, not to preach, but to listen to others preach while his new church was being built. One Sunday morning he was prevailed upon to preach in a London pulpit. But, somehow, the spiritual atmosphere was lacking. He confessed afterwards that he had never had such a hard time preaching in his life; everything was perfectly dead, and, as he vainly tried to preach, he said to himself, "What a fool I was to consent to preach! I came here to listen, and here I am preaching."

Then the awful thought came to him that he had to preach again that night, and only the fact that he had given the promise to do so kept him faithful to the engagement. But when Mr. Moody entered the pulpit at night, and faced the crowded congregation, he was conscious of a new atmosphere. "The powers of an unseen world seemed to have fallen upon the audience," he said. As he drew near the close of his sermon, he became emboldened to give out an invitation, and as he concluded he said, "If there is a man or woman here who will tonight accept Jesus Christ, please stand up."

At once about five hundred people rose to their feet. Thinking that there must be some mistake, he asked the people to be seated, and then, in order that there might be no possible misunderstanding, he repeated the invitation, couching it in even more definite and difficult terms. Again the same number rose. Still thinking that something must be wrong, Mr. Moody, for the second time, asked the standing men and women to be seated, and then he invited all who really meant to accept Christ to pass into the vestry. Fully five hundred people did as requested, and that was the beginning of a revival in that church and neighborhood, which brought Mr. Moody back from Dublin, a few days later, that he might assist the wonderful work of God.

The sequel, however, must be given, or my purpose in relating the incident will be defeated. When Mr. Moody preached at the morning service, there was a woman in the congregation who had an invalid sister. On her return home, she told the invalid that the preacher had been a Mr. Moody from Chicago, and on hearing this she turned pale.

"What," she said, "Mr. Moody from Chicago! I read about him some time ago in an American paper, and I have been praying that God would send him to London, and to our church. If I had known he was going to preach this morning, I would have eaten no breakfast. I would have spent the whole time in prayer. Now, sister, go out of the room, lock the door, send me no dinner; no matter who comes, don't let them see me. I am going to spend the whole afternoon and evening in prayer."

And so, while Mr. Moody stood in the pulpit that had been like an ice chamber in the morning, the bedridden saint was holding him up before God; and God, who ever delights to answer prayer, poured out His Spirit in mighty power.

The God of revivals who answered the prayer of His child for Mr. Moody, is willing to hear and to answer the faithful, believing prayers of His people today. Wherever God's conditions are met, there the revival is sure to fall. Professor Thomas Nicholson, of Cornell University, related an experience he had, on his first circuit, that impresses anew the old lesson of the place of prayer in the work of God:

> There had not been a revival on that circuit in years, and things were not spiritually hopeful. For more than four weeks, I had preached faithfully, visited from house to house, in stores, shops, and out-of-the-way places, and had done everything I could. The fifth Monday night saw many of the official members at lodges, but only a corporal's guard at the church.
>
> From that meeting, I went home, cast down, but not in despair. (See 2 Corinthians 4:8.) I resolved to spend that night in prayer. Locking the door, I took Bible and hymn book and began to inquire more diligently of the Lord, though the meetings had been the subject of hours of earnest prayer. Only God knows the anxiety and the faithful, prayerful study of that night. Near the dawn, a great peace and a full assurance came that God would surely bless the plan that had been decided upon, and a text was chosen that I felt sure was of the Lord. Dropping upon the bed, I slept about two hours, then rose, hastily breakfasted, and went nine miles to the far side of the circuit to visit some sick people. All day the assurance increased.
>
> Toward night, a pouring rain set in. The roads were heavy, and I reached home, wet, hungry, and a little late, only to find no fire in the church, the lights unlit, and no signs of service. The janitor had concluded that the rain would prevent the service. So I changed the order, rang the bell, and prepared for war. Three young men formed the congregation, but in that "full assurance," I delivered the message that had been prayed out on the preceding night, as earnestly and as fully as if the house had been crowded. I then made a personal appeal to each young man in turn. Two yielded, and they testified before the meeting closed.
>
> Tired from the long day, I went to a sweet rest, and the next morning, rising a little later than usual, I learned that

one of the young men was going from store to store throughout the town telling of his wonderful deliverance, and exhorting the people to salvation. Night after night conversions
occurred, until, after two weeks, one hundred and forty-four
people testified before the church in forty-five minutes. All
three points of that circuit saw a blaze of revival that winter,
and family after family came into the church, until the membership was more than tripled.

Out of that meeting, one convert became a successful
pastor in the Michigan Conference, another became the wife
of one of our best pastors, and a third was in the ministry for
a number of years, and then went to another denomination,
where he is faithful to this day. Probably none of the members ever knew about my night of prayer, but I certainly believe that God somehow does for the man who thus prays,
what He does not do for the man who does not pray. And I
am certain that "more things are wrought by prayer than this
world dreams of."

All the true revivals have been born in prayer. When God's
people become so concerned about the state of religion that they lie
on their faces day and night in earnest supplication, the blessing
will be sure to fall. Through prayer Hannah found her relief. Everywhere the church was backslidden and apostate; its foes were
victorious. Hannah gave herself to prayer, and in sorrow she multiplied her praying. She saw a great revival born out of her praying.
When the whole nation was oppressed, Samuel, prophet and priest,
was born to establish a new line of priesthood, and Hannah's
praying warmed into existence a new life for God. Religion revived
and flourished everywhere. Though the praying came from a
woman's broken heart, God, true to His promise, *Ask of Me,* heard
and answered, sending a new day of holy gladness to revive His
people.

It is the same all down the ages. Every revival of which we
have any record has been bathed in prayer. Take, for example, the
wonderful revival in Shotts, Scotland, in 1630. It was during this
time that it became known that several of the then persecuted
ministers were to take part in a solemn convocation. As a result, a
vast gathering of godly persons assembled on this occasion from all
quarters of the country, and several days were spent in joint
prayer, in preparation for the service. In the evening, instead of
retiring to rest, the multitude divided themselves into little bands,

and spent the whole night in supplication and praise. The following Monday was consecrated to thanksgiving, a practice not then common, and it proved to be one of the great days of the feast.

After much entreaty, John Livingston, chaplain to the Countess of Wigtown, a young man and not ordained, agreed to preach to this congregation. He had spent the night in prayer and conference; but as the hour of assembling approached, his heart quailed at the thought of addressing so many aged and experienced saints, and he actually fled from the duty he had undertaken.

But just as the church of Shotts was vanishing from his view, the following words were borne in upon his mind with such a force that he was compelled to return to the work: "Was I ever a barren wilderness or a land of darkness?" (See Jeremiah 2:31.) He took for his text Ezekiel 36:25–26, and discoursed with great power for about two hours. Five hundred conversions were believed to have occurred as a result of that one sermon, thus prefaced by prayer. And this was the report of that revival: "It was the sowing of a seed through Clydesdale, so that many of the most eminent Christians of that country [Scotland] could date their conversion, or some remarkable confirmation of their case, from that day."

Of Richard Baxter it has been said that "he stained his study walls with praying breath; and after becoming thus anointed with the unction of the Holy Ghost, he sent a river of living water over Kidderminster."

George Whitefield once prayed, "O Lord, give me souls or take my soul." It has been said that, after much closet pleading, "he once went to the Devil's fair and took more than a thousand souls out of the paw of the lion in a single day."

Charles Finney has said,

> I once knew a minister who had a revival fourteen winters in succession. I did not know how to account for it until I saw one of his members get up in a prayer meeting and make a confession. "Fellow believers," he said, "I have long been in the habit of praying every Saturday night till after midnight for the descent of the Holy Ghost among us. And now [and he began to weep], I confess that I have neglected it for two or three weeks." The secret was out. That minister had a praying church.

H. C. Fish has told the following account of how the prayers of one man brought about a revival:

An aged saint once came to the pastor at night and said, "We are about to have a revival." He was asked why he knew so. His answer was, "I went into the stable to take care of my cattle two hours ago, and there the Lord has kept me in prayer until just now. And I feel that we are going to be revived." It was the commencement of a revival.

And so we might go on multiplying illustration upon illustration to show the place of prayer in revival and to demonstrate that every mighty movement of the Spirit of God has had its source in the prayer chamber. The lesson of it all is this, that as workers together with God, we must regard ourselves as in not a little measure responsible for the conditions that prevail around us today. Are we concerned about the coldness of the church? Do we grieve over the lack of conversions? Do our souls go out to God in midnight cries for the outpouring of His Spirit? If not, part of the blame lies at our door. If we will do our part, God will do His.

Little prayer is the characteristic of a backslidden age and of a backslidden church. Whenever there is little praying in the pulpit or in the pew, spiritual bankruptcy is imminent and inevitable. Around us is a world lost in sin, above us is a God willing and able to save. It is our duty to build the bridge that links heaven and earth, and prayer is the mighty instrument that does the work.

Spurgeon has said, "If any minister can be satisfied without conversions, he shall have no conversions." And so the old cry comes to us with insistent voice: "Pray, brethren, pray."

13

Our Passport
to Assurance

An hour of solitude passed in sincere and earnest prayer,
or the conflict with and conquest over a single passion or sub-
tle bosom sin, will teach us more of thought, will more effectu-
ally awaken the faculty and form the habit of reflection, than a
year's study in the schools without these.   *—Coleridge*

THE example of our Lord in the matter of prayer is one that His followers might do well to copy. Christ prayed much, and He taught much about prayer. His life and His works, as well as His teaching, are illustrations of the nature and necessity of prayer. He lived and worked to answer prayer. But the necessity of importunity in prayer was the point He emphasized in His teaching about prayer. He taught not only that men must pray, but that they must persevere in prayer. For, as Robert Hall has said, "the prayer of faith is the only power in the universe to which the great Jehovah yields. Prayer is the sovereign remedy."

In both command and precept, Christ taught us to have energy and earnestness in praying. He also provided us with specific steps, aiding our efforts toward their climax, which is the answering of our prayers. We are to ask, but to the asking we must add seeking, and seeking must pass into the full force of effort in knocking. "Strive and endeavor to pray," one man has said, "even when thou thinkest thou canst not pray." We must put forth the effort to pray.

The pleading soul must be aroused to effort by God's silence. Denial, instead of abating or abashing, must arouse the soul's latent energies and kindle anew its highest ardor.

In the Sermon on the Mount, in which Christ lays down the cardinal duties of His religion, He not only gives prominence to prayer in general and secret prayer in particular, but He also sets apart a distinct and different section to give weight to importunate prayer. To prevent any discouragement in praying, He lays down as a basic principle the fact of God's great fatherly willingness—that God's willingness to answer our prayers exceeds our willingness to give good and necessary things to our children, just as far as God's ability, goodness, and perfection exceed our infirmities and evil.

As a further assurance and stimulant to prayer, Christ gives the most positive and iterated assurance of answer to prayers. He declares, *"Ask, and it shall be given you; seek, and ye shall find; knock, and it shall be opened unto you"* (Matt. 7:7). And to make assurance doubly sure, He adds, "For every one that asketh, receiveth; and he that seeketh findeth; and to him that knocketh it shall be opened" (v. 8).

Why does He unfold to us the Father's loving readiness to answer the prayers of His children? Why does He affirm so strongly that prayer will be answered? Why does He repeat that positive affirmation six times? Why does Christ, on two distinct occasions, go over the same strong promises, iterations, and reiterations in regard to the certainty of prayer being answered? Because He knew that there would be delay in many an answer, which would call for importunate pressing, and that if our faith did not have the strongest assurance of God's willingness to answer, delay would break it down.

He also knew that our spiritual sloth would come in, under the guise of submission, and say it is not God's will to give what we ask, and so we would cease praying and lose our case. After Christ had put in a very clear and strong light God's willingness to answer prayer, He then urged us to importunity, and He emphasized that every unanswered prayer, instead of abating our pressure, should only increase our intensity and energy. If asking does not obtain the answer, let asking pass into the settled attitude and spirit of seeking. If seeking does not secure the answer, let seeking pass on to the more energetic and clamorous plea of knocking. We must persevere until we get it. There will be no failure here if our faith does not break down.

But let me clarify my meaning with the words of J. Kennedy Maclean:

I do not mean that every prayer we offer is answered exactly as we desire it to be. Were this the case, it would mean that we would be dictating to God, and prayer would degenerate into a mere system of begging. Just as an earthly father knows what is best for his children's welfare, so does God take into consideration the particular needs of His human family, and meets them out of His wonderful storehouse. If our petitions are in accordance with His will, and if we seek His glory in the asking, the answers will come in ways that will astonish us and fill our hearts with songs of thanksgiving. God is a rich and bountiful Father, and He does not forget His children, nor withhold from them anything that it would be to their advantage to receive.

As our great example in prayer, our Lord presents love as a primary condition—a love that has purified the heart from all the elements of hate, revenge, and ill will. Love, or a life inspired by love, is the supreme condition of prayer. Recall that Fénelon said, "Perfect prayer is only another name for love." The thirteenth chapter of 1 Corinthians is the law of prayer as well as the law of love. The law of love is the law of prayer, and to master this chapter from Paul's epistle is to learn the first and fullest condition of prayer.

Christ taught us also to approach the Father in His name. That is our passport. It is in His name that we are to make our petitions known.

> *Verily, verily, I say unto you, He that believeth on me, the works that I do shall he do also; and greater works than these shall he do; because I go unto my Father. And whatsoever ye shall ask in my name, that will I do, that the Father may be glorified in the Son. If ye shall ask any thing in my name, I will do it.* (John 14:12–14)

How wide and comprehensive is that *"whatsoever."* There is no limit to the power of that name. *"Whatsoever ye shall ask."* That is the divine declaration, and it opens up to every praying child a vista of infinite resource and possibility.

And that is our heritage. The relationship of God and the Son is an eternal relationship of a Father to His Son. It is also a relationship of asking and giving—the Son always asking, the Father always giving. There is also a relationship between Christ and His people. All that Christ has may become ours if we obey the conditions. The one secret is prayer. The place of revealing and of equipment, of grace and of power, is the prayer chamber; and as we meet there with God, we will not only win our triumphs, but we will also grow in the likeness of our Lord and become His living witnesses to men.

Without prayer, the Christian life, robbed of its sweetness and its beauty, becomes cold and formal and dead; but when rooted in the secret place where God meets and walks and talks with His own, it will grow into such a testimony of divine power that all men will feel its influence and be touched by the warmth of its love. Thus, resembling our Lord and Master, we will be used for the glory of God and the salvation of our fellowmen.

And that, surely, is the purpose of all real prayer and the goal of all true service.

Book
Two

The Necessity of
Prayer

1

Prayer and Faith

A dear friend of mine who was quite a lover of the hunt, told me the following story. "Rising early one morning," he said, "I heard the barking of a number of dogs chasing deer. Looking at a large open field in front of me, I saw a young fawn making its way across the field and giving signs that its race was almost run. It leaped over the rails of the enclosed place and crouched within ten feet of where I stood. A moment later two of the hounds came over, and the fawn ran in my direction and pushed its head between my legs. I lifted the little thing to my breast, and, swinging round and round, fought off the dogs. Just then I felt that all the dogs in the West could not and would not capture that fawn after its weakness had appealed to my strength." So is it, when human helplessness appeals to Almighty God. I remember well, when the hounds of sin were after my soul, that at last I ran into the arms of Almighty God. —A. C. Dixon

WHENEVER a study of the principles of prayer is made, lessons concerning faith must accompany it. Faith is the essential quality in the heart of any man who desires to communicate with God. He must believe and stretch out the hands of faith for that which he cannot see or prove. Prayer is actually faith claiming and taking hold of its natural, immeasurable inheritance. True godliness is just as important in the realm of faith as it is in the area of prayer. Moreover, when faith ceases to pray, it ceases to live.

Faith does the impossible because it lets God undertake for us, and nothing is impossible with God. How great—without qualification or limitation—the power of faith is! If doubt can be banished from the heart and unbelief is made a stranger there, what we ask from God will surely come to pass. A believer has granted to him *"whatsoever he saith"* (Mark 11:23).

Prayer throws faith on God and God on the world. Only God can move mountains, but faith and prayer move God. In the cursing of the fig tree, our Lord demonstrated His power. (See Matthew 21:19–22.) Following that, He went on to say that large powers were committed to faith and prayer, not to kill but to make alive, not to blast but to bless.

At this point in our study, we need to emphasize some words of Jesus that are the very keystone of the arch of faith and prayer. The first is found in Mark 11:24: *"Therefore I say unto you, What things soever ye desire, when ye pray, believe that ye receive them, and ye shall have them."* We should think about that statement: *"Believe that ye receive them, and ye shall have them."* A faith that realizes, appropriates, and *takes is* described here. This faith is an awareness of God, an experienced communion, a real fact.

Is faith growing or declining as the years go by? Does faith stand strong and firm as sin abounds and the love of many grows cold? Does faith keep its hold, as religion becomes a mere formality and worldliness becomes victorious? The question our Lord asked may appropriately be ours. *"When the Son of man cometh,"* He asked, *"shall he find faith on the earth?"* (Luke 18:8). We believe that He will, and it is our job today to see to it that the lamp of faith is trimmed and burning, until He comes.

Faith is the foundation of Christian character and the security of the soul. When Jesus was looking toward Peter's denial and cautioning him against it, He said to His disciple, *"Simon, Simon, behold, Satan hath desired to have you, that he may sift you as wheat: but I have prayed for thee, that thy faith fail not"* (Luke 22:31–32).

Our Lord was stating a central truth. It was Peter's faith He was seeking to guard. He knew that when faith breaks down, the foundations of spiritual life give way, and the entire structure of religious experience falls. It was Peter's faith that needed guarding. That is why Christ was concerned for the welfare of His disciple's soul and was determined to strengthen Peter's faith by His own victorious prayer.

Peter, in his second epistle, had this same idea in mind when he wrote of growing in grace as a measure of safety in the Christian life and as fruitfulness. *"And beside this,"* he declared, *"giving all diligence, add to your faith virtue; and to virtue knowledge; and to knowledge temperance; and to temperance patience; and to patience godliness"* (2 Pet. 1:5–6).

In this addition process, faith was the starting point, the basis of the other graces of the Spirit. Faith was the foundation on which other things were built. Peter did not urge his readers to add to works or gifts or virtues but to *faith.* In this business of growing in grace, much depends on starting right. There is a divine order. Peter was aware of it. He went on to say that we are to give constant care to making our calling and election secure (2 Pet. 1:10). This election is made sure by adding to faith that which is done by constant, earnest praying. Faith is kept alive by prayer. Every step in this adding of grace to grace is accompanied by prayer.

Faith that creates powerful praying is the faith that centers itself on a powerful Person. Faith in Christ's ability to *do* and to do *greatly* is the faith that prays greatly. In this way the leper laid hold of the power of Christ. *"Lord, if thou wilt,"* he cried, *"thou canst make me clean"* (Matt. 8:2). In this instance, we are shown how a faith centered in Christ's ability to *do* obtained the healing power.

It was concerning this very point that Jesus questioned the blind men who came to Him for healing: *"Believe ye that I am able to do this?"* He asked. *"They said unto Him, Yea, Lord. Then touched he their eyes, saying, According to your faith be it unto you"* (Matt. 9:28-29).

It was because He wanted to inspire faith in His ability to *do* that Jesus left behind Him that last, great statement, which, in the final analysis, is a ringing challenge to faith. *"All power,"* He declared, *"is given unto me in heaven and in earth"* (Matt. 28:18).

Again, faith is obedient. It goes when commanded, as did the nobleman who came to Jesus, in the day of His flesh, when his son was grievously sick.

Likewise, such faith acts. Like the man who was born blind, it goes to wash in the pool of Siloam when *told* to wash. Like Peter on the Sea of Galilee, it instantly casts the net where Jesus commands, without question or doubt. Such faith promptly takes away the stone from the grave of Lazarus. A praying faith keeps the commandments of God and does those things that are pleasing in His sight. It asks, "Lord, what will you have me to do?" and answers quickly, "Speak, Lord, your servant hears." Obedience helps faith, and faith helps obedience. To do God's will is essential to true faith, and faith is necessary to absolute obedience.

Yet faith is often called upon to wait patiently before God and is prepared for God's seeming delays in answering prayer. Faith does not grow disheartened because prayer is not immediately honored. It takes God at His Word and lets Him take what time He chooses in fulfilling His purposes and in carrying on His work. There is bound to be delay and long days of waiting for true faith, but faith accepts the conditions. It knows there will be delays in answering prayer and regards such delays as times of testing where it is privileged to show that it is made of courage and stern stuff.

The case of Lazarus was an instance where there was delay and where the faith of two good women was sorely tried. Lazarus was critically ill, and his sisters sent for Jesus. But, without any known reason, our Lord delayed going to the relief of His sick friend. The plea was urgent and touching: *"Lord, behold, he whom thou lovest is sick"* (John 11:3). But the Master was not moved by it, and the women's earnest request seemed to fall on deaf ears. What a trial of faith! Furthermore, our Lord's delay appeared to bring about hopeless disaster. While Jesus tarried, Lazarus died.

But the delay of Jesus was used in the interest of a greater good. Finally, He made His way to the home in Bethany.

"Then said Jesus unto them plainly, Lazarus is dead. And I am glad for your sakes, that I was not there, to the intent ye may believe; nevertheless let us go unto him" (John 11:14–15).

Fear not, O tempted and tried believer, Jesus *will* come, if patience is exercised and faith holds fast. His delay will serve to make His coming more richly blessed. Pray on. Wait on. You cannot fail. If Christ delays, wait for Him. In His own good time, He *will* come and will not be late.

Delay is often the test and the strength of faith. How much patience is required when these times of testing come! Yet faith gathers strength by waiting and praying. Patience has its perfect work in the school of delay. In some instances, delay is of the very nature of the prayer. God has to do many things before He gives the final answer. They are things that are essential to the lasting good of the person who is requesting the favor from Him.

Jacob prayed with purpose and eagerness to be delivered from Esau. But, before that prayer could be answered, there was much to be done with and for Jacob. He had to be changed as well as Esau. Jacob had to be made into a new man before Esau could be. Jacob had to be converted to God before Esau could be converted to Jacob.

Among the brilliant sayings of Jesus concerning prayer, none is more interesting than this:

Verily, verily, I say unto you, He that believeth on me, the works that I do shall he do also; and greater works than these shall he do; because I go unto my Father. And whatsoever ye shall ask in my name, that will I do, that the Father may be glorified in the Son. If ye shall ask anything in my name, I will do it. (John 14:12–14)

How wonderful these statements are of what God will do in answer to prayer! What great importance these ringing words have when prefaced with solemn truth! Faith in Christ is the basis of all working and all praying. All wonderful works depend on wonderful praying, and all praying is done in the name of Jesus Christ. The amazing, simple lesson is this praying in the name of the Lord Jesus! All other conditions are of little value. Everything else is given up except Jesus. The name of Christ—the person of our Lord and Savior Jesus Christ—must be supremely sovereign in the hour of prayer.

If Jesus dwells at the source of my life—if the flow of His life has replaced all of my life—then He can safely commit the praying to my will. If absolute obedience to Him is the inspiration and force of every movement of my life, then He will pledge Himself, by a duty as deep as His own nature, that whatever is asked will be granted. Nothing can be clearer, more distinct, more unlimited both in application and extent, than the plea and urgency of Christ, *"Have faith in God"* (Mark 11:22).

Faith covers worldly as well as spiritual needs. Faith scatters excessive anxiety and needless care about what will be eaten, what will be drunk, what will be worn. Faith lives in the present and regards the day as being sufficient unto the evil thereof. (See Matthew 6:34.) It lives day by day and scatters all fears for tomorrow. Faith brings great peace of mind and perfect peace of heart.

"Thou wilt keep him in perfect peace, whose mind is stayed on thee: because he trusteth in thee" (Isa. 26:3).

When we pray, *"Give us this day our daily bread"* (Matt. 6:11), we are, in a measure, shutting tomorrow out of our prayer. We do not live for tomorrow, but for today. We do not look for tomorrow's grace or tomorrow's bread. Those who live in the present thrive best and get the most out of life. Those who pray best pray for today's, not tomorrow's, needs. Our prayer for tomorrow's needs may be unnecessary because they may not exist at all!

111

True prayers are born out of present trials and present needs. Bread for today is enough. Bread given for today is the strongest pledge that there will be bread tomorrow. Victory today is the assurance of victory tomorrow. Our prayers need to be focused on the present. We must trust God today and leave tomorrow entirely with Him. The present is ours; the future belongs to God. Prayer is the task and duty of each new day—daily prayer for daily needs.

As every day demands its bread, so every day demands its prayer. No amount of praying done today will be sufficient for tomorrow's praying. On the other hand, no praying for tomorrow is of any great value to us today. Today's manna is what we need; tomorrow God will see that our needs are supplied. This is the faith that God seeks to inspire.

So leave tomorrow, with its cares, needs, and troubles, in God's hands. There is no storing up of tomorrow's grace or tomorrow's praying. We cannot lay hold of today's grace to meet tomorrow's needs. We cannot have tomorrow's grace; we cannot eat tomorrow's bread; we cannot do tomorrow's praying. *"Sufficient unto the day is the evil thereof"* (Matt. 6:34). And, certainly, if we possess faith, sufficient also will be the good.

2

Prayer That Gets Results

The guests at a certain hotel were being made uncomfortable by the repeated banging on a piano by a little girl who possessed no musical knowledge. They complained to the owner with the hope of having the annoyance stopped. "I am sorry you are annoyed," he said. "But the girl is the child of one of my very best guests. I can hardly ask her not to touch the piano. But her father, who is away for a day or so, will return tomorrow. You can approach him and have the matter settled." When the father returned, he found his daughter in the reception room thumping on the piano. He walked up behind the child, put his arms over her shoulders, took her hands in his, and produced some beautiful music. So may it be with us, and so will it be someday. Just now, we can produce only clamor and disharmony; but, one day, the Lord Jesus will take hold of our hands of faith and prayer and use them to bring forth the music of the skies.   *—Anonymous*

GENUINE, authentic faith must be definite and free of doubt. It is not general in character or a mere belief in the being, goodness, and power of God. It is a faith that believes that the things that *"he saith, shall come to pass"* (Mark 11:23). As faith is specific, so the answer will also be definite. *"He shall have whatsoever he saith"* (v. 23). Faith and prayer select the things, and God pledges Himself to do the very things that faith and persistent prayer name and ask Him to accomplish.

We might also translate Mark 11:24 this way: "All things whatsoever you pray and ask for, believe that you receive them, and you shall have them." Perfect faith always has in its keeping what perfect prayer asks for. How large and unqualified this area of operation is—*"all things whatsoever"*! How definite and specific the promise is—*"ye shall have them"*!

Our major concern is our faith—the problems of its growth and the actions of its strong development. A faith that holds onto the very things it asks for, without wavering, doubt, or fear—that is the faith we need. We need faith, like a pearl of great price, in the process and practice of prayer.

The above statement about faith and prayer is of supreme importance. *Faith must be definite and specific.* It must be an unqualified, unmistakable request for the things asked for. It should not be a vague, indefinite, shadowy thing. It must be something more than an ideal belief in God's willingness and ability to do something for us. It should be a definite, specific asking for and expecting the things for which we ask. Note Mark 11:23: *"Whosoever...shall not doubt in his heart, but shall believe that those things which he saith shall come to pass; he shall have whatsoever he saith."*

Just as the faith and the request is definite, so the answer will be definite. The giving is not something other than the things prayed for, but the actual things sought and named. *"He shall have whatsoever he saith."* It is a certainty: *"he shall have."* The granting is unlimited both in quality and quantity.

Faith and prayer select the subjects to be prayed for, thus determining what God is to do. *"He shall have whatsoever he saith."* Christ is ready to supply exactly and fully all the demands of faith and prayer. If the order to God is clear, specific, and definite, God will fill it exactly in agreement with the terms put before Him.

Faith is not an abstract belief in the Word of God or a mere mental belief. It is not a simple agreement of the understanding and will or a passive belief in facts, no matter how sacred or thorough. Faith is an operation of God, a divine illumination, a holy energy planted by the Word of God and the Spirit in the human soul. It is a spiritual, divine principle that takes from the supernatural and makes it an understandable thing by the faculties of time and sense.

Faith deals with God and is conscious of God. It deals with the Lord Jesus Christ and sees Him as a Savior. It deals with God's Word and lays hold of the truth. It deals with the Spirit of God and is energized and inspired by its holy fire. God is the great objective of faith, for faith rests its whole weight on His Word. Faith is not an aimless act of the soul, but a looking to God and a resting on His promises. Just as love and hope always have an objective, so, also, has faith. Faith is not believing just *anything*. It is believing God, resting in Him, and trusting His Word.

Faith gives birth to prayer. It grows stronger, strikes deeper, and rises higher in the struggles and wrestling of mighty petitioning. Faith is the substance of things hoped for (see Hebrews 11:1), the confidence and reality of the inheritance of the saints. Faith, too, is humble and persistent. It can wait and pray. It can stay on its knees or lie in the dust. It is the one great condition of prayer. The lack of it lies at the root of all poor, feeble, little, unanswered praying.

The nature and meaning of faith is proven more in what it does than by any definition it is given. So, if we turn to the record of faith given to us in that great honor roll in Hebrews 11, we see something of the wonderful results of faith.

What a glorious list it is of these men and women of faith! What marvelous achievements are recorded there and set to faith's credit! The inspired writer, exhausting his resources in cataloging the Old Testament saints who were such notable examples of wonderful faith, finally said,

> *And what shall I more say? for the time would fail me to tell of Gedeon, and of Barak, and of Samson, and of Jephthae; of David also, and Samuel, and of the prophets.*   (Heb. 11:32)

Then the writer of Hebrews went on to tell of the unrecorded exploits brought about through the faith of the men of old, *"of whom the world was not worthy"* (v. 38). All these, he said, *"obtained a good report through faith"* (v. 39).

If we could only reproduce a race of saints with mighty faith and wonderful praying, what a glorious period of achievements would begin for the church and the world! The church does not need the intellectually great. The times do not demand wealthy men. It is not people of great social influence that is required. Above everybody and everything else, the church and the whole wide world of humanity need men of faith and mighty prayer. We need men and women like the saints and heroes counted in Hebrews 11 who *"obtained a good report through faith."*

Today, many men obtain a good report because of their monetary donations and their great mental gifts and talents. But there are few who obtain a good report because of their great faith in God or because of the wonderful things that come about through their great praying. Today, as much as at any time, we need men of great faith and men who are great in prayer. These are the two chief virtues that make men great in the eyes of God. These two things create conditions of real spiritual success in the life and work of the church. It is our main concern to see that we keep this kind of quality faith before God. This kind of faith grasps and holds in its keeping the things for which it asks without doubt and fear.

Doubt and fear are the twin enemies of faith. Sometimes they actually take the place of faith, and, although we pray, it is a restless, disquieted, uneasy, complaining prayer that we offer. Peter failed to walk on the waters of Galilee because he allowed the waves to break over him and swamp the power of his faith. Taking his eyes off the Lord and looking at the water around him, he began to sink and cry for help—"Lord, save me, or I perish!"

Doubts and fears should never be cherished or hidden. No one should cherish the false idea that he is a martyr to fear and doubt. It is of no credit to man's mental ability to cherish doubt of God. No comfort can possibly be gotten from such a thought. Our eyes should be taken off ourselves. They should be removed from our own weakness and allowed to rest totally on God's strength. *"Cast not away therefore your confidence, which hath great recompense of reward"* (Heb. 10:35). A simple, confiding faith, living day by day, will drive fear away. A faith that casts its burden on the Lord, each hour of the day, will drive away misgiving and deliver from doubt.

"Be careful for nothing; but in every thing by prayer and supplication with thanksgiving let your requests be made known unto God" (Phil. 4:6). That is the divine cure for all fear, anxiety, and excessive concern for the soul. All these are closely related to doubt and unbelief. This is the divine prescription for securing the peace that passes all understanding and keeps the heart and mind in quietness and peace.

All of us need to pay attention and heed the caution given in Hebrews 3:12: *"Take heed, brethren, lest there be in any of you an evil heart of unbelief, in departing from the living God."* We need to guard against unbelief as we would against an enemy. Faith needs to be cultivated. We need to keep on praying, *"Lord, Increase our faith"* (Luke 17:5), for faith is capable of increasing. Paul's tribute to the Thessalonians was that their faith grew exceedingly. (See 2 Thessalonians 1:3.) Faith is increased by exercise, by being put to use. It is nourished by painful trials.

> *That the trial of your faith, being much more precious than of gold that perisheth, though it be tried with fire, might be found unto praise and honour and glory at the appearing of Jesus Christ.* *(1 Pet. 1:7)*

Faith grows by reading and meditating upon the Word of God. Most of all, faith thrives in an atmosphere of prayer.

It would be good if we stop and ask ourselves, "Do I have faith in God? Do I have *real* faith—faith that keeps me in perfect peace about the things of the earth and heaven?" This is the most important question a man can propose and expect to be answered. And there is another question closely related to it in significance and importance: "Do I really pray to God so that He hears me and answers my prayers? And do I truly pray to God so that I get directly from God the things I ask of Him?"

It was said that Augustus Caesar found Rome a city of wood and left it a city of marble. The pastor who succeeds in changing his people from a prayerless to a prayerful people has done a greater work than Augustus did in changing a city from wood to marble. After all, this is the major work of the preacher. Primarily, he is dealing with prayerless people, of whom it is said, *"God is not in all* [their] *thoughts"* (Ps. 10:4).

The pastor meets such people everywhere all the time. His main business is to turn them from being forgetful about God, from lacking faith, from being prayerless, into people who habitually pray, believe in God, remember Him, and do His will. The preacher is not sent simply to persuade men to join the church or to get them to do better. He is sent to get them to pray, to trust God, and to keep God ever before their eyes so that they may not sin against Him.

The work of the ministry is to change unbelieving sinners into praying, believing saints. The call goes out by divine authority, *"Believe on the Lord Jesus Christ, and thou shalt be saved"* (Acts 16:31). We catch a glimpse of the tremendous importance of faith and the great value God has put on it, when we remember that He has made it the one essential condition of being saved. *"For by grace are ye saved through faith"* (Eph. 2:8). So, when we think about the great importance of prayer, we find faith standing immediately by its side. By faith are we saved, and by faith we *stay* saved. Prayer introduces us to a life of faith. Paul declared that the life he lived, he lived by faith in the Son of God, who loved him and gave Himself for him (see Galatians 2:20)—that he walked by faith and not by sight. (See 2 Corinthians 5:7.)

Prayer is absolutely dependent on faith. It has virtually no existence apart from it and accomplishes nothing unless it is faith's inseparable companion. Faith makes prayer effective and, in a certain important sense, must precede it. *"For he that cometh to God must believe that he is, and that he is a rewarder of them that diligently seek him"* (Heb. 11:6).

Before prayer ever starts toward God, before its petition is chosen and its requests made known, faith must have gone on ahead. It must have had its belief in the existence of God stated. It must have given its consent to the gracious truth that God is a rewarder of those who diligently seek His face.

This is the primary step in praying. In this regard, while faith does not bring the blessing, it puts prayer in a position to ask for it. It leads to another step of understanding by helping the petitioner believe that God is able and willing to bless.

Faith starts prayer to work. It clears the way to the mercy seat. It gives assurance, first of all, that there is a mercy seat, and that the High Priest waits there for us to come with our prayers. Faith opens the way for prayer to approach God. But it does more. It accompanies prayer with every step she takes. It is her inseparable companion. When requests are made to God, faith turns the asking into obtaining. And faith follows prayer, since the spiritual life into which a believer is led by prayer is a life of faith. Faith, not a life of works, is the one prominent characteristic of the experience that believers are brought into through prayer.

Faith makes prayer strong and gives it patience to wait on God. Faith believes that God is a rewarder. No truth is more clearly revealed and none is more encouraging in Scripture than this. Even the prayer closet has its promised reward: *"Thy Father which seeth in secret himself shall reward thee openly"* (Matt. 6:4). The most insignificant service given to a disciple in the name of the Lord surely receives its reward. Faith gives its hearty consent to this precious truth.

Yet, faith is narrowed down to one particular thing. It does not believe that God will reward everybody. It does not believe that He is a rewarder of all who pray, but that He is a rewarder of them that *"diligently seek Him"* (Heb. 11:6). Faith rests its case on diligent prayer. It gives assurance and encouragement to diligent seekers after God, for it is they alone who are richly rewarded when they pray.

We constantly need to be reminded that faith is the one inseparable condition of successful praying. There are other conditions, but faith is the final, essential condition of true praying, as it is written: *"But without faith it is impossible to please him"* (v. 6).

James put this truth very plainly:

> *If any of you lack wisdom, let him ask of God, that giveth to all men liberally, and upbraideth not; and it shall be given him. But let him ask in faith, nothing wavering. For he that wavereth is like a wave of the sea driven with the wind and tossed. For let not that man think that he shall receive any thing of the Lord.* (James 1:5–7)

Doubting is always forbidden because it stands as an enemy to faith and hinders effective praying. Paul gave us a priceless truth relative to the conditions of successful praying. He said, *"I will therefore that men pray every where, lifting up holy hands, without wrath and doubting"* (1 Tim. 2:8).

All questioning must be guarded against and avoided. Fear and doubt have no place in true praying. Faith must assert itself and tell these enemies of prayer to depart.

Faith cannot be assigned too much authority, but prayer is the scepter that signals power. There is much spiritual wisdom in the following advice written by a famous saint:

> Do you want to be free from the bondage of corruption? Do you want to grow in grace in general and grow in grace in particular? If you do, your way is plain. Ask God for more faith. Beg Him morning, noon, and night, while you walk by the road, while you sit in the house, when you lie down, and when you rise up. Beg Him simply to impress divine things more deeply on your heart, to give you more and more of *"the substance of things hoped for"* and of *"the evidence of things not seen"* (Heb. 11:1).

Great incentives to pray are furnished in Scripture. Our Lord closes His teaching about prayer with the assurance and promise of heaven. The presence of Jesus Christ in heaven and the preparation He is making there for His saints help the weariness of praying. The assurance that He will come again to receive the saints strengthens and sweetens its difficult work! These things are the star of hope to prayer. They are the wiping away of its tears and the putting of the sweet odor of heaven into the bitterness of its cry. The spirit of a pilgrim makes praying easier. An earthbound, earth-satisfied spirit cannot pray. The flame of spiritual desire in such a heart has either gone out or is smoldering in a faint glow. The wings of its faith are clipped, its eyes are filmed, its tongue is silenced. But they who, in immovable faith and unceasing prayer, wait continually upon the Lord *do* renew their strength, *do* mount up with wings as eagles, *do* run and are not weary, *do* walk and not faint (Isa. 40:31).

3

Prayer and Trusting God

One evening I left my office in New York with a bitterly cold wind in my face. I had with me (as I thought) my thick, warm muffler, but when I proceeded to button up against the storm, I found that it was gone. I turned back, looked along the streets, searched my office, but in vain. I realized that I must have dropped it, and I prayed to God that I would find it; for such was the state of the weather that it would be running a great risk to proceed without it. I looked again up and down the surrounding streets, but without success. Suddenly, I saw a man on the opposite side of the road holding out something in his hand. I crossed over and asked him if that was my muffler. He handed it to me saying, "It was blown to me by the wind." He who rides upon the storm, had used the wind as a means of answering prayer.
—William Horst

PRAYER does not stand alone. It is not an isolated duty or an independent principle. It lives in fellowship with other Christian duties. It is married to other principles and is a partner with other graces. But prayer is firmly joined to faith. Faith gives it color and tone, shapes its character, and secures its results.

Trust is faith that has become absolute, approved, and accomplished. When all is said and done, there is a sort of risk in faith and its exercise. But trust is firm belief; it is faith in full bloom. Trust is a conscious act, a fact of which we are aware. According to the scriptural concept, it is the eye of the newborn soul and the ear of the renewed soul. It is the feeling of the soul—the spiritual sight, hearing, taste, and feeling. All these have to do with trust. How bright, distinct, conscious, powerful, and scriptural such a trust is! How different, feeble, dry, and cold it is from many forms of modern beliefs!

These modern beliefs do not bring awareness of their presence. They do not bring *"joy unspeakable and full of glory"* (1 Pet. 1:8) from their exercise. They are, for the most part, adventures in the doubts of the soul. There is no safe, sure trust in anything. The whole transaction takes place in the area of *maybe* and *perhaps*.

Trust, like life, is feeling, though much more. An unfelt life is a contradiction. An unfelt trust is a misnaming and a false belief. Trust is the most felt of all qualities. It is *all* feeling, and it only works by love. An unfelt love is as impossible as an unfelt trust. The trust we are speaking about is a conviction. An unfelt conviction? How absurd!

Trust sees God doing things here and now. Yes, and more. It rises to a high place and looks into the invisible and the eternal. It realizes that God has done things and regards them as being already done. Trust brings eternity into the history and happenings of time. It transforms hope into the reality of fulfillment and changes promise into present possession. We know when we trust, just as we know when we see. We are conscious of our sense of touch. Trust sees, receives, holds. Trust is its own witness.

Yet, quite often, faith is too weak to obtain God's greatest good, immediately. It has to wait in loving, strong, prayerful, pressing obedience, until it grows in strength and is able to bring down the eternal into the areas of experience and time.

Up to this point, trust shapes all its forces. Here it holds. In the struggle, trust's grasp becomes mightier, and it grasps for itself all that God has done for it in His eternal wisdom and fullness of grace.

In the matter of waiting in mighty prayer, faith rises to its highest level and becomes the gift of God. It becomes the blessed character and expression of the soul that is secured by a constant fellowship with and tireless request to God.

Jesus Christ clearly taught that faith was the condition on which prayer was answered. When our Lord cursed the fig tree, the disciples were very surprised that its withering had actually taken place. Their remarks indicated their unbelief. It was then that Jesus said to them:

> *Have faith in God. For verily I say unto you, That whosoever shall say unto this mountain, Be thou removed, and be thou cast into the sea; and shall not doubt in his heart, but shall believe that those things which he saith shall come to pass; he*

shall have whatsoever he saith. Therefore I say unto you,
What things soever ye desire, when ye pray, believe that ye re-
ceive them, and ye shall have them.   *(Mark 11:22–24)*

There is no place where trust grows so readily and richly as in
the prayer closet. Its unfolding and development are rapid and
wholesome when they are kept regularly and well. When these ap-
pointments are sincere, full, and free, trust grows increasingly. The
eye and presence of God give active life to trust, just like the eye
and presence of the sun make fruit and flower grow and all things
glad and bright with fuller life.

Faith and trust in the Lord form the keynote and foundation
of prayer. Primarily, it is not trust in the Word of God, but rather
trust in the person of God. For trust in the person of God must
precede trust in the Word of God. *"Ye believe in God, believe also in
me"* (John 14:1) is the demand our Lord makes on the personal
trust of His disciples. The person of Jesus Christ must be central to
the eye of trust. Jesus sought to impress this great truth on Martha when her brother lay dead in their home at Bethany. Martha
stated her belief in the resurrection of her brother: *"Martha saith
unto him, I know that he shall rise again in the resurrection at the
last day"* (John 11:24).

Jesus lifts her trust above the mere fact of the resurrection, to
His own person, by saying,

*I am the resurrection, and the life: he that believeth in me,
though he were dead, yet shall he live: and whosoever liveth
and believeth in me shall never die. Believest thou this? She
saith unto him, Yea, Lord: I believe that thou art the Christ,
the Son of God, which should come into the world.*
                                         (John 11:25–27)

Trust in a historical fact or a mere record may be a very passive thing, but trust in a person strengthens the quality. It bears
fruit and supplies it with love. The trust that supplies prayer centers in a Person.

Trust goes even further than this. The trust that inspires our
prayer must not only be one in the person of God, and of Christ,
but in their ability and willingness to grant the thing prayed for. It
is not only, *"Trust in the LORD"* (Ps. 37:3), but also, *"for in the
LORD JEHOVAH is everlasting strength"* (Isa. 26:4).

The trust that our Lord taught as a condition of effective prayer is not from the head but from the heart. It is trust that does not doubt. Such trust has the divine assurance that it will be honored with large and satisfying answers. The strong promise of our Lord brings faith down to the present and counts on a present answer.

Do we believe without a doubt? When we pray, do we believe that we will receive the things we ask for, not on a future day, but then and there? This is the teaching of this inspiring scripture. How we need to pray, *"Lord, Increase our faith"* (Luke 17:5) until doubt is gone, and absolute trust claims the promised blessings as its very own.

This is no easy condition. It is only reached after many failures, much praying, many wailings, and much trial of faith. May our faith increase until we realize and receive all the fullness that there is in the name of Jesus, which guarantees to do so much.

Our Lord puts forth trust as the very foundation of praying. The background of prayer is trust. The whole purpose of Christ's ministry and work was dependent on absolute trust in His Father. The center of trust is God. Mountains of difficulties and all other hindrances to prayer are moved out of the way by trust and its strong follower, faith.

When trust is perfect and there is no doubt, prayer is simply the outstretched hand ready to receive. Trust perfected is prayer perfected. Trust looks to receive the thing asked for and gets it. Trust is not a belief that God *can* bless or that He *will* bless, but that He *does* bless, here and now. Trust always operates in the present tense. Hope looks toward the future. Trust looks to the present. Hope expects. Trust possesses. Trust receives what prayer acquires. So, what prayer needs, at all times, is abiding and abundant trust.

The disciples' unfortunate lack of trust and resulting failure to do what they were sent out to do is seen in the case of the lunatic son. His father brought him to nine of them while their Master was on the Mount of Transfiguration. The boy, sadly tormented, was brought to these men to be cured of his sickness. They had been commissioned to do this very kind of work. This was part of their mission. They tried to cast the devil from the boy but noticeably failed. The devil was too much for them. They were humiliated at their failure while their enemies were victorious.

During the incident, Jesus drew near. He was informed of the circumstances and conditions connected with it. Here is the account of what followed:

*Then Jesus answered and said, O faithless and perverse gen-
eration, how long shall I be with you? how long shall I suffer
you? bring him hither to me. And Jesus rebuked the devil; and
he departed out of him: and the child was cured from that
very hour. Then came the disciples to Jesus apart, and said,
Why could not we cast him out?...Howbeit this kind goeth not
out but by prayer and fasting.* (Matt. 17:17–19, 21)

Where was the difficulty of these men? They had been careless
in cultivating their faith by prayer, and, as a result, their trust utterly failed. They did not trust God, Christ, or the authenticity of
His mission or their own. It has been the same since, in many a
crisis in the church of God. Failure has resulted from a lack of
trust, a weakness of faith, and a lack of prayerfulness. Many failures in revival efforts have been traceable to the same cause. Faith
has not been nurtured and made powerful by prayer. Neglect of the
inner chamber is the solution of most spiritual failure. This is also
true of our personal struggles with the Devil when we attempt to
cast out devils. Being on our knees in private fellowship with God
is our only assurance that we will have Him with us in our personal
struggles or in our efforts to convert sinners.

When people came to Him, our Lord put their trust in Him
and the divinity of His mission in the forefront. He did not give a
definition of trust. He did not furnish a theological discussion or
analysis of it. He knew that men would see what faith was by what
faith *did*. They would see from its free exercise that trust grew up,
automatically, in His presence. It was the product of His work, His
power, and His person. These furnished and created a favorable
atmosphere for its exercise and development. Trust is altogether
too simple for verbal definition. It is too sincere and spontaneous
for theological terms. The very simplicity of trust is what staggers
many people. They look for some great thing to come to pass, while
all the time *"the word is nigh thee, even in thy mouth, and in thy
heart"* (Rom. 10:8).

When the sad news of his daughter's death was brought to
Jairus, our Lord interrupted saying, *"Fear not: believe only, and she
shall be made whole"* (Luke 8:50). To the woman with the issue of
blood, who stood tremblingly before Him, He said, *"Daughter, be of
good comfort: thy faith hath made thee whole; go in peace"* (v. 48).

As the two blind men followed Him, pressing their way into
the house, He said, *"According to your faith be it unto you. And*

their eyes were opened" (Matt. 9:29–30). When the paralytic was let down by four of his friends through the roof of the house where Jesus was teaching and placed before Him, it is recorded: *"And Jesus seeing their faith said unto the sick of the palsy; Son, be of good cheer; thy sins be forgiven thee"* (v. 2).

When Jesus dismissed the centurion whose servant was seriously ill, He did it in a particular manner. The centurion had come to Jesus with the prayer that He speak the healing word without even going to his house. Jesus did the following: *"And Jesus said unto the centurion, Go thy way; and as thou hast believed, so be it done unto thee. And his servant was healed in the selfsame hour"* (Matt. 8:13). When the poor leper fell at Jesus' feet and cried out for relief saying, *"Lord, if thou wilt, thou canst make me clean"* (v. 2), Jesus immediately granted his request, and the man glorified Him with a loud voice.

The Syrophenician woman came to Jesus about her troubled daughter. Making the case her own, she prayed, *"Lord, help me"* (Matt. 15:25). Jesus honored her faith and prayer, saying, *"O woman, great is thy faith: be it unto thee even as thou wilt. And her daughter was made whole from that very hour"* (v. 28).

After the disciples had utterly failed to cast the devil out of the epileptic boy, the father of the boy came to Jesus with a sad, despairing cry, *"If thou canst do any thing, have compassion on us, and help us"* (Mark 9:22). But Jesus replied, *"If thou canst believe, all things are possible to him that believeth"* (v. 23).

Blind Bartimaeus, sitting by the wayside, heard our Lord as He passed by and cried out pitifully, *"Jesus, thou son of David, have mercy on me"* (Mark 10:47). The keen ears of our Lord immediately caught the sound of prayer. He said to the beggar, *"Go thy way; thy faith hath made thee whole. And immediately he received his sight, and followed Jesus in the way"* (v. 52).

Jesus spoke cheerful, soul-comforting words to the weeping, penitent woman who washed His feet with her tears and wiped them with her hair: *"Thy faith hath saved thee; go in peace"* (Luke 7:50).

One day Jesus healed ten lepers at one time, in answer to their united prayer, *"Jesus, Master, have mercy on us"* (Luke 17:13). He told them to go and show themselves to the priests. *"And it came to pass, that, as they went, they were cleansed"* (v. 14).

4

Prayer and Desire

There are those who will mock me and tell me to stick to my trade as a cobbler. They will tell me to not trouble my mind with philosophy and theology. But the truth of God did so burn in my bones, that I took my pen in hand and began to set down what I had seen. —*Jacob Behmen*

DESIRE is not merely a simple wish. It is a deep-seated desire and an intense longing for accomplishment. In the realm of spiritual affairs, it is an important addition to prayer. It is so important that one could almost say desire is an absolute essential of prayer. Desire precedes and accompanies prayer. Desire goes before prayer and is created and intensified by it. Prayer is the oral expression of desire. If prayer is asking God for something, then prayer must be expressed. Prayer comes out into the open. Desire is silent. Prayer is heard. The deeper the desire, the stronger the prayer. Without desire, prayer is a meaningless mumble of words. Such uninterested, formal praying, with no heart, feeling, or real desire accompanying it, is to be avoided like a plague. Its exercise is a waste of precious time, and no real blessing results from it.

Yet, even if it is discovered that desire is honestly absent, we should pray anyway. We ought to pray. The *ought* comes in, in order that desire and expression are produced. God's Word commands it. Our judgment tells us we ought to pray—whether we feel like it or not—and not allow our feelings to determine our prayer habits. In such circumstances, we ought to pray for the *desire* to pray. This desire is God-given and heaven-born. We should pray for desire. Then, when desire has been given, we should pray according to its principles. The lack of spiritual desire should grieve us and

127

lead us to mourn its absence. We should earnestly seek for its prize so that our praying would be an expression of "the soul's sincere desire."

A sense of need creates, or should create, earnest desire. The stronger the need before God, the greater should be the desire and more earnest the prayer. The "poor in spirit" are highly competent to pray.

Hunger is an active sense of physical need. It prompts the request for food. In like manner, the inward awareness of spiritual need creates desire, and desire creates prayer. Desire is an inward longing for something that we do not possess and need. It is something that God has promised and that can be secured by earnest prayer at His throne of grace.

Spiritual desire, carried to a higher degree, is the evidence of the new birth. It is born in the renewed soul: *"As newborn babes, desire the sincere milk of the word, that ye may grow thereby"* (1 Pet. 2:2).

The absence of this holy desire in the heart is proof that there has been a decline in spiritual joy or that the new birth has never taken place. *"Blessed are they which do hunger and thirst after righteousness: for they shall be filled"* (Matt. 5:6).

These heaven-given appetites are proof of a renewed heart and the evidence of a stirring spiritual life. Physical appetites are the characteristics of a living body, not a corpse. Spiritual desires belong to a soul made alive to God. As the renewed soul hungers and thirsts after righteousness, these holy, inward desires break out into earnest, petitioning prayer.

In prayer we are dependent on the name and power of Jesus Christ, our great High Priest. Searching the accompanying conditions and forces in prayer, we find its vital basis, which is seated in the human heart. It is not simply our need; it is the heart's desire for what we need and for what we feel urged to pray about. *Desire is the will in action.* It is a strong, conscious longing that is excited in the inner man for some great good. Desire exalts the object of its longing and sets the mind on it. It has choice, attitude, and fire in it. Prayer, based on these, is genuine and specific. It knows its need, feels and sees the thing that will meet it, and hurries to acquire it.

Holy desire is helped by devout study. Meditation on our spiritual need and on God's readiness and ability to correct it helps desire to grow. Serious thought practiced before praying increases desire. It makes prayer more insistent and tends to save us from the danger of private prayer—wandering thought. We fail much more in desire than in its outward expression. We keep the form while the inner life fades and almost dies.

One might ask whether the feebleness of our desire for God, the Holy Spirit, and all the fullness of Christ is the cause of our lack of prayer. Do we really feel this inward hunger and desire for heavenly treasures? Do the inborn groanings of desire stir our souls to mighty wrestlings? Oh, the fire burns entirely too low. The flaming heat of the soul has been toned down to a lukewarmness. This, we should remember, was the major cause of the sad, desperate condition of the Laodicean Christians. Because of this condition, the awful condemnation is written about them: "[You are] *rich, and increased with goods, and* **have need of nothing;** *and knowest not that thou art wretched, and miserable, and poor, and blind, and naked"* (Rev. 3:17, emphasis added).

Again, we might ask, do we have that desire which presses us to close communion with God? Do we have the desire that is filled with silent pain that keeps us there through the agony of an intense, soul-stirred prayer? Our hearts need to be worked over, not only to get the evil out of them, but to get the good into them. They need to be worked over so that the foundation and inspiration to the incoming good is strong, moving desire. This holy, fervent flame in the soul awakens the interest of heaven, attracts God's attention, and places at the disposal of those who exercise it, the inexhaustible riches of divine grace.

The dampening of the flame of holy desire is destructive to the vital, aggressive forces in church life. God expects to be represented by a fiery church or He is not, in any proper sense, represented at all. God Himself is all fire; and His church, if it is to be like Him, must also be like white heat. The only things that His church can afford to be on fire about are the great, eternal interests of heaven-born, God-given faith.

Yet, holy desire does not have to be fussy in order to be consuming. Our Lord was the incarnate opposite of nervous excitability, the absolute opposite of intolerant or noisy speech. Yet, the zeal of God's house consumed Him. And the world is still feeling the glow of His fierce, consuming flame. They are responding to it with an ever increasing readiness and an even larger response.

A lack of passion in prayer is a sure sign of the lack of depth and the intensity of desire. The absence of intense desire is a sure sign of God's absence from the heart! To reduce fervor is to retire from God. He can, and does, tolerate in His children many things in the areas of weakness and mistakes. He can and will pardon sin when the repentant one prays.

But two things are intolerable to Him—insincerity and lukewarmness. Lack of heart and heat are two things He hates. He said to the Laodiceans, in unmistakable severity and condemnation: *"I would thou wert cold or hot. So then because thou art lukewarm, and neither cold nor hot, I will spue thee out of my mouth"* (Rev. 3:15–16).

This was God's precise judgment on the lack of fire in one of the seven churches. It is His accusation against individual Christians for the fatal lack of sacred zeal. Fire is the motivating power in prayer. Religious principles that do not come out of fire have neither force nor effect. Fire is the wing on which faith ascends. Passion is the soul of prayer. It is the *"effectual fervent prayer of a righteous man* [that] *availeth much"* (James 5:16). Love is kindled in a flame, and zeal is its life. Flame is the air that true Christian experience breathes. It feeds on fire. It can withstand anything except a weak flame. It dies, chilled and starved.

True prayer *must* be aflame. The Christian life and character need to be on fire. Lack of spiritual heat creates more unbelief than lack of faith does. If man is not wholly interested in the things of heaven, he is not interested in them at all. The fiery souls are those who conquer in the day of battle. They are those from whom the kingdom of heaven suffers violence and who take it by force (Matt. 11:12). The stronghold of God is taken only by those who storm it in worshipful earnestness and besiege it with fiery, unshaken zeal.

Nothing short of being red hot for God can keep the glow of heaven in our hearts during these chilly days. The early Methodists had no heating in their churches. They said that the flame in the pew and the fire in the pulpit must be sufficient to keep them warm. And we, today, need to have the live coal from God's altar and the consuming flame from heaven glowing in our hearts. This flame is not mental power or fleshly energy. It is divine, intense, dross-consuming fire in the soul. It is the very being of the Spirit of God.

No scholarship, pure speech, breadth of mental outlook, fluent language, or elegance can make up for the lack of fire. Prayer ascends by fire. Flame gives prayer access as well as wings. It gives prayer acceptance as well as energy. There is no incense without fire, no prayer without flame.

Ardent desire is the basis of unceasing prayer. It is not a shallow, fickle tendency, but a strong yearning, an unquenchable desire that permeates, glows, burns, and fixes the heart. It is the flame of a present and active principle ascending up to God. It is ardor propelled by desire that burns its way to the throne of mercy and gets its request. It is the determination of desire that gives victory in a great struggle of prayer. It is the burden of a weighty desire that sobers, makes restless, and reduces to quietness the soul just emerged from its mighty wrestlings. It is the inclusive character of desire that arms prayer with a thousand requests. It clothes it with an indestructible courage and an all-conquering power.

The Syrophenician woman is an object lesson of desire. The demanding widow represents desire gaining its end, overcoming obstacles that would be insurmountable to weaker instincts.

Prayer is not the rehearsal of a mere performance. It is not an indefinite, widespread demand. Desire, while it ignites the soul, holds it to the object sought. Prayer is a necessary phase of spiritual habit, but it ceases to be prayer when it is carried on by habit alone. It is depth and strength of spiritual desire that gives intensity and depth to prayer. The soul cannot be unconcerned when some great desire heats and inflames it. The urgency of our desire holds us to the thing desired with a courage that refuses to be lessened or loosened. It stays, pleads, persists, and refuses to let go until the blessing has been given.

> Lord, I cannot let Thee go,
> Till a blessing Thou bestow;
> Do not turn away Thy face;
> Mine's an urgent, pressing case.

The secret of cowardice, the lack of demanding, and the scarcity of courage and strength in prayer lie in the weakness of spiritual desire. The failure of prayer is the fearful evidence of that desire having ceased to live. That soul whose desire for Him no longer pushes into the inner room, has turned from God. There is no successful prayer without consuming desire. Of course, there can be much *seeming* to pray, without desire of any kind.

Many things may be listed and much ground covered. But does desire make up the list? Does desire map out the region to be covered? The answer hangs on the issue of whether our petitioning is babbling or prayer. Desire is intense, but narrow. It cannot spread itself over a wide area. It wants a few things and wants them badly. It wants them so badly that nothing but God's willingness to answer can bring it ease or contentment.

Desire shoots at its objective. There may be many things that are desired, but they are specifically and individually felt and expressed. David did not yearn for everything. He did not allow his desires to spread out everywhere and hit nothing. Here is the way his desires ran and found expression:

One thing have I desired of the Lord, that will I seek after; that I may dwell in the house of the Lord all the days of my life, to behold the beauty of the Lord, and to inquire in His temple.   *(Ps. 27:4)*

It is this singleness of desire, this definite yearning, that counts in praying and drives prayer directly to the core and center of supply.

In the Beatitudes, Jesus voiced the words that bear directly upon the inborn desires of a renewed soul with the promise that they will be granted. *"Blessed are they which do hunger and thirst after righteousness: for they shall be filled"* (Matt. 5:6).

This, then, is the basis of prayer that expects an answer. It is that strong, inward desire that has entered the spiritual appetite and demands to be satisfied. For us, it is entirely true and frequent that our prayers operate in the dry area of a mere wish or in the lifeless area of a memorized prayer. Sometimes our prayers are merely stereotyped expressions of set phrases and standardized dimensions. The freshness and life has gone out long ago.

Without desire, there is no burden of the soul, no sense of need, no enthusiasm, no vision, no strength, and no glow of faith. There is no strong pressure, no holding on to God with a deathless, despairing grasp—*"I will not let thee go, except thou bless me"* (Gen. 32:26). There is no total surrender as there was with Moses. Lost in the agony of a desperate, stubborn, and all-consuming request, he cried, *"Yet now, if thou wilt forgive their sin—; and if not, blot me, I pray thee, out of thy book which thou hast written"* (Exod. 32:32). Or, there was also John Knox when he pleaded, "Give me Scotland, or may I die!"

God draws very close to the praying soul. To see God, know God, and live for God—these form the objective of all true praying.

So, praying is, after all, inspired to seek after God. Prayer desire is ignited to see God and have a clearer, fuller, sweeter, and richer revelation of God. So, to those who pray this way, the Bible becomes a new Bible and Christ a new Savior by the light and revelation of the prayer closet.

We affirm and reaffirm that burning desire because the best and most powerful gifts and graces of the Spirit of God are the real heritage of true praying. Self and service cannot be divorced. They cannot possibly be separated. More than that, desire must be made intensely personal. It must be centered on God with an insatiable hungering and thirsting after Him and His righteousness. *"My soul thirsteth for God, for the living God"* (Ps. 42:2). The essential prerequisite for all true praying is a deep-seated desire that seeks after God Himself. It remains unsatisfied until the choice gifts in heaven have been richly and abundantly given.

5

Prayer and Enthusiasm

St. Teresa rose off her deathbed to finish her work. She inspected, with all her quickness of eye and love of order, the whole house where she had been carried to die. She saw everything put in its proper place and everyone answering to their proper order. After that she attended to the divine offices of the day. Then she went back to her bed, summoned her daughter around her...and, with David's penitential prayers on her tongue, Teresa of Jesus went forth to meet her Bridegroom.
—Alexander Whyte

PRAYER without burning enthusiasm stakes nothing on the issue, because it has nothing to stake. It comes with empty hands. These hands are listless, empty, and have never learned the lesson of clinging to the cross.

Prayer without enthusiasm has no heart in it. It is an empty thing, an unfit vessel. Heart, soul, and life must find a place in all real praying. Heaven must be made to feel the force of this crying unto God.

Paul was a notable example of the man who possesses a fervent spirit of prayer. His petitioning was all-consuming. It centered immovably upon the object of his desire and the God who was able to meet it.

Prayers must be red hot. It is the fervent prayer that is effective and profitable. Coldness of spirit hinders praying. It takes fire to make prayers go. A warm soul creates a favorable atmosphere to prayer because it is favorable to fervency. Prayer ascends to heaven by fire. Yet, fire is not fuss, heat, or noise. Heat is intensity—something that glows and burns.

God wants warmhearted servants. The Holy Spirit comes *as a fire* to dwell in us. We are to be baptized with the Holy Spirit and with fire. (See Luke 3:16.) Fervency is warmth of soul. A phlegmatic temperament is detestable to vital experience. If our faith does not set us on fire, it is because we have frozen hearts. God dwells in a flame; the Holy Spirit descends in fire. To be absorbed in God's will and to be so in earnest about doing it that our whole being takes fire are the qualifying conditions of the man who would engage in effective prayer.

Our Lord warns us against feeble praying. *"Men ought always to pray, and not to faint"* (Luke 18:1), said Christ to His disciples. This means that we are to possess enough enthusiasm to carry us through the severe and long periods of pleading prayer. Fire makes one alert, vigilant, and brings him out more than a conqueror. The atmosphere about us is too heavily charged with resisting forces for limp and languid prayers to make headway. It takes heat, fervency, and meteoric fire to push through to the upper heavens where God dwells with His saints in light.

Many of the great Bible characters were notable examples of fervency of spirit when they were seeking God. The psalmist declared with great earnestness, *"My soul breaketh for the longing that it hath unto thy judgments at all times"* (Ps. 119:20). What strong heart desires are here! What earnest soul longings there are for the Word of the living God! An even greater fervency is expressed by him in another place:

> As the hart panteth after the water brooks, so panteth my soul after thee, O God. My soul thirsteth for God, for the living God: when shall I come and appear before God? (Ps. 42:1–2)

This is the word of a man who lived in a state of grace and had been deeply and supernaturally fulfilled in his soul.

Fervency before God counts in the hour of prayer and finds a speedy and rich reward at His hands. The psalmist gave us this statement of what God had done for the king, as his heart turned toward his Lord: *"Thou hast given him his heart's desire, and hast not withholden the request of his lips"* (Ps. 21:2).

At another time, he expressed himself directly to God in making his request: *"Lord, all my desire is before thee; and my groaning is not hid from thee"* (Ps. 38:9). What a cheerful thought! Our inward groanings, our secret desires, our heart longings are not hidden from the eyes of Him with whom we deal in prayer.

The incentive to fervency of spirit before God is precisely the same as it is for continued and earnest prayer. While fervency is not prayer, yet it comes out of an earnest soul and is precious in the sight of God. Fervency in prayer is the forerunner of what God will do by way of an answer. When we seek His face in prayer, God stands pledged to give us the desire of our hearts in proportion to the fervency of spirit we exhibit.

Fervency has its seat in the heart, not in the brain or intellectual faculties of the mind. Fervency, therefore, is not an expression of the intellect. Fervency of spirit is something far above poetical fancy or sentimental imagery. It is something besides preference, which contrasts likes with dislikes. Fervency is the pulse and movement of the emotional nature.

It is not our job to create fervency of spirit at will, but we can ask God to implant it. Then, it is ours to nourish and cherish, guard against extinction, and prevent its lessening or decline. The process of personal salvation is not just to pray and express our desires to God. But it is to acquire a fervent spirit and seek to cultivate it. It is never wrong to ask God to create in us and keep alive the spirit of fervent prayer.

Fervency has to do with God, just as prayer has to do with Him. Desire always has an objective. If we desire at all, we desire *something*. The degree of enthusiasm with which we form our spiritual desires will always serve to determine the earnestness of our praying. In this relation, Adoniram Judson has said,

> A travailing spirit, the throes of a great burdened desire, belongs to prayer. A fervency strong enough to drive away sleep, which devotes and inflames the spirit, and which retires all earthly ties, all this belongs to wrestling, prevailing prayer. The Spirit, the power, the air, and food of prayer is in such a spirit.

Prayer must be clothed with fervency, strength, and power. It is the force that, centered on God, determines the amount of Himself given out for earthly good. Men who are fervent in spirit are bent on attaining righteousness, truth, grace, and all other sublime, powerful graces that adorn the character of the authentic, unquestioned child of God.

God once declared the following message by the mouth of the prophet Hanani to Asa. Asa, at one time, had been true to God. But, through success and material prosperity, he lost his faith.

The eyes of the Lord run to and fro throughout the whole earth, to show himself strong in the behalf of them whose heart is perfect toward him. Herein thou hast done foolishly: therefore from henceforth thou shalt have wars. (2 Chron. 16:9)

God had heard Asa's prayer in early life; but because he had given up the life of prayer and simple faith, disaster and trouble came to him.

In Romans 15:30 we have the word *strive* in the request that Paul made for prayerful cooperation. In Colossians 4:12 we have the same word, but translated differently: *"Epaphras...always labouring fervently for you in prayers."* Paul charged the Romans to strive together with him in prayer, that is, to help him with his struggle in prayer. The word *strive* means "to enter into a contest, to fight against adversaries." It means "to engage with fervent zeal to endeavor to obtain."

These recorded instances of the exercise and reward of faith allow us to see that, in almost every instance, faith was blended with trust until the former was swallowed up in the latter. It is hard to properly distinguish the specific activities of these two qualities, faith and trust. But there is a point at which faith is relieved of its burden, so to speak, and trust comes along and says, "You have done your part. The rest is mine!"

In the incident of the barren fig tree, our Lord transfers the marvelous power of faith to His disciples. To their exclamation, *"How soon is the fig tree withered away!"* (Matt. 21:20), He said,

If ye have faith, and doubt not, ye shall not only do this which is done to the fig tree, but also if ye shall say unto this mountain, Be thou removed, and be thou cast into the sea; it shall be done. And all things, whatsoever ye shall ask in prayer, believing, ye shall receive. (vv. 21–22)

When a believer achieves these magnificent proportions of faith, he steps into the realm of absolute trust. He stands without a tremor at the height of his spiritual outreaching. He has attained faith's top stone, which is unswerving, unalterable, unquestionable trust in the power of the living God.

6

Prayer That Is Persistent

How glibly we talk of praying without ceasing! Yet, we are quite ready to quit if our prayer remains unanswered but one week or month! We assume that by a stroke of His arm or an action of His will, God will give us what we ask. It never seems to dawn on us that He is the Master of nature, as of grace, and that sometimes He chooses one way, and sometimes another, to do His work. It takes years, sometimes, to answer a prayer. When it is answered, we can look back to see that it did take years. But God knows all the time. It is His will that we pray, and pray, and still pray, and so come to know indeed what it is to pray without ceasing. —*Anonymous*

OUR Lord Jesus declared that *"men ought always to pray, and not to faint"* (Luke 18:1). The parable that comes after these words was taught with the intention of saving men from faintheartedness and weakness in prayer. Our Lord wanted to teach us to guard against negligence, and encourage and bring about persistence. We cannot have two opinions regarding the importance of the exercise of this indispensable quality in our praying.

Persistent prayer is a mighty move of the soul toward God. It is a stirring of the deepest forces of the soul toward the throne of heavenly grace. It is the ability to hold on, press on, and wait. Restless desire, restful patience, and strength to hold on are all embraced in it. It is not an incident or a performance, but a passion of soul. It is not something half-needed, but a sheer necessity.

The wrestling quality in persistent prayer does not spring from physical violence or fleshly energy. It is not an impulse of energy or a mere earnestness of the soul. It is an inward force or ability planted and aroused by the Holy Spirit. Virtually, it is the

138

intercession of the Spirit of God in us. It is *"the effectual fervent prayer* [that] *availeth much"* (James 5:16). The divine Spirit supplies every part of us with the energy of His own striving. This is the essence of the persistence that urges our praying at the mercy seat to continue until the fire falls and the blessing descends. This wrestling in prayer is not loud or vehement, but quiet, firm, and urgent. When there are no visible outlets for its mighty forces, it may be silent.

Nothing distinguishes the children of God so clearly and strongly as prayer. It is the one infallible mark and test of being a Christian. Christian people are prayerful. The worldly minded are prayerless. Christians call on God. The world ignores God and does not call on His name. But even the Christian has to cultivate *continual* prayer. It must be habitual, but it must be much more than a habit. It is duty, yet it is one that rises far above and goes beyond the ordinary implications of the term. It is the expression of a relationship with God, a yearning for divine communion. It is the outward and upward flow of the inner life toward its original fountain. It is a statement of the soul's origin, a claiming of sonship that links man to the eternal.

Prayer has everything to do with molding the soul into the image of God. It also has everything to do with elevating and enlarging the measure of divine grace. It has everything to do with bringing the soul into complete communion with God. It has everything to do with enriching, broadening, and maturing the soul's experience of God. A man who does not pray cannot possibly be called a Christian. There is no possible way that he can claim any right to the term or its implied significance. If he does not pray, he is a sinner, pure and simple. Prayer is the only way the soul of man can enter into fellowship and communion with the source of all Christlike spirit and energy. Therefore, if he does not pray, he is not of the household of faith.

In this study, however, we will turn our attention to one phase of prayer—persistence. It is the pressing of our desires on God with urgency and perseverance. It is praying with that courage and tension that neither relaxes nor stops until its cry is heard and its cause is won.

The man who has clear views of God, has scriptural conceptions of the divine character, appreciates his privilege of approach to God, and understands his inward need of all that God has for him, will be eager, outspoken, and persistent. In Scripture, the duty of prayer is advocated in terms that are barely stronger than those in which the necessity for its persistence is mentioned. Praying that influences God is said to be the outpouring of the fervent, effectual righteous man. It is prayer on fire. It does not have a feeble, flickering flame or a momentary flash, but shines with a vigorous, steady glow.

The repeated intercessions of Abraham for the salvation of Sodom and Gomorrah present an early example of the necessity for and benefit derived from persistent prayer. The case of Jacob, wrestling all night with the angel, gives significant emphasis to the power of a dogged perseverance in prayer. It shows how, in spiritual things, persistence succeeds just as effectively as it does in matters relating to time and sense.

Moses prayed forty days and forty nights to stop the wrath of God against Israel. His example and success are a stimulus to present-day faith in its darkest hour. Elijah repeated his prayer seven times before the rain clouds appeared above the horizon and heralded the success of his prayer and the victory of his faith. On one occasion, Daniel, though faint and weak, pressed his case for three weeks before the answer and the blessing came.

During His earthly life, the blessed Savior spent many nights in prayer. In Gethsemane He presented the same petition three times with unshaken, urgent, yet submissive persistence. This called on every part of His soul and brought about tears and bloody sweat. His life crises were distinctly marked, and His life victories were all won in hours of persistent prayer. So, the servant is not greater than his Lord.

The parable of the persistent widow is a classic example of insistent prayer. We would do well to refresh our memories, at this point in our study, by reading the account from Scripture.

And he spake a parable unto them to this end, that men ought always to pray, and not to faint; saying, There was in a city a judge, which feared not God, neither regarded man: and there was a widow in that city; and she came unto him, saying, Avenge me of my adversary. And he would not for a while: but afterward he said within himself, Though I fear not God, nor regard man; yet because this widow troubleth me, I will avenge her, lest by her continual coming she weary me. And the Lord said, Hear what the unjust judge saith. And shall not God avenge his own elect, which cry day and night unto

him, though he bear long with them? I tell you he will avenge
them speedily. (Luke 18:1–8)

This parable stresses the central truth of persistent prayer. The widow presses her case until the unjust judge yields. If this parable does not teach the necessity for persistence, it does not have any purpose or teaching. Take this one thought away and you have nothing left worth recording. Beyond objection, Christ intended it to stand as evidence of the need that exists for insistent prayer.

We have the same teaching emphasized in the incident of the Syrophenician woman, who came to Jesus on behalf of her daughter. Here, persistence is shown, not as rudeness, but as the persuasive equipment of humility, sincerity, and fervency. We are given a glimpse of a woman's clinging faith, her bitter grief, and her spiritual insight. The Master went to that Sidonian country so that this truth could be shown for all time: There is no cry as effective as persistent prayer, and there is no prayer to which God surrenders Himself so fully and so freely.

The persistence of this distressed mother won her the victory and brought about her request. Instead of being an offense to the Savior, it drew from Him a word of wonder and glad surprise: *"O woman, great is thy faith: be it unto thee even as thou wilt"* (Matt. 15:28).

He who does not push his plea does not pray at all. Cold prayers have no claim on heaven and no hearing in the courts above. Fire is the life of prayer, and heaven is reached by fiery persistence rising in an ascending scale. Going back to the case of the persistent widow, we see that her widowhood, friendlessness, and weakness did not count for anything with the unjust judge. Persistence was everything. *"Because this widow troubleth me,"* he said, *"I will avenge her* [speedily], *lest...she weary me."* Because the widow imposed upon the time and attention of the unjust judge, her case was won.

God waits patiently as, day and night, His elect cry to Him. He is moved by their requests a thousand times more than this unjust judge was. A limit is set to His waiting by the persistent praying of His people, and the answer is richly given. God finds faith in His praying child. He honors this faith that stays and cries by permitting its further exercise, so that it is strengthened and enriched. Then He rewards it in abundance.

141

The case of the Syrophenician woman is a notable instance of successful persistence. It is one that is highly encouraging to all who pray successfully. It is a remarkable example of insistence and perseverance to ultimate victory in the face of insurmountable obstacles and hindrances. But the woman overcame them all by heroic faith and persistent spirit. Jesus had gone over into her country, *"and would have no man know it"* (Mark 7:24). But she breaks through His purpose, violates His privacy, attracts His attention, and pours out to Him a distressing appeal of need and faith. Her heart was in her prayer.

At first, Jesus appears to pay no attention to her agony and ignores her cry for relief. He gives her neither eye, nor ear, nor word. Silence, deep and chilling, greets her impassioned cry. But she is not turned aside or disheartened. She holds on. The disciples, offended at her unseemly noise, intercede for her, but they are silenced by the Lord's declaring that the woman is entirely outside the scope of His mission and His ministry.

But neither the failure of the disciples to gain her a hearing, nor the despairing knowledge that she is barred from the benefits of His mission, stop her. They serve only to lend intensity and increased boldness in her approach to Christ. She came closer, cutting her prayer in half, and fell at His feet. Worshipping Him, she made her daughter's case her own and cries with pointed brevity— *"Lord, help me!"* (Matt. 15:25). This last cry won her case. Her daughter was healed the same hour. Hopeful, urgent, and unwearied, she stays near the Master, insisting and praying until the answer is given. What a study in persistence, in earnestness. They were promoted and propelled under conditions that would have disheartened any but a heroic, constant soul.

In these parables of persistent praying, our Lord states, for our information and encouragement, the serious difficulties that stand in the way of prayer. At the same time, He teaches that persistence conquers all unfavorable circumstances and gets itself a victory over a whole host of obstacles.

He teaches that an answer to prayer is conditional upon the amount of faith that goes into the petition. To test this, He delays the answer. The superficial pray-er sinks into silence when the answer is delayed. But the man of prayer hangs on and on. The Lord recognizes and honors his faith and gives him a rich, abundant answer to his faith-evidencing, persistent prayer.

7

Prayer That Motivates God

Two thirds of the praying we do is for that which would give us the greatest possible pleasure to receive. It is a sort of spiritual self-indulgence in which we engage and, as a consequence, is the exact opposite of self-discipline. God knows all this and keeps His children asking. In the process of time— His time—our petitions take on another aspect, and we, another spiritual approach. God keeps us praying until, in His wisdom, He is ready to answer. And no matter how long it may be before He speaks, it is, even then, far earlier than we have a right to expect or hope to deserve. —Anonymous

THE purpose of Christ's teachings is to declare that men are to pray earnestly. They are to pray with an earnestness that cannot be denied. Heaven has listening ears only for the wholehearted and the deeply earnest. Energy, courage, and perseverance must back the prayers that heaven respects and that God hears.

All these qualities of soul, so essential to effectual praying, are brought out in the parable of the man who went to his friend for bread at midnight. (See Luke 11:5–10.) This man went on his errand with confidence. Friendship promised him success. His cry was pressing. Truly, he could not go back empty-handed. The flat refusal shamed and surprised him. Here even friendship failed! But there was still something to be tried—stern resolution and fixed determination. He would stay and pursue his demand until the door was opened and the request granted. He proceeded to do this and, by persistence, secured what ordinary requesting had failed to obtain.

The success of this man, achieved in the face of a flat denial, was used by the Savior to illustrate the need for insistence in humble prayer before the throne of heavenly grace. When the answer is not immediately given, the praying Christian must gather courage at each delay. He must urgently go forward until the answer comes. The answer is assured, if he has the faith to press his petition with vigorous faith.

Negligence, faintheartedness, impatience, and fear will be fatal to our prayers. The Father's heart, hand, infinite power, and infinite willingness to hear and give to His children is waiting for the start of our insistence.

Persistent praying is the earnest, inward movement of the heart toward God. It is throwing the entire force of the spiritual man into the exercise of prayer. Isaiah lamented that no one stirred himself to take hold of God. There was much praying done in Isaiah's time, but it was too easy, indifferent, and complacent. There were no mighty moves by souls toward God. There was no array of sanctified energies bent on reaching and grappling with God. There was no energy to draw the treasures of His grace from Him. Forceless prayers have no power to overcome difficulties, win marked results, or gain complete victories. We must win God before we can win our plea.

Isaiah looked with hopeful eyes to the day when faith would flourish and there would be times of real praying. When those times came, the watchmen would not weaken their vigilance, but cry day and night. And those who were the Lord's remembrancers would give Him no rest. Their urgent, persistent efforts would keep all spiritual interests busy and make increasing demands on God's exhaustless treasures.

Persistent praying never faints or grows weary. It is never discouraged. It never yields to cowardice, but is lifted up and sustained by a hope that knows no despair and a faith that will not let go. Persistent praying has patience to wait and strength to continue. It never prepares itself to quit praying, and it refuses to get up from its knees until an answer is received.

The familiar words of the great missionary Adoniram Judson are the testimony of a man who was persistent at prayer. He said,

> I was never deeply interested in any object, never prayed sincerely and earnestly for it, but that it came at some time, no matter how distant the day. Somehow, in some shape, probably the last I would have devised, it came.

"Ask, and it shall be given you; seek, and ye shall find; knock, and it shall be opened unto you" (Matt. 7:7). These are the ringing challenges of our Lord in regard to prayer. These challenges are His explanation that true praying must stay and advance in effort and urgency until the prayer is answered and the blessing sought is received.

In the three words *ask, seek,* and *knock,* Jesus, by the order in which He places them, urges the necessity of persistence in prayer. Asking, seeking, and knocking are ascending rungs in the ladder of successful prayer. No principle is more definitely enforced by Christ than that successful prayer must have in it the quality that waits and perseveres. It must have in it the courage that never surrenders, the patience that never grows tired, and the resolution that never wavers.

In the parable of the friend at midnight, a most significant and instructive lesson in this respect is outlined. Chief among the qualities included in Christ's estimate of the highest and most successful form of praying are the following: unbeatable courage, ceaseless courage, and stability of purpose.

Persistence is made up of intensity, perseverance, and patience. The apparent delay in answering prayer is the ground and demand of persistence. In Matthew we have the first recorded instance of the miracle of healing the blind. We have an illustration of the way in which our Lord did not seem to hear immediately those who sought Him. But the two blind men continued their crying and followed Him with their continual petition saying, *"Thou son of David, have mercy on us"* (Matt. 9:27). But He did not answer them and went into the house. The needy ones followed Him and, finally, gained their eyesight and their plea.

The case of blind Bartimaeus is a notable one in many ways. (See Mark 10:46–52.) It is especially remarkable for the show of persistence that this blind man exhibited in appealing to our Lord. His first crying, as it seems, was done as Jesus entered Jericho, and he continued it until Jesus came out of the place. It is a strong illustration of the necessity of persistent prayer. It is also an illustration of the success that comes to those who stake their all on Christ and do not give Him any peace until He grants them their hearts' desire.

Mark put the entire incident clearly before us. At first, Jesus seems not to hear. The crowd rebukes the noisy babbling of Bartimaeus. Despite the apparent unconcern of our Lord and the rebuke of an impatient, quick-tempered crowd, the blind beggar still cries. He increases the loudness of his cry until Jesus is impressed and moved. Finally, the crowd, as well as Jesus, listens to the beggar's cry and speaks in favor of his cause. He wins his case. His persistence wins even in the face of apparent neglect on the part of Jesus and despite opposition and rebuke from the surrounding crowd. His persistence won where halfhearted indifference would surely have failed.

Faith functions in connection with prayer and, of course, has its inseparable association with persistence. But the latter quality *drives* the prayer to the believing point. A persistent spirit brings a man to the place where faith takes hold, claims, and appropriates the blessing.

The absolute necessity of persistent prayer is plainly stated in the Word of God and needs to be stated and restated today. We are inclined to overlook this vital truth. Love of ease, spiritual laziness, and religious indifference all operate against this type of petitioning. Our praying, however, needs to be coaxed and pursued with an energy that never tires. It needs to have a persistency that will not be denied and a courage that never fails.

We also need to give thought to that mysterious fact of prayer— the certainty that there will be delays, denials, and seeming failures in connection with its exercise. We are to prepare for these and to permit them. However, we must not cease in our urgent praying. The praying Christian is like a brave soldier who, as the conflict grows more severe, exhibits a more superior courage than in the earlier stages of the battle. When delay and denial face him, he increases his earnest asking and does not stop until prayer prevails.

Moses furnished us with an excellent example of persistence in prayer. Instead of allowing his intimacy with God to release him from the necessity for persistence, he regards it as something better to fit him for its exercise.

When Israel set up the golden calf, the wrath of God increased fiercely against them. Jehovah, bent on executing justice, said to Moses when He told him what He purposed to do, *"Let me alone"* (Exod. 32:10). But Moses would not let Him alone. He threw himself down before the Lord in an agony of intercession on behalf of the sinning Israelites. For forty days and nights he fasted and prayed. What a season of persistent prayer that was!

Jehovah was also angry with Aaron, who had acted as leader in this idolatrous business of the golden calf. But Moses prayed for

Aaron as well as for the Israelites. If he had not prayed, both Israel and Aaron would have perished under the consuming fire of God's wrath.

That long period of pleading before God left a mighty impression on Moses. He had been in close relationship with God before, but his character never attained the greatness that marked it in the days and years following this long season of persistent intercession.

There can be no question about persistent prayer moving God and heightening human character. If we were more in agreement with God in this great command of intercession, our faces would shine more brightly. Our lives and service would possess richer qualities that earn the goodwill of humanity and bring glory to the name of God.

8

Prayer and
Christian Conduct

*General Charles James Gordon, the hero of Khartoum,
was a truly Christian soldier. Shut up in the Sudanese town,
he gallantly held out for one year, but finally was overcome
and slain. On his memorial in Westminster Abbey are these
words: "He gave his money to the poor, his sympathy to the
sorrowing, his life to his country, and his soul to God."*
—Homer W. Hodge

PRAYER governs conduct, and conduct makes character. Conduct is what we do. Character is what we are. Conduct is the outward life. Character is the unseen life, hidden within, yet is evidenced by that which is seen. Conduct is external, seen from without. Character is internal, operating within. In the economy of grace, conduct is the offspring of character. Character is the state of the heart. Conduct is its outward expression. Character is the root of the tree. Conduct is the fruit it bears.

Prayer is related to all the gifts of grace. Its relationship to character and conduct is that of a helper. Prayer helps to establish character and to fashion conduct. Both, for their successful continuance, depend on prayer. There may be a certain degree of moral character and conduct independent of prayer, but there cannot be any distinctive religious character and Christian conduct without it. Prayer helps where all other aids fail. The more we pray, the better we are, and the purer and better our lives become.

The very end and purpose of the atoning work of Christ is to create religious character and make Christian conduct.

> *Who gave himself for us, that he might redeem us from all iniquity, and purify unto himself a peculiar people, zealous of good works.* (Titus 2:14)

In Christ's teaching, it is not simply works of charity and deeds of mercy that He insists upon, but inward spiritual character. This much is demanded, and nothing short of it will suffice.

In the study of Paul's epistles, there is one thing that stands out clearly and unmistakably—the insistence on holiness of heart and righteousness of life. Paul does not seek to promote what is termed "personal work." The leading theme of his letters is not deeds of charity. Rather, it is the condition of the human heart and the blamelessness of the personal life that form the burden of Paul's writings.

It is character and conduct that are most important elsewhere in the Scriptures, too. The Christian religion deals with men who are lacking spiritual character and are unholy in life. It aims to change them so that they become holy in heart and righteous in life. It aims to change bad men into good men.

Here is where prayer enters and demonstrates its wonderful ability and fruit. Prayer drives toward this specific end. In fact, without prayer, no such supernatural change in moral character can ever be effected. The change from badness to goodness is not brought about *"by works of righteousness which we have done,"* but according to God's mercy, which saves us *"by the washing of regeneration"* (Titus 3:5). This marvelous change is brought to pass through earnest, persistent, faithful prayer. Any assumed form of Christianity that does not effect this change in the hearts of men is a delusion and a snare.

The office of prayer is to change the character and conduct of men. In countless instances, change has been brought about by prayer. At this point, prayer, by its credentials, has proven its divinity. Just as it is the office of prayer to effect this, it is the major work of the church to take hold of evil men and make them good. Its mission is to change human nature and character, influence behavior, and revolutionize conduct. The church is presumed to be righteous and should be engaged in turning men to righteousness.

The church is God's factory on earth. Its primary duty is to create and foster righteous character. This is its very first business. Primarily, its work is not to acquire members or amass numbers. Its aim is not to get money or engage in deeds of charity and works of mercy. Its work is to produce righteousness of character and purity of the outward life.

A product reflects and partakes of the character of the manufacturer that makes it. A righteous church with a righteous purpose makes righteous men. Prayer produces cleanliness of heart and purity of life. It can produce nothing else. Unrighteous conduct is born in prayerlessness. The two go hand in hand. Prayer and sinning cannot keep company with each other. One or the other must, of necessity, stop. Get men to pray, and they will quit sinning, because prayer creates a distaste for sinning. It works so much upon the heart, that evildoing becomes repugnant. It lifts the entire nature to a reverent contemplation of high and holy things.

Prayer is based on character. What we are with God determines our influence with Him. It was the inner character, not the outward appearance, of such men as Abraham, Job, David, Moses, and others, that had such great influence with God in the days of old. Today, it is not so much our words, but what we really are that counts with God. Conduct affects character, of course, and counts for much in our praying.

At the same time, character affects conduct to a far greater extent and has a superior influence over prayer. Our inner life gives color to our praying.

Bad living means bad praying and, in the end, no praying at all. We pray feebly because we live feebly. The stream of prayer cannot rise higher than the fountain of living. The force of the prayer closet is made up of the energy that emerges from the flowing streams of life. The weakness of living grows out of the shallowness and shoddiness of character.

Feebleness of living reflects its weakness in the praying hours. We simply cannot talk strongly, intimately, and confidently to God unless we are living for Him, faithfully and truly. The prayer closet cannot become sanctified to God when the life is alien to His laws and purpose. We must learn this lesson well. Righteous character and Christlike conduct give us a peculiar and preferential standing in prayer before God. The Word gives special emphasis to the part that conduct has in imparting value to our praying.

Then shalt thou call and the Lord shall answer; thou shalt cry, and he shall say, Here I am. If thou take away from the midst of thee the yoke, the putting forth of the finger, and speaking vanity. (Isa. 58:9)

The wickedness of Israel and their heinous practices were definitely cited by Isaiah as the reason why God would turn His ears away from their prayers. *"And when ye spread forth your hands, I will hide mine eyes from you: yea, when ye make many prayers, I will not hear: your hands are full of blood"* (Isa. 1:15).

The same sad truth was declared by the Lord through the mouth of Jeremiah: *"Therefore pray not thou for this people, neither lift up a cry or prayer for them: for I will not hear them in the time that they cry unto me for their trouble"* (Jer. 11:14). Here, it is plainly stated that unholy conduct is a hindrance to successful praying. It is clearly suggested that, in order to have full access to God in prayer, there must be a total abandonment of conscious and premeditated sin.

We are commanded to pray, *"lifting up holy hands, without wrath and doubting"* (1 Tim. 2:8). We must pass the time we live here in a rigorous abstaining from evil if we are to keep our privilege of calling upon the Father. We cannot, by any process, divorce praying from conduct. *"And whatsoever we ask, we receive of Him because we keep His commandments, and do those things which are pleasing in His sight"* (1 John 3:22).

James declared that men ask and receive not because they ask amiss and seek only the gratification of selfish desires. (See James 4:3.)

Our Lord's command to watch and pray always is to cover and guard all our conduct. Then we may come to our prayer closet with all its force secured by a vigilant guard kept over our lives.

And take heed to yourselves, lest at any time your hearts be overcharged with surfeiting, and drunkenness, and cares of this life, and so that day come upon you unawares.
(Luke 21:34)

Quite often, Christian experience collapses on the rock of conduct. Beautiful theories are marred by ugly lives. The most difficult thing about piety, because it is the most impressive, is to be able to live it. It is the life that counts. Our praying suffers, as do other phases of our religious experience, from bad living.

In early times, preachers were ordered to preach by their lives or not preach at all. Christians everywhere ought to be reminded to pray by their lives or not pray at all. The most effective preaching is not that which is heard from the pulpit, but that which is proclaimed quietly, humbly, and consistently. It is preaching that exhibits its excellencies in the home and in the community. Example preaches a far more effective sermon than instruction. The best preaching, even in the pulpit, is that which is strengthened by the preacher living a godly life.

The most effective work done by people sitting in the pews is preceded by, and accompanied with, holiness of life, separation from the world, and severance from sin. Some of the strongest appeals are made with mute lips by godly fathers and saintly mothers. These parents, around the fireside, fear God, love His cause, and daily show their children and others around them the beauties and excellencies of Christian life and conduct.

The best prepared, most eloquent sermon can be marred and rendered ineffective by questionable practices in the preacher. The most active church worker can have the labor of his hands weakened by worldliness of spirit and inconsistency of life. Men preach by their lives, not by their words. Sermons are delivered, not so much in and from a pulpit, as in tempers, actions, and the thousand and one incidents that crowd the pathway of daily life.

Of course, the prayer of repentance is acceptable to God. He delights in hearing the cries of penitent sinners. But repentance involves not only sorrow for sin, but turning away from wrongdoing and learning to do well. A repentance that does not produce a change in character and conduct is a mere sham that should deceive no one. Old things *must* pass away. All things *must* become new. (See 2 Corinthians 5:17.)

Praying that does not result in right thinking and right living is a farce. We have missed the whole office of prayer if it fails to purge character and correct conduct. We have failed entirely to understand the virtue of prayer, if it does not bring about the revolutionizing of the life. In the very nature of things, we must either quit praying or quit our bad conduct. Cold, formal praying may exist side by side with bad conduct, but such praying, in God's estimation, is no praying at all. Our praying advances in power just as much as it rectifies the life. A prayerful life will grow in purity and devotion to God.

The character of the inner life is a condition of effectual praying. As the life is, so the praying will be. An inconsistent life hinders praying and neutralizes what little praying we may do. Always, it is the prayer of the righteous man that avails much. (See James 5:16.) Indeed, one may go further and say that it is only the prayer of the righteous that avails anything at all, at any time. To have an eye to God's glory and to be possessed by an earnest desire to please Him in all our ways gives weight, influence, and power to prayer. To possess hands busy in His service, and to have feet swift to run in the way of His commandments, insures an audience with God. The oppression of our lives often breaks the force of our praying and, not infrequently, is as a door of brass in the face of prayer.

Praying must come out of a clean heart and be presented and urged with the *"lifting up* [of] *holy hands"* (1 Tim. 2:8). It must be strengthened by a life aiming, unceasingly, to obey God, to attain conformity to the divine law, and to come into submission to the divine will.

Let it not be forgotten, that, while life is a condition of prayer, prayer is also the condition of righteous living. Prayer promotes righteous living and is the one great aid to uprightness of heart and life. The fruit of real praying is right living. Praying sets him who prays to the great business of working out his salvation with fear and trembling. (See Philippians 2:12.) It causes him to watching his temper, conversation, and conduct. It leads him to walk circumspectly and redeem the time. (See Ephesians 5:15–16.) It enables him to walk worthy of the vocation wherewith he is called, with all lowliness and meekness. (See Ephesians 4:1–2.) It gives him a high incentive to pursue his pilgrimage consistently by shunning every evil way to walk in the good. (See Psalm 199:101.)

9

Prayer and Obedience

An obedience discovered itself in John Fletcher, which I wish I could describe or imitate. It produced in him a mind ready to embrace every cross with alacrity and pleasure. He had a singular love for the lambs of the flock and applied himself with the greatest diligence to their instruction for which he had a peculiar gift....All his fellowship with me was so mingled with prayer and praise that every employment and every meal was, as it were, perfumed therewith. —John Wesley

UNDER the Mosaic law, to obey was looked upon as being *"better than sacrifice, and to hearken than the fat of rams"* (1 Sam. 15:22). In Deuteronomy 5:29, Moses represented Almighty God declaring the importance He laid upon the exercise of this quality. Referring to the waywardness of His people, He cried,

O that there were such an heart in them, that they would fear me, and keep all my commandments always, that it might be well with them, and with their children for ever!

Unquestionably, obedience is a high virtue, the quality of a soldier. To obey belongs, preeminently, to the soldier. It is his first and last lesson. He must learn how to practice it without questioning or complaining at all times. Obedience is faith in action. It is the outflow, the very test of love. *"He that hath My commandments, and keepeth them, he it is that loveth me"* (John 14:21).

Furthermore, obedience is love. *"If ye keep My commandments, ye shall abide in My love; even as I have kept My Father's commandments, and abide in His love"* (John 15:10). What a marvelous statement of the relationship created and maintained by obedience! The Son of God is held in the bosom of the Father's love by virtue of His obedience! The fact that allows the Son of God to ever abide in His Father's love is revealed in His own statement, *"For I do always those things that please him"* (John 8:29).

The gift of the Holy Spirit in full measure and in richer experience depends on loving obedience. *"If ye love me, keep my commandments"* is the Master's word. *"And I will pray the Father, and he shall give you another Comforter, that he may abide with you for ever"* (John 14:15–16).

Obedience to God is a condition of spiritual thrift, inward satisfaction, stability of heart. Obedience opens the gates of the Holy City and gives access to the Tree of Life. *"Blessed are they that do his commandments, that they may have right to the tree of life, and may enter in through the gates into the city"* (Rev. 22:14).

What is obedience? It is doing God's will. It is keeping His commandments. How many of the commandments require obedience? To keep half of them and break the other half—is that real obedience? To keep all the commandments but one—is that obedience? James the apostle was very explicit on this point. *"Whosoever shall keep the whole law, and yet offend in one point, he is guilty of all"* (James 2:10).

The spirit that prompts a man to break one commandment is the spirit that may move him to break them all. God's commandments are a unit. To break one strikes at the principle that underlies and runs through the whole. He who does not hesitate to break a single commandment probably would, under the same stress and surrounded by the same circumstances, break them all.

Universal obedience of the race is demanded. Nothing short of absolute obedience will satisfy God. The keeping of all His commandments is the demonstration of obedience that God requires. But can we keep all of God's commandments? Can a man receive moral ability that helps him to obey every one of them? Certainly he can. By the same token, man can, through prayer, obtain ability to do this very thing.

Does God give commandments that men cannot obey? Is He so arbitrary, so severe, so unloving, that He issues commandments that cannot be obeyed? The answer is that, in all of Scripture, not a single instance is recorded of God having commanded any man to do a thing that was beyond his power. Is God so unjust and so inconsiderate to require of man something that he is unable to do? Certainly not. To infer it is to slander the character of God.

Let us think about this thought for a moment. Do earthly parents require their children to perform duties that they cannot do? Where is the father who would even think of being so unjust and so tyrannical? Is God less kind and just than faulty earthly parents? Are they better and more just than a perfect God? What a foolish and inconsistent thought!

In principle, obedience to God is the same quality as obedience to earthly parents. It implies, in general, the giving up of one's own way to follow that of another. It requires the surrender of the will to the will of another. It implies the submission of oneself to the authority and requirements of a parent. Commands, either from our heavenly Father or our earthly father, are directed by love. All such commands are in the best interests of those who are commanded. God's commands are not issued in severity or tyranny. They are always issued in love and in our interests. So, it is important for us to pay attention and obey them. In other words, God has issued His commands to us in order to promote our good.

It pays, therefore, to be obedient. Obedience brings its own reward. God has ordained it so. Since He has, even human reason can realize that He would never demand that which is out of our power to perform.

Obedience is love fulfilling every command. It is love expressing itself. Obedience, therefore, is not a hard demand made on us. It is not any more than the service a husband renders his wife or a wife renders her husband. Love delights to obey and please whom it loves. There are no hardships in love. There may be demands, but no irritations. There are no impossible tasks for love.

How simply and matter-of-factly John said, *"And whatsoever we ask, we receive of him, because we keep his commandments, and do those things that are pleasing in his sight"* (1 John 3:22). This is obedience, running ahead of every command. It is love, obeying by anticipation. They greatly err, and even sin, who say that men are bound to commit sin because of environment, heredity, or tendency. God's commands are not grievous (1 John 5:3). Their ways are pleasant, and their paths are peace. The task that falls to obedience is not a hard one. *"For my yoke is easy, and my burden is light"* (Matt. 11:30).

Far be it from our heavenly Father to demand impossibilities of His children. It is possible to please Him in all things, for He is not hard to please. He is neither a hard master, nor an austere lord, *"taking up that* [he] *laid not down, and reaping that* [he] *did not sow"* (Luke 19:22). Thank God it is possible for every child of God to please his heavenly Father! It is really much easier to please Him than to please men. Moreover, we may *know* when we please Him. This is the witness of the Spirit—the inward, divine assurance given to all the children of God that they are doing their Father's will and that their ways are well pleasing in His sight.

God's commandments are righteous and founded in justice and wisdom. *"Wherefore the law is holy, and the commandment holy, and just, and good"* (Rom. 7:12). *"Just and true are thy ways, thou King of saints"* (Rev. 15:3). God's commandments, then, can be obeyed by all who seek supplies of grace that enable them to obey. These commandments must be obeyed. God's government is at stake. God's children are under obligation to obey Him. Disobedience cannot be permitted. The spirit of rebellion is the very essence of sin. It is denial of God's authority that God cannot tolerate. He has never done so. A declaration of His attitude was part of the reason why the Son of the Highest was made manifest among men.

> *For what the law could not do, in that it was weak through the flesh, God sending his own Son in the likeness of sinful flesh, and for sin, condemned sin in the flesh: that the righteousness of the law might be fulfilled in us, who walk not after the flesh, but after the Spirit.* (Rom. 8:3–4)

If anyone complains that man under the Fall is too weak and helpless to obey these high commands of God, the answer is that, through the atonement of Christ, man is able to obey. The Atonement is God's enabling act. God works in us, through regeneration and the agency of the Holy Spirit, the enabling grace sufficient for all that is required of us under the Atonement. This grace is furnished without measure in answer to prayer.

So, while God commands, He, at the same time, stands pledged to give us all the necessary strength of will and grace of soul to meet His demands. Because this is true, man has no excuse for disobedience. He is immediately criticized for refusing or failing to secure necessary grace, whereby he may serve the Lord with reverence and godly fear.

Those who say it is impossible to keep God's commandments overlook one important consideration. It is the vital truth that, through prayer and faith, man's nature is changed and made partaker of the divine nature. All reluctance to obey God is taken out of him. His natural inability to keep God's commandments, growing out of his fallen and helpless state, is gloriously removed. By this radical change in his moral nature, a man receives power to obey God in every way and to yield full and glad allegiance. Then he can say, *"I delight to do thy will, O my God"* (Ps. 40:8). Not only is rebellion of the natural man removed, but he also receives a heart that gladly obeys God's Word.

There is no denying that the unrenewed man cannot obey God. But to declare that—after one is renewed by the Holy Spirit, has received a new nature, and become a child of the King—he *cannot* obey God is to assume a ridiculous attitude. It is to show a lamentable ignorance of the work and implications of the Atonement.

Absolute and perfect obedience is the state to which the man of prayer is called. *"Lifting up holy hands, without wrath and doubting"* (1 Tim. 2:8) is the condition of obedient praying. Here inward loyalty and love, together with outward cleanliness, are set forth as accompaniments of acceptable praying.

John gave the reason for answered prayer in the passage previously quoted: *"And whatsoever we ask we receive of him, because we keep his commandments, and do those things that are pleasing in his sight"* (1 John 3:22). Because we have said that keeping God's commandments is the reason why He answers prayer, it is reasonable to assume that we *can* keep God's commandments. We *can* do those things that are pleasing to Him. Do you think God would make the keeping of His commandments a condition of effectual prayer if He knew we could not keep His statutes? *Certainly not!*

Obedience can ask with boldness at the throne of grace. Those who exercise it are the only ones who can ask after that fashion. The disobedient folk are timid in their approach and hesitant in their supplication. They are stopped by their wrongdoing. The requesting, obedient child comes into the presence of his Father with confidence and boldness. His very consciousness of obedience gives him courage and frees him from the dread born of disobedience.

To do God's will without hesitation is the joy and the privilege of the successful praying man. He who has clean hands and a pure heart can pray with confidence. In the Sermon on the Mount, Jesus said, *"Not every one that saith unto me, Lord, Lord, shall enter into the kingdom of heaven, but he that doeth the will of my Father which is in heaven"* (Matt. 7:21). To this great deliverance may be added another: *"If ye keep my commandments, ye shall abide in my love: even as I have kept my Father's commandments, and abide in his love"* (John 15:10).

"The Christian's trade," said Martin Luther, "is prayer." But the Christian has another trade to learn before he proceeds to learn the secrets of the trade of prayer. He must learn well the trade of perfect obedience to the Father's will. Obedience follows love, and prayer follows obedience. The business of *real* obedience to God's commandments inseparably accompanies the business of *real* praying.

One who has been disobedient may pray. He may pray for pardoning mercy and the peace of his soul. He may come to God's feet with tears, confession, and a penitent heart. God will hear him and answer his prayer. This kind of praying does not belong to the child of God, but to the penitent sinner, who has no other way to approach God. It is the possession of the unjustified soul, not him who has been saved and reconciled to God.

An obedient life helps prayer. It speeds prayer to the throne. God cannot help hearing the prayer of an obedient child. He has always heard His obedient children when they have prayed. Unquestioning obedience counts much in the sight of God, at the throne of heavenly grace. It acts like the flowing tides of many rivers. It gives volume and fullness of flow, as well as power, to the prayer closet. An obedient life is not simply a reformed life. It is not the old life primed and repainted. It is not a superficial churchgoing life or a flurry of activities. Neither is it an external conformation to the dictates of public morality. Far more than all this is combined in a truly obedient Christian God-fearing life.

A life of full obedience, a life that is settled on the most intimate terms with God, offers no hindrance to the prayer closet. Where the will is in full conformity to God's will and the outward life shows the fruit of righteousness like Aaron and Hur, such a life lifts up and sustains the hands of prayer.

If you have an earnest desire to pray well, you must learn how to obey well. If you have a desire to learn to pray, then you must have an earnest desire to learn how to do God's will. If you desire to pray to God, you must first have a consuming desire to obey

Him. If you want to have free access to God in prayer, then every obstacle in the nature of sin or disobedience must be removed.

God delights in the prayers of obedient children. Requests coming from the lips of those who delight to do His will, reach His ears with great speed. They incline Him to answer them promptly and abundantly. In themselves, tears are not rewarding. Yet, they have their uses in prayer. Tears should baptize our place of supplication.

The person who has never wept concerning his sins has never really prayed over his sins. Tears, sometimes, are a prodigal's only plea. But tears are for the past, for the sin and wrongdoing. There is another step and stage waiting to be taken. That step is unquestioning obedience. Until it is taken, prayer for blessing and continued sustenance will be of no avail.

Everywhere in Scripture, God is represented as disapproving disobedience and condemning sin. This is as true in the lives of His elect as it is in the lives of sinners. Nowhere does He approve of sin or excuse disobedience. Always, God puts the emphasis upon obedience to His commands. Obedience to them brings blessing. Disobedience meets with disaster. This is true in the Word of God from the beginning to the end. It is because of this that the men of prayer in the Bible had such influence with God. Obedient men have always been the closest to God. They are the ones who have prayed well and have received great things from God. They have brought great things to pass.

Obedience to God counts tremendously in the realm of prayer. This fact cannot be emphasized too much or too often. To plead for a faith that tolerates sinning is to cut the ground out from under the feet of effectual praying. To excuse sinning by the plea that obedience to God is not possible to unregenerate men is to discount the character of the new birth and to place men where effective praying is not possible. At one time Jesus spoke out with a very pertinent and personal question that strikes right to the core of disobedience. He said, *"Why call ye me, Lord, Lord, and do not the things which I say?"* (Luke 6:46).

He who prays must obey. The person who wants to get anything out of his prayers must be in perfect harmony with God. Prayer puts in those who sincerely pray a spirit of obedience. The spirit of disobedience is not of God and does not belong to God's praying people.

An obedient life is a great help to prayer. In fact, an obedient life is a necessity to prayer. The absence of an obedient life makes prayer an empty performance. A penitent sinner seeks pardon and salvation and has an answer to his prayers, even with a life stained with sin. But God's royal intercessors come before Him with royal lives. Holy living promotes holy praying. God's intercessors *"lifting up holy hands"* (1 Tim. 2:8), are the symbols of righteous, obedient lives.

10

Prayer and Full Surrender

Many exemplary men have I known, holy in heart and life, within my four score years. But one equal to John Fletcher—one so inwardly and outwardly obedient and devoted to God—I have not known. —*John Wesley*

IT is important to note that the praying that is given such a transcendent position, and from which great results are attributed, is not simply the saying of prayers, but holy praying. It is the *"prayers of the saints"* (Rev. 8:4). It is the prayers of the holy men of God. Behind such praying, giving to it energy and flame, are men and women who are wholly devoted to God. They are entirely separated from sin and fully separated unto God. They always give energy, force, and strength to praying.

Our Lord Jesus Christ excelled in praying because He was supreme in saintliness. Entire dedication to God and full surrender, which carry the whole being in a flame of holy consecration, give wings to faith and energy to prayer. Full surrender opens the door to the throne of grace. It brings strong influence to bear on Almighty God.

The *"lifting up [of] holy hands"* (1 Tim. 2:8) is essential to Christlike praying. It is not, however, a holiness that only dedicates a closet to God. It does not merely set apart an hour to Him. It is a consecration that takes hold of the entire man. It dedicates the whole life to God.

Our Lord Jesus Christ, who was *"holy, harmless, undefiled, separate from sinners"* (Heb. 7:26), had ready access to God in prayer. He had this free, full access because of His unquestioning obedience to His Father. Throughout His earthly life His supreme care and desire was to do the will of His Father. This fact, coupled with another—the consciousness of having so ordered His life—gave Him confidence and assurance. It enabled Him to draw near to the throne of grace with unlimited confidence born of obedience, promised acceptance, audience, and answer.

Loving obedience puts us where we can ask anything in His name. It gives us the assurance that He will do it. (See John 14:14.) Loving obedience brings us into the prayer realm. It makes us beneficiaries of the wealth of Christ. We receive the riches of His grace through the Holy Spirit, who will abide with us and be in us. Cheerful obedience to God qualifies us to pray effectually.

This obedience that qualifies and is the forerunner of prayer must be loving and constant. It is always doing the Father's will and cheerfully following the path of God's commands.

In King Hezekiah's situation, it was a potent plea that changed God's decree that he should die and not live. The stricken ruler called upon God to remember how he had walked before Him in truth and with a perfect heart. With God, this counted. He listened carefully to the petition. As a result, death found its approach to Hezekiah barred for fifteen years.

Jesus learned obedience in the school of suffering. At the same time, He learned prayer in the school of obedience. Just as it is the prayer of a righteous man that avails much, so it is righteousness that is obedience to God. A righteous man is an obedient man. He can pray effectually. He can accomplish great things when he goes to his knees.

Remember that true praying is not mere sentiment, poetry, or eloquent speech. It does not consist of saying in sweet tones, "Lord, Lord." Prayer is not a mere form of words. It is not just calling upon a name. *Prayer is obedience.* It is founded on the unbending rock of obedience to God. Only those who obey have the right to pray. Behind the praying must be the doing. It is the constant doing of God's will in daily life that gives prayer its potency.

Our Lord plainly taught,

Not every one that saith unto me, Lord, Lord, shall enter the kingdom of heaven; but he that doeth the will of my Father which is in heaven. Many will say to me in that day, Lord, Lord, have we not prophesied in thy name? and in thy name have we cast out devils? and in thy name done many wonderful

163

works? And then will I profess unto them, I never knew you: depart from me, ye that worketh iniquity. (Matt. 7:21–23)

No name, however precious and powerful, can protect and give efficiency to prayer that is unaccompanied by doing God's will. Neither can the doing, without the praying, protect from divine disapproval. If the will of God does not master the life, the praying will be nothing but sickly sentiment. If prayer does not inspire, sanctify, and direct our work, then self-will enters and ruins both the work and worker.

How many great misconceptions there are of the true elements and functions of prayer! There are many who earnestly desire to obtain an answer to their prayers, but who go unrewarded and unblessed. They fix their minds on some promise of God. Then they endeavor by stubborn perseverance to summon enough faith to lay hold of it and claim it. This fixing the mind on some great promise may help in strengthening faith. But persistent and urgent prayer—prayer that expects and waits until faith grows exceedingly—must be added to this promise. Who is able and competent to do such praying except the man who readily, cheerfully, and continually *obeys God?*

Faith, in its highest form, is the attitude as well as the act of a soul surrendered to God. His Word and His Spirit dwell in that soul. It is true that faith must exist in some form or another in order to prompt praying. But in its strongest form and in its greatest results, faith is the fruit of prayer. It is true that faith increases the ability and efficiency of prayer. It is likewise true that prayer increases the ability and efficiency of faith. Prayer and faith work, act, and react one upon the other.

Obedience to God helps faith as no other attribute possibly can. When there is absolute recognition of the validity and supremacy of the divine commands, faith ceases to be an almost superhuman task. It requires no straining to exercise it. Obedience to God makes it easy to believe and trust God. Where the spirit of obedience totally saturates the soul, and the will is perfectly surrendered to God, faith becomes a reality. It also does this where there is a fixed, unalterable purpose to obey God. Faith then becomes almost involuntary. After obedience it is the next natural step. It is easily and readily taken. The difficulty in prayer then is not with faith but with obedience, which is faith's foundation.

If we want to pray well and get the most out of our praying, we must look at our obedience. We must look at the secret springs of action and the loyalty of our heart to God. Obedience is the groundwork of effective praying. This brings us near to God.

The lack of obedience in our lives breaks down our praying. Quite often our lives are in rebellion. This places us where praying is almost impossible, except for pardoning mercy. Disobedient living produces extremely poor praying. Disobedience shuts the door of the prayer closet. It bars the way to the Holy of Holies. No man can pray—really pray—who does not obey.

Our will must be surrendered to God as a primary condition to all successful praying. Everything about us receives its coloring from our innermost character. Our secret will determines our character and controls our conduct. Our will, therefore, plays an important part in all successful praying. There can be no rich, true praying when the will is not wholly and fully surrendered to God. This unswerving loyalty to God is an utterly indispensable condition of the best, truest, and most effective praying. We have "simply got to trust and obey. *There's no other way,* to be happy in Jesus—but to trust and *obey!*"

11

Prayer and
Spiritual Warfare

*David Brainerd was pursued by unearthly adversaries
who were resolved to rob him of his reward. He knew he must
never take off his armor, but lie down to rest with his corselet
laced. The stains that marred the perfection of his lustrous
dress and the spots of rust on his gleaming shield are imper-
ceptible to us, but they were to him the source of much sorrow
and ardency of yearning.* —The Life of David Brainerd

THE description of the Christian soldier given by Paul in Ephesians 6 is compact and comprehensive. He is seen as always being in
the conflict, which has many fluctuating seasons. There are seasons
of prosperity and adversity, lightness and darkness, victory and defeat. He is to pray in all seasons and with all prayer. This is to be
added to the armor when he goes into battle. At all times, he is to
have the full armor of prayer. The Christian soldier, if he fights to
win, must pray much. Only by this means is he able to defeat his
long-standing enemy, the Devil, and his many agents. *"Praying always with all prayer"* (Eph. 6:18) is the divine direction given to him.
This covers all seasons and includes all manner of praying.

Christian soldiers, fighting the good fight of faith (see 1 Timothy 6:12), have access to a place of retreat where they continually
go for prayer. *"Praying always with all prayer"* is a clear statement
of the essential need of much praying. It is also a statement of
many kinds of praying, by him who, fighting the good fight of faith,
wins out, in the end, over all his foes.

The Revised Standard Version puts it this way:

> *Pray at all times in the Spirit, with all prayer and supplication...for all the saints, and also for me, that utterance may be given me in opening my mouth boldly to proclaim the mystery of the gospel, for which I am an ambassador in chains; that I may declare it boldly, as I ought to speak.*   (Eph. 6:18–20)

It cannot be said too often that the life of a Christian is warfare, an intense conflict, a lifelong contest. It is a battle fought against invisible foes who are ever alert and seeking to entrap, deceive, and ruin the souls of men. The Bible calls men to life, not a picnic or holiday. It is no pastime or pleasure excursion. It entails effort, wrestling, and struggling. It demands putting out the full energy of the spirit in order to frustrate the foe and to come out, at last, more than a conqueror. It is no primrose path, no rose-scented flirting. From start to finish, it is war. The Christian warrior is compelled from the hour he first draws his sword to *"endure hardness, as a good soldier"* (2 Tim. 2:3).

What a misconception many people have of the Christian life! How little the average church member appears to know of the character of the conflict and of its demands on him! How ignorant he seems to be of the enemies he must encounter if he is to serve God faithfully, succeed in getting to heaven, and receive the crown of life! He scarcely seems to realize that the world, the flesh, and the Devil will oppose his onward march. He hardly realizes that they will defeat him utterly, unless he gives himself to constant vigilance and unceasing prayer.

The Christian soldier wrestles not against flesh and blood, but against spiritual wickedness in high places. (See Ephesians 6:12.) Or, as the scriptural margin reads, *"wicked spirits in high places."* What a fearful array of forces that are set against him! They desire to impede his way through the wilderness of this world to the doors of the Celestial City! It is no surprise, therefore, to find Paul, who understood the character of the Christian life so well, carefully and plainly urging Christians to *"put on the whole armour of God"* (v. 11). It is not surprising that Paul, who was so thoroughly informed as to the malignity and number of the foes that the disciple of the Lord must encounter, would urge us to pray *"with all prayer and supplication in the Spirit"* (v. 18) The present generation would be wise if all professors of our faith could be persuaded to realize this all-important, vital truth, which is absolutely indispensable to a successful Christian life.

It is just at this point in today's Christianity that one may find its greatest defect. There is little or nothing of the soldier element in it. The discipline, self-denial, spirit of hardship, determination, so prominent in and belonging to the military life, are lacking. Yet, the Christian life is warfare, all the way.

How comprehensive, pointed, and striking are all Paul's directions to the Christian soldier who is bent on defeating the Devil and saving his soul alive. First of all, he must possess a clear idea of the character of the life into which he has entered. Then, he must know something of his foes—the adversaries of his immortal soul—their strength their skill, their viciousness.

Knowing something of the character of the enemy and realizing the need of preparation to overcome them, he is prepared to hear the apostle's decisive conclusion:

> *Finally, my brethren, be strong in the Lord, and in the power of his might. Put on the whole armour of God, that ye may be able to stand against the wiles of the devil....Wherefore, take unto you the whole armour of God, that ye may be able to withstand in the evil day, and having done all, to stand.*
>
> *(Eph. 6:10–11, 13)*

All these directions end in a climax, and that climax is prayer. How can the brave warrior for Christ be made braver still? How can the strong soldier be made stronger still? How can the victorious fighter be made still more victorious?

Here are Paul's explicit directions to that end: *"Praying always with all prayer and supplication in the Spirit, and watching thereunto with all perseverance and supplication for all saints"* (Eph. 6:18).

Prayer, and more prayer, adds to the fighting qualities and the more certain victories of God's good, fighting men. The power of prayer is most forceful on the battlefield in the midst of the noise and strife of the conflict. Paul was preeminently a soldier of the cross. For him, life was no flowery bed of ease. He was no parading, holiday soldier, whose only business was to put on a uniform for special occasions. His was a life of intense conflict, the facing of many adversaries, the exercise of unsleeping vigilance and constant effort. And in sight of the end, we hear him as he chanted his final song of victory, *"I have fought a good fight"* (2 Tim. 4:7). Reading between the lines, we see that he is more than a conqueror!

Paul indicated the nature of his soldier life, giving us some views of the kind of praying needed for such a career. He wrote,

Now I beseech you, brethren, for the Lord Jesus Christ's sake, and for the love of the Spirit, that ye strive together with me in your prayers to God for me; that I may be delivered from them that do not believe in Judaea.   (Rom. 15:30–31)

Paul *had* foes in Judea—foes who surrounded and opposed him in the form of unbelieving men, and this, added to other weighty reasons, led him to urge the Roman Christians to strive with him in prayer. That word *strive* indicates wrestling, the putting forth of great effort. This is the kind of effort and spirit that must possess the Christian soldier.

Here is a great soldier, in the great struggle, faced by malignant forces who seek his ruin. His strength is almost gone. What reinforcements can he count on? What can give help and bring success to a warrior in such a pressing emergency? It is a critical moment in the conflict. What strength can be added to the energy of his own prayers? The answer is—the prayers of others, even the prayers of his fellow believers who were at Rome. These, he believes, will bring him additional aid. He can then win his fight, overcome his adversaries, and, ultimately, prevail.

The Christian soldier is to pray in all seasons and under all circumstances. His praying must be arranged in order to cover his times of peace as well as his hours of active conflict. It must be available in his marching and his fighting. Prayer must diffuse all effort, impregnate all ventures, decide all issues. The Christian soldier must be as intense in his praying as in his fighting, for his victories will depend much more on his praying than on his fighting.

Fervent supplication must be added to steady resolve. Prayer and supplication must supplement the armor of God. The Holy Spirit must aid the supplication with His own strenuous plea. And the soldier must pray in the Spirit. In this, as in other forms of warfare, eternal vigilance is the price of victory. Thus, watchfulness and perseverance must mark every activity of the Christian warrior.

The soldier's prayer must reflect his profound concern for the success and well-being of the whole army. The battle is not altogether a personal matter. Victory cannot be achieved for self alone. There is a sense in which the entire army of Christ is involved. The cause of God, His saints, their woes and trials, their duties and crosses, all should find a pleading voice in the Christian soldier when he prays. He dare not limit his praying to himself. Nothing dries up spiritual blessings so certainly and completely, nothing poisons the fountain of spiritual life so effectively, and nothing acts in such deadly fashion as selfish praying.

Note carefully that the Christian's armor will avail him nothing unless prayer is added. This is the pivot, the connecting link of the armor of God. This holds it together and renders it effective. God's true soldier plans his campaigns, arranges his battle forces, and conducts his conflicts with prayer. Prayer is all-important and absolutely essential to victory. Prayer should so impregnate the life, that every breath becomes a petition, every sigh a supplication. The Christian soldier must always be fighting. He should, of sheer necessity, be always praying.

The Christian soldier is compelled to constant guard duty. He is faced by a foe who never sleeps, who is always alert, and who is ever prepared to take advantage of the fortunes of war. Watchfulness is a fundamental principle with Christ's warrior; *"watch and pray"* (Matt. 26:41) is forever sounding in his ears. He cannot dare to be asleep at his post. Such a lapse brings him not only under the displeasure of the Captain of his salvation, but also exposes him to added danger. Watchfulness, therefore, imperatively constitutes the duty of the soldier of the Lord.

In the New Testament, there are three different words that are translated "watch." The first means "absence of sleep" and implies a wakeful frame of mind, as opposed to listlessness. It is a command to keep awake, attentive, and vigilant. The second word means "fully awake"—a state induced by some rousing, active, cautious effort lest, through carelessness or laziness, some destructive calamity should suddenly evolve. The third word means "to be calm and collected in spirit," unemotional, untouched by confusing circumstances, cautious against all pitfalls and diversions.

All three definitions are used by Paul. Two of them are used in connection with prayer. Watchfulness intensified is a necessity for prayer. Watchfulness must guard and cover the whole spiritual man and prepare him for prayer. Everything resembling unpreparedness or non-vigilance is death to prayer.

In Ephesians 6:18, Paul gave prominence to the duty of constant watchfulness, *"watching thereunto with all perseverance and supplication."* "Watch," he said, *"watch,* WATCH!"

Sleepless alertness is the price one must pay for victory over his spiritual foes. Rest assured that the Devil never falls asleep. He ever *"walketh about, seeking whom he may devour"* (1 Pet. 5:8). Just as a shepherd must never be careless or unwatchful lest the wolf devour his sheep, so the Christian soldier must have his eyes wide open, implying his possession of a spirit that neither slumbers nor grows careless. The inseparable companions and safeguards of prayer are vigilance and watchfulness. In writing to the Colossians, Paul bracketed these inseparable qualities together: *"Continue in prayer, and watch in the same with thanksgiving"* (Col. 4:2).

When will Christians more thoroughly learn the twofold lesson that they are called to a great warfare and that, in order to get the victory, they must give themselves to unsleeping watchfulness and unceasing prayer? *"Be sober, be vigilant; because your adversary the devil, as a roaring lion, walketh about, seeking whom he may devour"* (1 Pet. 5:8).

God's church is a militant host. Its warfare is with unseen forces of evil. God's people compose an army fighting to establish His kingdom in the earth. Their aim is to destroy the sovereignty of Satan and, over its ruins, erect the kingdom of God, which is *"righteousness, and peace, and joy in the Holy Ghost"* (Rom. 14:17). This militant army is composed of individual soldiers of the cross. The armor of God is needed for defense, and added prayer crowns the entire army.

Prayer is too simple, too obvious a duty, to need definition. Necessity gives being and shape to prayer. Its importance is so absolute that the Christian soldier's life, in all the breadth and intensity of it, should be one of prayer. The entire life of a Christian soldier—its being, intention, implication, and action—are all dependent on its being a life of prayer. Without prayer—no matter what else he has—the Christian soldier's life will be feeble and ineffective. Without prayer, he is an easy prey for his spiritual enemies.

Unless prayer has an important place in a Christian's life, his experience and influence will be powerless. Without prayer the Christian graces will wither and die. Without prayer, we may add, preaching is futile and fruitless. Christ is the lawgiver of prayer,

171

and Paul is His apostle of prayer. Both declare its primary importance and demonstrate the fact of its necessity. Their prayer directions cover all places, include all times, and comprehend all things. How, then, can the Christian soldier hope or dream of victory, unless he is fortified by its power? How can he fail if in addition to putting on the armor of God he is, at all times and seasons, *"watching thereunto with all perseverance and supplication for all saints"* (Eph. 6:18)?

12

Prayer and God's Promises

In the Scriptures, we constantly encounter such words as "field," "seed," "sower," "reaper," "seedtime," "harvest." Employing such metaphors interprets a fact of nature by a parable of grace. The field is the world and the good seed is the Word of God. Whether the Word be spoken or written, it is the power of God unto salvation. In our work of evangelism, the whole world is our field, every creature the object of effort, and every book and tract, a seed of God. —David Fant, Jr.

GOD'S Word is a record of prayer—of praying men and their achievements, of the divine warrant of prayer, and of the encouragement given to those who pray. No one can read the instances, commands, and examples of statements that concern themselves with prayer, without realizing that the cause of God and the success of His work in this world are committed to prayer. Praying men have been God's appointed officers on earth. Prayerless men have never been used of Him.

A reverence for God's holy name is closely related to a high regard for His Word. This hallowing of God's name, the ability to do His will on earth as it is done in heaven, and the establishment and glory of God's kingdom are as much involved in prayer as when Jesus taught men the universal prayer. That *"men ought always to pray, and not to faint"* (Luke 18:1) is as fundamental to God's cause today as when Jesus Christ enshrined that great truth in the immortal setting of the parable of the persistent widow.

As God's house is called *"the house of prayer"* (Matt. 21:13), because prayer is the most important of its holy offices, so, by the same token, the Bible may be called the book of prayer. Prayer is the great theme and content of its message to mankind.

God's Word is the basis of, the directory of, and the prayer of faith. Paul said,

Let the word of Christ dwell in you richly in all wisdom; teaching and admonishing one another in psalms and hymns and spiritual songs, singing with grace in your hearts to the Lord. *(Col. 3:16)*

As the Word of Christ dwells richly in us, we become transformed. The result is that we become praying Christians. Faith is constructed of the Word and the Spirit, and faith is the body and substance of prayer.

In many of its aspects, prayer is dependent on the Word of God. Jesus says, *"If ye abide in me, and my words abide in you, ye shall ask what ye will, and it shall be done unto you"* (John 15:7).

The Word of God is the support upon which the lever of prayer is placed, and by which things are mightily moved. God has committed Himself, His purpose, and His promise to prayer. His Word becomes the basis and the inspiration of our praying. Under certain circumstances, persistent prayer may bring additional assurance of His promises. It is said of the old saints that they *"through faith...obtained promises"* (Heb. 11:33). There would seem to be the capacity in prayer for going beyond the Word, beyond His promise, and into the very presence of God Himself.

Jacob wrestled, not so much with a promise, as with the Promiser. We must take hold of the Promiser, or else the promise is useless. Prayer may well be defined as the force that vitalizes and energizes the Word of God, by taking hold of God Himself. By taking hold of the Promiser, prayer releases the personal promise. *"There is none...that stirreth up himself to take hold of* [me]*"* (Isa. 64:7) is God's sad lament. *"Let him take hold of my strength, that he may make peace with me"* (Isa. 27:5) is God's recipe for prayer.

By scriptural authority, prayer may be divided into the petition of faith and that of submission. The prayer of faith is based on the written Word, for *"faith cometh by hearing, and hearing by the word of God"* (Rom. 10:17). It inevitably receives its answer—the very thing for which it prays.

The prayer of submission is without a definite word of promise, so to speak. But it takes hold of God with a lowly and contrite spirit and asks and pleads with Him for that which the soul desires. Abraham had no definite promise that God would spare Sodom.

Moses had no definite promise that God would spare Israel. On the contrary, there was the declaration of His wrath and of His purpose to destroy. But the devoted leader gained his plea with God when he interceded for the Israelites with incessant prayers and many tears. Daniel had no definite promise that God would reveal to him the meaning of the king's dream; but he prayed specifically, and God answered definitely.

The Word of God is made effectual and operative by the process and practice of prayer. The Word of the Lord came to Elijah, *"Go, show thyself unto Ahab; and I will send rain upon the earth"* (1 Kings 18:1). Elijah showed himself to Ahab, but the answer to his prayer did not come until he had pressed his fiery prayer upon the Lord seven times.

Paul had the definite promise from Christ, that He would deliver him *"from the people, and from the Gentiles"* (Acts 26:17). But we find that he exhorted the Romans in an urgent and solemn manner concerning this very matter:

> *Now I beseech you, brethren, for the Lord Jesus Christ's sake, and for the love of the Spirit, that ye strive together with me in your prayers to God for me; that I may be delivered from them that do not believe in Judaea; and that my service which I have for Jerusalem may be accepted of the saints.*
>
> *(Rom. 15:30–31)*

The Word of God is a great help in prayer. If it is lodged and written in our hearts, it will form an outflowing current of prayer, full and irresistible. Promises, stored in the heart, are to be the fuel from which prayer receives life and warmth. Just as coal, which has been stored in the earth, gives us comfort on stormy days and wintry nights, the Word of God stored in our hearts is the food by which prayer is nourished and made strong. Prayer, like man, cannot live by bread alone, *"but by every word that proceedeth out of the mouth of God"* (Matt. 4:4).

Unless the vital forces of prayer are supplied by God's Word, prayer, though earnest, even vociferous in its urgency, is, in reality, flabby and void. The absence of vital force in praying can be traced to the absence of a constant supply of God's Word to repair the waste and renew the life. He who wants to learn to pray well, must first study God's Word and store it in his memory and thought.

When we consult God's Word, we find that no duty is more binding, more exacting, than that of prayer. On the other hand, we discover that no privilege is more exalted, no habit more richly owned of God. No promises are more radiant, more abounding, more explicit, more often reiterated, than those that are attached to prayer. "All things whatsoever" are received by prayer because "all things whatsoever" are promised. (See Matthew 21:22.) There is no limit to the provisions included in the promises to prayer, and no exclusion from its promises. *"For every one that asketh receiveth"* (Luke 11:10). The word of our Lord is to this all-embracing effect: *"If ye shall ask any thing in my name, I will do it"* (John 14:14).

Here are some of the comprehensive and exhaustive statements of the Word of God about prayer, the things to be taken in by prayer, and the strong promise made in answer to prayer: *"Pray without ceasing"* (1 Thess. 5:17); *"continue in prayer"* (Col. 4:2); *"continuing instant in prayer"* (Rom. 12:12); *"in every thing by prayer...let your requests be made known unto God"* (Phil. 4:6); *"always to pray, and not to faint"* (Luke 18:1); *"men* [should] *pray every where"* (1 Tim. 2:8); *"praying always with all prayer and supplication"* (Eph. 6:18).

What clear and strong statements those are that are put in the divine record to furnish us with a sure basis of faith and to urge, constrain, and encourage us to pray! How wide the range of prayer in the divine revelation! How these Scriptures incite us to seek the God of prayer, with all our needs, with all our burdens!

In addition to these statements left on record for our encouragement, the sacred pages teem with facts, examples, incidents, and observations, stressing the importance and the absolute necessity of prayer and putting emphasis on its all-prevailing power.

The greatest benefit of the rich promises of the Word of God should humbly be received by us and put to the test. The world will never receive the full benefits of the Gospel until this is done. Neither Christian experience nor Christian living will be what they ought to be until these divine promises have been fully tested by those who pray. By prayer, we bring these promises of God's holy will into the realm of the actual and the real.

If asked what is to be done in order to render God's promises real, the answer is that we must pray, until the words of the promise are fulfilled.

God's promises are too large to be mastered by aimless praying. When we examine ourselves, we discover that our praying does not rise to the demands of the situation. It is so limited that it is little more than a mere oasis amid the waste and desert of the world's sin. Who of us, in our praying, measures up to the promises of our Lord? *"Verily, verily, I say unto you, He that believeth on me, the works that I do shall he do also; and greater works than these shall he do; because I go unto my Father"* (John 14:12).

How comprehensive, how far reaching, how all-embracing! How much is here, for the glory of God, how much for the good of man! How much for the manifestation of Christ's enthroned power, how much for the reward of abundant faith! How great and gracious are the results that grow from the exercise of believing prayer!

Look at another of God's great promises and discover how we may be strengthened by the Word as we pray, and on what firm ground we may stand to make our petitions to our God: *"If ye abide in me, and my words abide in you, ye shall ask what ye will, and it shall be done unto you"* (John 15:7). In these comprehensive words, God turns Himself over to the will of His people. When Christ becomes our all in all, prayer lays God's treasures at our feet.

Early Christianity had an easy and practical solution to the situation. The first Christians received all that God had to give. That simple, short solution is recorded in 1 John 3:22: *"Whatsoever we ask, we receive of him, because we keep his commandments, and do those things that are pleasing in his sight."*

Prayer coupled with loving obedience is the answer to all ends and all things. Prayer joined to the Word of God hallows and makes sacred all God's gifts. Prayer is not simply to receive things from God, but to make holy those things that already have been received of Him. It is not merely to *receive* a blessing, but also to be able to *give* a blessing. Prayer makes common things holy and secular things sacred. It receives things from God with thanksgiving and hallows them with thankful hearts and devoted service.

In 1 Timothy 4:4–5, Paul gave us these words: *"For every creature of God is good, and nothing to be refused, if it be received with thanksgiving: for it is sanctified by the word of God and prayer."* God's good gifts are to be holy, not only by God's creative power, but because they are made holy to us by prayer. We receive them, appropriate them, and sanctify them by prayer.

Doing God's will—having His Word abiding in us—is an imperative of effectual praying. But, it may be asked, how are we to know what God's will is? The answer is by studying His Word (see 2 Timothy 2:15), by hiding it in our hearts (see Psalm 119:11), and by letting the Word dwell in us richly. (See Colossians 3:16.) *"The entrance of thy words giveth light"* (Ps. 119:130).

To know God's will in prayer, we must be filled with God's Spirit, who makes intercession for the saints according to the will of God. (See Romans 8:27.) To be filled with God's Spirit, to be filled with God's Word, is to know God's will. It is to be put in such a frame of mind and state of heart that it will enable us to read and correctly interpret the purposes of the infinite. Such filling of the heart with the Word and the Spirit gives us an insight into the will of the Father. It enables us to rightly discern His will and puts a disposition of mind and heart within us to make it the guide and compass of our lives.

Epaphras prayed that the Colossians might stand *"perfect and complete in all the will of God"* (Col. 4:12). This is proof positive that not only can we know the will of God, but that we can know *all* the will of God. And not only can we know all the will of God, but we can *do* all the will of God. In addition, we can do all the will of God as an established habit instead of an occasional impulse. Still further, it shows us that we not only can do the will of God externally, but from the heart, cheerfully, without holding back from the intimate presence of the Lord.

13

Prayer and the Word of God

Some years ago a man was traveling in the wilds of Kentucky. He had with him a large sum of money and was well armed. He stayed at a log house one night, but was much concerned with the rough appearance of the men who came and went from this abode. He retired early, but not to sleep. At midnight he heard the dogs barking furiously and the sound of someone entering the cabin. Peering through a chink in the boards of his room, he saw a stranger with a gun in his hand. Another man sat before the fire. The traveler concluded they were planning to rob him and prepared to defend himself and his property. Presently the newcomer took down a copy of the Bible, read a chapter aloud, and then knelt down and prayed. The traveler dismissed his fears, put his revolver away, and lay down to sleep peacefully until morning light. And all because a Bible was in the cabin, and its owner a man of prayer.
—Rev. F. F. Shoup

PRAYER means the success of the preaching of the Word. Paul clearly taught this in that familiar and pressing request he made to the Thessalonians: *"Finally, brethren, pray for us, that the word of the Lord may have free course, and be glorified"* (2 Thess. 3:1).

Prayer opens the way for the Word of God to run without hindrance. It creates the atmosphere that is favorable for the Word to accomplish its purpose. Prayer puts wheels under God's Word and gives wings to the angel of the Lord *"having the everlasting gospel to preach unto them that dwell on the earth, and to every nation, and kindred, and tongue, and people"* (Rev. 14:6). Prayer greatly helps the Word of the Lord.

The parable of the sower is a notable study of preaching, showing its differing effects and describing the diversity of hearers. The wayside hearers are many. The soil lies unprepared either by previous thought or prayer. As a consequence, the Devil easily takes away the seed (which is the Word of God). Dissipating all good impressions, Satan renders the work of the sower futile. If only the hearers would prepare the ground of their hearts beforehand by prayer and meditation, much of the current sowing would be fruitful.

The same applies to the stony-ground and thorny-ground hearers. Although the Word lodges in their hearts and begins to sprout, yet all is lost, chiefly because there is no prayer or watchfulness or cultivation following. The good-ground hearers are profited by the sowing, simply because their minds have been prepared for the reception of the seed. After hearing, they have cultivated the seed sown in their hearts by the exercise of prayer. All this gives particular emphasis to the conclusion of this striking parable: *"Take heed therefore how ye hear"* (Luke 8:18). In order that we can heed how we hear, we must give ourselves continually to prayer.

We have to believe that the success and effect of God's Word depend on prayer. *"So shall my word be that goeth forth out of my mouth: it shall not return unto me void, but it shall...prosper in the thing whereto I sent it"* (Isa. 55:11).

In Psalm 19, David magnified the Word of God in six statements concerning it. The Word converts the soul, makes wise the simple, rejoices the heart, enlightens the eyes, endures eternally, and is true and righteous altogether. The Word of God is perfect, sure, right, pure. It is heart-searching and, at the same time, purifying in its effect.

It is no surprise that after considering the deep spirituality of the Word of God, its power to search the inner nature of man, and its deep purity, the psalmist should close his dissertation with this passage:

> *Who can understand his errors? Cleanse thou me from secret faults. Keep back thy servant also from presumptuous sins; let them not have dominion over me....Let the words of my mouth, and the meditation of my heart, be acceptable in thy sight, O Lord, my strength, and my redeemer.* (Ps. 19:12–14)

James recognized the deep spirituality of the Word and its inherent saving power in the following exhortation: *"Wherefore lay apart all filthiness and superfluity of naughtiness, and receive with meekness the engrafted word, which is able to save your souls"* (James 1:21).

And Peter talked along the same line when describing the saving power of the Word of God: *"Being born again, not of corruptible seed, but of incorruptible, by the word of God, which liveth and abideth for ever"* (1 Pet. 1:23). Not only did Peter speak of being born again by the incorruptible Word of God, but he informed us that to grow in grace we must be like newborn babes, desiring or feeding upon the *"sincere milk of the word"* (1 Pet. 2:2).

Prayer invariably generates a love for the Word of God. Prayer leads people to obey the Word of God and puts into the obedient heart a joy unspeakable. Praying people and Bible-reading people are the same sort of folk. The God of the Bible and the God of prayer are one. God speaks to man in the Bible; man speaks to God in prayer. One reads the Bible to discover God's will. He prays in order to receive power to do that will. Bible reading and praying are the distinguishing traits of those who strive to know and please God.

Just as prayer generates a love for the Scriptures and causes people to begin to read the Bible, so does prayer cause men and women to visit the house of God to hear the Scriptures expounded. Churchgoing is closely connected with the Bible, primarily because the Bible cautions us against *"forsaking the assembling of ourselves together, as the manner of some is"* (Heb. 10:25). Churchgoing also results because God's chosen minister explains and enforces the Scriptures upon his hearers. Prayer germinates a resolve in those who practice it to not forsake the church.

Prayer generates a churchgoing conscience, a church-loving heart, and a church-supporting spirit. Praying people take delight in the preaching of the Word and the support of the church. Prayer exalts the Word of God and gives it preeminence in those who faithfully and wholeheartedly call upon the name of the Lord.

Prayer draws its very life from the Bible. It places its security on the firm ground of Scripture. Its very existence and character depend on revelation made by God to man in His holy Word. Prayer, in turn, exalts this same revelation and turns men toward that Word. The nature, necessity, and all-comprehending character of prayer are based on the Word of God.

Psalm 119 is a directory of God's Word. With three or four exceptions, each verse contains a word that identifies or locates the

Word of God. Quite often, the author broke out into supplication, several times praying, *"Teach me thy statutes"* (Ps. 119:12). So deeply impressed was he with the wonders of God's Word, and with the need for divine illumination to see and understand the wonderful things recorded within, that he fervently prayed, *"Open thou mine eyes, that I may behold wondrous things out of thy law"* (Ps. 119:18).

From the opening of this wonderful psalm to its close, prayer and God's Word are intertwined. Almost every phase of God's Word is touched upon by this inspired writer. So thoroughly convinced was the psalmist of the deep spiritual power of the Word of God that he made this declaration: *"Thy word have I hid in mine heart, that I might not sin against thee"* (v. 11).

Here the psalmist found his protection against sinning. By having God's Word hidden in his heart and his whole being thoroughly impregnated with that Word, he was able to walk to and fro on the earth. He was safe from the attack of the Evil One and strengthened from wandering away.

We find, furthermore, that the power of prayer creates a real love for the Scriptures and puts within men a nature that will take pleasure in the Word. In holy ecstasy the psalmist cried, *"O how I love thy law! It is my meditation all the day"* (v. 97). And again: *"How sweet are thy words unto my taste! yea, sweeter than honey to my mouth!"* (v. 103).

Do we relish God's Word? If so, then let us give ourselves continually to prayer. He who would have a heart for the reading of the Bible must not—dare not—forget to pray. A man who loves the Bible will also love to pray. A man who loves to pray will delight in the law of the Lord.

Our Lord was a man of prayer. He magnified the Word of God and often quoted the Scriptures. Right through His earthly life, Jesus observed Sabbath keeping, churchgoing, and the reading of the Word of God. His prayer intermingled with them all: *"And he came to Nazareth, where he had been brought up: and, as his custom was, he went into the synagogue on the sabbath day, and stood up for to read"* (Luke 4:16).

Let it be said, that no two things are more essential to a Spirit-filled life than Bible reading and secret prayer. They will help you to grow in grace, to obtain joy from living a Christian life, and to be established in the way of eternal peace. To neglect these all-important duties means leanness of soul, loss of joy, absence of peace, dryness of spirit, and decay in all that pertains to spiritual life. Neglecting these things paves the way for apostasy and gives the Evil One an advantage such as he is not likely to ignore.

Reading God's Word regularly and praying habitually in the secret place of the Most High puts one where he is absolutely safe from the attacks of the Enemy of souls. It guarantees him salvation and final victory through the overcoming power of the Lamb.

14

Prayer and the
House of God

And dear to me the loud "Amen,"
Which echoes through the blest abode—
Which swells, and sinks, then swells again,
Dies on the walls—but lives with God!

PRAYER affects places, times, occasions, and circumstances. It has to do with God and with everything that is related to God. It has an intimate and special relationship to His house. A church should be a sacred place, set apart from all unhallowed and secular uses, for the worship of God. As worship is prayer, the house of God is a place set apart for worship. It is no common place. It is where God dwells, where He meets with His people, and where He delights in the worship of His saints.

Prayer is always proper in the house of God. When prayer is a stranger there, it ceases to be God's house at all. Our Lord put particular emphasis on what the church is to be, when He cast out the buyers and sellers in the temple. He repeated the words from Isaiah: *"It is written, My house shall be called the house of prayer"* (Matt. 21:13). He makes prayer preeminent above all else in the house of God. Those who sidetrack prayer or seek to minimize it pervert the church of God and make it something less than it is ordained to be.

Prayer is perfectly at home in the house of God. It is no stranger, no mere guest; it belongs there. It has a peculiar affinity for the place. It has a divine appointment to be there.

The inner chamber is a sacred place for personal worship. The house of God is a holy place for united worship. The prayer closet is for individual prayer. The house of God is for mutual, united prayer. Yet even in the house of God, there is the element of private worship. God's people are to worship Him and pray to Him, personally, even in public worship. The church is for the united prayer of kindred, yet individual, believers.

The life, power, and glory of the church is prayer. The life of its members is dependent on prayer. The presence of God is secured and retained by prayer. The very place is made sacred by its ministry. Without it, the church is lifeless and powerless. Without it, even the building itself is nothing more than any other structure. Prayer converts even the bricks, mortar, and lumber into a sanctuary, a Holy of Holies, where the Shekinah dwells. Prayer separates it, in spirit and in purpose, from all other buildings. Prayer gives a peculiar sacredness to the building, sanctifies it, sets it apart for God, and conserves it from all common and mundane affairs.

With prayer, the house of God becomes a divine sanctuary. So the tabernacle, moving about from place to place, became the Holy of Holies, because God and prayer were there. Without prayer, the building may be costly, perfect in its structure, attractive to the eye, but it comes down to the human, with nothing divine in it, and is on a level with all other buildings.

Without prayer, a church is like a body without spirit; it is a dead, inanimate thing. A church with prayer in it has God in it. When prayer is set aside, God is outlawed. When prayer becomes an unfamiliar exercise, then God Himself is a stranger there.

As God's house is a house of prayer, the divine intention is that people should leave their homes and go to meet Him in His own house. The building is set apart for prayer. God has made special promise to meet His people there. It is their duty to go there for that specific end. Prayer should be the chief attraction for all spiritually-minded churchgoers. While it is conceded that the preaching of the Word has an important place in the house of God, yet prayer is its predominant, distinguishing feature. Not that all other places are sinful or evil in themselves or in their uses. But they are secular and human, having no special conception of God in them.

The church is, essentially, spiritual and divine. The work belonging to other places is done without special reference to God. He is not specifically recognized nor called upon. In the church, however, God is acknowledged, and nothing is done without Him.

Prayer is the one distinguishing mark of the house of God. As prayer distinguishes the Christian from unsaved people, so prayer distinguishes God's house from all other houses. It is a place where faithful believers meet with their Lord.

As God's house is a house of prayer, prayer should enter into and underlie everything that is done there. Prayer belongs to every sort of work relating to the church. As God's house is a house where the business of praying is carried on, so is it a place where the business of making praying people out of prayerless people is done. The house of God is a divine workshop, and there the work of prayer goes on. Or the house of God is a divine schoolhouse, in which the lesson of prayer is taught, where men and women learn to pray, and where they graduate from the school of prayer.

Any church that calls itself the house of God but fails to magnify and teach the great lesson of prayer, should change its teaching to conform to the divine prayer pattern; or, it should change the name of its building to something other than a church.

On an earlier page, I referred to the finding of the Book of the Law that was given to Moses from the Lord. How long that book had been there, we do not know. But when tidings of its discovery were carried to Josiah, he tore his clothes and was greatly disturbed. He lamented the neglect of God's Word and saw, as a natural result, the iniquity that abounded throughout the land.

And then, Josiah thought of God and commanded Hilkiah, the priest, to go and make inquiry of the Lord. Such neglect of the word of the law was too serious a matter to be treated lightly. God must be sought. Josiah and his nation needed to repent.

Go ye, inquire of the Lord for me, and for the people, and for all Judah, concerning the words of this book that is found: for great is the wrath of the Lord that is kindled against us, because our fathers have not hearkened unto the words of this book, to do according unto all that which is written concerning us. (2 Kings 22:13)

But that was not all. Josiah was bent on promoting a revival of religion in his kingdom. He gathered all the elders of Jerusalem end Judah together for that purpose. When they had come together, the king went into the house of the Lord and read all the words of the Book of the Covenant that was found in the house of the Lord.

With this righteous king, God's Word was of great importance. He esteemed it at its proper worth. He counted it to be of grave importance and consulted God in prayer about it. He gathered together the notables of his kingdom, so that they, together with himself, could be instructed out of God's Book concerning God's law.

When Ezra was seeking the reconstruction of his nation, the people assembled themselves together as one man before the water gate.

> *And they spake unto Ezra the scribe to bring the book of the law of Moses, which the Lord had commanded to Israel. And Ezra the priest brought the law before the congregation both of men and women, and all that could hear with understanding....And he read therein before the street that was before the water gate from the morning until midday...and the ears of all the people were attentive unto the book of the law.*
>
> *(Neh. 8:1–3)*

This was Bible reading-day in Judah—a real revival of Scripture study. The leaders read the Law before the people. Their ears were keen to hear what God had to say to them out of the Book of the Law. But it was not only a Bible reading-day. It was a time when real preaching was done, as the following passage indicates: *"So they read in the book in the law of God distinctly, and gave the sense, and caused them to understand the reading"* (Neh. 8:8).

Here is the scriptural definition of preaching. No better definition can be given. To read the Word of God distinctly, so that the people could hear and understand the words presented boldly and clearly—that was the method followed in Jerusalem on this auspicious day. The sense of the words was made clear in the meeting held before the water gate. The people were treated to a high type of expository preaching. That was true preaching—preaching of a sort that is sorely needed today so that God's Word may have the same effect on the hearts of the people. This meeting in Jerusalem surely contains a lesson that all present-day preachers should learn and heed.

No one, having any knowledge of the existing facts, will deny the comparative lack of expository preaching in the pulpit today. And no one should do other than lament the lack. Topical, controversial, and historical preaching have, one supposes, their rightful place. But expository preaching, the prayerful expounding of the Word of God, is preaching that *is* preaching—pulpit effort *par excellence.*

For its successful accomplishment, however, a preacher must be a man of prayer. For every hour spent in study, he will have to spend two upon his knees. For every hour devoted to wrestling with an obscure passage of Holy Scripture, he must have two hours in which he is found wrestling with God. Prayer and preaching! Preaching and prayer! They cannot be separated. The ancient cry was, *"To your tents, O Israel!"* (1 Kings 12:16). The modern cry should be, "To your knees, O preachers, to your knees!"

Book
Three

The Possibilities
of Prayer

1

The Ministry of Prayer

Prayer should be the breath of our breathing, the thought of our thinking, the soul of our feeling, and the life of our living, the sound of our hearing, the growth of our growing. Prayer in its magnitude is length without end, width without bounds, height without top, and depth without bottom. Illimitable in its breadth, exhaustless in height, fathomless in depths, and infinite in extension. —Homer W. Hodge

THE ministry of prayer has been the peculiar distinction of all of God's saints. This has been the secret of their power. The energy and the soul of their work has been the prayer closet. The need of help outside of man being so great, given man's natural inability to always judge kindly, justly, and truly and to act out the Golden Rule, prayer is enjoined by Christ to enable man to act in all these things according to the divine will. By prayer, the ability is secured to feel the law of love, to speak according to the law of love, and to do everything in harmony with the law of love.

God can help us. God is a Father. We need God's good things to help us to *"do justly, and to love mercy, and to walk humbly with* [our] *God"* (Mic. 6:8). We need divine aid to act brotherly, wisely, and nobly, and to judge truly and charitably. God's help to do all these things in God's way is secured by prayer. *"Ask, and it shall be given you; seek, and ye shall find; knock, and it shall be opened unto you"* (Matt. 7:7).

Regarding the marvelous output of Christian graces and duties that are the result of giving ourselves wholly to God, we find these words recorded in Romans: *"Continuing instant in prayer,"* preceded by *"rejoicing in hope; patient in tribulation,"* and followed by *"distributing to the necessity of the saints; given to hospitality"* (Rom. 12:12–13). Paul thus wrote as if these rich and rare graces and unselfish duties—so sweet, bright, generous, and unselfish—had for their center and source the ability to pray.

The same word, *continue,* is used of the prayer of the disciples that ushered in Pentecost with all of its rich and glorious blessings of the Holy Spirit. In Colossians, Paul pressed the word into the service of prayer, saying, *"Continue in prayer, and watch in the same with thanksgiving"* (Col. 4:2). The word in its background and root means "to hold fast and firm, to give constant attention to." It connotes strength and the ability to stay and persevere with steadfastness.

Acts 6:4 is translated, *"Give ourselves continually to prayer."* Here there is constancy, courage, unfainting perseverance. It means giving such marked attention to and such deep concern to a thing that it will be conspicuous and controlling.

This is an advance in demand on the word *continue.* Prayer is to be incessant, without intermission, assiduous, having no check in desire, in spirit, or in act, the spirit and the life always in the attitude of prayer. The knees may not always be bent, the lips may not always be vocal with words of prayer, but the spirit is always in the act and communication of prayer.

There ought to be no adjustment of life or spirit for the hours spent in the prayer closet. The closet spirit should sweetly rule and adjust all times and occasions. Our activities and work should be performed in the same spirit that makes our devotion and that makes our closet time sacred. "Without intermission, incessantly, assiduously," describes an opulence, an energy, and unabated and ceaseless strength and fullness of effort—like the full, inexhaustible, and spontaneous flow of an artesian stream. Touch the man of God who thus understands prayer, at any point, at any time, and a full current of prayer is seen flowing from him.

But all these untold benefits, of which the Holy Spirit is made to us the conveyor, go back in their disposition and results to prayer. The coming of the Holy Spirit and His great grace are not conditioned on a little process and a mere performance of prayer, but on prayer set on fire by an unquenchable desire. This prayer must be accompanied by such a sense of need that it cannot be denied, and by a fixed determination that will not let go and that will never faint until it wins the greatest good and gets the best and last blessing God has in store for us.

The First Christ, Jesus, our Great High Priest, forever blessed and adored be His name, was a gracious Comforter, a faithful Guide, a gifted Teacher, a fearless Advocate, a devoted Friend, and an all-powerful Intercessor. The other, *"another Comforter"* (John 14:16), the Holy Spirit, comes into all these blessed relations of fellowship, authority, and aid with all the tenderness, sweetness, fullness, and efficiency of Christ.

Was the First Christ the Christ of prayer? Did He offer *"prayers and supplications with strong crying and tears"* (Heb. 5:7) unto God? Did He seek the silence, the solitude, and the darkness that He might pray, unheard and unwitnessed except by heaven, in His wrestling agony for man with God? Does He ever live, enthroned above at the Father's right hand, there to pray for us?

Then how truly does the other Christ, the other Comforter, the Holy Spirit, represent Jesus Christ as the Christ of prayer! This other Christ, the Comforter, plants Himself not in the waste of the mountain, nor far into the night, but in the chill and the night of the human heart, to rouse it to the struggle and to teach it the need and form of prayer. How the Divine Comforter, the Spirit of Truth, puts into the human heart the burden of earth's almighty need, and makes human lips give voice to its mute and unutterable groaning!

What a mighty Christ of prayer is the Holy Spirit! How He quenches every flame in the heart but the flame of heavenly desire! How He quiets, like a weaned child, all the self-will, until in will, in brain, in heart, and by mouth, we pray only as He prays, making *"intercession for the saints, according to the will of God"* (Rom. 8:27).

2

Prayer and the Promises

You need not utterly despair even of those who for the present "turn again and rend you." For if all your arguments and persuasives fail, there is yet another remedy left, and one that is frequently found effectual when no other method avails. This is prayer. Therefore, whatsoever you desire or want, either for others or for your own soul, "Ask, and it shall be given you." —John Wesley

WITHOUT the promise, prayer is eccentric and baseless. Without prayer, the promise is dim, voiceless, shadowy, and impersonal. The promise makes prayer dauntless and irresistible. The apostle Peter declared that God has given to us *"exceeding great and precious promises"* (2 Pet. 1:4). Precious and great promises they are, and for this very cause we are to *"add to* [our] *faith"* (v. 5) and supply virtue. It is the addition that makes the promises current and beneficial to us. It is prayer that makes the promises weighty, precious, and practical. The apostle Paul did not hesitate to declare that God's grace, so richly promised, was made operative and efficient by prayer. *"Ye also helping together by prayer for us"* (2 Cor. 1:11).

The promises of God are *"exceeding great and precious,"* words that clearly indicate their great value and their broad reach, as grounds upon which to base our expectations in praying. However exceeding great and precious they are, their realization, and the possibility and condition of that realization, are based on prayer. How glorious are these promises to the believing saints and to the whole church! How the brightness and bloom, the fullness and cloudless midday glory of the future beam on us through the

194

promises of God! Yet these promises never brought hope to bloom or fruit to a prayerless heart. Neither could these promises, were they increased thousandfold in number and preciousness, bring millennium glory to a prayerless church. Prayer makes the promise rich, fruitful, and a conscious reality.

Prayer as a spiritual energy, and, illustrated in its enlarged and mighty working, makes way for and brings into practical realization the promises of God.

God's promises cover all things that pertain to life and godliness, that relate to body and soul, that have to do with time and eternity. These promises bless the present and stretch out in their benefactions to the illimitable and eternal future. Prayer holds these promises in keeping and in fruition. Promises are God's golden fruit, to be plucked by the hand of prayer. Promises are God's incorruptible seed, to be sown and tilled by prayer.

Prayer and the promises are interdependent. The promise inspires and energizes prayer, but prayer locates the promise and gives it realization and location. The promise is like the blessed rain falling in full showers, but prayer, like the pipes that transmit, preserve, and direct the rain, localizes and precipitates these promises until they become local and personal, and until they bless, refresh, and fertilize. Prayer takes hold of the promise and conducts it to its marvelous ends, removes the obstacles, and makes a highway for the promise to its glorious fulfillment.

While God's promises are *"exceeding great and precious,"* they are specific, clear, and personal. How pointed and plain was God's promise to Abraham:

> *And the angel of the Lord called unto Abraham out of heaven the second time, and said, By myself have I sworn, saith the Lord, for because thou hast done this thing, and hast not withheld thy son, thine only son: that in blessing I will bless thee, and in multiplying I will multiply thy seed as the stars of heaven, and as the sand which is upon the sea shore; and thy seed shall possess the gate of his enemies; and in thy seed shall all the nations of the earth be blessed; because thou hast obeyed my voice.*   *(Gen. 22:15–18)*

Rebekah, through whom the promise was to flow, was childless. Her barren womb formed an invincible obstacle to the fulfillment of God's promise. But, in the course of time, children were born to her. Isaac became a man of prayer through whom the promise was to be realized, and so we read: *"And Isaac entreated the Lord for his wife, because she was barren: and the Lord was entreated of him, and Rebekah his wife conceived"* (Gen. 25:21).

Isaac's praying opened the way for the fulfillment of God's promise, carried it on to its marvelous fulfillment, and made the promise effectual in bringing forth marvelous results.

God also spoke to Jacob and made definite promises to him: *"Return unto the land of thy fathers, and to thy kindred; and I will be with thee"* (Gen. 31:3). Jacob promptly moved out on the promise, but Esau confronted him with his awakened vengeance and his murderous intention, which were more dreadful because of the long years that had passed unappeased and waiting. Jacob threw himself directly on God's promise by a night of prayer. First in quietude and calmness, and then when the stillness, the loneliness, and the darkness of the night were upon him, he made the all-night wrestling prayer.

> With thee I mean all night to stay,
> And wrestle till the break of day.

God's being was involved, His promise was at stake, and much was involved in the issue. Esau's temper, his conduct, and his character were involved. It was a notable occasion. Much depended on it. Jacob pursued his case and pressed his plea with great struggles and hard wrestling. His was the highest form of troublesome persistence. But the victory was gained at last. His name and nature were changed, and he became a new and different man.

Jacob himself was saved, first of all. He was blessed in his life and soul. But, still more was accomplished. Esau underwent a radical change of mind. He who came forth with hate and revenge in his heart against his own brother, seeking Jacob's destruction, was strangely and wonderfully affected, and he was changed and his whole attitude toward his brother became radically different. And when the two brothers met, love took the place of fear and hate, and they vied with each other in showing true brotherly affection.

The promise of God was fulfilled. But it took that whole night of importunate praying to do the deed. It took that fearful night of wrestling on Jacob's part to make the promise sure and to cause it to bear fruit. Prayer worked the marvelous deed. So prayer of the same kind will produce like results in this day. It was God's promise and

Jacob's praying that crowned and crowded the results so wondrously.

"Go, show thyself unto Ahab; and I will send rain on the earth"
(1 Kings 18:1) was God's command and promise to his servant Elijah after the sore famine had cursed the land. Many glorious results marked that day of heroic faith and dauntless courage on
Elijah's part. The sublime issue with Israel had been successful,
the fire had fallen, Israel had been reclaimed, the prophets of Baal
had been killed, but there was no rain. The one thing, the only
thing, that God had promised, had not been given. The day was
declining, and the awestruck crowds were faint, and yet held by an
invisible hand.

Elijah turned from Israel to God and from Baal to the one
source of help for a final issue and a final victory. But seven times
the restless eagerness of the prophet was stayed. Not until the sev-
enth time was his vigilance rewarded and the promise pressed to
its final fulfillment. Elijah's fiery, relentless praying bore to its triumphant results the promise of God, and rain descended in full
showers.

> Thy promise, Lord, is ever sure,
> And they that in Thy house would dwell
> That happy station to secure,
> Must still in holiness excel.

Our prayers are too little and feeble to execute the purposes or
to claim the promises of God with appropriating power. Marvelous
purposes need marvelous praying to execute them. Miracle-making
promises need miracle-making praying to realize them. Only divine
praying can operate divine promises or carry out divine purposes.
How great, how sublime, and how exalted are the promises God
makes to His people! How eternal are the purposes of God! Why are
we so impoverished in experience and so low in life when God's
promises are so *"exceeding great and precious"*? Why do the eternal
purposes of God move so slowly? Why are they so poorly executed?
Our failure to appropriate the divine promises, to rest our faith on
them, and to pray with belief is the answer. *"Ye have not, because
ye ask not. Ye ask, and receive not, because ye ask amiss"* (James
4:2–3).

Prayer is based on the purpose and promise of God. Prayer is
submission to God. Prayer has no sigh of disloyalty against God's

will. It may cry out against the bitterness and the dread weight of an hour of unutterable anguish: *"If it be possible, let this cup pass from me"* (Matt. 26:39). But it is surcharged with the sweetest and promptest submission. *"Nevertheless not my will, but thine, be done"* (Luke 22:42).

But prayer in its usual uniform and deep current is conscious conformity to God's will, based upon the direct promise of God's Word, and under the illumination and application of the Holy Spirit. Nothing is surer than that the Word of God is the sure foundation of prayer. We pray just as we believe God's Word. Prayer is based directly and specifically upon God's revealed promises in Christ Jesus. It has no other ground upon which to base its plea. All else is shadowy, shifty, fickle. Not our feelings, not our merits, not our works, but God's promise is the basis of faith and the solid ground of prayer.

> Now I have found the ground wherein
> Sure my soul's anchor may remain;
> The wounds of Jesus—for my sin,
> Before the world's foundation slain.

The converse of this proposition is also true. God's promises are dependent and conditioned upon prayer to appropriate them and make them a conscious realization. The promises are implanted in us, appropriated by us, and held in the arms of faith by prayer. Let it be noted that prayer gives the promises their efficiency, localizes and appropriates them, and utilizes them. Prayer puts the promises to practical and present uses. Prayer makes the promises as the seed in the nourishing soil. Promises, like the rain, are general. Prayer embodies, precipitates, and locates them for personal use. Prayer goes by faith into the great orchard of God's *"exceeding great and precious promises,"* and with hand and heart picks the ripest and richest fruit. The promises, like electricity, may sparkle and dazzle and yet be impotent for good until these dynamic, life-giving currents are chained by prayer and are made the mighty forces that move and bless.

3

More Prayer Promises

Every promise of Scripture is a writing of God, which may be pleaded before Him with this reasonable request: "Do as thou hast said." The Creator will not cheat His creature who depends upon His truth; and, far more, the heavenly Father will not break His word to His own child. "Remember the word unto thy servant, upon which thou hast caused me to hope," is most prevalent pleading. It is a double argument: It is Your Word, will You not keep it? Why have You spoken of it if You will not make it good? You have caused me to hope in it; will You disappoint the hope that You have Yourself begotten in me?
—Charles Spurgeon

THE great promises find their fulfillment along the lines of prayer. They inspire prayer, and through prayer the promises flow out to their full realization and bear their ripest fruit.

The magnificent and sanctifying promise in Ezekiel, a promise finding its full, ripe, and richest fruit in the New Testament, is an illustration of how the promise waits on prayer.

Then will I sprinkle clean water upon you, and ye shall be clean: from all your filthiness, and from all your idols, will I cleanse you. A new heart also will I give you, and a new spirit will I put within you: and I will take away the stony heart out of your flesh, and I will give you an heart of flesh. And I will put my spirit within you, and cause you to walk in my statutes, and ye shall keep my judgments, and do them. And ye shall dwell in the land that I gave to your fathers; and ye shall be my people, and I will be your God. (Ezek. 36:25–28)

Concerning this promise and this work, God definitely says, *"I will yet for this be inquired of by the house of Israel, to do it for them"* (v. 37). The more truly men have prayed for these rich things, the more fully have they entered into this exceeding great and precious promise. In its initial and final results, as well as in all of its processes, the promise realized is entirely dependent on prayer.

> Give me a new, a perfect, heart,
> > From doubt and fear and sorrow free;
> The mind that was in Christ impart,
> > And let my spirit cleave to Thee.
>
> Oh, take this heart of stone away!
> > Thy sway it doth not, cannot own;
> In me no longer let it stay;
> > Oh, take away this heart of stone!

No new heart ever throbbed with its pulsations of divine life in one whose lips had never in prayer with contrite spirit sought that precious privilege of a perfect heart of love and cleanness. God has never put His Spirit into the realm of a human heart that had never invoked by ardent praying the coming and indwelling of the Holy Spirit. A prayerless spirit has no affinity for a clean heart. Prayer and a pure heart go hand in hand. Purity of heart follows praying, while prayer is the natural, spontaneous outflowing of a heart made clean by the blood of Jesus Christ.

In this connection, let it be noted that God's promises are always personal and specific. They are not general, indefinite, vague. They do not have to do with multitudes and classes of people in a mass, but are directed to individuals. They deal with people. Each believer can claim the promise as his own. God deals with each one personally, so that every saint can put the promises to the test. *"Prove me now herewith, saith the LORD"* (Mal. 3:10). No need for generalizing, nor for being lost in vagueness. The praying saint has the right to put his hand upon the promise and claim it as his own, one made especially for him, and one intended to embrace all his needs, present and future.

> Though troubles assail,
> > And dangers affright,
> Though friends should all fail,
> > And foes all unite,

> Yet one thing secures us,
> Whatever betide,
> The promise assures us,
> The Lord will provide.

Jeremiah once said, speaking of the captivity of Israel and of its ending, speaking for Almighty God, *"After seventy years be accomplished at Babylon I will visit you, and perform my good word toward you, in causing you to return to this place"* (Jer. 29:10). But this strong and definite promise of God was accompanied by these words, coupling the promise with prayer:

> *Then shall ye call upon me, and ye shall go and pray unto me, and I will hearken unto you. And ye shall seek me, and find me, when ye shall search for me with all your heart.*   *(vv. 12–13)*

This seems to indicate very clearly that the promise was dependent on prayer for its fulfillment.

In Daniel we have this record:

> *I Daniel understood by books the number of the years, whereof the word of the LORD came to Jeremiah the prophet, that he would accomplish seventy years in the desolations of Jerusalem. And I set my face unto the Lord God, to seek by prayer and supplications, with fasting, and sackcloth, and ashes.*
> *(Dan. 9:2–3)*

So Daniel, as the time of the captivity was expiring, set himself in mighty prayer in order that the promise should be fulfilled and the captivity be brought to an end. It was God's promise by Jeremiah and Daniel's praying that broke the chains of Babylonian captivity, set Israel free, and brought God's ancient people back to their native land. The promise and prayer went together to carry out God's purpose and to execute His plans.

God had promised through His prophets that the coming Messiah should have a forerunner. How many homes and wombs in Israel had longed for the coming to them of this great honor? Perhaps Zacharias and Elizabeth were the only ones who were trying to realize by prayer this great dignity and blessing. At least we do know that the angel said to Zacharias, as he announced to him the coming of this great personage, *"Thy prayer is heard"* (Luke 1:13).

It was then that the word of the Lord, as spoken by the prophets, and the prayers of the old priest and his wife brought John the Baptist into the withered womb and into the childless home of Zacharias and Elizabeth.

The promise given to Paul, engraved on his apostolic commission, as related by him after his arrest in Jerusalem when he was making his defense before King Agrippa, was on this line: *"Delivering thee from the people, and from the Gentiles, unto whom I now send thee"* (Acts 26:17). How did Paul make this promise efficient? How did he make the promise real? Here is the answer. In trouble by men, Jew and Gentile, pressed by them sorely, he wrote to his brethren at Rome, with a pressing request for prayer:

> *Now I beseech you, brethren, for the Lord Jesus Christ's sake, and for the love of the Spirit, that ye strive together with me in your prayers to God for me; that I may be delivered from them that do not believe in Judaea.* (Rom. 15:30)

Their prayers, united with his prayer, were to secure his deliverance and secure his safety, and were also to make the apostolic promise vital and cause it to be fully realized.

All is to be sanctified and realized by the Word of God and prayer. God's deep and wide river of promise will turn into the deadly miasma or be lost in the morass, if we do not utilize these promises by prayer and receive their full and life-giving waters into our hearts.

The promise of the Holy Spirit to the disciples was in a very marked way the *"promise of the Father"* (Acts 1:4), but it was only realized after many days of continued and persistent praying. The promise was clear and definite that the disciples should be endowed with power from on high; but as a condition of receiving that power of the Holy Spirit, they were instructed to *"tarry...in the city of Jerusalem, until* [they were] *endued with power from on high"* (Luke 24:49). The fulfillment of the promise depended upon the tarrying. The promise of this enduement of power was made sure by prayer. Prayer sealed it to glorious results. So we find it written, *"These all continued with one accord in prayer and supplication, with the women"* (Acts 1:14). And it is significant that it was while they were praying, resting their expectations on the surety of the promise, that the Holy Spirit fell upon them and they were all *"filled with the Holy Ghost"* (Acts 2:4). The promise and the prayer went hand in hand.

After Jesus Christ made this large and definite promise to His disciples, He ascended on high, and was seated at His Father's right hand of exaltation and power. Yet the promise given by Him of sending the Holy Spirit was not fulfilled by His enthronement merely, nor by the promise only, nor by the fact that the prophet Joel had foretold with transported raptures of the bright day of the Spirit's coming. Neither was it that the Spirit's coming was the only hope of God's cause in this world.

All these all-powerful and all-engaging reasons were not the immediate operative cause of the coming of the Holy Spirit. The solution is found in the attitude of the disciples. The answer is found in the fact that the disciples, with the women, spent several days in that upper room, in earnest, specific, continued prayer. It was prayer that brought to pass the famous day of Pentecost. And, as it was then, so it can be now. Prayer can bring a Pentecost in this day if there is the same kind of praying, for the promise has not exhausted its power and vitality. The *"promise of the Father"* (Acts 1:4) still holds good for the present-day disciples.

Prayer, mighty prayer, united, continued, earnest prayer, for nearly two weeks, brought the Holy Spirit to the church and to the world in Pentecostal glory and power. And mighty, continued, and united prayer will do the same now.

> Lord God, the Holy Ghost,
>   In this accepted hour;
> As on the Day of Pentecost,
>   Descend in all Thy power.
>
> We meet with one accord,
>   In our appointed place,
> And wait the promise of our Lord,
>   The Spirit of all grace.

Nor must it be passed by that the promises of God to sinners of every kind and degree are equally sure and steadfast, and are made real and true by the earnest cries of all true penitents. It is just as true with the divine promises made to the unsaved when they repent and seek God, that they are realized in answer to the prayers of brokenhearted sinners, as it is true that the promises to believers are realized in answer to their prayers. The promise of pardon and peace was the basis of the prayers of Saul of Tarsus during those days of darkness and distress in the house of Judas, when the Lord told Ananias in order to allay his fears, *"Behold, he prayeth"* (Acts 9:11).

Isaiah told how the promise of mercy and an abundant pardon was tied up with seeking God and calling upon Him:

> *Seek ye the Lord while he may be found, call ye upon him while he is near: let the wicked forsake his way, and the unrighteous man his thoughts: and let him return unto the Lord, and he will have mercy upon him; and to our God, for he will abundantly pardon.*　　　　　　　　　(Isa. 55:6–7)

The praying sinner receives mercy because his prayer is grounded on the promise of pardon made by Him whose right it is to pardon guilty sinners. The penitent seeker after God obtains mercy because there is a definite promise of mercy to all who seek the Lord in repentance and faith. Prayer always brings forgiveness to the seeking soul. The abundant pardon is dependent upon the promise made real by the promise of God to the sinner.

While salvation is promised to him who believes, the believing sinner is always a praying sinner. God has no promise of pardon for a prayerless sinner just as He has no promise for the prayerless professor of religion. *"Behold he prayeth"* is not only the unfailing sign of sincerity and the evidence that the sinner is proceeding in the right way to find God, but it is the unfailing prophecy of an abundant pardon. Get the sinner to pray according to the divine promise, and he then is near the kingdom of God. The very best sign of the returning prodigal is that he confesses his sins and begins to ask for the lowliest place in his father's house.

It is the divine promise of mercy, of forgiveness, and of adoption that gives the poor sinner hope. This encourages him to pray. This moves him in distress to cry out, *"Jesus, thou Son of David, have mercy on me"* (Mark 10:47).

> Thy promise is my only plea,
> 　With this I venture nigh;
> Thou callest the burdened soul to Thee,
> 　And such, O Lord, am I.

How large are the promises made to the saint! How great the promises given to poor, hungry-hearted, lost sinners, ruined by the fall! Prayer has arms sufficient to encompass them all and prove them. How great the encouragement to all souls, these promises of God! How firm the ground on which to rest our faith! How stimulating to prayer! What firm ground on which to base our pleas in praying!

> The Lord hath promised good to me,
> His word my hope secures;
> He will my shield and portion be
> As long as life endures.

4

Prayer Possibilities

The Holy Spirit comes down into our hearts sometimes in prayer with a beam from heaven, whereby we see more at once of God and His glory, more astounding thoughts and enlarged apprehensions of God, many beams meeting in one and falling to the center of our hearts. By these coming downs or divine influxes, God slides into our hearts by beams of Himself; we come not to have communion with God by way of many broken thoughts put together, but there is a contraction of many beams from heaven, which is shed into our souls, so that we know more of God and have more communion with Him in a quarter-hour than we could know in a year by the way of wisdom only. —Thomas Goodwin

HOW vast are the possibilities of prayer! How wide is its reach! What great things are accomplished by this divinely appointed means of grace! It lays its hand on Almighty God and moves Him to do what He would not otherwise do if prayer were not offered. It brings things to pass that would never otherwise occur.

The story of prayer is the story of great achievements. Prayer is a wonderful power placed by Almighty God in the hands of His saints, which may be used to accomplish great purposes and to achieve unusual results. Prayer reaches to everything, taking in all things great and small that are promised by God to the children of men. The only limit to prayer is the promises of God and His ability to fulfill those promises. *"Open thy mouth wide, and I will fill it"* (Ps. 81:10).

The records of prayer's achievements are encouraging to faith, cheering to expectations of saints, and an inspiration to all who would pray and test its value. Prayer is no mere untried theory. It is not some strange, unique scheme, concocted in the brains of men and set on foot by them, an invention that has never been tried nor put to the test. Prayer is a divine arrangement in the moral government of God, designed for the benefit of men, intended as a means for furthering the interests of His cause on earth, and carrying out His gracious purposes in redemption and providence.

Prayer proves itself. It is susceptible of proving its virtue by those who pray. Prayer needs no proof other than its accomplishments. *"If any man will do his will, he shall know of the doctrine"* (John 7:17). If any man will know the virtue of prayer, if he will know what it will do, let him pray. Let him put prayer to the test.

What a breadth is given to prayer! What heights it reaches! It is the breathing of a soul inflamed for God and inflamed for man. It goes as far as the Gospel goes, and is as wide, compassionate, and prayerful as is that Gospel.

How much of prayer do all these unpossessed, alienated provinces of earth demand in order to enlighten them, to impress them, and to move them toward God and His Son, Jesus Christ? Had the professed disciples of Christ only prayed in the past as they ought to have done, the centuries would not have found these provinces still bound in death, in sin, and in ignorance.

Alas, how the unbelief of men has limited the power of God to work through prayer! What limitations have disciples of Jesus Christ put upon prayer by their prayerlessness! How the church, with her neglect of prayer, has hedged about the Gospel and shut up doors of access!

Prayer possibilities open doors for the entrance of the Gospel: *"Withal praying also for us, that God would open unto us a door of utterance"* (Col. 4:3). Prayer opened doors of utterance, created opportunities, and made openings to preach the Gospel for the apostles. The appeal by prayer was to God, because God was moved by prayer. God was thereby moved to do His own work in an enlarged way and by new ways. Prayer possibility gives not only great power and opens doors to the Gospel, but it also gives facility to the Gospel. Prayer makes the Gospel go fast and move with glorious speed. The Gospel projected by the mighty energies of prayer is neither slow, lazy, nor dull. It moves with God's power, with God's brilliance, and with angelic swiftness.

"Brethren, pray for us, that the word of the Lord may have free course, and be glorified" (2 Thess. 3:1) was the request of the apostle

Paul, whose faith reached to the possibilities of prayer for the preached Word. The Gospel moves altogether too slowly, often timidly, and with feeble steps. What will make this Gospel go rapidly, like a runner in a race? What will give this Gospel divine brightness and glory, and cause it to move worthy of God and of Christ? The answer is at hand. Prayer, more prayer, better prayer will do the deed. This means of grace will give swiftness, splendor, and divinity to the Gospel.

The possibilities of prayer reach to all things. Whatever concerns man's highest welfare and whatever has to do with God's plans and purposes concerning men on earth can be a subject for prayer. *"Whatsoever ye shall ask"* (Matt. 21:22) embraces all that concerns us or the children of men and God. And whatever is left out of *"whatsoever"* is left out of prayer. Where will we draw the lines that leave out or that will limit the word *whatsoever?* Define it, and search out and publish the things that the word does not include. If *"whatsoever"* does not include all things, then substitute for it the word *anything.* *"If ye shall ask **any thing** in my name, I will do it"* (John 14:14, emphasis added).

What riches of grace, what blessings, spiritual and temporal, what good for time and eternity would have been ours had we learned the possibilities of prayer and if our faith had taken in the wide range of the divine promises to us to answer prayer! What blessings on our times and what furtherance to God's cause could we have seen had we but learned how to pray with large expectations! Who will rise up in this generation and teach the church this lesson? It is a child's lesson in simplicity, but who has learned it well enough to put prayer to the test? It is a great lesson in its matchless and universal good. The possibilities of prayer are unspeakable, but who has learned the lesson of prayer that realizes and measures up to these possibilities? In His discourse in John, our Lord seems to connect friendship for Him with that of prayer, and His choosing of His disciples seemed to have been with a design that through prayer they should bear much fruit:

> *Ye are my friends, if ye do whatsoever I command you....Ye have not chosen me, but I have chosen you, and ordained you, that ye should go and bring forth fruit, and that your fruit should remain; that whatsoever ye shall ask the Father in my name, he may give it you.*   *(John 15:14, 16)*

Jesus states that bearing fruit—ripe, unwithered, and rich fruit that remains—is essential so that prayer might come to its full possibilities in order that the Father might give. Here we have again the undefined and unlimited word *whatsoever,* covering the rights and the things for which we are to pray in the possibilities of prayer.

We still have another declaration from Jesus:

> *Verily, verily, I say unto you, Whatsoever ye shall ask the Father in my name, he will give it you. Hitherto have ye asked nothing in my name: ask, and ye shall receive, that your joy may be full.* (John 16:23–24)

Here is a very definite exhortation from our Lord to largeness in praying. Here we are definitely urged by Him to ask for large things. He announces this opportunity with the dignity and solemnity indicated by the double amen, *"Verily, verily."* Why are these marvelous urgencies in this last-recorded, vital conversation of our Lord with His disciples? The answer is, that our Lord might prepare them for the new dispensation, in which prayer was to have such marvelous results and prayer was to be the chief agency to conserve and make aggressive His Gospel.

In our Lord's affluent statement to His disciples about choosing them that should bear fruit, He clearly teaches us that this matter of praying and fruit bearing is not a petty business of our choice, or a secondary matter in relation to other matters, but that He has chosen us for this very business of praying. He had specially in mind our praying; He has chosen us of His own divine selection; and He expects us to do this one thing of praying, and to do it intelligently and well. For He states before, that He had made us His friends, had brought us into bosom confidence with Him, and also into free and full conference with Him. The main object of choosing us as His disciples and of friendship with Him was that we might be the better fitted to bear the fruit of prayer.

Let us not forget that we are noting the possibilities for the true, praying believers. *Anything* is the word of area and circumference. How far it reaches we cannot know. How wide it spreads, our minds fail to discover. What is there that is not within its reach? Why does Jesus repeat and exhaust these words, all-inclusive and boundless words, if He does not desire to emphasize the unbounded magnificence and illimitable benevolence of prayer?

Why does He press men to pray, except that our very poverty might be enriched and our limitless inheritance be secured by prayer?

We affirm with absolute certainty that Almighty God answers prayer. The vast possibilities and the urgent necessity of prayer lie in this stupendous fact that God hears and answers prayer. And God hears and answers all prayer. He hears and answers every prayer where the true conditions of praying are met. Either this is so or it is not. If not, then there is nothing in prayer. Then prayer becomes but the recitation of words, a mere verbal performance, an empty ceremony. Then prayer is an altogether useless exercise. But if what we have said is true, then there are vast possibilities in prayer. Then is it far-reaching in its scope and wide in its range. Then it is true that prayer can lay its hand upon Almighty God and move Him to do great and wonderful things.

The benefits, the possibilities, and the necessity of prayer are not merely subjective but are peculiarly objective in their character. Prayer aims at a definite object. Prayer has a direct design in view. Prayer always has something specific before the mind's eye. There may be some subjective benefits that accrue from praying, but this is altogether secondary and incidental. Prayer always drives directly at an object and seeks to secure a desired end. Prayer is asking, seeking, and knocking at a door for something we do not have, but that we desire, and that God has promised to us.

Prayer is a direct address to God. *"In every thing...let your requests be made known unto God"* (Phil. 4:6). Prayer secures blessings and makes men better because it reaches the ear of God. Prayer is only for the betterment of men when it has affected God and moved Him to do something for men. Prayer affects men by affecting God. Prayer moves men because it moves God to move men. Prayer influences men by influencing God to influence them. Prayer moves the hand that moves the world.

> The power is prayer, that soars on high,
>   Through Jesus to the throne;
> It moves the hand which moves the world,
>   To bring salvation down.

The utmost possibilities of prayer have rarely been realized. The promises of God are so great to those who truly pray, when He puts Himself so fully into the hands of the praying ones, that it almost staggers our faith and causes us to hesitate with astonishment. His promise to answer, to do, and to give *"all things," "any thing," "whatsoever,"* and *"all things whatsoever"* are so large, so great, so exceedingly broad, that we stand back in amazement and give ourselves over to questioning and doubt. We stagger at the promises through unbelief. (See Romans 4:20.) In reality, we have pared down the promises of God about prayer to match our little faith, and have been brought down to the low level of our narrow notions about God's ability, liberality, and resources.

Let us ever keep in mind and never for one moment allow ourselves to doubt the statement that God means what He says in all of His promises. God's promises are His own word. His veracity is at stake in them. To question them is to doubt His veracity. He cannot afford to prove faithless to His word. *"In hope of eternal life, which God, that cannot lie, promised before the world began"* (Titus 1:2). His promises are for ordinary people, and He means to do for all who pray just what He says He will do. *"For he is faithful that promised"* (Heb. 10:23).

Unfortunately, we have failed to expend ourselves in praying. We have limited the Holy One of Israel. The ability to pray can be secured by the grace and power of the Holy Spirit, but it demands so strenuous and high a character that it is a rare thing for a man or woman to be on "praying ground and on pleading terms with God." It is as true today as it was in the days of Elijah, that *"the effectual, fervent prayer of a righteous man availeth much"* (James 5:16). How much such a prayer avails, who can tell.

The possibilities of prayer are the possibilities of faith. Prayer and faith are Siamese twins. One heart animates them both. Faith is always praying. Prayer is always believing. Faith must have a tongue by which it can speak. Prayer is the tongue of faith. Faith must receive. Prayer is the hand of faith stretched out to receive. Prayer must rise and soar. Faith must give prayer the wings to fly and ascend. Prayer must have an audience with God. Faith opens the door, and access and audience are given. Prayer asks. Faith lays its hand on the thing asked for.

God's omnipotent power is the basis of omnipotent faith and omnipotent praying. *"All things are possible to him that believeth"* (Mark 9:23), and *"all things whatsoever"* are given to him who prays. God's decree and death yield readily to Hezekiah's faith and prayer. When God's promise and man's praying are united by faith, then *"nothing shall be impossible"* (Matt. 17:20). Persistent prayer is so all-powerful and irresistible that it obtains promises and wins where the prospect and the promise seem to be against it. In fact, the New Testament promise includes all things in heaven and in earth. God, by promise, puts all things He possesses into man's hands. Prayer and faith put man in possession of this boundless inheritance.

Prayer is not an indifferent or a small thing. It is not a sweet, little privilege. It is a great prerogative, far-reaching in its effects. Failure to pray entails losses far beyond the person who neglects it. Prayer is not a mere episode of the Christian life. Rather, the whole life is a preparation for and the result of prayer. In its condition, prayer is the sum of religion. Faith is but a channel of prayer. Faith gives it wings and swiftness. Prayer is the lungs through which holiness breathes. Prayer is not only the language of spiritual life, but prayer also makes its very essence and forms its innermost, real character.

> Oh, for a faith that will not shrink
> Though pressed by every foe;
> That will not tremble on the brink
> Of any earthly woe.
>
> Lord, give us such a faith as this,
> And then, whatever may come,
> We'll taste e'en here, the hallowed bliss
> Of our eternal home.

5

Prayer Possibilities
(Continued)

He who has the spirit of prayer has the highest interest in the court of heaven. And the only way to retain it is to keep it in constant employment. Apostasy begins in the closet. No man ever backslid from the life and power of Christianity who continued constant and fervent in private prayer. He who prays without ceasing is likely to rejoice evermore.

—Adam Clarke

AFTER a comprehensive and cursory view of the possibilities of prayer, as mapped out in what has been said, it is important to focus on particulars—on Bible facts and principles in regard to this great subject. What are the possibilities of prayer as disclosed by divine revelation? The necessity of prayer and its being are coexistent with man. Nature, even before a clear and full revelation, cries out in prayer. Man is; therefore, prayer is. God is; therefore, prayer is. Prayer is born of the instincts, the needs, the cravings, and the very being of man.

The prayer of Solomon at the dedication of the temple is the product of inspired wisdom and piety, and gives a lucid and powerful view of prayer in the width of its range, the minuteness of its details, its abounding possibilities, and its urgent necessity. How minute and exactly comprehending is this prayer! National and individual blessings are in it, and temporal and spiritual good is embraced by it. National calamities, sins, enemies, exile, famine, war, pestilence, mildew, drought, insects, damage to crops, whatever affects agriculture, as well as individual needs—whatever sickness, one's own sore, one's own guilt, one's own sin—one and all are in this prayer, and all are for prayer.

For all these evils, prayer is the one universal remedy. Pure praying remedies all ills, cures all diseases, relieves all situations, however dire, calamitous, fearful, or despairing. Prayer to God, pure praying, relieves dire situations because God can relieve when no one else can. Nothing is too difficult for God. No cause is hopeless that God undertakes. No case is mortal when Almighty God is the physician. No conditions are despairing that can deter or defy God.

Almighty God heard this prayer of Solomon, and committed Himself to undertake, to relieve, and to remedy if real praying were done, despite all adverse and inexorable conditions. He will always relieve, answer, and bless if men will pray from the heart, and if they will give themselves to real, true praying. After Solomon had finished his magnificent, all-comprehending prayer, this is the record of what God said to him:

> *And the Lord appeared to Solomon by night, and said unto him, I have heard thy prayer, and have chosen this place to myself for an house of sacrifice. If I shut up heaven that there be no rain, or if I command the locusts to devour the land, or if I send pestilence among my people; if my people, which are called by my name, shall humble themselves, and pray, and seek my face, and turn from their wicked ways; then will I hear from heaven, and will forgive their sin, and will heal their land. Now mine eyes shall be open, and my ears attent unto the prayer that is made in this place. For now I have chosen and sanctified this house, that my name may be there for ever.* (2 Chron. 7:12)

God put no limitation on His ability to save through true praying. No hopeless conditions, no accumulation of difficulties, no desperation in distance or circumstance can hinder the success of real prayer. The possibilities of prayer are linked to the infinite rectitude and to the omnipotent power of God. There is nothing too hard for God to do. God is pledged that if we ask, we shall receive. God can withhold nothing from faith and prayer.

> The thing surpasses all my thought,
> But faithful is my Lord;

> Through unbelief I stagger not,
>   For God has spoken the word!
>
> Faith, mighty faith, the promise sees,
>   And looks to that alone;
> Laughs at impossibilities,
>   And cries, "It shall be done!"

The many statements of God's Word fully set forth the possibilities and far-reaching nature of prayer. How full of pathos! *"Call upon me in the day of trouble: I will deliver thee, and thou shalt glorify me"* (Ps. 50:15). Again, read the cheering words: *"He shall call upon me, and I will answer him: I will be with him in trouble; I will deliver him, and honour him"* (Ps. 91:15).

How diversified the range of trouble! How almost infinite its extent! How universal and dire its conditions! How despairing its waves! Yet the range of prayer is as great as trouble, as universal as sorrow, as infinite as grief. And prayer can relieve all these evils that come to the children of men. There is no tear that prayer cannot wipe away or dry up. There is no depression of spirits that it cannot relieve and elevate. There is no despair that it cannot dispel.

"Call unto me, and I will answer thee, and show thee great and mighty things, which thou knowest not." (Jer. 33:3). How broad are these words of the Lord, how great the promise, how cheering to faith! They really challenge the faith of the saint. Prayer always brings God to our relief to bless and to aid, and brings marvelous revelations of His power. What impossibilities are there with God? Name them. He says, *"For with God nothing shall be impossible"* (Luke 1:37). And all the possibilities in God are in prayer.

Samuel, under the judges of Israel, fully illustrates the possibility and the necessity of prayer. He himself was the beneficiary of the greatness of faith and prayer in a mother who knew what praying meant. Hannah, his mother, was a woman of distinction, both in character and in piety, who was childless. That privation was a source of worry and weakness and grief. She sought God for relief, and prayed and poured out her soul before the Lord. She continued her praying; in fact, she multiplied her praying to such an extent that to old Eli she seemed to be intoxicated, almost beside herself in the intensity of her supplications. She was specific in her prayers. She wanted a child. For a man-child she prayed.

215

And God was specific in His answer. A man-child God gave her; a man indeed he became. Samuel was the creation of prayer and grew to become a man of prayer himself. He was a mighty intercessor, especially in emergencies in the history of God's people. The epitome of his life and character is found in the statement, *"Samuel cried unto the LORD for Israel; and the LORD heard him"* (1 Sam. 7:9). The victory was complete, and the Ebenezer was the memorial of the possibilities and necessity of prayer. (See 1 Samuel 7:12.)

Again, at another time, Samuel called unto the Lord, and thunder and rain came out of season in wheat harvest. Samuel was a mighty intercessor, who knew how to pray and whom God always regarded when he prayed. *"Samuel cried unto the LORD all night"* (1 Sam. 15:11).

At another time, in speaking to the Lord's people, he said, *"Moreover as for me, God forbid that I should sin against the LORD in ceasing to pray for you"* (1 Sam. 12:23).

These great occasions show how this notable ruler of Israel made prayer a habit, and that this was a notable and conspicuous characteristic of his dispensation. Prayer was no strange exercise to Samuel. He was accustomed to it. He was in the habit of praying, knew the way to God, and received answers from God. Through him and his praying, God's cause was brought out of its low, depressed condition and a great national revival began, of which David was one of its fruits.

Samuel was one of the notable men of the Old Testament who stood out prominently as one who had great influence with God in prayer. God could not deny him anything he asked of Him. Samuel's praying always affected God and moved God to do what would not have otherwise been done had he not prayed. Samuel stands out as a striking illustration of the possibilities of prayer. He shows conclusively the achievements of prayer.

Jacob is an illustration for all time of the commanding and conquering forces of prayer. God came to him as an antagonist. He grappled with Jacob and shook him as if he were in the embrace of a deadly foe. Jacob, the deceitful supplanter, the wily, unscrupulous trader, had no eyes to see God. His perverted principles and his deliberate overreaching and wrongdoing had blinded his vision.

To reach God, to know God, and to conquer God—that was the demand of this critical hour. Jacob was alone, and only the night witnessed the intensity of the struggle, its changing issues, and its veering fortunes, as well as the receding and advancing lines in the conflict. Here was the strength of weakness, the power of self-despair, the energy of perseverance, the elevation of humility, and the victory of surrender. Jacob's salvation issued from the forces that he massed in that all-night conflict.

He prayed and wept and clamored until the fiery hate of Esau's heart died and softened into love. A greater miracle was worked in Jacob than in Esau. His name, his character, and his destiny were all changed by that all-night praying. Here is the record of the results of that night's praying struggle: *"As a prince hast thou power with God and with men, and hast prevailed"* (Gen. 32:28). *"By his strength he had power with God: yea, he had power over the angel, and prevailed"* (Hos. 12:3–4). What forces lie in unrelenting prayer! What mighty results are gained by it in one night's struggle in praying! God is affected and changed in attitude, and two men are transformed in character and destiny!

6

The Viability of Prayer

Satan dreads nothing but prayer. The church that lost its Christ was full of good works. Activities are multiplied that meditation may be ousted, and organizations are increased that prayer may have no chance. Souls may be lost in good works, as surely as in evil ways. The one concern of the Devil is to keep the saints from praying. He fears nothing from prayerless studies, prayerless work, prayerless religion. He laughs at our toil, mocks at our wisdom, but trembles when we pray. —Samuel Chadwick

THE possibilities of prayer are seen in its accomplishments in temporal matters. Prayer reaches to everything that concerns man, whether it be his body, his mind, or his soul. Prayer embraces the very smallest things of life. Prayer takes in the wants of the body, food, raiment, business, finances, in fact everything that belongs to this life, as well as those things that have to do with the eternal interests of the soul. The achievements of prayer are seen not only in the large things of earth, but more especially in what might be called the little things of life. It brings to pass not only large things, speaking after the manner of men, but also the small things.

Temporal matters are of a lower order than the spiritual, but they concern us greatly. Our temporal interests make up a great part of our lives. They are the main source of our cares and worries. They have much to do with our religion. We have bodies with their wants, their pains, their disabilities, and their limitations. That which concerns our bodies necessarily engages our minds. These are subjects of prayer. Prayer takes in all of them, and large are the accomplishments of prayer in this realm of our being.

Our temporal matters have much to do with our health and happiness. They form our relations. They are tests of honesty and belong to the sphere of justice and righteousness. Not to pray about temporal matters is to leave God out of the largest sphere of our being. He who cannot pray about everything, as we are charged to do by Paul in Philippians, has never learned in any true sense the nature and worth of prayer.

To leave business and time out of prayer is to leave religion and eternity out of it. He who does not pray about temporal matters cannot pray with confidence about spiritual matters. He who does not put God in his struggling toil for daily bread will never put Him in his struggle for heaven. He who does not cover and supply the needs of the body by prayer will never cover and supply the needs of his soul. Both body and soul are dependent on God, and prayer is but the crying expression of that dependence.

The Old Testament is the record of God in dealing with His people through the divine appointment of prayer. Abraham prayed that Sodom might be saved from destruction. Abraham's servant prayed and received God's direction in choosing a wife for Isaac. Hannah prayed, and Samuel was given unto her. Elijah prayed, and no rain came for three years. He prayed again, and the clouds gave rain. Hezekiah was saved from a mortal sickness by his praying. Jacob's praying saved him from Esau's revenge. The Old Testament is the history of prayer for temporal blessings as well as for spiritual blessings.

In the New Testament, we have the same principles illustrated and enforced. Prayer in this section of God's Word covers the whole realm of good, both temporal and spiritual. Our Lord, in His universal prayer—the prayer for humanity in every climate, in every age, and for every condition—puts in it the petition, *"Give us this day our daily bread"* (Matt. 6:11). This embraces all necessary earthly good.

In the Sermon on the Mount, a whole paragraph is taken up by our Lord about food and clothing, where He cautions against undue care or anxiety for these things, and at the same time He encourages a faith that takes in and claims all these necessary bodily comforts. And this teaching stands in close connection with His teachings about prayer. Food and clothing are taught as subjects of prayer. Not for one moment is it even hinted that they are things beneath the notice of a great God, nor that they are too material and earthly for such a spiritual exercise as prayer.

The Syrophenician woman prayed for the health of her daughter. Peter prayed for Dorcas to be brought back to life. Paul prayed for the father of Publius on his way to Rome, when cast on the island by a shipwreck, and God healed the man who was sick with a fever. He urged the Christians at Rome to strive with him together in prayer that he might be delivered from evil men.

When Peter was put in prison by Herod, the church was instant in prayer that Peter might be delivered from the prison, and God honored the praying of these early Christians. John prayed that Gaius might *"prosper and be in health, even as* [his] *soul prospere*[d]" (3 John 1:2).

The divine directory in James says, *"Is any among you afflicted? let him pray....Is any sick among you? let him call for the elders of the church; and let them pray over him"* (James 5:13–14).

Paul, in writing to the Philippians, said, *"Be careful for nothing; but in every thing by prayer and supplication with thanksgiving let your requests be made known unto God"* (Phil. 4:6). This provides for all kinds of cares—business cares, home cares, body cares, and soul cares. All are to be brought to God by prayer. At the mercy seat our minds and souls are to be unburdened of all that affects us or causes anxiety or uneasiness. These words of Paul stand in especially close connection with what he said about temporal matters:

> *But I rejoiced in the Lord greatly, that now at the last your care of me hath flourished again; wherein ye were also careful, but ye lacked opportunity. Not that I speak in respect of want: for I have learned, in whatsoever state I am, therewith to be content.*   *(Phil. 4:10–11)*

Paul closed his epistle to these Christians with the words that embrace all temporal needs as well as spiritual wants: *"But my God shall supply all your need according to his riches in glory by Christ Jesus"* (v. 19).

Unbelief in the doctrine that prayer covers all things that have to do with the body and business affairs breeds undue anxiety about earth's affairs, causes unnecessary worry, and creates very unhappy states of mind. How much needless care would we save ourselves if we but believed in prayer as the means of relieving those cares, and would learn the happy art of casting all our cares in prayer upon God, who cares for us! (See 1 Peter 5:7.) Disbelief that God is concerned about even the smallest affairs that affect our happiness and comfort limits the Holy One of Israel, and makes our lives altogether devoid of real happiness and sweet contentment.

We have, in the instance of the failure of the disciples to cast the devil out of the lunatic son, who was brought to them by his father while Jesus was on the Mount of Transfiguration, a suggestive lesson of the union of faith, prayer, and fasting, and the failure to reach the possibilities and obligations of an occasion. The disciples ought to have cast the devil out of the boy. They had been sent out to do this very work and had been empowered by their Lord and Master to do it. And yet they strikingly failed. Christ reproved them with sharp upbraiding for not doing it. They had been sent out on this very specific mission. This one thing was specified by our Lord when He sent them out. Their failure brought shame and confusion on them, and discounted their Lord and Master and His cause. They brought Him into disrepute and reflected very seriously upon the cause that they represented. Their faith to cast out the devil had failed simply because it had not been nurtured by prayer and fasting. Failure to pray broke the ability of faith, and failure came because they did not have the energy of a strong, authoritative faith.

The promise reads (and we cannot too often refer to it, for it is the very basis of our faith and the ground on which we stand when we pray): *"All things, whatsoever ye shall ask in prayer, believing, ye shall receive"* (Matt. 21:22). What enumeration table can tabulate, itemize, and aggregate *"all things whatsoever"*? The possibilities of prayer and faith go to the length of the endless chain and cover the immeasurable area.

In Hebrews, the revered writer, wearied with trying to specify the examples of faith and to recite the wonderful exploits of faith, paused a moment and then cried out, giving us almost unheard-of achievements of prayer and faith as exemplified by the saints of the older times. Here is what he said:

> *And what shall I say more? for the time would fail me to tell of Gideon, and of Barak, and of Samson, and of Jephthae; of David also, and Samuel, and of the prophets: who through faith subdued kingdoms, wrought righteousness, obtained promises, stopped the mouths of lions, quenched the violence of fire, escaped the edge of the sword, out of weakness were*

made strong, waxed valiant in fight, turned to flight the ar-
mies of the aliens. Women received their dead raised to life
again: and others were tortured, not accepting deliverance;
that they might obtain a better resurrection.   *(Heb. 11:32–35)*

What an illustrious record this is! What marvelous accomplishments, wrought not by armies, nor by man's superhuman strength, nor by magic, but all accomplished simply by men and women noted alone for their faith and prayer! Hand in hand with these records of faith's limitless range are the illustrious records of prayer, for they are all one. Faith has never won a victory nor gained a crown where prayer was not the weapon of the victory, and where prayer did not jewel the crown. If *"all things are possible to him that believeth"* (Mark 9:23), then all things are possible to him that prays.

> Depend on Him; thou cannot fail;
>   Make all thy wants and wishes known.
> Fear not; His merits must prevail;
>   Ask but in faith, it shall be done.

7

The Wide Range of Prayer

Nothing so pleases God in connection with our prayer as our praise, and nothing so blesses the man who prays as the praise that he offers. I got a great blessing once in China in this connection. I had received bad and sad news from home, and deep shadows had covered my soul. I prayed, but the darkness did not vanish. I summoned myself to endure, but the darkness only deepened. Just then I went to an island station and saw on the wall of the mission home these words: "Try Thanksgiving." I did, and in a moment every shadow was gone, not to return. Yes, the psalmist was right: "It is a good thing to give thanks unto the LORD." —Henry W. Frost

THE possibilities of prayer are gauged by faith in God's ability to do. Faith is the one prime condition by which God works. Faith is the one prime condition by which man prays. Faith draws on God to its full extent. Faith gives character to prayer. A feeble faith has always brought forth feeble praying. Vigorous faith creates vigorous praying. At the close of a parable in which He stressed the necessity of vigorous praying, Christ asked this pointed question: *"When the Son of man cometh, shall he find faith on the earth?"* (Luke 18:8).

In the case of the lunatic child whom the father brought first to the disciples, who could not cure him, and then to the Lord Jesus Christ, the father cried out with all the pathos of a declining faith and of a great sorrow, *"If thou canst do any thing, have compassion on us, and help us"* (Mark 9:22). And Jesus said unto him, *"If thou canst believe, all things are possible to him that believeth"* (v. 23). The healing depended on the faith in the ability of Christ to heal the boy. The ability to do was in Christ essentially and eternally, but the doing of the thing depended on the ability of the faith. Great faith enables Christ to do great things.

We need a quickening faith in God's power. We have hedged God in until we have little faith in His power. We have conditioned the exercise of His power until we have a little God, and a little faith in a little God.

The only condition that restrains God's power and that disables Him to act, is lack of faith. He is not limited in action nor restrained by the conditions that limit men.

The conditions of time, place, nearness, ability, and all others that could possibly be named, upon which the actions of men hinge, have no bearing on God. If men will look to God and cry to Him with true prayer, He will hear and can deliver, no matter how dire the state may be or how remediless the conditions may be.

It is strange how God has to school His people in His ability to do! He made a promise to Abraham and Sarah that Isaac would be born. Abraham was then nearly one hundred years old, and Sarah was barren by natural defect, having passed into a barren, wombless age. She laughed at the thought of having a child as preposterous. God asked, *"Wherefore did Sarah laugh...? Is any thing too hard for the LORD?"* (Gen. 18:13–14). And God fulfilled His promise to these old people to the letter. Moses hesitated to undertake God's purpose to liberate Israel from Egyptian bondage, because of his inability to talk well. God checks him at once by an inquiry:

> *And Moses said unto the Lord, O my Lord, I am not eloquent, neither heretofore, nor since thou hast spoken unto thy servant: but I am slow of speech, and of a slow tongue. And the Lord said unto him, Who hath made man's mouth? or who maketh the dumb, or deaf, or the seeing, or the blind? have not I the Lord? Now therefore go, and I will be with thy mouth, and teach thee what thou shalt say.* (Exod. 4:10–12)

When God said He would feed the children of Israel a whole month with meat, Moses questioned His ability to do it. The Lord said unto Moses, *"Is the LORD'S hand waxed short? thou shalt see now whether my word shall come to pass unto thee or not"* (Num. 11:23).

Nothing is too hard for the Lord to do. As Paul declared, "He *'is able to do exceeding abundantly above all that we ask or think'*

(Eph. 3:20)." Prayer has to do with God, with His ability to do. The possibility of prayer is the measure of God's ability to do.

The *"all things,"* the *"all things whatsoever,"* and the *"any thing,"* are all covered by the ability of God. The urgent entreaty reads, *"Ask what ye will"* (John 15:7), because God is able to do anything and all things that the desire may yearn for, and that He has promised. In God's ability to do, He goes far beyond man's ability to ask. Human thoughts, human words, human imaginations, human desires, and human needs cannot in any way measure God's ability to do.

Prayer in its legitimate possibilities goes forward by the power of God Himself. Prayer goes forth with faith, not only in the promise of God, but also in God Himself and in God's ability to do. Prayer goes ahead not merely on the promise, but obtains promises and creates promises.

Elijah had the promise that God would send the rain, but no promise that He would send the fire. But by faith and prayer he obtained the fire as well as the rain, but the fire came first.

Daniel had no specific promise that God would make known to him the dream of the king, but he and his associates joined in united prayer, and God revealed to Daniel the king's dream and the interpretation. Their lives were spared thereby.

Hezekiah had no promise that God would cure him of his desperate sickness that threatened his life. On the contrary, the word of the Lord came to him by the mouth of the prophet, that he should die. However, he prayed against this decree of Almighty God in faith, and he succeeded in obtaining a reversal of God's word, and lived.

God makes it marvelous when He says by the mouth of His prophet, *"Thus saith the LORD, the Holy One of Israel, and his Maker, Ask me of things to come concerning my sons, and concerning the work of my hands command ye me"* (Isa. 45:11). And in this strong promise in which He commits Himself into the hands of His praying people, He appeals in it to His great creative power: *"I have made the earth, and created man upon it: I, even my hands, have stretched out the heavens, and all their hosts have I commanded"* (v. 12).

The majesty and power of God in making man and man's world, and constantly upholding all things, are ever kept before us as the basis of our faith in God and as an assurance and urgency to prayer. Then God calls us away from what He Himself has done and turns our minds to Himself personally. The infinite glory and power of His person are set before our contemplation: *"Remember ye not the former things, neither consider the things of old"* (Isa. 43:18). He declares that He will do *"a new thing"* (v. 19), that He does not have to repeat Himself, that all He has done neither limits His doing nor the manner of His doing. Therefore, if we have prayer and faith, He will so answer our prayers and so work for us, that His former work will not be remembered nor come into mind.

If men would pray as they ought to pray, the marvels of the past would be more than reproduced. The Gospel would advance with a facility and power it has never known. Doors would be thrown open to the Gospel, and the Word of God would have a conquering force rarely if ever known before.

If Christians prayed as Christians ought—with strong commanding faith, with earnestness and sincerity—men, God-called men, God-empowered men everywhere, would be burning to go and spread the Gospel worldwide. The Word of the Lord would run and be glorified as never known heretofore. The God-influenced men, the God-inspired men, the God-commissioned men, would go and kindle the flame of sacred fire for Christ, salvation, and heaven, everywhere in all nations. Soon all men would hear the glad tidings of salvation and have an opportunity to receive Jesus Christ as their personal Savior.

Let us read another one of those large, limitless statements in God's Word, which are a direct challenge to prayer and faith. *"He that spared not his own Son, but delivered him up for us all, how shall he not with him also freely give us all things?"* (Rom. 8:32).

What a basis we have here for prayer and faith, illimitable, measureless in breadth, in depth, and in height! The promise to give us all things is backed up by the fact that God freely gave His only begotten Son for our redemption. His giving His Son is the assurance and guarantee that He will freely give all things to him who believes and prays.

What confidence we have in this divine statement for inspired asking! What holy boldness we have here for the largest asking! No commonplace tameness should restrain our largest asking. Large, larger, and largest asking magnifies grace and adds to God's glory. Feeble asking impoverishes the asker, restrains God's purposes for the greatest good, and obscures His glory.

How enthroned, magnificent, and royal the intercession of our Lord Jesus Christ at His Father's right hand in heaven! The benefits of His intercession flow to us through our intercessions. Our intercession ought to catch by contagion and by necessity the inspiration and largeness of Christ's great work at His Father's right hand. His business and His life are to pray. Our business and our lives ought to be to pray, and to *"pray without ceasing"* (1 Thess. 5:17).

Failure in our intercession affects the fruits of His intercession. Lazy, heartless, feeble, and indifferent praying by us mars and hinders the effects of Christ's praying.

8

Prayer Facts and History

The particular value of private prayer consists in being able to approach God with more freedom, and unbosom ourselves more fully than in any other way. Between us and God there are private and personal interests, sins to confess, and wants to be supplied, which it would be improper to disclose to the world. This duty is enforced by the example of good men in all ages. —Amos Binney

THE possibilities of prayer are established by the facts and the history of prayer. Facts are stubborn things. Facts are the true things. Theories may be but speculations. Opinions may be wholly at fault. But facts must be deferred to. They cannot be ignored. What are the possibilities of prayer judged by the facts? What is the history of prayer? What does it reveal to us? Prayer has a history, written in God's Word and recorded in the experiences and lives of God's saints. History is truth teaching by example. We may miss the truth by perverting the history, but the truth is in the facts of history.

> He spake with Abraham at the oak,
> He called Elisha from the plow;
> David He from the sheepfolds took,
> Thy day, thine hour of grace, is now.

God reveals the truth by the facts. God reveals Himself by the facts of religious history. God teaches us His will by the facts and examples of Bible history. God's facts, God's Word, and God's history are all in perfect harmony and have much of God in them all. God has ruled the world by prayer; and God still rules the world by the same divinely ordained means.

The possibilities of prayer cover not only individuals but also cities and nations. They take in classes and peoples. The praying of Moses was the one thing that stood between the wrath of God against the Israelites, along with His declared purpose to destroy them, and the execution of that divine purpose; yet the Hebrew nation still survived. Notwithstanding, Sodom was not spared, because ten righteous men could not be found inside its limits. By comparison, the little city of Zoar was spared because Lot prayed for it as he fled from the storm of fire and brimstone that burned up Sodom. Nineveh was saved because the king and its people repented of their evil ways and gave themselves to prayer and fasting.

Paul, in his remarkable prayer in Ephesians, honored the illimitable possibilities of prayer and glorified the ability of God to answer prayer. Closing that memorable prayer, so far-reaching in its petitions, and setting forth the very deepest religious experience, he declared that God *"is able to do exceeding abundantly above all that we ask or think"* (Eph. 3:20). Prayer is all-inclusive, encompassing all things, great and small. There is no time or place that prayer does not cover and sanctify. All things in earth and in heaven, everything for time and for eternity, all are embraced in prayer. Nothing is too great and nothing is too small to be the subject of prayer. Prayer reaches down to the least things of life and includes the greatest things that concern us.

> If pain afflict or wrongs oppress,
> If cares distract, or fears dismay;
> If guilt deject, or sin distress,
> In every case, still watch and pray.

One of the most important, far-reaching, peace-giving, necessary, and practical prayer possibilities we have is in Paul's words in Philippians and deals with prayer as a cure for undue care:

> *Be careful for nothing; but in every thing by prayer and supplication with thanksgiving let your requests be made known unto God. And the peace of God, which passeth all understanding, shall keep your hearts and minds through Christ Jesus.* (Phil. 4:6–7)

Cares are the epidemic evil of mankind. They are universal in their reach. They belong to man in his fallen condition. The predisposition to undue anxiety is the natural result of sin. Care comes in all shapes, at all times, and from all sources. It comes to all of every age and station. There are the cares of the home, from which there is no escape except in prayer. There are the cares of business, the cares of poverty, and the cares of riches.

Ours is an anxious world, and ours is an anxious race. The caution of Paul is well addressed, *"Be careful for* [anxious about] *nothing"* (v. 6). This is the divine injunction, so that we might be able to live above anxiety and freed from undue care. *"In every thing by prayer and supplication let your requests be made known unto God"* (v. 6). This is the divinely prescribed remedy for all anxious cares, for all worry, for all inward fretting.

The word *careful* implies being drawn in different directions, distracted, anxious, disturbed, annoyed in spirit. Jesus had warned against this very thing in the Sermon on the Mount, where He had earnestly urged His disciples, *"Take therefore no thought for the morrow"* (Matt. 6:34), in things concerning the needs of the body. He was endeavoring to show them the true secret of a quiet mind, freed from anxiety and unnecessary care about food and clothing. Tomorrow's evils were not to be considered. He was simply teaching the same lesson found in Psalm 37:3: *"Trust in the LORD, and do good; so shalt thou dwell in the land, and verily thou shalt be fed."* In cautioning against the fears of tomorrow's prospective evils and the material wants of the body, our Lord was teaching the great lesson of an implicit and childlike confidence in God. *"Commit thy way unto the LORD; trust also in him; and he shall bring it to pass"* (v. 5).

> "Day by day," the promise reads,
>   Daily strength for daily needs
> Cast foreboding fears away;
>   Take the manna of today.

Paul's direction was very specific: *"Be careful for nothing."* Be careful for not one thing. Do not be careful for anything, for any condition, chance, or happening. Do not be troubled about anything that creates disturbing anxiety for anyone. Have a mind freed from all anxieties, all cares, all fretting, and all worries. Cares divide, distract, bewilder, and destroy unity and quietness of mind. Cares are fatal to weak piety and are enfeebling to strong piety. What great need to guard against them and learn the one secret of their cure, which is prayer!

What boundless possibilities there are in prayer to remedy the situation of mind of which Paul spoke! Prayer about everything can quiet every distraction, hush every anxiety, and lift every care from care-enslaved lives and from care-bewildered hearts. The specific prayer is the perfect cure for all anxieties, cares, and worries. Only prayer in everything can drive dull care away, relieve of unnecessary heart burdens, and save from the besetting sin of worrying over things that we cannot help. Only prayer can bring into the heart and mind the *"peace of God, which passeth all understanding"* (Phil. 4:7), and keep mind and heart at ease, free from burdensome care.

Oh, the needless heart-burdens borne by fretting Christians! How few know the real secret of a happy Christian life, filled with perfect peace, hidden from the storms and billows of a fretting, careworn life! Prayer has a possibility of saving us from "carefulness," the bane of human lives. Paul, in writing to the Corinthians, said, *"I would have you without carefulness"* (1 Cor. 7:32), and this is the will of God. Prayer has the ability to do this very thing. *"Casting all your care upon him; for he careth for you"* (1 Pet. 5:7) is the way Peter put it, while the psalmist said, *"Fret not thyself in any wise to do evil"* (Ps. 37:8). Oh, the blessedness of a heart at ease from all inward care, exempt from undue anxiety, in the enjoyment of the peace of God that passes all understanding!

Paul's injunction that includes both God's promise and His purpose, and that immediately precedes his entreaty to be *"careful for nothing,"* reads as follows: *"Rejoice in the Lord alway: and again I say, Rejoice. Let your moderation be known unto all men. The Lord is at hand"* (Phil. 4:4–5).

In a world filled with cares of every kind, where temptation is the rule, where there are so many things to try us, how is it possible to rejoice always? We look at the naked, dry command, and we accept it and reverence it as the Word of God, but no joy comes. How are we to let our moderation, our mildness, and our gentleness be universally and always known? We resolve to be benign and gentle. We remember the nearness of the Lord, but still we are hasty, quick, hard, and salty.

We listen to the divine charge, *"Be careful for nothing,"* yet still we are anxious, careworn, care-eaten, and care-tossed. How can we fulfill the divine Word, so sweet and so large in promise, so beautiful in the eye, and yet so far from being realized? How can we enter upon the rich patrimony of being true, honest, just, pure, and possess lovely things? The recipe is infallible, the remedy is universal, and the cure is unfailing. It is found in the words of Paul that I have so often referred to here: *"Be careful for nothing; but in every thing by prayer and supplication with thanksgiving let your requests be made known unto God"* (Phil. 4:6).

This joyous, carefree, peaceful experience bringing the believer into a joyousness, living simply by faith day by day, is the will of God. Writing to the Thessalonians, Paul told them, *"Rejoice evermore. Pray without ceasing. In every thing give thanks: for this is the will of God in Christ Jesus concerning you"* (1 Thess. 5:16–18). Not only is it God's will that we should find full deliverance from all care and undue anxiety, but He has ordained prayer as the means by which we can reach that happy state of heart.

The Revised Version makes some changes in the Philippians 4 passage. The reading there is, *"In nothing be anxious,"* and, *"the peace of God...shall guard your hearts and your thoughts"* (vv. 6–7). Only a few verses before that, Paul wrote, *"Rejoice in the Lord alway"* (v. 4 RV). That is, be always glad in the Lord, and be happy with Him. So that you may thus be happy, *"Be careful for nothing."* This rejoicing is the doorway for prayer, and its pathway, too. The sunshine and buoyancy of joy in the Lord are the strength and boldness of prayer, the peace of its victory.

"Moderation" makes the rainbow of prayer. The word denotes mildness, fairness, gentleness, sweet reasonableness. The Revised Version changes it to *"forbearance,"* with the margin reading *"gentleness."* What rare ingredients and beautiful colorings, which make a strong and beautiful character and a wide and positive reputation! A rejoicing, gentle spirit, positive in reputation, is well fitted for prayer, rid of the distractions and unrest of care!

9

Prayer Facts and History
(Continued)

The neglect of prayer is a grand hindrance to holiness. We have not, because we ask not. Oh, how meek and gentle, how lowly in heart, how full of love both to God and to man, might you have been at this day, if you had only asked! If you had continued instant in prayer! Ask, that you may thoroughly experience and perfectly practice the whole of that religion that our Lord has so beautifully described in the Sermon on the Mount. —John Wesley

IT is to the prayer closet that Paul directed us to go. The unfailing remedy for all burdensome, distressing care is prayer. The place where the Lord is at hand is the closet of prayer. There He is always found, and there He is at hand to bless, to deliver, and to help. The one place where the Lord's presence and power will be more fully realized than any other place is the closet of prayer.

Paul set forth the various terms of prayer, supplication, and giving of thanks as the complement of true praying. The soul must be in all of these spiritual exercises. There must be no halfhearted praying, no abridging its nature, and no abating its force if we would be freed from this undue anxiety that causes friction and internal distress, and if we would receive the rich fruit of that peace that passes all understanding. He who prays must be an earnest soul, well-rounded in spiritual attributes.

"In every thing...let your requests be made known unto God" (Phil. 4:6), said Paul. Nothing is too great to be handled in prayer or to be sought in prayer. Nothing is too small to be weighed in the

secret councils of the closet, and nothing is too little for its final arbitration. As care comes from every source, so prayer goes to every source. As there are no small things in prayer, so there are no small things with God. He who counts the hairs of our head, and who is not too lofty and high to notice the little sparrow that falls to the ground, is not too great and high to note everything that concerns the happiness, the needs, and the safety of His children. Prayer brings God into what men are pleased to term the little affairs of life. The lives of people are made up of these small matters, and yet how often do great consequences come from small beginnings.

> There is no sorrow, Lord, too light
> To bring in prayer to Thee;
> There is no anxious care too slight
> To wake Thy sympathy.
>
> There is no secret sigh we breathe,
> But meets Thine ear divine,
> And every cross grows light beneath
> The shadow, Lord, of Thine.

As everything by prayer is to be brought to the notice of Almighty God, so we are assured that whatever affects us concerns Him. How comprehensive is this direction about prayer? *"In every thing by prayer."* There is no distinction here between temporal and spiritual things. Such a distinction is against faith, wisdom, and reverence. God rules everything in nature and in grace. Man is affected for time and eternity by things secular as well as by things spiritual. Man's salvation hangs on his business as well as on his prayers. A man's business hangs on his prayers just as it hangs on his diligence.

The chief hindrances to piety, the wiliest and the deadliest temptations of the Devil, are in business and lie alongside the things of time. The heaviest, the most confusing, and the most stupefying cares lie beside secular and worldly matters. So, in everything that comes to us and that concerns us, in everything that we want to come to us, and in everything that we do not want to come to us, prayer is to be made for all things. Prayer blesses all things, brings all things, relieves all things, and prevents all things. Everything as well as every place and every hour is to be ordered by prayer. Prayer has in it the possibility to affect everything that affects us. Here are the vast possibilities of prayer.

How the bitter of life is sweetened by prayer! How the feeble are made strong by prayer! Sickness flees before the health of prayer. Doubts, misgivings, and trembling fears retire before prayer. Wisdom, knowledge, holiness, and heaven are at the command of prayer. Nothing is outside of prayer. It has the power to gain all things in the provision of our Lord Jesus Christ. Paul covered all departments and swept the entire field of human concern, conditions, and happenings by saying, *"In every thing by prayer."*

Supplications and thanksgiving are to be joined with prayer. It is not the dignity of worship, the gorgeousness of ceremonials, the magnificence of its ritual, nor the plainness of its sacraments that avail. It is not simply the soul's hallowed and lowly abasement before God, neither is it the speechless awe, that benefits in this prayer service, but the intensity of supplication, the looking and the lifting of the soul in ardent plea to God for the things desired and for which request is made.

The radiance and gratitude and utterance of thanksgiving must be there. This is not simply the poetry of praise, but the deep-toned words and the prose of thanks. There must be hearty thanks that remembers the past, sees God in it, and voices that recognition in sincere thanksgiving. The hidden depths within must have utterance. The lips must speak the music of the soul. A heart enthused with God, a heart illumined by His presence, a life guided by His right hand, must have something to say for God in gratitude. Such is to recognize God in the events of one's past, to exalt God for His goodness, and to honor God who has honored it.

Make known your requests to God. The *requests* must be made known unto God. Silence is not prayer. Prayer is asking God for something that we do not have, that we desire, and that He has promised to give in answer to prayer. Prayer is really verbal asking. Words are in prayer. Strong words and true words are found in prayer. Desires in prayer are put in words. The praying one is a pleader. He urges his prayer by arguments, promises, and needs.

Sometimes loud words are in prayer. The psalmist said, *"Evening, and morning, and at noon, will I pray, and cry aloud"* (Ps. 55:17). The praying one wants something that he does not have. He wants something that God has in His possession and that he can get by praying. He is beggared, bewildered, oppressed, and

235

confused. He is before God in supplication, in prayer, and in thanksgiving. These are the attitudes, the incense, the equipment, and the fashion of this hour, the court attendance of his soul before God.

Requests are things sought for oneself. The man is in a bind. He needs something, and he needs it badly. Other help has failed. A request is a plea for something to be given that has not been done. The request is for the Giver—not alone His gifts, but Himself. The requests of the praying one are to be made known unto God. The requests are to be brought to the knowledge of God. It is then that cares fly away, anxieties disappear, worries depart, and the soul is set at ease. Then *"the peace of God, which passeth all understanding"* (Phil. 4:7) steals into the heart.

> Peace! doubting heart, my God's I am,
>   Who formed me man, forbids my fear;
> The Lord hath called me by my name;
>   The Lord protects, forever near;
> His blood for me did once atone,
> And yet He loves and guards His own.

In James 5, we have another marvelous description of prayer and its possibilities. It has to do with sickness and health, sin and forgiveness, and rain and drought. Here we have James' direction for praying:

Is any among you afflicted? let him pray. Is any merry? let him sing psalms. Is any sick among you? let him call for the elders of the church; and let them pray over him, anointing him with oil in the name of the Lord: and the prayer of faith shall save the sick, and the Lord shall raise him up; and if he have committed sins, they shall be forgiven him. Confess your faults one to another, and pray one for another, that ye may be healed. The effectual fervent prayer of a righteous man availeth much. Elias was a man subject to like passions as we are, and he prayed earnestly that it might not rain: and it rained not on the earth by the space of three years and six months. And he prayed again, and the heaven gave rain, and the earth brought forth her fruit. (James 5:13–18)

Here is prayer for one's own needs and intercessory prayer for others, prayer for physical needs and prayer for spiritual needs, prayer for drought and prayer for rain, prayer for temporal matters and prayer for spiritual things. How vast the reach of prayer! How wonderful are its possibilities!

Here is the remedy for affliction and depression of every sort, and here we find the remedy for sickness and for rain in the time of drought. Here is the way to obtain forgiveness of sins. A stroke of prayer paralyzes the energies of nature, stays its clouds, rain, and dew, and blasts field and farm like the typhoon. Prayer brings clouds, rain, and fertility to the famished and wasted earth.

The general statement, *"The effectual fervent prayer of a righteous man availeth much"* (v. 16), is a statement of prayer as an energetic force. Two words are used. One signifies power in exercise, operative power, while the other is power as an endowment. Prayer is power and strength, a power and strength that influences God, and is most salutary, widespread, and marvelous in its gracious benefits to man. Prayer influences God. The ability of God to do for man is the measure of the possibility of prayer.

> Thou art coming to a king,
> Large petitions with thee bring;
> For His grace and power are such
> None can ever ask too much.

10

Answered Prayer

In his "Soldier's Pocket Book," Lord Wolseley says if a young officer wishes to succeed, he must volunteer for the most hazardous duties and take every possible chance of risking his life. It was a spirit and courage like that which was shown in the service of God by a good soldier of Jesus Christ named John McKenzie. One evening when he was a lad and eager for work in the foreign mission field he knelt down at the foot of a tree in the Ladies' Walk on the banks of the Lossie at Elgin and offered up this prayer: "O Lord, send me to the darkest spot on earth." And God heard him and sent him to South Africa where he labored many years first under the London Missionary Society and then under the British Government as the first Resident Commissioner among the natives of Bechuanaland. —J. O. Struthers

ANSWERED prayer brings praying out of the realm of dry, dead things and makes praying a thing of life and power. It is the answer to prayer that brings things to pass, changes the natural trend of things, and orders all things according to the will of God. It is the answer to prayer that takes praying out of the regions of fanaticism, and saves it from being utopian, or from being merely fanciful. It is the answer to prayer that makes praying a power for God and for man, and makes praying real and divine. Unanswered prayers are training schools for unbelief, an imposition and a nuisance, an impertinence to God and to man.

Answers to prayer are the only surety that we have prayed aright. What marvelous power there is in prayer! What untold miracles it works in this world! What untold benefits to men does it secure to those who pray! Why is it that the average prayer goes begging for an answer?

The millions of unanswered prayers are not to be solved by the mystery of God's will. We are not the sport of His sovereign power. He is not playing at "make-believe" in His marvelous promises to answer prayer. The whole explanation is found in our wrong praying. We ask and do not receive because we ask amiss. (See James 4:3.) If all unanswered prayers were dumped into the ocean, they would come very near filling it.

Child of God, can you pray? Are your prayers answered? If not, why not? Answered prayer is the proof of your real praying.

The efficacy of prayer from a Bible standpoint lies solely in the answer to prayer. The benefit of prayer has been well and popularly maximized by the saying, "It moves the arm that moves the universe."

To get unquestioned answers to prayer is not only important as to the satisfying of our desires, but is the evidence of our abiding in Christ. Thus, it becomes more important still. The mere act of praying is no test of our relationship to God. The act of praying may be a dead performance. It may be the routine of habit. But to pray and receive clear answers, not once or twice, but daily, is the sure test and is the gracious point of our vital connection with Jesus Christ. Read our Lord's words in this connection: *"If ye abide in me, and my words abide in you, ye shall ask what ye will, and it shall be done unto you"* (John 15:7).

To God and to man, the answer to prayer is the all-important part of our praying. The answer to prayer, direct and unmistakable, is the evidence of God's being. It proves that God lives, that there is a God, an intelligent being, who is interested in His creatures, and who listens to them when they approach Him in prayer. There is no proof so clear and demonstrative that God exists than prayer and its answer. This was Elijah's plea: *"Hear me, O LORD, hear me, that this people may know that thou art the LORD God"* (1 Kings 18:37).

The answer to prayer is the part of prayer that glorifies God. Unanswered prayers are dumb oracles that leave the praying ones in darkness, doubt, and bewilderment, and that carry no conviction to the unbeliever. It is not the act or the attitude of praying that gives efficacy to prayer. It is not abject prostration of the body before God, the vehement or quiet utterance to God, or the exquisite beauty and poetry of the diction of our prayers that do the deed. It is not the marvelous array of argument and eloquence in praying that makes prayer effectual. Not one or all of these are the things that glorify God. It is the answer that brings glory to His name.

Elijah might have prayed on Carmel's heights until this day, with all the fire and energy of his soul, but if no answer had been given, no glory would have come to God. Peter might have shut himself up with Dorcas' dead body until he himself died on his knees, but if no answer had come, no glory to God nor good to man would have followed. Only doubt, blight, and dismay would be the result.

Answer to prayer is the convincing proof of our right relations to God. Jesus said at the grave of Lazarus,

> *Father, I thank thee that thou hast heard me. And I knew that thou hearest me always: but because of the people which stand by I said it, that they may believe that thou hast sent me.*
> *(John 11:41–42)*

The answer to His prayer was the proof of His mission from God, just as the answer to Elijah's prayer was made to the woman whose son he raised to life. She said, *"Now by this I know that thou art a man of God"* (1 Kings 17:24). He is highest in the favor of God who has the readiest access and the greatest number of answers to prayer from Almighty God.

Prayer ascends to God by an invariable law, even by more than law—by the will, the promise, and the presence of a personal God. The answer comes back to earth by all the promise, the truth, the power, and the love of God. Not to be concerned about the answer to prayer is not to pray. What a world of waste there is in praying! What myriads of prayers have been offered for which no answer is returned, no answer is longed for, and no answer is expected!

We have been nurturing a false faith and hiding the shame of our loss and inability to pray by the false, comforting plea that God does not answer directly or objectively, but indirectly and subjectively. We have persuaded ourselves that by some kind of hocus-pocus, of which we are wholly unconscious about its process and its results, we have been made better.

Fully aware that God has not answered us directly, we have solaced ourselves with the delusive balm that God has in some impalpable way, and with unknown results, given us something better. Or, we have comforted and nurtured our spiritual sloth by saying that it is not God's will to give it to us.

Faith teaches God's praying ones that it is God's will to answer prayer. God answers all prayers and every prayer of His children who truly pray.

> Prayer makes darkened clouds withdraw,
> Prayer climbs the ladder Jacob saw;
> Gives exercise to faith and love,
> Brings every blessing from above.

The emphasis in the Scriptures is always given to the answer to prayer. All things from God are given in answer to prayer. God Himself, His presence, His gifts, and His grace, one and all, are secured by prayer. The medium by which God communicates with men is prayer. The most real thing in prayer, its very essential end, is the answer it secures. The mere repetition of words in prayer, the counting of beads, the multiplying of mere words as works of uncalled-for obligation—as if there were virtue in the number of prayers to avail—is a vain delusion, an empty thing, a useless service. Prayer looks directly to securing an answer. This is its design. It has no other end in view.

Communion with God, of course, is in prayer. There is sweet fellowship with our God through His Holy Spirit. Enjoyment of God is in praying—sweet, rich, and strong. The graces of the Spirit in the inner soul are nurtured by prayer, kept alive and promoted in their growth by this spiritual exercise. But not one or even all of these benefits of prayer have in them the essential end of prayer. The divinely appointed channel through which all good and all grace flows to our souls and bodies is prayer.

> Prayer is appointed to convey
> The blessings God designs to give.

Prayer is divinely ordained as the means by which all temporal and spiritual good are directed to us. Prayer is not an end in itself. It is not something done to be rested in, not something we have done, about which we are to congratulate ourselves. It is a means to an end. It is something we do that brings us something in return, without which the praying is valueless. Prayer always aims at securing an answer.

We are rich and strong, good and holy, generous and kind by answered prayer. It is not the mere performance, the attitude, or the words of prayer that bring benefit to us, but it is the answer sent directly from heaven. Conscious, real answers to prayer bring real good to us. This is not praying merely for self or simply for selfish ends. The selfish character cannot exist when the prayer conditions are fulfilled.

It is by these answered prayers that human nature is enriched. The answered prayer brings us into constant, conscious communion with God, awakens and enlarges gratitude, and excites the melody and lofty inspiration of praise. Answered prayer is the mark of God in our praying. It is the exchange with heaven, and it establishes and realizes a relationship with the unseen. We give our prayers in exchange for the divine blessing. God accepts our prayers through the atoning blood and gives Himself, His presence, and His grace in return.

All holy attitudes are affected by answered prayers. By the answers to prayer all holy principles are matured, and faith, love, and hope have their enrichment by answered prayer. The answer is found in all true praying. The answer is strongly in prayer as an aim, a desire expressed; and its expectation and realization give importunity and realization to prayer. It is the fact of the answer that makes the prayer and that enters into its very being.

To seek no answer to prayer takes the desire, the aim, and the heart out of prayer. It makes praying a dead, stockish thing, fit only for dumb idols. It is the answer that brings praying into biblical regions and makes it a desire realized, a pursuit, an interest. The answer clothes it with flesh and blood, and makes it a prayer, throbbing with all the true life, affluent with all the paternal relations of giving and receiving, of asking and answering.

God holds all good in His own hands. That good comes to us through our Lord Jesus Christ, only because of His atoning merits, by asking it in His name. The only and the sole command in which all the others of its class belong, is, *"Ask...seek...knock"* (Matt 7:7). And the promise is its counterpart, its necessary equivalent, and its result: *"It shall be given...ye shall find...it shall be opened unto you"* (v. 7). God is so much involved in prayer and its hearing and answering that all of His attributes and His whole being are centered in that great fact. It distinguishes Him as particularly beneficent, wonderfully good, and powerfully attractive in His nature. *"O thou that hearest prayer, unto thee shall all flesh come"* (Ps. 65:2).

Faithful, O Lord, Thy mercies are
A rock that cannot move;
A thousand promises declare
Thy constancy of love.

Not only does the Word of God stand as assurance for the answer to prayer, but all the attributes of God conspire to the same end. God's veracity is at stake in the engagements to answer prayer. His wisdom, His truthfulness, and His goodness are involved. God's infinite and inflexible rectitude is pledged to the great end of answering the prayers of those who call upon Him in time of need. Justice and mercy blend into oneness to secure the answer to prayer. It is significant that the very justice of God comes into play and stands hard by God's faithfulness in the strong promise God makes of the pardon of sins and of cleansing from sin's pollution: *"If we confess our sins, he is faithful and just to forgive us our sins, and to cleanse us from all unrighteousness"* (1 John 1:9).

God's kingly relation to man, with all of its authority, unites with the fatherly relation and with all of its tenderness to secure the answer to prayer.

Our Lord Jesus Christ is most fully committed to the answer of prayer. *"Whatsoever ye shall ask in my name, that will I do, that the Father may be glorified in the Son"* (John 14:13). How well assured the answer to prayer is, when that answer is to glorify God the Father! And how eager Jesus Christ is to glorify His Father in heaven! So eager is He to answer prayer that always and everywhere brings glory to the Father, that no prayer offered in His name is denied or overlooked by Him. Says our Lord Jesus Christ again, giving fresh assurance to our faith, *"If ye shall ask any thing in my name, I will do it"* (v. 14). So says He once more, *"Ask what ye will, and it shall be done unto you"* (John 15:7).

Come, my soul, thy suit prepare,
Jesus loves to answer prayer;
He Himself has bid thee pray,
Therefore will not say thee nay.

11

Answered Prayer
(Continued)

Constrained at the darkest hour to confess humbly that without God's help I was helpless, I vowed in the forest of solitude that I would confess His aid before men. A silence as death was around me; it was midnight, I was weakened by illness, prostrated with fatigue and worn with anxiety for my white and black companions, whose fate was a mystery. In this physical and mental distress I besought God to give me back my people. Nine hours later we were exulting with rapturous joy. In full view of all was the crimson flag with the crescent and beneath its waving folds was the long-lost rear column. —Henry M. Stanley

GOD has committed Himself to us by His Word in our praying. The Word of God is the basis, the inspiration, and the heart of prayer. Jesus Christ stands as the illustration of God's Word and its unlimited good in promise as well as in realization. God takes nothing by halves. He gives nothing by halves. We can have the whole of Him when He has the whole of us.

His words of promise are so far-reaching and so all-encompassing that they seem to have deadened our comprehension and have paralyzed our praying. This appears when we consider those large words, when He almost exhausts human language in promises, as in *"whatever," "anything,"* and the all-inclusive *"whatsoever"* and *"all things."* These oft-repeated promises, so very great, seem to daze us, and instead of allowing them to move us to asking, testing, and receiving, we turn away full of wonder, but empty-handed and with empty hearts.

Let me quote another passage from our Lord's teaching about prayer. By the most solemn verification, He declares as follows:

And in that day ye shall ask me nothing; verily, verily, I say unto you, Whatsoever ye shall ask the Father in my name, he will give it you. Hitherto have ye asked nothing in my name: ask, and ye shall receive, that your joy may be full.

(John 16:23–24)

Twice in this passage He declares the answer, pledging His Father, *"He will give it you,"* and declaring with impressive and most suggestive repetition, *"Ask, and ye shall receive."* So strong and so often did Jesus declare the answer as an inducement to pray and as an inevitable result of prayer, that the apostles held it as fully and invincibly established that prayer would be answered, and that their main duty was to urge and command men to pray. So firmly were they established as to the truth of the law of prayer as laid down by our Lord, that they were led to affirm that the answer to prayer was involved in and necessarily bound up with all right praying. God the Father and Jesus Christ, His Son, are both strongly committed by all the truth of their word and by the fidelity of their character to answer prayer.

Not only do these and all the promises pledge Almighty God to answer prayer, but they assure us that the answer will be specific, and that the very thing for which we pray will be given. Our Lord's invariable teaching was that we receive that for which we ask, obtain that for which we seek, and have that door opened at which we knock. This is according to our heavenly Father's direction to us and His giving to us for our asking. He will not disappoint us by not answering; neither will He deny us by giving us some other thing for which we have not asked, or by letting us find some other thing that we have not sought, or by opening to us the wrong door at which we were not knocking. If we ask for bread, He will give us bread. If we ask for an egg, He will give us an egg. If we ask for a fish, He will give us a fish. Not something like bread, but bread itself will be given unto us. Not something like a fish, but a fish will be given. Not evil will be given to us in answer to prayer, but good.

Earthly parents, though evil in nature, give for the asking and respond to the crying of their children. The encouragement to pray is transferred from our earthly father to our heavenly Father, from the evil to the good, to the supremely good; from the weak to the omnipotent, our heavenly Father, centering in Himself all the highest conceptions of fatherhood—abler, readier, and much more than the best, and much more than the ablest earthly father. *"How much more"* (Matt. 7:11), who can tell? Much more than our earthly fathers will He supply all our needs, give us all good things, and enable us to meet every difficult duty and fulfill every law, though hard to flesh and blood, but made easy under the full supply of our Father's beneficent and exhaustless help.

Here we have more than an intimation of the necessity, not only of perseverance in prayer, but of the progressive stages of intention and effort in the outlay of increasing spiritual force—asking, seeking, and knocking. Here is an ascending scale from the mere words of asking to a settled attitude of seeking, resulting in a determined, clamorous, and vigorous direct effort of praying.

Just as God has commanded us to pray always, to pray everywhere, and to pray in everything, so He will answer always, everywhere, and in everything. God has plainly and with directness committed Himself to answer prayer. If we fulfill the conditions of prayer, the answer is bound to come. The laws of nature are not so invariable and so inexorable as the promised answer to prayer. The ordinances of nature might fail, but the ordinances of grace can never fail. There are no limitations, no adverse conditions, no weakness, no inability that can or will hinder the answer to prayer. God's doing for us when we pray has no limitations and is not hedged about by provisos in Himself or in the peculiar circumstances of any particular case. If we really pray, God masters and defies all things and is above all conditions.

God explicitly says, *"Call unto me, and I will answer"* (Jer. 33:3). There are no limitations, no hedges, no hindrances in the way of God's fulfilling the promise. His word is at stake. His word is involved. God solemnly engages to answer prayer. Man is to look for the answer, be inspired by the expectation of the answer, and may with humble boldness demand the answer. God, who cannot lie (Titus 1:2), is bound to answer. He has voluntarily placed Himself under obligation to answer the prayer of those who truly pray.

> To God your every want
>> In instant prayer display;
> Pray always; pray, and never faint;
>> Pray, without ceasing, pray.
>
> In fellowship, alone,
>> To God with faith draw near;

Approach His courts, beseech His throne,
With all the power of prayer.

The prophets and the men of God of Old Testament times were unshaken in their faith in the absolute certainty of God's fulfilling His promises to them. They rested in security on the Word of God and had no doubt whatever either as to the fidelity of God in answering prayer or of His willingness or ability. Thus, their history is marked by repeated asking and receiving at the hands of God.

The same is true of the early church. They received without question the doctrine their Lord and Master had so often affirmed that the answer to prayer was sure. The certainty of the answer to prayer was as fixed as God's Word is true. The Holy Spirit dispensation was ushered in by the disciples carrying this faith into practice. When Jesus told them to *"tarry [at] Jerusalem, until ye be endued with power from on high"* (Luke 24:49), they received it as a sure promise that if they obeyed the command, they would certainly receive the divine power. So they tarried in the upper room in prayer for ten days, and the promise was fulfilled. The answer came just as Jesus said.

When Peter and John were arrested for healing the man who sat at the Beautiful Gate of the temple, after being threatened by the rulers in Jerusalem, they were released. *"And being let go, they went to their own company"* (Acts 4:23); they went to those with whom they were in affinity, those of like minds, and not to men of the world. Still believing in prayer and its efficacy, they gave themselves to prayer, the prayer itself being recorded in Acts 4. They recited some things to the Lord, and

> *when they had prayed, the place was shaken where they were assembled together; and they were filled with the Holy Ghost, and they spake the word of God with boldness.* (Acts 4:31)

Here they were filled for this special occasion with the Holy Spirit. The answer to prayer was a response to their faith and prayer. The fullness of the Spirit always brings boldness. The cure for fear in the face of threatening enemies of the Lord is being filled with the Spirit. This gives power to speak the word of the Lord with boldness. This gives courage and drives away fear.

12

Answered Prayer
(Continued)

A young man had been called to the foreign field. He had not been in the habit of preaching, but he knew one thing, how to prevail with God; and going one day to a friend he said, "I don't see how God can use me on the field. I have no special talent." His friend said, "My brother, God wants men on the field who can pray. There are too many preachers now and too few pray-ers." He went. In his own room in the early dawn a voice was heard weeping and pleading for souls. All through the day, the shut door and the hush that prevailed made you feel like walking softly, for a soul was wrestling with God. Yet to this home, hungry souls would flock, drawn by some irresistible power. Ah, the mystery was unlocked. In the secret chamber lost souls were pleaded for and claimed. The Holy Ghost knew just where they were and sent them along.

—J. Hudson Taylor

WE display it at the front. We unfold it on a banner never to be lowered or folded, that God does hear and answer prayer. God has always heard and answered prayer. God will forever hear and answer prayer. He is the same yesterday, today, and forever, ever blessed, ever to be adored. Amen. He changes not. As He has always answered prayer, so will He ever continue to do so!

To answer prayer is God's universal rule. It is His unchangeable and irrepealable law to answer prayer. It is His invariable, specific, and inviolate promise to answer prayer. The few denials to prayer in the Scriptures are the exceptions to the general rule, suggestive and startling by their fewness, exception, and emphasis.

The possibilities of prayer, then, lie in the great truth, unlimited in its broadness, fathomless in its depths, exhaustless in its fullness, that God answers every prayer from every true soul who truly prays. God's Word does not say, "Call unto me, and you will thereby be trained into the happy art of knowing how to be denied. Ask, and you will learn sweet patience by getting nothing." Far from it. But it is definite, clear, and positive: *"Ask, and it shall be given you"* (Matt. 7:7).

We have this case in the Old Testament:

Jabez called on the God of Israel, saying, Oh that thou wouldest bless me indeed, and enlarge my coast, and that thine hand might be with me, and that thou wouldest keep me from evil, that it may not grieve me.   (1 Chron. 4:10)

And God readily granted him the things that he had requested.

Hannah, distressed in soul because she was childless, and desiring a man child, went back to the house of prayer and prayed. This is the record she makes of the direct answer she received: *"For this child I prayed; and the LORD hath given me my petition which I asked of him"* (1 Sam. 1:27).

God's promises and purposes go directly to the fact of giving for the asking. The answer to our prayers is the motive constantly presented in the Scriptures to encourage us to pray and to quicken us in this spiritual exercise. Read the following strong, clear Scriptures:

Call unto me, and I will answer thee. (Jer. 33:3)

He shall call upon me, and I will answer. (Ps. 91:15)

Ask, and it shall be given you; seek, and ye shall find; knock, and it shall be opened unto you. (Matt. 7:7)

This is Jesus Christ's law of prayer. He does not say, "Ask, and something shall be given you." Nor does He say, "Ask, and you will be trained into piety." Rather, when you ask, the very thing asked for will be given. Jesus does not say, "Knock, and some door will be opened." Instead, the very door at which you are knocking will be opened. To make this doubly sure, Jesus Christ duplicates and reiterates the promise of the answer: *"For every one that asketh, receiveth; and he that seeketh findeth; and to him that knocketh it shall be opened"* (Matt. 7:8).

Answered prayer is the spring of love, and is the direct encouragement to pray.

I love the Lord, because he hath heard my voice and my supplications. Because he hath inclined his ear unto me, therefore will I call upon him as long as I live. (Ps. 116:1–2)

The certainty of the Father's giving is assured by the Father's relation, and by the ability and goodness of the Father. Earthly parents, frail, infirm, and limited in goodness and ability, give when the child asks and seeks. The parental heart responds most readily to the cry for bread. The hunger of the child touches and wins the father's heart. So God, our heavenly Father, is as easily and strongly moved by our prayers as the earthly parent.

If ye then, being evil, know how to give good gifts unto your children, how much more shall your Father which is in heaven give good things unto them that ask him? (Matt. 7:11)

"Much more," just as much more does God's goodness, tenderness, and ability exceed that of man's.

Just as the asking is specific, so also is the answer specific. The child does not ask for one thing and get another. He does not cry for bread, but get a stone. He does not ask for an egg and receive a scorpion. He does not ask for a fish and get a serpent. Christ demands specific asking. He responds to specific praying by specific giving.

To give the very thing prayed for, and not something else, is fundamental to Christ's law of praying. No prayer for the cure of blind eyes did He ever answer by curing deaf ears. The very thing prayed for is the very thing that He gives. The exceptions to this are confirming of this great law of prayer. He who asks for bread gets bread, and not a stone. If he asks for a fish, he receives a fish, and not a serpent.

No cry is so pleading and so powerful as the child's cry for bread. The hunger cravings, the appetite felt, and the need realized, all create and propel the crying of the child. Our prayers must be as earnest, as needy, and as hungry as the starving child's cry for bread. Simple, artless, direct, and specific must be our praying, according to Christ's law of prayer and His teaching of God's fatherhood.

The illustration and enforcement of the law of prayer are found in the specific answers given to prayer. Gethsemane is an exception. The prayer of Jesus Christ in that awful hour of darkness and hell was conditioned on these words: *"If it be possible, let this cup pass from me"* (Matt. 26:39). But beyond these utterances of our Lord was the soul and life prayer of the willing, suffering, divine victim, *"Nevertheless not as I will, but as thou wilt"* (v. 39). The prayer was answered, the angel came, strength was imparted, and the meek sufferer in silence drank the bitter cup.

Two cases of unanswered prayer are recorded in the Scriptures in addition to the Gethsemane prayer of our Lord. The first was that of David for the life of his baby child, but for good reasons to Almighty God the request was not granted. The second was that of Paul for the removal of the thorn in the flesh, which was denied. But we are constrained to believe these must have been notable as exceptions to God's rule, as illustrated in the history of prophets, priests, apostles, and saints as recorded in the divine Word. There must have been unrevealed reasons that moved God to veer from His settled and fixed rule to answer prayer by giving the specific thing prayed for.

Our Lord did not hold the Syrophenician woman in the school of unanswered prayer in order to test and mature her faith. Neither did He answer her prayer by healing or saving her husband. She asked for the healing of her daughter, and Christ healed the daughter. She received the very thing for which she asked the Lord Jesus Christ. It was in the school of answered prayer that our Lord disciplined and perfected her faith, and it was by giving her a specific answer to her prayer. Her prayer centered on her daughter. She prayed for the one thing, the healing of her child. And the answer of our Lord centered likewise on the daughter.

We tread altogether too gingerly upon the great and precious promises of God, and too often we ignore them wholly. The promise is the ground on which faith stands in asking of God. This is the one basis of prayer. We limit God's ability. We measure God's ability and willingness to answer prayer by the standard of men. We limit the Holy One of Israel.

How full of loving-kindness and remedy to suffering mankind are the promises as given us in the fifth chapter of James! How personal and intimate do they make God in prayer! They are a direct challenge to our faith. They are encouraging to large expectations in all the requests we make of God. Prayer affects God in a direct manner, and has its aim and end in affecting Him. Prayer takes hold of God and induces Him to do large things for us, whether personal or relative, temporal or spiritual, earthly or heavenly.

The great gap between Bible promises to answer prayer and the income from praying is almost unspeakably great, so much so that it is a prolific source of unbelief. It breeds unbelief in prayer as a great moral force and begets doubt as to the efficacy of prayer.

Christianity needs today, above all else, men and women who can in prayer put God to the test and who can prove His promises. These are the sort of men and women needed in this modern day in the church. It is not educated men who are needed for the times. It is not more money that is required. It is not more machinery, more organization, more ecclesiastical laws, but it is men and women who know how to pray, who can in prayer move God to take hold of earth's affairs mightily and put life and power into the church and into all of its machinery!

The church and the world greatly need saints who can bridge this wide gap between the praying done and the small number of answers received. Saints are needed whose faith is bold enough and sufficiently far-reaching to put God to the test. The cry comes even now out of heaven to the people of the present church, as it sounded forth in the days of Malachi: *"Prove me now herewith, saith the LORD of hosts"* (Mal. 3:10). God is waiting to be put to the test by His people in prayer. He delights in being put to the test on His promises. It is His highest pleasure to answer prayer to prove the reliability of His promises. Nothing worthy of God nor of great value to men will be accomplished until this is done.

Our Gospel belongs to the miraculous. It was projected on the miraculous plane. It cannot be maintained except by the supernatural. Take the supernatural out of our holy religion, and its life and power are gone, and it degenerates into a mere mode of morals. The miraculous is divine power. Prayer has in it this same power. Prayer brings this divine power into the ranks of men and puts it to work. Prayer brings into the affairs of earth a supernatural element. Our Gospel, when truly presented, is the power of God.

Never was the church more in need of those who can and will test Almighty God. Never did the church need more than now those who can raise up everywhere memorials of God's supernatural power, memorials of answers to prayer, memorials of promises fulfilled. These would do more to silence the enemy of souls, the foe of God, and the adversary of the church than any modern scheme or present-day plan for the success of the Gospel. Such memorials reared by praying people would dumbfound God's foes, strengthen weak saints, and fill strong saints with triumphant rapture.

The most prolific source of unbelief, that which traduces and hinders praying, and that which obscures the being and glory of God most effectually, is unanswered prayer. Better not to pray at all than to go through a dead form that secures no answer, brings no glory to God, and supplies no good to man. Nothing so hardens the heart and nothing so blinds us to the unseen and the eternal, as this kind of prayerless praying!

13

Prayer Miracles

George Benfield, a driver on the Midland Railway, was standing on the footplate oiling his engine, the train being stationary, when his foot slipped. He fell on the space between the lines. He heard the express coming on, and had only time enough to lie full length on the "six-foot" when it rushed by, and he escaped unhurt. He returned to his home in the middle of the night and as he was going upstairs he heard one of his children, a girl about eight years old, crying and sobbing. "Oh, father," she said, "I thought somebody came and told me that you were going to be killed, and I got out of bed and prayed that God would not let you die." Was it only a dream, a coincidence? George Benfield and others believed that he owed his life to that prayer. —Dean Hole

THE earthly career of our Lord Jesus Christ was no mere episode or interlude in His eternal life. What He was and what He did on earth were neither abnormal nor divergent, but characteristic. What He was and what He did on earth are but the representation and the illustration of what He is and what He is doing in heaven. He is *"the same yesterday, and to day, and for ever"* (Heb. 13:8). This statement is the divine summary of the eternal unity and changelessness of His character. His earthly life was made up largely of hearing and answering prayer. His heavenly life is devoted to the same divine business. The Old Testament is really the record of God hearing and answering prayer. The whole Bible deals largely with this all-important subject.

Christ's miracles are object lessons. They are living pictures. They talk to us. They have hands that take hold of us. Many valuable lessons do these miracles teach us. In their diversity, they refresh us.

They show us the matchless power of Jesus Christ, and at the same time discover for us His marvelous compassion for suffering humanity. These miracles disclose to us His ability to endlessly diversify His operations.

God's method in working with man is not the same in all cases. He does not administer His grace in rigid ruts. There is endless variety in His movements. There is marvelous diversity in His operations. He does not fashion His creations in the same mold. Likewise, our Lord is not circumscribed in His working nor hampered by models. He works independently. He is His own architect. He furnishes His own patterns, which have unlimited variety.

When we consider our Lord's miracles, we discover that quite a number were performed unconditionally. At least there were no conditions accompanying them, so far as the divine record shows. At His own instance, without being solicited to do so, in order to glorify God and to manifest His own glory and power, this class of miracles was accomplished. Many of His mighty works were performed at the moving of His compassion and the call of suffering and need, as well as at the call of His power.

A number of them were performed by Him in answer to prayer. Some were in answer to the personal prayers of those who were afflicted. Others were performed in answer to the prayers of the friends of those who were afflicted. Those miracles worked in answer to prayer are very instructive in the uses of prayer.

In these conditional miracles, faith holds preeminence, and prayer is faith's administrator. We have an illustration of the importance of faith as the condition on which the exercise of Christ's power was based, or the channel through which it flowed, in the incident of a visit He made to Nazareth. Here is the record of the case, with its results, or rather its lack of results. *"And he could there do no mighty work, save that he laid his hands upon a few sick folk, and healed them. And he marvelled because of their unbelief"* (Mark 6:5–6).

Those people at Nazareth may have prayed that our Lord raise their dead, or open the eyes of the blind, or heal the lepers, but it was all in vain. The absence of faith, however much of performance may be seen, restrains the exercise of God's power, paralyzes the arm of Christ, and turns to death all signs of life. Unbelief is the one thing that seriously hinders Almighty God in doing mighty works. Matthew's record of this visit to Nazareth says, *"And he did not many mighty works there because of their unbelief"* (Matt. 13:58). Lack of faith ties the hands of Almighty God in His working among the children of men. Prayer to Christ must always be based, backed, and impregnated with faith.

The miracle of miracles in the earthly career of our Lord, the raising of Lazarus from the dead, was remarkable for its prayer accompaniment. It was really a prayer issue, something after the issue between the prophets of Baal and Elijah. It was not a prayer for help. It was one of thanksgiving and assured confidence. Let us read it.

> *And Jesus lifted up his eyes, and said, Father, I thank thee that thou hast heard me. And I knew that thou hearest me always: but because of the people which stand by I said it, that they may believe that thou hast sent me.*   *(John 11:41–42)*

It was a prayer mainly for the benefit of those who were present, that they might know that God was with Him because He had answered His prayers, and that faith in God might be radiated in their hearts.

Answered prayers are sometimes the most convincing and faith-creating forces. Unanswered prayers chill the atmosphere and freeze the soil of a faith. If Christians knew how to pray so as to have answers to their prayers—evident, immediate, demonstrative answers from God—faith would be more widely diffused, would become more general, would be more profound, and would be a much mightier force in the world.

What a valuable lesson of faith and intercessory prayer does the miracle of the healing of the centurion's servant bring to us! The simplicity and strength of the faith of this Roman officer are remarkable, for He believed that it was not necessary for our Lord to go directly to his house in order to have his request granted, *"But speak the word only, and my servant shall be healed"* (Matt. 8:8). And our Lord puts His mark upon this man's faith by saying, *"Verily I say unto you, I have not found so great faith, no, not in Israel"* (v. 10). This man's prayer was the expression of his strong faith, and such faith brought the answer promptly.

We get the same invaluable lesson from the prayer miracle of the case of the Syrophenician woman who went to our Lord on behalf of her stricken daughter, making her daughter's case her own, by pleading, *"Lord, help me"* (Matt. 15:25). Here was importunity, holding on, pressing her case, refusing to let go or to be denied. A strong case it was of intercessory prayer and its benefits. Our Lord seemingly held her off for a while but at last yielded, and put His seal upon her strong faith: *"O woman, great is thy faith: be it unto thee even as thou wilt"* (v. 28). What a lesson on praying for others and its large benefits!

Individual cases could be named where the afflicted persons interceded for themselves, illustrations of wonderful things brought about by our Lord in answer to the cries of those who were afflicted. As we read the evangelists' record, the pages fairly glisten with records of our Lord's miracles performed in answer to prayer, showing the wonderful things accomplished by the use of this divinely appointed means of grace.

If we turn back to Old Testament times, we have no lack of instances of prayer miracles. The saints of those days were well acquainted with the power of prayer to move God to do great things. Natural laws did not stand in the way of Almighty God when He was appealed to by His praying ones. What a marvelous record is that of Moses, when those successive plagues were visited upon Egypt in the effort to make Pharaoh let the children of Israel go that they might serve God! As one after another of these plagues came, Pharaoh beseeched Moses, *"Entreat the LORD your God, that he may take away from me this death"* (Exod. 10:17).

As the plagues themselves were miracles, prayer removed them as quickly as they were sent by Almighty God. The same hand that sent these destructive agencies upon Egypt was moved by the prayers of His servant Moses to remove these same plagues. The removal of the plagues in answer to prayer was as remarkable a display of divine power as was the sending of the plagues in the first place. The removal in answer to prayer did as much to show God's being and His power as did the plagues themselves. They were miracles of prayer.

All down the line in Old Testament days we see these prayer miracles. God's praying servants did not have the least doubt that prayer would work marvelous results and bring the supernatural into the affairs of earth. Miracles and prayer went hand in hand. They were companions. The one was the cause, the other was the effect. The one brought the other into existence. The miracle was the proof that God heard and answered prayer. The miracle was the divine demonstration that God, who was in heaven, interfered

in earth's affairs, intervened to help men, and worked supernaturally, if need be, to accomplish His purposes in answer to
prayer.

Passing to the days of the early church, we find the same divine record of prayer miracles. The sad news came to Peter that
Dorcas was dead and he was wanted at Joppa. He promptly made
his way to that place. Peter put everybody out of the room and then
knelt down and prayed with faith, saying, *"Tabitha, arise"* (Acts
9:40), at which she opened her eyes and sat up. Knee work on the
part of Peter did the job. Prayer brought things to pass and saved
Dorcas for further service on earth.

On that noted journey to Rome under guard, Paul had been
shipwrecked on an island. The chief man of the island was Publius,
and his old father was critically ill of a bloody flux. Paul laid his
hands on the old man and prayed for him, and God came to the
rescue and healed the sick man. Prayer brought the thing desired
to pass. God interfered with the laws of nature, either suspending
or setting them aside for a season, and answered the prayer of this
praying servant of His. And the answer to prayer among those heathen people convinced them that a supernatural power was at work
among them. In fact, so true was this that they seemed to think a
supernatural being had come among them.

Peter was put in prison by Herod after he had killed James
with the sword. The young church was greatly concerned, but they
neither lost heart nor gave themselves over to needless fretting and
worrying. They had learned before this from where their help
came. They had been schooled in the lesson of prayer. God had intervened before in the behalf of His servants and interfered when
His cause was at stake. *"Prayer was made without ceasing of the
church unto God for him"* (Acts 12:5).

An angel on swift wings came to the rescue, and in a marvelous and supernatural way released Peter and left the prison doors
locked. Locks and prison doors and an unfriendly king cannot
stand in the way of Almighty God when His people cry in prayer
unto Him. Miracles, if need be, will be worked in their behalf to
fulfill His promises and to carry forward His plans. After this order
does the Word of God illustrate and enlarge and confirm the possibilities of prayer by what may be termed "prayer miracles."

How quickly, when we are distressed and troubled, God releases us from difficulty! God wrought a wonderful work through

Samson in enabling him with a crude instrument, the jawbone of a donkey, to slay a thousand men, giving him a great deliverance. Shortly afterward, he was abnormally thirsty, and he was unable to obtain any water. It seemed as if he would perish with thirst. God had saved him from the hands of the Philistines. Could he not as well save him from thirst? So Samson cried unto the Lord, and *"God clave a hollow place that was in the jaw, and there came water thereout; and when he had drunk, his spirit came again, and he revived"* (Judg. 15:19). God could bring water out of the jawbone just as well as He could give victory by it to Samson. God could change that which had been death-dealing to His enemies and make it life-giving to His servant. God can and will work a miracle in answer to prayer in order to deliver His friends, sooner than He will work one to destroy His enemies. He does both, however, in answer to prayer.

All natural forces are under God's control. He did not create the world, put it under law, and then retire from it to work out its own destiny, irrespective of the welfare of His intelligent creatures. Natural laws are simply God's laws, by which He governs and regulates all things in nature. Nature is nothing but God's servant. God is above nature; God is not the slave of nature. This being true, God can and will suspend the working of nature's laws, can hold them in abeyance by His almighty hand, can for the time being set them aside, to fulfill His higher purposes in redemption. It is no violation of nature's laws when, in answer to prayer, He who is above nature makes nature His servant and causes nature to carry out His plans and purposes.

This is the explanation of that wonderful prayer miracle of Old Testament times, when Joshua, in the strength and power of the Lord God, commanded the sun and moon to stand still in order to give time to complete the victory over the enemies of Israel. Why should it be thought an incredible thing that the God of nature and of grace should interfere with His own natural laws for a short season in answer to prayer, and for the good of His cause? Is God tied hand and foot? Has He so circumscribed Himself that He cannot operate the law of prayer? Is the law of nature superior to the law of prayer? Not by any means. He is the God of prayer as well as the God of nature. Both prayer and nature have God as their Maker, their Ruler, and their Executor! And prayer is God's servant, just as nature is His servant.

The prayer force in God's government is as strong as any other force, and all natural and other forces must give way before the force of prayer. Sun, moon, and stars are under God's control in answer to prayer. Rain, sunshine, and drought obey His will. *"Fire, and hail; snow, and vapours; stormy wind fulfilling his word"* (Ps. 148:8). Disease and health are governed by Him. All things in heaven and earth are absolutely under the control of Him who made heaven and earth, and who governs all things according to His own will.

Prayer still works miracles among men and brings to pass great things. It is as true now as when James wrote, *"The effectual fervent prayer of a righteous man availeth much"* (James 5:16). And when the records of eternity are read out to an assembled world, then will it appear how much prayer has wrought in this world. Little is now seen of the fruits of prayer compared with all that it has accomplished and is accomplishing. At the Judgment Day, God will disclose the things that were brought to pass in this world through the prayers of the saints. Many occurrences that are now taken as a matter of course will then be seen to have happened because of the Lord's praying ones.

The work of George Müller in Bristol, England, was a miracle of the nineteenth century. It will take the opening of the books at the Great Judgment Day to disclose all he brought about through prayer. His orphanage, in which hundreds of fatherless and motherless children were cared for—to sustain which this godly man never asked anyone for money with which to pay its running expenses—is a marvel of modern times. His practice was always to ask God for just what was needed, and the answers that came to him read like a record of apostolic times. He prayed for everything and trusted God implicitly to supply all his needs. And it is a matter of record that never did he and the orphans lack any good thing.

At the grave of a holy man who had done so much for Christ and suffering humanity, it was said about him,

> He prayed up the walls of a hospital, and the hearts of the nurses. He prayed mission stations into being, and missionaries into faith. He prayed open the hearts of the rich, and gold from the most distant lands.

Luther is quoted as once saying, "The Christian's trade is praying." Certainly, for a great reason, the preacher's trade should be praying. We fear greatly that many preachers know nothing of this trade of praying, and hence they never succeed at this trade. A severe apprenticeship in the trade of praying must be served in order to be come a journeyman in it. Not only is it true that there are few journeymen at work at this praying trade, but numbers have never even been apprentices at praying. No wonder so little is accomplished by them! God and the supernatural are left out of their programs.

Many do not understand this trade of praying because they have never learned it and hence do not work at it. Many miracles ought to be worked by our praying. Why not? Is the arm of the Lord shortened that He cannot save? Is His ear deaf that He cannot hear? (See Isaiah 59:1.) Has prayer lost its power because iniquity abounds and the love of many has grown cold (Matt. 24:12)? Has God changed from what He once was? To all these queries we enter an emphatic negative. God can as easily today work miracles by praying as He did in the days of old. *"I am the LORD; I change not"* (Mal. 3:6). *"Is any thing too hard for the LORD?"* (Gen. 18:14).

He who works miracles by praying will first of all work the chief miracle on himself. Oh, that we might fully understand the Christian's trade of praying, follow the trade day by day, and thus make for ourselves great spiritual wealth!

14

Wonders of God through Prayer

Take a weak understanding (but one that is exceedingly holy), having little knowledge of God by way of discursive wisdom: such poor soul is oftentimes hardly able to speak wisely, but he often knows more of God in one prayer than a great scholar (though also very holy) has known of Him in all his life. God often deals thus with the weak who are very holy; for if such were shut up to knowing God by way of a sanctified reason, large understandings would have infinite advantage over them, and they would grow little in grace and holiness. Therefore, God makes a supply by breaking in upon their spirits by such irradiations as these. —Thomas Goodwin

A fearful contest exists in this world between God and the Devil, between good and evil, and between heaven and hell. Prayer is the mighty force for overcoming Satan, giving dominion over sin, and defeating hell. Only praying leaders are to be counted on in this dreadful conflict. Praying men alone are to be put to the front. These are the only sort who are able to successfully contend with all the evil forces.

The *"prayers of all saints"* (Rev. 8:3) are a perpetual force against all the powers of darkness. These prayers are a mighty energy in overcoming the world, the flesh, and the Devil, and in shaping the destiny of God's movements to overcome evil and get the victory over the Devil and all his works. The character and energy of God's movements lie in prayer. Victory is to come at the end of praying.

The wonders of God's power are to be kept alive, made real and present, and repeated only by prayer. God is not so evident in the world now or so almighty in manifestation as of old, not because miracles have passed away or because God has ceased to work, but because prayer has been shorn of its simplicity, its majesty, and its power. God still lives, and miracles still live while God lives and acts, for miracles are God's ways of acting. Prayer is dwarfed, withered, and petrified when faith in God is staggered by doubts of His ability or through the shrinking caused by fear. When faith has a telescopic, far-off vision of God, prayer works no miracles and brings no marvels of deliverance. But when God is seen by faith's closest, fullest eye, prayer makes a history of wonders.

Think about God. Make much of Him, until He broadens and fills the horizon of faith. Then prayer will come into its marvelous inheritance of wonders. The marvels of prayer are seen when we remember that God's purposes are changed by prayer, God's vengeance is stayed by prayer, and God's penalty is remitted by prayer. The whole range of God's dealing with man is affected by prayer. Prayer is a force that must be increasingly used, a force to which all the events of life ought to be subjected.

To *"pray without ceasing"* (1 Thess. 5:17), to pray in everything, and to pray everywhere—these commands of continuity are expressive of the sleepless energy of prayer, of the exhaustless possibilities of prayer, and of its exacting necessity. Prayer can do all things. Prayer must do all things.

> Prayer is the simplest form of speech
>> That infant lips can try;
> Prayer the sublimest strains that reach
>> The majesty on high.

Prayer is asking God for something, and for something that He has promised. Prayer is using the divinely appointed means for obtaining what we need and for accomplishing what God proposes to do on earth.

> Prayer is appointed to convey
>> The blessings God designs to give;
> Long as they live should Christians pray,
>> They learn to pray when first they live.

Prayer brings to us blessings that we need, that only God can give, and that prayer alone can convey to us. In their broadest fullness, the possibilities of prayer are to be found in the very nature of prayer! This service of prayer is not a mere rite, a ceremony through which we go, a sort of performance. Prayer is going to God for something needed and desired. Prayer is simply asking God to do for us what He has promised us He will do if we ask Him.

The answer is a part of prayer, God's part of it. God's doing the thing asked for is as much a part of the prayer as the asking of the thing is prayer. Asking is man's part. Giving is God's part. The praying belongs to us. The answer belongs to God.

Man makes the plea, and God makes the answer. The plea and the answer compose the prayer. God is more ready, more willing, and more anxious to give the answer than man is to do the asking. The possibilities of prayer lie in the ability of man to ask large things and in the ability of God to give large things.

God's only condition and limitation of prayer is found in the character of the one who prays. The measure of our faith and praying is the measure of His giving. As our Lord said to the blind men, *"According to your faith be it unto you"* (Matt. 9:29), so it is the same in praying, "According to the measure of your asking, be it unto you." God measures the answer according to the prayer. He is limited by the law of prayer in the measure of the answers He gives to prayer. As is the measure of prayer, so will be the answer.

If the person praying has the characteristics that warrant praying, then the possibilities are unlimited. They are declared to be *"all things whatsoever."* Here there is no limitation in circumference or condition, in character or kind. The man who prays can pray for anything and for everything, and God will give anything and everything. If we limit God in the asking, He will be limited in the giving.

Looking ahead, God declares in His Word that the wonder of wonders will be so great in the last days that everything animate and inanimate will be excited by His power.

> *For, behold, I create new heavens and a new earth: and the former shall not be remembered, nor come into mind. But be ye glad and rejoice for ever in that which I create: for, behold, I create Jerusalem a rejoicing, and her people a joy.*
> (Isa. 65:17–18)

But these days of God's mighty working, the days of His magnificent and wonder-creating power, will be days of magnificent praying. *"And it shall come to pass, that before they call, I will answer; and while they are yet speaking, I will hear"* (v. 24).

It has ever been so. God's marvelous, miracle-working times have been times of marvelous, miracle-working praying. The greatest thing in God's worship by His own estimate is praying! Its chief service and its distinguishing feature is prayer.

Even them will I bring to my holy mountain, and make them joyful in my house of prayer: their burnt offering and their sacrifices shall be accepted upon mine altar; for mine house shall be called an house of prayer for all people.   *(Isa. 56:7)*

This was true under all the gorgeous rites and parade of ceremonies under the Jewish worship. Sacrifice, offering, and the atoning blood were all to be impregnated with prayer. The smoke of burnt offerings and perfumed incense that filled God's house was to be but the flame of prayer, and all of God's people were to be anointed priests to minister at His altar of prayer. So all things were to be done with mighty prayer, because mighty prayer was the fruit and inspiration of mighty faith. But much more is it now true in every way under the more simple service of the Gospel.

The course of nature, the movements of the planets and the clouds, have yielded to the influence of prayer, and God has changed and checked the order of the sun and the seasons under the mighty energies of prayer. It is only necessary to note the remarkable incident when Joshua, through this divine means of prayer, caused the sun and the moon to stand still in order that a more complete victory could be given to the armies of Israel in the contest with the armies of the Amorites.

If we believe God's Word, we are bound to believe that prayer affects God, and affects Him mightily; that prayer avails, and that prayer avails mightily. There are wonders in prayer because there are wonders in God. Prayer has no talismanic influence. It is no mere fetish. It has no so-called powers of magic. It is simply making known our requests to God for things agreeable to His will in the name of Christ. It is just yielding our requests to a Father, who knows all things, who has control of all things, and who is able to do all things. Prayer is infinite ignorance trusting in the wisdom of God. Prayer is the voice of need crying out to Him who is inexhaustible in resources. Prayer is helplessness reposing with childlike confidence on the word of its Father in heaven. Prayer is but the verbal expression of the heart of perfect confidence in the infinite wisdom, the power, and the riches of Almighty God, who has placed at our command in prayer everything we need.

We are taught in God's Word how all the gracious results of such gracious times are to come to the world through prayer. God's heart seems to overflow with delight at the prospect of thus blessing His people. By the mouth of the prophet Joel, God said,

Fear not, O land; be glad and rejoice; for the Lord will do great things. Be not afraid, ye beasts of the field: for the pastures of the wilderness do spring, for the tree beareth her fruit, the fig tree and the vine do yield their strength. Be glad then, ye children of Zion, and rejoice in the Lord your God: for he hath given you the former rain moderately, and he will cause to come down for you the rain, the former rain, and the latter rain in the first month. And the floors shall be full of wheat, and the vats shall overflow with wine and oil. And I will restore to you the years that the locust hath eaten, the cankerworm, and the caterpillar, and the palmerworm, my great army which I sent among you. And ye shall eat in plenty, and be satisfied, and praise the name of the Lord your God, that hath dealt wondrously with you: and my people shall never be ashamed. And ye shall know that I am in the midst of Israel, and that I am the Lord your God, and none else: and my people shall never be ashamed. (Joel 2:21–27)

What wonderful, material things are these that God proposes to bestow upon His people! They are marvelous temporal blessings He promises to bestow on them. They almost astonish the mind when they are studied. But God does not restrict His large blessings to temporal things. Looking down the ages, He foresaw Pentecost and made these exceedingly great and precious promises concerning the outpouring of the Holy Spirit, these very words being quoted by Peter on that glad Day of Pentecost:

And it shall come to pass afterward, that I will pour out my Spirit upon all flesh; and your sons and your daughters shall prophesy, your old men shall dream dreams, your young men shall see visions: and also upon the servants and upon the handmaids in those days will I pour out my spirit. And I will show wonders in the heavens and in the earth, blood, and fire, and pillars of smoke. The sun shall be turned into darkness, and the moon into blood, before the great and the terrible day

266

of the Lord come. And it shall come to pass, that whosoever shall call on the name of the Lord shall be delivered; for in mount Zion and in Jerusalem shall be deliverance, as the Lord hath said, and in the remnant whom the Lord shall call.

(Joel 2:28–32)

But these marvelous blessings will not be bestowed upon the people by sovereign power, nor will they be given unconditionally. God's people must do something preceding such glorious results. Fasting and prayer must play an important part as conditions of receiving such large blessings. By the mouth of the same prophet, God thus spoke:

Therefore also now, saith the LORD, turn ye even to me with all your heart, and with fasting, and with weeping, and with mourning: and rend your heart, and not your garments, and turn unto the LORD your God: for he is gracious and merciful, slow to anger, and of great kindness, and repenteth him of the evil. Who knoweth if he will turn and repent, and leave a blessing behind him; even a meat offering and a drink offering unto the LORD your God? Blow the trumpet in Zion, sanctify a fast, call a solemn assembly: gather the people, sanctify the congregation, assemble the elders, gather the children, and those that suck the breasts: let the bridegroom go forth of his chamber, and the bride out of her closet. Let the priests, the ministers of the LORD, weep between the porch and the altar, and let them say, Spare thy people, O LORD, and give not thine heritage to reproach, that the heathen should rule over them: wherefore should they say among the people, Where is their God? Then will the LORD be jealous for his land, and pity his people. Yea, the LORD will answer and say unto his people, Behold I will send you corn, and wine, and oil, and ye shall be satisfied therewith: and I will no more make you a reproach among the heathen. (Joel 2:12–19)

Prayer reaches even as far as the presence of God goes. It reaches everywhere because God is everywhere. Let us read from Psalm 139:8–10.

If I ascend up into heaven, thou art there: if I make my bed in hell, behold, thou art there. If I take the wings of the morning, and dwell in the uttermost parts of the sea; even there shall thy hand lead me, and thy right hand shall hold me.

This may be said as truly of prayer as it is said of the God of prayer. The mysteries of death have been fathomed by prayer, and its victims have been brought back to life by the power of prayer, because God holds dominion over death, and prayer reaches where God reigns. Elisha and Elijah both invaded the realms of death by their prayers, and asserted and established the power of God as the power of prayer. Peter by prayer brought back to life the saintly Dorcas to the early church. Paul doubtless exercised the power of prayer as he fell upon and embraced Eutychus, who fell out of the window when Paul preached at night.

Our Lord several times explicitly declared the far-reaching possibilities and the unlimited nature of prayer as covering *"all things whatsoever."* The conditions of prayer are exalted into a personal union with Himself. That successful praying glorified God was the condition upon which laborers of first quality and of sufficient numbers were to be secured in order to press forward God's work in the world.

The giving of all good things is conditioned upon asking for them. The giving of the Holy Spirit to God's children is based upon the asking of the children of God. God's will on earth can only be secured by prayer. Daily bread is obtained and sanctified by prayer. Reverence, forgiveness of sins, deliverance from the Evil One, and salvation from temptation are in the hands of prayer.

The first jeweled foundation Christ put forth as the basic principle of His religion in the Sermon on the Mount reads like this: *"Blessed are the poor in spirit: for theirs is the kingdom of heaven"* (Matt. 5:3). As prayer follows from the inner sense of need, and prayer is the utterance of a deep poverty-stricken spirit, so it is evident that being *"poor in spirit"* is where a person can pray and where he does pray.

Prayer is a tremendous force in the world. Consider this picture of prayer and its wonderful possibilities. God's cause is quiet and motionless on the earth. An angel, strong and impatient to be of service, waits around the throne of God in heaven. In order to move things on earth and give impetus to the movements of God's cause in this world, he gathers all the prayers of all God's saints in all ages, and puts them before God just as Aaron used to perfume himself with the delicious incense when he entered the holy sanctuary, made awesome by the immediate presence of God. The angel impregnates all the air with that holy offering of prayers, and then takes its fiery body and casts it on the earth.

Note the remarkable result. *"There were voices, and thunderings, and lightnings, and an earthquake"* (Rev. 8:5). What tremendous force is this that has thus convulsed the earth? The answer is that it is the *"prayers of the saints"* (v. 4), turned loose by the angel around the throne, who has charge of those prayers. This mighty force is prayer, like the power of earth's mightiest dynamite.

Take another fact showing the wonders worked by Almighty God in answer to the praying of His true prophet. The nation of God's people was fearfully apostate in head and heart and life. A man of God went to the apostate king with the fearful message that meant so much to the land: *"There shall not be dew nor rain these years, but according to my word"* (1 Kings 17:1). From where comes this mighty force that can stay the clouds, seal up the rain, and hold back the dew? Who is this who speaks with such authority? Is there any force that can do this on earth? Only one, and that force is prayer, wielded in the hands of a praying prophet of God. It is he who has influence with God in prayer, who thus dares to assume such authority over the forces of nature. This man Elijah is skilled in the use of that tremendous force. And Elijah *"prayed earnestly...and it rained not on the earth by the space of three years and six months"* (James 5:17).

But this is not the whole story. He who could by prayer lock up the clouds and seal up the rain, could also unlock the clouds and unseal the rain by the same mighty power of prayer. *"And he prayed again, and the heaven gave rain, and the earth brought forth her fruit"* (v. 18).

Mighty is the power of prayer. Wonderful are its fruits. Remarkable things are brought to pass by men of prayer. Many are the wonders of prayer performed by an almighty hand. The evidences of prayer's accomplishments almost stagger us. They challenge our faith. They encourage our expectations when we pray.

From a cursory overview like this, we get a bird's-eye view of the large possibilities of prayer and the urgent necessity of prayer. We see how God commits Himself into the hands of those who truly pray. Great are the wonders of prayer because great is the God who hears and answers prayer. Great are these wonders because great are the rich promises made by a great God to those who pray.

We have seen prayer's far-reaching possibilities and its absolute, unquestioned necessity. We have also seen that the foregoing particulars and elaboration were requisite in order to bring the subject more clearly, truly, and strongly before our minds. The church more than ever needs profound convictions of the vast importance of prayer in prosecuting the work committed to it. More praying and better praying must be done if the church is to be able to perform the difficult, delicate, responsible task given to her by her Lord and Master.

Defeat awaits a non-praying church. Success is sure to follow a church given to much prayer. The supernatural element in the church, without which it must fail, comes only through praying. More time in this bustling age must be given to prayer by a God-called church. More thought must be given to prayer in this thoughtless, silly age of superficial religion. More heart and soul must be in the praying that is done if the church would go forth in the strength of her Lord and perform the wonders that is her heritage by divine promise.

> O Spirit of the living God,
> In all Thy plenitude of grace,
> Where'er the foot of man hath trod,
> Descend on our apostate race.
>
> Give tongues of fire and hearts of love,
> To preach the reconciling word,
> Give power and unction from above,
> Where'er the joyful sound is heard.

It might be in order to give an instance or two in the life of John Wesley, showing some remarkable displays of spiritual power. Many times it has been stated this noted man gathered his company together and prayed all night, or until the mighty power of God came upon them. It was at a watch night service at Fetter Lane, December 31, 1738, when Charles and John Wesley, with George Whitefield, sat up until after midnight singing and praying. This is the account:

> About three o'clock in the morning, as we were continuing instant in prayer, the power of God came mightily upon us, so that many cried out for exceeding joy, and many fell to the ground. As soon as we had recovered a little from that awe and amazement at the presence of His majesty, we broke out with one voice, "We praise thee, O God! We acknowledge thee to be the Lord!"

On another occasion, Mr. Wesley gave us this account: "After midnight, about a hundred of us walked home together, singing, rejoicing, and praising God."

Often did this godly man make the record to this effect: "We continued in ministering the Word and in prayer and praise till morning." One of his all-night wrestlings in prayer alone with God is said to have greatly affected a Catholic priest, who was really awakened by the occurrence to a realization of his spiritual condition.

As often as God manifested His power in scriptural times in working wonders through prayer, He has not left Himself without witness in modern times. Prayer brings the Holy Spirit upon men today in answer to persistent, continued prayer just as it did before Pentecost. The wonders of prayer have not ceased.

15

Prayer and Divine Providence

When a soul is tempted to doubt the existence of God, arguments by way of reason and wisdom may convince him; he may get a little light from them. But sometimes God will come into his soul with an immediate beam and scatter all his doubts, more than a thousand arguments can do. As for knowing there is a God, the way of wisdom unties the knot; but the other cuts it in pieces. So it is in all temptations, when a man goes the way of wisdom and reason and looks into his own heart and there sees the work of grace and argues from all God's dealings with him. Yet all these cannot satisfy a man, unless God comes with a light in his spirit, and all his bolts and shackles are knocked off in a moment. Here lies the contrast between the way of wisdom and the way of revelation.
—Thomas Goodwin

PRAYER and the divine providence are closely related. They stand in close companionship. They cannot possibly be separated. So closely connected are they that to deny one is to abolish the other. Prayer supposes a providence, while providence is the result of and belongs to prayer. All answers to prayer are but the intervention of the providence of God in the affairs of men. Providence has to do especially with a praying people. Prayer, providence, and the Holy Spirit form a triune relationship, cooperate with each other, and are in perfect harmony with one another. Prayer is but the request of man for God through the Holy Spirit to interfere on the behalf of him who prays.

What is termed *providence* is the divine superintendence over earth and its affairs. It implies gracious provisions that Almighty

God makes for all His creatures, animate and inanimate, intelligent or otherwise. Once we admit that God is the creator and preserver of all men and concede that He is wise and intelligent, logically we are driven to the conclusion that Almighty God has a direct superintendence over those whom He has created and whom He preserves. In fact, creation and preservation assume a superintending providence. What is called divine providence is simply Almighty God governing the world for its best interests and overseeing everything for the good of mankind.

Men talk about a "general providence" as separate from a "special providence." There is no general providence but what is made up of special providences. A general supervision on the part of God supposes a special and individual supervision of each person, even every creature, animal and all alike.

God is everywhere, watching, superintending, overseeing, governing everything in the highest interest of man, and carrying forward His plans and executing His purposes in creation and redemption. He is not an absentee God. He did not make the world with all that is in it, turn it over to so-called natural laws, and then retire into the secret places of the universe, having no regard for it or for the working of His laws. His hand is still on the throttle. The work is not beyond His control. Earth's inhabitants and its affairs are not running independently of Almighty God.

Any and all providences are special providences, and prayer and this sort of providence work hand in hand. God's hand is in everything. None are beyond Him or beneath His notice. This is not to imply that God orders everything that comes to pass. Man is still a free agent, but the wisdom of Almighty God comes out when we remember that while man is free, and the Devil is abroad in the land, God can superintend and overrule earth's affairs for the good of man and for His glory, and cause even the wrath of man to praise Him.

Nothing occurs by accident under the superintendence of an all-wise and perfectly just God. Nothing happens by chance in God's moral or natural government. God is a God of order, a God of law, but nonetheless a superintendent in the interest of His intelligent and redeemed creatures. Nothing can take place without the knowledge of God!

> His all surrounding sight surveys
> Our rising and our rest;

Our public walks, our private ways,
The secrets of our breasts.

Jesus Christ set this matter at rest when He said,

*Are not two sparrows sold for a farthing? and one of them
shall not fall on the ground without your Father. But the very
hairs of your head are all numbered. Fear ye not therefore, ye
are of more value than many sparrows.* (Matt. 10:29–31)

God cannot be ruled out of the world. The doctrine of prayer brings
Him directly into the world and moves Him to a direct interference
with all of this world's affairs.

To rule Almighty God out of the providences of life is to strike
a direct blow at prayer and its effectiveness. Nothing takes place in
the world without God's consent, yet not in a sense that He either
approves everything or is responsible for all things that happen.
God is not the author of sin.

The question is sometimes asked, "Is God in everything?" as if
there are some things that are outside of the government of God,
beyond His attention, with which He is not concerned. If God is not
in everything, what is the Christian doing praying according to
Paul's directions, *"Be careful for nothing; but in every thing by
prayer and supplication with thanksgiving let your requests be
made known unto God"* (Phil. 4:6)?

Are we to pray for some things and about things with which
God has nothing to do? According to the doctrine that God is not in
everything, then we are outside the realm of God when we *"in
every thing"* make our requests unto God. Then what will we do
with that large promise, so comforting to all of God's saints in all
ages and in all climates, a promise that belongs to prayer and that
is embraced in a special providence: *"And we know that all things
work together for good to them that love God"* (Rom. 8:28)?

If God is not in everything, then what are the things we are to
expect from the *"all things"* that *"work together for good to them
that love God"*? And if God is not in everything in His providence,
what are the things that are to be left out of our praying?

We can lay it down as a proposition, borne out by Scripture,
which has a sure foundation, that nothing ever comes into the life
of God's saints without His consent. God is always there when it
occurs. He is not far away. He whose eyes are on the sparrow has

His eyes also upon His saints. His presence that fills immensity is always where His saints are. *"Certainly I will be with thee"* (Exod. 3:12) is the word of God to every child of His.

"The angel of the LORD encampeth round about them that fear him, and delivereth them" (Ps. 34:7). Nothing can touch those who fear God, except with the permission of the angel of the Lord. Nothing can break through the encampment without the permission of the captain of the Lord's hosts. Sorrows, afflictions, want, trouble, or even death cannot enter this divine encampment without the consent of Almighty God, and even then it is to be used by God in His plans for the good of His saints and for carrying out His purposes.

> *For I am persuaded, that neither death, nor life, nor angels, nor principalities, nor powers, nor things present, nor things to come, nor height, nor depth, nor any other creature, shall be able to separate us from the love of God, which is in Christ Jesus our Lord.*　　　　　　　　　　　　　　*(Rom. 8:38–39)*

These evil things, unpleasant and afflictive, may come with divine permission, but God is on the spot, His hand is in all of them, and He sees to it that they are woven into His plans. He causes them to be overruled for the good of His people, and eternal good is brought out of them. These things, with hundreds of others, belong to the disciplinary processes of Almighty God in administering His government for the children of men.

The providence of God reaches as far as the realm of prayer. It has to do with everything for which we pray. Nothing is too small for the eye of God, nothing too insignificant for His notice and His care. God's providence has to do with even the stumbling of the feet of His saints. *"For he shall give his angels charge over thee, to keep thee in all thy ways. They shall bear thee up in their hands, lest thou dash thy foot against a stone"* (Ps. 91:11–12).

Read again our Lord's words about the sparrow, for He says, *"Five sparrows [are] sold for two farthings, and not one of them is forgotten before God"* (Luke 12:6). Paul asked the pointed question, *"Doth God take care for oxen?"* (1 Cor. 9:9). His care reaches to the smallest things and has to do with the most insignificant matters that concern men. He who believes in the God of providence is prepared to see His hand in all things that come to him and can pray about everything.

275

Not that the saint who trusts the God of providence and who takes all things to God in prayer can explain the mysteries of divine providence, but the praying ones recognize God in everything, see Him in all that comes to them, and are ready to say as John said to Peter at the Sea of Galilee, *"It is the Lord"* (John 21:7).

Praying saints do not presume to interpret God's dealings with them nor undertake to explain God's providences, but they have learned to trust God in the dark as well as in the light, to have faith in God even when "cares like a wild deluge come, and storms of sorrow fall."

"Though he slay me, yet will I trust in him" (Job 13:15). Praying saints rest themselves upon the words of Jesus to Peter: *"What I do thou knowest not now; but thou shalt know hereafter"* (John 13:7). None but the praying ones can see God's hands in the providences of life. *"Blessed are the pure in heart: for they shall see God"* (Matt. 5:8), shall see God here in His providences, in His Word, in His church. These are they who do not rule God out of earth's affairs, and who believe God intervenes for them in matters of earth.

While God's providence is over all men, yet His supervision and administration of His government are particularly in the interest of His people. Prayer brings God's providence into action. Prayer puts God to work in overseeing and directing earth's affairs for the good of men. Prayer opens the way when it is shut up or hampered.

Providence deals with temporalities most especially. It is in this realm that the providence of God shines brightest and is most apparent. It has to do with food and clothing, with business difficulties, with interposing and saving from danger, and with helping in emergencies at opportune and critical times.

The feeding of the Israelites during the wilderness journey is a striking illustration of the providence of God in taking care of the temporal wants of His people. His dealings with those people show how He provided for them in that long pilgrimage.

> Day by day the manna fell,
> Oh, to learn this lesson well!
> Still by constant mercy fed,
> Give me, Lord, my daily bread.
>
> "Day by day" the promise reads,
> Daily strength for daily needs;

> Cast foreboding fears away,
> Take the manna of today.

Our Lord teaches this same lesson of providence that clothes and feeds His people in the Sermon on the Mount, when He says, *"Take no thought...what ye shall eat, or what ye shall drink; nor yet for your body, what ye shall put on"* (Matt. 6:25). He directs attention to the fact that it is God's providence that feeds the fowls of the air and clothes the lilies of the field. Then He asks, if God does all this for birds and flowers, will He not care for His children?

All of this teaching leads up to the need of a childlike, implicit trust in an overruling providence, which looks after the temporal needs of the children of men. And let it be noted especially that all this teaching stands closely connected in the utterances of our Lord with what He says about prayer, thus closely connecting a divine oversight with prayer and its promises.

We have an impressive lesson on divine providence in the case of Elijah when he was sent to the brook Cherith, where God actually employed the ravens to feed His prophet. Here was an interposition so plain that God cannot be ruled out of life's temporalities. Before God will allow His servant to lack bread, He moves the birds of the air to do His bidding and take care of His prophet.

Nor was this all. When the brook ran dry, God sent him to a poor widow, who had just enough meal and oil for the urgent needs of the good woman and her son. Yet she divided with him her last morsel of bread. What was the result? The providence of God intervened, and as long as the drought lasted, the cruse of oil never failed, nor did the meal in the barrel give out. The Old Testament sparkles with illustrations of the provisions of Almighty God for His people and shows clearly God's overruling providence. In fact, the Old Testament is largely the account of a providence that dealt with a peculiar people, that anticipated their every temporal need, that ministered to them when in emergencies, and that sanctified to them their troubles.

It is worthwhile to read that old hymn of Newton's, which has in it so much of the providence of God:

> Though troubles assail, and dangers affright,
> Though friends should all fail, and foes all unite,
> Yet one thing secures me, whatever betide,
> The promise assures us, the Lord will provide!

The birds without barns or storehouse are fed,
From them let us learn, to trust for our bread;
His saints what is fitting, shall ne'er be denied,
So long as it's written, the Lord will provide.

In fact, many of our old hymns are filled with sentiments in song about a divine providence, which are worthwhile to be read and sung even in these days.

God is in the most afflictive and sorrowing events of life. All such events are subjects of prayer, and this is so for the reason that everything that comes into the life of the praying one is in the providence of God and takes place under His overseeing hand. Some would rule God out of the sad and hard things of life. They tell us that God has nothing to do with certain events that bring such grief to us. They say that God is not in the death of children, that they die from natural causes, and that it is but the working of natural laws.

Let us ask what are nature's laws but the laws of God, the laws by which God rules the world? And what is nature anyway? And who made nature? How great the need to know that God is above nature, is in control of nature, and is in nature! We need to know that nature or natural laws are but the servants of Almighty God who made these laws, that He is directly in them, and they are but the divine servants to carry out God's gracious designs and are made to execute His gracious purposes. The God of providence, the God to whom Christians pray, the God who interposes in behalf of the children of men for their good, is above nature, in perfect and absolute control of all that belongs to nature. And no law of nature can crush the life out of even a child without God giving His consent, and without such a sad event occurring directly under His all-seeing eye, and without His being immediately present.

David believed this doctrine when he fasted and prayed for the life of his child, for why pray and fast for a baby to be spared if God has nothing to do with his death if he should die?

Moreover, is it possible that God, who *"doth...care for oxen"* (1 Cor. 9:9) and has a direct oversight of the sparrows that fall to the ground, could yet have nothing to do with the going out of this world of an immortal child? Still further, the death of a child, no matter if it should come alone, as some people claim, by the operation of the laws of nature, is a great affliction to the parents of the child. Where do these innocent parents come in under any such doctrine? It becomes a great sorrow to mother and father. Are they not to recognize the hand of God in the death of the child? Is there no providence or divine oversight to them in the taking away of their child?

David recognized clearly that God had to do with keeping his child in life, that prayer might avail in saving his child from death, and that when the child died it was because God had allowed it. Prayer and providence in all this affair worked in harmonious co-operation, and David thoroughly understood it. No child ever dies without the direct permission of Almighty God, and such an event takes place in His providence for wise and beneficent ends. God works it into His plans concerning the child himself, the parents, and all concerned. Moreover, it is a subject of prayer whether the child lives or dies.

> In each event of life how clear,
>   Thy ruling hand I see;
> Each blessing to my soul most dear,
>   Because conferred by Thee.

16

Prayer and Divine Providence
(Continued)

A proper idea of prayer is the pouring out of the soul before God, with the hand of faith placed on the head of the Sacrificial Offering, imploring mercy, and presenting itself as a free-will offering unto God, giving up body, soul, and spirit, to be guided and governed as may seem good to His heavenly wisdom, desiring only perfectly to love Him and to serve Him with all its powers, at all times, while He has a being.
—Adam Clarke

Two kinds of providences are seen in God's dealings with men: direct providences and permissive providences. God orders some things, and others He permits. But when He permits an afflictive dispensation to come into the life of His saint, even though it may originate in a wicked mind and be the act of a sinner, yet before it strikes His saint and touches him, it becomes God's providence to the saint.

In other words, God consents to some things in this world without in the least being responsible for them, or in the least excusing him who originates them, many of them very painful and afflictive. However, such events or things always become to the saint of God the providence of God to him, so that the saint can say in each and all of these sad and distressing experiences, *"It is the LORD: let him do what seemeth him good"* (1 Sam. 3:18). Or with the psalmist, he may say, *"I was dumb, I opened not my mouth; because thou didst it"* (Ps. 39:9).

This was the explanation of all of Job's severe afflictions. They came to him in the providence of God, even though they had their origin in the mind of Satan, who devised them and put them into execution. God gave Satan permission to afflict Job, to take away his property, and to rob him of his children. But Job did not attribute these things to blind chance, nor to accident, neither did he charge them to satanic agency, but said, *"The LORD gave, and the LORD hath taken away; blessed be the name of the LORD"* (Job 1:21). He took these things as coming from God, whom he feared, served, and trusted.

Job's words to his wife when she left God out of the question and wickedly told her husband, *"Curse God, and die"* (Job 2:9), have the same effect. Job replied, *"Thou speakest as one of the foolish women speaketh. What? shall we receive good at the hand of God, and shall we not receive evil?"* (v. 10).

It is no surprise under such a view of God's dealings with Job that it should be recorded of this man of faith, *"In all this did not Job sin with his lips"* (v. 10), and in another place was it said, *"In all this Job sinned not, nor charged God foolishly"* (Job 1:22). In nothing concerning God and the events of life do men talk more foolishly and even wickedly than when they ignorantly make their judgments on the providences of God in this world. Oh, that we had men after the type of Job who, even though afflictions and privations become extremely severe, they see the hand of God in providence and openly recognize God in it.

The sequel to all these painful experiences goes to illustrate that familiar text of Paul: *"And we know that all things work together for good to them that love God"* (Rom. 8:28). Job received back more in the end than was ever taken away from him. He emerged from under these tremendous troubles with victory and became, to this day, the exponent and example of great patience and strong faith in God's providences. *"Ye have heard of the patience of Job"* (James 5:11) rings down the line of divine revelation. God took hold of the evil acts of Satan, worked them into His plans, and brought great good out of them. He made evil work out for good without in the least endorsing the evil or contributing to it.

We have the same gracious truth of divine providence evidenced in the story of Joseph and his brothers, who sold him wickedly into Egypt and forsook him and deceived their old father. All this had its origin in their evil minds. Yet, when it reached God's plans and purposes, it became God's providence both to Joseph and to the future of Jacob's descendants. Hear Joseph as he spoke to his brothers after he had disclosed himself to them down in Egypt—in which he traced all the painful events back to the mind of God and made them have to do with fulfilling God's purposes concerning Jacob and his posterity:

> *Now therefore be not grieved, nor angry with yourselves, that ye sold me hither: for God did send me before you to preserve life....And God sent me before you to preserve you a posterity in the earth, and to save your lives by a great deliverance. So now it was not you that sent me hither, but God.*
>
> *(Gen. 45:5, 7–8)*

Cowper's well-known hymn might well be read in this connection, one verse of which is sufficient just now:

> God moves in a mysterious way,
> His wonders to perform;
> He plants His footsteps in the sea,
> And rides upon the storm.

The very same line of argument appears in the betrayal of our Lord by Judas. Of course it was the wicked act of an evil man, but it never touched our Lord until the Father gave His consent. God then took the evil design of Judas and worked it into His own plans for the redemption of the world. It did not excuse Judas in the least that good came out of his wicked act, but it does magnify the wisdom and greatness of God in so overruling it in a manner in which man's redemption was secured. It is always so in God's dealings with man. Things that come to us from second causes are no surprise to God, nor are they beyond His control. His hand can take hold of them in answer to prayer, and He can make afflictions from whatever quarter they may come, work *"for us a far more exceeding and eternal weight of glory"* (2 Cor. 4:17).

The providence of God goes before His saints, opens the way, removes difficulties, solves problems, and brings deliverance when escape seems hopeless. God brought Israel out of Egypt by the hand of Moses, His chosen leader of that people. They came to the Red Sea, but there were the waters in front, with no crossing or bridges. On one side were high mountains, and behind came the hosts of Pharaoh. Every avenue of escape was closed. There seemed to be no hope. Despair almost reigned. But there was one way open that men overlooked, the upward way.

A man of prayer as well as the man of faith in God, Moses was on the ground. This man of prayer, who recognized God in providence, with commanding force, spoke to the people like this: *"Fear ye not, stand still, and see the salvation of the LORD"* (Exod. 14:13). With this he lifted up his rod, and according to divine command, he stretched his hand over the sea. The waters divided, and the command issued forth, *"Speak unto the children of Israel, that they go forward"* (v. 15). And Israel went over the sea on dry ground. God had opened a way, and what seemed an impossible emergency was remarkably turned into a wonderful deliverance.

Nor is this the only time that God has interposed on behalf of His people when their way was shut up. The whole history of the Jews is the story of God's providence. The Old Testament cannot be accepted as true without receiving the doctrine of a divine, overruling providence.

The Bible is preeminently a divine revelation. It reveals things. It discovers, uncovers, and brings to light things concerning God, His character, and His manner of governing this world and its inhabitants that are not discoverable by human reason, by science, or by philosophy. The Bible is a book in which God reveals Himself to men. And this is particularly true when we consider God's care of His creatures, His oversight of the world, and His superintendence of its affairs. And to dispute the doctrine of providence is to discredit the entire revelation of God's Word. Everywhere this Word discovers God's hand in man's affairs.

The Old Testament especially, but also the New Testament, is the story of prayer and providence. It is the tale of God's dealings with men of prayer and faith, of His direct interference in earth's affairs, and of God's manner of superintending the world in the interest of His people and in carrying forward His work in His plans and purposes in creation and redemption.

Praying men and God's providence go together. This was thoroughly understood by the praying people of the Scripture. They prayed over everything because God was involved with everything. They took all things to God in prayer because they believed in a divine providence that had to do with all things.

They believed in an ever present God who had not retired into the secret recesses of space, leaving His saints and His creatures to the mercy of a tyrant, called nature, and its laws—blind, unyielding, with no regard for anyone who stood in its way. If that were the correct concept of God, why would anyone pray to Him? That God would be too far away to hear their prayers, and too unconcerned to trouble Himself about those on earth.

These men of prayer had an implicit faith in a God of special providence, who would gladly, promptly, and readily respond to their cries for help in times of need and in seasons of distress. The so-called "laws of nature" did not trouble them in the least. God is above nature, in control of nature, while nature is but the servant of Almighty God. Nature's laws are but His own laws, since nature is but the offspring of the divine hand. Laws of nature may be suspended, and no evil would result.

Every intelligent person is familiar with this every day when he sees man overruling and overcoming the law of gravity, and no one is surprised or raises his hand or voice in horror at the thought of nature's laws being violated. God is a God of law and order, and all His laws in nature, in providence, and in grace work together in perfect accord with no clash or disharmony.

God suspends or overcomes the laws of disease and rain often without or independent of prayer. But quite often He does this in answer to prayer. Prayer for rain or for dry weather is not outside the moral government of God, nor is it asking God to violate any law that He has made, but only asking Him to give rain in His own way, according to His own laws. So also the prayer for the rebuking of disease is not a request at war with natural law, but is a prayer in accordance with law, even the law of prayer, a law set in operation by Almighty God, just as the so-called natural law that governs rain or that controls disease.

The believer in the law of prayer has strong grounds on which to base his plea; the believer in divine providence, the companion of prayer, stands equally on strong granite foundations, from which he need not be shaken. These twin doctrines stand fast and will abide forever.

> In every condition, in sickness, in health,
> In poverty's vale or abounding in wealth;
> At home or abroad, on the land or the sea,
> As thy days may demand shall thy strength ever be.

Book
Four

Essentials of
Prayer

1

Prayer and the Entire Man

Henry Clay Trumbull spoke forth the Infinite in terms of our world, and the Eternal in the forms of our human life. Some years ago, on a ferry boat, I met a gentleman who knew him, and I told him that when I had last seen Dr. Trumbull, a fortnight before, he had spoken of him. "Oh, yes," said my friend, "he was a great Christian, so real, so intense. He was at my home years ago and we were talking about prayer. 'Why, Trumbull,' I said, 'you don't mean to say if you lost a pencil you would pray about it, and ask God to help you find it.' 'Of course I would; of course I would,' was his instant and excited reply." Of course he would. Was not his faith a real thing? Like the Savior, he put his doctrine strongly by taking an extreme illustration to embody his principle, but the principle was fundamental. He did trust God in everything. And the Father honored the trust of his child.

—Robert E. Speer

PRAYER has to do with the entire man. Prayer takes in man in his whole being—mind, soul, and body. It takes the whole man to pray, and prayer affects the entire man in its gracious results. As the whole nature of man enters into prayer, so also all that belongs to man is the beneficiary of prayer. All of man receives benefits in prayer. The whole man must be given to God in praying.

The largest results in praying come to him who gives himself—all of himself, all that belongs to himself—to God. This is the secret of full consecration (a condition of successful praying) and the sort of praying that brings the largest fruits.

The men of olden times who were very successful in prayer, who brought the largest things to pass, who moved God to do great things, were those who were entirely given over to God in their praying. God wants, and must have, all that there is in man in answering his prayers. He must have wholehearted men through whom to work out His purposes and plans concerning men. God must have men in their entirety. No double-minded man need apply. No vacillating man can be used. No man with a divided allegiance to God, the world, and self, can do the praying that is needed.

Holiness is wholeness, and so God wants holy men, men wholehearted and true, for His service and for the work of praying.

And the very God of peace sanctify you wholly; and I pray God your whole spirit and soul and body be preserved blameless unto the coming of our Lord Jesus Christ.   (1 Thess. 5:23)

These are the sort of men God wants for leaders of the hosts of Israel, and these are the kind out of which the praying class is formed.

Man is a trinity in one, and yet man is neither a trinity nor a dual creature when he prays, but a unit. Man is one in all the essentials and acts and attitudes of piety. Soul, spirit, and body are to unite in all things pertaining to life and godliness.

The body, first of all, engages in prayer, since it assumes the praying attitude in prayer. Prostration of the body becomes us in praying as well as prostration of the soul. The attitude of the body counts much in prayer, although it is true that the heart may be haughty and lifted up, and the mind listless and wandering, and the praying a mere form, even while the knees are bent in prayer.

Daniel knelt upon his knees three times a day in prayer. Solomon knelt in prayer at the dedication of the temple. Our Lord in Gethsemane prostrated Himself in that memorable season of praying just before His betrayal. Where there is earnest and faithful praying, the body always takes on the form most suited to the state of the soul at the time. In that way the body joins the soul in praying.

The entire man must pray. The whole man—life, heart, temper, mind—are in it. Each and all join in the prayer exercise. Doubt, double-mindedness, division of the affections are all foreign to the prayer closet. Character and conduct, undefiled, made whiter than snow, are mighty potencies and are the most seemly beauties for the closet hour and for the struggles of prayer.

A loyal intellect must conspire and add the energy and fire of its undoubting and undivided faith to that kind of hour, the hour of prayer. Necessarily the mind enters into the praying. First of all, it takes thought to pray. The intellect teaches us that we ought to pray. By serious thinking beforehand, the mind prepares itself for approaching the throne of grace. Thought goes before entrance into the prayer closet and prepares the way for true praying. It considers what will be asked for in the closet hour.

True praying does not leave to the inspiration of the hour what will be the requests of that hour. Praying is asking for something definite of God; therefore, the thought arises beforehand: "What shall I ask for at this hour?" All vain and evil and frivolous thoughts are eliminated, and the mind is given over entirely to God, thinking of Him, of what is needed, and of what has been received in the past.

By every token, prayer, in taking hold of the entire man, does not leave out the mind. The very first step in prayer is a mental one. The disciples took that first step when they said to Jesus, *"Lord, teach us to pray"* (Luke 11:1). We must be taught through the intellect, and only as far as the intellect is given up to God in prayer will we be able to learn well and readily the lesson of prayer.

Paul knew that the nature of prayer is spread over the whole man. It must be so. It takes the whole man to embrace in its godlike sympathies the entire race of man—the sorrows, the sins, and the death of Adam's fallen race. It takes the whole man to run parallel with God's high and sublime will in saving mankind. It takes the whole man to stand with our Lord Jesus Christ as the one Mediator between God and sinful man. This is the doctrine Paul taught in his prayer directory found in 1 Timothy 2.

Nowhere does it appear so clearly that it requires the entire man in all departments of his being to pray than in this teaching of Paul. It takes the whole man to pray, until all the storms that agitate his soul are calmed to a great calm, until the stormy winds and waves cease as by a godlike spell. It takes the whole man to pray, until cruel tyrants and unjust rulers are changed in their natures and lives, as well as in their governing qualities, or until they cease to rule. It requires the entire man in praying, until high and proud and unspiritual ecclesiastics become gentle, lowly, and religious, until godliness and gravity bear rule in church and in state, in home and in business, in public as well as in private life.

It is man's business to pray, and it takes manly men to do it. It is godly business to pray, and it takes godly men to do it. And it is godly men who give themselves over entirely to prayer. Prayer is far-reaching in its influence and in its gracious effects. It is intense and profound business that deals with God and His plans and purposes, and it takes wholehearted men to do it. No halfhearted, half-brained, half-spirited effort will do for this serious, all-important, heavenly business. The whole heart, the whole brain, and the whole spirit must be engaged in the matter of praying, which is so mightily to affect the characters and destinies of men.

The answer of Jesus to the scribe as to what was the first and greatest commandment was as follows: *"Thou shalt love the Lord thy God with all thy heart, and with thy soul, and with all thy strength, and with all thy mind"* (Luke 10:27). In other words, the entire man must love God without reservation. So it takes the same entire man to do the praying that God requires of men. All the powers of man must be engaged in it. God cannot tolerate a divided heart in the love He requires of men, neither can He bear with a divided man in praying.

The psalmist taught this very truth: *"Blessed are they that keep his testimonies, and that seek him with the whole heart"* (Ps. 119:2). It takes wholehearted men to keep God's commandments, and it demands the same sort of men to seek God. These are they who are counted *"blessed."* Upon these wholehearted ones, God's approval rests.

Bringing the case closer home to himself, the psalmist made this declaration as to his own personal practice: *"With my whole heart have I sought thee: O let me not wander from thy commandments"* (v. 10). And, further on, giving us his prayer for a wise and understanding heart, he told us his purposes concerning the keeping of God's law: *"Give me understanding and I shall keep thy law; yea, I shall observe it with my whole heart"* (v. 34).

Just as it requires a whole heart given to God to gladly and fully obey God's commandments, so it takes a whole heart to do effectual praying. Because it requires the whole man to pray, praying is no easy task. Praying is far more than simply bending the knee and saying a few words by rote.

> 'Tis not enough to bend the knee,
> And words of prayer to say;

> The heart must with the lips agree,
> Or else we do not pray.

Praying is no light and trifling exercise. While children should be taught early to pray, praying is no child's task. Prayer draws upon the whole nature of man. Prayer engages all the powers of man's moral and spiritual nature. It is this that explains somewhat the praying of our Lord as described in Hebrews:

Who in the days of his flesh, when he had offered up prayers and supplications with strong crying and tears unto him that was able to save him from death, and was heard in that he feared.   *(Heb. 5:7)*

It takes only a moment's thought to see how such praying of our Lord drew mightily upon all the powers of His being and called into exercise every part of His nature. This is the praying that brings the soul close to God and that brings God down to earth.

Body, soul, and spirit are taxed and brought under tribute to prayer. David Brainerd made this record of his praying: "God enabled me to agonize in prayer until I was wet with perspiration, though in the shade and in a cool place."

The Son of God in Gethsemane was in an agony of prayer, which engaged His whole being:

And when he was at the place, he said unto them, Pray that ye enter not into temptation. And he was withdrawn from them about a stone's cast, and kneeled down, and prayed, saying, Father, if thou be willing, remove this cup from me: nevertheless, not my will, but thine, be done. And there appeared an angel unto him from heaven, strengthening him. And being in an agony he prayed more earnestly: and his sweat was as it were great drops of blood falling down to the ground.
    (Luke 22:40–44)

Here was praying that laid its hands on every part of our Lord's nature, that called forth all the powers of His soul, His mind, and His body. This was praying that took in the entire man.

Paul was acquainted with this kind of praying. In writing to the Roman Christians, he urged them to pray with him after this fashion: *"Now I beseech you, brethren, for the Lord Jesus Christ's sake, and for the love of the Spirit, that ye strive together with me in your prayers to God for me"* (Rom. 15:30).

The words *strive together with me* tell of Paul's praying and how much he put into it. It is not a docile request, not a little thing, this sort of praying, this "striving with me." It has the nature of a great battle, a conflict to win, a great battle to be fought. As the soldier, the praying Christian fights a life-and-death struggle. His honor, his immortality, and eternal life are all in it. This is praying as the athlete struggles for the mastery and for the crown, and as he wrestles or runs a race. Everything depends on the strength he puts in it. Energy, ardor, swiftness, every power of his nature is in it. Every power is quickened and strained to its very utmost. Littleness, halfheartedness, weakness, and laziness are all absent.

Just as it takes the whole man to pray successfully, so in turn the whole man receives the benefits of such praying. As every part of man's complex being enters into true praying, so every part of that same nature receives blessings from God in answer to such praying. This kind of praying engages our undivided hearts, our full consent to be the Lord's, our whole desires.

God sees to it that when the whole man prays, in turn the whole man will be blessed. His body takes in the good of praying, for much praying is done specifically for the body. Food and raiment, health and bodily vigor come in answer to praying. Clear mental action, right thinking, an enlightened understanding, and safe reasoning powers come from praying. Divine guidance means God so moving and impressing the mind, that we will make wise and safe decisions. *"The meek will he guide in judgment"* (Ps. 25:9).

Many a praying preacher has been greatly helped just at this point. The unction of the Holy One that comes upon the preacher invigorates the mind, loosens up thought, and gives utterance. This is the explanation of former days, when men of very limited education had such wonderful liberty of the Spirit in praying and in preaching. Their thoughts flowed as a stream of water. Their entire intellectual machinery felt the impulse of the divine Spirit's gracious influences.

And, of course, the soul receives large benefits in this sort of praying. Thousands can testify to this statement. So we repeat, that as the entire man comes into play in true, earnest, effectual praying, so the entire man—soul, mind, and body—receives the benefits of prayer.

2

Prayer and Humility

*If two angels were to receive at the same moment a com-
mission from God, one to go down and rule earth's grandest
empire, the other to go and sweep the streets of its meanest village, it would be a matter of entire indifference to each which
service fell to his lot, the post of ruler or the post of scavenger;
for the joy of the angels lies only in obedience to God's will,
and with equal joy they would lift a Lazarus in his rags to
Abraham's bosom, or be a chariot of fire to carry an Elijah
home.*   —*John Newton*

TO be humble is to have a low estimate of oneself. It is to be
modest, lowly, with a disposition to seek obscurity. Humility retires
itself from the public gaze. It does not seek publicity or hunt for
high places, neither does it care for prominence. Humility is retiring in its nature. Self-abasement belongs to humility. It is given to
self-depreciation. It never exalts itself in the eyes of others or even
in the eyes of itself. Modesty is one of its most prominent characteristics.

In humility there is the total absence of pride, and it is at the
very farthest distance from anything like self-conceit. There is no
self-praise in humility. Rather, it has the disposition to praise others. *"In honour preferring one another"* (Rom. 12:10). It is not
given to self-exaltation. Humility does not love the uppermost seats
or aspire to the high places. It is willing to take the lowliest seat
and prefers those places where it will be unnoticed. The prayer of
humility is after this fashion:

> Never let the world break in,
> Fix a mighty gulf between;

293

Keep me humble and unknown,
Prized and loved by God alone.

Humility does not have its eyes on self, but rather on God and others. It is poor in spirit, meek in behavior, lowly in heart. *"With all lowliness and meekness, with longsuffering, forbearing one another in love"* (Eph. 4:2).

The parable of the Pharisee and publican is a sermon in brief on humility and self-praise. The Pharisee, given over to self-conceit, wrapped up in himself, seeing only his own self-righteous deeds, catalogs his virtues before God, despising the poor publican who stands afar off. He exalts himself, gives himself over to self-praise, is self-centered, and goes away unjustified, condemned, and rejected by God.

The publican sees no good in himself and is overwhelmed with self-depreciation. Far removed from anything that would take any credit for any good in himself, he does not presume to lift his eyes to heaven; but with downcast countenance he smites himself, crying out, *"God be merciful to me a sinner"* (Luke 18:13).

Our Lord, with great precision, gave us the sequel of the story of these two men, one utterly devoid of humility, the other utterly submerged in the spirit of self-depreciation and lowliness of mind.

I tell you, this man went down to his house justified rather than the other: for every one that exalteth himself shall be abased; and he that humbleth himself shall be exalted.
(Luke 18:14)

God puts a great price on humility of heart. It is good to be clothed with humility as with a garment. It is written, *"God resisteth the proud, but giveth grace unto the humble"* (James 4:6). That which brings the praying soul near to God is humility of heart. That which gives wings to prayer is lowliness of mind. That which gives ready access to the throne of grace is self-depreciation. Pride, self-esteem, and self-praise effectually shut the door of prayer. He who would come to God must approach the Lord with self hidden from his eyes. He must not be puffed up with self-conceit, nor can he be possessed with an overestimate of his virtues and good works.

Humility is a rare Christian grace of great price in the courts of heaven, entering into and being an inseparable condition of effectual praying. It gives access to God when other qualities fail. It takes many descriptions to describe it and many definitions to define it. It is a rare and retiring grace. Its full portrait is found only in the Lord Jesus Christ. Our prayers must be set low before they can ever rise high. Our prayers must have much of the dust on them before they can ever have much of the glory of the skies in them. In our Lord's teaching and system of religion, humility has such prominence and is such a distinguishing feature of His character, that to leave it out of His lesson on prayer would be very unseemly, would not comport with His character, and would not fit into His religious system.

The parable of the Pharisee and publican stands out in such bold relief that we must again refer to it. The Pharisee seemed to be accustomed to prayer. Certainly he should have known by that time how to pray, but, alas, like many others, he seemed never to have learned this invaluable lesson. He leaves business and business hours and walks with steady and fixed steps up to the house of prayer. The position and place are well chosen by him. There is the sacred place, the sacred hour, and the sacred name—each and all invoked by this seemingly praying man. But this praying ecclesiastic, though schooled in prayer by training and by habit, does not really pray. Words are uttered by him, but words are not prayer. God hears his words only to condemn him. A death chill has come from those formal lips of prayer—a death curse from God is on his words of prayer. A solution of pride has entirely poisoned the prayer offering of that hour. His entire praying has been impregnated with self-praise, self-congratulation, and self-exaltation. That season of temple going has had no worship whatever in it.

On the other hand, the publican, smitten with a deep sense of his sins and his inward sinfulness, realizing how poor in spirit he is, how utterly void of anything like righteousness, goodness, or any quality that would commend him to God, his pride within utterly blasted and dead, falls down with humiliation and despair before God while he utters a sharp cry for mercy for his sins and his guilt. A sense of sin and a realization of utter unworthiness have fixed the roots of humility deep down in his soul, and have oppressed self and eye and heart downward to the dust. This is the picture of humility in praying, as opposed to pride in praying. Here we see, by sharp contrast, the utter worthlessness of self-righteousness, self-exaltation, and self-praise in praying, and the great value, the beauty, and the divine commendation that comes to humility of heart, self-depreciation, and self-condemnation when a soul comes before God in prayer.

Happy are they who have no righteousness of their own to plead and no goodness of their own of which to boast. Humility flourishes in the soil of a true and deep sense of our sinfulness and our nothingness. Nowhere does humility grow so rankly and so rapidly and shine so brilliantly, as when it feels all guilty, confesses all sin, and trusts all grace. "I the chief of sinners am, but Jesus died for me." That is praying ground, the ground of humility, low down, far away seemingly, but in reality brought near by the blood of the Lord Jesus Christ. God dwells in the lowly places. He makes such lowly places really the high places to the praying soul.

> Let the world their virtue boast,
>   Their works of righteousness;
> I, a wretch undone and lost,
>   Am freely saved by grace;
> Other title I disclaim,
>   This, only this, is all my plea,
> I the chief of sinners am,
>   But Jesus died for me.

Humility is an indispensable requisite of true prayer. It must be an attribute, a characteristic of prayer. Humility must be in the praying character as light is in the sun. Prayer has no beginning, no ending, no being, without humility. As a ship is made for the sea, so prayer is made for humility, and so humility is made for prayer.

Humility is not abstraction from self, nor does it ignore thought about self. It is a many-phased principle. Humility is born by looking at God and His holiness, and then looking at self and man's unholiness. Humility loves obscurity and silence, dreads applause, esteems the virtues of others, excuses their faults with mildness, easily pardons injuries, fears contempt less and less, and sees the baseness and falsehood in pride. A true nobleness and greatness are in humility. It knows and reveres the inestimable riches of the cross and the humiliations of Jesus Christ. It fears the luster of those virtues admired by men and loves those that are more secret and that are prized by God. It draws comfort even from its own defects, through the abasement that they occasion. It prefers any degree of conscience before all the light in the world.

Somewhat after this order of description is that definable grace of humility, so perfectly drawn in the publican's prayer and so entirely absent from the prayer of the Pharisee. It takes many sittings to make a good picture of it.

Humility holds in its keeping the very life of prayer. Neither pride nor vanity can pray. Humility, though, is much more than the absence of vanity and pride. It is a positive quality, a substantial force, that energizes prayer. There is no power in prayer to ascend without it. Humility springs from a lowly estimate of ourselves and of our deserving. The Pharisee did not truly pray, though he was well schooled and habituated to pray, because there was no humility in his praying. The publican prayed, though banned by the public and receiving no encouragement from church sentiment, because he prayed in humility.

To be clothed with humility is to be clothed with a praying garment. Humility is just feeling little because we are little. Humility is realizing our unworthiness because we are unworthy, the feeling and declaring ourselves sinners because we are sinners. Kneeling suits us very well as the physical posture of prayer because it speaks of humility.

The Pharisee's proud estimate of himself and his supreme contempt for his neighbor closed the gates of prayer to him, while humility opened wide those gates to the defamed and reviled publican. That fearful saying of our Lord about the works of big, religious workers in the latter part of the Sermon on the Mount, is called out by proud estimates of work and wrong estimates of prayer:

> *Many will say to me in that day, Lord, Lord, have we not prophesied in thy name? and in thy name have cast out devils? and in thy name done many wonderful works? And then will I profess unto them, I never knew you: depart from me, ye that work iniquity.* (Matt. 7:22–23)

Humility is the first and last attribute of Christlike religion, and the first and last attribute of Christlike praying. There is no Christ without humility. There is no praying without humility. If you wish to learn well the art of praying, then learn well the lesson of humility.

How graceful and imperative does the attitude of humility become to us! Humility is one of the unchanging and exacting attitudes of prayer. Dust, ashes, earth upon the head, sackcloth for the body, and fasting for the appetites were the symbols of humility for the Old Testament saints. Sackcloth, fasting, and ashes brought Daniel a lowliness before God and brought Gabriel to him. The angels are fond of the sackcloth-and-ashes men.

How lowly the attitude of Abraham, the friend of God, when pleading for God to stay His wrath against Sodom, *"which am but dust and ashes"* (Gen. 18:27). With what humility did Solomon appear before God! His grandeur was abased, and his glory and majesty were retired, as he assumed the rightful attitude before God: *"I am but a little child: I know not how to go out or come in"* (1 Kings 3:7).

The pride of doing sends its poison all though our praying. The same pride of being infects all our prayers, no matter how beautifully worded they may be. This lack of humility, this self-applauding, this self-exaltation, kept the most religious man of Christ's day from being accepted by God. The same thing will keep us in this day from being accepted by Him.

> Oh that now I might decrease!
> Oh that all I am might cease!
> Let me into nothing fall!
> Let my Lord be all in all.

3

Prayer and Devotion

Once as I rode out into the woods for my health, in 1737, having alighted from my horse in a retired place, as my manner commonly had been to walk for divine contemplation and prayer, I had a view that for me was extraordinary, of the glory of the Son of God. As near as I can judge, this continued about an hour, and kept me the greater part of the time in a flood of tears and weeping aloud. I felt an ardency of soul to be what I know not otherwise how to express, emptied and annihilated; to love Him with a holy and pure love; to serve and follow Him; to be perfectly sanctified and made pure with a divine and heavenly purity.   —Jonathan Edwards*

DEVOTION has great religious significance. The root meaning of *devotion* is "to devote to a sacred use." Thus, devotion, in its true sense, has to do with religious worship. It stands intimately connected with true prayer. Devotion is the particular frame of mind found in one entirely devoted to God. It is the spirit of reverence, of awe, of godly fear. It is a state of heart that appears before God in prayer and worship. It is foreign to everything like lightness of spirit and is opposed to levity, noise, and bluster. Devotion dwells in the realm of quietness and is still before God. It is serious, thoughtful, meditative.

Devotion belongs to the inner life and lives in the closet, but it also appears in the public services of the sanctuary. It is a part of the very spirit of true worship and is of the nature of the spirit of prayer.

Devotion belongs to the devout man whose thoughts and feelings are devoted to God. Such a man has a mind given up wholly to religion and possesses a strong affection for God and an ardent love for His house. Cornelius was *"a devout man, and one that feared God with all his house, which gave much alms to the people, and prayed to God alway"* (Acts 10:2). *"Devout men carried Stephen to his burial"* (Acts 8:2). *"And one Ananias, a devout man according to the law"* (Acts 22:12), was sent to Saul when he was blind, to tell him what the Lord would have him do. God can wonderfully use such men, for devout men are His chosen agents in carrying forward His plans.

Prayer promotes the spirit of devotion, while devotion is favorable to the best praying. Devotion furthers prayer and helps to drive prayer home to the object that it seeks. Prayer thrives in the atmosphere of true devotion. It is easy to pray when in the spirit of devotion. The attitude of mind and the state of heart implied in devotion make prayer effectual in reaching the throne of grace. God dwells where the spirit of devotion resides. All the graces of the Spirit are nourished and grow well in the environment created by devotion. Indeed, these graces grow nowhere else but here. The absence of a devotional spirit means death to the graces born in a renewed heart. True worship finds congeniality in the atmosphere made by a spirit of devotion. While prayer is helpful to devotion, at the same time devotion reacts on prayer and helps us to pray.

Devotion engages the heart in prayer. It is not an easy task for the lips to try to pray while the heart is absent from it. The charge that God at one time made against His ancient Israel was that they honored Him with their lips while their hearts were far from Him. (See Isaiah 29:13.)

The very essence of prayer is the spirit of devotion. Without devotion, prayer is an empty form, a vain round of words. Sad to say, much of this kind of prayer prevails in the church today. This is a busy age, bustling and active, and this bustling spirit has invaded the church of God. Its religious performances are many.

The church works at religion with the order, precision, and force of real machinery. But too often it works with the heartlessness of the machine. There is much of the treadmill movement in our ceaseless round and routine of religious doings. We pray without praying. We sing without singing with the Spirit and the understanding. (See 1 Corinthians 14:15.) We have music without the praise of God being in it or near it. We go to church by habit and come home all too gladly when the benediction is pronounced. We read our accustomed chapter in the Bible and feel quite relieved when the task is done. We say our prayers by rote, as a schoolboy recites his lesson, and are not sorry when the *Amen* is uttered.

Religion has to do with everything but our hearts. It engages our hands and feet, it takes hold of our voices, it lays its hands on our money, it affects even the postures of our bodies, but it does not take hold of our affections, our desires, our zeal, and make us serious, desperately in earnest, and cause us to be quiet and worshipful in the presence of God. Social affinities attract us to the house of God, not the spirit of the occasion. Church membership keeps us after a fashion decent in outward conduct and with some shadow of loyalty to our baptismal vows, but the heart is not in the thing. It remains cold, formal, and unimpressed amid all this outward performance, while we give ourselves over to self-congratulation that we are doing wonderfully well religiously.

Why all these sad defects in our piety? Why this modern perversion of the true nature of the religion of Jesus Christ? Why is the modern type of religion so much like a jewel case with the precious jewels gone? Why so much of this handling religion with the hands, often not too clean or unsoiled, and so little of it felt in the heart and witnessed in the life?

The great lack of modern religion is the spirit of devotion. We hear sermons in the same spirit with which we listen to a lecture or hear a speech. We visit the house of God just as if it were a common place, on a level with the theater, the lecture hall, or the forum. We look upon the minister of God not as the divinely called man of God, but merely as a sort of public speaker, on a plane with the politician, the lawyer, or the average speech maker or lecturer. Oh, how the spirit of true and genuine devotion would radically change all this for the better! We handle sacred things just as if they were the things of the world. Even the sacrament of the Lord's Supper becomes a mere religious performance, with no preparation for it beforehand and no meditation and prayer afterward. Even the sacrament of baptism has lost much of its solemnity and degenerated into a mere form with nothing specially in it.

We need the spirit of devotion, not only to be salt in our secular activities, but to make our prayers real prayers. We need to put the spirit of devotion into Monday's business as well as in Sunday's worship. We need the spirit of devotion to recollect always the presence of God, to be always doing the will of God, to direct all things always to the glory of God.

The spirit of devotion puts God in all things. It puts God not merely in our praying and churchgoing, but in all the concerns of life. *"Whether therefore ye eat or drink, or whatsoever ye do, do all to the glory of God"* (1 Cor. 10:31). The spirit of devotion makes the common things of earth sacred, and the little things great. With this spirit of devotion, we go to the workplace on Monday directed and inspired by the very same influence by which we went to church on Sunday. The spirit of devotion makes a Sabbath out of Saturday and transforms the shop or the office into a temple of God.

The spirit of devotion removes religion from being a thin veneer and puts it into the very life and being of our souls. With it, religion ceases to be merely doing a work and becomes a heart, sending its rich blood through every artery and beating with the pulsations of vigorous and radiant life.

The spirit of devotion is not merely the aroma of religion, but the stalk and stem on which religion grows. It is the salt that penetrates and makes savory all religious acts. It is the sugar that sweetens duty, self-denial, and sacrifice. It is the bright coloring that relieves the dullness of religious performances. It dispels frivolity, drives away all skin-deep forms of worship, and makes worship a serious and deep-seated service that impregnates body, soul, and spirit with its heavenly infusion. Let us ask in all seriousness: Has this highest angel of heaven, this heavenly spirit of devotion, this brightest and best angel of earth, left us? When the angel of devotion has gone, the angel of prayer has lost its wings, and it becomes a deformed and loveless thing.

The ardor of devotion is in prayer. In Revelation 4:8 we read: *"And they rest not day and night, saying, Holy, holy, holy, Lord God Almighty, which was, and is, and is to come."* The inspiration and center of their rapturous devotion is the holiness of God. That holiness of God claims their attention and inflames their devotion. There is nothing cold, nothing dull, nothing wearisome about them or their heavenly worship. *"They rest not day and night."* What zeal! What unfainting ardor and ceaseless rapture! The ministry of prayer, if it be anything worthy of the name, is a ministry of ardor, a ministry of unwearied and intense longing after God and after His holiness.

The spirit of devotion pervades the saints in heaven and characterizes the worship of heaven's angelic intelligences. No devotionless creatures are in that heavenly world. God is there, and His very presence begets the spirit of reverence, of awe, and of filial fear. If we would be partakers with them after death, we must first learn the spirit of devotion on earth before we get there.

These living creatures, in their relentless, tireless attitude toward God and their rapt devotion to His holiness, are the perfect symbols and illustrations of true prayer and its ardor. Prayer must be aflame. Its ardor must consume us. Prayer with out fervor is as a sun without light or heat, or as a flower without beauty or fragrance. A soul devoted to God is a fervent soul, and prayer is the creature of that flame. He only can truly pray who is all aglow for holiness, for God, and for heaven.

Activity is not strength. Work is not zeal. Moving about is not devotion. Activity often is the unrecognized symptom of spiritual weakness. It may be hurtful to piety when made the substitute for real devotion in worship. The colt is much more active than its mother, but she is the wheelhorse of the team, pulling the load without noise or bluster or show. The child is more active than the father, who may be bearing the rule and burdens of an empire on his heart and shoulders. Enthusiasm is more active than faith, though it cannot remove mountains nor call into action any of the omnipotent forces that faith can command.

A feeble, lively, showy religious activity may spring from many causes. There is much running around, much stirring about, much going here and there, in present-day church life. However, sad to say, the spirit of genuine, heartfelt devotion is strangely lacking. If there is real spiritual life, a deep-toned activity will spring from it. But it is an activity springing from strength and not from weakness. It is an activity that has deep roots, many and strong.

In the nature of things, religion must show much of its growth above ground. Much will be seen and be evident to the eye. The flower and fruit of a holy life, abounding in good works, must be seen. It cannot be otherwise. But the surface growth must be based on a vigorous growth of unseen life and hidden roots. The roots of religion must go down deep in the renewed nature to be seen on the outside. The external must have a deep internal groundwork. There must be much of the invisible and the underground growth, or else the life will be feeble and short-lived, and the external growth sickly and fruitless.

In the book of the prophet Isaiah these words are written:

303

They that wait upon the Lord shall renew their strength; they shall mount up with wings as eagles; they walk shall run, and not be weary; and they shall walk, and not faint. (Isa. 40:31)

This is the genesis of the whole matter of activity and strength of the most energetic, exhaustless, and untiring nature. All this is the result of waiting on God.

There may be much of activity induced by drill or created by enthusiasm, the product of the weakness of the flesh and the inspiration of volatile, short-lived forces. Activity continues often at the expense of more solid, useful elements and generally to the total neglect of prayer. To be too busy with God's work to commune with God, to be busy with doing church work without taking time to talk to God about His work, is the highway to backsliding. Many people have walked there to the hurt of their immortal souls. Notwithstanding great activity, great enthusiasm, and much hurrah for the work, the work and the activity will be but blindness without the cultivation and the maturity of the graces of prayer.

4

Prayer, Praise, and Thanksgiving

Dr. A. J. Gordon describes the impression made upon his mind by speaking with Joseph Rabinowitz, whom Dr. Delitzsch considered the most remarkable Jewish convert since Saul of Tarsus: "We shall not soon forget the radiance that would come into his face as he expounded the Messianic psalms at our morning or evening worship, and how, as here and there he caught a glimpse of the suffering or glorified Christ, he would suddenly lift his hands and his eyes to heaven in a bust of adoration, exclaiming with Thomas after he had seen the nail-prints, 'My Lord, and my God.'"

—*D. M. McIntyre*

PRAYER, praise, and thanksgiving all go in company. A close relationship exists among them. Praise and thanksgiving are so nearly alike that it is not easy to distinguish between them or to define them separately. The Scriptures join these three things together. Many are the causes for thanksgiving and praise. The Psalms are filled with many songs of praise and hymns of thanksgiving, all pointing back to the results of prayer.

Thanksgiving includes gratitude. In fact, thanksgiving is but the expression of an inward, conscious gratitude to God for mercies received. Gratitude is an inward emotion of the soul, involuntarily arising therein, while thanksgiving is the voluntary expression of gratitude.

Thanksgiving is oral, positive, active. It is the giving out of something to God. Thanksgiving comes out into the open. Gratitude is secret, silent, passive, not showing its being until expressed in praise and thanksgiving. Gratitude is felt in the heart. Thanksgiving is the expression of that inward feeling.

Thanksgiving is just what the word itself signifies—the giving of thanks to God. It is giving something to God in words that we feel at heart for blessings received. Gratitude arises from a contemplation of the goodness of God. It is bred by serious meditation on what God has done for us. Gratitude and thanksgiving both point to and have to do with God and His mercies. The heart is consciously grateful to God. The soul gives expression to that heartfelt gratitude to God in words or acts.

Gratitude is born of meditation on God's grace and mercy. *"The LORD hath done great things for us, whereof we are glad"* (Ps. 126:3). Here we see the value of serious meditation. *"My meditation of him shall be sweet"* (Ps. 104:34). Praise is begotten by gratitude and a conscious obligation to God for mercies given. As we think of mercies past, the heart is inwardly moved to gratitude.

> I love to think on mercies past,
>   And future good implore;
> And all my cares and sorrows cast
>   On Him whom I adore.

Love is the child of gratitude. Love grows as gratitude is felt and then breaks out into praise and thanksgiving to God. I love the Lord because He *"hath heard the voice of my weeping…*[and] *my supplication"* (Ps. 6:8–9). Answered prayers cause gratitude, and gratitude brings forth a love that declares it will not cease praying: *"Because he hath inclined his ear unto me, therefore will I call upon him as long as I live"* (Ps. 116:2). Gratitude and love move to larger and increased praying.

Paul appealed to the Romans to dedicate themselves wholly to God, a living sacrifice, and the constraining motive was the mercies of God:

> *I beseech you therefore, brethren, by the mercies of God, that ye present your bodies a living sacrifice, holy, acceptable unto God, which is your reasonable service.*   (Rom. 12:1)

Consideration of God's mercies not only begets gratitude, but induces a large consecration to God of all that we have and are.

Thus, prayer, thanksgiving, and consecration are all inseparably linked together. Gratitude and thanksgiving always look back at the past, though they may also take in the present. But prayer always looks to the future. Thanksgiving deals with things already received. Prayer deals with things desired, asked for, and expected. Prayer turns to gratitude and praise when the things asked for have been granted by God. As prayer brings things to us that beget gratitude and thanksgiving, so praise and gratitude promote prayer and induce more praying and better praying.

Gratitude and thanksgiving forever stand opposed to all murmuring at God's dealings with us, and all complaining at our lot. Gratitude and murmuring never abide in the same heart at the same time. An unappreciative spirit has no standing beside gratitude and praise. True prayer corrects complaining and promotes gratitude and thanksgiving. Dissatisfaction at one's lot, and a disposition to be discontented with things that come to us in the providence of God, are foes to gratitude and enemies to thanksgiving.

Murmurers are ungrateful people. Appreciative men and women have neither the time nor disposition to stop and complain. The bane of the wilderness journey of the Israelites on their way to Canaan was their proneness to murmur and complain against God and Moses. For this, God was several times greatly grieved, and it took the strong praying of Moses to avert God's wrath because of those murmuring. The absence of gratitude left neither room nor disposition for praise and thanksgiving, just as it always happens. But when these same Israelites were brought through the Red Sea dry, while their enemies were destroyed, there was a song of praise led by Miriam, the sister of Moses. One of the leading sins of these Israelites was forgetfulness of God and His mercies, and ingratitude of soul. This brought forth murmuring and lack of praise, as it always does.

When Paul wrote to the Colossians to let the word of Christ dwell in their hearts richly and to let the peace of God rule therein, he said to them, *"And be ye thankful,"* and added, *"Admonishing one another in psalms and hymns and spiritual songs, singing with grace in your hearts to the Lord"* (Col. 3:15–16).

Further on, in writing to these same Christians, he joined prayer and thanksgiving together: *"Continue in prayer, and watch in the same with thanksgiving"* (Col. 4:2).

And, writing to the Thessalonians, he again joined them: *"Rejoice evermore. Pray without ceasing. In everything give thanks: for this is the will of God in Christ Jesus concerning you"* (1 Thess. 5:16–18).

> We thank Thee, Lord of heaven and earth,
> Who hast preserved us from our birth;
> Redeemed us oft from death and dread,
> And with Thy gifts our table spread.

Wherever there is true prayer, there thanksgiving and gratitude stand by, ready to respond to the answer when it comes. As prayer brings the answer, so the answer brings forth gratitude and praise. As prayer sets God to work, so answered prayer sets thanksgiving to work. Thanksgiving follows answered prayer just as day succeeds night. True prayer and gratitude lead to full consecration, and consecration leads to more praying and better praying. A consecrated life is a life of both prayer and thanksgiving.

The spirit of praise was once the boast of the early church. This spirit rested on the tabernacles of these early Christians, as a cloud of glory out of which God shone and spoke. It filled their temples with the perfume of costly, flaming incense. That this spirit of praise is sadly deficient in our present-day congregations must be evident to every careful observer. That it is a mighty force in projecting the Gospel, and its body of vital forces, must be equally evident. To restore the spirit of praise to our congregations should be one of the main points with every true pastor. The normal state of the church is set forth in this declaration: *"Praise waiteth for thee, O God, in Sion: and unto thee shall the vow be performed"* (Ps. 65:1).

Praise is so distinctly and definitely wedded to prayer, so inseparably joined, that they cannot be divorced. Praise is dependent on prayer for its full volume and its sweetest melody. Singing is one method of praise—not the highest, it is true—but it is the ordinary and usual form. The singing service in our churches has much to do with praise, for according to the character of the singing will be the genuineness or the measure of praise. The singing may be so directed as to have in it elements that deprave and debauch prayer. It may be so directed as to drive away everything like thanksgiving and praise. Much of modern singing in our churches is entirely foreign to anything like hearty, sincere praise to God.

The spirit of prayer and of true praise go hand in hand. Both are often entirely dissipated by the flippant, thoughtless, light singing in our congregations. Much of the singing lacks serious thought and is devoid of everything like a devotional spirit. Its lustiness and sparkle may not only dissipate all the essential features of worship, but may substitute the flesh for the spirit.

Giving thanks is the very life of prayer. It is its fragrance and music, its poetry and its crown. Prayer, bringing the desired answer, breaks out into praise and thanksgiving. Whatever interferes with and injures the spirit of prayer necessarily hurts and dissipates the spirit of praise.

The heart must have in it the grace of prayer to sing the praises of God. Spiritual singing is not to be done by musical taste or talent, but by the grace of God in the heart. Nothing helps praise so mightily as a gracious revival of true religion in the church. The conscious presence of God inspires song. The angels and the glorified ones in heaven do not need artistic precentors to lead them, nor do they care for paid choirs to chime in with their heavenly doxologies of praise and worship. They are not dependent on singing schools to teach them the notes and scale of singing. Their singing involuntarily breaks forth from the heart.

God is immediately present in the heavenly assemblies of the angels and the spirits of *"just men made perfect"* (Heb. 12:23). His glorious presence creates the song, teaches the singing, and impregnates their notes of praise. It is so on earth. God's presence begets singing and thanksgiving, while the absence of God from our congregations is the death of song, or makes the singing lifeless, cold, and formal, which amounts to the same. His conscious presence in our churches would bring back the days of praise and would restore the full chorus of song.

Where grace abounds, song abounds. When God is in the heart, heaven is present and melody is there, and the lips overflow out of the abundance of the heart. This is as true in the private life of the believer as it is so in the congregations of the saints. The decay of singing, the dying down and out of the spirit of praise in song, means the decline of grace in the heart and the absence of God's presence from the people.

The main purposes of all singing are for God's ear, to attract His attention and to please Him. It is unto the Lord, for His glory, and to His honor. Certainly it is not for the glorification of the paid choir, to exalt the wonderful musical prowess of the singers, nor to draw people to the church, but it is for the glory of God and the good of the souls of the congregation.

Alas! How far has the singing of choirs of churches of modern times departed from this idea! It is no surprise that there is no life, no power, no unction, and no spirit in much of the church singing heard in this day. It is sacrilege for any but sanctified hearts and holy lips to direct the singing part of the service of God's house of prayer. Much of the singing in churches would do credit to the opera house and might satisfy as mere entertainments, pleasing the ear; but as a part of real worship, having in it the spirit of praise and prayer, it is a fraud, an imposition on spiritually-minded people, and entirely unacceptable to God. The cry should go out afresh, *"Let the people praise thee, O God"* (Ps. 67:5), for *"it is good to sing praises unto our God; for it is pleasant; and praise is comely"* (Ps. 147:1).

The music of praise—for there is real music of soul in praise— is too hopeful and happy to be denied. All these are in the giving of thanks. In Philippians 4:6, prayer is called *requests. "Let your requests be made known unto God"* describes prayer as an asking for a gift, giving prominence to the thing asked for, making it emphatic, something to be given by God and received by us, not something to be done by us. All this is closely connected with gratitude to God: *"With thanksgiving let your requests be made known unto God"* (Phil. 4:6).

God does much for us in answer to prayer, but we need from Him many gifts, and for them we are to make special prayer. According to our special needs, so must our praying be. We are to be specific and particular and bring to the knowledge of God by prayer, supplication, and thanksgiving, our particular requests, the things we need, the things we greatly desire. And with it all, accompanying all these requests, there must be thanksgiving.

It is indeed a pleasing thought that what we are called upon to do on earth, to praise and give thanks, the angels in heaven and the redeemed spirits of the saints are doing also. It is still further pleasing to contemplate the glorious hope that what God wants us to do on earth, we will be engaged in doing throughout an unending eternity. Praise and thanksgiving will be our blessed employment while we remain in heaven. Nor will we ever grow weary of this pleasing task.

Joseph Addison set before us this pleasing prospect in verse:

> Through every period of my life
> Thy goodness I'll pursue;
> And after death, in distant worlds,
> The pleasing theme renew.
> Through all eternity to Thee
> A grateful song I'll raise;
> But, oh! eternity's too short
> To utter all Thy praise.

5

Prayer and Trouble

"He will." It may not be today,
That God Himself shall wipe our tears away,
Nor, hope deferred, may it be yet tomorrow
He'll take away our cup of earthly sorrow;
But, precious promise, He has said He will,
If we but trust Him fully—and be still.

We, too, as He, may fall, and die unknown;
And e'en the place we fell be all unshown,
But eyes omniscient will mark the spot
Till empires perish and the world's forgot.
Then they who bore the yoke and drank the cup
In fadeless glory shall the Lord raise up.
God's word is ever good; His will is best:—
The yoke, the heart all broken—and then rest.
                              —Claudius L. Chilton

TROUBLE and prayer are closely related to each other. Prayer is of great value to trouble. Trouble often drives men to God in prayer, while prayer is but the voice of men in trouble. There is great value in prayer in the time of trouble. Prayer often delivers one out of trouble and, more often, gives strength to bear trouble, ministers comfort in trouble, and begets patience in the midst of trouble. Wise is he in the day of trouble who knows his true source of strength and who fails not to pray.

Trouble belongs to the present state of man on earth. *"Man that is born of a woman is of few days, and full of trouble"* (Job 14:1). Trouble is common to man. There is no exception in any age or climate or station. Rich and poor alike, the learned and the ignorant,

312

one and all, are partakers of this sad and painful inheritance of the fall of man. *"There hath no temptation taken you but such as is common to man"* (1 Cor. 10:13). The *"day of trouble"* (Ps. 20:1) dawns on everyone at some time in his life. The evil days come and the years draw near when the heart feels its heavy pressure.

The view of life that expects nothing but sunshine and looks only for ease, pleasure, and flowers, is an entirely false view and shows supreme ignorance. It is this class who are so sadly disappointed and surprised when trouble breaks into their lives. These are the ones who know not God, who know nothing of His disciplinary dealings with His people, and who are prayerless.

What an infinite variety there is in the troubles of life! How diversified the experiences of men in the school of trouble! No two people have the same troubles under like environments. God deals with no two of His children in the same way. Just as God varies His treatment of His children, so trouble is varied. God does not repeat Himself; He does not run in a rut. He does not have one pattern for every child. Each trouble is proportioned to each child. Each one is dealt with according to his own peculiar case.

Trouble is God's servant, doing His will unless He is defeated in the execution of that will. Trouble is under the control of Almighty God and is one of His most efficient agents in fulfilling His purposes and in perfecting His saints. God's hand is in every trouble that breaks into the lives of men. This is not to say that He directly and arbitrarily orders every unpleasant experience of life or that He is personally responsible for every painful and afflicting thing that comes into the lives of His people. However, no trouble is ever turned loose in this world and comes into the life of saint or sinner, but that it comes with divine permission and is allowed to exist and do its painful work with God's hand involved, carrying out His gracious designs of redemption.

All things are under divine control. Trouble is neither above God nor beyond His control. It is not something in life independent of God. No matter from what source it springs or from where it arises, God is sufficiently wise and able to lay His hand upon it, without assuming responsibility for its origin, and work it into His plans and purposes concerning the highest welfare of His saints. This is the explanation of that gracious statement, so often quoted, but the depth of whose meaning has rarely been sounded, *"And we*

know that all things work together for good to them that love God"
(Rom. 8:28).

Even the evils brought about by the forces of nature are His
servants, carrying out His will and fulfilling His designs. God even
claims the locusts, the cankerworm, the caterpillar are His servants: *"My great army"* (Joel 2:25), used by Him to correct His
people and discipline them.

Trouble belongs to the disciplinary part of the moral government of God. This is a life of probation, where the human race is on
probation. It is a season of trial. Trouble is not penal in its nature.
It belongs to what the Scriptures call "chastening." *"Whom the
Lord loveth he chasteneth, and scourgeth every son whom he receiveth"* (Heb. 12:6). Speaking accurately, punishment does not belong
to this life. Punishment for sin will take place in the next world.
God's dealings with people in this world are of the nature of discipline. They are corrective processes in His plans concerning man.
It is because of this that prayer comes in when trouble arises.
Prayer belongs to the discipline of life.

As trouble is not sinful in itself, neither is it the evidence of
sin. Good and bad alike experience trouble. As the rain falls alike
on the just and unjust (see Matthew 5:45), so drought likewise
comes to the righteous and the wicked. Trouble is no evidence
whatever of the divine displeasure. Scriptural instances without
number disprove any such idea. Job is a case in point, where God
bore explicit testimony to his deep piety, and yet God permitted
Satan to afflict him beyond any other man for wise and beneficent
purposes. Trouble has no power in itself to interfere with the relations of a saint to God.

> *Who shall separate us from the love of Christ? shall tribula-*
> *tion, or distress, or persecution, or famine, or nakedness, or*
> *peril, or sword?*   *(Rom. 8:35)*

Three words that are practically the same are used in the descriptions of divine discipline: temptation, trial, and trouble; and
yet there is a difference between them. Temptation is really a so-
licitation to evil arising from the Devil or born in the carnal nature
of man.

Trial is testing. It is that which proves us, tests us, and makes
us stronger and better when we submit to the trial and work together with God in it. *"My brethren, count it all joy when ye fall*

into divers temptations; knowing this, that the trying of your faith worketh patience" (James 1:2–3).

Peter spoke along the same line:

> *Wherein ye greatly rejoice, though now for a season, if need be, ye are in heaviness through manifold temptations: that the trial of your faith, being much more precious than that of gold that perisheth, though it be tried with fire, might be found unto praise and honour and glory at the appearing of Jesus Christ.*   *(1 Pet. 1:6–7)*

The third word is trouble itself, which covers all the painful, sorrowing, grievous events of life. Yet temptations and trials might really become troubles, so that all evil days in life might well be classed under the heading of *"the time of trouble"* (Ps. 37:39). Such days of trouble are the lot of all men. It is enough to know that trouble, no matter from what source it comes, becomes in God's hand His own agent to accomplish His gracious work concerning those who submit patiently to Him, who recognize Him in prayer, and who work together with God.

Let us settle down at once to the idea that trouble does not arise by chance, nor does it occur by what men call accident.

> *Although affliction cometh not forth of the dust, neither doth trouble spring out of the ground; yet man is born unto trouble, as the sparks fly upward.*   *(Job 5:6–7)*

Trouble naturally belongs to God's moral government and is one of His invaluable agents in governing the world.

When we realize this, we can the better understand much that is recorded in the Scriptures and can have a clearer conception of God's dealings with His ancient Israel. In God's dealings with them, we find what is called a history of divine providence, and providence always embraces trouble. No one can understand the story of Joseph and his father Jacob unless he takes into the account trouble and its varied offices. God takes account of trouble when He urges His prophet Isaiah thus:

> *Comfort ye, comfort ye my people, saith your God. Speak ye comfortably to Jerusalem, and cry unto her that her warfare is accomplished, that her iniquity is pardoned.*   *(Isa. 40:1–2)*

There is a distinct note of comfort in the Gospel for the praying saints of the Lord, and he is a wise scribe in divine things who knows how to minister this comfort to the brokenhearted and sad ones of earth. Jesus Himself said to His sad disciples, *"I will not leave you comfortless"* (John 14:18).

All the foregoing has been said so that we may rightly appreciate the relationship of prayer to trouble. In the time of trouble, where does prayer come in? The psalmist told us, *"Call upon me in the day of trouble: I will deliver thee, and thou shalt glorify me"* (Ps. 50:15). Prayer is the most appropriate thing for a soul to do in the time of trouble. Prayer recognizes God in the day of trouble. *"It is the LORD; let him do what seemeth him good"* (1 Sam. 3:18). Prayer sees God's hand in trouble and prays about it. Nothing more truly shows us our helplessness than when trouble comes. It brings the strong man low, it discloses our weakness, it brings a sense of helplessness. Blessed is he who knows how to turn to God in the time of trouble.

If trouble is of the Lord, then the most natural thing to do is to carry the trouble to the Lord and seek grace, patience, and submission. It is the time to inquire in the trouble, *"Lord, what wilt thou have me to do?"* (Acts 9:6). How natural and reasonable for the oppressed, broken, bruised soul to bow low at the footstool of mercy and seek the face of God! Where could a soul in trouble more likely find solace?

Alas! Trouble does not always drive men to God in prayer. Sad is the case of him who, when trouble bends his spirit down and grieves his heart, yet knows not from where the trouble comes nor knows how to pray about it. Blessed is the man who is driven by trouble to his knees in prayer!

> Trials must and will befall;
> But with humble faith to see
> Love inscribed upon them all—
> This is happiness to me.
>
> Trials make the promise sweet,
> Trials give new life to prayer;
> Bring me to my Savior's feet,
> Lay me low, and keep me there.

Prayer in the time of trouble brings comfort, help, hope, and blessings that, while not removing the trouble, enable the saint the better to bear it and to submit to the will of God. Prayer opens the eyes to see God's hand in trouble. Prayer does not interpret God's providences, but it does justify them and recognize God in them. Prayer enables us to see wise ends in trouble. Prayer in trouble drives us away from unbelief, saves us from doubt, and delivers from all vain and foolish questioning because of our painful experiences. Let us not lose sight of the tribute paid to Job when all his troubles came to the culminating point: *"In all this Job sinned not, nor charged God foolishly"* (Job 1:22).

Alas for vain, ignorant men, without faith in God and knowing nothing of God's disciplinary processes in dealing with men, who charge God foolishly when troubles come, and who are tempted to *"curse God"* (Job 2:9). How silly and vain are the complaining, the murmuring, and the rebellion of men in the time of trouble! What need to read again the story of the children of Israel in the wilderness! And how useless is all our fretting, our worrying over trouble, as if such unhappy doings on our part could change things! *"And which of you with taking thought can add to his stature one cubit?"* (Luke 12:25). How much wiser, how much better, how much easier to bear life's troubles when we take everything to God in prayer!

Trouble has wise ends for the praying ones, and these find it so. Happy is he who, like the psalmist, finds that his troubles have been blessings in disguise.

> *It is good for me that I have been afflicted; that I might learn thy statutes. I know, O LORD, that thy judgments are right, and that thou in faithfulness hast afflicted me. (Ps. 119:71, 75)*

The writer of the following poem also saw the value of trouble:

> O who could bear life's stormy doom,
>   Did not Thy wing of love
> Come brightly wafting through the gloom
>   Our peace branch from above.
>
> Then sorrow, touched by Thee, grows bright,
>   With more than rapture's ray;
> As darkness shows us worlds of light
>   We never saw by day.

Of course, it may be conceded that some troubles are really imaginary. They have no existence other than in the mind. Some are anticipated troubles that never arrive at our door. Others are past troubles, and there is much folly in worrying over them. Present troubles are the ones requiring attention and demanding prayer. *"Sufficient unto the day is the evil thereof"* (Matt. 6:34). Some troubles are self-originated; we are their authors. Some of these originate involuntarily with us; some arise from our ignorance; some come from our carelessness.

All this can be readily admitted without breaking the force of the statement that troubles are the subjects of prayer and should drive us to prayer. What father casts off his child who cries to him when the little one, from its own carelessness, has stumbled and fallen and hurt himself? Does not the cry of the child attract the ears of the father even though the child is to blame for the accident? *"What things soever ye desire"* (Mark 11:24) takes in every event of life, even though we are responsible for some.

Some troubles are human in their origin. They arise from secondary causes. They originate with others, but we are the sufferers. This is a world where often the innocent suffer the consequences of the acts of others. This is a part of life's incidents. Who has not at some time suffered at the hands of others? But even these are allowed to come in the order of God's providence, are permitted to break into our lives for beneficent ends, and may be prayed over. Why should we not carry our hurts, our wrongs, and our privations, caused by the acts of others, to God in prayer? Are such things outside the realm of prayer? Are they exceptions to the rule of prayer? Not at all. God can and will lay His hand upon all such events in answer to prayer and cause them to work for us *"a far more exceeding and eternal weight of glory"* (2 Cor. 4:17). Nearly all of Paul's troubles arose from wicked and unreasonable men. (See 2 Corinthians 11:23–33.)

So also some troubles are directly of satanic origin. Quite all of Job's troubles were the offspring of the Devil's scheme to break down Job's integrity, to make him charge God foolishly, and to make him curse God. But are these not to be recognized in prayer? Are they to be excluded from God's disciplinary processes? Job did not do so. Hear him in those familiar words: *"The LORD gave, and the LORD hath taken away; blessed be the name of the LORD"* (Job 1:21).

Oh, what a comfort to see God in all of life's events! What a relief to a broken, sorrowing heart to see God's hand in sorrow! What a source of relief is prayer in unburdening the heart in grief.

O Thou who driest the mourner's tear,
　　How dark this world would be,
If, when deceived and wounded here,
　　We could not fly to Thee?

The friends who in our sunshine live,
　　When winter comes are flown,
And he who has but tears to give,
　　Must weep those tears alone.

But Thou wilt heal the broken heart,
　　Which, like the plants that throw
Their fragrance from the wounded part,
　　Breathes sweetness out of woe.

But when we survey all the sources from which trouble comes, it all resolves itself into two invaluable truths: first, our troubles, in the end, are of the Lord. They come with His consent. He is in all of them and is interested in us when they press and bruise us. Secondly, in our troubles, no matter what the cause, whether of ourselves, or men, or devils, or even God Himself, we are warranted in taking them to God in prayer, in praying over them, and in seeking to get the greatest spiritual benefits out of them.

Prayer in the time of trouble tends to bring the spirit into perfect subjection to the will of God, saves from all murmuring over our lot, and delivers from everything like a rebellious heart or a spirit critical of the Lord. Prayer sanctifies trouble to our highest good. Prayer so prepares the heart that it softens under the disciplining hand of God. Prayer places us where God can bring to us the greatest good, spiritual and eternal. Prayer allows God to freely work with us and in us in the day of trouble. Prayer removes everything in the way of trouble, bringing to us the sweetest, the highest, and greatest good. Prayer permits God's servant, trouble, to accomplish its mission in us, with us, and for us.

The end of trouble is always good in the mind of God. If trouble fails in its mission, it is either because of prayerlessness or unbelief, or both. Being in harmony with God in the dispensations of His providence, always makes trouble a blessing. The good or evil of trouble is always determined by the spirit in which it is received. Trouble proves a blessing or a curse, just according as it is received and treated by us. It either softens or hardens us. It either draws us to prayer and God or drives us away from God and the prayer closet. Trouble hardened Pharaoh until, finally, it had no effect on him, only to make him more desperate and to drive him further from God. The same sun softens the wax and hardens the clay. The same sun melts the ice and dries out the moisture from the earth.

As there is infinite variety of trouble, so also there is infinite variety in the relationship of prayer to other things. How many things are the subject of prayer! It has to do with everything that concerns us, with everybody with whom we deal, and with all times. But prayer especially has to do with trouble. *"This poor man cried, and the LORD heard him, and saved him out of all his troubles"* (Ps. 34:6). Oh, the blessedness, the help, the comfort of prayer in the day of trouble! How marvelous the promises of God to us in troubled times!

> *Because he hath set his love upon me, therefore will I deliver*
> *him: I will set him on high, because he hath known my name.*
> *He shall call upon me, and I will answer him: I will be with*
> *him in trouble; I will deliver him, and honour him.*
> *(Ps. 91:14–15)*

As one poet put it,

> If pain afflict, or wrongs oppress,
> If cares distract, or fears dismay;
> If guilt deject, if sin distress,
> In every case, still watch and pray.

How rich in its sweetness, how cheering to faith, and how far-reaching in the realm of trouble are the words of promise that God delivers to His believing, praying ones by the mouth of Isaiah:

> *But now thus saith the LORD that created thee, O Jacob, and*
> *he that formed thee, O Israel, Fear not: for I have redeemed*
> *thee, I have called thee by thy name; thou art mine. When thou*
> *passest through the waters, I will be with thee; and through*
> *the rivers, they shall not overflow thee: when thou walkest*
> *through the fire, thou shalt not be burned; neither shall the*
> *flame kindle upon thee. For I am the LORD thy God, the Holy*
> *One of Israel, thy Saviour.*   *(Isa. 43:1–3)*

6

Prayer and Trouble
(Continued)

My first message for heavenly relief went singing over millions of miles of space in 1869, and brought relief to my troubled heart. But, thanks be to Him, I have received many delightful and helpful answers during the last fifty years. I would think the commerce of the skies had gone into bankruptcy if I did not hear frequently, since I have learned how to ask and how to receive. —Homer W. Hodge

IN the New Testament there are three words used that embrace trouble. These are tribulation, suffering, and affliction. These words differ somewhat, and yet, practically, each of them means trouble of some kind. Our Lord gave His disciples notice that they might expect tribulation in this life, teaching them that tribulation belonged to this world, that they could not hope to escape it, and that they would not be carried through this life on flowery beds of ease. How hard to learn this plain and patent lesson! *"In the world ye shall have tribulation: but be of good cheer; I have overcome the world"* (John 16:33). There is the encouragement. As He had overcome the world and its tribulations, so might they do the same.

Paul taught the same lesson throughout his ministry, when in confirming the souls of the brethren and exhorting them to continue in the faith, he told them that *"we must through much tribulation enter into the kingdom of God"* (Acts 14:22). He himself knew this by his own experience, for his pathway was anything but smooth and flowery.

Paul used the word *sufferings* to describe the troubles of life in that comforting passage in which he contrasted life's troubles with the final glory of heaven, which shall be the reward of all who patiently endure the ills of divine providence: *"For I reckon that the sufferings of this present time are not worthy to be compared with the glory which shall be revealed in us"* (Rom. 8:18). Further, he spoke of the afflictions that come to the people of God in this world, and he regarded them as nearly weightless when compared with the weight of glory awaiting all who are submissive, patient, and faithful in all their troubles: *"For our light affliction, which is but for a moment, worketh for us a far more exceeding and eternal weight of glory"* (2 Cor. 4:17).

But these present afflictions can work for us only as we cooperate with God in prayer. As God works through prayer, it is only through this means that He can accomplish His highest ends for us. His providence works with greatest effect with His praying ones. These know the uses of trouble and its gracious designs. The greatest value in trouble comes to those who bow lowest before the throne.

Paul, in urging patience in tribulation, connected it directly with prayer, as if prayer alone would place us where we could be patient when tribulation comes: *"Rejoicing in hope; patient in tribulation; continuing instant in prayer"* (Rom. 12:12). He here coupled tribulation and prayer, showing their close relationship and the worth of prayer in begetting and culturing patience in tribulation. In fact, there can be no patience exemplified when trouble comes except as it is secured through instant and continued prayer. The school of prayer is where patience is learned and practiced.

Prayer brings us into that state of grace where tribulation is not only endured, but where there is under it a spirit of rejoicing. In showing the gracious benefits of justification, Paul said,

> *And not only so, but we glory in tribulations also: knowing that tribulation worketh patience; and patience, experience; and experience, hope: and hope maketh not ashamed; because the love of God is shed abroad in our hearts by the Holy Ghost which is given unto us.* (Rom. 5:3)

What a chain of graces are here set forth as flowing from tribulation! What successive steps to a high state of religious experience! And what rich fruits result from even painful tribulation!

To the same effect are the words of Peter in his strong prayer for those Christians to whom he wrote. He showed that suffering and the highest state of grace are closely connected, and he intimated that it is through suffering that we are to be brought to those higher regions of Christian experience:

But the God of all grace, who hath called us into his eternal glory by Christ Jesus, after that ye have suffered a while, make you perfect, stablish, strengthen, settle you. (1 Pet. 5:10)

It is in the fires of suffering that God purifies His saints and brings them to the highest things. It is in the furnace that their faith is tested, their patience is tried, and they are developed in all those rich virtues that make up Christian character. It is while they are passing through deep waters that He shows how close He can come to His praying, believing saints. It takes faith of a high order and a Christian experience far above the average religion of this day to count it joy when we are called to pass through tribulation. (See James 1:2.)

God's highest aim in dealing with His people is in developing Christian character. He is after infusing in us those rich virtues that belong to our Lord Jesus Christ. He is seeking to make us like Himself. It is not so much work that He wants in us. It is not greatness. It is the presence in us of patience, meekness, submission to the divine will, prayerfulness that brings everything to Him. He seeks to implant His own image in us. And trouble in some form tends to do this very thing, for this is the end and aim of trouble. This is its work. This is the task it is called to perform. It is not a chance incident in life, but has a design in view, just as it has an all-wise Designer back of it, who makes trouble His agent to bring forth the largest results.

The writer of the letter to the Hebrews gave us a perfect directory of trouble—comprehensive, clear, and worthwhile to be studied. Here we find *chastisement,* another word for trouble, coming from a Father's hand, showing God is in all the sad and afflictive events of life. Here is its nature and its gracious design. It is not punishment in the accurate meaning of that word, but rather the means God employs to correct and discipline His children in dealing with them on earth. Then we have the fact of the evidence of being His people, namely, the presence of chastisement. The ultimate end is that we *"might be partakers of his holiness"* (Heb. 12:10), which is but another way of saying that all this disciplinary process is to the end that God may make us like Himself. What an encouragement, too, that chastisement is no evidence of anger or displeasure on God's part, but is the strong proof of His love. Let us read the entire directory on this important subject:

> *And ye have forgotten the exhortation which speaketh unto you as unto children, My son, despise not thou the chastening of the Lord, nor faint when thou art rebuked of him: for whom the Lord loveth he chasteneth, and scourgeth every son whom he receiveth. If ye endure chastening, God dealeth with you as with sons; for what son is he whom the father chasteneth not? But if ye be without chastisement, whereof all are partakers, then are ye bastards, and not sons. Furthermore we have had fathers of our flesh which corrected us, and we gave them reverence: shall we not much rather be in subjection to the Father of spirits, and live? For they verily for a few days chastened us after their own pleasure; but he for our profit, that we might be partakers of his holiness. Now no chastening for the present seemeth to be joyous, but grievous; nevertheless afterward it yieldeth the peaceable fruit of righteousness unto them which are exercised thereby.*
> *(Heb. 12:5–11)*

Just as prayer is wide in its range, taking in everything, so trouble is infinitely varied in its uses and designs. It takes trouble sometimes to arrest attention, to stop men in the busy rush of life, and to awaken them to a sense of their helplessness and their need and sinfulness. Not until King Manasseh was bound with thorns and carried away into a foreign land when he got into deep trouble was he awakened and brought back to God. It was then that he humbled himself and began to call upon God.

The prodigal son was independent and self-sufficient when in prosperity. But, when money and friends departed and he began to be in need, then he *"came to himself"* (Luke 15:17) and decided to return to his father's house, with prayer and confession on his lips. Through trouble many a man who has forgotten God has been arrested, caused to consider his ways, and brought to remember God and pray. Blessed is trouble when it accomplishes this in men!

It is for this, among other reasons, that Job declared,

Behold, happy is the man whom God correcteth: therefore despise not thou the chastening of the Almighty. For he maketh sore, and bindeth up: he woundeth, and his hands make whole. He shall deliver thee in six troubles; yea, in seven there shall no evil touch thee. *(Job 5:17–19)*

One thing more might be named. Trouble makes earth undesirable and causes heaven to loom up large in the horizon of hope. There is a world where trouble never comes. But the path of tribulation leads to that world. Those who are there went there through tribulation. What a world is set before our longing eyes, which appeals to our hopes as sorrows like a cyclone sweep over us! Hear John as he talked about it and those who are there:

What are these which are arrayed in white robes? and whence came they?...And he said to me, These are they which came out of great tribulation, and have washed their robes, and made them white in the blood of the Lamb....And God shall wipe away all tears from their eyes. *(Rev. 7:13–14, 17)*

A poet expressed it in these words:

> There I shall bathe my weary soul,
> In seas of heavenly rest,
> And not a wave of trouble roll,
> Across my peaceful breast.

Oh, children of God, you who have suffered, who have been sorely tried, whose sad experiences have often produced broken spirits and bleeding hearts, cheer up! God is in all your troubles, and He will see that all will *"work together for good"* (Rom. 8:28) if you will but be patient, submissive, and prayerful.

7

Prayer and God's Work

If Jacob's desire had been given him in time for him to get a good night's sleep, he might never have become the prince of prayers we know today. If Hannah's prayer for a son had been answered at the time she set for herself, the nation might never have know the mighty man of God it found in Samuel. Hannah wanted only a son, but God wanted more. He wanted a prophet, and a savior, and a ruler for His people. Someone said that "God had to get a woman before He could get a man." This woman He got in Hannah. Precisely by those weeks and months and years there came a woman with a vision like God's, with tempered soul and gentle spirit and a seasoned will, prepared to be the kind of a mother for the kind of a man God knew the nation needed. —W. E. Biederwolf

GOD has a great work on hand in this world. This work is involved in the plan of salvation. It embraces redemption and providence. God is governing this world, including its intelligent beings, for His own glory and for their good.

What, then, is God's work in this world? Moreover, what is the end He seeks in His great work? It is nothing short of holiness of heart and life in the children of fallen Adam. Man is a fallen creature, born with an evil nature, with an evil bent, unholy propensities, sinful desires, wicked inclinations. Man is born so by nature. *"They go astray as soon as they be born, speaking lies"* (Ps. 58:3). God's entire plan is to take hold of fallen man and to seek to change him and make him holy. God's work is to make holy men out of unholy men. This is the very reason Christ came into the world: *"For this purpose the Son of God was manifested, that he might destroy the works of the devil"* (1 John 3:8).

God is holy in nature and in all His ways, and He wants to make man like Himself: *"As he which hath called you is holy, so be ye holy in all manner of conversation; because it is written, Be ye holy; for I am holy"* (1 Pet. 1:15–16).

This is being Christlike. This is following Jesus Christ. This is the aim of all Christian effort. This is the earnest, heartfelt desire of every truly regenerated soul. This is what is to be constantly and earnestly prayed for—that we may be made holy. Not that we must make ourselves holy, but we must be cleansed from all sin by the precious, atoning blood of Christ and be made holy by the direct agency of the Holy Spirit. Not that we are to do holy, but rather to be holy. Being must precede doing. First be, then do. First, obtain a holy heart, then live a holy life. And for this high and gracious end, God has made the most ample provisions in the atoning work of our Lord and through the agency of the Holy Spirit.

The work of God in the world is the implantation, the growth, and the perfection of holiness in His people. Keep this always in mind. But we might ask just now, Is this work advancing in the church? Are men and women being made holy? Is the present-day church engaged in the business of making holy men and women? This is not a vain and speculative question. It is practical, pertinent, and all-important.

The present-day church has vast machinery. Her activities are great, and her material prosperity is unparalleled. The name of religion is widely spread and well known. Much money comes into the Lord's treasury and is paid out. But here are the questions: Does the work of holiness keep pace with all this? Is the burden of the prayers of church people to be made holy? Are our preachers really holy men, or, to go back a little further, are they hungering and thirsting after righteousness (see Matthew 5:6), desiring the sincere milk of the Word that they may grow thereby? (See 1 Peter 2:2.) Are they really seeking to be holy men? Of course, men of intelligence are greatly needed in the pulpit; but, prior to that and primary to it, is the fact that we need holy men to stand before dying men and proclaim the salvation of God to them.

Ministers, like laymen and no more so than laymen, must be holy men in life, in conversation, and in temper. They must be examples to the flock of God in all things. By their lives they are to preach as well as to speak. Men in the pulpit are needed who are spotless in life, circumspect in behavior, *"blameless and...without rebuke, in the midst of a crooked and perverse nation, among whom* [they are to] *shine as lights in the world"* (Phil. 2:15). Are our present-day preachers this type of men? We are simply asking the question. Let the reader make his own judgment. Is the work of holiness making progress among our preachers?

Again let us ask, Are our leading laymen examples of holiness? Are they seeking holiness of heart and life? Are they praying men, ever praying that God would fashion them according to His pattern of holiness? Are their business ways without stain of sin, and their gains free from the taint of wrongdoing? Have they the foundation of solid honesty, and does uprightness bring them into elevation and influence? Does business integrity and probity run parallel with religious activity and with Christian observance?

Then, while we are pursuing our investigation, seeking light as to whether the work of God among His people is making progress, let us ask further as to our women. Are the leading women of our churches dead to the fashions of this world, separated from the world, not conformed to the world's maxims and customs? Is their behavior such that becomes holiness, teaching the young women by word and life the lessons of soberness, obedience, and home-keeping? Are our women noted for their praying habits? Are they models of prayer?

How searching are all these questions? Will anyone dare say they are impertinent and out of place? If God's work is to make men and women holy—and He has made ample provisions in the law of prayer of doing this very thing—why should it be thought impertinent and useless to propound such personal and pointed questions as these? They have to do directly with the work and with its progress and its perfection. They go to the very center of the disease. They hit the spot.

We might as well face the situation at the first as at the last. There is no use in shutting our eyes to real facts. If the church does not do this sort of work, if the church does not advance its members in holiness of heart and life, then all our show of activities and all our display of church work are a delusion and a snare.

But let us ask about another large, important class of people in our churches. They are the hope of the future church. To them all eyes are turned. Are our young men and women growing in sober-mindedness and reverence, and in all those graces that have their root in the renewed heart, that mark solid and permanent advance in the divine life? If we are not growing in holiness, then we are doing nothing religious or abiding.

Material prosperity is not the infallible sign of spiritual prosperity. The former may exist while the latter is significantly absent. Material prosperity may easily blind the eyes of church leaders, so much so that they will make it a substitute for spiritual prosperity. How great the need to watch at that point! Prosperity in monetary matters does not signify growth in holiness. The seasons of material prosperity are rarely seasons of spiritual advance, either to the individual or to the church. It is so easy to lose sight of God when goods increase. It so easy to lean on human agencies and cease praying and relying upon God when material prosperity comes to the church.

If it is contended that the work of God is progressing and that we are growing in holiness, then some perplexing questions arise that will be hard to answer. If the church is making advances on the lines of deep spirituality—if we are a praying people, noted for our prayer habits, and if our people are hungering after holiness—then let us ask, why do we now have so few mighty outpourings of the Holy Spirit on our chief churches and our principal appointees? Why is it that so few of our revivals spring from the life of the pastor, who is noted for his deep spirituality, or from the life of the church? *"Behold, the LORD'S hand is not shortened, that it cannot save; neither his ear heavy, that it cannot hear"* (Isa. 59:1). Why is it that in order to have so-called revivals we must have outside pressure, by the reputation and sensationalism of some renowned evangelist? This is generally true in our larger charges and with our leading men. Why is it that the pastor is not sufficiently spiritual, holy, and in communion with God, that he cannot hold his own revival services and have large outpourings of the Holy Spirit on the church, on the community, and on himself?

There can be but one answer for all this state of things. We have cultivated other things, to the neglect of the work of holiness. We have permitted our minds to be preoccupied with material things in the church. Unfortunately, whether purposefully or not, we have substituted the external for the internal. We have put that which is seen to the front and shut out that which is unseen. It is all too true as to the church, that we are much further advanced in material matters than in spiritual matters.

But the cause of this sad state of things may be traced further back. It is largely due to the decay of prayer. With the decline of the work of holiness has come the decline of the business of praying. As praying and holiness go together, so the decline of one means the decay of the other. We may excuse it, we may try to justify the present state of things, yet it is all too clear that the emphasis in the work of the present-day church is not put on prayer. And just as this has occurred, the emphasis has been taken from the great work of God that was begun in the Atonement—holiness of heart and life. The church is not turning out praying men and women because the church is not intently engaged in the one great work of holiness.

At one time, John Wesley saw that there was a perceptible decline in the work of holiness, and he stopped short to inquire into the cause. If we are as honest and spiritual as he was, we will now see the same causes operating to hold back God's work among us. In a letter to his brother, Charles, at one time, he came directly to the point and made short, incisive work of it. Here is how he began his letter:

> What has hindered the work? I want to consider this. And must we not first say, we are the chief. If we were more holy in heart and life, thoroughly devoted to God, would not all the preachers catch fire, and carry it with them, throughout the land?
>
> Is not the next hindrance the littleness of grace (rather than of gifts) in a considerable part of our preachers? They do not have the whole mind that was in Christ. They do not steadily walk as He walked. And, therefore, the hand of the Lord is stayed, though not altogether; though He does work still. But it is not in such a degree as He surely desires, were they holy as He who sent them is holy. (See 1 Peter 1:15–16.)
>
> Is not the third hindrance the littleness of grace in the majority of our people? Therefore, they pray little, and with little fervency for a general blessing. And, therefore, their prayer has little power with God. It does not, as once, shut and open heaven.
>
> Add to this, that as there is much of the spirit of the world in their hearts, so there is much conformity to the world in their lives. They ought to be bright and shining lights, but they neither burn nor shine. They are not true to the rules they profess to observe. They are not holy in all manner of conversation. Nay, many of them are salt that has lost its savor, the little savor they once had. Wherewith then

shall the rest of the land be seasoned? (See Luke 14:34.) What wonder that their neighbors are as unholy as ever?

He strikes the spot. He hits the center. He catalogs the sources of the trouble. He freely confesses that he and Charles are the first cause in this decline of holiness. The chief leaders occupy positions of responsibility. As they go, so goes the church. They give color to the church. They largely determine its character and its work. What holiness should mark these chief men? What zeal should ever characterize them? What prayerfulness should be seen in them! How influential they ought to be with God! If the head is weak, then the whole body will feel the stroke.

The pastors come next in his catalog. When the chief shepherds and those who are under them, the associate pastors, cease their advance in holiness, the panic will reach to all other levels. As a rule, as the pastors are, so will the people be. If the pastors are prayerless, then the people will follow in their footsteps. If the preacher is silent about the work of holiness, then there will be no hungering and thirsting after holiness in the laymen. If the preacher is careless about obtaining the highest and best that God has for him in religious experience, then the people will take after him.

One statement of Wesley needs to be repeated with emphasis. The littleness of grace, rather than the smallness of gifts, is largely the case with the preachers. It may be stated as an axiom: The work of God fails, as a general rule, more for the lack of grace than for the want of gifts. It is more than this, for a full supply of grace brings an increase of gifts. It may be repeated that small results, a low experience, a low religious life, and pointless, powerless preaching always flow from a lack of grace. And a lack of grace flows from a lack of praying. Great grace comes from great praying.

> What is our calling's glorious hope
> But inward holiness?
> For this to Jesus I look up,
> I calmly wait for this.
>
> I wait till He shall touch me clean,
> Shall life and power impart;
> Give me the faith that casts out sin,
> And purifies the heart.

In carrying on His great work in the world, God works through human agents. He works through His church collectively and through His people individually. In order that they may be effective agents, they must be *"vessel[s] unto honour, sanctified, and meet for the master's use, and prepared unto every good work"* (2 Tim. 2:21). God works most effectively through holy men. His work makes progress in the hands of praying men. Peter told us that husbands who might not be reached by the Word of God might be won by the conversation of their wives. (See 1 Peter 3:1.) It is those who are *"blameless and harmless, the sons of God,"* who can hold forth the *"word of life...in the midst of a crooked and perverse nation"* (Phil. 2:15–16).

The world judges religion not by what the Bible says, but by how Christians live. Christians are the Bible that sinners read. These are the epistles to be read by all men. *"By their fruits ye shall know them"* (Matt. 7:20). The emphasis, then, is to be placed upon holiness of life. But, unfortunately, in the present-day church, emphasis has been placed elsewhere. In selecting church workers and choosing ecclesiastical officers, the quality of holiness is not considered. One's fitness in prayer seems not to be taken into account, when it is just the opposite in all of God's movements and in all of His plans. He looks for holy men, those noted for their praying habits. But prayer leaders are scarce. Prayer conduct is not counted as the highest qualification for offices in the church.

We cannot wonder that so little is accomplished in the world for the great work that God has in hand. The fact is that it is surprising that so much has been done with such feeble, defective agents. *"HOLINESS TO THE LORD"* (Exod. 28:36) needs again to be written on the banners of the church. Once more it needs to be sounded out in the ears of modern Christians: *"Follow peace with all men, and holiness, without which no man shall see the Lord"* (Heb. 12:14).

Let it be said again and again that this is the divine standard of religion. Nothing short of this will satisfy the divine requirement. Oh, the danger of deception at this point! How near one can come to being right and yet be wrong! Some men can come very near to pronouncing the test word, "Shibboleth," but they miss it. (See Judges 12:6.) *"Many will say to me in that day, Lord, Lord,"* says Jesus Christ, but He further states that then will He say unto them, *"I never knew you: depart from me, ye that work iniquity"* (Matt. 7:22–23).

Men can do many good things and yet not be holy in heart and righteous in conduct. They can do many good things and yet lack that spiritual quality of heart called holiness. Men need to hear the words of Paul guarding us against self-deception in the great work of personal salvation: *"Be not deceived; God is not mocked: for whatsoever a man soweth, that shall he also reap"* (Gal. 6:7).

> O may I still from sin depart;
>   A wise and understanding heart,
> Jesus, to me to be given;
>   And let me through Thy Spirit know
> To glorify my God below,
>   And find my way to heaven.

8

Prayer and Consecration

Eudamidas, a citizen of Corinth, died in poverty; but having two wealthy friends, Arctaeus and Charixenus, left the following testament: "In virtue of my last will, I bequeath to Arctaeus my mother and to Charixenus my daughter to be taken home to their houses and supported for the remainder of their lives." This testament occasioned much mirth and laughter. The two legatees were pleased and affectionately executed the will. If heathens trusted each other, why should not I cherish a greater confidence in my beloved Master, Jesus? I hereby, therefore, nominate Him my sole heir, consigning to Him my soul and my children and sisters, that He may adopt, protect, and provide for them by His mighty power unto salvation. The whole residue of the estate shall be entrusted to His holy counsel. —Gotthold*

WHEN we study the many-sidedness of prayer, we may be surprised at the number of things with which it is connected. There is no phase of human life that it does not affect, and it has to do with everything affecting human salvation. Consecration is one of these things to which prayer is closely related. Prayer leads up to and governs consecration. Prayer is precedent to consecration, accompanies it, and is a direct result of it.

Much goes under the name of consecration that has no consecration in it. Much consecration of the present day is defective, superficial, and spurious, worth nothing so far as the office and ends of consecration are concerned. Popular consecration is sadly at fault because it has little or no prayer in it. No consecration is worth a thought that is not the direct fruit of much praying and that fails to bring one into a life of prayer. Prayer is the one prominent thing in a consecrated life.

Consecration is much more than a life of so-called service. It is a life of personal holiness, first of all. It is that which brings spiritual power into the heart and enlivens the entire inner man. It is a life that ever recognizes God, and a life given up to true prayer.

Full consecration is the highest type of a Christian life. It is the one divine standard of experience, of living, and of service. It is the one thing for which the believer should aim. Nothing short of entire consecration must satisfy him. Never is he to be contented until he is fully, entirely the Lord's by his own consent. His praying naturally and involuntarily leads up to this one act of his.

Consecration is the voluntary, set dedication of oneself to God, an offering definitely made, and made without any reservation whatsoever. It is the setting apart of all we are, all we have, and all we expect to have or be, to God first of all. It is not so much the giving of ourselves to the church or the mere engaging in some one line of church work. Almighty God is in view, and He is the end of all consecration. It is a separation of oneself to God, a devoting of all that he is and has to a sacred use. Some things may be devoted to a special purpose, but it is not consecration in the true sense. Consecration has a sacred nature. It is devoted to holy ends. It is the voluntary putting of oneself into God's hands to be used sacredly, with sanctifying ends in view.

Consecration is not so much setting oneself apart from sinful things and wicked ends, but rather it is the separation of self for holy uses from worldly, secular, and even legitimate things, if they come in conflict with God's plans. It is the devoting of all we have to God for His own specific use. It is a separation from things questionable, or even legitimate, when the choice is to be made between the things of this life and the claims of God.

The consecration that meets God's demands and that He accepts is to be full, complete, with no mental reservation, with nothing withheld. It cannot be partial, any more than a whole burnt offering in Old Testament times could have been partial. The whole animal had to be offered in sacrifice. To reserve any part of the animal would have seriously debased the offering. To make a halfhearted, partial consecration is to make no consecration at all and is to fail utterly in securing the divine acceptance. It involves our whole being, all we have and all that we are. Everything is definitely and voluntarily placed in God's hands for His supreme use.

Consecration is not all there is in holiness. Many make serious mistakes at this point. Consecration makes us relatively holy. We are holy only in the sense that we are now closely related to God and we were not related heretofore. Consecration is the human side of holiness. In this sense, it is self-sanctification, and only in this sense. But sanctification, or holiness in its truest and highest sense, is divine, the act of the Holy Spirit working in the heart, making it clean, and putting therein a higher degree the fruits of the Spirit.

This distinction was clearly set forth and kept in view by Moses in Leviticus, where he showed the human and the divine sides of holiness: *"Sanctify yourselves, therefore, and be ye holy: for I am the LORD your God. And ye shall keep my statutes, and do them: I am the LORD which sanctify you"* (Lev. 20:7–8).

Here we are told to sanctify ourselves, and then in the next word we are taught that it is the Lord who sanctifies us. Here is the two-fold meaning of sanctification, and a distinction that needs to be always kept in mind. God does not consecrate us to His service; we must wholeheartedly commit or consecrate ourselves to Him. But we do not sanctify ourselves in this highest sense; that is the work of the Spirit in us.

Consecration being the intelligent, voluntary act of the believer, this act is the direct result of prayer. No prayerless man ever conceives the idea of a full consecration. Prayerlessness and consecration have nothing in common whatsoever. A life of prayer naturally leads to full consecration. It leads nowhere else. In fact, a life of prayer is satisfied with nothing else but an entire dedication of oneself to God. Consecration recognizes fully God's ownership of us. It cheerfully assents to the truth set forth by Paul: *"Ye are not your own. For ye are bought with a price: therefore glorify God in your body, and in your spirit, which are God's"* (1 Cor. 6:19–20).

True praying leads that way. It cannot reach any other destination. It is bound to run into this depot. This is its natural result. This is the sort of work that praying turns out. Praying makes consecrated people. It cannot make any other sort. It drives to this end. It aims at this very purpose.

As prayer leads up to and brings forth full consecration, so prayer entirely impregnates a consecrated life. The prayer life and the consecrated life are intimate companions. They are Siamese twins, inseparable. Prayer enters into every phase of a consecrated life. A prayerless life that claims consecration is a misnomer, false, counterfeit.

Consecration is really the setting apart of oneself to a life of prayer. It means not only to pray, but to pray habitually, and to pray more effectively. It is the consecrated man who accomplishes most by his praying. God must hear the man wholly given up to Him. God cannot deny the requests of the man who has renounced all claims to himself and who has wholly dedicated himself to God and His service. This act of the consecrated man puts him on praying ground and pleading terms with God. It puts Him in reach of God in prayer. It places him where he can get hold of God, and where he can influence God to do things that He would not otherwise do.

Consecration brings answers to prayer. God can depend upon consecrated men. God can afford to commit Himself to those who have fully committed themselves to Him in prayer. He who gives all to God will get all from God. Having given all to God, he can claim all that God has for him.

As prayer is the condition of full consecration, so prayer is the habit, the rule, of him who has dedicated himself wholly to God. Prayer is the most appropriate thing in the consecrated life; it is no strange thing in such a life. There is a peculiar affinity between prayer and consecration, for both recognize God, both submit to God, and both have their aim and end in God. Prayer is part and parcel of the consecrated life. Prayer is the constant, the inseparable, the intimate companion of consecration. They walk and talk together.

There is much talk today of consecration, and many are termed consecrated people who do not know even the alphabet of it. Much modern consecration falls far below the scriptural standard. There is really no real consecration in it. Just as there is much praying without any real prayer in it, so there is much so-called consecration present in the church today that has no real consecration in it. Much passes for consecration in the church that receives the praise and plaudits of superficial, formal professors but that is wide of the mark. There is much hurrying to and fro, here and there, much fuss and feathers, much going about and doing many things, and those who busy themselves after this fashion are called consecrated men and women.

The central trouble with all this false consecration is that there is no prayer in it, nor is it in any sense the direct result of praying. People can do many excellent and commendable things in the church and be utter strangers to a life of consecration, just as they can do many things and be prayerless.

Here is the true test of consecration: it is a life of prayer. Unless prayer is preeminent, unless prayer is in the forefront, the consecration is faulty, deceptive, falsely named. Does he pray? That is the test question of every so-called consecrated man. Is he a man of prayer? No consecration is worth a thought if it is devoid of prayer, but even more so if it is not preeminently and primarily a life of prayer.

God wants consecrated men because they can pray and will pray. He can use consecrated men because He can use praying men. As prayerless men are in His way, hinder Him and prevent the success of His cause, so likewise unconsecrated men are useless to Him and hinder Him in carrying out His gracious plans and in executing His noble purposes in redemption. God wants consecrated men because He wants praying men. Consecration and prayer meet in the same man. Prayer is the tool with which the consecrated man works. Consecrated men are the agents through whom prayer works. Prayer helps the consecrated man in maintaining his attitude of consecration, keeps him alive to God, and aids him in doing the work to which he is called and to which he has given himself. Consecration helps one to pray effectually. Consecration enables one to get the most out of his praying.

> Let Him to whom we now belong
> His sovereign right assert;
> And take up every thankful song,
> And every loving heart.
>
> He justly claims us for His own,
> Who bought us with a price;
> The Christian lives to Christ alone,
> To Christ alone he dies.

We must insist that the prime purpose of consecration is not service in the ordinary sense of that word. Service, in the minds of many, means nothing more than engaging in some of the many forms of modern church activities. There is a multitude of such activities, enough to engage the time and mind of anyone, even more than enough. Some of these may be good, others not so good. The present-day church is filled with machinery, organizations, committees, and societies, so much so that the power it has is altogether insufficient to run the machinery or to furnish life sufficient to do all this external work. Consecration has a much nobler end than merely to expend itself in external things.

Consecration aims at the right sort of service, the scriptural kind. It seeks to serve God, but in an entirely different sphere than that which is in the minds of present-day church leaders and workers. The very first sort of service mentioned by Zacharias, father of John the Baptist, in his wonderful prophecy and statement was this:

> *That he would grant unto us, that we being delivered out of the hand of our enemies might serve him without fear, in holiness and righteousness before him, all the days of our life.*
> *(Luke 1:74–75)*

Here we have the idea of consecration as *"serving God in holiness and righteousness all the days of our* [lives]." The same kind of service is mentioned in Luke's strong tribute to the father and mother of John the Baptist before the latter's birth: *"And they were both righteous before God, walking in all the commandments and ordinances of the Lord blameless"* (Luke 1:6).

In writing to the Philippians, Paul struck the same keynote in putting the emphasis on blamelessness of life:

> *Do all things without murmurings and disputings: that ye may be blameless and harmless, the sons of God, without rebuke, in the midst of a crooked and perverse nation, among whom ye shine as lights in the world; holding forth the word of life.*
> *(Phil. 2:14–16)*

I must mention a truth that is strangely overlooked in these days by what are called personal workers. In the Epistles, it is not what are called church activities that are brought to the front, but rather the personal life. It is good behavior, righteous conduct, godly conversation, holy living, right tempers—things that belong primarily to the personal life in religion. Everywhere this is emphasized, put in the forefront, made much of, and insisted on. Religion puts one to living right. Religion shows itself in the life. In this way religion proves its reality, its sincerity, and its divinity.

> So let our lips and lives express
> The holy Gospel we profess;
> So let our works and virtues shine
> To prove the doctrine all Divine.
>
> Thus shall we best proclaim abroad
> The honors of our Saviour God;
> When the salvation reigns within
> And grace subdues the power of sin.

The first great end of consecration is holiness of heart and of life. It is to glorify God, and this can be done in no more effective way than by a holy life flowing from a heart cleansed from all sin. The great burden of heart pressed on everyone who becomes a Christian lies right here. This he is to ever keep in mind. To further this kind of life and this kind of heart, he is to watch, to pray, and to bend all his diligence in using all the means of grace. He who is truly and fully consecrated lives a holy life. He seeks after holiness of heart. He is not satisfied without it. For this very purpose he consecrates himself to God. He gives himself entirely over to God in order to be holy in heart and in life.

As holiness of heart and life is thoroughly impregnated with prayer, so consecration and prayer are closely allied in personal religion. It takes prayer to bring one into such a consecrated life of holiness to the Lord, and it takes prayer to maintain such a life. Without much prayer, such a life of holiness will break down. Holy people are praying people. Holiness of heart and life puts people to praying. Consecration puts people to praying in earnest.

Prayerless people are strangers to anything like holiness and cleanness of heart. Those who are unfamiliar with the prayer closet are not at all interested in consecration and holiness. Holiness thrives in the place of secret prayer. The environment of the prayer closet is favorable to its being and its culture. In the closet, holiness is found. Consecration brings one into holiness of heart, and prayer stands by when it is done.

The spirit of consecration is the spirit of prayer. The law of consecration is the law of prayer. Both laws work in perfect harmony without the slightest jarring or discord. Consecration is the practical expression of true prayer. People who are consecrated are known by their praying habits. Consecration thus expresses itself in prayer. He who is not interested in prayer has no interest in consecration. Prayer creates an interest in consecration, then prayer brings one into a state of heart where consecration is a subject of delight, bringing joy of heart, satisfaction of soul, and contentment of spirit. The consecrated soul is the happiest soul. There is no friction whatsoever between God's will and the man who is fully given over to God. There is perfect harmony between the will of such a man and God and His will. And that the two wills are in perfect accord brings rest of soul, absence of friction, and the presence of perfect peace.

> Lord, in the strength of grace,
>   With a glad heart and free,
> Myself, my residue of days,
>   I consecrate to Thee.
>
> Thy ransomed servant, I
>   Restore to Thee Thy own;
> And from this moment, live or die,
>   To serve my God alone.

9

Prayer and Definite Standards

The Angel Gabriel described Him as "that holy thing" before He was born. As He was, so are we, in our measure, in this world. — Alexander Whyte

MUCH of the feebleness, barrenness, and paucity of religion results from the failure to have a scriptural, reasonable standard in religion by which to shape character and measure results. This largely results from the omission of prayer or the failure to put prayer in the standard.

We cannot possibly mark our advances in religion if there is no point to which we are definitely advancing. Always there must be something definite before the mind's eye at which we are aiming and to which we are driving. We cannot contrast shapeliness with unshapeliness if there is no pattern after which to model. Neither can there be inspiration if there is no high end to stimulate us.

Many Christians are disjointed and aimless because they have no pattern before them after which conduct and character are to be shaped. They just move on aimlessly, their minds in a cloudy state, no pattern in view, no point in sight, no standard after which they are striving. There is no standard by which to value and gauge their efforts. No magnet is there to fill their eyes, quicken their steps, draw them, and keep them steady.

This vague idea of religion grows out of loose notions about prayer. That which helps to make the standard of religion clear and definite is prayer. That which aids in placing that standard high is prayer. The prayerful ones are those who have something definite in view. In fact, prayer itself is a very definite thing; it aims at something specific, it has a mark at which it aims. Prayer aims at

342

the most definite, the highest, and the sweetest religious experience.

The praying ones want all that God has in store for them. They are not satisfied with anything like a low religious life, superficial, vague, and indefinite. The praying ones are not only after a deeper work of grace, but want the very deepest work of grace possible and promised. They are not after being saved from some sin, but saved from all sin, both inward and outward. They are after not only deliverance from sinning, but from sin itself, from its being, its power, and its pollution. They are after holiness of heart and life.

Prayer believes in and seeks for the very highest religious life set before us in the Word of God. Prayer is the condition of that life. Prayer points out the only pathway to such a life. The standard of a religious life is the standard of prayer. Prayer is so vital, so essential, so far-reaching that it enters into all religion and sets the standard clear and definite before the eye. The degree of our estimate of prayer fixes our ideas of the standard of a religious life. The standard of Bible religion is the standard of prayer. The more there is of prayer in the life, the more definite and the higher our notions of religion.

The Scriptures alone comprise the standard of life and experience. When we make our own standards, there is delusion and falsity for our desires, convenience and pleasure form the rule, and that is always a fleshly and a low rule. From it, all the fundamental principles of a Christ-centered religion are left out. Whatever standard of religion that makes in it provision for the flesh is unscriptural and hurtful.

Nor will it do to leave it to others to set the standard of religion for us. When we allow others to set our standard of religion, it is generally deficient because, in imitation, defects are transferred to the imitator more readily than virtues, and a second edition of a man is marred by its defects.

The most serious damage in determining what religion is according to what others say is in allowing current opinion, the contagion of example, the grade of religion current among us, to shape our religious opinions and characters. Adoniram Judson once wrote to a friend, "Let me beg you, not to rest contented with the commonplace religion that is now so prevalent." Commonplace religion is pleasing to flesh and blood. There is no self-denial in it, no crossbearing, no self-crucifixion. It is good enough for our neighbors. Why should we be singular and straightlaced? Others are living on a low plane, on a compromising level, living as the world lives. Why should we be peculiar, zealous of good works? (See Titus 2:14.) Why should we fight to win heaven while so many are sailing there on flowery beds of ease? But, are the easygoing, careless, sauntering crowd, who are living prayerless lives, going to heaven? Is heaven a fit place for non-praying, loose-living, ease-loving people? That is the supreme question.

Paul gave the following caution about making for ourselves the jolly, pleasure-seeking religious company all about us the standard of our measurement:

> *For we dare not make ourselves of the number, or compare ourselves with some that commend themselves: but they measuring themselves by themselves, and comparing themselves among themselves, are not wise. But we will not boast of things without our measure, but according to the measure of the rule which God hath distributed to us, a measure to reach even unto you.*   *(2 Cor. 10:12–13)*

No standard of religion is worth a moment's consideration that leaves prayer out of the account. No standard is worth any thought that does not make prayer the main thing in religion. So necessary is prayer, so fundamental in God's plan, so all-important to everything pertaining to a religious life, that it enters into all Bible religion. Prayer itself is a standard—definite, emphatic, scriptural. A life of prayer is the divine rule. This is the pattern, just as our Lord, being a Man of prayer, is the one pattern for us after whom to copy. Prayer fashions the pattern of a religious life. Prayer is the measure. Prayer molds the life.

The vague, indefinite, popular view of religion has no prayer in it. In its program, prayer is entirely left out or put so low down and made so insignificant that it is hardly worth mentioning. Man's standard of religion has no prayer about it.

It is God's standard at which we are to aim, not man's. Our goal should be set not by the opinions of men, not by what they say, but by what the Scriptures say. Loose notions of religion grow out of low notions of prayer. Prayerlessness begets loose, cloudy, and indefinite views of what religion is. Aimless living and prayerlessness go hand in hand. Prayer sets something definite in the mind. Prayer seeks after something specific. The more definite our views as to the nature and need for prayer, the more definite will be our views of Christian experience and right living, and the less vague our views of religion. A low standard of religion lives by a low standard of praying.

Everything in a religious life depends upon being definite. The definiteness of our religious experiences and of our living will depend on the definiteness of our views of what religion is and of the things of which it consists. The Scriptures ever set before us the one standard of full consecration to God. This is the divine rule. This is the human side of this standard. The sacrifice acceptable to God must be a complete one—entire, a whole burnt offering. This is the measure laid down in God's Word. Nothing less than this can be pleasing to God.

Nothing halfhearted can please Him. *"A living sacrifice, holy"* (Rom. 12:1), and perfect in all its parts, is the measurement of our service to God. A full renunciation of self, a free recognition of God's right to us, and a sincere offering of all to Him—this is the divine requirement. Nothing is indefinite in that. Nothing in that is governed by the opinions of others or affected by how men live around us.

While a life of prayer is embraced in such a full consecration, at the same time prayer leads up to the point where a complete consecration is made to God. Consecration is but the silent expression of prayer. And the highest religious standard is the measure of prayer and selfless dedication to God. The prayer life and the consecrated life are partners in religion. They are so closely allied that they are never separated. The prayer life is the direct fruit of entire consecration to God. Prayer is the natural outflow of a really consecrated life. The measure of consecration is the measure of real prayer.

No consecration is pleasing to God that is not perfect in all its parts, just as no burnt offering of a Jew was ever acceptable to God unless it was a *"whole burnt offering"* (Ps. 51:19). A consecration of this sort, according to this divine measurement, has in it as a basic principle the business of praying. Consecration is made to God. Prayer has to do with God. Consecration is putting oneself entirely at the disposal of God. And God wants and commands all His consecrated ones to be praying ones. This is the one definite standard at which we must aim. We cannot afford to seek anything lower than this.

A scriptural standard of religion includes a clear religious experience. Religion is nothing if not experiential. Religion appeals to the inner consciousness. It is an experience, if anything at all, and an experience in addition to a religious life. There is the internal part of religion as well as the external. Not only are we to *"work out* [our] *own salvation with fear and trembling,"* but *"it is God which worketh in* [us] *to will and do of his good pleasure"* (Phil. 2:12–13). There is a *"good work in you"* (Phil. 1:6), as well as a life outside to be lived.

The new birth is a definite Christian experience, proved by infallible marks, appealing to the inner consciousness. The witness of the Spirit is not an indefinite, vague *something*, but is a definite, clear, inward assurance given by the Holy Spirit that we are the children of God. In fact, everything belonging to religious experience is clear and definite, bringing conscious joy, peace, and love. This is the divine standard of religion, a standard attained by earnest, constant prayer and a religious experience kept alive and enlarged by the same means of prayer.

An end to be gained, to which effort is to be directed, is important in every pursuit in order to give unity, energy, and steadiness to it. In the Christian life, such an end is all-important. Without a high standard before us to be gained, for which we are earnestly seeking, lassitude will unnerve effort, and past experience will deteriorate into mere sentiment or will be hardened into cold, loveless principle.

We must go on. *"Therefore leaving the principles of the doctrine of Christ, let us go on unto perfection"* (Heb. 6:1). The present ground we occupy must be held by making advances, and all the future must be covered and brightened by it. In religion, we must not only go on, but we must also know where we are going. This is all-important. It is essential, in going on in religious experience, that we have something definite in view and that we strike out for that one point. To always go on and not know where we are going is altogether too vague and indefinite. It is the condition of a man who starts out on a journey and does not have any destination in mind. It is important that we do not lose sight of the starting point in a religious life, and that we measure the steps already trod. But it is likewise necessary that the end be kept in view and that the steps necessary to reach the standard be always in sight.

10

Prayer Born of Compassion

Open your New Testament, take it with you to your knees, and set Jesus Christ out of it before you. Are you like David in the sixty-third Psalm? Is your soul thirsting for God, and is your flesh longing for God in a "dry and thirsty land, where no water is"? Then set Jesus at the well of Samaria before the eyes of your thirsty heart. And, again, set Him before your heart when He stood on the last day, that great day of the feast, and cried, saying, "If any man thirst, let him come unto me, and drink." Or, are you like David after the matter of Uriah? "For, day and night thy hand was heavy upon me: my moisture is turned into the drought of summer." Then set Him before you who says: "I am not come to call the righteous, but sinners to repentance....They that be whole need not a physician, but they that are sick." Or are you the unhappy father of a prodigal son? Then, set your Father in heaven always before you: and set the Son of God always before you, as He composes and preaches the parable of all parables for you and your son.
                                            —*Alexander Whyte*

WE are speaking here particularly about spiritual compassion, that which is born in a renewed heart and which finds hospitality there. This compassion has in it the quality of mercy, is of the nature of pity, and moves the soul with tenderness of feeling for others. Compassion is moved at the sight of sin, sorrow, and suffering. It stands at the other extreme to indifference to the wants and woes of others. It is far removed from insensibility and hardness of heart in the midst of need and trouble and wretchedness. Compassion stands beside sympathy for others, is interested in them, and is concerned about them.

That which excites and develops compassion and puts it to work is the sight of multitudes in want and distress, helpless to relieve themselves. Helplessness especially appeals to compassion. Compassion is silent but does not remain secluded. It reaches out at the sight of trouble, sin, and need. First of all, compassion flows out in earnest prayer for those for whom it feels and has a sympathy for them. Prayer for others is born of a sympathetic heart. Prayer is natural and almost spontaneous when compassion is begotten in the heart. Prayer belongs to the compassionate man.

There is a certain compassion that belongs to the natural man, that expends its force in simple gifts to those in need, not to be despised. But spiritual compassion, the kind born in a renewed heart, which is Christlike in its nature, is deeper, broader, and more prayerlike. The compassion of Christ always moves to prayer. This sort of compassion goes beyond the relief of mere bodily wants to say, *"Be ye warmed and filled"* (James 2:16). It reaches deeper down and goes much further.

Compassion is not blind. Rather, I should say that compassion is not born of blindness. He who has compassion of soul has eyes, first of all, to see the things that excite compassion. He who has no eyes to see the exceeding sinfulness of sin, the wants and the sorrows of humanity, will never have compassion for humanity. It is written of our Lord that *"when he saw the multitudes, he was moved with compassion on them"* (Matt. 9:36). First, He saw the multitudes with their hunger, their woes, and their helpless condition; then He experienced compassion that moved Him to pray for the multitudes. Hard is the man, and far from being Christlike, who sees the multitudes but is unmoved at the sight of their sad state, their unhappiness, and their peril. He has no heart of prayer for men.

Compassion may not always move men, but is always moved toward men. Compassion may not always turn men to God, but it will, and does, turn God to man. And where it is most helpless to relieve the needs of others, it can at least break out into prayer to God for others. Compassion is never indifferent, selfish, or forgetful of others. Compassion has to do with others only. The fact that the multitudes were as sheep having no shepherd was the one thing that appealed to our Lord's compassionate nature. Then their hunger moved Him, and the sight of the sufferings and diseases of these multitudes stirred the pity of His heart.

> Father of mercies, send Thy grace
> All powerful from above,
> To form in our obedient souls
> The image of Thy love.
>
> Oh, may our sympathizing breasts
> That generous pleasure know;
> Kindly to share in others' joy,
> And weep for others' woe.

But compassion has not only to do with the body and its disabilities and needs. The soul's distressing state, its needs, and its danger, all appeal to compassion. The highest state of grace is known by the infallible mark of compassion for poor sinners.

This sort of compassion belongs to grace and sees not only the bodies of men, but their immortal spirits—soiled by sin, unhappy in their condition without God, and in imminent peril of being forever lost. When compassion beholds this sight of dying men hurrying to the bar of God, then it breaks out into intercessions for sinful men. Then it is that compassion speaks out after this fashion:

> But feeble my compassion proves,
> And can but weep where most it loves;
> Thy own all-saving arm employ,
> And turn these drops of grief to joy.

The prophet Jeremiah declared this about God, giving the reason why sinners are not consumed by His wrath: *"It is of the LORD'S mercies that we are not consumed, because his compassions fail not"* (Lam. 3:22).

This divine quality in us is what makes us so much like God. So we find the psalmist described the righteous man who is pronounced blessed by God: *"He is gracious, and full of compassion, and righteous"* (Ps. 112:4).

As if giving great encouragement to penitent, praying sinners, the psalmist thus recorded some of the striking attributes of the divine character: *"The LORD is gracious, and full of compassion; slow to anger, and of great mercy"* (Ps. 145:8).

It is no wonder, then, that we find it recorded several times of our Lord while on earth that He *"was moved with compassion"* (Matt. 9:36; 14:14; Mark 1:41; 6:34). Can anyone doubt that His compassion moved Him to pray for those suffering, sorrowing ones who came across His pathway?

Paul was wonderfully interested in the religious welfare of his Jewish brethren; he was concerned over them, and his heart was strangely warmed with tender compassion for their salvation, even though mistreated and sorely persecuted by them. In writing to the Romans, he thus expressed himself:

> *I say the truth in Christ, I lie not, my conscience also bearing me witness in the Holy Ghost, that I have great heaviness and continual sorrow in my heart. For I could wish that myself were accursed for my brethren, my kinsmen according to the flesh.*   *(Rom. 9:1–3)*

What marvelous compassion is here described for Paul's own nation! No wonder that a little later on he recorded this: *"Brethren, my heart's desire and prayer to God for Israel is, that they might be saved"* (Rom. 10:1).

We have an interesting case in Matthew that gives us an account of what excited so largely the compassion of our Lord one time:

> *But when he saw the multitudes, he was moved with compassion on them, because they fainted, and were scattered abroad, as sheep having no shepherd. Then saith he unto his disciples, The harvest truly is plenteous, but the labourers are few. Pray ye therefore the Lord of the harvest, that he will send forth labourers into his harvest.*   *(Matt. 9:36–38)*

It seems from parallel statements that our Lord had called His disciples aside to rest awhile, exhausted as He and they were by the excessive demands on them, by the ceaseless contact with the persons who were ever coming and going, and by their exhaustive toil in ministering to the immense multitudes. But the multitudes precede Him, and instead of finding solitude, quiet, and repose, He finds great multitudes eager to see, to hear, and to be healed. His compassions are moved. The ripened harvests need laborers. He did not call these laborers all at once, by sovereign authority, but He charged the disciples to take themselves to God in prayer, asking Him to send forth laborers into His harvest.

Here is the urgency of prayer enforced by the compassions of our Lord. It is prayer born of compassion for perishing humanity.

The church is urged to pray for laborers to be sent into the harvest of the Lord. The harvest will go to waste and perish without the laborers, while the laborers must be God-chosen, God-sent, and God-commissioned. But God does not send these laborers into His harvest without prayer. The failure of the laborers is owing to the failure of prayer. The scarcity of laborers in the harvest is due to the fact that the church fails to pray for laborers according to His command.

The ingathering of the harvests of earth for the granaries of heaven is dependent on the prayers of God's people. Prayer secures laborers sufficient in quantity and in quality for all the needs of the harvest. God's chosen laborers, God's endowed laborers, and God's thrust-forth laborers are the only ones who will truly go, filled with Christlike compassion and endued with Christlike power. They are the only ones whose going will avail, and these are secured by prayer. Christ's people on their knees, with Christ's compassion in their hearts for dying men and for needy souls, exposed to eternal peril, is the pledge of laborers in numbers and character to meet the needs of earth and the purposes of heaven.

God is the Sovereign of earth, of heaven, and of the choice of laborers in His harvest. He delegates to no one else. Prayer honors Him as sovereign and moves Him to His wise and holy selection. We will have to put prayer to the front before the fields of paganism will be successfully tilled for Christ. God knows His men, and He likewise knows full well His work. Prayer gets God to send forth the best men and the most fit men and the men best qualified to work in the harvest. Moving the missionary cause by forces on this side of God has been its bane, its weakness, and its failure. Compassion for the world of sinners, fallen in Adam but redeemed in Christ, will move the church to pray for them and stir the church to pray the Lord of the harvest to send forth laborers into the harvest.

> Lord of the harvest hear
>   Thy needy servants' cry;
> Answer our faith's effectual prayer,
>   And all our wants supply.
>
> Convert and send forth more
>   Into Thy church abroad;
> And let them speak Thy word of power,
>   As workers with their God.

What a comfort and what hope there is to fill our hearts when we think of one in heaven who ever lives to intercede for us (see Hebrews 7:25), because *"his compassions fail not"* (Lam. 3:22). Above everything else, we have a compassionate Savior, one *"who can have compassion on the ignorant, and on them that are out of the way; for that he himself is compassed with infirmity"* (Heb. 5:2). The compassion of our Lord well fits Him for being the Great High Priest of Adam's fallen, lost, and helpless race.

Moreover, if He is filled with such compassion that it moves Him at the Father's right hand to intercede for us, then by every token we should have the same compassion on the ignorant and those out of the way, exposed to divine wrath, as would move us to pray for them. Just insofar as we are compassionate will we be prayerful for others. Compassion does not expend its force in simply saying, *"Be ye warmed and filled"* (James 2:16), but drives us to our knees in prayer for those who need Christ and His grace.

> The Son of God in tears
> The wondering angels see;
> Be thou astonished, O my soul!
> He shed those tears for thee.
>
> He wept that we might weep;
> Each sin demands a tear;
> In heaven alone no sin is found,
> And there's no weeping there.

Jesus Christ was altogether man. While He was the divine Son of God, yet at the same time He was the human son of God. Christ had a preeminently human side, and here compassion reigned. He *"was in all points tempted like as we are, yet without sin"* (Heb. 4:15). At one time how the flesh seems to have weakened under the fearful strain upon Him, and how He must have inwardly shrunk under the pain and pull! Looking up to heaven, He prays, *"Father, save me from this hour."* How the spirit nerves and holds on, as He continues, *"but for this cause came I unto this hour"* (John 12:27). Only one who has followed his Lord in straits and gloom and pain, who has realized that the *"spirit indeed is willing, but the flesh is weak"* (Matt. 26:41), can solve this mystery.

All this fitted our Lord to be a compassionate Savior. It is no sin to feel the pain and realize the darkness on the path into which

God leads. It is only human to cry out against the pain, the terror, and desolation of that hour. It is divine to cry out to God in that hour, even while shrinking and sinking down, *"For this cause came I unto this hour"* (John 12:27). Will I fail through the weakness of the flesh? No. *"Father, glorify thy name"* (v. 28). How strong it makes us, and how true, to have one polestar to guide us to the glory of God!

11

Concerted Prayer

*A tourist, in climbing an Alpine summit, finds himself tied by a strong rope to his trusty guide, and to three of his fellow tourists. As they skirt a perilous precipice, he cannot pray, "Lord hold up **my** goings in a safe path, that **my** footsteps slip not, but as to my guide and companions, they must look out for themselves." The only proper prayer in such a case is, "Lord, hold up **our** goings in a safe path; for if one slips all of us may perish."*
        —Henry Clay Trumbull

THE pious Quesnel said that "God is found in union and agreement. Nothing is more efficacious than this in prayer."

Intercessions combine with prayers and supplications. The word *intercession* does not necessarily mean "prayer in relation to others." It means "a coming together, a falling in with a most intimate friend for free, unrestrained communion." It implies prayer—free, familiar, and bold.

Our Lord deals with this question of the concert of prayer in Matthew. He deals with the benefit and energy resulting from the aggregation of prayer forces. The prayer principle and the prayer promise will be best understood in the connection in which it was made by our Lord:

Moreover if thy brother shall trespass against thee, go and tell him his fault between thee and him alone: if he shall hear thee, thou hast gained thy brother. But if he will not hear thee, then take with thee one or two more, that in the mouth of two or three witnesses, every word may be established. And if he shall neglect to hear them, tell it unto the church: but if he neglect to hear the church, let him be unto thee as a heathen man and a publican. Verily I say unto you, Whatsoever ye shall bind on earth shall be bound in heaven: and whatsoever ye shall loose on earth shall be loosed in heaven. Again I say unto you, That if two of you shall agree on earth as touching any thing that they shall ask, it shall be done for them of my Father which is in heaven. For where two or three are gathered together in my name, there am I in the midst of them.   (Matt. 18:15–20)

This passage represents the church in prayer, enforcing discipline in order that its members who have been overtaken by faults may yield readily to the disciplinary process. In addition, it represents the church called together in a concert of prayer, in order to repair the waste and friction ensuing upon the cutting off of a church offender. The last instruction in this passage is given so that the whole matter may be referred, in concerted prayer, to Almighty God for His approval and ratification.

All of this means that the main, the concluding, and the all-powerful agency in the church is prayer, whether it be, as we have seen in Matthew, to thrust out laborers into God's earthly harvest fields or to exclude from the church a violator of unity, law, and order, who will neither listen to his brethren nor repent and confess his fault.

It means that church discipline, now a lost art in the modern church, must go hand in hand with prayer. The church that has no disposition to separate wrongdoers from the church, and that does not excommunicate incorrigible offenders against law and order, will have no communication with God. Church purity must precede the church's prayers. The unity of discipline in the church precedes the unity of prayers by the church.

Let it be noted with emphasis that a church that is careless of discipline will be careless in praying. A church that tolerates evil-doers in its communion will cease to pray, will cease to pray with agreement, and will cease to be a church gathered together in prayer in Christ's name. This matter of church discipline is an important one in the Scriptures. The need of watchfulness over the lives of its members belongs to the church of God.

The church is an organization for mutual help, and it is charged with the watchful care of all of its members. Disorderly conduct cannot be passed by unnoticed. The course of procedure in such cases is clearly given in the eighteenth chapter of Matthew, which has been previously referred to. Furthermore, Paul gave explicit directions as to those who fall into sin in the church:

> *Brethren, if a man be overtaken in a fault, ye which are spiritual, restore such an one in the spirit of meekness; considering thyself, lest thou also be tempted.*　　　*(Gal. 6:1)*

The work of the church is not just to seek members, but it is to watch over and guard them after they have entered the church. If any are overtaken by sin, they must be sought out; but if they cannot be cured of their faults, then excision must take place. This is the doctrine our Lord lays down.

It is somewhat striking that the church at Ephesus, though it had left its first love and had sadly declined in vital godliness and in those things that make up spiritual life, yet it received credit for this good quality: *"Thou canst not bear them which are evil"* (Rev. 2:2).

At the same time, the church at Pergamos was admonished because it had among its membership those who taught hurtful doctrines that were a stumbling block to others. The rebuke was not so much that such characters were in the church, but that they were tolerated. The impression is that the church leaders were blind to the presence of such hurtful characters, and hence were indisposed to administer discipline. This indisposition was an unfailing sign of prayerlessness in the membership. There was no concerted prayer effort to cleanse the church and keep it clean.

This disciplinary idea stands out prominently in the apostle Paul's writings to the churches. The church at Corinth had a notorious case of fornication, where a man had been intimate with his stepmother, and this church had been careless about this iniquity. Paul rather sharply reproved this church and gave explicit command to this effect: *"Therefore put away from among yourselves that wicked person"* (1 Cor. 5:13). Here Paul demanded a concerted action on the part of praying people.

The church at Thessalonica also needed instruction and caution on this matter of looking after disorderly persons, as good as that church was. So Paul said to them, *"Now we command you, brethren, in the name of our Lord Jesus Christ, that ye withdraw yourselves from every brother that walketh disorderly"* (2 Thess. 3:6).

Mark this. It is not the mere presence of disorderly persons in a church that merits the displeasure of God. It is when they are tolerated under the mistaken plea of "bearing with them," and no steps are taken either to cure them of their evil practices or exclude them from the fellowship of the church. This glaring neglect of its wayward members on the part of the church is but a sad sign of a lack of praying; a praying church that is given to mutual, agreed praying is keen to discern when a brother is overtaken in a fault and seeks either to restore him or to cut him off if he is incorrigible.

Much of this dates back to the lack of spiritual vision on the part of church leaders. The Lord, by the mouth of the prophet Isaiah, once asked the very pertinent, suggestive question, *"Who is blind, but my servant?"* (Isa. 42:19). This blindness in leadership in the church is no more exposed than in this question of seeing evildoers in the church, in caring for them, and, when the effort to restore them fails, in withdrawing fellowship from them and letting them be *"as a heathen man and a publican"* (Matt. 18:17). The truth is, there is such a lust for members in the church in these modern times, that the officials and preachers have entirely lost sight of the members who have violated baptismal covenants and who are living in open disregard of God's Word. The idea now is quantity in membership, not quality. The purity of the church is put in the background in the craze to secure numbers, to pad the church rolls, and to make large figures in statistical columns. Prayer—much prayer, mutual prayer—would bring the church back to scriptural standards and would purge the church of many wrongdoers, while it might cure more than a few of their evil lives.

Prayer and church discipline are not new revelations of the Christian dispensation. These two things had a high place in the Jewish practice. Instances are too numerous to mention all of them. Ezra is a case in point. When he returned from the captivity, he found a sad and distressing condition of things among the Lord's people who were left in the land. They had not separated themselves from the surrounding heathen people and had intermarried with them, contrary to divine commands. Those high in authority were involved, the priests and the Levites, along with others. Ezra was greatly moved at the account given him, tore his garments, wept, and prayed. Evildoers in the congregation did not meet his approval, nor did he shut his eyes to them nor excuse them, neither did he compromise the situation. When he had finished confessing the sins of the people and had finished his prayers, the people assembled themselves before him, joined him in a covenant agreement to put away from themselves their evildoings, wept, and prayed in company with Ezra. The result was that the people thoroughly repented of their transgressions, and Israel was reformed.

Praying and a good man, who was neither blind nor unconcerned, did the deed. Of Ezra it is written: *"For he mourned because of the transgression of them that had been carried away"* (Ezra 10:6). So it is with every praying man in the church when he has eyes to see the transgression of evildoers in the church, who has a heart to grieve over them, and who has a spirit in him so concerned about the church that he prays about it.

Blessed is that church that has praying leaders who can see what is disorderly in the church, who are grieved about it, and who put forth their hands to correct the evils that harm God's cause as a weight to its progress.

One point in the indictment against those who *"are at ease in Zion"* (Amos 6:1) is that *"they are not grieved for the affliction of Joseph"* (v. 6). This same indictment could be brought against church leaders of modern times. They are not grieved because the members are engulfed in a craze for worldly, carnal things, nor when there are those in the church walking openly in disorder, whose lives scandalize religion. Of course, such leaders do not pray over the matter, for praying would foster a spirit of solicitude in them for these evildoers, and would drive away the spirit of unconcern that possesses them.

It would be well for prayerless church leaders and careless pastors to read the account of the man with the inkhorn in Ezekiel, where God instructed the prophet to send through the city certain men who would destroy those in the city because of the great evils found there. But certain persons were to be spared. These were they who *"sigh and* [who] *cry for all the abominations that be done in the midst* [of the city]" (Ezek. 9:4). The man with the inkhorn was to mark every one of these sighers and mourners so that they would escape the impending destruction. Note that the instructions were that the slaying of those who did not mourn and sigh should *"begin at my sanctuary"* (v. 6).

What a lesson for non-praying, unconcerned officials of the modern church! How few there are who "sigh and cry" for present-day abominations in the land and who are grieved over the desolations of Zion! What need for *"two or three...gathered together"*

(Matt. 18:20) in a concert of prayer over these conditions, who in the secret place weep and pray for the sins in Zion!

This concert of prayer, this agreement in praying, taught by our Lord in Matthew, finds proof and illustration elsewhere. This was the kind of prayer that Paul referred to in his request to his fellow believers in Rome:

> *Now I beseech you, brethren, for the Lord Jesus Christ's sake, and for the love of the Spirit, that ye strive together with me in your prayers to God for me; that I may be delivered from them that do not believe in Judaea.* *(Rom. 15:30)*

Here is unity in prayer, prayer by agreement, and prayer that drives directly at deliverance from unbelieving and evil men. It is the same kind of prayer urged by our Lord, and the end practically the same—deliverance from unbelieving men, that deliverance wrought either by bringing them to repentance or by exclusion from the church.

The same idea is found in 2 Thessalonians 3:1:

> *Finally, brethren, pray for us that the word of the Lord may have free course, and be glorified, even as it is with you: and that we may be delivered from unreasonable and wicked men.*

Here, united prayer is requested by an apostle, for, among other things, deliverance from wicked men, the same deliverance that the church of God needs in this day. By joining their prayers to his, there was the desired objective of riddance from men who were hurtful to the church of God and who were a hindrance to the running of the Word of the Lord. Let us ask, are there not in the present-day church those who are a definite hindrance to the ongoing of the Word of the Lord? What better course is there than to jointly pray over the question, at the same time using the Christ-given course of discipline first to save them, but failing in that course, to excise them from the body?

Does that seem a harsh course? Then our Lord was guilty of harshness Himself, for He ends these directions by saying, *"But if he neglect to hear the church, let him be unto thee as a heathen man and a publican"* (Matt. 18:17).

This is no more harsh than the act of the skillful surgeon, who sees the whole body and its members endangered by a gangrenous limb and severs the limb from the body for the good of the whole. Nor was it harshness on the part of the captain and crew of the vessel on which Jonah was found, when the storm arose threatening destruction to all on board, to cast the fleeing prophet overboard. What seems to be harsh is actually obedience to God, is for the welfare of the church, and is wise in the extreme.

12

The Universality of Prayer

*It takes more of the power of the Spirit to make the farm,
the home, the office, the store, the shop holy than it does to
make the church holy. It takes more of the power of the Spirit
to make Saturday holy than to make Sunday holy. It takes
much more of the power of the Spirit to make money for God
than it does to make a talk for God. Much more to live a great
life for God than to preach a great sermon.   —E. M. Bounds*

PRAYER is far-reaching in its influence and worldwide in its
effects. It affects all men, affects them everywhere, and affects
them in all things. It touches man's interest in time and eternity.
It lays hold of God and moves Him to interfere in the affairs of
earth. It moves the angels to minister to men in this life. It restrains and defeats the Devil in his schemes to ruin man.

Prayer goes everywhere and lays its hand upon everything.
There is a universality in prayer. When we talk about prayer and
its work, we must use universal terms. It is individual in its application and benefits, but it is general and worldwide at the same
time in its good influences. It blesses man in every event of life,
furnishes him help in every emergency, and gives him comfort in
every trouble. There is no experience through which man is called
to go but prayer is there as a helper, a comforter, and a guide.

When we speak of the universality of prayer, we discover many
sides to it. First, it may be remarked that all men ought to pray.
Prayer is intended for all men, because all men need God and need
what God has and what only prayer can secure. As men are called
upon to pray everywhere, by consequence all men must pray for men
everywhere. Universal terms are used when men are commanded to

pray, while there is a promise in universal terms to all who call upon
God for pardon, for mercy and help:

> *For there is no difference...for the same Lord over all is rich*
> *unto all that call upon him. For whosoever shall call upon the*
> *name of the Lord shall be saved.*   *(Rom. 10:12–13)*

As there is no difference in the state of sin in which men are
found, all men need the saving grace of God that alone can bless
them. Further, as this saving grace is obtained only in answer to
prayer, therefore all men are called on to pray because of their very
needs.

It is a rule of scriptural interpretation that whenever a command comes forth with no limitation, it is universal in binding
force. So the words of the Lord in Isaiah are to the point:

> *Seek ye the LORD while he may be found, call ye upon him*
> *while he is near: let the wicked forsake his way, and the un-*
> *righteous man his thoughts: and let him return unto the*
> *LORD, and he will have mercy upon him, and to our God, for*
> *he will abundantly pardon.*   *(Isa. 55:6–7)*

Since wickedness is universal and pardon is needed by all men,
all men must seek the Lord while he may be found and must call
upon Him while he is near. Prayer belongs to all men because all
men are redeemed in Christ. It is a privilege for every man to pray,
but it is no less a duty for them to call upon God. No sinner is
barred from the mercy seat. All are welcomed to approach the
throne of grace with all their wants and woes, with all their sins
and burdens.

> Come all the world, come, sinner thou,
> All things in Christ are ready now.

Whenever a poor sinner turns his eyes to God, no matter
where he is or what his guilt and sinfulness, the eye of God is upon
him, and His ear is opened to his prayers.

But men may pray everywhere, since God is accessible in every
climate and under all circumstances. *"I will therefore that men pray*
every where, lifting up holy hands, without wrath and doubting" (1
Tim. 2:8).

No locality on earth is too distant from God to reach heaven. No place is so remote that God cannot see and hear one who looks toward Him and seeks His face. Oliver Holden put into a hymn these words:

> Then, my soul, in every strait,
> To thy Father come and wait;
> He will answer every prayer;
> God is present everywhere.

There is just one modification of the idea that a person can pray everywhere. Some places exist in which evil business is conducted. The intrinsic environments of these settings grow out of the places themselves, out of the moral character of those who carry on the business, and out of those who support them. In such localities, prayer would not be appropriate. We might cite the saloon, the theater, the gambling hall, the dance hall, and other places of worldly amusement. Prayer is so much out of place at such places that no one would ever presume to pray. Prayer would be regarded by the owners, the patrons, and the supporters of such places as an intrusion. Furthermore, those who attend such places are not praying people. They belong almost entirely to the prayerless crowd of worldlings.

While we are to pray everywhere, it unquestionably means that we are not to frequent places where we cannot pray. To pray everywhere is to pray in all legitimate places, and to attend especially those places where prayer is welcome and is given a gracious hospitality. To pray everywhere is to preserve the spirit of prayer in places of business, in our dealings with men, and in the privacy of the home amid all of its domestic cares.

The model prayer of our Lord, familiarly called the Lord's Prayer, is the universal prayer because it is peculiarly adapted to all men everywhere, in all circumstances, and in all times of need. It can be put in the mouths of all people in all nations and in all times. It is a model of praying that needs no amendment or alteration for every family, people, and nation.

Furthermore, prayer has its universal application in that all men are to be the subjects of prayer. All men everywhere are to be prayed for. Prayer must take in all of Adam's fallen race because all men are fallen in Adam, are redeemed in Christ, and benefit from prayers for them. This is Paul's doctrine in his prayer directory: *"I exhort therefore, that, first of all, supplications, prayers, intercessions, and giving of thanks, be made for all men"* (1 Tim. 2:1).

There is strong scriptural warrant, therefore, for reaching out and embracing all men in our prayers. Not only are we commanded thus to pray for them, but the reason given is that Christ gave Himself a ransom for all men (see verse 6), and all men are provisionally beneficiaries of the atoning death of Jesus Christ.

Lastly, and more at length, prayer has a universal side in that all things that concern us are to be prayed about, while all things that are for our good—physical, social, intellectual, spiritual, and eternal—are subjects of prayer.

However, before we consider this phase of prayer, let us stop and look again at the universal prayer for all men. As a special class to be prayed for, we may mention those who have control in state or who bear rule in the church. Prayer has mighty potencies. It makes good rulers, and makes good rulers better rulers. It restrains the lawless and the despotic. Rulers are to be prayed for. They are not out of the reach and the control of prayer, because they are not out of the reach and control of God. Wicked Nero was on the throne of Rome when Paul wrote these words to Timothy urging prayer for those in authority.

Christian lips are to breathe prayers for the cruel and infamous rulers in state as well as for the righteous and the benign governors and princes. Prayer is to be as far-reaching as the race—*"for all men"* (1 Tim. 2:1). Humanity is supposed to burden our hearts as we pray, and all men are to engage our thoughts in approaching the throne of grace. In our praying hours, all men must have a place. The wants and woes of the entire race are to broaden and make tender our sympathies and inflame our petitions.

No little man can pray. No man with narrow views of God, of His plan to save men, and of the universal needs of all men can pray effectually. It takes a broad-minded man who understands God and His purposes in the Atonement to pray well. No cynic can pray. Prayer is the most divine philanthropy, as well as giant greatheartedness. Prayer comes from a big heart, filled with thoughts about all men and with sympathies for all men.

Prayer runs parallel with the will of God, *"who will have all men to be saved, and to come unto the knowledge of the truth"* (1 Tim. 2:4). Prayer reaches up to heaven and brings heaven down to earth. Prayer has in its hands a double blessing. It rewards him who prays and blesses him who is prayed for. It brings peace to warring passions and calms warring elements. Tranquility is the happy fruit of true praying. There is an inner calm that comes to him who prays and an outer calm as well. Prayer creates the environment for *"a quiet and peaceable life in all godliness and honesty"* (v. 2).

Right praying not only makes life beautiful in peace, but infused with righteousness and weighty in influence. Honesty, gravity, integrity, and strength of character are the natural and essential fruits of prayer.

This kind of worldwide, largehearted, unselfish praying pleases God well and is acceptable in His sight, because it cooperates with His will and runs in gracious streams to all men and to each man. It is this kind of praying that the Man Christ Jesus did when on earth, and the same kind that He is now doing at His Father's right hand in heaven as our mighty Intercessor. He is the pattern of prayer. He is between God and man, the one Mediator, who gave Himself as a ransom for all men and for each man.

So it is that true prayer links itself to the will of God and runs in streams of solicitude, compassion, and intercession for all men. As Jesus Christ died for everyone involved in the fall, so prayer girdles everyone and gives itself for the benefit of everyone. Like our one Mediator between God and man, he who prays stands midway between God and man, with *"prayers and supplications with strong crying and tears"* (Heb. 5:7). Prayer holds in its grasp the movements of the race of man and embraces the destinies of men for all eternity. The king and the beggar are both affected by it. It touches heaven and moves earth. Prayer holds earth to heaven and brings heaven in close contact with earth.

> Your guides and brethren bear
> Forever on your mind;
> Extend the arms of mighty prayer
> In grasping all mankind.

13

Prayer and Missions

One day, about this time, I heard an unusual bleating amongst my few remaining goats, as if they were being killed or tortured. I rushed to the goat-house and found myself instantly surrounded by a band of armed men. The snare had caught me, their weapons were raised, and I expected the next moment to die. But God moved me to talk to them firmly and kindly; I warned them of their sin and its punishment; I showed them that only my love and pity led me to remain there seeking their good, and that if they killed me they killed their best friend. I further assured them I was not afraid to die, for at death my Savior would take me to heaven and that I would be far happier than on earth; and that my only desire to live was to make them happy by teaching them to love Jesus Christ my Lord. I then lifted up my hands and eyes to the heavens and prayed aloud for Jesus to bless all my Tannese and to protect me or take me to heaven as He saw to be for the best. One after another they slipped away from me and Jesus restrained them again. Did ever a mother run more quickly to protect her crying child in danger's hour than the Lord Jesus hastens to answer believing prayer and send help to His servants in His own good time and way, so far as it shall be for their good and His glory. —John G. Paton

MISSIONS means the giving of the Gospel to those of Adam's fallen race who have never heard of Christ and His atoning death. It means the giving to others the opportunity to hear of salvation through our Lord Jesus Christ, and allowing others to have a chance to receive and accept the blessings of the Gospel as we have it in Christianized lands. It means that those who enjoy the benefits of the Gospel give these same religious advantages and gospel privileges to all of mankind.

Prayer has a great deal to do with missions. Prayer is the handmaid of missions. The success of all real missionary effort is dependent on prayer. The life and spirit of missions are the life and spirit of prayer. Both prayer and missions were born in the divine Mind. Prayer and missions are bosom companions. Prayer creates and makes missions successful, while missions leans heavily on prayer.

Psalm 72, which deals prophetically with the Messiah, states, *"Prayer shall be made for him continually"* (v. 15). Prayer would be made for His coming to save man, and prayer would be made for the success of the plan of salvation that He would come to set in motion.

The Spirit of Jesus Christ is the spirit of missions. Our Lord Jesus Christ was Himself the first missionary. His promise and advent composed the first missionary movement. The missionary spirit is not simply a phase of the Gospel, not a mere feature of the plan of salvation, but is its very spirit and life. The missionary movement is the church of Jesus Christ marching in militant array, with the design of possessing the whole world of mankind for Christ. Whoever is touched by the Spirit of God is fired by the missionary spirit.

An anti-missionary Christian is a contradiction in terms. We might say that it would be impossible to be an anti-missionary Christian because of the impossibility for the divine and human forces to put men in such a state as not to align them with the missionary cause. Missionary impulse is the heartbeat of our Lord Jesus Christ sending His own vital forces through the whole body of the church. The spiritual life of God's people rises or falls with the force of those heartbeats. When these life forces cease, then death ensues. Likewise, anti-missionary churches are dead churches, just as anti-missionary Christians are dead Christians.

If Satan cannot prevent a great movement for God, his craftiest wile is to debauch the movement. If he can put the movement in the forefront and the spirit of the movement in the background, he has materialized and thoroughly debauched the movement. Only mighty prayer will save the movement from being materialized and keep the spirit of the movement strong and controlling. The key of all missionary success is prayer.

That key is in the hands of the home churches. The trophies won by our Lord in heathen lands will be won by praying missionaries, not by professional workers in foreign lands. More especially will this success be won by saintly praying in the churches at home. The home church on her knees, fasting and praying, is the great base of spiritual supplies, the sinews of war, and the pledge of victory in this dire and final conflict. Financial resources are not the real muscles of war in this fight. Machinery in itself carries no power to break down heathen walls, open effectual doors, and win heathen hearts to Christ. Prayer alone can do the deed.

Just as Aaron and Hur surely gave victory to Israel through Moses, so a praying church through Jesus Christ will give victory on every battlefield in heathen lands. It is as true in foreign fields as it is in homelands. The praying church wins the contest. The home church has done but a paltry thing when she has furnished the money to establish missions and support her missionaries. Money is important, but money without prayer is powerless in the face of the darkness, the wretchedness, and the sin in unchristianized lands. Prayerless giving breeds barrenness and death. Poor praying at home is the solution for poor results in the foreign field. Prayerless giving is the secret of all crises in the missionary movements of the day and is the occasion of the accumulation of debts in missionary boards.

It is all right to urge men to give of their means to the missionary cause, but it is much more important to urge them to give their prayers to the movement. Today, foreign missions have more need of the power of prayer than the power of money. Prayer can make even poverty in the missionary cause move on amid difficulties and hindrances. Much money without prayer is helpless and powerless in the face of the utter darkness, sin, and wretchedness on the foreign field.

The present is particularly a missionary age. Protestant Christianity is stirred as it never was before in the line of aggression in pagan lands. The missionary movement has taken on proportions that awaken hope, kindle enthusiasm, and demand the attention, if not the interest, of the coldest and the most lifeless. Nearly every church has caught the contagion, and the sails of their proposed missionary movements are spread wide to catch the favoring breezes. Here is the danger just now—that the missionary movement will go ahead of the missionary spirit. This has always been the peril of the church, losing the substance in the shade, losing the spirit in the outward shell, and contenting itself in the mere parade of the movement, putting the force of effort in the movement and not in the spirit.

The magnificence of this movement may not only blind us to the spirit of it, but the spirit that should give life and shape to the movement may be lost in the wealth of the movement, just as the ship, borne by favoring winds, may be lost when these winds swell to a storm.

Many of us have heard eloquent and earnest speeches stressing the imperative need of money for missions while we have heard perhaps one stressing the imperative need of prayer. All our plans and devices drive toward the one end of raising money, not to quicken faith and promote prayer. The common idea among church leaders is that if we get the money, prayer will come as a matter of course.

The very reverse is the truth. If we get the church involved in the business of praying, and thus secure the spirit of missions, money will more than likely come as a matter of course. Spiritual agencies and spiritual forces never come as a matter of course. Spiritual duties and spiritual factors, left to the "matter of course" law, will surely fall out and die. Only the things that are stressed live and rule in the spiritual realm.

The people who give will not necessarily pray. Many in our churches are liberal givers who are noted for their prayerlessness. One of the evils of the present-day missionary movement lies just there. Giving is entirely removed from prayer. Prayer receives scant attention, while giving stands out prominently. Those who truly pray will be moved to give. Praying creates the giving spirit. The praying ones will give liberally and self-denyingly. He who enters his closet in prayer to God will also open his purse to God. But mechanical, reluctant giving kills the very spirit of prayer. Emphasizing the material to the neglect of the spiritual, by an inexorable law, retires and discounts the spiritual.

It is truly astonishing how great a part money plays in the modern religious movements and how little prayer plays in them. In striking contrast with that statement, it is marvelous how little part money played in primitive Christianity as a factor in spreading the Gospel, and how wonderful a part prayer played in it.

The grace of giving is nowhere cultured to a richer growth than in the prayer closet. If all our missionary boards and secretaryships were turned into praying bands, until the agony of real prayer and travail with Christ for a perishing world came on them, real estate, bank stocks, and United States bonds would be in the market for the spreading of Christ's Gospel among men. If the spirit of prayer prevailed, missionary boards whose individual members are worth millions would not be staggering under a load of debt, and great churches would not have a yearly deficit and a yearly grumbling, grudging pressure to pay a beggarly assessment to support a mere handful of missionaries, with the additional humiliation of debating the question of recalling some of them. The ongoing of Christ's kingdom is locked up in the closet of prayer by Christ Himself, and not in the contribution box.

The prophet Isaiah, looking down the centuries with the vision of a seer, thus expressed his purpose to continue in prayer and give God no rest until Christ's kingdom was established among men:

For Zion's sake will I not hold my peace, and for Jerusalem's sake I will not rest, until the righteousness thereof go forth as brightness, and the salvation thereof as a lamp that burneth.
(Isa. 62:1)

Then, foretelling the final success of the Christian church, he said, *"And the Gentiles shall see thy righteousness, and all kings thy glory: and thou shalt be called by a new name, which the mouth of the LORD shall name"* (v. 2).

Then the Lord Himself, by the mouth of this evangelical prophet, declares as follows:

I have set watchmen upon thy walls, O Jerusalem, which shall never hold their peace day nor night: ye that make mention of the LORD, keep not silence. And give him no rest, till he establish, and till he make Jerusalem a praise in the earth.
(Isa. 62:6–7)

In the margin of our Bible, it reads, *"Ye who remember the Lord."* The idea is, these praying ones are those who are the Lord's remembrancers, those who remind Him of what He has promised, and who give Him no rest until God's church is established in the earth.

One of the leading petitions in the Lord's Prayer deals with this same question of the establishing of God's kingdom and the progress of the Gospel in the short, pointed petition, *"Thy kingdom come,"* with the added words, *"Thy will be done on earth, as it is in heaven"* (Matt. 6:10).

The missionary movement in the apostolic church was born in an atmosphere of fasting and prayer. The very movement looking to offer the blessings of the Christian church to the Gentiles was born on the housetop on the occasion when Peter went up there to pray. God showed him His divine purpose to extend the privileges of the Gospel to the Gentiles and to break down the middle wall of partition between Jew and Gentile.

Even more specifically, Paul and Barnabas were definitely called and set apart to the missionary field at Antioch when the church there had fasted and prayed. It was then that the Holy Spirit answered from heaven, *"Separate me Barnabas and Saul for the work whereunto I have called them"* (Acts 13:2).

Note this was not the call to the ministry of Paul and Barnabas, but more particularly their definite call to the foreign field. Paul had been called to the ministry years before this, even at his conversion. This was a subsequent call to a work born of special and continued prayer in the church at Antioch. God calls men not only to the ministry but to be missionaries. Missionary work is God's work. It is the God-called men who are to do it. These are the missionaries that have worked well and successfully in the foreign field in the past, and the same kind of missionaries will do the work in the future, or it will not be done.

Praying missionaries are needed for the work, and only a praying church can send them out. These are prophecies of the success that is promised. The sort of religion to be exported by missionaries is of the praying sort. The religion to which the heathen world is to be converted is a religion of prayer, and a religion of prayer to the true God. The heathen world already prays to its idols and false gods. But they are to be taught by praying missionaries who have been sent out by a praying church to cast away their idols and to begin to call upon the name of the Lord Jesus Christ. No prayerless church can transport to heathen lands a praying religion. No prayerless missionary can bring heathen idolaters who do not know our God to their knees in true prayer until he becomes preeminently a man of prayer. Just as it takes praying men at home to do God's work, it takes praying missionaries to bring those who sit in darkness to the light.

The most noted and most successful missionaries have been preeminently men of prayer. David Livingstone, William Taylor,

Adoniram Judson, Henry Martyn, Hudson Taylor, and many others form a band of illustrious praying men whose impress and influence still abide where they labored. No prayerless man is wanted for this job. Above everything else, the primary qualification for every missionary is prayer. Let him be, above all else, a man of prayer. Finally, when the crowning day comes and the records are made up and read at the Great Judgment Day, then it will appear how well praying men worked in the hard pagan fields and how much was due to them in laying the foundations of Christianity in those fields.

The only condition that is to give worldwide power to this Gospel is prayer, and the spread of this Gospel will depend on prayer. The energy that is to give it marvelous momentum and conquering power over all its malignant and powerful foes is the energy of prayer.

The fortunes of the kingdom of Jesus Christ are not made by the feebleness of its foes. They are strong and bitter, have ever been strong and ever will be. But mighty prayer is the one great spiritual force that will enable the Lord Jesus Christ to enter into full possession of His kingdom, and secure for Him the heathen as His inheritance and the uttermost part of the earth for His possession. (See Psalm 2:8.)

It is prayer that will enable Him to break His foes with a rod of iron, that will make these foes tremble in their pride and power, who are but frail potter's vessels to be broken in pieces by one stroke of His hand. (See Revelation 2:27.) A person who can pray is the mightiest instrument Christ has in this world. A praying church is stronger than all the gates of hell.

God's decree for the glory of His Son's kingdom is dependent on prayer for its fulfillment: *"Ask of me, and I will give thee the heathen for thine inheritance, and the uttermost part of the earth for thy possession"* (Ps. 2:8). God the Father gives nothing to His Son except through prayer. And the reason why the church has not received more in the missionary work in which it is engaged is the lack of prayer. *"Ye have not, because ye ask not"* (James 4:2).

Every dispensation foreshadowing the coming of Christ, after the world has been evangelized, rests upon these constitutional provisions, God's decree, His promises, and the prayers of the church. However far away that day of victory is by distance or time, or however remote the shadowy type, prayer is the essential condition on which the dispensation becomes strong, typical, and representative. From Abraham, the first of the nation of the Israelites, the friend of God, down to this dispensation of the Holy Spirit, this has been true.

> The nations call! From sea to sea
>   Extends the thrilling cry,
> "Come over, Christians, if there be,
>   And help us, ere we die."
>
> Our hearts, O Lord, the summons feel;
>   Let hand with heart combine,
> And answer to the world's appeal,
>   By giving what is Thine.

Our Lord's plan for securing workers in the foreign missionary field is the same plan He has set for obtaining preachers. It is by the process of praying. It is the prayer plan as distinguished from all man-made plans. These mission workers are to be "sent men." God must send them. They are God-called, divinely moved to this great work. They are inwardly moved to enter the harvest fields of the world and gather sheaves for the heavenly garners. Men do not choose to be missionaries any more than they choose to be preachers. God sends out laborers in His harvest fields in answer to the prayers of His church. Here is the divine plan as set forth by our Lord:

> *But when he saw the multitudes, he was moved with compassion on them, because they fainted, and were scattered abroad, as sheep having no shepherd. Then saith he unto his disciples, The harvest truly is plenteous, but the labourers are few; pray ye therefore the Lord of the harvest, that he will send forth labourers into his harvest.* (Matt. 9:36–38)

It is the business of the home church to do the praying. It is the Lord's business to call and send forth the laborers. The Lord does not do the praying. The church does not do the calling. Just as our Lord's compassions were aroused by the sight of multitudes—weary, hungry, and scattered, exposed to evils, as sheep having no shepherd—so whenever the church has eyes to see the vast multitudes of earth's inhabitants, descendants of Adam—weary in soul, living in darkness, wretched and sinful—will it be moved to compassion and begin to pray the Lord of the harvest to send forth laborers into His harvest.

373

Missionaries, like ministers, are born of praying people. A praying church begets laborers in the harvest field of the world. The scarcity of missionaries argues a non-praying church. It is all right to send trained men to the foreign field, but first of all they must be God-sent. The sending is the fruit of prayer. As praying men are the occasion of sending them, so in turn the workers must be praying men. The prime mission of these praying missionaries is to convert prayerless, heathen men into praying men. Prayer is the proof of their calling, their divine credentials, and their work.

He who is not a praying man here at home needs to develop fitness in prayer in order to become a missions worker abroad. He who does not have the spirit that moves him toward sinners at home will hardly have a spirit of compassion for sinners abroad. Missionaries are not made of men who are failures at home. He who will be a man of prayer abroad must, before anything else, be a man of prayer in his home church. If he is not engaged in turning sinners away from their prayerless ways at home, he will hardly succeed in turning away the heathen from their prayerless ways. In other words, it takes the same spiritual qualifications for being a home worker as it does for being a foreign worker.

God in His own way, in answer to the prayers of His church, calls men into His harvest fields. Sad will be the day when missionary boards and churches overlook that fundamental fact and send out their own chosen men, independent of God's call.

Is the harvest great? Are the laborers few? Then *"pray ye therefore the Lord of the harvest, that he will send forth labourers into his harvest"* (Matt. 9:38). Oh, that a great wave of prayer would sweep over the church, asking God to send out a great army of laborers into the needy harvest fields of the earth! There is no danger of the Lord of the harvest sending out too many laborers and crowding the fields. He who calls will most certainly provide the means for supporting those whom He calls and sends forth.

The one great need in the modern missionary movement is intercessors. They were scarce in the days of Isaiah. This was his complaint: *"And he saw that there was no man, and wondered that there was no intercessor"* (Isa. 59:16). So today there is great need of intercessors: first, for the needy harvest fields of earth, born of a Christlike compassion for the thousands without the Gospel, and, then, for laborers to be sent forth by God into the needy fields of earth.

374

Book
Five

Obtaining Answers
to Prayer

1

Faith in Prayer

*The Holy Spirit will give the praying saint the brightness
of an immortal hope, the music of a deathless song. In His
baptism and communion with the heart, He will give sweeter
and more enlarged visions of heaven until the taste for other
things will fade, and other visions will grow dim and distant.
He will put notes of other worlds in human hearts until all
earth's music is discord and songless.* —E. M. Bounds

THE men and women of the Old Testament saw God as their
Father and felt that prayerful communion with Him was a natural
part of life. Israel's leaders were noted for their habit of coming to
their Father in prayer. Prayer and God's loving and powerful answer to it are major themes of the Old Testament.

The tenth chapter of Joshua describes God's powerful intervention in a prolonged battle between the Israelites and their enemies as a result of prayer. Night was rapidly coming on, and the
Israelites discovered that they needed a few more hours of daylight
to ensure victory. Joshua, that sturdy man of God, stepped into the
breach with prayer for the Lord's army.

The sun was setting too rapidly for God's people to reap the
full fruits of a great victory. Joshua, seeing how much depended on
the occasion, cried out in the sight and hearing of Israel, *"Sun,
stand thou still upon Gideon; and thou, Moon, in the valley of Aja-
lon"* (Josh. 10:12). The sun actually stood still, and the moon
stopped in its course, at the command of this praying man of God,
until the Lord's people had avenged themselves upon His enemies.

Jacob's life was not a strict pattern of righteousness, prior to
his all-night praying. Yet, he was a man of prayer, and he trusted

in the God of prayer. He was swift to call upon God in prayer when he was in trouble because he knew God would answer him. For example, as Jacob fled from Esau, he prayed. As night came on, he found a special place where he could sleep peacefully. That night he had a wonderful dream in which he saw the angels of God ascending and descending on a ladder that stretched from earth to heaven. It was no wonder that he awoke exclaiming, *"Surely the LORD is in this place; and I knew it not"* (Gen. 28:16).

As a result of this dream, he entered into a very definite covenant with Almighty God. In prayer, Jacob made a vow to the Lord, saying,

If God will be with me, and will keep me in this way that I go, and will give me bread to eat, and raiment to put on, so that I come again to my father's house in peace; then shall the Lord be my God: and this stone, which I have set for a pillar, shall be God's house; and of all that thou shalt give me I will surely give the tenth unto thee. (Gen. 28:20–22)

With a deep sense of his utter dependence on God, Jacob conditioned his prayer for protection, blessing, and guidance with a solemn vow. Thus Jacob supported his prayer to God with a vow.

Twenty years passed while Jacob stayed at Laban's house. He married two of Laban's daughters, and God gave him children. God had generously answered Jacob's prayer. Becoming very wealthy, Jacob decided to leave Laban's house and return home. When he was nearing home, it occurred to him that he must meet his brother Esau, whose anger had not abated despite the passage of time. God, however, had said to him, *"Return unto the land of thy fathers, and to thy kindred; and I will be with thee"* (Gen. 31:3).

In this dire emergency, no doubt God's promise and the vow he had made long ago came to mind. As a result, he prayed all night. We notice that this is the night of that strange, inexplicable incident of the angel struggling with Jacob all night long, until Jacob at last obtained the victory. *"I will not let thee go, except thou bless me"* (Gen. 32:26). Immediately in answer to his fervent prayer, God responded by blessing Jacob richly and changing his name. God, knowing the desire of Jacob's heart, blessed Jacob further by removing Esau's angry nature. When Jacob and Esau met the next day, Esau greeted the brother who had wronged him with kindness and generosity. The remarkable change in the heart of Esau could only have come through prayer.

Samuel, a mighty intercessor for Israel and a man of God, was the product of his mother's prayer. Hannah is a memorable example of the nature and benefits of persistent praying. She had no children, and she especially yearned for a son. Her whole soul was in her desire. So she went to the house of worship and saw Eli, God's priest.

Staggering under the weight of her longing, she could not articulate her desires. Nonetheless, she poured out her soul in prayer before the Lord. (See 1 Samuel 1:10–17.) Her silent prayer was so fervent that Eli thought she was drunk. When Eli learned the truth about Hannah's prayer, he said, *"And the God of Israel grant thee thy petition"* (v. 17). Soon Samuel was hers by a conscious faith, and a nation was restored by faith.

Samuel was born in answer to the faithful Hannah's prayer. The solemn covenant that she made with God if He would grant her request must not be left out of this investigation of a praying woman and the answer she received. Prayer in its highest form of faith is prayer that carries the whole man as a sacrificial offering. Thus, devoting the whole man to God—with a quenchless and impassioned desire for heaven—mightily helps praying.

Samson is somewhat of a paradox when we examine his religious character. Despite all of his extreme faults, he knew the God who hears prayer, and he knew how to talk to God.

Israel could never slip so far away, fall into sin so deeply, or be bound so strongly that God could not easily span the distance, fathom the depths, and break the chains at their cry. The lesson they were always learning and always forgetting was that prayer continually brought God to their deliverance and that there was nothing too hard for God to do for His people.

We find all of God's saints in distress at different times in some way or another. Their troubles are, however, often the heralds of their great triumphs. But no matter what the reason, the kind, the degree, or the source, no difficult circumstances could keep God from answering prayer. Not even the great strength of Samson could relieve him of his distress. The Scriptures say,

And when he came unto Lehi, the Philistines shouted against him: and the spirit of the Lord came mightily upon him, and

*the cords that were upon his arms became as flax that was
burnt with fire, and his bands loosed from off his hands. And
he found a new jawbone of an ass, and put forth his hand,
and took it, and slew a thousand men therewith. And Samson
said, With the jawbone of an ass, heaps upon heaps, with the
jawbone of an ass have I slain a thousand men. And it came to
pass, when he had made an end of speaking, that he cast away
the jawbone out of his hand, and called that place Ramath-
lehi. And he was sore athirst, and called on the Lord, and
said, Thou hast given this great deliverance into the hand of
thy servant: and now shall I die for thirst, and fall into the
hand of the uncircumcised? But God clave a hollow place that
was in the jaw, and there came water thereout; and when he
had drunk, his spirit came again, and he revived.*

(Judg. 15:14–19)

Another incident in Samson's life shows how, during a great
trial, a saint's mind involuntarily turns to God in prayer. However
checkered their spiritual lives, however far from God they depart,
however sinful they might be, when trouble came upon these men
they invariably called upon God for deliverance, knowing He would
answer them. As a rule, when they repent God hears their cries
and grants their requests.

The incident in question comes at the close of Samson's life.
Read the record in the sixteenth chapter of Judges. Samson had
formed an alliance with Delilah, a heathen woman. In connivance
with the Philistines, she sought to discover the source of his immense strength. Three successive times she failed.

At last, by her persistence, she persuaded Samson to divulge
the wonderful secret. In an unsuspecting hour he told her that the
source of his strength was in his hair that had never been cut. That
night she robbed him of his great physical power by cutting off his
hair. She then called for the Philistines who came, tortured him,
and put out his eyes.

Later, when the Philistines were gathered together to offer a
great sacrifice to Dagon, their idol god, they called for Samson to
entertain them. The following is the account as he stood there presumably the laughingstock of his enemies and God's enemies.

*And Samson said unto the lad that held him by the hand, Suf-
fer me that I may feel the pillars whereupon the house*

standeth, that I may lean upon them. Now the house was full of men and women; and all the lords of the Philistines were there; and there were upon the roof about three thousand men and women, that beheld while Samson made sport. And Samson called unto the Lord, and said, O Lord God, remember me, I pray thee, and strengthen me, I pray thee, only this once, O God, that I may be at once avenged of the Philistines for my two eyes. And Samson took hold of the two middle pillars upon which the house stood, and on which it was borne up, of the one with his right hand, and of the other with his left. And Samson said, Let me die with the Philistines. And he bowed himself with all his might; and the house fell upon the lords, and upon all the people that were therein. So the dead which he slew at his death were more than they which he slew in his life.   *(Judg. 16:26–30)*

God's praying saints of the Old Testament found their comfort and their strength in their believing petitions to the Father. Prayer and God's answers compose a vital part of the Old Testament.

2

Mighty Answers to Prayer

Bishops Lambeth and Wainwright had a great mission meeting in Osaka, Japan. One day the order came from Japanese officials that Christian meetings were no longer allowed in the city. Lambeth and Wainwright did all they could, but the officials were unrelenting. The bishops then retired to the prayer room. Supper time arrived and the Japanese servant girl came to summon them to their meal, and she fell under the power of prayer. Mrs. Lambeth came to find out was happening, and she fell under the same power. They then rose, went to the mission hall, and immediately started a prayer meeting. God fell upon the assembly, causing two sons of the city officials to come to the altar and be saved. The next morning one of the officials in authority came to the mission and said, "Go on with your meetings, you will not be interrupted." The Osaka daily paper came out with the headline, "The Christian's God Came to Town Last Night."

—Rev. H. C. Morrison

JONAH, the man who prayed in the whale's belly, brings to mind another remarkable instance of Old Testament saints who were convinced of the power of prayer. Jonah, a prophet of the Lord, was a fugitive from God running from his place of duty. He had been sent on a mission to warn the wicked city of Nineveh. He was commanded to cry out against them; *"for their wickedness is come up before me,"* said God (Jonah 1:2).

But Jonah, through fear or otherwise, decided not to obey God. He boarded a ship leaving for Tarshish, thinking he could flee from God. Jonah overlooked the fact that the same God who had sent him on that alarming mission had His eye upon him as he hid himself on board the vessel.

A storm arose as the vessel was on its way to Tarshish. The crew decided to throw Jonah overboard in order to appease God and to avert the destruction of the boat and everyone on board. God, however, was still there with Jonah, as He had been from the beginning. God had prepared a whale to swallow Jonah in order to stop his flight from his post of duty, and to save Jonah so he would carry out His will.

Jonah, while in the whale's belly, suffered a strange and terrifying experience and called upon God. God heard him and caused the whale to vomit Jonah out on dry land. What possible force could have rescued him from this fearful place? He seemed hopelessly lost, in *"the belly of hell"* (Jonah 2:2). But he prayed—what else could he do? He had been accustomed to doing this when he was in trouble.

> *I cried by reason of mine affliction unto the Lord, and he heard me; out of the belly of hell cried I, and thou heardest my voice....And the Lord spake unto the fish, and it vomited out Jonah upon the dry land.* (Jonah 2:2, 10)

Like others, he joined prayer to a vow he had made, as he said in his prayer: *"But I will sacrifice unto thee with the voice of thanksgiving; I will pay that that I have vowed. Salvation is of the LORD"* (Jonah 2:9).

Prayer was the mighty force that brought Jonah from *"the belly of hell."* Prayer, mighty prayer, secured the end. Prayer brought God to the rescue of unfaithful Jonah, despite his sin of fleeing from duty. God could not deny his prayer. Nothing is beyond the reach of prayer because no prayer is too hard for God to answer.

The mighty results of Jonah's prayer became an Old Testament type of the miraculous power displayed in the resurrection from the dead of Jesus Christ.

Through these stories, the Bible clearly points out that prayer is only significant because God hears and answers it. The Old Testament saints strongly believed this fact. The belief that God would answer prayer is the one characteristic that stands out prominently and continuously in their lives. They were essentially men of prayer.

How we need a school to teach the art of praying! Prayer, the simplest of all arts and mightiest of all forces, is always in danger of being forgotten or corrupted. As we grow older, worldly influences constantly attempt to break down our childhood prayer lessons. Old Testament people, however, because of their simpler culture, had less difficulty praying. These men and women had a childlike faith in God.

In citing Old Testament saints noted for their praying habits, David must not be overlooked. David is the most noted of Old Testament saints for his communication with God in prayer. Prayer was a habit to him. We hear him say, *"Evening, and morning, and at noon, will I pray, and cry aloud"* (Ps. 55:17). Prayer, for the gentle psalmist of Israel, was no strange occupation. He knew the way to God and was often found in fellowship with Him.

It is no wonder we hear his clear and impressive call, *"O come, let us worship and bow down: let us kneel before the LORD our maker"* (Ps. 95:6). He knew God was the one being who could answer prayer. *"O thou that hearest prayer, unto thee shall all flesh come"* (Ps. 65:2).

When God struck down Bathsheba's child because David's grievous sins gave God's enemies an opportunity to blaspheme, it is no surprise that David spent an entire week praying and fasting for his child's recovery. God's denial of his request, however, did not affect David's habit of praying or his faith in God. While God did not give David the life of this son, He later gave David another son named Solomon.

In close connection with this season of prayer was David's penitential praying. Nathan, by God's command, uncovered David's two great sins of adultery and murder. David immediately acknowledged his wickedness by saying to Nathan, *"I have sinned"* (2 Sam. 12:13). Psalm 51 is his heart's cry of deep grief and genuine repentance.

David knew where to find God, who would pardon his sins. God received him back, and he had the joys of salvation restored to him by earnest, sincere, penitential praying. In the same way, God answers all sinners' repentant prayers and brings them back into divine favor, pardoning them and giving them a new heart.

The entire book of Psalms brings prayer to the forefront, showing how personal communication with God can bristle with life and feeling.

Solomon must not be overlooked, either, in the catalog of Old Testament praying men. While in his later life Solomon departed from God, he often prayed at the beginning of his reign. On one occasion, Solomon went to Gibeon to offer a sacrifice. While offering the sacrifice, Solomon prayed. That night the Lord appeared to Solomon in a vision saying, *"Ask what I shall give thee"* (1 Kings 3:5). The following account of his request shows the quality of Solomon's character:

> *O Lord my God, thou hast made thy servant king instead of David my father: and I am but a little child: I know not how to go out or come in. And thy servant is in the midst of thy people which thou hast chosen, a great people, that cannot be numbered nor counted for multitude. Give therefore thy servant an understanding heart to judge thy people, that I may discern between good and bad: for who is able to judge this thy so great a people?*   *(1 Kings 3:7–9)*

It is no wonder that, as a result of such praying, the Lord responded in a generous and powerful way:

> *And the speech pleased the Lord, that Solomon had asked this thing. And God said unto him, Because thou hast asked this thing, and hast not asked for thyself long life; neither hast asked riches for thyself, nor hast asked the life of thine enemies; but hast asked for thyself understanding to discern judgment; behold, I have done according to thy words: lo, I have given thee a wise and an understanding heart; so that there was none like thee before thee, neither after thee shall any arise like unto thee. And I have also given thee that which thou hast not asked, both riches, and honour: so that there shall not be any among the kings like unto thee all thy days.*   *(1 Kings 3:10–13)*

What powerful prayer! What self-deprecation and simplicity! *"I am but a little child"* (v. 7). He really specified what he needed! Because of his attitude, God answered with more than what Solomon asked!

The remarkable prayer at the dedication of the temple is another example. This could be the longest recorded prayer in God's Word. How comprehensive, direct, and intense it was! Solomon could not afford to lay the foundation of God's house without prayer. God heard this prayer as He heard them before, *"for the glory of the LORD filled the house"* (1 Kings 8:11). Thus God confirmed acceptance of this house of worship and of Solomon, the praying king.

The list of Old Testament saints who were devoted to prayer is too long to discuss at length. However, as one who reads the Scriptures examines other praying men of God, he will want to include Isaiah and Jeremiah. Careful readers will see how great a place prayer occupied in the minds and lives of the men of those early days.

3

Beginning with Prayer

*Oh, for determined men and women, who will rise early
and really burn out for God. Oh, for a faith that will sweep
into heaven with the early dawn and have ships from a shore-
less sea loaded in the soul's harbor ere the ordinary laborer
has knocked the dew from his scythe or the peddler has turned
from his pallet of straw to spread nature's treasures of fruit
before the early buyers.* —*Homer W. Hodge*

PRAYER reaches back to man's first existence on earth. We see
how the energy of prayer is required in the simplest as well as the
most complex provision of God's grace.

Abraham, the friend of God, is a striking illustration of one of
the Old Testament saints who strongly believed in prayer. Abraham was not by any means a shadowy figure. God called Abraham
to journey to an unknown land, taking his entire household. Whenever Abraham stopped for the night or longer, he always erected an
altar and *"called on the name of the LORD"* (Gen. 13:4).

This man of faith and prayer was one of the first to erect a
family altar, around which he gathered his household and offered
sacrifices of worship, praise, and prayer. Abraham's altars were
essentially altars where he gathered his household, as distinguished from secret prayer.

It was Abraham's rule to stand before the Lord in prayer. His
life was surcharged with prayer, and Abraham's blessing was sanctified by prayer. Wherever he halted in his pilgrimage, he always
asked for God's blessing through prayer. Side by side with the sacrifice altar was the prayer altar. He arose early in the morning and
went to stand before the Lord in prayer.

As God's revelations became fuller, Abraham's prayerfulness increased, and it was during one of these spiritual meetings that Abraham *"fell on his face: and God talked with him"* (Gen. 17:3). On still another occasion, we find this man, "the father of the faithful," praying on his face before God, astonished at the answers, purposes, and revelations of Almighty God for him. God was promising him a son in his old age as well as great honor for this son.

Even Ishmael's destiny was shaped by Abraham's prayer when he prayed, *"O that Ishmael might live before thee!"* (v. 18).

What a remarkable story of Abraham's standing before God, repeating his intercessions for the wicked city of Sodom! Sodom was the home of his nephew, Lot, and was doomed by God's decision to destroy it. Sodom's fate was delayed for a while by Abraham's praying, and it was almost entirely relieved by the humility and insistence of his prayers. Abraham believed strongly in prayer and knew how to pray. No other recourse was open to Abraham to save Sodom but prayer.

Perhaps the failure to ultimately rescue Sodom from her doom of destruction was due to Abraham's optimistic view of the spiritual condition of things in that city. Perhaps if Abraham had entreated God once more, asking Him to spare the city even if He found only one righteous man, for Lot's sake, God might have heeded Abraham's request.

Another instance in the life of Abraham shows how he was a man of prayer and had power with God. Abraham had journeyed to and was lodging in Gerar. Fearing that Abimelech might kill him and appropriate Sarah his wife for his own lustful uses, he deceived Abimelech by claiming that Sarah was his sister. God appeared to Abimelech in a dream and warned him not to touch Sarah, telling him that she was Abraham's wife, not his sister. He said unto Abimelech, *"Now therefore restore the man his wife; for he is a prophet, and he shall pray for thee, and thou shalt live"* (Gen. 20:7).

The conclusion of the incident is recorded in Genesis 20:17–18:

So Abraham prayed unto God: and God healed Abimelech, and his wife, and his maidservants; and they bare children. For the Lord had fast closed up all the wombs of the house of Abimelech because of Sarah Abraham's wife.

This case is similar to that of Job's at the close of his fearful experience and terrible trials. His friends, neither understanding him nor comprehending God's dealings with His servant, falsely charged Job with being in sin. They cited this presumed sin as the cause of his troubles. God said to Job's friends, *"My servant Job shall pray for you: for him will I accept.... And the LORD turned the captivity of Job, when he prayed for his friends"* (Job 42:8, 10).

Almighty God knew His servant Job as a man of prayer, and He could afford to send Job's friends to him for prayer in order to carry out and fulfill His plans and purposes.

4

Intercessory Prayer Moves God

Intercessory prayer is a powerful means of grace for the praying man. The English missionary Henry Martyn observed that at times of inward dryness and depression, he often found a delightful revival in the act of praying for others, for their conversion, their sanctification, or their prosperity in the work of the Lord. His intercessions with God about these gifts and blessings were, for him, the divinely natural channel of a renewed insight into his own part and lot in Christ. Christ was his own rest and power, into the "perfect freedom" of an entire yielding of himself to his Master for His work.
—Bishop Handley C. G. Moule

PRAYER unites with God's purposes and lays itself out to secure those purposes. How often would the wise and benign will of God fail in its rich and beneficent ends by the sins of the people if prayer had not come in to arrest wrath and make the promise sure! Israel as a nation would have met their just destruction after their apostasy with the golden calf, had it not been for the unfainting intercession of Moses' forty days and forty nights of praying!

Moses' character was greatly affected by his praying. His forty days of close interaction in prayer with God worked a greater change in his character than did his exchanges with God when he received the law. When he came down from the mountain after his long prayer, his face shone with dazzling brightness. (See Exodus 34:29–30.) Our heights of transfiguration and loving character and conduct are born of seasons of prayer. God has responded to all-night praying by changing many a Jacob, a supplanter, into an Israel, a prince, who has power with God and men.

No mission was more majestic in purpose and results than that of Moses. None was more responsible, diligent, or difficult. His mission teaches us the noble ministry of prayer. Not only is prayer the medium of supply and support, but it is a compassionate agency through which the pitying, long-suffering God has an out-flow. Prayer is a medium to restrain God's wrath, allowing mercy to rejoice against judgment.

Moses himself and his mission were the answer to prayer. In 1 Samuel 12:8 the Scriptures record,

> *When Jacob was come into Egypt, and your fathers cried unto the LORD, then the LORD sent Moses and Aaron, which brought forth your fathers out of Egypt, and made them dwell in this place.*

This was the beginning of the great deliverance of the Hebrews from Egyptian bondage.

The great movements of God originate with and are shaped by the prayers of men. Prayer deals directly with God. He is pleased to order His policy and base His actions on the prayers of His saints. Prayer influences God greatly. Moses could not do God's great work, even though it was God-commissioned, without praying. Moses could not govern God's people and carry out the divine plans without having his censer full of the incense of prayer. The work of God cannot be done unless the fire and fragrance of prayer are always burning, ascending, and perfuming.

Moses prayed often to relieve the terrible stroke of God's wrath. Four times Pharaoh solicited the prayers of Moses for relief from the fearful blow of God's wrath. *"Entreat the LORD"* (Exod. 8:8) begged Pharaoh while the loathsome frogs were upon him. *"And Moses cried unto the LORD because of the frogs which he had brought against Pharaoh. And the LORD did according to the word of Moses"* (Exod. 8:12–13). God answered his prayers.

When the grievous plague of flies had corrupted the whole land, Pharaoh again piteously cried out to Moses, *"Entreat for me"* (v. 28). Moses left Pharaoh and begged the Lord, and again the Lord answered and did as Moses asked.

The plague of fiery hail, which destroyed all of Egypt's crops, brought Pharaoh to Moses with the same earnest appeal, *"Entreat the LORD"* (Exod. 9:28). Moses went into the privacy of the wilderness alone with Almighty God. He *"spread abroad his hands unto the LORD: and the thunders and hail ceased, and the rain was not poured upon the earth"* (v. 33).

Though Moses was the man of law, prayer with him still asserted its mighty force. As in the more spiritual dispensation, Moses could have said, literally, *"My house is the house of prayer"* (Luke 19:46). Moses accepted the foundation principle of praying at its full face value.

Prayer deals directly with God. With Abraham we saw this clearly and strongly enunciated. With Moses it is still clearer and stronger, if that is possible. The principle is this: prayer affects God. God's conduct is influenced by prayer. A continuation of this principle is that God hears and answers prayer, even when the hearing and answering might change His conduct and reverse His action. The decree, *"Call unto me, and I will answer thee"* (Jer. 33:3), is stronger than all other laws and more inflexible than any other decree.

Moses had bold, free, and unhindered access to God. Familiarity and closeness to God gives delight, frequency, focus, and potency to prayer. Those who know God the best are the richest and most powerful in obtaining answers to prayer. Prayer becomes a rare thing for those unacquainted with God.

Moses sometimes found himself reduced to extreme conditions that God decided not to relieve. However, there are no circumstances too extreme for God to relieve.

Moses' mission was divine. It was ordered, directed, and planned by God. The more there is of God in a movement, the more prayer is conspicuous. Moses urgently prayed for the salvation of the Lord's people for forty days and forty nights. His concern was so intense for them that his physical infirmities and appetites were taken away during long seasons of prayer.

Evidence of the strange effect a righteous man's prayers have on God can be seen in God's exclamation to Moses: *"Now therefore let me alone, that my wrath may wax hot against them, that I may consume them; and I will make of thee a great nation"* (Exod. 32:10). The presence of such an influence over God fills us with astonishment, awe, and fear. How bold, lofty, and devoted is such a pleader!

Read this from the divine record:

And Moses returned unto the Lord, and said, Oh, this people have sinned a great sin, and have made them gods of gold. Yet

now, if thou wilt forgive their sin—; and if not, blot me, I pray
thee, out of thy book which thou hast written. And the Lord
said unto Moses, Whosoever hath sinned against me, him will
I blot out of my book. Therefore now go, lead the people unto
the place of which I have spoken unto thee: behold mine Angel
shall go before thee.   *(Exod. 32:31–34)*

At the rebellion of Korah, God's anger flamed out against everyone in Israel who sympathized with the rebels. Again Moses appeared on the stage of action, and this time Aaron joined him in
intercession for these sinners. In a serious time like this, Moses
knew where to go for relief. He knew to pray that God would answer by holding back His wrath to spare Israel. Here is what Scripture says about the situation:

And the Lord spake unto Moses and unto Aaron, saying,
Separate yourselves from among this congregation, that I may
consume them in a moment. And they fell on their faces, and
said, O God, the God of the spirits of all flesh, shall one man
sin, and wilt thou be wroth with all the congregation?
                                       (Num. 16:20–22)

The assumption, pride, and rebellion of Miriam, the sister of
Moses, in which she had the presence and sympathy of Aaron, put
the praying and the spirit of Moses in the noblest and most amiable
light. Because of her sin, God smote her with leprosy. But Moses
made tender and earnest intercession for his sister who had so
grievously offended God. His prayer was answered, and God saved
her from the fearful and incurable malady. The record of this is
very interesting:

And the anger of the Lord was kindled against them; and he
departed. And the cloud departed from off the tabernacle; and
behold, Miriam became leprous, white as snow: and Aaron
looked upon Miriam, and, behold, she was leprous. And
Aaron said unto Moses, Alas, my lord, I beseech thee, lay not
the sin upon us, wherein we have done foolishly, and wherein
we have sinned. Let her not be as one dead, of whom the flesh
is half consumed when he cometh out of his mother's womb.
And Moses cried unto the Lord, saying, Heal her now, O God,
I beseech thee. And the Lord said unto Moses, If her father
had but spit in her face, should she not be ashamed seven

days? let her be shut out from the camp seven days, and after
that let her be received again. *(Num. 12:9–14)*

The murmurings of the children of Israel furnished conditions
that called into play the full force of prayer. These conditions im-
pressively bring out the intercessory feature of prayer and disclose
Moses in his great office as an intercessor. It was at Marah that the
waters were bitter, and it was here that the people grievously
murmured against Moses and God. Here is the Scripture account:

And when they came to Marah, they could not drink of the wa-
ters of Marah, for they were bitter: therefore the name of it was
called Marah. And the people murmured against Moses, say-
ing, What shall we drink? And he cried unto the Lord; and
the Lord showed him a tree, which when he had cast into the
waters, the waters were made sweet: there he made for them a
statute and an ordinance, and there he proved them.
(Exod. 15:23–25)

The records of eternity alone will disclose how many bitter places
of the earth have been sweetened by answers to prayer.

Again at Taberah, the people complained, and God became angry with them. Moses again came to the front, stepped into the
breach, and prayed for them. Here is the brief account:

And when the people complained, it displeased the Lord: and
the Lord heard it; and his anger was kindled; and the fire of
the Lord burnt among them, and consumed them that were in
the uttermost part of the camp. And the people cried unto
Moses; and when Moses prayed unto the Lord, the fire was
quenched. *(Num. 11:1–2)*

Moses got what he asked for. His praying was specific, and
God's answer was likewise specific. Almighty God always heard
and always answered Moses when he prayed. Once, however, the
answer was not specific. Moses had prayed to go into Canaan. The
answer came, but it was not what he asked for. He was given a vision of the Promised Land, but he was not allowed to cross the Jordan into that land.

Moses' prayer was a prayer on the order of Paul's, when he
prayed three times for the removal of the thorn in the flesh. In this

case, the thorn was not removed, and, like Moses, Paul did not get what he asked for. However, God did provide grace that made the thorn a blessing.

The ninetieth Psalm, though it is incorporated with the Psalms of David, is attributed to Moses. It gives us a sample of the prayers of God's lawgiver. It is a prayer worth studying. It is sacred because it has been the requiem uttered over our dead for years. However, its very familiarity may cause us to lose its full meaning.

We would be wise if we digested it, not for the dead, but for the living, and let it teach us how to live, how to pray while living, and how to die. *"So teach us to number our days, that we may apply our hearts to wisdom....Establish thou the work of our hands upon us; yea, the work of our hands establish thou it"* (Ps. 90:12, 17).

5

Prayer: The Prophet's Link to God

I have known men who came to God for no other reason than to come to Him, they so loved Him. They refused to soil either Him or themselves with any other purpose than to simply be alone with Him. Friendship is best kept up, even among men, by frequent visits; and the more free from impurity those frequent visits are, and the less brought about by business, necessity, or custom, the more friendly and welcome they are.
—Thomas Goodwin

ELIJAH is considered the preeminent elder of the prophets. The crown, the throne, and the scepter are his. His garments are white with flame. He seems exalted in his fiery and prayerful nature, like a superhuman being. But the New Testament places him alongside us as a man with a nature similar to ours. (See James 5:17–18.) Instead of placing him outside the sphere of humanity, in the marvelous fruit of his praying, Scripture points to him as an example to be imitated and as an inspiration to stimulate us. To pray and have results as Elijah did is the crying need of our times.

Elijah learned the lesson of prayer, and he graduated from that divine school before Scripture mentions him. Somewhere in the secret places, on a mountain or a plain, he had been alone with God as an intercessor against the debasing idolatry of Ahab. His prayers prevailed mightily with God. He was certain that his prayers were answered.

He had been talking with God about vengeance. He was the embodiment of his times—times of vengeance. The intercessor was not to be clothed with an olive branch—the symbol of a suppliant for mercy—but with fire—the symbol of justice and the messenger of wrath. Elijah prayed earnestly that he might take a message of vengeance to Ahab, and God did not deny his prayer. Self-assured and with holy boldness, he declared to the astonished, cowering king his fearful message: *"As the* LORD *God of Israel liveth, before whom I stand, there shall not be dew nor rain these years, but according to my word"* (1 Kings 17:1).

The secret of his praying and his close relationship with God is found in the words *before whom I stand.* Gabriel's words to Zacharias, informing this priest of the coming of a son, are similar: *"I am Gabriel that stand in the presence of God"* (Luke 1:19). Even the archangel Gabriel had little more unflinching devotion, courage, readiness of obedience, and zeal for God's honor than Elijah.

What answers to prayer! What lasting power was in Elijah's prayer! Elijah prayed, *"and it rained not on earth by the space of three years and six months"* (James 5:17). What a man who dared utter such a claim and assert such power! Elijah's praying was no mere sham or performance, no spiritless, soulless, official praying. Elijah was in Elijah's praying. The whole man, with all his fiery forces, prayed unceasingly. Almighty God was real to him. Prayer to him was the means of projecting God in full force on the world, in order to vindicate His name, establish His own being, avenge His blasphemed name and violated law, and vindicate His servants.

Instead of *"prayed earnestly,"* in James 5:17, the margin of the Revised Standard Version has it, *"He prayed with prayer."* That is, he prayed with all the combined energies of prayer.

Elijah's praying was strong, insistent, and resistless in its elements of power. Feeble praying secures no results and brings neither glory to God nor good to man.

Elijah learned new and higher lessons of prayer with God while hidden away by the brook Cherith. He was doubtless communing with God while Ahab was searching everywhere for him. After a while God ordered him to Sarepta, where He had commanded a widow to sustain Elijah.

He went there for the widow's good as well as for his own. While this woman provided for him, he provided for the woman, yet Elijah's prayers did more for the woman than the woman's hospitality did for Elijah. Great trials and sorrows awaited the widow—yet, great answers, too. Her widowhood and her poverty told of her struggles and her sorrows. Elijah was there to relieve her poverty and to assuage her griefs. Here is the account:

> *And it came to pass after these things, that the son of the woman, the mistress of the house, fell sick; and his sickness was so sore, that there was no breath left in him. And she said unto Elijah, What have I to do with thee, O thou man of God? art thou come unto me to call my sin to remembrance, and to slay my son? And he said unto her, Give me thy son. And he took him out of her bosom, and carried him up into a loft, where he abode, and laid him down upon his own bed. And he cried unto the Lord, and said, O Lord my God, hast thou also brought evil upon the widow with whom I sojourn, by slaying her son? And he stretched himself upon the child three times, and cried unto the Lord, and said, O Lord my God, I pray thee, let this child's soul come into him again. And the Lord heard the voice of Elijah; and the soul of the child came into him again, and he revived. And Elijah took the child, and brought him down out of the chamber into the house, and delivered him unto his mother: and Elijah said, See, thy son liveth. And the woman said to Elijah, Now by this I know that thou art a man of God, and that the word of the LORD in thy mouth is truth.*   *(1 Kings 17:17–24)*

Elijah's prayer entered a region where prayer had never gone before. The awful, mysterious, and powerful regions of the dead were invaded by the presence and demands of prayer. God's answers to Elijah's praying kept the woman from starving and brought her son back from death. Surely no sorrow is like the bitterness of the loss of an only son.

Elijah faced these conditions full of confidence. There was no hesitancy in his actions, and there was no pause in his faith. He took the dead son to his own room, and alone with God he prayed. In that room, God met him. The encounter was too intense and too sacred for a third party to share.

The prayer was made to God, and the issue was with God. God took the child, and only God rules the realms of death. In His hands are the issues of life and death. Elijah believed that God took the child's spirit, and that God could also restore that spirit.

God answered Elijah's prayer. The answer was proof of Elijah's mission and the truth of God's Word. The dead child brought to life was a sure conviction of this truth: *"Now by this I know that thou art a man of God, and that the word of the* LORD *in thy mouth is truth"* (v. 24). Answers to prayer are evidences of God and the truth of His Word.

The unforgettable test of Elijah—made in the presence of an apostate king, in the face of a backslidden nation that was ruled by an idolatrous priesthood—is a sublime exhibition of faith and prayer. The prophets of Baal lost the contest. No fire from heaven fell in answer to their frantic cries.

Elijah, in great quietness of spirit and with confident assurance, called Israel to himself. He repaired the wasted altar of God, the altar of sacrifice and of prayer, and put the pieces of bullock in order on the altar. He then took action to prevent any charge of deception. He flooded the altar with water. Then Elijah prayed a model prayer, remarkable for its clarity, simplicity, and candor. It is also noted for its brevity and faith. Read the account given in Scripture:

> *And it came to pass at the time of the offering of the evening sacrifice, that Elijah the prophet came near, and said, Lord God of Abraham, Isaac, and of Israel, let it be known this day that thou art God in Israel, and that I am thy servant, and that I have done all these things at thy word. Hear me, O Lord, hear me, that this people may know that thou art the Lord God, and that thou hast turned their heart back again. Then the fire of the Lord fell, and consumed the burnt sacrifice, and the wood, and the stones, and the dust, and licked up the water that was in the trench. And when all the people saw it, they fell on their faces: and they said, The Lord, he is the God; the Lord, he is the God.* (1 Kings 18:36–39)

Elijah was dealing directly with God, for true prayer always deals directly with God. Elijah's prayer was to determine the existence of the true God. The answer, direct from God, settled the question. The answer is also the proof of Elijah's divine mission and the evidence that God deals with men. If we had more of Elijah's praying, marvels would be greater than those things we call marvels today. God would not seem so strange, so far away, and so feeble in action. Everything is tame and feeble to us because our praying is so tame and feeble.

God said to Elijah, *"Go, show thyself unto Ahab; and I will send rain upon the earth"* (1 Kings 18:1). Elijah acted promptly on the divine order and showed himself to Ahab. He made his issue with Ahab, Israel, and Baal. The whole current of national feeling turned back to God. The day faded into the evening shades. No rain had come. But Elijah did not fold his arms and say the promise had failed. He emphasized the promise and saw God fulfill it. Here is the Scripture record with the result given:

> *And Elijah said unto Ahab, Get thee up, eat and drink; for there is a sound of abundance of rain. So Ahab went up to eat and to drink. And Elijah went up to the top of Carmel; and he cast himself down upon the earth, and put his face between his knees, and said to his servant, Go up now, look toward the sea. And he went up, and looked, and said, There is nothing. And he said, Go again seven times. And it came to pass at the seventh time, that he said, Behold, there ariseth a little cloud out of the sea, like a man's hand. And he said, Go up say unto Ahab, Prepare thy chariot, and get thee down, that the rain stop thee not. And it came to pass in the mean while, that the heaven was black with clouds and wind, and there was a great rain. And Ahab rode, and went to Jezreel. And the hand of the Lord was on Elijah.* (1 Kings 18:41–46)

Then, as James recorded, *"he prayed again, and the heaven gave rain, and the earth brought forth her fruit"* (James 5:18).

Elijah's persistent, fiery praying and God's promise brought the rain. Prayer carries the promise to its gracious fulfillment. It takes persistent and persevering prayer to give the promise its largest and most gracious results. In this instance, it was expectant prayer, watchful of results, looking for the answer. Elijah's answer was the small cloud that was like a man's hand. He had the inward assurance of the answer even before he had the rain.

Elijah's praying shames our feeble praying. His praying made things happen! It vindicated God's existence, brought conviction to dull and sluggish consciences, and proved that God was still Master of the nation. Elijah's praying turned a whole nation back to God, ordered the moving of the clouds, and directed the falling of the rain. It called down fire from heaven to prove God's existence or destroy His enemies.

Elijah, the elder prophet of Israel's praying, was clothed in fire. He wore a golden crown, and his censer was full of burning, fragrant prayer. No wonder Elisha cried out, as the fiery chariot separated him from the fiery prophet of the Lord, *"My father, my father, the chariot of Israel, and the horsemen thereof"* (2 Kings 2:12). But chariots and armies could not begin to do as much for Israel as the praying Elijah, who could not touch anything except through prayer. God was with him mightily because he was mighty in prayer. Today we need saints who dare to pray with the fire, force, and fragrance of Elijah's prayers!

In the contest with the prophets of Baal, the issue was clearly to determine the true God. Does God live? Is the Bible a revelation from Him? How often do those questions arise? How often do they need to be settled? An appeal by prayer is the only way to settle them. The trouble is not in God, but in our praying. The proof that God exists is answered prayers.

Where are the Elijahs in today's church? Where are the men with his fervor, who can pray as he prayed? We have thousands of intense men, but where are the men who will pray as he prayed? Notice the calm, assured confidence that Elijah displayed as he staked the issue and built the altar. His prayer was clear and calm on that occasion.

Elijah's praying follows New Testament prayer principles and illustrates the nature of prayer. It also proves what prayer can do for the person who prays with confidence and faith. Elijah's results could be secured today if we had more men praying as Elijah did.

Elijah obtained his answers by praying truly and earnestly. So much of today's praying is not real praying, but a mere shell, mere words! Most of it could be called non-praying. It goes nowhere and accomplishes nothing. In fact, very often no results are even expected.

True prayer that wins an answer must be backed up by a scriptural, vital, personal religion. This is essential to real Christian service in this life. It is most important that in serving, we serve. So, in praying, we must talk with God. Truth and reality of the heart—these are the core, the substance, the sum, the heart of prayer. Prayer has no potential unless we pray with simplicity, sincerity, and truth. Prayerless praying—how popular, yet what a useless delusion!

6

Even Kings Must Pray

One can form a habit of study until the will seems to be at rest and only the intellect is engaged, the will having retired altogether from exercise. This is not true of real praying. If the affections are laggard, cold, indifferent; if the intellect is furnishing no material to clothe the petition, then nothing worthwhile is accomplished. —Homer W. Hodge

THE great religious reformation under King Hezekiah and the prophet Isaiah was thoroughly saturated with prayer during various stages. The story of King Hezekiah serves as an illustration of a praying elder of Israel, white-robed and gold-crowned. He had genius and strength, wisdom and piety. He was a statesman, a general, a poet, and a religious reformer. He surprises us, not so much because of his strength and genius—they were to be expected—but because of his piety under all the circumstances connected with him.

The rare statement, *"He did that which was right in the sight of the LORD"* (2 Chron. 29:2), is a thrilling surprise when we consider all his antecedents and his environments. Where did he come from? Under what circumstances was his childhood spent? Who were his parents, and what was their religious character?

Worldliness, halfheartedness, and utter apostasy marked the reign of his father, grandfather, and great-grandfather. As he grew up, his home surroundings were far from being a foundation for godliness and faith in God. One thing, however, favored him. He was fortunate to have Isaiah for his friend and counselor when he assumed the crown of Judah. It is extremely valuable for a ruler to have a God-fearing man for his counselor and associate!

Hezekiah interceded on behalf of a number of people who were unfit to participate in the Passover Feast. These people were not prepared with the required ceremonial cleansing, and it was important that they be allowed to eat the Passover Feast with everyone. Here is the brief account, with special reference to Hezekiah's praying and God's response:

> *For there were many in the congregation that were not sanctified: therefore the Levites had the charge of the killing of the passovers for every one that was not clean, to sanctify them unto the Lord. For a multitude of the people...had not cleansed themselves, yet did they eat the passover otherwise than it was written. But Hezekiah prayed for them, saying, The good Lord pardon every one that prepareth his heart to seek God, the Lord God of his fathers, though he be not cleansed according to the purification of the sanctuary. And the Lord hearkened to Hezekiah, and healed the people.*
> *(2 Chron. 30:17–20)*

So the Lord heard his prayer, and even the violation of the most sacred law of the Passover was forgiven to answer this praying, God-fearing king. Law must yield its scepter to prayer.

The strength, directness, and foundation of Hezekiah's faith and prayer are found in his words to his army. They are memorable words, stronger and mightier than all the armies of Sennacherib:

> *Be strong and courageous, be not afraid nor dismayed for the king of Assyria, nor for all the multitude that is with him: for there be more with us than with him: with him is an arm of flesh; but with us is the Lord our God to help us, and to fight our battles. And the people rested themselves upon the words of Hezekiah king of Judah.*   *(2 Chron. 32:7–8)*

Hezekiah's defense against the mighty enemies of God was prayer. His enemies cowered and were destroyed by God's answers to his prayers, even when his own armies were powerless. God's people were always safe when their princes were princes in prayer.

One momentous occasion really tested Hezekiah's faith, furnishing him with an opportunity to try prayer as a means to deliverance. Judah was sorely pressed by the Assyrians, and, humanly speaking, defeat and captivity seemed imminent. The king of Assyria sent a commission to defy and blaspheme the name of God and to insult King Hezekiah publicly. Note what Hezekiah did without hesitation: *"And it came to pass when king Hezekiah heard it, that he rent his clothes, and covered himself with sackcloth, and went into the house of the LORD"* (Isa. 37:1).

His very first reflex was to turn to God by entering the house of prayer. God was in his thoughts, and prayer was the first action to be taken. He sent messengers to Isaiah, asking Isaiah to join him in prayer. Isaiah and Hezekiah appealed to God for deliverance from these blasphemous enemies.

Just at this particular point in time, the Assyrian king's forces, which were besieging Hezekiah, were diverted from an immediate attack on Jerusalem. This was God's answer. The king of Assyria, however, sent Hezekiah a defaming and blasphemous letter.

For the second time, as he was insulted by the forces of this heathen king, Hezekiah entered the Lord's house, the house of prayer. He knew exactly where he should go and to whom he should appeal.

> *And Hezekiah received the letter from the hand of the messengers, and read it: and Hezekiah went up unto the house of the Lord, and spread it before the Lord. And Hezekiah prayed unto the Lord, saying, O Lord of hosts, God of Israel, that dwellest between the cherubims, thou art the God, even thou alone, of all the kingdoms of the earth: thou hast made heaven and earth....Now therefore, O Lord our God, save us from his hand, that all the kingdoms of the earth may know that thou art the Lord, even thou only.*   *(Isa. 37:14–16, 20)*

Note the speedy answer and the marvelous results of such praying by this God-fearing king. First, Isaiah gave the king full assurance that he need fear nothing. God heard the prayer and would give a great deliverance. Secondly, the angel of the Lord came with swift wings and smote one hundred and eighty-five thousand Assyrians. The king was vindicated, God was honored, and the people of God were saved.

The united prayers of the praying king and the praying prophet were mighty forces in bringing God's deliverance and destroying His enemies. Armies were at their mercy. Angels, swift-winged and armed with almighty power and vengeance, were their allies.

Hezekiah served his people in prayer to destroy idolatry and reform his kingdom. Prayer was his chief weapon. He later tried its power against the set and declared plan of Almighty God. When Hezekiah was very sick, God sent his close friend, wise counselor, and prophet, Isaiah, to warn him of his approaching end. Isaiah also told him to arrange his affairs in preparation for his final departure. This is the scriptural statement:

> *In those days was Hezekiah sick unto death. And the prophet Isaiah the son of Amoz came to him, and said unto him, Thus saith the Lord, Set thine house in order; for thou shalt die, and not live.*   *(2 Kings 20:1)*

The decree came directly from God, and Hezekiah wondered what could reverse that divine decree. He had never been in a situation so insurmountable, with a decree so direct and definite from God. Could prayer change the purposes of God? Could prayer snatch from the jaws of death one who was destined to die? Could prayer save a man from an incurable sickness? These were the questions with which he had to deal.

But his faith did not waver one moment. His faith did not stagger one minute when the Lord's prophet suddenly gave him the definite news. Hezekiah did not let any untrusting, unbelieving thoughts enter his mind—as believers might today. Instantly he started to pray. Immediately, without delay, he petitioned God, who had issued the edict. He could not go to anyone else. God could change His own purposes if He so chose.

Note what Hezekiah did in this emergency and the gracious result.

> *Then he turned his face to the wall, and prayed unto the Lord, saying, I beseech thee, O Lord, remember now how I have walked before thee in truth and with a perfect heart, and have done that which is good in thy sight. And Hezekiah wept sore.*   *(2 Kings 20:2–3)*

He did not offer God a self-righteous plea for recovery. He wanted God to remember his sincerity, fidelity, and service—which was legitimate. This prayer was directly in line with that of David in Psalm 26:1: *"Judge me, O LORD; for I have walked in mine integrity."* This was not a prayer test with Hezekiah, nor was it a faith cure, but it was testing God. It had to be God's cure if a cure was to come at all.

Hezekiah hardly finished his prayer, and Isaiah was just about to go home, when God gave another message for Hezekiah. This time the message was more pleasant and encouraging. The mighty force of prayer had affected God and had changed His edict, reversing His purpose concerning Hezekiah. Prayer can accomplish anything. A praying man can accomplish anything through prayer.

> *And it came to pass, afore Isaiah was gone out into the middle court, that the word of the Lord came to him, saying, Turn again, and tell Hezekiah the captain of my people, Thus saith the Lord, the God of David thy father, I have heard thy prayer, I have seen thy tears: behold, I will heal thee: on the third day thou shalt go up unto the house of the Lord. And I will add unto thy days fifteen years; and I will deliver thee and this city out of the hand of the king of Assyria; and I will defend this city for mine own sake, and for my servant David's sake.*
>
> *(2 Kings 20:4–6)*

The prayer was to God. It asked God to reconsider and change His mind. Doubtless Isaiah returned to his house with a lighter heart than when he delivered his original message. This sick king prayed to God, asking Him to revoke His decree, and God condescended to grant the request. God sometimes changes His mind in answer to prayer. He has a right to do so. His reasons for changing His mind are strong reasons. His servant Hezekiah wanted it done.

Hezekiah had been a dutiful servant for God. Truth, perfection, and goodness were the elements of Hezekiah's service and the rule of his life. Hezekiah's tears and prayer were in the way of God's executing His decree to take away His servant's life. Prayer and tears are mighty things with God. They mean much more to Him than consistency and decrees. *"I have heard thy prayer, I have seen thy tears: behold, I will heal thee"* (v. 5).

Health comes in answer to prayer. God answered by giving more than what Hezekiah asked. Hezekiah prayed only for his life.

God not only gave him life, but He also promised him protection and security from his enemies.

Isaiah also had something to do with the recovery of this praying king. Isaiah's praying was changed into the skill of the physician. *"And Isaiah said, Take a lump of figs. And they took and laid it on the boil, and he recovered"* (v. 7).

Isaiah and Hezekiah prayed further for concrete proof of God's healing:

> *And Hezekiah said unto Isaiah, What shall be the sign that the Lord will heal me, and that I shall go up into the house of the Lord the third day? And Isaiah said, This sign shalt thou have of the Lord, that the Lord will do the thing that he hath spoken: shall the shadow go forward ten degrees, or go back ten degrees? And Hezekiah answered, It is a light thing for the shadow to go down ten degrees: nay, but let the shadow return backward ten degrees. And Isaiah the prophet cried unto the Lord: and he brought the shadow ten degrees backward, by which it had gone down in the dial of Ahaz. (2 Kings 20:8–11)*

Life was sweet to Hezekiah, and he wanted to live. Nothing but the energy of faith could have impelled God to act so powerfully. Hezekiah's heart was broken, and his tears added force and volume to his prayer. He pleaded with great strivings and strong arguments. God heard Hezekiah praying, saw his tears, and changed His mind.

Hezekiah lived to praise God and be an example of God's answers to mighty praying. His prayer was born in the fire of great desire, and it pursued through the deepest agony of conflict and opposition to find success.

Spiritual cravings must be strong enough to give life to the mighty conflicts of prayer. They must be absorbing enough to stop business, arrest worldly pursuits, awaken us before daybreak, and send us to solitude with God. With this powerful reinforcement, prayer will conquer every opposing force and win victories from the jaws of hell.

We need men and women who will pray with power and with confidence that they can reach out, grapple with God, and draw out His treasures for spiritual uses. Forceless prayers have no power to obtain answers, overcome difficulties, or gain complete and wonderful victories.

There are four things to remember when praying: God hears prayer, God considers prayer, God answers prayer, and God delivers by prayer. These things cannot be repeated too often. Prayer breaks all bars, dissolves all chains, opens all prisons, and widens all straits that bind God's saints.

7

Reformation
through Prayer

*Before the Civil War, there were many signs of a new in-
terest in prayer and new hope from its exercise. These signs
have multiplied. The war has already done for us this one
thing, at least, that is good. Let us not miss our opportunity.
Prayer is not an easy exercise. It requires encouragement, ex-
position, and training. There was never a time when men and
women were more sincerely anxious to be told how to pray.
Prayer is our mightiest weapon if we use it as God has encouraged us. We must do everything in our power to bring it
into exercise.* —James Hastings

EZRA, a priest and one of God's great reformers, was an Old
Testament praying man who knew that God's answer to prayer
would overcome difficulties and bring good things to pass. He returned from Babylon under the patronage of the king of Babylon,
who was strangely moved toward Ezra and who favored him in
many ways.

Ezra had been in Jerusalem only a few days when the princes
came to him with the distressing information that Israel had not
separated themselves from the people of Babylon and were prac-
ticing the abominations of the heathen nations surrounding them.
What was worse was that the princes and rulers in Israel had been
leaders in the trespass.

It was a sad state of affairs facing Ezra when he found Israel
hopelessly involved with the world. God demands that His people, in
all ages, keep themselves separated from the world—a separation so

sharp that it can inspire antagonism. To this end, He put Israel in the Promised Land and cut them off from other nations by mountains, deserts, and seas. He immediately commanded them not to form any alliance with foreign nations, whether marital, social, or business.

Ezra found Israel, as he returned from Babylon, paralyzed and thoroughly prostrated by the violation of this principle. They had intermarried, forming the closest and most sacred ties in family, social, and business life. Everyone was involved—priests, Levites, princes, and the populace. The families, businesses, and religious lives of God's people were in violation of His law. What was to be done? What could be done? These were the important questions facing this leader of Israel, this man of God.

Everything appeared to be against Israel's recovery. Ezra could not preach to them, because the whole city would be inflamed, and the people would chase him out. What force was there that could recover them to God so that they would dissolve business partnerships, divorce wives and husbands, cut acquaintances, and dissolve friendships?

The first thing about Ezra that is worthy of remark was that he saw the situation and realized how serious it was. He was not a blind-eyed optimist who never saw anything wrong in Israel. By the mouth of Isaiah God had proposed the very pertinent question, *"Who is blind, but my servant?"* (Isa. 42:19). But it could not possibly have applied to Ezra.

Nor did he minimize the condition of things or seek to excuse the sins of the people or to minimize the enormity of their crimes. Their offense appeared in his eyes to be extremely serious. The leaders in Zion needed eyes to see the sins of Israel as well as the evils of the times. One great need of the modern church is for leaders like Ezra who are not blind and who are willing to see the real state of the church.

Naturally, seeing these dreadful evils in Israel and Jerusalem, he was distressed. The sad condition of things grieved him so much that he tore his garments, plucked his hair, and sat down in utter astonishment. All these things are evidences of his great distress at the terrible state of affairs. It was then, in that frame of mind, concerned, solicitous, and troubled in soul, that he gave himself to prayer, confessing the sins of the people and pleading for God's pardoning mercy. To whom should he go in a time like this but the

God who hears prayer, who is ready to pardon, and who can bring the unexpected thing to pass?

Ezra was amazed beyond expression at the wicked conduct of the people. He was so deeply moved that he began to fast and pray. Prayer and fasting obtains results. He prayed with a broken heart, for there was nothing else he could do. He prayed to God, deeply burdened, prostrate on the ground and weeping, and the city turned to unite with him in prayer.

Prayer was the only way to appease God. Ezra became a great mover through prayer in a great work for God, with marvelous results. The whole work, its principles and its results, are summarized in Ezra 10:1:

> *Now when Ezra had prayed, and when he had confessed, weeping and casting himself down before the house of God, there assembled unto him out of Israel a very great congregation of men and women and children: for the people wept very sore.*

That was simple, mighty, and persevering prayer. Intense and prevailing prayer had accomplished its end. Ezra's praying obtained results and brought a great work for God into being. It was mighty praying because it brought Almighty God to do His own work. Nothing but God and prayer could have changed this absolutely hopeless situation. But nothing is hopeless to prayer because nothing is hopeless to God.

Again we must say that prayer has only to do with God and only brings results if it has to do with God. Whatever influence the praying of Ezra had upon himself, prayer's chief result, if not its only result, followed because it affected God and moved Him to do the work.

A great and general repentance followed Ezra's praying, and a wonderful reformation occurred in Israel. Ezra's mourning and praying were the great factors that brought these great things to pass.

So thorough was the revival that Scripture notes that Israel's leaders came to Ezra with these words:

> *We have trespassed against our God, and have taken strange wives of the people of the land: yet now there is hope in Israel concerning this thing. Now therefore let us make a covenant*

with our God to put away all the wives, and such as are born of them, according to the counsel of my lord, and of those that tremble at the commandment of our God; and let it be done according to the law. Arise, for this matter belongeth unto thee: we also will be with thee: be of good courage, and do it.

(Ezra 10:2–4)

8

Prayer: The Builder's Blueprint

We do not care for your splendid abilities as a minister, or your natural endowment as an orator. We are sure that the truth of the matter is this: No one will or can command success and become a real praying soul unless intense application is the price. I am even now convinced that the difference between the saints like Wesley, Fletcher, Edwards, Brainerd, Bramwell, and ourselves is energy, perseverance, and invincible determination to succeed or die in the attempt. God help us.
                                                    —*Homer W. Hodge*

IN telling of the praying saints of the Old Testament who obtained answers to prayer, we must not leave out Nehemiah, the builder. He stands on an equal footing with the others who have already been considered here. In the story of the reconstruction of Jerusalem after the Babylonian captivity, he played a prominent role. Prayer was also prominent in his life during those years. He was a captive in Babylon and had an important position in the palace of the king—he was the cupbearer. There must have been considerable merit in him to cause the king to take a Hebrew captive and place him in such an office. He had responsibility for the king's life, because he was in charge of the wine that the king drank.

One day while Nehemiah was in Babylon, in the king's palace, some of his fellow Israelites came from Jerusalem. Very naturally, Nehemiah desired news about the people and information concerning the city itself. He heard the distressing news that the walls of Jerusalem were broken down, the gates were burned with fire, and those who were left at the beginning of the captivity were stigmatized and always in trouble.

Just one verse shows the effect of this sad news on this man of God: *"And it came to pass, when I heard these words, that I sat down and wept, and mourned certain days, and fasted, and prayed before the God of heaven"* (Neh. 1:4). Here was a man whose heart was in his native land, far away from where he lived. He loved Israel, was concerned for the welfare of Zion, and was true to God. Deeply distressed by the information concerning his fellow Israelites at Jerusalem, he mourned and wept. There are so few strong men today who can weep at the evils and abominations of the times! How rare are those who, seeing the desolations of God's people, are sufficiently interested and concerned for the welfare of the church to mourn!

Mourning and weeping over the decay of religion, the decline of revival power, and the fearful inroads of worldliness in the church are almost unknown. There is so much so-called optimism that leaders cannot see the breaking down of the walls of the church and the low spiritual state of modern Christians. They have less heart to mourn and cry about it. Nehemiah was a mourner in Zion.

In this state of heart, distressed beyond measure, he did what other praying saints have done—he went to God and made the problem the subject of prayer. The prayer is recorded in the first chapter of Nehemiah and is a model for our prayers. He began with adoration, confessed the sins of his nation, pleaded the promises of God, mentioned former mercies, and begged for pardoning mercy.

Then he prayed with an eye to the future—for unquestionably the next time he was summoned into the king's presence he planned to ask permission to visit Jerusalem to try to remedy the distressing situation. He prayed for something very special: *"And prosper, I pray thee, thy servant this day, and grant him mercy in the sight of this man. For* [he adds by way of explanation] *I was the king's cupbearer"* (Neh. 1:11).

It seemed all right to pray for his people. But how would a heathen king, with no sympathy whatever for the sad condition of Nehemiah's city and his people, consent to give up his faithful cupbearer, allowing him to be gone for months? Nehemiah believed in a God who could respond and touch even the mind of a heathen ruler and move him favorably toward the request of his praying servant.

When Nehemiah was summoned into the king's presence, God used the sad appearance of Nehemiah's countenance to gain the consent of Artaxerxes. This started the king's inquiry as to its cause, and the final result was that the king not only permitted Nehemiah to go back to Jerusalem, but furnished him with everything he needed for the journey and the success of the enterprise.

Nehemiah did not rest his case after he first prayed about this matter. He stated this significant fact as he talked to the king: *"So I prayed unto the God of heaven"* (Neh. 2:4). He gave the impression that while the king was inquiring about Nehemiah's request and the length of time he would be gone, he was then and there talking to God about the matter.

Nehemiah's intense, persistent praying prevailed. God can affect the mind of even a heathen ruler, and He can do this in answer to prayer without overturning the king's free choice or forcing his will. Esther's was a parallel case when she called upon her people to fast and pray for her as she went uninvited into the king's presence. As a result, at a very critical moment, his mind was touched by the Spirit of God, and he was favorably moved toward Esther, holding out the golden scepter to her.

Nor did Nehemiah's praying cease after he succeeded thus far. In building the wall of Jerusalem, he met great opposition from Sanballat and Tobiah, who ridiculed the efforts of the people to rebuild the city's walls. Unmoved by the derision and intense opposition of wicked opponents, he pursued his task. He mixed prayer with all he did: *"Hear, O our God; for we are despised: and turn their reproach upon their own head, and give them for a prey in the land of our captivity"* (Neh. 4:4). In continuing the account he said, *"Nevertheless we made our prayer unto our God"* (v. 9).

Prayer was prominent all through the accounts of the high and noble work that Nehemiah did. God's replies were also prominent. Even after the walls were completed, these same enemies of God's people opposed Nehemiah again. But he renewed his praying, and he himself recorded this significant prayer: *"Now therefore, O God, strengthen my hands"* (Neh. 6:9).

Still further on, when Sanballat and Tobiah hired an emissary to frighten and hinder Nehemiah, he set himself directly against this new attack. Again, he turned to God in prayer:

> *My God, think thou upon Tobiah and Sanballat according to these their works, and on the prophetess Noadiah, and the rest of the prophets, that would have put me in fear.* (Neh. 6:14)

God answered his faithful laborer and defeated the counsels and plans of Israel's wicked opponents.

Nehemiah discovered, to his dismay, that *"the portions of the Levites had not been given them"* (Neh. 13:10). As a result, the house of God was forsaken. He took steps to see that the lawful tithes were forthcoming, so that God's house would be opened to all religious services. He even appointed treasurers to take charge of this business. Prayer must not be overlooked, so we find his prayer recorded at this time: *"Remember me, O my God, concerning this, and wipe not out my good deeds that I have done for the house of my God, and for the offices thereof"* (Neh. 13:14).

Do not think that this was a self-righteous plea like that of the Pharisee in our Lord's time. The Pharisee declared he was going up to the temple to pray, and he paraded his self-righteous claims in God's sight. Rather, Nehemiah's prayer was a prayer like that of Hezekiah, who reminded God of his fidelity to Him and of his heart being right in His sight.

Once more Nehemiah found evil among the people of God. Just as he corrected the evil that had caused the closing of God's house, he discovered Sabbath breaking. At this time he not only had to counsel the people and seek to correct them by mild means, but he also proposed to exercise his authority if they did not cease their buying and selling on the Sabbath day. He closed this part of his work with prayer, knowing God would hear him, and he recorded his prayer on that occasion: *"Remember me, O my God, concerning this also, and spare me according to the greatness of thy mercy"* (Neh. 13:22).

Lastly, as a reformer, Nehemiah discovered another great evil among the people. They had intermarried with the men and women of Ashdod, Ammon, and Moab. Contending with them, he caused them to reform in this matter, and the close of his record has a prayer in it: *"Remember them, O my God, because they have defiled the priesthood, and the covenant of the priesthood, and of the Levites"* (v. 29).

Cleansing them from all strangers, he appointed the wards of the priests and the Levites. His recorded career closes with this brief prayer: *"Remember me, O my God, for good"* (v. 31).

Blessed is the church whose leaders are men of prayer. Happy is that congregation that contemplates the building of a church so that it will include leaders who will lay its foundations in prayer and whose walls go up side by side with prayer. Through prayer God builds churches and erects the walls of houses of worship. Through prayer God defeats the opponents of those who are prosecuting His enterprises. Prayer favorably touches minds, even those not connected with the church, and moves them in favor of church matters. Prayer helps mightily in all matters concerning God's cause. It wonderfully aids and encourages the hearts of those who have His work in hand in this world.

9

Raise Your Children for God

It was a grand action by Jerome, one of the Roman fathers. He laid aside all pressing engagements and went to fulfill the call God gave him, which was to translate the Holy Scriptures. His congregations were larger than many preachers' of today; but he said to his people, "Now it is necessary that the Scriptures be translated, you must find another minister. I am bound for the wilderness and shall not return until my task is finished." Away he went and labored and prayed until he produced the Latin Vulgate, which will last as long as the world stands. So we must say to our friends, "I must go away and take time for prayer and solitude." And though we do not write Latin Vulgates, our work will be immortal. Glory to God. —Charles Spurgeon

SAMUEL was born in direct answer to prayer. His praying mother's heart was full of earnest desire for a son. He came into life under prayer surroundings, and his first months in this world were spent in direct contact with a woman who knew how to pray. It was a prayer accompanied by the solemn vow that if he was given to her, he would be *"lent to the LORD"* (1 Sam. 1:28).

True to that vow, this praying mother put him directly in touch with the minister of the sanctuary and under the influence of the house of prayer. It was no wonder he developed into a man of prayer. We could not have expected otherwise with such a beginning in life and with such early environments. Such surroundings always make impressions upon children and tend to mold character and determine destiny.

Samuel was in a favorable place to hear God when He spoke to him, and he was in an atmosphere that nurtured his heeding the divine call that came to him. It was the most natural thing in the world when, at the third call from heaven, he recognized God's voice. His childish heart responded promptly, *"Speak; for thy servant heareth"* (1 Sam. 3:10). There was a quick response from his boyish spirit, of submission, willingness, and prayer.

If he had been born to a different sort of mother, if he had been placed in different surroundings, if he had spent his early days in contact with different influences, he may not have heard God's voice and so readily yielded his young life to God. Would a worldly home, with worldly surroundings, with a worldly-minded mother, separated from the will of God, have produced such a character as Samuel? It takes godly influences in early life to produce such praying men as Samuel.

Would you have your child called early into divine service and separated from the world to God? Would you have him situated so that he could be called in childhood by the Spirit of God? Put him under prayer influences. Place him near and directly under the influence of a man or woman of God and in close touch with the house of prayer. God will honor your action.

Samuel knew God in boyhood. As a consequence, he knew God in manhood. He recognized God in childhood, obeyed Him, and prayed to Him. The result was that he recognized God in manhood, obeyed Him, and prayed to Him. If more children were born of praying parents, brought up in direct contact with the house of prayer, and reared in prayer environments, more children would hear the voice of God's Spirit speaking to them. They would respond more quickly to those divine calls to a religious life.

Do we want to have praying men in our churches? We must have praying mothers to give them birth, praying homes to influence their lives, and praying surroundings to impress their minds and to lay the foundations for praying lives. Praying Samuels come from praying Hannahs. Praying priests come from the house of prayer. Praying leaders come from praying homes.

For years Israel was under bondage to the Philistines. The ark was housed in the home of Abinadab whose son, Eleazer, was appointed to keep this sacred testimony of God. The people had turned to idolatry, and Samuel was disturbed about the religious condition of the nation. The ark of the covenant was absent, the people worshipped idols, and there was a grievous departure from God.

Calling upon them to put away their strange gods, Samuel urged them to prepare their hearts for the Lord and begin to serve Him again. He promised them that the Lord would deliver them out of the hands of the Philistines. Samuel was a preacher of the times. He made a deep impression and bore rich fruits, as such preaching always does. *"Then the children of Israel did put away Baalim and Ashtaroth, and served the LORD only"* (1 Sam. 7:4).

But this was not enough. Prayer had to accompany their reformation. So Samuel, true to his convictions about prayer, said to the people, *"Gather all Israel to Mizpeh, and I will pray for you unto the LORD"* (v. 5). While Samuel was offering up prayer for these wicked Israelites, the Philistines were preparing for battle against the nation. But, in answer to prayer, the Lord intervened at the critical moment with a great thunderstorm, defeated the enemy, *"and they were smitten before Israel"* (v. 10).

Fortunately the nation had a man who could pray and who knew the worth of prayer. He was a leader who had God's ear and who could influence God.

But Samuel's praying did not stop there. He judged Israel all the days of his life. Every year he made a circuit through Bethel, Gilgal, and Mizpeh. Then he returned home to Ramah. *"And there he built an altar unto the LORD"* (1 Sam. 7:17). It was an altar of sacrifice, but it was also an altar of prayer.

While the altar may have been for the benefit of his community, it must have also been a family altar. At the altar, Almighty God was acknowledged in the home. The altar was the advertisement of a religious home. Here father and mother would call upon the Lord. The altar differentiated this home from all the worldly and idolatrous homes surrounding them. Blessed is that home where daily thanksgiving ascends to heaven and where praying is done at the altar morning and night.

Samuel was not only a praying priest, a praying leader, and a praying teacher, but he was also a praying father. The great need of these modern times is for Christian homes to have praying mothers and fathers. This is where the breakdown in religion occurs, where the religious life of a community first begins to decay, and where we must go first to raise praying men and women in God's church. The revival must start in the home.

A crisis came to this nation. The people were infatuated by the glory of a kingdom with a human king, and they were prepared to reject God as their King. God had always been their King. They came to Samuel with the bold request, *"Make us a king to judge us like all the nations"* (1 Sam. 8:5).

The idea displeased this man of God, who was jealous for the name, the honor, and the pleasure of the Lord God. How could it be otherwise? Who would not have been displeased if he thought as Samuel did? It grieved his soul. The Lord, however, came to him with comforting assurance: *"Hearken unto the voice of the people in all that they say unto thee: they have not rejected thee, but they have rejected me, that I should not reign over them"* (1 Sam. 8:7).

It was then that Samuel followed the bent of his mind, *"and Samuel prayed unto the LORD"* (v. 6). It seemed that in every matter concerning this people, Samuel had to pray over it. The need was greater when the people wanted an entire revolution in the form of government, replacing God with a human king. Samuel wanted to know what God thought about this. Praying men are needed to carry the affairs of government to God in prayer. Lawmakers, judges, and lawyers need leaders who know God to pray for them. There would be fewer mistakes if there was more praying done in civil matters.

But this was not to be the end of this matter. God had to show definitely and plainly His displeasure at such a request, that the people would know what a wicked thing they had done, even though God consented to their request. They had to know God still existed and was active in the lives of His people, their king, and the affairs of government.

So the prayers of Samuel were again brought into play to carry out the divine purposes. Samuel told the people to stand still, so he could show them what the Lord would do. He called upon God, and in answer God sent a tremendous thunderstorm that terrified the people and caused them to acknowledge their great sin.

The people were so afraid that they hastily called upon Samuel to pray for them and to spare them from what seemed to be destruction. Samuel prayed again; God heard and answered; and the thunder and rain ceased.

One more incident in the prayer life of Samuel is worth noticing. King Saul, whom Samuel had appointed at the request of the people, was ordered to destroy all the Amalekites, root and branch, and all of their goods. But Saul, contrary to divine instructions, spared King Agag and the best of the sheep and the cattle. He justified it by claiming that the people wanted it done.

God then brought this message to Samuel:

> *It repenteth me that I have set up Saul to be king: for he is turned back from following me, and hath not performed my commandments. And it grieved Samuel; and he cried unto the LORD all night.* (1 Sam. 15:11)

Such a sudden declaration was enough to produce grief in the soul of a man like Samuel, who loved his nation, who was true to God, and who above everything else desired the prosperity of Zion. Today such grief over the evils of the church should still drive a man to his knees in prayer.

Of course, Samuel carried the problem to God. It was a time for prayer. The circumstance was too serious for him not to be deeply moved to pray. The inner soul of Samuel was so greatly disturbed that he prayed all night about it. Too much was at stake for him to shut his eyes to the affair, to treat it indifferently, and to let it pass without taking God into the matter. The future welfare of Israel was in the balance. Samuel's childhood was greatly influenced by prayer. When he became a leader over Israel, he obtained answers to prayer because of his longtime communion with the Lord.

10

Praying in Captivity

It is a wonderful historical fact that men of prayer have always been men of power in the world. If you are debating with some friend in the workshop, be sure to ask him why it is that the men of power in the world have always been the men of prayer. —*Bishop Winnington Ingram*

DANIEL took a chance when he refused to obey the Babylonian king who ordered him not to petition God or king for thirty days. The penalty was to be thrown into the lion's den. However, Daniel paid no attention to the edict, for it is recorded,

Now when Daniel knew that the writing was signed, he went into his house; and his windows being open in his chamber toward Jerusalem, he kneeled upon his knees three times a day, and prayed, and gave thanks before his God, as he did aforetime. (Dan. 6:10)

Do not forget that this was Daniel's regular habit. *"He kneeled upon his knees...and prayed...as he did aforetime."* What was the result? He was thrown to the lions just as expected. God responded by sending an angel into the den of lions with Daniel, and He locked their mouths so that not a hair on his head was touched, and he was wonderfully delivered. Even so today, deliverance always comes to God's saints who tread the path of prayer as the saints of old.

Even though Daniel was away from the house of God and deprived of religious privileges, he did not forget God while he was in a foreign land. He is a striking illustration of a young man who was decidedly religious under the most unfavorable circumstances. He proved conclusively that one could definitely be a servant of God though his environment was anything but religious. He was among heathens as far as a God-fearing nation was concerned. There was no temple worship, no Sabbath day, no Word of God to be read. But he had one help that remained with him, and of which he could not be deprived. That was his secret prayers, and his assurance that God would answer him.

Resolving in his heart, without debating the question, not to eat the king's meat or drink the king's wine, he stood out in that ungodly country as a striking illustration of a young man who feared God. He was determined to be religious, no matter what the cost. But he did not have a flowery bed on which to rest or a smooth road on which to travel.

The whimsical, tyrannical, and unreasonable king, Nebuchadnezzar, put him to the test and proved his praying qualities. This king had a strange dream, the details of which he forgot, but the fact of the dream remained. He was so troubled about the dream that he called for all the soothsayers, astrologers, and sorcerers to recall the dream and then interpret it.

He classed Daniel and his three companions, Shadrach, Meshach, and Abednego, with these men, though there really was nothing they had in common with the others. The soothsayers knew that it was impossible to discover a dream like that. They then asked the king to tell the dream to them, saying they would interpret it. The king became very angry, and he ordered that all the wise men, including Daniel and his friends, be put to death.

But Daniel leaped into action. At his suggestion, the execution of the rash edict was held up. He immediately called his three companions into counsel. Urging them to unite with him in prayer, Daniel asked God to show him the dream as well as the interpretation. In answer to this united praying, it is recorded: *"Then was the secret revealed unto Daniel in a night vision. Then Daniel blessed the God of heaven"* (Dan. 2:19).

As a sequel to the praying session of these four men, Daniel revealed to the king his dream and its interpretation. As a result, the king acknowledged God and elevated Daniel and his three associates to high positions. It all came about because there was a praying man available at a critical time.

Blessed is that nation that has praying men who can aid civil rulers who are greatly perplexed and in great difficulty. Blessed is the nation composed of praying men who can be depended upon to pray for rulers of state and church.

Years afterward, while still in a foreign land, Daniel still had not forgotten the God of his fathers. He was given the noted vision of the ram and the he goat. Daniel, however, did not comprehend this strange vision, yet he knew it was from God and had a deep and future meaning for nations and people. So he followed the bent of his religious mind and prayed about it.

> *And it came to pass, when I, even I Daniel, had seen the vision, and sought for the meaning, then, behold, there stood before me as the appearance of a man. And I heard a man's voice...which called, and said, Gabriel, make this man to understand the vision.*   *(Dan. 8:15–16)*

And so Gabriel made Daniel understand the full meaning of this remarkable vision. But understanding only came in answer to Daniel's praying. Puzzling questions may often find the answer in prayer. And, as elsewhere, God employed angelic means to convey information and prayer answers. Angels are very involved with prayer. Praying men and the angels of heaven are in close communication with each other.

Some years thereafter, Daniel was studying the records of the nation, and he discovered that it was about time for the seventy years of captivity of his people to end. So he prayed,

> *And I set my face unto the Lord God, to seek by prayer and supplications, with fasting, and sackcloth, and ashes: and I prayed unto the Lord my God, and made my confession.*
>   *(Dan. 9:3–4)*

Then follows the record in Old Testament Scripture of Daniel's prayer. It was full of meaning, so simple in its delivery, so earnest in its spirit, and so direct in its confession and requests. It is worthy of being an example for our prayers.

It was while he was speaking in prayer that the same archangel, Gabriel, who seemed to have a direct interest in this man's praying, *"being caused to fly swiftly, touched me about the time of the evening oblation. And he informed me, and talked with me"* (vv. 21–22). And then Gabriel gave Daniel the valuable information.

The angels of God are much nearer to us in our intervals of prayer than we imagine. God employs these glorious, heavenly beings in the blessed work of hearing and answering prayer. Usually the prayer, as in the case of Daniel on this occasion, deals with the present and future welfare of His people.

One other praying incident in the life of this captive man in Babylon is noteworthy. Daniel had another revelation, but the time of its fulfillment appeared to be far in the future. *"In those days I Daniel was mourning three full weeks. I ate no pleasant bread, neither came flesh nor wine into my mouth...till three whole weeks were fulfilled"* (Dan. 10:2–3).

It was then that he had a very strange experience and that a strange angelic being gave him a still stranger revelation. It is worthwhile to read the Scripture account:

> *And, behold, an hand touched me, which set me upon my knees and upon the palms of my hands. And he said unto me, O Daniel, a man greatly beloved, understand the words that I speak unto thee, and stand upright: for unto thee am I now sent. And when he had spoken this word unto me, I stood trembling. Then said he unto me, Fear not, Daniel: for from the first day that thou didst set thine heart to understand, and to chasten thyself before thy God, thy words were heard, and I am come for thy words. But the prince of the kingdom of Persia withstood me one and twenty days: but, lo, Michael, one of the chief princes, came to help me; and I remained there with the kings of Persia.* (Dan. 10:10–13)

What all this means is difficult to comprehend, but enough appears on its face to lead us to believe that the angels in heaven are deeply interested in our praying and are sent to tell us the answers to our prayers. Further, it is very clear that some unseen forces or invisible spirits are operating to hinder the answers to our prayers. Exactly who the prince of Persia was who withstood this great angelic being is not divulged. But enough is revealed to know that there must be a contest in the unseen world around us, between spirits sent to minister to us in answer to our prayers and the Devil and his evil spirits who seek to defeat these good spirits.

The passage furthermore gives us some hint as to why we do not obtain answers to prayer immediately. For three full weeks, Daniel mourned and prayed, and for twenty-one days the divinely appointed angel was opposed by the *"prince of the kingdom of Persia."* Daniel was wise to continue praying, maintaining his courage, fortitude, and determination, and persisting in his praying for three weeks while the fearful conflict between good and evil spirits raged around him, unseen by mortal eyes. It would be well for us if we do not give up in our praying when God seems not to hear and the answer is not immediate. It takes time to pray, and it takes time to get the answer.

Delays in answering prayer are not denials.

Failure to receive an immediate answer is not evidence that God does not hear prayer. It takes not only courage and persistence to pray successfully, but a lot of patience as well. *"Wait on the LORD: be of good courage, and he shall strengthen thine heart: wait, I say, on the LORD"* (Ps. 27:14).

11

Faith of Sinners in Prayer

A certain preacher, whose sermons converted many souls, received a revelation from God. It said it was not his sermons or works, but the prayers of an illiterate lay brother who sat on the pulpit steps pleading for the success of the sermon. It was this brother's prayers that brought men to the Lord. This could be the case with us as well. It may be that after laboring long and wearily, without good prayer, all honor belongs to another builder whose prayers were gold, silver, and precious stones; while our sermonizing, being apart from prayer, are but hay and stubble.   —*Charles Spurgeon*

ONE of the peculiar features of prayer, as we study the Old Testament on this subject, is the faith of unrighteous and backslidden men in prayer. They had great confidence that God would answer the prayers of praying men of that day. The backslidden knew certain men were men of prayer who believed in God, who were favored by God, and who prayed to God. They recognized these men as having influence with God in averting wrath and in giving deliverance from evil.

Frequently, when in trouble, when God's wrath was threatened, and when evil fell upon them for their iniquities, the unrighteous showed their faith in prayer by appealing to the men who prayed. These sinners wanted God's favored ones to beg God to avert His displeasure and turn aside His wrath against them. Recognizing the value of prayer as a divine agency to save men, they implored the men who prayed to intercede with God for them. They knew God answered a righteous man's prayers.

One of the strange paradoxes of those early days is that while people departed from God, going into grievous sin, they did not become atheists or unbelievers in the existence of a prayer-answering God. Wicked men held fast to a belief in God's existence and to faith in the power of prayer to secure pardon for sin and to deliver them from His wrath.

It is worthy to note the influence of Christianity on sinners who believe in a Christian's prayer for them. It is an item of interest and an important event when a sinner on a dying bed calls for a praying man to come to his bedside to pray for him. It is meaningful when penitent sinners, under a sense of their guilt, feel the displeasure of God, approach a church altar, and say, "Pray for me, you praying men and women."

Little does the church understand its full impact or appreciate the full significance of prayer. This is especially true for the unsaved men and women who ask for prayer for their immortal souls. If the church was fully attuned to God's willingness to respond, and fully aware of the real peril of the unconverted all around it, more sinners would seek the altars of the church, crying out to praying people, "Pray for my soul!"

There may be much so-called praying for sinners, but it is cold, formal, official praying that never reaches God and that accomplishes nothing. Revivals begin when sinners seek the prayers of praying people and then begin to seek the God who answers those prayers.

Several things stand out in bold relief as we look at those Old Testament days.

First, there was the tendency of sinners against God to almost involuntarily turn to praying men for help and refuge when trouble drew near. They requested prayers for relief and deliverance. "Pray for us!" was their cry.

Second, there was the readiness with which those praying men responded to these appeals and prayed to God for those who desired deliverance. Moreover, it is impressive that these praying men were always in the spirit of prayer and ready at any time to seek God's reply. They were always excited about prayer.

Third, we note the wonderful influence these men of prayer had with God when they made their appeal to Him. God nearly always responded quickly and heard their praying for others. Intercessory prayer predominated in those early days of the church.

How far the present-day church is responsible for the unbelief of today's sinners in the value of prayer is a question worthy of earnest consideration.

The first illustration we notice showing the faith of wicked men in prayer, and their appeal for a man of God to intercede for them, is when the fiery serpents were sent upon the Israelites. They were journeying from Mount Hor by way of the Red Sea, seeking to circle the land of Edom, when they spoke against God and Moses:

> *Wherefore have ye brought us up out of Egypt to die in the wilderness? for there is no bread, neither is there any water; and our soul loatheth this light bread.* (Num. 21:5)

This complaining so displeased God that He sent fiery serpents among the people, causing many of the Israelites to die.

> *Therefore the people came to Moses, and said, We have sinned for we have spoken against the Lord, and against thee; pray unto the Lord, that he take away the serpents from us.*
> (Num. 21:7)

And Moses prayed for the people. God answered his prayer.

As far as these people had departed from God, and as great as their sin was in complaining against God's dealings with them, they had not lost faith in obtaining answers to prayer. Neither did they forget that there was a leader in Israel who had influence with God in prayer; nor did they forget that he could—by prayer—avert disaster and bring deliverance to them.

Jeroboam, the first king of the ten tribes when the kingdom was divided, is another case in point. This case is famous because of the notoriety of his departure from God, which was often referred to in the later history of Israel as *"the sins of Jeroboam the son of Nebat"* (2 Kings 10:29). His life shows that, despite his great wickedness, he did not lose his faith in the powerful effectiveness of prayer. He knew that God acted as a result of prayer.

This king presumed to take the place of the high priest and stood by the altar to burn incense. A man of God came out of Judah and cried against the altar and proclaimed, *"Behold, the altar shall be rent, and the ashes that are upon it shall be poured out"* (1 Kings 13:3). This angered Jeroboam, who saw that it was intended as a

430

public rebuke for him because it was contrary to the Levitical law to assume the office of God's priest. The king even put forth his hand with the apparent purpose of arresting or doing violence to the man of God and said, *"Lay hold on him"* (1 Kings 13:4)

Immediately God smote the king with leprosy so that he could not pull his hand back again. At the same time, the altar was rent. Astonished and afraid beyond measure at this lightning retribution for his sin, Jeroboam cried out to the man of God, *"Entreat now the face of the LORD thy God, and pray for me, that my hand may be restored me again"* (v. 6). And it is recorded that *"the man of God besought the LORD, and the king's hand was restored him again, and became as it was before"* (v. 6).

Let us keep in mind that we are not now considering the praying habits of the man of God or the possibilities of prayer, though both face us here. But, rather, we find here that a ruler in Israel, who is guilty of a serious sin, immediately calls upon a praying man to intercede with God in his behalf when God's wrath falls upon him. It is another case where a sinner showed his faith that God would answer the prayers of a holy man. Sad is the day in a Christian land when there is decay of prayer in the church and when sinners are so unaffected by the religion of the church that they have no faith in prayer and care little about the prayers of praying men.

King Jeroboam illustrated his faith in prayer again when his son fell sick and was about to die. This wicked, indifferent king sent his wife off to Ahijah, the prophet of God, to ask him to give the outcome of the child's illness. She attempted to deceive the old prophet, who was nearly blind, intending not to make herself known to him. But he had the vision of a prophet, even though nearly blind, and immediately revealed that he recognized her.

After telling her many important things concerning the kingdom and charging that her husband had not kept God's commandments, but had gone into idolatry, he said to her, *"Arise thou therefore, get thee down to thine own house: and when thy feet enter into the city, the child shall die"* (1 Kings 14:12).

How natural it is for a father in trouble to appeal to a praying prophet for relief! As in the first case, his sin did not blind his eyes to the value of having a man of God intercede for him. Jeroboam knew God would respond. It accomplished nothing, but it did prove our contention that in Old Testament times sinners, while they were not themselves praying men, believed strongly in the prayers of praying men.

Take for instance, Johanan who lived just as the children of Israel began their life of captivity in Babylon. Johanan and Jeremiah, with a small company, were left in their native land. Ishmael had conspired against Gedaliah, the appointed governor of the country, and had slain him. Johanan came to the rescue, delivering the people from Ishmael, who was taking them away from their land. But Johanan wanted to flee down into Egypt, contrary to the divine plan. At this point he assembled all the people, and they went to Jeremiah with the earnest appeal:

Let, we beseech thee, our supplication be accepted before thee, and pray for us unto the Lord thy God...that the Lord thy God may show us the way wherein we may walk, and the thing that we may do. (Jer. 42:2–3)

As in all other appeals to good men for prayer, Jeremiah interceded for these seekers of the right way. After ten days the answer came. Jeremiah informed them that God said they should not go down to Egypt, but remain in and about Jerusalem. But Johanan and the people refused to do as God told them. Their disobedience, however, does not disprove the fact that they had faith in prayer and in praying men.

Another case may be noticed as showing the truth of our proposition that Old Testament sinners had faith in prayer, thus indirectly proving the preeminence of prayer in those days. Zedekiah was king of Judah just as the captivity of God's people began. He was in charge of the kingdom when Jerusalem was besieged by the king of Babylon. It was just about this time that Zedekiah sent two chosen men to Jeremiah saying,

Inquire, I pray thee, of the Lord for us; for Nebuchadnezzar king of Babylon maketh war against us; if so be that the Lord will deal with us according to all His wondrous works, that he may go up from us. (Jer. 21:2)

And God told Jeremiah, in answer to this inquiry, what to do and what would occur. But as in the case of Johanan, Zedekiah proved unfaithful and would not do as God instructed. This turning to prayer proved conclusively that Zedekiah had not lost his faith in prayer as a means of finding out the mind of God, nor did it cause him to change his belief in the virtue of the prayers of a praying man.

These sinners believed that prayer brought results. Certainly prayer must have had a prominent place, and its necessity must have been generally recognized, when even sinners, by their actions, endorsed its virtue and necessity.

Surely, if sinners bore testimony to its worth, modern church people ought to have a deep sense of its need and should have strong faith in prayer and its virtue. If the men of Old Testament times had a reputation as praying men, then in this favored day, Christian men should prize prayer so that they would also have a wide reputation as praying men.

Truly, prayer had a preeminent place in all Old Testament history when not only the men of God were noted for obtaining answers to prayer, but even disloyal, sinful men testified to the virtue of prayer.

12

Lessons in Prayer

John Fletcher, a great teacher of the eighteenth century, used to lecture young theological students. He was a fellow worker with Wesley, and a man of most saintly character. When he lectured on one of the great topics of the Word of God, such as the fullness of God's Holy Spirit or on the power and blessing that He meant His people to have, he would close the lecture and say, "That is the theory. Now, will those who want the practice come along up to my room?" Again and again they closed their books and went away to his room, where the hour's theory would be followed by one or two hours of prayer. —Hubert Brooke

PAUL felt the urgent need for prayer so much that his encouragement to Christians to pray was often strenuous, pleading, and persistent. *"I exhort therefore,"* he wrote to Timothy, *"that, first of all, supplications, prayers, intercessions, and giving of thanks, be made for all men"* (1 Tim. 2:1). Prayer was to be the greatest security and truth for the church. First and foremost, the church of Christ was to be a praying church. It was to pray for all men.

Paul instructed the Philippians this way: *"Be careful for nothing; but in every thing by prayer and supplication with thanksgiving let your requests be made known unto God"* (Phil. 4:6). The church is to be anxious about nothing. Every need and request must be made through prayer. Nothing is too small for prayer. Nothing is too great for God to overcome. God will answer and take care of the church's needs.

Paul wrote a vital command to the church at Thessalonica: *"Rejoice evermore. Pray without ceasing. In everything give thanks:*

for this is the will of God in Christ Jesus concerning you" (1 Thess. 5:16–18). The church, in order to obtain answers, must devote itself to unceasing prayer. Never was prayer to cease in the church. This is God's will concerning His church on earth.

Paul was not only devoted to prayer himself, but he continually and earnestly urged it in a way that showed its vital importance. He not only insisted that the church pray, but he urged persistent praying. *"Continue in prayer, and watch in the same"* (Col. 4:2) was the keynote of all his exhortations on prayer. *"Praying always with all prayer and supplication"* (Eph. 6:18) was the way he pressed this important matter upon the people. He exhorted *"that men pray every where, lifting up holy hands, without wrath and doubting"* (1 Tim. 2:8). Because he prayed this way himself, he could justify encouraging those to whom he ministered.

Paul was an appointed leader and a leader by universal recognition and acceptance. He had many mighty miracles occur in his ministry. His conversion, so conspicuous and radical, was a great miracle. His call to the apostleship was clear, luminous, and convincing. But these were not the most divine manifestations of God that brought forth the largest results in his ministry. Paul's course was more distinctly shaped and his career rendered more powerfully successful because of his prayerful communication with God. He knew God would answer his prayers with guidance and provision.

It is no surprise, then, that he gave so much prominence to prayer in his preaching and writing. Because prayer was the highest exercise in his personal life, prayer assumed the same high place in his teaching. His personal example of prayer and its answers added force to his teaching. His practice and his teaching ran on parallel lines. There was no inconsistency between the two parts of his life.

Paul was the chief of the apostles and the chief in prayer. He was the foremost of the apostles because of his prayer life. Therefore, he was qualified to be a teacher on prayer. His praying fitted him to teach others what prayer was and what prayer could do. For this reason, he was capable of urging the people to not neglect prayer since so much depended upon it.

He who wants to teach others to receive answers to prayer must first himself be devoted to prayer. He who urges prayer on others must first tread the path of prayer himself. Preachers will encourage the practice of praying in proportion to the quality of their own prayer lives. The quality of their sermons will also depend on the quality of their prayer lives. Since that course of reasoning is true, it would be legitimate to draw the conclusion that the reason there is so little preaching on how to receive answers to prayer today is because preachers themselves do not know how.

We might stake the whole question of the absolute necessity and the possibilities of prayer in this dispensation on Paul's attitude toward prayer. If personal force, if the energy of a strong will, if profound convictions, if personal culture and talents, if any one of these, or all of them united, could direct the church of God without prayer, then, logically, prayer would be unnecessary.

If profound piety and unswerving consecration to a high purpose, if impassioned loyalty to Jesus Christ, if any or all of these could exist without devoted prayer, or lift a church leader above the necessity of prayer, then Paul was above its use. But prayer brings God's response and direction. Even Paul, the great, gifted, favored, and devoted apostle, felt the necessity of unceasing prayer. He realized that its practice was urgent and pressing, that the church should pray without ceasing. Today, also, the believers in the apostolate should be aided by universal and mighty praying.

Paul's praying, his commands, and the urgency with which he encouraged the church to pray, are the most convincing proof of the absolute necessity of prayer. Prayer is a great moral force in the world, an indispensable and inalienable factor in the progress and spread of the Gospel. Prayer is the means of communicating with God, asking His direction. It is also key in the development of personal piety. In Paul's view, no church could succeed without answered prayer.

Pray *"everywhere,"* pray *"in everything,"* and pray *"without ceasing,"* was Paul's reply to the question regarding unanswered prayer.

Timothy was very dear to Paul, and the attachment was mutual and intensified by all their similar characteristics. Paul found in Timothy those elements that enabled him to be his spiritual successor. Paul was the leader of the great spiritual principles that were essential to the establishment and prosperity of the church. These primary and vital truths he drilled into Timothy. Paul regarded Timothy as one to whom fundamental and vital truths might be committed, who would preserve them truly, and who would commit them, without corruption, to the future. So he gave Timothy this deposit of prayer for all ages.

Before we go any further, note that Paul wrote directly under the supervision of the Holy Spirit, who guarded Paul against error and who suggested the truths that Paul taught. We believe, without compromise in the least, in the absolute inspiration of the Scriptures, and Paul's writings are part of those sacred writings. This being true, the doctrine of prayer that Paul affirmed is the doctrine of the Holy Spirit. His epistles are of the Word of God—inspired, authentic, and of divine authority. Prayer, as taught by Paul, is the doctrine that Almighty God would have His church accept, believe, and practice. God does not want His church to be without His provision and direction as given through prayer.

These words to Timothy, therefore, were divinely inspired words. This section of Scripture is much more than suggestive and is far more than a broad, bare outline on prayer. It instructs about prayer, about how men ought to pray, how businessmen should pray, and the reasons why men ought to pray, and it needs to be strongly and insistently emphasized.

Here are Paul's words to Timothy on prayer:

> *I exhort therefore, that, first of all, supplications, prayers, intercessions, and giving of thanks, be made for all men; for kings, and for all that are in authority; that we may lead a quiet and peaceable life in all godliness and honesty. For this is good and acceptable in the sight of God our Saviour; who will have all men to be saved, and to come unto the knowledge of the truth. For there is one God, and one mediator between God and men, the man Christ Jesus; who gave himself a ransom for all, to be testified in due time....I will therefore that men pray every where, lifting up holy hands, without wrath and doubting.* (1 Tim. 2:1–6, 8)

In this prayer section, Paul illustrated the inheritance and practice of every Christian in all ages. He gave us a view of the energetic and multifaceted characteristics of prayer. Prayer comes first. It must be first in all occupations. So exacting and imperative in its significance and power is prayer that it stands first among spiritual values. He that prays not, is not at all. He is nothing, less than nothing. He is below zero, so far as Jesus Christ and God are concerned. How can a man's needs be met, or those of the church or those of the country, if he does not ask of the Lord?

Paul's teaching is that praying is the most important of all activities on earth. Everything else must be restrained, retired, to give it primacy. Put it first, and keep it first. Defeat, not victory, lies in making prayer secondary. Making prayer subordinate is to fetter and destroy its power. If God and prayer are put first, then victory is assured. Prayer must either reign in life or must abdicate. Which will it be?

According to Paul, *"supplications, prayers, intercessions, and giving of thanks"* (1 Tim. 2:1)—all these elements and forms of prayer—are to be offered in intercession for men. Prayer is offered for things, for all temporal good, and for all spiritual good and grace. But in these directions, Paul rose to the highest results and purposes of prayer. Men are to be affected by prayer. Their benefit, character, conduct, and destiny are all involved in answered prayer.

In this regard, prayer moves along the highest plane and pursues its loftiest goal. Since we live in the world, we must be concerned with such material things as our possessions and jobs. However, our main purpose in this life is to pray for other men. This broadens and ennobles prayer. Men, despite the range of their spiritual conditions, are to be held in the mighty grasp of prayer.

Paul's teaching states that prayer is essentially a thing of the inner nature. The Spirit within us prays. Note Paul's directions: *"I will therefore that men pray every where...without wrath"* (1 Tim. 2:8). *Wrath* is a term that denotes the natural, internal motion of plants and fruits swelling with juice. The natural juices are warmed into life and rise by the warmth of spring.

Man has in him natural juices that rise also. Warmth, heat, all stages of passions and desires, every degree of feeling—these spontaneously rise under provocation. Guard against and suppress them. Man cannot pray with these natural feelings rising in him, cultivated, cherished, and continued within.

Prayer is to be without these. *"Without wrath."* Higher, better, nobler inspirations are to lift prayer upward. Wrath depresses prayer, hinders it, suppresses it. The word *without* means "making no use of, having no association with, apart from, aloof from." The natural, unrenewed heart has no part in praying. Its heat and all of its natural juices poison and destroy praying. The essence of prayer

438

is deeper than nature. We cannot pray by nature, not even the kindliest and the best nature.

Prayer is the true test of character. Fidelity to our conditions and trueness to our relatives are often indicated by our prayerfulness. These qualities come as answers to prayer. Some conditions give birth to prayer. They are the soil that germinates and perfects prayer. To pray under some circumstances seems very fitting. Not to pray in some conditions seems heartless and discordant. The natural and providential conditions of prayer are the great storms of life—when we are helpless and without relief or are devoid of comfort, God is most willing to aid and comfort us.

Widowhood is a great sorrow. It comes to saintly women as well as to others. Widows are to be honored, especially because their sorrow is deep. Their piety is aromatic and lightened by their bruised hearts. Here is Paul's description of such widows:

Now she that is a widow indeed, and desolate, trusteth in God, and continueth in supplications and prayers night and day. But she that liveth in pleasure is dead while she liveth.
(1 Tim. 5:5–6)

Here is the striking contrast between two types of women. One devoted her time to supplication and prayer night and day. The other lived in sinful pleasure and was spiritually dead. Paul described a faithful widow as being great in prayer. Her prayers, born of her faith and desolation, are a mighty force. Day and night her prayers go up to God—unceasingly. The widowed heart receives help from God when that heart is found in the way of prayer, intense, unwearied prayer.

One of Paul's striking directions, worthy of study, is this: *"Continuing instant in prayer"* (Rom. 12:12), or, as the Revised Standard Version reads, *"Be constant in prayer."* This is Paul's description of prayer. The term means "to remain, to be steadfast and faithful without hesitating, to stick to it, to continue with strength to the end."

Praying is an occupation, a lifelong business to be followed with diligence, fervor, and toil. The Christian's foremost purpose is prayer. It is his most engaging, most heavenly, most lucrative business. Prayer is a commission of such high dignity and importance that it is to be performed without ceasing. In other words, without letup or breakdown, followed assiduously, and without intermission.

439

Prayer must cover all things, be in every place, find itself in all seasons, and embrace everything, always, and everywhere.

In the remarkable prayer in the third chapter of Ephesians, Paul prayed for wide reaches of religious experience. He bowed his knees before God, in the name of Jesus Christ, asking God to grant that the Ephesian believers would experience the fullness of Jesus' love, becoming saints through to their bones. *"Filled with all the fulness of God"* (Eph. 3:19) is an experience so great and so glorious that it makes the head of the modern saints so dizzy they are afraid to look up to those heavenly heights or peer down into the fathomless depths. Paul passed us on to Him *"that is able to do exceeding abundantly above all that we ask or think"* (v. 20). Paul knew how God answers prayer. This is a sample of his teaching on prayer.

In writing to the Philippian church, Paul recounted an event and showed the transmuting power of prayer as follows:

> *Some indeed preach Christ even of envy and strife; and some also of good will: the one preach Christ of contention, not sincerely, supposing to add affliction to my bonds: but the other of love, knowing that I am set for the defense of the gospel. What then? notwithstanding, every way, whether in pretence, or in truth, Christ is preached; and I therein do rejoice, yea, and will rejoice. For I know that this shall turn to my salvation through your prayer, and the supply of the Spirit of Jesus Christ, according to my earnest expectation and my hope, that in nothing I shall be ashamed, but that with all boldness, as always, so now also Christ shall be magnified in my body, whether it be by life, or by death.* (Phil. 1:15–20)

Boldness was to be secured by him in answer to their prayers. Christ was to be gloriously magnified by and through Paul, whether he lived or died.

Note that in all of these quotations in Corinthians, Ephesians, or Philippians, the Revised Standard Version gives us the most intense form of prayer and supplications. Paul requested intense, personal, strenuous, persistent praying by the saints. They must give special strength, interest, time, and heart to their praying in order to influence God to grant the most fruitful answers.

The general instruction about prayer to the Colossian Christians is made specific and is sharpened to the point of a personal appeal:

> *Continue in prayer, and watch in the same, with thanksgiving; withal praying also for us, that God would open unto us a door of utterance, to speak the mystery of Christ, for which I am also in bonds: that I may make it manifest, as I ought to speak.* *(Col. 4:2–4)*

Paul is credited with the authorship of the epistle to the Hebrews. This book gives the reader a reference to the character of Christ's praying, illustrating with authority the elements of true praying. How rich are His words! How heart-affecting and how sublime was His praying. He prayed as man never prayed before, and yet He prayed in order to teach man how to pray and how to receive from God.

> *Who in the days of his flesh, when he had offered up prayers and supplications with strong crying and tears unto him that was able to save him from death, and was heard in that he feared.* *(Heb. 5:7)*

The praying of Jesus Christ drew on the mightiest forces of His being. His prayers were His sacrifices, which He offered before He offered Himself on the cross for the sins of mankind. Prayer-sacrifice is the forerunner and pledge of self-sacrifice. We must die in our closets before we can die on the cross.

13

Examples of Effective Prayer

One day Frank Crossley said goodbye to his friends, General and Mrs. Booth, at the station. But before they steamed out, he handed a letter to them giving details of a sacrifice he had resolved to make for the Salvation Army. He came home and was praying alone. "As I was praying," he said, "there came over me the most extraordinary sense of joy. It was not exactly in my head, nor in my heart; it was almost a grasping of my chest by some strange hand that filled me with an ecstasy I never had before. This was the joy of the Lord." So this servant of God grew closer to Him. He thought it likely at the time that the Booths had read this letter in the train and his experience was God's answer to their prayer. He heard later that they had prayed for him in the train just after leaving Manchester.
—Edward Shillito

HE who studies Paul's praying, both his prayers and his commands about prayer, will find it covers a wide, diversified, and detailed area.

Famous spiritual leaders like Wesley, Brainerd, Luther, and others spent many hours in prayer. They committed all things—secular, religious, natural, and spiritual—to God in prayer. In this way they ordered their lives around God's provision and will. Yet, they were not superstitious fanatics. They were only following the great example and authority of the apostle Paul.

To seek God by prayer as Paul did, to commune with God as Paul did, to entreat Jesus Christ as Paul did, to seek the Holy Spirit by prayer as Paul did, to pray without ceasing—all this makes a saint, an apostle, and a leader for God. This kind of a life

442

engages, absorbs, enriches, and empowers with God and for God. Prayer, if successful, will always engage and absorb us. This kind of praying brings the results and gifts that Paul experienced. Praying like Paul costs a lot. It is death to self, the flesh, and the world. Yet, the benefits of praying like Paul are worth the expense. Prayer that costs nothing gets nothing. It is a beggarly effort at best.

Paul's respect of prayer is seen and enforced by the fact that Paul was a man of prayer. His high position in the church was not one of the dignity and position in which he could enjoy himself and luxuriate. It was not one of officialism, nor was it one of arduous and exhaustless drudgery, for Paul was preeminently a praying man who got answers.

He began his great career for Christ in the great struggle and school of prayer. God's convincing and wonderful argument to assure Ananias was, *"Behold, he prayeth"* (Acts 9:11). Three days he was without sight, neither eating nor drinking, but he learned the lesson well.

He went out on his first great missionary trip under the power of fasting and prayer. Paul and Barnabas established every church by the very same means—fasting and prayer. He began his work in Philippi *"where prayer was wont to be made"* (Acts 16:13). *"As we went to prayer"* (v. 16), God answered by casting the spirit of divination out of the young woman. And when Paul and Silas were put in prison, they prayed and sang praises to God at midnight. In response, God took them out of prison.

Paul made praying a habit, a business, and a life. He literally gave himself to prayer. So with him praying was not a mere coloring, a paint, or a polish. Praying supplied the substance, the bone, and the marrow of his religious life. His conversion was a marvel of grace and power. His apostolic commission was full and royal. Paul knew that answered prayer was the key to making his ministry successful. Even though he had a dramatic conversion, Paul knew his apostolic mission was sealed by divine authority. Through prayer Paul accomplished his work, crowned his work, his life, and his death with martyr principles and with martyr glory.

Paul's marked spiritual trait was a strong tendency to pray. He had a profound conviction that prayer was a great and solemn duty. Prayer was a royal privilege. Prayer gauged piety and made faith mighty. God expected Christians to pray, so He made prayer the key to Christian success through His answers.

Paul took it for granted that men who knew God would pray. He also knew that men who did not pray did not live for God. He revered prayer and knew its full value. Paul was in the habit of praying because he loved God, and such love in the heart always finds its expression in regular prayer. He felt his need for grace, knowing that God only supplies grace through prayer. Grace only abounds as prayer abounds.

Paul, though in the habit of praying, did not pray by mere force of habit. Man is such a creature of habit that he is always in danger of doing things without thinking, in a routine, perfunctory manner. Paul's habit was regular and hearty. To the Romans he wrote, *"For God is my witness...that without ceasing I make mention of you always in my prayers"* (Rom. 1:9).

Prison doors are opened and earthquakes take place by praying such as Paul's. All things are opened to the kind of praying that was done by Paul and Silas. They could stop Paul from preaching, but they could not keep him from praying.

And the Gospel could win its way by Paul's praying as well as by Paul's preaching. The apostle may have been in prison, but the Word of God was free and went like the mountain air, while the apostle was bound in prison and abounded in prayer.

How profound was their joy in Jesus—their joy that expressed itself so happily and so sweetly in praise and prayer, under conditions so painful and so depressing! Prayer brought them into full communion with God, which made all things radiant with the divine presence. Prayer also enabled them to be *"rejoicing that they were counted worthy to suffer shame for his name"* (Acts 5:41), and to *"count it all joy when they* [fell] *into divers temptations"* (James 1:2). Prayer sweetens all things and sanctifies all things. A praying saint will be a praising saint. Praise is prayer set to music and song.

After Paul's notable charge to the elders at Ephesus, as he visited there before continuing on his way to Jerusalem, this characteristic record is made: *"And when he had thus spoken, he kneeled down, and prayed with them all. And they all wept sore, and fell on Paul's neck, and kissed him"* (Acts 20:36–37).

"He kneeled down, and prayed." Note those words. Kneeling in prayer was Paul's favorite position, the fitting posture of an earnest, humble servant. Humility and intensity are appropriate for answered prayer from Almighty God. It is the proper attitude of

man before God, of a sinner before a Savior, and of a beggar before his benefactor. To seal his sacred and living charge to those Ephesian elders by prayer was that which made the charge efficient, benign, and abiding.

Paul's religion was born in the throes of the three days' struggle of prayer while he was in the house of Ananias. There he received a divine impetus that never slackened till it brought him to the gates of the eternal city. That spiritual history and religious experience, coupled with unceasing prayer, brought him to the highest spiritual altitudes and yielded the largest spiritual results.

Paul lived in the very atmosphere of prayer. His first missionary trip was projected by prayer. It was in answer to prayer and fasting that he was called into the foreign missionary field. By the same means, the church at Antioch was moved to send forth Paul and Barnabas on their first missionary journey. Here is the Scripture record of it:

> *Now there were in the church that was at Antioch certain prophets and teachers; as Barnabas, and Simeon that was called Niger, and Lucius of Cyrene, and Manaen, which had been brought up with Herod the tetrarch, and Saul. As they ministered to the Lord, and fasted, the Holy Ghost said, Separate me Barnabas and Saul for the work whereunto I have called them. And when they had fasted and prayed, and laid their hands on them, they sent them away.* (Acts 13:1-3)

Here is a model, a forerunner of success, for all missionary journeys. The Holy Spirit, in answer to prayer, directed an obedient church into divine leadership. This condition of things brought forth the very largest possible results in the mission of these two men of God. We may confidently assert that no church in which Paul was prominent was a prayerless church. Paul lived, worked, and suffered in an atmosphere of prayer. To him, prayer was the very heart and life of religion, its meat and bone, the motor and the sign by which it conquered. Here is the divine record of Paul's work and the important role prayer played in establishing churches:

> *Confirming the souls of the disciples, and exhorting them to continue in the faith, and that we must through much tribulation enter into the kingdom of God. And when they had ordained them elders in every church, and had prayed with*

fasting, they commended them to the Lord, on whom they be-
lieved. (Acts 14:22–23)

In obedience to a heavenly vision, Paul landed in Europe and found himself at Philippi. There was no synagogue, and few if any Jews lived there. A few pious women, however, had a meeting place for prayer, and Paul was drawn by spiritual guidance to the place *"where prayer was wont to be made"* (Acts 16:13). And Paul's first planting of the Gospel in Europe was at that little prayer meeting. He was the chief person who prayed and the leading speaker. Lydia was the first convert at that prayer meeting. They extended the meeting, and they called it a meeting for prayer.

It was on the way to that extended prayer meeting that Paul performed the miracle of casting the devil of divination out of a poor demon-possessed girl. This poor girl had been made a source of gain by some covetous men. The results of Paul's deeds by the magistrate's orders was scourging and imprisonment. The result by God's orders was the conversion of the jailer and his whole household. The praying apostle allowed no discouragement.

In this last incident, we have a picture of Paul at midnight. He was in the inner prison, dark and deadly. He had just been severely whipped, his clothing was covered with blood, and there were blood clots on his torn body. His feet were in the stocks, and every nerve was feverish, swollen, and sensitive.

But, even under these very unfavorable and suffering conditions, he was absorbed in his favorite pursuit, confident of obtaining an answer. Paul was praying with Silas, his companion, in joyous, triumphant agreement.

And at midnight Paul and Silas prayed, and sang praises
unto God: and the prisoners heard them. And suddenly there
was a great earthquake, so that the foundations of the prison
were shaken: and immediately all the doors were opened, and
every one's bands were loosed. And the keeper of the prison
awaking out of his sleep, and seeing the prison doors open, he
drew out his sword, and would have killed himself, supposing
that the prisoners had been fled. But Paul cried out with a
loud voice, saying, Do thyself no harm: for we are all here.
(Acts 16:25–28)

Never was prayer so beautiful, never more productive. Paul was adept at prayer. He was a lover of prayer who could pursue it with joy, even under conditions of despondency and despair. What a mighty weapon of defense was prayer to Paul! How songful! The angels doubtless stilled their highest and sweetest notes to listen to the music that bore those prayers to heaven. The earthquake trod along the path made by the mighty forces of Paul's praying.

He did not escape when his chains were loosed and the stocks fell off. God answered Paul's prayers by showing him nobler purposes that night than his own individual freedom. His praying and the earthquake alarm were to bring salvation to that prison, freedom from the slavery of sin that was foreshadowed by his physical emancipation. God's mighty providence opened his prison door and broke his prison bands, not only to give Paul freedom, but to give the jailer freedom as well. God's providential openings are often to test our ability to stay rather than to go. This instance tested Paul's ability to stay.

14

Benefiting from
Persistent Prayer

*William Law has said, "When you begin your petitions,
use such various expressions of the attributes of God as may
make you most aware of the greatness and power of His divine
nature." I want to emphasize and commend the principle of it,
which is that our fellowship should begin with the primary
elements of adoration and praise.* —*J. H. Jowett*

THERE are two occasions when, although Scripture does not
explicitly say that Paul was in prayer, the circumstances and Paul's
praying habit make it evident that the results obtained were God's
answer to his prayer. The first occasion was when Paul sailed from
Philippi and came to Troas, where he stayed seven days. On the
first day of the week, when the disciples came together to break
bread, Paul preached to them late in the night, expecting to depart
the next morning.

Sitting in the window was a young man named Eutychus, who
fell asleep and fell out of the high window. (See Acts 20:9–12.) Everyone believed he was dead. Paul went down to where the young
man had fallen, and, embracing him, he told the people that they
need not be troubled, for life was still in the body. Paul returned to
the upper room, where he had been preaching, and talked with the
disciples until morning. The young man lived, and, as a consequence, all were greatly comforted.

The natural conclusion, without the fact being specifically
stated, is that Paul must have prayed for the young man when he
embraced him. His prayer was answered in the quick recovery of
the young man.

The second occasion was in the long perilous storm that overtook the vessel in which Paul was being carried, as a prisoner, to Rome. They were tossed about in the great storm and neither sun nor stars appeared as they struggled against wind and storm. All hope of survival seemed gone. But after a long fast, Paul stood in the midst of those on board and spoke particularly to the officers of the vessel, saying,

> *Sirs, ye should have hearkened unto me, and not have loosed from Crete, and to have gained this harm and loss. And now I exhort you to be of good cheer: for there shall be no loss of any man's life among you, but of the ship. For there stood by me this night the angel of God, whose I am, and whom I serve, saying, Fear not, Paul; thou must be brought before Caesar: and, lo, God hath given thee all them that sail with thee. Wherefore, sirs, be of good cheer: for I believe God, that it shall be even as it was told me.* (Acts 27:21–25)

It requires no strained interpretation to read into this simple record that Paul must have been praying when the angel appeared to him with that message of encouragement and assurance of safety. Paul's habit of prayer and his strong belief in prayer must have driven him to his knees. Such an emergency would necessarily move him to pray, especially since he was certain that God would respond to him.

After the shipwreck, while on the island of Melita, Paul prayed again. He was praying for a very sick man. While a fire was being made, a deadly, poisonous snake fastened itself on his hand. The barbarians immediately concluded this was a case of retribution for some crime Paul had committed. But they soon discovered that Paul did not die. They then changed their minds, concluding that he was a sort of god.

During his stay on the island, Publius' father was near death, suffering from a hemorrhage and fever. Paul went to him, laid his hands upon him, and, with simple confidence in God, he prayed. Immediately, the disease was rebuked, and the man was healed. When the natives of the island saw this remarkable incident, they brought others to Paul, and they, too, were healed in answer to Paul's praying.

Earlier in Paul's life, when he was traveling from Ephesus on his way to Jerusalem, he stopped at Tyre. Before leaving Ephesus he had prayed with the Christians. But he did not trust in his words alone. God had to be recognized, invoked, and sought. Paul did not take it for granted, after he had done his best, that God simply would bless his efforts to do good. Paul sought God. God does not do things simply as a matter of course. God must first be asked and consulted, then He will respond.

Following his visit to Ephesus, Paul arrived at Tyre, where he rested a few days. Here Paul found some disciples who begged him not to go to Jerusalem, saying through the Spirit that he should not go up to that city. But Paul adhered to his original purpose to go to Jerusalem. The account says,

> *And when we had accomplished those days, we departed and went our way; and they all brought us on our way, with wives and children, till we were out of the city: and we kneeled down on the shore, and prayed.* (Acts 21:5)

What a sight to see on that seashore! Here is a picture of family love and devotion, where husbands, wives, and even children are present and praying out in the open air. What an impression it must have made upon those children! The boat was ready to depart, but prayer had to cement their affections, sanctify their wives and children, and bless their parting—a parting that was final so far as this world was concerned. The scene was beautiful and honored the head and heart of Paul. It showed the tender affection in which he was held. His devoted habit of sanctifying all things by prayer came directly to light. *"We kneeled down on the shore, and prayed"* (v. 5). Never did anyone see a grander picture or witness a lovelier sight—Paul on his knees on the sands of that shore, invoking God's blessing upon these men, women, and children.

When Paul was arraigned at Jerusalem, he referred to two instances of his praying in making his public defense. One instance was when he was in the house of Judas, in Damascus, after Jesus struck him to the earth and brought him under conviction. He was in Damascus three days when Ananias came to lay his hand upon him. This is the Scriptural record, and the words are those of Ananias addressed to Paul: *"And now why tarriest thou? arise, and be baptized, and wash away thy sins, calling on the name of the Lord"* (Acts 22:16).

The Lord had emboldened the timid Ananias to go and minister to Paul, by telling him, *"Behold, he prayeth"* (Acts 9:11). And so

450

we have in this reference Paul's prayerfulness intensified by the exhortation of Ananias. Prayer precedes pardon of sins. Prayer fits those who seek God. Prayer belongs to the earnest, sincere inquirer after God. Pardon of sin and acceptance with God always come in answer to earnest praying. The evidence of sincerity in a true seeker of Jesus is that it can be said of him, *"Behold, he prayeth."*

The other reference in his defense lets us see the prayerful intensity with which his whole religious life had been fashioned. It shows how, in the absorbing ecstasy of prayer, the vision came and directions were given by which his toilsome life was to be guided. We also see the familiar terms on which he stood and talked with his Lord:

> *And it came to pass, that, when I was come again to Jerusalem, even while I prayed in the temple, I was in a trance; and saw him saying unto me, Make haste, and get thee quickly out of Jerusalem: for they will not receive thy testimony concerning me. And I said, Lord, they know that I imprisoned and beat in every synagogue them that believed on thee: and when the blood of thy martyr Stephen was shed, I also was standing by, and consenting unto his death, and kept the raiment of them that slew him. And he said unto me, Depart: for I will send thee far hence unto the Gentiles.* (Acts 22:17–21)

Prayer always brings directions from heaven as to what God would have us do. If we prayed more directly, we would make fewer mistakes in life as to duty. God's will concerning us is revealed in answer to prayer. If we prayed more, prayed better and sweeter, then we would receive clearer and more entrancing vision, and our walk with God would be of the most intimate, free, and bold order.

It is difficult to itemize or classify Paul's praying. His prayers were so comprehensive and detailed that it is no easy task to classify them. Paul taught a lot about prayer in his didactics. He specifically enforced the duty and necessity of prayer upon the church. He practiced what he preached. He tested the exercise of prayer that he urged upon the people of his day.

To the church at Rome he plainly, specifically, and solemnly affirmed his habit of praying. He wrote this to those Roman believers: *"For God is my witness, whom I serve with my spirit in the gospel of his Son, that without ceasing I make mention of you always in my prayers"* (Rom. 1:9). Paul not only prayed for himself, but he also made a practice of praying and seeking God's answers for others. He was first and foremost an intercessor. As he urged intercessory prayer on others, so he interceded for others.

He began that remarkable epistle to the Romans with prayer. He then closed it with this solemn charge: *"Now I beseech you, brethren, for the Lord Jesus Christ's sake, and for the love of the Spirit, that ye strive together with me in your prayers to God for me"* (Rom. 15:30).

But this was not all. In the very heart of that epistle, he commanded, *"continuing instant in prayer"* (Rom. 12:12). That is, give constant attention to prayer. Make it the business of life. Be devoted to it. He recommended just what he did himself, for Paul was a standing example of the doctrine of prayer that he advocated and pressed upon the people.

In his epistles to the Thessalonians, how all-inclusive and wonderful the praying! He wrote in his first epistle to this church, *"We give thanks to God always for you all, making mention of you in our prayers; remembering without ceasing your work of faith, and labour of love, and patience of hope"* (1 Thess. 1:2–3).

Not to quote all that Paul said, it is worthwhile to read his words to this same church of true believers further on:

> *Night and day praying exceedingly that we might see your face, and might perfect that which is lacking in your faith. Now God himself...direct our way unto you. And the Lord make you to increase and abound in love one toward another...even as we do toward you: to the end he may stablish your hearts unblameable in holiness before God, even our Father.*   *(1 Thess. 3:10–13)*

And this sort of praying for these Thessalonian Christians was in direct line with that closing prayer for those same believers in this epistle, where he recorded that striking prayer for their entire sanctification:

> *And the very God of peace sanctify you wholly; and I pray God your whole spirit and soul and body be preserved blameless unto the coming of our Lord Jesus Christ.*   *(1 Thess. 5:23)*

How Paul prayed for those early Christians! They were in his mind and on his heart, and he was *"night and day praying exceedingly"* (1 Thess. 3:10). Oh, if only we had a legion of preachers, in these days of superficial piety and these times of prayerlessness, who would pray for their churches as Paul did for those early churches! Praying men are needed. Likewise praying preachers are demanded in this age.

At the conclusion of the remarkable prayer in the third chapter of Ephesians, Paul declared that God *"is able to do exceeding abundantly above all that we ask or think"* (Eph. 3:20). In other words, God answers prayer abundantly. Paul earnestly desired to pray parallel to God's will, taking full advantage of His power in order to bless and greatly enrich His church.

Paul and his friends prayed for the saints everywhere. With what solemnity did Paul call the attention of the Roman Christians to the important fact of praying for them—believers whom he had never seen! *"God is my witness...that without ceasing I make mention of you always in my prayers"* (Rom. 1:9). To the churches he said, *"Praying always for you"* (Col. 1:3).

Again, on the same theme, we hear him articulating clearly, *"Always in every prayer of mine for you all making request with joy"* (Phil. 1:4). Again he wrote, *"[I] do not cease to pray for you"* (Col. 1:9). Once more we read the record, *"Wherefore also we pray always for you"* (2 Thess. 1:11). And again it is written, *"Cease not to give thanks for you, making mention of you in my prayers"* (Eph. 1:16). And then he said, *"I have remembrance of thee in my prayers night and day"* (2 Tim. 1:3).

Paul's declaration, *"night and day praying exceedingly"* (1 Thess. 3:10), is a condensed record of the engrossing nature of the praying done by this apostle. It shows conclusively how important praying and receiving answers was to him and to his ministry. It further shows how prayer was an agony of *earnest striving,* seeking blessings from God that could be secured no other way.

15

Church Body Prayers
Are Necessary

I desire above all things to learn to pray. We want to sound the trumpet for the Christian warriors. We desire to find out why there is a lack of real praying. What is it? Why is it? Why so little time spent in prayer when Christ, who had command of His time, chose to spend the great part of it in intercession? "He ever liveth to make intercession for us." We believe the answer is that the desire exists in the heart, but the will is undisciplined. The motive is present, but the affections have not melted under hours of heavenly meditation. The intellect is keen, yet not sharp enough for hours of tireless research. The intellect and the affections have never been linked together by the sealing of the blessed Holy Spirit for God's glory in the secret places, with doors shut, lusts crucified.
—Homer W. Hodge

PAUL'S many requests for prayer for himself, from those to whom he ministered, showed that Paul had a high regard for prayer because he knew the source of help. Paul prayed often himself and tried hard to teach Christians the extreme importance of the work of prayer. He felt the need of receiving answers to prayer so deeply that he believed firmly in the habit of personal praying. Realizing this for himself, he urged this invaluable duty upon others. Intercessory prayer, or prayer for others, was the most valuable type of prayer to Paul. It was no surprise, therefore, when he threw himself upon the prayers of the churches to whom he wrote.

Because of their devotion to Jesus Christ, their interest in the advancement of God's kingdom on earth, and the ardor of their personal attachment to Jesus, he charged them to pray often. He wanted them to pray unceasingly in all things. Then, realizing his own dependence on prayer to support his difficult duties, severe trials, and heavy responsibilities, he urged those to whom he wrote to pray especially for him.

The chief of the apostles needed answers to prayer. He needed the prayers of others, and he admitted this when asking for their prayers. His call to the apostleship did not lift him above this need. He realized and acknowledged his dependence on prayer. He craved and prized the prayers of all Christians. He was not ashamed to solicit prayers for himself nor to urge the believers everywhere to pray for him.

In writing to the Hebrews, he based his request for prayer on two things: his honesty and his desire to visit them. If he were insincere, he could lay no claim to their prayers. Praying for him was a powerful agent in facilitating his visit to them. They touched the secret place of the wind and the waves, and, through prayer, God arranged all secondary agencies, making them minister to this end.

Paul's frequent request of his fellow believers was that they would pray for him. One can judge the value of a thing by the frequency of its request and the urgent plea made for it. Since that was true with Paul, the prayers of the saints were among his greatest assets. By the urgency and reiteration of the request, "Pray for me," Paul showed conclusively the great value he put on prayer as a means of grace. Paul had no need more pressing than his need of prayer. He claimed prayer was the greatest factor behind the success of his work. Thus the most powerful and far-reaching energy, in Paul's estimation, was prayer. The intensity of his belief showed itself in these requests. In this entreaty for prayer he was writing to the Romans: *"I beseech you, brethren, for the Lord Jesus Christ's sake, and for the love of the Spirit, that ye strive together with me in your prayers to God for me"* (Rom. 15:30).

Prayers by others for Paul were valuable because they helped him. Nothing gives us so much aid in our need as real prayers. Through prayers, God supplies our needs and delivers us from difficulties. Paul's faith, so he wrote to the Corinthians, was often tested. He was comforted by his confidence that God would always deliver and strengthen him, especially in response to prayer. *"Ye also helping together by prayer"* (2 Cor. 1:11). God has done marvelous things for His favored saints through the prayers of others! The saints can help each other more by fervent praying than in any other way.

In the midst of envy, backbiting, and perils at the hands of false brethren, Paul wrote to the Philippians,

> *For I know that this shall turn to my salvation through your*
> *prayer, and the supply of the Spirit of Jesus Christ, according*
> *to my earnest expectation and my hope, that in nothing I shall*
> *be ashamed, but that with all boldness, as always, so now also*
> *Christ shall be magnified in my body, whether it be by life, or*
> *by death.* (Phil. 1:19–20)

Shame was taken away, holy boldness secured, and life and death made glorious in answer to the prayers of the saints at Philippi for Paul.

Paul had many mighty events occur during his ministry. His remarkable conversion was a great event, a powerful point of thrust. Yet, he did not secure results in his ministry because of the force of his astounding conversion. His call to the apostleship was clear, luminous, and all-convincing, but he knew he had to pray in order to bring the largest results in his ministry. Paul's course was more clearly marked out and his career rendered more powerfully successful by prayer than by any other force.

Paul urged the Roman Christians to pray for him, so that he could be delivered from the negative effect of unbelieving men. Prayer is a defense and protection against the slander of evil men. Paul not only had unbelieving enemies with whom to contend, but there were many Christians who were prejudiced against him so much that it was doubtful whether they would accept any Christian service at his hands. This was especially the case at Jerusalem. Prayer, powerful prayer, had to be used to remove the mighty and pernicious force of inflamed and deep-seated prejudice. The Romans prayed that Paul would have a safe and prosperous journey so that God's answer would result in their mutual blessing and refreshment.

Paul's prayer requests were many-sided and all-comprehensive. How many things did his request to the Roman church include! The request for their prayers, like the church to whom it was directed, was cosmopolitan. He entreated them, a term indicating intensity and earnestness, for the sake of Jesus Christ, to strive with him in their prayers for him. (See Romans

15:30.) These prayers helped to deliver him from the evil men who could have hindered and embarrassed him in his mission. He wanted all of the brethren to accept his service to the poor saints, and he wanted to have the opportunity to visit the Roman church.

How full of earnestness was his request! How tender and loving was his appeal! How touching and high was the motive for the highest and truest form of prayer, *"for the Lord Jesus Christ's sake"* (v. 30)! Also pray out of the love we bear for the Holy Spirit, the love that the Holy Spirit bears for us, and by the ties of the Christian brotherhood. He urged them to pray with these noble motives and to strive with him in their mutual praying. Paul was in the greatest prayer struggle, a struggle in which the mightiest issues were involved and imperiled. He was committed to the struggle because Christ was in it. He needed the help that comes only through answered prayer. So he pleaded with his fellow believers to pray for him and with him.

Prayer will sweep enemies out of the way. Prayer will drive out the prejudices in the hearts of good men. Paul's way to Jerusalem was cleared of difficulties, the success of his mission was secured, and the will of God and the good of the saints was accomplished. All these marvelous ends were secured in answer to marvelous praying. Wonderful and worldwide are the results to be gained by mighty praying. If all apostolic successors had prayed as Paul did, if all Christians in all ages had placed the same value on prayer as did the apostolic men, how marvelous and divine the history of God's church would have been! How unparalleled its success would have been! The glory of its millennium would have brightened and blessed the world ages ago.

We see in Paul's request his belief in the far-reaching power of prayer. Not that prayer is a talismanic magical force, nor that it is a fetish, but that it moves God to do things that it suggests. Prayer has no magic, potent charm in itself, but it is all-powerful because it gets the omnipotent God to grant its request. A forerunner basic to all prayer, as expressed or understood by Paul, is that *"ye strive together with me in your prayers to God for me"* (Rom. 15:30). Paul needed reinforcements in this prayer struggle, as well as divine help in his striving. He was in the midst of the struggle and bore the brunt, but he solicited the help of others. Their prayers were needed to help him offer intense prayers.

Prayer is not inaptly called *wrestling,* because it is an intense struggle. Prayer has the greatest hindrances, and it has the most persistent foes. Mighty, evil forces surge around the closets of prayer. Powerful enemies who are strongly entrenched are near where praying is done. Paul's praying was no feeble, listless act. In this thing he *"put away childish things"* (1 Cor. 13:11). The commonplace and the tame were retired. Paul had to pray mightily to receive an answer, or he had to pray not at all. Hell had to feel the mightiness of his prayer stroke and stagger under it, or he would not strike at all. The strongest graces and the manliest efforts were required.

Paul needed strength for his praying. Courage was at a premium. Timid touches and fainthearted desires accomplished nothing in the mind of Paul. Enemies had to be faced and routed. Fields were to be won. In order to receive answers to prayer, the Christian must pray with unflagging force, just as the apostle Paul prayed.

16

Principles for Prayer

We announce the law of prayer as follows: A Christian's prayer is a joint agreement of the will, the mind, the emotions, the conscience, the intellect, working in harmony at white heat. The body cooperates under certain conditions to make the prayer long enough and at a high voltage to insure tremendous supernatural and unearthly results.

—Homer W. Hodge

To the church at Ephesus, Paul made a request that is found in the latter part of chapter six of his epistle to those Christians:

Praying always with all prayer and supplication in the Spirit, and watching thereunto with all perseverance and supplication for all saints; and for me that utterance may be given unto me, that I may open my mouth boldly, to make known the mystery of the gospel, for which I am an ambassador in bonds: that therein I may speak boldly, as I ought to speak.

(Eph. 6:18–20)

He labored and prayed for this church night and day. As he drew a vivid picture of the Christian soldier, with his foes harassing him, he gave the churches the duty of praying especially for him.

To these Ephesian Christians he gave a comprehensive statement of the necessity, nature, and special benefits of prayer. The most important was that God answered prayer. Prayer was to be urgent, covering all times and embracing all kinds of places. Supplication had to be intense, the Holy Spirit had to be invoked, vigilance and perseverance were necessary, and the whole family of saints had to be involved.

The purpose behind his request for prayer centered on his need to be able to talk with power, fluency, direction, and courage. Paul did not depend upon his natural gifts, but on those that came to him in answer to prayer. He was afraid he would be a dull, dry speaker or a hesitating stammerer. He urged these believers to pray that he might not only speak clearly, but freely and fully.

He wanted them to pray for his boldness. No quality seems more important for a preacher than boldness. It is that positive quality that does not take consequences into too much account, but with freedom and fullness meets the crisis, faces a present danger, and performs a present duty without fear. Boldness was one of the marked characteristics of apostolic preachers and apostolic preaching. They were brave men; they were fearless preachers. The record of their trials is the applause of their faith.

There are many chains that enslave the preacher. His very tenderness makes him weak. His attachment to his people tends to bring him into bondage. His personal fellowship, his obligations to his people, and his love for them all tend to hamper his freedom and restrain his delivery in the pulpit. Thus, there is constant need to be continually praying for the preacher's ability to speak boldly as he ought to speak! A congregation must pray, seeking God's answers to their prayers for their preacher.

The prophets of old were charged not to be afraid of the faces of men. Unafraid of the frowns of men, they were to declare the truth of God without apology, timidity, hesitancy, or compromise. The warmth and freedom of conviction and sincerity, the fearlessness of a vigorous faith, and, above all, the power of the Holy Spirit were all wonderful helpers and elements of boldness. These things should be sought with all earnestness by modern ministers of the Gospel!

Meekness and humility are high virtues of utmost importance in the preacher, but these qualities do not at all negate boldness. This boldness is not the freedom of furious speech. It is not scolding or rashness. It speaks the truth in love. (See Ephesians 4:15.) Boldness is not rudeness. Roughness dishonors boldness. Boldness is as gentle as a mother with a babe, but as fearless as a lion standing before its foe. Fear, in the mild and innocent form of timidity, or in the offensive form of cowardice, has no place in the true ministry. Humble but holy boldness is of the very first importance.

What hidden, mysterious, mighty entity can add courage to apostolic preaching and give bolder utterances to apostolic lips?

There is one answer, and that is knowing that God has chosen to respond to prayer.

What can so affect and dominate evil that the very results of evil will be changed into good? We have the answer in Paul's words again: *"Who delivered us from so great a death, and doth deliver: in whom we trust that he will yet deliver us; ye also helping together by prayer for us"* (2 Cor. 1:10–11). *"What then? notwithstanding every way, whether in pretence, or in truth, Christ is preached; and I therein do rejoice, yea, and will rejoice"* (Phil. 1:18).

We can see how the promises of God become real and personal with prayer. *"All things work together for good to them that love God"* (Rom. 8:28). Here is a jeweled promise. Paul loved God, but he did not usually rest on that promise alone to work out its blessed results. For example, he wrote to the Corinthians describing his escape from peril: "[God] *delivered us from so great a death...we trust that he will yet deliver us; ye also helping together by prayer"* (2 Cor. 1:10–11). In other words, helping me by prayer, you help God make the promise strong and rich in realization.

Paul's prayer requests embraced *"supplication for all saints"* (Eph. 6:18) but especially for apostolic courage for himself. He needed this courage, just as all preachers called of God need it! God responded to prayer and opened doors for the apostles' labors, but at the same time He opened apostolic lips to utter, with bravery and truth, the Gospel message.

Here he spoke to the church at Colossae:

> *Withal praying also for us, that God would open unto us a door of utterance, to speak the mystery of Christ, for which I am also in bonds: that I may make it manifest, as I ought to speak.* (Col. 4:3–4)

It would be appropriate for such a request to be made by a modern preacher to his congregation! Present-day preachers need those things that Paul desired for himself!

As in his request to the Ephesians, Paul wanted a *"door of utterance"* to be given him, so that he could preach with the liberty of the Spirit, and be delivered from being hampered in thought or delivery. Furthermore, he desired the ability to present the Gospel in the clearest terms, without confusion of thought, and with force. Every preacher today should and could speak with these attributes if the church prayed expecting God to answer. Happy is that

461

preacher who ministers to a people who pray like this for him! He would be still happier if he inwardly felt—as he faced his responsible task, realizing how much he needed these things—that he encouraged his people to pray for him!

God answers prayer and changes crosses, trials, and oppositions into blessings, causing them to work for good. *"This shall turn to my salvation through your prayer"* (Phil. 1:19), said Paul. Today the same things in the life of the preacher are changed into gracious blessings in the end, *"ye also helping together by prayer"* (2 Cor. 1:11). Saintly praying really helped apostolic preaching and rescued apostolic men from many dire circumstances. This kind of praying in these days will bring similar results in faithful preaching done by brave, fearless ministers.

Prayer for the preacher produces results as prayer by the preacher produces results. Two things are always factors in the life and work of a good preacher. First, he prays constantly, fervently, and persistently for those to whom he preaches. Secondly, the congregation prays continually for their preacher. What a blessed set of circumstances when the preacher and congregation pray for each other!

Paul sent this pressing request to the church at Thessalonica:

Finally, brethren, pray for us, that the word of the Lord may have free course, and be glorified, even as it is with you: and that we may be delivered from unreasonable and wicked men.
                                                                    (2 Thess. 3:1–2)

Paul had a racecourse in mind, where the racer pushed himself to reach the goal. Hindrances were in the way of his success and had to be removed, so that the racer could finally succeed and obtain the reward. The Word of the Lord is this racer, as preached by Paul. This Word is personified and there are serious impediments that hamper the running of the Word. It must have a free course. Everything in the way, opposing its running, had to be taken out.

These impediments to the Word of the Lord running and being glorified are found in the preacher himself, in the church to whom he ministers, and in the sinners around him. The Word runs and is glorified when it has unobstructed access to the minds and hearts of those to whom it is preached. When sinners are convicted of sin, when they seriously consider the claims of God's Word on them, and when they are induced to pray for themselves, asking for pardoning mercy, the Word is glorified. The Word is glorified when saints are instructed in religious experience, when they are corrected of doctrinal errors and mistakes in practice, when they are led to seek higher things, and when they pray for deeper experiences in the divine life.

Note that it is not the preacher who is glorified because of the wonderful success brought through the Word. It is not when people praise the preacher unduly and make much out of him because of his wonderful sermons, great eloquence, and remarkable gifts. The preacher must remain in the background in all this work of glorification, even though he is the foremost object of all this praying.

Prayer is to do all these things. This is why Paul urged, entreated, and insisted, *"Pray for us"* (Heb. 13:18). It was not so much prayer for Paul personally in his Christian life and religious experience as it was for him officially. He needed God to answer the prayers for his work as a minister of the Gospel. His tongue had to be unloosed in preaching, his mouth unstopped, and his mind set free. Answers to prayer were not to help "work out his own salvation" (see Philippians 2:12), but to help him live correctly and to effectively advertise the Word of the Lord. They would also keep him from hindering the Word as he preached, as he desired that no hindrance should be in himself that would defeat his own preaching.

He also wanted all hindrances taken away from the churches to whom he ministered, so that church people would not stand in the way or weigh down the Word as it ran the racecourse, attempting to reach the minds and hearts of people. Furthermore, Paul prayed that hindrances in the unsaved would be set aside so that, when he preached God's Word, it would reach their hearts and be glorified in their salvation.

Thinking all of these things, Paul sent his pressing request to the believers at Thessalonica, *"Pray for us"* (2 Thess. 3:1), because praying by true Christians would greatly help to spread the Word of the Lord.

The preacher who sees these things, realizing that his success depends largely on this kind of praying from his people, is wise. We need churches now that, having the preacher in mind and the Word on their hearts, pray for him that *"the word of the Lord may have free course, and be glorified"* (v. 1).

One other item in this request is worth noting: *"That we may be delivered from unreasonable and wicked men"* (v. 2). Such men are hindrances in the way of the Word of the Lord. Many preachers are harassed by them and need to be delivered from them. Prayer helps to bring such a deliverance. Paul was annoyed by such characters, and for this reason he urged prayer for himself that he might find deliverance from them.

Summing it all up, we find that Paul felt the success of the Word, its liberty and largeness, were bound up in prayers, and he found that failure to pray would restrict the Word's influence and glory. His deliverance from unreasonable and wicked men, as well as his safety, depended on people's prayers and God's answers. These prayers, while they greatly helped him preach, at the same time protected him from the cruel plans of wicked and unreasonable men.

Book
Six

Power through Prayer

1

The Divine Channel
of Power

Study universal holiness of life. Your whole usefulness depends on this, for your sermons last only an hour or two; your life preaches all week. If Satan can make you a covetous minister, a lover of praise, of pleasure, of good eating, he has ruined your ministry. Give yourself to prayer, and get your texts, your thoughts, your words from God. Luther spent his best three hours in prayer.   —Robert Murray McCheyne

WE are continually striving to create new methods, plans, and organizations to advance the church. We are ever working to provide and stimulate growth and effectiveness for the Gospel.

This trend of the day has a tendency to lose sight of the man. Or else he is lost in the workings of the plan or organization. God's plan is to make much of the man, far more of him than of anything else. Men are God's method.

The church is looking for better methods; God is looking for better men. *"There was a man sent from God, whose name was John"* (John 1:6). The dispensation that heralded and prepared the way for Christ was bound up in that man John. *"Unto us a child is born, unto us a son is given"* (Isa. 9:6). The world's salvation comes out of that cradled Son.

When Paul appealed to the personal character of the men who rooted the Gospel in the world, he solved the mystery of their success. The glory and effectiveness of the Gospel depend on the men who proclaim it. When God declares that *"the eyes of the LORD run to and fro throughout the whole earth, to show himself strong in the behalf of them whose heart is perfect toward him"* (2 Chron. 16:9), He declares the necessity of men. He acknowledges His dependence on them as a channel through which He can exert His power on the world.

This vital, urgent truth is one that this age of machinery is apt to forget. The forgetting of it is as detrimental to the Word of God as removing the sun from its sphere would be. Darkness, confusion, and death would ensue.

What the church needs today is not more or better machinery, not new organizations or more and novel methods. She needs men whom the Holy Spirit can use—men of prayer, men mighty in prayer. The Holy Spirit does not flow through methods, but through men. He does not come on machinery, but on men. He does not anoint plans, but men—men of prayer!

An eminent historian has said that the accidents of personal character have more to do with the revolutions of nations than either philosophic historians or democratic politicians will allow. This truth fully applies to the Gospel of Christ, and the character and conduct of the followers of Christ. Christianize the world, and you transfigure nations and individuals. It is eminently true of the preachers of the Gospel.

The character as well as the fortunes of the Gospel are committed to the preacher. He either makes or mars the message from God to man. The preacher is the golden pipe through which the divine oil flows. The pipe must not only be golden, but open and flawless. This way the oil may have a full, unhindered, and unwasted flow.

The man makes the preacher. God must make the man. The messenger is, if possible, more than the message. The preacher is more than the sermon. The preacher *makes* the sermon. As life-giving milk from the mother's bosom is no more than the mother's life, so all the preacher *says* is tinctured, impregnated, by what the preacher *is*. The treasure is in earthen vessels, and the taste of the vessel may permeate and discolor the treasure.

The man—the whole man—lies behind the sermon. Preaching is not the performance of an hour. It is the outflow of a life. It takes twenty years to make a sermon, because it takes twenty years to make the man. The true sermon is a thing of life. The sermon grows because the man grows. The sermon is forceful because the man is forceful. The sermon is holy because the man is holy. The sermon is full of the divine anointing because the man is full of the divine anointing.

Paul termed it *"my gospel"* (Rom. 2:16). It was not that he had slanted it with his personal eccentricities or selfish understanding. But, the Gospel was laid up in the heart and lifeblood of Paul as a personal trust to be executed by his Pauline traits—to be set aflame and empowered by the fiery energy of his fiery soul. Paul's sermons—what were they? Where were they? Skeletons, scattered fragments, afloat on the sea of inspiration! But the man Paul—greater than his sermons—lives forever, in full form, feature, and stature, with his molding hand on the church. The preacher is only a voice. The voice in silence dies; the text is forgotten; the sermon fades from memory, but the preacher lives.

In its life-giving forces, the sermon cannot rise above the man. Dead men preach dead sermons, and dead sermons kill. Everything depends on the spiritual character of the preacher. Under the Jewish dispensation, the high priest had "Holiness to the Lord" inscribed in jeweled letters on a golden frontlet. So every preacher in Christ's ministry must be molded into and mastered by this same holy motto. It is a shame that the Christian ministry has less holiness of character and aim than the Jewish priesthood. Jonathan Edwards, the famous missionary, said, "I went on with my eager pursuit after more holiness and conformity to Christ. The heaven I desired was a heaven of holiness."

The Gospel of Christ does not move by popular waves. It has no self-propagating power. It moves as the men who have charge of it move. The preacher must live the Gospel. Its divine, most distinctive features must be embodied in him. The constraining power of love must be in the preacher as a projecting, extraordinary, all-commanding, and self-oblivious force. The energy of self-denial must be his being—his heart, blood, and bones. He must go forth as a man among men, clothed with humility, abiding in meekness, wise as a serpent, and harmless as a dove. He must wear the bonds of a servant with the spirit of a king, and the simplicity and sweetness of a child.

The preacher must throw himself—with all the abandon of a perfect, self-emptying faith and a self-consuming zeal—into his work for the salvation of men. The men who take hold of and shape a generation for God must be hearty, heroic, compassionate, and fearless martyrs. If they are timid timeservers, place-seekers, men-pleasers, men-fearers, if their faith in God or His Word is weak, and if their denial may be broken by any phrase of self or the world, they cannot take hold of the church or the world for God.

The preacher's sharpest and strongest preaching should be to himself. His most difficult, delicate, laborious, and thorough work must be with himself. The training of the twelve was the great, difficult, and enduring work of Christ. Preachers are not sermon makers, but men makers, and saint makers. Only he who has made himself a man and a saint is well trained for this business. God does not need great talents, great learning, or great preachers, but men great in holiness, great in faith, great in love, great in fidelity, great for God. He needs men who are always preaching holy sermons in the pulpit, and living holy lives out of it. These can mold a great generation for God.

After this order, the early Christians were formed. They were men of solid mold, preachers after the heavenly type—heroic, stalwart, soldierly, saintly. To them, preaching meant self-denying, self-crucifying, serious, toilsome, martyr business. They applied themselves to it in a way that influenced their generation, and formed in its womb a generation yet unborn for God. The preaching man is to be the praying man. Prayer is the preacher's mightiest weapon. An almighty force in itself, it gives life and force to all.

The real sermon is made in the closet. The man—God's man—is made in the closet. His life and his most profound convictions are born in his secret communion with God. The burdened and tearful agony of his spirit, his weightiest and sweetest messages, are received when alone with God. Prayer makes the man; prayer makes the preacher; prayer makes the pastor.

The pulpit of this day is weak in praying. The pride of learning is in opposition to the dependent humility of prayer. In the pulpit, prayer is all too often only official—a performance for the routine of service. In the modern pulpit, prayer is not the mighty force it was in Paul's life or ministry. Every preacher who does not make prayer a mighty factor in his own life and ministry is weak as a factor in God's work, and is powerless to advance God's cause in this world.

2

Our Sufficiency Is of God

But, above all, George Fox excelled in prayer. The inwardness and weight of his spirit, the reverence and solemnity of his address and behavior, and the fewness and fullness of his words have often struck even strangers with admiration as they used to reach others with consolation. The most awful living, reverend frame I ever felt or beheld, I must say, was his prayer. And truly it was a testimony. He knew and lived nearer to the Lord than other men, for they that know Him most will see most reason to approach Him with reverence and fear. —William Penn

BY a slight perversion, the sweetest graces may bear the bitterest fruit. The sun gives life, but sunstrokes are death. Preaching is to give life, but it may kill. The preacher holds the keys; he may lock as well as unlock. Preaching is God's great institution for the planting and maturing of spiritual life. When properly executed, its benefits are untold. When wrongly executed, no evil can exceed its damaging results.

It is an easy matter to destroy the flock if the shepherd is unwary or the pasture is destroyed. It is easy to capture the citadel if the watchmen are asleep or the food and water are poisoned. The preacher is invested with gracious prerogatives, exposed to great evils, involving so many grave responsibilities. It would be a parody on the shrewdness of the Devil—a libel on his character and reputation—if he did not use his master influences to adulterate the preacher and the preaching. In the face of all this, Paul's exclamatory question, *"Who is sufficient for these things?"* (2 Cor. 2:16), is never out of place.

Paul said,

Our sufficiency is of God; who also hath made us able minis-
ters of the new testament; not of the letter, but of the spirit: for
the letter killeth, but the spirit giveth life. (2 Cor. 3:5–6)

The true ministry is God-touched, God-enabled, and God-made. The Spirit of God is on the preacher in anointing power. The fruit of the Spirit is in his heart. The Spirit of God has vitalized the man and the Word; his preaching gives life, gives life as the spring gives life. His words give life as the resurrection gives life. His sermons give ardent life as the summer gives ardent life. His preaching gives fruitful life as the autumn gives fruitful life. The life-giving preacher is a man of God, whose soul is continually following after God. His eye looks only to God; and in him, by the power of God's Spirit, the flesh and the world have been crucified. His ministry is like the generous flood of a life-giving river.

The preaching that kills is unspiritual preaching. The ability of the preaching is not from God. Lower sources than God have given it energy and stimulant. The Spirit is not evident in the preacher, nor his preaching. Many kinds of forces may be projected and stimulated by preaching that kills, but they are not spiritual forces. They may resemble spiritual forces, but are only the shadow, the counterfeit. They may seem to have life, but the life is false. The preaching that kills is the letter. It may be shapely and orderly, but it is the letter still—the dry, husky letter, the empty, bald shell. The letter may have the germ of life in it, but it has no breath of spring to evoke it. They are winter seeds, as hard as the winter's soil, as icy as the winter's air. They will neither thaw nor germinate.

This letter-preaching has the truth. But even divine truth has no life-giving energy alone. It must be energized by the Spirit, with all God's forces behind it. Truth unquickened by God's Spirit deadens as much as, or more than, error. It may be the truth, but without the Spirit its shade and touch are deadly. Its truth is error, its light darkness. The letter-preaching is unanointed, neither mellowed nor oiled by the Spirit.

There may be tears, but tears cannot run God's machinery. Tears may be nothing but superficial expression. There may be feelings and earnestness, but it is the emotion of the actor and the earnestness of the attorney. The preacher may be moved by the kindling of his own sparks, be eloquent over his own exegesis, and be earnest in delivering the product of his own brain, but the message of his words may be dead and fruitless. The professor may imitate the fire of the apostles; brains and nerves may feign the work of God's Spirit, and by these forces the letter may glow and sparkle like an illuminated text, but the glow and sparkle will be as barren of life as the field sown with pearls. The death-dealing element lies behind the words, behind the sermon, behind the occasion, behind the manner, behind the action.

The great hindrance is in the preacher himself. He does not find within himself the mighty, life-creating forces. There may be no deficiency in his orthodoxy, honesty, cleanness, or earnestness. But, somehow the man—the inner man—in his secret places has never broken down and surrendered to God. His inner life is not a great highway for the transmission of God's message, God's power.

Somehow, self, not God, rules in the holy of holiest. Somewhere, all unconscious to himself, some spiritual nonconductor has touched his inner being. The divine current has been arrested. His inner being has never felt its thorough spiritual bankruptcy, its utter powerlessness. He has never learned to cry out with an ineffable cry of self-despair and helplessness until God's power and fire come in, fill, purify, and empower. Self-esteem—self-ability in some wicked form—has defamed and violated the temple that should be held sacred for God.

Life-giving preaching costs the preacher much—death to self, crucifixion to the world, the travail of his own soul. Only crucified preaching can give life. Crucified preaching can only come from a crucified man.

3

Man's Most Noble Exercise

During this affliction I examined my life in relation to eternity closer than I had done when in the enjoyment of health. In the examination relative to the discharge of my duties toward my fellowmen as a man, a Christian minister, and an officer of the church, I stood approved by my own conscience. But, in relation to my Redeemer and Savior, the result was different. My returns of gratitude and loving obedience bear no proportion to my obligations for redeeming, preserving, and supporting me through the vicissitudes of life from infancy to old age. The coldness of my love to Him who first loved me and has done so much for me overwhelmed and confused me. And, to complete my unworthy character, I had not only neglected to improve the grace given to the extent of my duty and privilege, but for want of that improvement had, while abounding in perplexing care and labor, declined from first zeal and love. I was confounded, humbled myself, implored mercy, and renewed my covenant to strive and devote myself unreservedly to the Lord. —Bishop McKendree

THE preaching that kills may be, and often is, orthodox—dogmatically, inviolably orthodox. We love orthodoxy. It is good. It is the best. It is the clean, clear-cut teaching of God's Word. It is the trophies won by truth in its conflict with error, the levees that faith has raised against the desolating floods of honest or reckless misbelief or unbelief. But, orthodoxy, clear and hard as a crystal, suspicious and militant, may be nothing but the letter, well shaped, well named, and well learned—the letter that kills. Nothing is so dead as a dead orthodoxy—too dead to speculate, too dead to think, study, or pray.

The preaching that kills may have insight and grasp of principle. It may be scholarly and critical in taste. It may be fluent in all the minor details of the derivation and grammar of the letter. It may be able to trim the letter into its perfect pattern, and illuminate it as Plato and Cicero may have done. It may study the letter as a lawyer studies his textbooks to form his brief or to defend his case. And yet, it may still be like a frost, a killing frost. Letter-preaching may be eloquent, embellished with poetry and rhetoric, sprinkled with prayer, spiced with sensation, illuminated by genius, and yet these may merely be the chaste, costly mountings—the rare and beautiful flowers—that coffin the corpse.

The preaching that kills may be without scholarship. It may be unmarked by any freshness of thought or feeling, clothed in tasteless generalities or dull specialities. It may be slovenly, savoring neither closet nor study, graced neither by thought, nor expression, nor prayer. Under such preaching, how wide and utter the desolation! How profound the spiritual death!

This letter-preaching deals with the surface and shadow of things, not the things themselves. It does not penetrate the inner part. It has no deep insight into, no strong grasp of, the hidden life of God's Word. It is true to the outside. But, the outside is the hull that must be broken and penetrated to obtain the kernel. The letter may be dressed so as to attract and be fashionable, but the attraction is not toward God, nor is the fashion for heaven.

The failure is in the preacher. God has not made him. He has never been in the hands of God like clay in the hands of the potter. He has been busy working on the sermon, its thought and finish, its drawing and impressive forces. But, the deep things of God have never been sought, studied, fathomed, experienced by him. He has never stood before the *"throne, high and lifted up"* (Isa. 6:1). He has never heard the seraphim song or seen the vision, nor has he felt the rush of that awesome holiness. He has never cried out in utter abandon and despair under the sense of weakness and guilt. He has never had his life renewed or his heart touched, purged, and inflamed by the live coal from God's altar.

His ministry may draw people to him, to the church, and to the form and ceremony. But, no true drawings to God, no sweet, holy, divine communion, is induced. The church has been adorned, but not edified. It has pleased, but not sanctified. Life is suppressed. The city of our God becomes the city of the dead—the church a graveyard, not an embattled army. Praise and prayer are stifled; worship is dead. The preacher and the preaching have helped sin, not holiness. They have populated hell, not heaven.

Preaching that kills is prayerless preaching. Without prayer, the preacher creates death and not life. The preacher who is feeble in prayer is feeble in life-giving forces. The preacher who has retired from prayer as a conspicuous and largely prevailing element in his own character has stripped his preaching of its distinctive, life-giving power. There is and will be professional praying, but professional praying helps the preaching to do its deadly work. Professional praying chills and kills both preaching and praying.

Much of the lax devotion and lazy, irreverent attitudes in congregational praying is attributable to professional praying in the pulpit. The prayers in many pulpits are long, discursive, dry, and inane. Without anointing or heart, they fall like a killing frost on all the graces of worship. Death-dealing prayers they are. Every trace of devotion has perished under their breath. The more dead they are, the longer they grow.

A plea for short praying, live praying, real heart praying, praying by the Holy Spirit—direct, specific, ardent, simple, anointed in the pulpit—is in order. A school to teach preachers how to pray, as God counts praying, would be more beneficial to true piety, true worship, and true preaching than all theological schools.

Stop! Pause! Consider! Where are we? What are we doing? Preaching to kill? Praying to kill? Praying to God! The great God, the Maker of all worlds, the Judge of all men! What reverence! What simplicity! What sincerity! What truth in the inward parts is demanded! How real we must be! How hearty! Prayer to God: the most noble exercise, the loftiest effort of man, the most real thing! We will forever discard accursed preaching and prayer that kills, and we will do the real thing. Life-giving preaching brings the mightiest force to bear on heaven and earth. It draws on God's exhaustless and open treasure for the need and beggary of man.

4

Talking to God for Men

Let us often look at Brainerd, an American missionary to the native Indians, in the woods of America, pouring out his very soul before God for the perishing heathen without whose salvation nothing could make him happy. Prayer—secret, fervent, believing prayer—lies at the root of all personal godliness. A competent knowledge of the language where a missionary lives, a mild and winning temper, a heart given up to God in close religion—these, these are the attainments that, more than all knowledge or all other gifts, will fit us to become the instruments of God in the great work of human redemption. —Carey's Brotherhood

THERE are two extreme tendencies in the ministry. The one is to shut itself out from fellowship with the people. The monk and the hermit are illustrations of this. They shut themselves out from men to be more with God. They failed, of course. Our being with God is of use only as we expend its priceless benefits on men.

Too often Christian leaders shut themselves in their studies and become students—bookworms, Bible experts, and sermon makers. They are noted for literature, thought, and sermons; but the people and God, where are they? Out of heart, out of mind. Preachers who are great thinkers, great students, must be the greatest of pray-ers. If they are not, they will be the greatest of backsliders, heartless professionals, rationalistic, less than the least of preachers in God's estimate.

The other tendency is to popularize the ministry thoroughly. It is no longer God's, but a ministry of affairs, of the people. The minister does not pray because his mission is to the people. If he can move the people, create a sensation in favor of religion, and an interest in church work—he is satisfied. His personal relationship to God is no factor in his work. Prayer has little or no place in his plans. The disaster and ruin of such a ministry cannot be computed by earthly mathematics. What the preacher is in prayer to God—for himself, for his people—so is his power for real good to men, his true fruitfulness, and his true fidelity to God—for time and for eternity.

It is impossible for the preacher to keep his spirit in harmony with the divine nature of his high calling without much and constant prayer. It is a serious mistake to think that the preacher, by duty and laborious fidelity to the work and routine of the ministry, can keep himself trim and fit for his high calling. Even sermon making—incessant and taxing as an art, as a duty, as a work, or as a pleasure—will engross, harden, and estrange the heart from God by neglect of prayer. The scientist loses God in nature. The preacher may lose God in his sermon.

Prayer freshens the heart of the preacher, keeps it in tune with God and in sympathy with the people. It lifts his ministry out of the chilly air of a profession, revitalizes routine, and moves every wheel with the ease and power of a divine anointing.

Charles Spurgeon has said,

> Of course the preacher is above all others distinguished as a man of prayer. He prays as an ordinary Christian, else he were a hypocrite. He prays more than ordinary Christians, else he were disqualified for the office he has undertaken. If you as ministers are not very prayerful, you are to be pitied. If you become lax in sacred devotion, not only will you need to be pitied, but your people also, and the day approaches in which you will be ashamed and confounded. All our libraries and studies are mere emptiness compared with our prayer closets. Our seasons of fasting and prayer at the tabernacle have been high days indeed; never has heaven's gate stood wider; never have our hearts been nearer the central glory.

The praying that makes a prayerful ministry is not the meager praying added only as flavoring to give it a pleasant taste. But, the praying must be in the body, form, blood, and bones. Prayer is no petty duty put into a corner. It is no piecemeal performance made out of the fragments of time that have been snatched from business and other engagements of life. The best of our time, and the heart of our time and strength, must be given to prayer. This does not mean that the closet is absorbed in the study or swallowed up in the activities of ministerial duties. But, it means the closet first, the study and activities second. In this way, both the study and the activities are freshened and made efficient by the closet.

Prayer that affects one's ministry must touch one's life. The praying that gives color and bent to character is no pleasant, hurried pastime. It must enter as strongly into the heart and life as Christ's *"strong crying and tears"* (Heb. 5:7) did. It must draw the soul into an agony of desire as Paul's did. It must be an inwrought fire and force like the *"effectual fervent prayer"* (James 5:16) of James. The praying must be of that quality that, when put into the golden censer and incensed before God, works mighty, spiritual struggles and revolutions.

Prayer is not a little habit pinned onto us while we were tied to our mother's apron strings. Neither is it a little, decent quarter-of-a-minute's grace said over an hour's dinner. But, it is a most serious work of our most serious years. It engages more of time and appetite than our longest dinings or richest feasts. The prayer that makes much of our preaching must itself be made much of. The character of our praying will determine the character of our preaching. Light praying will make light preaching. Prayer makes preaching strong, gives it an anointing, and makes it stick. In every ministry that is righteously working for good, prayer has always been a serious business.

The preacher must primarily be a man of prayer. In the school of prayer, only the heart can learn to preach. No learning can make up for the failure to pray. No earnestness, no diligence, no study, no gifts will supply its lack.

Talking to men for God is a great thing, but talking to God for men is still greater. He who has not learned well how to talk to God for men will never talk well—with real success—to men for God. More than this, prayerless words, both in and out of the pulpit, are deadening.

5

How to Get
Results for God

You know the value of prayer: it is precious beyond all price. Never, never neglect it.　　　　　*—Sir Thomas Buxton*

Prayer is the first thing, the second thing, the third thing necessary to a minister. Pray, then, my dear brother; pray, pray, pray.　　　　　*—Edward Payson*

PRAYER, in the preacher's life, study, and pulpit, must be a conspicuous and all-impregnating force, an all-coloring ingredient. It must play no secondary role, be no mere coating. The preacher is called to be with his Lord *"all night in prayer"* (Luke 6:12). To train himself in self-denying prayer, he is charged to look to his Master, who, *"rising up a great while before day...went out, and departed into a solitary place, and there prayed"* (Mark 1:35).

The preacher's study ought to be a closet, a Bethel, an altar, a vision, and a ladder, so that every thought might ascend heavenward before it goes manward. Likewise, every part of the sermon should be scented by the air of heaven and made serious, because God was in the study.

Just as the steam engine never moves until the fire is kindled, so preaching—with all its machinery, perfection, and polish—is at a dead standstill, spiritually, until prayer has kindled and created the steam. The texture, fineness, and strength of the sermon are rubbish unless the mighty impulse of prayer is in it, through it, and behind it. The preacher must, by prayer, put God in the sermon. The preacher must, by prayer, move God toward the people before he can move the people to God by his words. The preacher must have had audience and ready access to God before he can have access to the people. An open way to God for the preacher is the surest pledge of an open way to the people.

It is necessary to iterate and reiterate that prayer, as a mere habit, as a performance gone through by routine or in a professional way, is a dead and rotten thing. Such praying has no connection with the praying for which we plead. We stress true praying that engages and sets on fire every high element of the preacher's being. We emphasize prayer that is born of vital oneness with Christ in the fullness of the Holy Spirit, and that springs from the deep, overflowing fountains of His tender compassion.

We seek prayer composed of undying solicitude for man's eternal good, and a consuming zeal for the glory of God. The preacher needs a thorough conviction of his difficult and delicate work and of his imperative need of God's mightiest help. Praying grounded on these solemn and profound convictions is the only true praying. Preaching backed by such praying is the only preaching that sows the seeds of eternal life in human hearts, and builds men up for heaven.

It is true that—with little or no praying—there may be popular, pleasant, captivating, and intellectual preaching that avails a small amount of good. But, the preaching that secures God's end must be born of prayer from the initial conception to the actual presentation. It must be delivered with the energy and spirit of prayer. It must be followed, made to germinate, and kept in vital force in the hearts of the hearers by the preacher's prayers, long after the occasion has passed.

We may excuse the spiritual poverty of our preaching in many ways. But, the true reason for it is the lack of urgent prayer for God's presence in the power of the Holy Spirit. There are innumerable preachers who can deliver masterful sermons, but the effects are short-lived. They do not affect the regions of the spirit where the fearful war between God and Satan, heaven and hell, is being waged, because they are not made powerfully militant and spiritually victorious by prayer.

The preachers who gain mighty results for God are the men who have prevailed in their pleadings with God *before* venturing to plead with men. The preachers who are the mightiest in their closets with God are the mightiest in their pulpits with men.

Preachers are human, and are often exposed to or involved in the strong currents of human emotions and problems. Praying is spiritual work, and human nature does not like taxing, spiritual work. Human nature wants to sail to heaven under a pleasant breeze and a full, smooth sea. Prayer is humbling work. It abases intellect and pride, crucifies vainglory, and signals our spiritual bankruptcy. All these are hard for flesh and blood to bear. It is easier not to pray than to bear them. So, we come to one of the crying evils of these times, maybe of all times: little or no praying. Of these two evils, perhaps little praying is worse than no praying. Little praying is a kind of make-believe, a salve for the conscience, a farce and a delusion.

The little regard we give prayer is evident from the little time we spend in it. The time given to prayer by the average preacher scarcely counts in light of how the remaining time is delegated to daily chores. Not infrequently, the preacher's only praying is by his bedside—in his nightdress, ready for bed. Perchance, he gets in a few additional prayers before he is dressed in the morning. How feeble, vain, and little is such praying compared with the time and energy devoted to praying by holy men in and out of the Bible! How poor and meager our petty, childish praying is beside the habits of the true men of God in all ages! God commits the keys of His kingdom to men who think that praying is their main business, and devote time to it according to this high estimate of its importance. By these men, He works His spiritual wonders in this world. Great praying is the sign and seal of God's great leaders. It is the most earnest of the conquering forces with which God will crown their labors.

The preacher is commissioned to pray as well as to preach. His mission is incomplete if he does not do both well. The preacher may speak with all the eloquence of men and of angels, but unless he can pray with a faith that draws all heaven to his aid, his preaching will be *"as sounding brass, or a tinkling cymbal"* (1 Cor. 13:1). It will be useless for permanent, God-honoring, soul-saving purposes.

6

Great Men of Prayer

The principal cause of my leanness and unfruitfulness is due to an unaccountable backwardness to pray. I can write or read or converse or hear with a ready heart. But, prayer is more spiritual and inward than any of these, and the more spiritual any duty is, the more my carnal heart is apt to stray from it. Prayer and patience and faith are never disappointed. I have long since learned that if ever I was to be a minister, faith and prayer must make me one. When I can find my heart dissolved in prayer, everything else is comparatively easy.
—Richard Newton

IT may be considered a spiritual axiom that, in every truly successful ministry, prayer is an evident and controlling force. It is evident and controlling in the life of the preacher, evident and controlling in the deep spirituality of his work. A ministry may be a very thought-provoking ministry without prayer. The preacher may secure fame and popularity without prayer. The whole machinery of the preacher's life and work may be run without the oil of prayer, or with scarcely enough to grease one cog. But, no ministry can be a spiritual one—securing holiness in the preacher and in his people—without prayer being made an evident and controlling force.

Indeed, the preacher who prays puts God into the work. God does not come into the preacher's work as a matter of course or on general principle. But, He comes in by prayer and special urgency. It is as true of the preacher as of the penitent, that God will be found the day that we seek Him with the whole heart. (See Jeremiah 29:13.) A prayerful ministry is the only ministry that brings the preacher into sympathy with the people. As essentially as prayer unites the human, it does the divine. A prayerful ministry is the only ministry qualified for the high offices and responsibilities of the preacher. Colleges, knowledge, books, theology, and preaching do not make a preacher, but praying does. The apostles' commission to preach was nothing until it was filled up by the praying that Pentecost resulted from. A prayerful minister has passed beyond the regions of the popular—beyond the man of mere affairs, secularities, and pulpit attractiveness. He has passed beyond the ecclesiastical organizer or leader, and has entered into a more sublime and mightier region—the region of the spiritual.

Holiness is the product of the prayerful preacher's work. Transfigured hearts and lives emblazon the reality of his work, its trueness and substantial nature. God is with him. His ministry is not based or built on worldly, surface principles. He is highly experienced and deeply learned in the things of God. His long, deep communings with God about His people, and the agony of his wrestling spirit, have crowned him as a prince in the things of God. The iciness of mere professionalism has long since melted under the intensity of his praying.

The superficial results of many a ministry, and the deadness of others, are to be found in the lack of praying. No ministry can succeed without much praying, and this praying must be fundamental, ever abiding, ever increasing. The text—the sermon—should be the result of prayer. The study should be bathed in prayer, all its duties impregnated with prayer, its whole spirit the spirit of prayer.

"I am sorry that I have prayed so little," was the deathbed regret of one of God's chosen ones. That is a sad and remorseful regret for a preacher. "I want a life of greater, deeper, truer prayer," said the late Archbishop Tait. So may we all say, and this may we all secure.

God's true preachers can be distinguished by one great feature: they are men of prayer. Often differing in many things, they always have a common center. They may start from different points, and travel by different roads, but they converge to one point: they are one in prayer. To them, God is the center of attraction, and prayer is the path that leads to God. These men do not pray occasionally—not a little or at odd times. But, they pray in such a way that their prayers enter into and shape their very characters. They pray so as to affect their own lives and the lives of others, and to cause the history of the church to influence the current of the times. They spend much time in prayer, not because they watch the shadow on the dial or the hands on the clock, but because it is to them so momentous and engaging a business that they can scarcely quit.

Prayer is to them what it was to Paul—a striving with earnest effort of soul. It is to them what it was to Jacob—a wrestling and prevailing. It is to them what it was to Christ—strong crying and tears. They pray *"always with all prayer and supplication in the Spirit, and watching thereunto with all perseverance"* (Eph. 6:18). *"The effectual fervent prayer"* (James 5:16) has been, and still is, the mightiest weapon of God's mightiest soldiers.

The statement that James made in regard to Elijah—that he *"was a man subject to like passions as we are, and he prayed earnestly that it might not rain: and it rained not on the earth by the space of three years and six months. And he prayed again, and the heaven gave rain, and the earth brought forth her fruit"* (vv. 17–18)—applies to all prophets and preachers who have moved their generation for God, and shows the instrument by which they worked their wonders.

Many private prayers must be short. Public prayers, as a rule, ought to be short and condensed. Also, there is often need for spontaneous, exclamatory prayer. However, in our private communions with God, time is essential to the value of the prayer. Much time spent with God is the secret of all successful praying.

Prayer that produces a powerful influence is the immediate product of much time spent with God. Our short prayers are effective and efficient because long ones have preceded them. The short, prevailing prayer cannot be prayed by one who has not prevailed with God in a mightier struggle of long continuance. Jacob's victory of faith could not have been gained without that all-night wrestling.

God's acquaintance is not made hurriedly. He does not bestow His gifts on the casual or hasty comer and goer. To be much alone with God is the secret of knowing Him and of having influence with Him. God yields to the persistency of a faith that knows Him. He bestows His richest gifts on those who declare their desire for and appreciation of those gifts by the constancy as well as the earnestness of their importunity.

Christ, who in this as well as in other things is our example, spent many whole nights in prayer. His custom was to pray much. He had His habitual place to pray. Many long seasons of praying make up His history and character. Paul prayed day and night. Daniel's three daily prayers took time away from other important interests. David's morning, noon, and night praying was doubtless on many occasions very long and involved. While we have no specific account of the time these Bible saints spent in prayer, the indications are that they devoted much time to prayer, and on some occasions long seasons of praying were their custom.

We would not want anyone to think that the value of their prayers is measured by the clock. Our purpose is to impress on our minds the necessity of being much alone with God. And, if this feature has not been produced by our faith, then our faith is feeble and superficial.

The men who have most fully imitated Christ in their character, and have most powerfully affected the world for Him, have been men who spent so much time with God as to make it a notable feature of their lives. Charles Simeon, the English revivalist, devoted the hours from four to eight in the morning to God. John Wesley spent two hours a day in prayer. He began at four in the morning. One who knew him well wrote, "He thought prayer to be more his business than anything else, and I have seen him come out of his closet with a serenity of face next to shining."

John Fletcher, an English clergyman and author, stained the walls of his room by the breath of his prayers. Sometimes he would pray all night—always frequently and with great earnestness. His whole life was a life of prayer. "I would not rise from my seat," he said, "without lifting my heart to God." His greeting to a friend was always: "Do I meet you praying?" Martin Luther said, "If I fail to spend two hours in prayer each morning, the Devil gets the victory through the day. I have so much business, I cannot get on without spending three hours daily in prayer." He had a motto: "He that has prayed well has studied well."

Archbishop Leighton was so much alone with God that he seemed to be in a perpetual meditation. "Prayer and praise were his business and his pleasure," said his biographer. Bishop Thomas Ken was so much with God that his soul was said to be God-enamored. He was with God before the clock struck three every morning. Bishop Francis Asbury said, "I propose to rise at four o'clock as often as I can and spend two hours in prayer and meditation." Samuel Rutherford, the fragrance of whose piety is still rich, rose at three in the morning to meet God in prayer. Joseph Alleine, an English clergyman, arose at four o'clock for his business of praying until eight. If he heard other tradesmen going about their business before he was up, he would exclaim, "Oh, how this shames me! Does my Master not deserve more than theirs?" He who has well learned this practice of prayer draws to it at will, on sight, and with the acceptance of heaven's unfailing bank.

One of the holiest and most gifted of Scottish preachers said, "I ought to spend the best hours in communion with God. It is my noblest and most fruitful employment, and is not to be thrust into a corner. The morning hours, from six to eight, are the most uninterrupted and should be thus employed. After tea is my best hour, and that should be solemnly dedicated to God. I ought not to give up the good and old habit of prayer before going to bed; but guard must be kept against sleep. When I awake in the night, I ought to rise and pray. A little time after breakfast might be given to intercession." This was the praying plan of Robert Murray McCheyne. In their praying, the memorable Methodists shame us. "From four to five in the morning, private prayer; from five to six in the evening, private prayer."

John Welch, the holy and wonderful Scottish preacher, thought the day was ill spent if he did not spend eight or ten hours in prayer. He kept a blanket near his bed so that he might wrap himself when he arose to pray at night. His wife would complain when she found him lying on the ground weeping. He would reply, "O woman, I have the souls of three thousand to answer for, and I know not how it is with many of them!"

Bishop Wilson said, "In Henry Martyn's journal, the spirit of prayer—the time he devoted to the duty—and his fervor in it are the first things that strike me."

Edward Payson wore grooves into the hardwood floor where his knees pressed so often and so long. His biographer said,

> His continuing time in prayer, regardless of his circumstances, is the most noticeable fact in his history. It points out the duty of all who would rival his eminency. His distinguished and almost uninterrupted success must no doubt be ascribed in a great measure to his ardent and persevering prayers.

The Marquis DeRenty, to whom Christ was most precious, ordered his servant to call him from his devotions at the end of half an hour. The servant at the time saw his face through an opening. It was marked with such holiness that he hated to arouse him. His lips were moving, but he was perfectly silent. The servant waited until an hour and a half had passed, then he called to him. The Marquis arose from his knees, saying that half an hour was so short when he was communing with Christ.

David Brainerd said, "I love to be alone in my cottage, where I can spend much time in prayer."

William Bramwell, famous in Methodist records for personal holiness, for his wonderful success in preaching, and for the marvelous answers to his prayers, would pray for hours at a time. He almost lived on his knees. He went over his circuits like a flame of fire. The fire was kindled by the time he spent in prayer. He often spent as much as four hours in a single season of prayer in retirement.

Bishop Andrewes spent the greatest part of five hours every day in prayer and devotion.

Sir Henry Havelock, a distinguished British soldier, always spent the first two hours of each day alone with God. If they were to break camp at six o'clock, he would rise at four.

Earl Cairns, an Irish lawyer, rose daily at six o'clock to spend an hour and a half in Bible study and prayer, before conducting family worship at a quarter to eight.

Dr. Adoniram Judson's success in God's work, as an American missionary in India, is attributable to the fact that he gave much time to prayer. He said on this point,

> Arrange your affairs, if possible, so that you can leisurely devote two or three hours every day, not merely to devotional exercises, but to the very act of secret prayer and communion with God. Endeavor seven times a day to withdraw from business and company, and lift up your soul to God in private retirement. Begin the day by rising after midnight and devoting some time amid the silence and darkness of the night to this sacred work. Let the hour of opening dawn find you at the same work. Let the hours of nine, twelve, three, six, and nine at night witness the same. Be resolute in His cause. Make all practical sacrifices to maintain it. Consider that your time is short and that business and company must not be allowed to rob you of your God.

Impossible! we say. Fanatical directions! Yet Adoniram Judson impressed an empire for Christ. He laid the foundations of God's kingdom with imperishable granite in the heart of Burma. He was successful—one of the few men who mightily impressed the world for Christ. Many men of greater gifts and genius and learning than he have made no such impression. Their religious work resembles footsteps in the sand. But, his work endures, as if it were engraved in stone. The secret of its profoundness and endurance is found in the fact that he gave time to prayer. He kept the iron red-hot with prayer, and God's skill molded it with enduring power. No man who is not a man of prayer can do a great and enduring work for God. And no man can be a man of prayer without giving much time to prayer.

Is it true that prayer is simply a compliance with habit—dull and mechanical? Is it petty performance into which we are trained until tameness, shortness, and superficiality are its chief elements?

Canon Liddon, the English orator, has asked,

> Is it true that prayer is, as is assumed, little else than the half-passive play of sentiment that flows languidly on through the minutes or hours of easy reverie? Let those who have really prayed give the answer. They sometimes describe prayer as a wrestling together with an unseen power that may last late into the night hours, or even to the break of day, as it was with Jacob. And, like St. Paul, they sometimes refer to common intercession as a concerted struggle. They have, when praying, their eyes fixed on the Great Intercessor in Gethsemane, on the drops of blood that fall to the ground in that agony of resignation and sacrifice. Importunity is the essence of successful prayer. Importunity means not dreaminess but sustained work. It is through prayer especially that the kingdom of heaven suffers violence and the violent take it by force. (See Matthew 11:12.)

It was a saying of the late Bishop Hamilton that

> a man is not likely to do much good in prayer if he does not begin by looking on it in the light of a work to be prepared for and persevered in with all the earnestness that we bring to bear on subjects that in our opinion are at once more interesting and most necessary.

7

"Early Will I Seek Thee"

I ought to pray before seeing anyone. Often when I sleep long, or meet with others early, it is eleven or twelve o'clock before I begin secret prayer. This is a wretched system. It is unscriptural. Christ arose before day and went into a solitary place. David said, "Early will I seek thee," and, "My voice shalt thou hear in the morning." Family prayer loses much of its power and sweetness, and I can do no good to those who come to seek from me. My conscience feels guilty, my soul unfed, my lamp not trimmed. Then, when in secret prayer, the soul is often out of tune. I feel it is far better to begin with God—to see His face first—to get my soul near Him before it is near another. —*Robert Murray McCheyne*

THE men who have done the most for God in this world have been early on their knees. He who fritters away the early morning—its opportunity and freshness—in other pursuits than seeking God will make poor headway seeking Him the rest of the day. If God is not first in our thoughts and efforts in the morning, He will be last during the remainder of the day.

Behind this early rising and early praying is the intense desire that urges us into this pursuit after God. Morning listlessness indicates a listless heart. The heart that is lax in seeking God in the morning has lost its relish for God. David's heart was ardent after God. He hungered and thirsted after God. He sought God early, before daylight. The bed and sleep could not chain his soul in its eagerness after God. Christ longed for communion with God; and so, rising a great while before day, He would go out to the mountain to pray. The disciples, when fully awake and ashamed of their indulgence, knew where to find Him. We could list men who have mightily impressed the world for God, and we would find that they were early in seeking after God.

A desire for God that cannot break the chains of sleep is a weak thing and will do little good for God. The desire for God that stays far behind the Devil and the world at the beginning of the day will never catch up.

It is not simply getting up that has brought men to the front and has made them leaders in God's hosts. It is the overwhelming desire that stirs and breaks all self-indulgent chains that does so. But getting up gives vent, increase, and strength to the desire. If they had lain in bed and indulged themselves, the desire would have been quenched. The desire aroused them and inspired them to reach out for God.

This heeding and acting on the call gave their faith its grasp on God, and their hearts the sweetest and fullest revelation of Him. This strength of faith and fullness of revelation made them saints by eminence. The halo of their sainthood has come down to us, and we have entered into the enjoyment of their conquests. But we take our fill in enjoyment of them, and not in imitating them. We build their tombs and write their epitaphs, but are careful not to follow their examples.

We need a generation of preachers who seek God and seek Him early. We need men who give the freshness and dew of effort to God, and in return secure the freshness and fullness of His power, that He may be as the dew to them—full of gladness and strength through all the heat and labor of the day. Our laziness after God is our crying sin. The children of this world are far wiser than we. They are at it early and late. We do not seek God with ardor and diligence. No man receives God who does not follow hard after Him. And no soul follows hard after God who is not after Him in early morn.

8

The Secret of Power

There is a manifest want of spiritual influence on the ministry of the present day. I feel it in my own case and I see it in that of others. I am afraid there is too much of a low, managing, contriving, maneuvering temper of mind among us. We are laying ourselves out more than is expedient to meet one man's taste and another man's prejudices. The ministry is a grand and holy affair, and it should find in us a simple habit of spirit and a holy but humble indifference to all consequences. The leading defect in Christian ministers is want of a devotional habit.　　　　　　　　　　　　*—Richard Cecil*

NEVER was there a greater need for saintly men and women. More imperative still is the call for saintly, God-devoted preachers. The world moves with gigantic strides. Satan has his hold and rule on the world, and labors to make all its movements subserve his ends. Christianity must do its best work, present its most attractive and perfect models. By every means, modern sainthood must be inspired by the loftiest ideals and by the largest possibilities through the Spirit.

Paul lived on his knees, so that the Ephesian church might measure the heights, breadths, and depths of an unmeasurable saintliness, and *"be filled with all the fulness of God"* (Eph. 3:18–19). Epaphras spent himself with the exhaustive toil and strenuous conflict of fervent prayer, so that the Colossian church might *"stand perfect and complete in all the will of God"* (Col. 4:12). Everywhere and everything in apostolic times was growing, so that the people of God might each and *all come in the unity of faith, and of the knowledge of the Son of God, unto a perfect man, unto the measure of the stature of the fulness of Christ.* (Eph. 4:13)

No premium was given to those who fell short of God's calling. No encouragement was offered to an old babyhood. The babies were to grow. The old, instead of feebleness and infirmities, were to bear fruit in old age, and be fat and flourishing. The most divine thing in Christianity is holy men and women.

No amount of money, genius, or culture can move things for God. Holiness energizing the soul—the whole man aflame with love, with desire for more faith, more prayer, more zeal, more consecration—this is the secret of power. These we need and must have, and men must be the incarnation of this God-inflamed devotedness. God's advance has been stayed, His cause crippled, His name dishonored for their lack. Genius (though the loftiest and most gifted), education (though the most learned and refined), position, dignity, place, and honored names cannot move this chariot of our God. It is a fiery one, and only fiery forces can move it.

The genius of a Milton fails. The imperial strength of a Leo fails. But, Brainerd's spirit could move it. Brainerd's spirit was on fire for God, on fire for souls. Nothing earthly, worldly, or selfish was able to quench the intensity of this all-impelling and all-consuming force and name.

Prayer is the creator as well as the channel of devotion. The spirit of devotion is the spirit of prayer. Prayer and devotion are united as soul and body are united, as life and heart are united. There is no real prayer without devotion, no devotion without prayer. The preacher must be surrendered to God in the holiest devotion. He is not a professional man; his ministry is not a profession. It is a divine institution, a divine devotion. He is devoted to God. His aim, aspirations, and ambitions are for God and to God; and to such, prayer is as essential as food is to life.

The preacher, above everything else, must be devoted to God. The preacher's relationship to God is the insignia and credentials of his ministry. These must be clear, conclusive, and unmistakable. He must not possess a common, superficial piety. If he does not excel in grace, he does not excel at all. If he does not preach by life, character, and conduct, he does not preach at all. His piety may be light, his preaching as soft and as sweet as music, yet, its weight will be a feather's weight—visionary, fleeting as the morning cloud or the early dew.

Devotion to God—there is no substitute for this in the preacher's character and conduct. Devotion to a church, to opinions, to an organization, to orthodoxy—these are paltry, misleading, and vain when they become the source of inspiration. God must be the mainspring of the preacher's effort, the fountain and crown of all his toil. The name and honor of Jesus Christ, the advance of His cause, must be all in all. The preacher must have no inspiration but the name of Jesus Christ, no ambition but to have Him glorified, no toil but for Him. Then, prayer will be the source of his illuminations, the means of perpetual advancement, the gauge of his success. The continual aim, the only ambition the preacher can cherish, is to have God with him.

Never has God's cause been in greater need of the perfect example of the possibilities of prayer than in this age. No age, no person, will demonstrate the gospel power except the ages or persons of deep and earnest prayer. A prayerless age will have only scant models of divine power. Prayerless hearts will never rise to these glorious heights. The age may be a better age than the past. But, there is an infinite distance between the betterment of an age by the force of an advancing civilization and its betterment by the increase of holiness and Christlikeness by the energy of prayer.

The Jews were much better off when Christ came than in the ages before. It was the golden age of their pharisaical religion. Their golden, religious age crucified Christ. During the time of Christ, there was never more so-called piety, never less praying; never more indulgence, never less sacrifice; never more idolatry, never less devotion to God; never more temple worship, never less God worship; never more lip service, never less heart service; never more churchgoers, never fewer saints.

It is the prayer force that makes saints. Holy characters are formed by the power of real praying. The more true saints, the more praying; the more praying, the more true saints.

God has now, and has had in the past, many of these devoted, prayerful preachers—men in whose lives prayer has been a mighty, controlling, conspicuous force. The world has felt their power. God has felt and honored their power. God's cause has moved mightily and swiftly by their prayers; holiness has shone out in their characters with a divine effulgence. God found one of the men he was looking for in David Brainerd, whose work and name have gone into history. He was no ordinary man, but was capable of shining in any company. He was the peer of the wise and gifted ones, eminently suited to fill the most attractive pulpits and to labor among the most refined and cultured who were so anxious to secure him for their pastor.

Jonathan Edwards, the famous missionary and clergyman, bears testimony that Brainerd was

> a young man of distinguished talents, had extraordinary knowledge of men and things, had rare conversational powers, excelled in his knowledge of theory, and was truly, for one so young, an extraordinary divine, and especially in all matters relating to practical Christianity. I never knew his equal of his age and standing for clear and accurate notions of the nature and essence of true Christianity. His manner in prayer was almost inimitable, such as I have very rarely known equaled. His learning was very considerable, and he had extraordinary gifts for the pulpit.

No more noble or inspiring a story has ever been recorded in earthly annals than that of David Brainerd. No miracle attests the truth of Christianity with more divine force than the life and work of such a man. Alone in the savage wilds of America, struggling day and night with a mortal disease, unschooled in the care of souls, he fully established the worship of God. Hindered by having only a pagan interpreter through whom he preached to the Indians, strengthened by the Word of God in his heart and in his hands, he seized many for God's service. With his soul fired by the divine flame, and his mouth, heart, and mind always in prayer, he secured all the gracious results of his divine calling and devotion.

The Indians experienced a great change, from the very lowest form of an ignorant and debased heathenism to pure, devout, intelligent Christianity. All vice was reformed; the external duties of Christianity were at once embraced and acted on. Family prayer was set up; the Sabbath was instituted and joyously observed. The internal graces of Christianity were exhibited with growing sweetness and strength.

The cause of these results is found in David Brainerd himself—not in the conditions or accidents, but in the man Brainerd. He was God's man, acting for God, first and last and all the time.

God could flow unhindered through him. The omnipotence of grace was neither arrested nor hindered by the conditions of his heart. The whole channel was broadened and cleaned out for God's fullest and most powerful passage. Thus, God, with all His mighty forces, could come down on the hopeless, savage wilderness and transform it into His blooming and fruitful garden. Nothing is too hard for God to do if He can get the right kind of man to do it.

Brainerd lived a life of holiness and prayer. His diary is full of the record of his seasons of fasting, meditation, and retirement. The time he spent in private prayer amounted to many hours daily. "When I return home," he said,

> and give myself to meditation, prayer, and fasting, my soul longs for mortification, self-denial, humility and divorcement from all things of the world. I have nothing to do with earth, but only labor in it honestly for God. I do not desire to live one minute for anything that earth can afford.

It was prayer that gave marvelous power to his life and ministry. He prayed after this high order:

> Feeling somewhat of the sweetness of communion with God and the constraining force of His love and how admirably it captivates the soul and makes all the desires and affections to center in God, I set apart this day for secret fasting and prayer to God, to direct and bless me with regard to the great work that I have in view of preaching the Gospel and to ask that the Lord would return to me and show me the light of His countenance. I had little life and power in the forenoon. Near the middle of the afternoon, God enabled me to wrestle ardently in intercession for my absent friends, but just at night the Lord visited me marvelously in prayer. I think my soul was never in such agony before. I felt no restraint, for the treasures of divine grace were opened to me. I wrestled for absent friends, for the ingathering of souls, for multitudes of poor souls, and for many that I thought were the children of God, personally in many distant places. I was in such agony from sun half an hour high until near dark that I was wet all over with sweat, but yet it seemed to me I had done nothing. Oh, my dear Savior did sweat blood for poor souls! I longed for more compassion toward them. I felt still in a sweet frame, under a sense of divine love and grace, and went to bed in such a frame, with my heart set on God.

The men of mighty prayer are men of spiritual strength. Prayers never die. Brainerd's whole life was a life of prayer. By day and by night he prayed. Before preaching and after preaching he prayed. Riding through the interminable solitudes of the forest he prayed. On his bed of straw he prayed. Retiring to the dense and lonely forest he prayed. Hour by hour, day after day, early morn and late at night, he was praying and fasting, pouring out his soul, interceding, communing with God. He was with God mightily in prayer; God was with him mightily, and because of this, he who is dead yet speaks and works and will continue to do so until the end comes. Among the glorious ones of that glorious day, he will be with the first.

Jonathan Edwards said of David Brainerd,

> His life shows the right way to success in the works of the ministry. He sought it as the soldier seeks victory in a siege or battle; or as a man that runs a race for a great prize. Animated with love to Christ and souls, how did he labor? Always fervently, not only in word and doctrine, in public and in private, but in prayers by day and night, wrestling with God in secret and travailing in birth with unutterable groans and agonies, until Christ was formed in the hearts of the people to whom he was sent. Like a true son of Jacob, he persevered in wrestling through all the darkness of the night, until the breaking of the day!

9

Power through Prayers

For nothing reaches the heart but what is from the heart,
or pierces the conscience but what comes from a living con-
science. —*William Penn*

In the morning I was more engaged in preparing the
head than the heart. This has been frequently my error, and I
have always felt the evil of it, especially in prayer. Reform it,
then, O Lord! Enlarge my heart, and I shall preach.
—*Robert Murray McCheyne*

A sermon that has more head infused into it than heart
will not come home with efficacy to the hearers.
—*Richard Cecil*

PRAYER, with its manifold and many-sided forces, helps the
mouth to utter the truth in its fullness and freedom. The preacher
is to be prayed for, because the preacher is made by prayer. The
preacher's mouth is to be prayed for—his mouth is to be opened
and filled by prayer. A holy mouth is made by praying, by much
praying. A brave mouth is made by praying, by much praying. The
church and the world, God and heaven, owe much to Paul's
mouth. Paul's mouth owed its power to prayer.

How manifold, illimitable, valuable, and helpful prayer is to
the preacher in so many ways, at so many points, in every way!
One great value is, it helps his heart.

Praying makes the preacher a heart-preacher. Prayer puts the
preacher's whole heart into the preacher's sermon. Prayer puts
the preacher's sermon into the preacher's heart.

The heart makes the preacher. Men of great hearts are great preachers. Men of bad hearts may do a measure of good, but this is rare. The hireling and the stranger may help the sheep at some points, but it is the good shepherd with the good shepherd's heart who will bless the sheep, and fill the full measure of the shepherd's place.

We have emphasized sermon preparation until we have lost sight of the important thing to be prepared—the heart. A prepared heart is much better than a prepared sermon. A prepared heart will *make* a prepared sermon.

Volumes have been written stating the detailed mechanics of sermon making. We have become possessed with the idea that this scaffolding is the building. The young preacher has been taught to exhaust all of his strength on the form, taste, and beauty of his sermon as a mechanical and intellectual product. We have thereby cultivated a vicious taste among the people and raised the clamor for talent instead of grace. We have emphasized eloquence instead of piety, rhetoric instead of revelation, reputation and brilliance instead of holiness. By it, we have lost the true idea of preaching. We have lost preaching power, and the pungent conviction for sin. We have also lost the rich experience, the elevated Christian character, and the divine authority over consciences and lives that always results from genuine preaching.

It would not do to say that preachers study too much. Some of them do not study at all; others do not study enough. Many do not study the right way to show themselves workmen approved of God. (See 2 Timothy 2:15.) But our great lack is not in the head culture, but in heart culture. Not lack of knowledge, but lack of holiness is our sad and telling defect—not that we know too much, but that we do not meditate enough on God and His Word, and we do not watch and fast and pray enough. The heart is the great hindrance to our preaching. Words pregnant with divine truth find our hearts to be nonconducive. Arrested, they fall flat and powerless.

Can ambition that lusts after praise and position preach the Gospel of Him who made Himself of no reputation and took on the form of a servant? (See Philippians 2:7.) Can the proud, the vain, the egotistical preach the Gospel of Him who was meek and lowly? (See Matthew 11:29.) Can the bad-tempered, passionate, selfish, hard, worldly man preach the doctrine that is based on long-suffering, self-denial, tenderness, and that imperatively demands separation from enmity and crucifixion to the world? Can the hireling official, heartless, perfunctory, preach the Gospel that demands that the Shepherd give His life for the sheep? Can the covetous man, who counts salary and money, preach the Gospel until he has cleansed his heart and can say in the spirit of Christ and Paul in the words of Wesley: "I count it dung and dross; I trample it under my feet; I (yet not I, but the grace of God in me) esteem it just as the mire of the streets, I desire it not, I seek it not"?

God's revelation does not need the light of human genius, the polish and strength of human culture, the brilliancy of human thought, the force of human brains to adorn or enforce it. But, it does demand the simplicity, docility, humility, and faith of a child's heart.

It was this surrender and subordination of intellect and genius to the divine and spiritual forces that made Paul peerless among the apostles. It was this that gave Wesley his power.

Our great need is heart preparation. Luther held it as an axiom: "He who has prayed well has studied well."

I am not saying that men are not to think and use their intellects. But, he who cultivates his heart the most will use his intellect the best. I am not saying that preachers should not be students. But, I am saying that their great study should be the Bible; and he who has kept his heart with diligence studies the Bible best. I am not saying that the preacher should not know men. But, he who has fathomed the depths and intricacies of his own heart will be more adept in the knowledge of human nature.

I am saying that while the channel of preaching is the mind, its fountain is the heart. You may broaden and deepen the channel, but if you do not look well to the purity and depth of the fountain, you will have a dry or polluted channel. Almost any man of average intelligence has sense enough to preach the Gospel, but very few have grace enough to do so. He who has struggled with his own heart and conquered it; who has taught it humility, faith, love, truth, mercy, sympathy, courage; who can pour the rich treasures of the human heart thus trained, all surcharged with the power of the Gospel, on the consciences of his hearers—such a person will be the truest, most successful preacher in the esteem of his Lord.

The heart is the savior of the world. Heads do not save. Genius, brains, brilliancy, strength, natural gifts do not save. The Gospel flows through hearts. All the mightiest forces are heart forces. All the sweetest and loveliest graces are heart graces. Great hearts make great characters; great hearts make divine characters. God is love. There is nothing greater than love, nothing greater than God. Hearts make heaven; heaven is love. There is nothing higher, nothing sweeter, than heaven. It is the heart and not the head that makes God's great preachers. The heart counts for much in every way in Christianity. The heart must speak from the pulpit. The heart must hear in the pew. In fact, we serve God with our hearts. Head homage does not conduct current in heaven.

We believe that one of the serious and most popular errors of the modern pulpit is the inclusion of more thought than prayer—more head than heart—in its sermons. Big hearts make big preachers; good hearts make good preachers. A theological school to enlarge and cultivate the heart is the golden desire of the Gospel. The pastor binds his people to him and rules his people by his heart. They may admire his gifts; they may be proud of his ability; they may be affected for the time by his sermons. But, the stronghold of his power is his heart. The throne of his power is his heart. His scepter is love.

The Good Shepherd gives His life for the sheep. Heads never make martyrs. It is the heart that surrenders the life to love and fidelity. It takes great courage to be a faithful pastor, but the heart alone can supply this courage. Gifts and genius may be brave, but they are the gifts and genius of the heart and not of the head.

It is easier to fill the head than it is to prepare the heart. It is easier to make a brain sermon than a heart sermon. It was heart that drew the Son of God from heaven. It is heart that will draw men to heaven. The world needs men of heart to sympathize with its woe, to kiss away its sorrows, to feel compassion for its misery, and to alleviate its pain. Christ was eminently the man of sorrows (see Isaiah 53:3), because He was preeminently the man of heart.

"Give Me your heart" is God's requisition of men. "Give me your heart!" is man's demand of man.

A professional ministry is a heartless ministry. When salary plays a great part in the ministry, the heart plays little part. We may make preaching our business and not put our hearts in the business. He who puts self to the front in his preaching puts heart to the rear. He who does not sow with his heart in his study will never reap a harvest for God. The closet is the heart's study. We will learn more about how to preach and what to preach there than we can learn in our libraries.

"Jesus wept" (John 11:35) is the shortest and biggest verse in the Bible. It is he who goes forth weeping (not preaching great sermons), *"bearing precious seed,* [who will] *come again with rejoicing, bringing his sheaves with him"* (Ps. 126:6).

Praying gives sense, brings wisdom, and broadens and strengthens the mind. The prayer closet is a perfect schoolteacher and schoolhouse for the preacher. Thought is not only brightened and clarified in prayer, but thought is born in prayer. We can learn more in an hour of praying, when praying indeed, than from many hours of rigorous study. There are books in the closet that can be found and read nowhere else. Revelations are made in the closet that are made nowhere else.

10

Under the Dew of Heaven

One bright blessing that private prayer brings down upon the ministry is an indescribable and inimitable something— an anointing from the Holy One. If the anointing that we bear comes not from the Lord of hosts, we are deceivers, since only in prayer can we obtain it. Let us continue instant, constant, fervent in supplication. Let your fleece lie on the thresh-ing-floor of supplication until it is wet with the dew of heaven.
—Charles Spurgeon

ALEXANDER Knox, a Christian philosopher in the days of Wesley, during the time of the great Methodist revival, wrote,

It is strange and lamentable, but I truly believe that except among Methodists and Methodistic clergymen, there is not much interesting preaching in England. The clergy, too generally, have absolutely lost the art. When I was in this country two years ago, I did not hear a single preacher who taught me as my own great masters did, but such as are deemed Methodistic. And I now despair of getting an atom of heart instruction from any other quarter. The Methodist preachers (although I may not always approve of all their expressions) do most assuredly diffuse this religion, true and undefiled.

I felt real pleasure last Sunday. I can bear witness that the preacher did at once speak the words of truth and soberness. There was no eloquence—the honest man never dreamed of such a thing—but there was far better: a cordial communication of vitalized truth. I say *vitalized* because what he declared to others it was impossible not to feel he lived himself. He was truly anointed.

This anointing is the art of preaching. The preacher who never had this anointing never had the art of preaching. The preacher who has lost this anointing has lost the art of preaching. Whatever other arts he may have and retain—the art of sermon making, the art of eloquence, the art of great, clear thinking, the art of pleasing an audience—he has lost the divine art of preaching. This anointing makes God's truth powerful and interesting, draws, attracts, edifies, convicts, and saves.

This same anointing, or unction, vitalizes God's revealed truth, makes it living and life-giving. God's truth, spoken without this anointing, is too light; it is dead and deadening. Though abounding in truth, though weighty with thought, though sparkling with rhetoric, though pointed by logic, though powerful by earnestness, without this divine anointing it issues death, not life. Spurgeon has said,

> I wonder how long we might beat our brains before we could plainly put into words what is meant by preaching with unction. Yet, he who preaches knows its presence, and he who hears soon detects its absence. Samaria, in famine, typifies a discourse without it. Jerusalem, with her feast of fat things, full of marrow (see Isaiah 25:6), may represent a sermon enriched with it. Everyone knows what the freshness of the morning is when orient pearls abound on every blade of grass, but who can describe it, much less produce it of itself? Such is the mystery of spiritual anointing. We know, but we cannot tell others, what it is. It is as easy as it is foolish to counterfeit it. Unction is a thing that you cannot manufacture, and its counterfeits are worse than worthless. Yet it is, in itself, priceless, and beyond measure needful if you wish to edify believers and bring sinners to Christ.

Anointing is that indefinable, indescribable something that an old, renowned Scottish preacher explained in this manner:

> There is sometimes something in preaching that cannot be described either in matter or expression, and cannot be described what it is, or from where it comes, but with a sweet violence it pierces into the heart and affections and comes immediately from the Lord; but if there is any way to obtain such a thing it is by the heavenly disposition of the speaker.

We call it *unction,* or *anointing.* It is this anointing that makes the Word of God

> *quick, and powerful, and sharper than any two-edged sword, piercing even to the dividing asunder of soul and spirit, and of the joints and marrow, and...a discerner of the thoughts and intents of the heart.*   *(Heb. 4:12)*

It is this anointing that gives the words of the preacher such point, sharpness, and power, and that creates such friction and stir in many a dead congregation.

The same truths have been told in the strictness of the letter, smooth as human oil could make them. But, no signs of life—not a pulse—are evident. All is as peaceful as the grave and equally as dead. The same preacher, in the meanwhile, receives a baptism of this anointing; divine inspiration is on him. The letter of the Word has been embellished and fired by this mysterious power, and the throbbings of life begin—life that receives or life that resists. The anointing pervades and convicts the conscience and breaks the heart.

This divine anointing is the feature that separates and distinguishes true gospel preaching from all other methods of presenting the truth. It creates a wide spiritual chasm between the preacher who has it and the one who does not. It supports and impregnates revealed truth with all the energy of God. Anointing is simply allowing God to be in His own Word and on His own preacher. By mighty, great, and continual prayerfulness, it is the preacher's entire potential. It inspires and clarifies his intellect, gives insight, grasp, and projecting power. It gives the preacher heart power, which is greater than head power. And, tenderness, purity, and force flow from the heart by it. Growth, freedom, fullness of thought, directness, and simplicity of utterance are the fruits of this anointing.

Often, earnestness is mistaken for this anointing. He who has the divine anointing will be earnest in the very spiritual nature of things. But, there may be a great deal of earnestness without the least bit of anointing.

Earnestness and anointing look alike from some points of view. Earnestness may be readily and without detection substituted or mistaken for unction. It requires a spiritual eye and a spiritual taste to discriminate.

Earnestness may be sincere, serious, ardent, and persevering. It goes at a thing with a good will, pursues it with perseverance, and urges it with vehemence—puts force in it. But all these forces do not rise higher than the mere human. The *man* is in it, the whole man, with all that he has of will and heart, of brains and genius, of planning, working, and talking. He has set himself to some purpose that has mastered him, and he pursues to master it. There may be none of God in it. There may be little of God in it, because there is so much of the man in it. He may present pleas in support of his earnest purpose that please, touch, move, or overwhelm with the conviction of their importance. In all this earnestness, he may move along earthly ways, being propelled by human forces only. Its altar is made by earthly hands, and its fire kindled by earthly flames.

It was once said of a rather famous preacher of gifts, who interpreted Scripture to fit his fancy or purpose, that he "grows very eloquent over his own exegesis." Oftentimes men grow exceedingly earnest over their own plans or movements. Earnestness may be selfishness in disguise.

What, then, is the anointing? It is the indefinable aspect of preaching that makes it preaching. It is that which distinguishes and separates preaching from all mere human speeches and presentations. It is the divine quality in preaching. It makes the preaching sharp to those who need sharpness. It cleanses as the dew those who need to be refreshed. It is well described as

> ...a two-edged sword
> Of heavenly temper keen.
> And double were the wounds it made
> Where'er it glanced between.
> 'Twas death to sin; 'twas life
> To all who mourned for sin.
> It kindled and it silenced strife,
> Made war and peace within.

This anointing comes to the preacher not in the study but in the closet. It is heaven's distillation in answer to prayer. It is the sweetest exhalation of the Holy Spirit. It impregnates, suffuses, softens, percolates, cuts, and soothes. It carries the Word like dynamite. It makes the Word a soother, an arraigner, a revealer, a searcher. It makes the hearer a culprit or a saint, makes him weep like a child and live like a giant. It opens his heart and his purse as gently, yet as strongly, as the spring opens the leaves. This anointing is not the gift of genius. It not found in the halls of learning. No eloquence can woo it. No industry can win it. No orthodox hands can bestow it. It is the gift of God, the signet sent to His own messengers. It is heaven's knighthood given to the chosen, true, and brave ones who have sought this anointed honor through many hours of tearful, wrestling prayer.

Earnestness is good and impressive; genius is gifted and great. Thought kindles and inspires, but it takes a divine endowment—a more powerful energy than earnestness, genius, or thought—to break the chains of sin. It takes more to win estranged and depraved hearts to God, to repair the breaches, and to restore the church to her old ways of purity and power. Nothing but holy anointing can do this.

In the Christian system, unction is the anointing of the Holy Spirit, separating the believer for God's work and qualifying him for it. This anointing is the one divine enablement by which the preacher accomplishes the unique and saving ends of preaching. Without it, no true spiritual results are accomplished. The results and forces in preaching do not rise above the results of unsanctified speech. Without anointing, the preacher is as potent as the pulpit itself.

This divine anointing on the preacher generates, through the Word of God, the spiritual results that flow from the Gospel. Without this anointing, these results are not secured. Many pleasant impressions may be made, but these all fall far below the ends of gospel preaching. This anointing may be simulated. There are many things that look like it. There are many results that resemble its effects. But, they are foreign to its results and to its nature. The fervor or softness excited by a pathetic or emotional sermon may look like the movements of the divine anointing. But, it has no pungent, penetrating, heartbreaking force. No heart-healing balm exists in these superficial, sympathetic, emotional movements. They are not radical—neither sin-searching nor sin-curing.

This divine anointing is the one distinguishing feature that separates true gospel preaching from all other methods of presenting truth. It supports and interpenetrates the revealed truth with all the force of God. It illumines the Word, broadens and enriches the intellect, and empowers it to grasp and understand the

Word. It qualifies the preacher's heart, and brings it to that condition of tenderness, purity, force, and light necessary to secure the highest results. This anointing gives the preacher liberty and enlargement of thought and soul—a freedom, fullness, and directness of utterance that can be secured by no other process.

Without this anointing on the preacher, the Gospel has no more power to propagate itself than any other system of truth. This is the seal of its divinity. Anointing on the preacher puts God in the Gospel. Without the anointing, God is absent, and the Gospel is left to the low and unsatisfactory forces that the ingenuity, interest, or talents of men can devise to enforce and project its doctrines.

It is in this element that the pulpit more often fails than in any other element. It lapses just at this all-important point. It may be full of knowledge, brilliance, eloquence, and charm. Sensationalism, or even less offensive methods, may attract large crowds. Mental power may impress and enforce truth with all its resources. But, without this anointing, each and all of these will merely be like the fretful assault of the waters on a Gibraltar. Spray and foam may cover and spangle, but the rocks are still there, unimpressed and immovable. The human heart can no more be rid of its hardness and sin by these human forces than these rocks can be swept away by the ocean's ceaseless flow.

This anointing is the consecration force, and its presence the continuous test of that consecration. It is this divine anointing of the preacher that secures his consecration to God and His work. Other forces and motives may call him to the work, but only this is consecration. A separation to God's work by the power of the Holy Spirit is the only consecration recognized by God as legitimate.

The anointing—the divine unction, this heavenly anointing—is what the pulpit needs and must have. This divine and heavenly oil put on it by the imposition of God's hand must soften and lubricate the whole man—heart, head, and spirit. It must mightily separate him from all earthly, secular, worldly, selfish motives and aims, separating him to everything that is pure and godlike.

It is the presence of this anointing in the preacher that creates the stir and friction in many a congregation. The same truths have been told in the strictness of the letter, but no effect has been seen, no pain or pulsation felt. All is as quiet as a graveyard. Another preacher comes, and this mysterious influence is on him.

The letter of the Word has been tried by the Spirit; the throes of a mighty movement are felt. It is the unction that pervades and stirs the conscience, and breaks the heart. Unctionless preaching makes everything hard, dry, acrid, and dead.

This anointing is more than a memory or an era of the past. It is a present, realized, conscious fact. It belongs to the experience of the man as well as to his preaching. It is that which transforms him into the image of his divine Master, as well as that by which he declares the truths of Christ with power. It is so much the power in the ministry that it makes all else seem feeble and vain without it. By its presence, it atones for the absence of all other forces.

This anointing is not an inalienable gift. It is a conditional gift. Its presence is perpetuated and increased by the same process by which it was at first secured—by unceasing prayer to God, by impassioned desires after God, by seeking it with tireless zeal, by deeming all else loss and failure without it.

This anointing comes directly from God in answer to prayer. Only praying hearts are filled with this holy oil. Only praying lips are anointed with this divine unction.

Prayer, much prayer, is the price of the anointing on preaching. Prayer, much prayer, is the sole condition of keeping this anointing. Without unceasing prayer, the anointing never comes to the preacher. Without perseverance in prayer, the anointing, like overkept manna, breeds worms.

11

The Example of the Apostles

Give me one hundred preachers who fear nothing but sin, and desire nothing but God, and I care not a straw whether they be clergymen or laymen; such alone will shake the gates of hell and set up the kingdom of heaven on earth. God does nothing but in answer to prayer.   —*John Wesley*

THE apostles knew the necessity and worth of prayer to their ministry. They knew that their high commission as apostles— instead of relieving them from the necessity of prayer—committed them to it by a more urgent need. They were exceedingly jealous when some other important work exhausted their time and prevented their praying as they ought. As a result, they appointed laymen to look after the delicate and engrossing duties of ministering to the poor, so that they might, unhindered, give themselves *"continually to prayer, and to the ministry of the word"* (Acts 6:4). Prayer was put first, and their relation to prayer was strongly stated—they gave themselves to it. They made a business of it, surrendering themselves to praying, putting fervor, urgency, perseverance, and time into it.

How holy, apostolic men devoted themselves to this divine work of prayer! *"Night and day praying exceedingly"* (1 Thess. 3:10), said Paul. The consensus of apostolic devotedness is, "We will give ourselves continually to prayer."

How these New Testament preachers spent themselves in prayer for God's people! How they put God in full force into their churches by their praying! These holy apostles did not vainly think that they had met their high and solemn duties by faithfully delivering God's Word. But, their preaching was made effective and lasting by the fervor and insistence of their praying.

Apostolic praying was as taxing, toilsome, and imperative as apostolic preaching. They prayed mightily day and night to bring their people to the highest regions of faith and holiness. They prayed even mightier still to hold them to this high spiritual altitude. The preacher who has never learned in the school of Christ the high and divine art of intercession for his people will never learn the art of preaching. Though homiletics be poured into him by the ton, and though he may be the most gifted genius in sermon making and sermon delivery, he will never preach as the apostles did if he does not pray as they did.

The prayers of apostolic, saintly leaders do much in making saints of those who are not apostles. If the church leaders in later years had been as particular and fervent in praying for their people as the apostles were, the sad, dark times of worldliness and apostasy would not have marred the history of the world and arrested the advance of the church. Apostolic praying makes apostolic saints, and keeps apostolic times of purity and power in the church.

12

What God Would Have

If some Christians who have been complaining of their ministers had said and acted less before men and had applied themselves with all their might to cry to God for their ministers—had, as it were, risen and stormed heaven with their humble, fervent, and incessant prayers for them—they would have been much more in the way of success.

—Jonathan Edwards

SOMEHOW the practice of praying for the preacher has fallen into disuse, or become discounted. Occasionally, we have heard the practice referred to as a discredit of the ministry. Some think of it as being a public declaration of the inefficiency of the ministry. Perhaps praying for the preacher offends the pride of learning and self-sufficiency. But, these *ought* to be offended and rebuked if a ministry is so derelict as to allow them to exist.

Prayer, to the preacher, is not simply a duty or a privilege of his profession. It is a necessity. Air is not more necessary to the lungs than prayer is to the preacher. It is absolutely necessary for the preacher to pray. It is an absolute necessity that the preacher be prayed for. These two propositions are wedded into a union that ought never to know any divorce. *The preacher must pray; the preacher must be prayed for.* It will take all the praying he can do, and all the praying he can get done, to meet the fearful responsibilities and gain the largest, truest success in his great work. The true preacher, next to the cultivation of the spirit and fact of prayer in himself in their most intense form, greatly covets the prayers of God's people.

The more holy a man is, the more he values prayer. He sees clearly that God gives Himself to the praying ones, and that the measure of God's revelation to the soul is proportionate to the soul's longing, importunate prayer for God. Salvation never finds its way to a prayerless heart. The Holy Spirit never abides in a prayerless spirit. Preaching never edifies a prayerless soul. Christ knows nothing of prayerless Christians. The Gospel cannot be extended by a prayerless preacher. Gifts, talents, education, eloquence, and God's call cannot lessen the demand of prayer, but only intensify the necessity for the preacher to pray and to be prayed for. The more the preacher's eyes are opened to the nature, responsibility, and difficulties in his work, the more he will see. And, if he is a true preacher, he will feel the necessity of prayer even more strongly. He will not only feel the increasing demand to pray himself, but he will also feel compelled to call on others to help him by their prayers.

What loftiness of soul, what purity and elevation of motive, what unselfishness, what self-sacrifice, what exhaustive toil, what enthusiasm of spirit, what divine tact are necessary to be an intercessor for men!

The preacher is to spend himself in prayer for his people—not that they might simply be saved, but that they be mightily saved. The apostles spent themselves in prayer so that their sights might be perfect. They did this not because they wanted a meager relish for the things of God, but so that they *"might be filled with all the fulness of God"* (Eph. 3:19). Paul did not rely on his apostolic preaching to secure this end. For this cause, he bowed his knees to the Father of our Lord Jesus Christ. (See verse 14.) Paul's praying carried Paul's converts farther along the highway of sainthood than Paul's preaching did.

Epaphras did as much or more by prayer for the Colossian saints than by his preaching. He labored fervently, always in prayer for them, that they might *"stand perfect and complete in all the will of God"* (Col. 4:12).

Preachers are preeminently God's leaders. They are primarily responsible for the condition of the church. They shape its character, give tone and direction to its life.

Much depends on these leaders. They shape the times and the institutions. The church is divine; the treasure it encases is heavenly. But, it bears the imprint of the human. The treasure is in earthen vessels, and it tastes of the vessel. The church of God makes, or is made by, its leaders. In any case, the church will be what its leaders are: spiritual if they are spiritual; secular if they are secular; conglomerate if its leaders are a mixture of the two.

Israel's kings gave character to Israel's piety. A church rarely revolts against or rises above the religion of its leaders. Strong spiritual leaders—men of holy might—at the lead are tokens of God's favor. Disaster and weakness follow the wake of feeble or worldly leaders. Israel fell low when God gave them children for princes and babes to rule over them. The prophets predict unhappiness when children oppress God's Israel and enemies rule over them. Times of spiritual leadership are times of great spiritual prosperity to the church.

Prayer is one of the eminent characteristics of strong spiritual leadership. Men of mighty prayer are men of might, and they shape the outcome of things. Their power with God has the conquering tread.

How can a man who does not get his message fresh from God in the closet expect to preach? How can he preach without having his faith quickened, his vision cleared, and his heart warmed by his closeting with God? Alas for the pulpit lips that are untouched by this closet flame! (See Isaiah 6:1–7.) They will forever be dry and without the anointing. Divine truths will never come with power from such lips. As far as the real interests of Christianity are concerned, a pulpit without a prayer closet will always be a barren thing.

A preacher may preach in an official, entertaining, or learned way, without prayer. But, there is an immeasurable distance between this kind of preaching and the sowing of God's precious seed with holy hands and prayerful, weeping hearts.

Paul was an illustration of these things. If any man could extend or advance the Gospel by personal force, by brainpower, by culture, by personal grace, by God's apostolic commission, God's extraordinary call, that man was Paul. Paul exemplified the fact that the preacher must be a man given to prayer. Paul preeminently demonstrated that the true apostolic preacher must have the prayers of other good people to give to his ministry its full quota of success. Paul asked, he coveted, he pleaded in an impassioned way for the help of all God's saints.

Paul knew that in the spiritual realm—as elsewhere—in union there is strength. He knew that the concentration and aggregation of faith, desire, and prayer increased the volume of spiritual force until it became overwhelming and irresistible in its power. Units of prayer combined, like drops of water, make an ocean that defies resistance. So Paul, with his clear and full understanding of spiritual dynamics, decided to make his ministry as impressive, eternal, and irresistible as the ocean by gathering all the scattered units of prayer and precipitating them on his ministry.

The reason for Paul's prominence in labors and results, and his impact on the church and the world, may be that he was able to center more prayer on himself and his ministry than others. To his brethren at Rome he wrote,

> *Now I beseech you, brethren, for the Lord Jesus Christ's sake, and for the love of the Spirit, that ye strive together with me in your prayers to God for me.*   *(Rom. 15:30)*

To the Ephesians he said,

> *Praying always with all prayer and supplication in the Spirit, and watching thereunto with all perseverance and supplication for all saints; and for me, that utterance may be given unto me, that I may open my mouth boldly, to make known the mystery of the gospel.*   *(Eph. 6:18–19)*

To the Colossians he emphasized,

> *Withal praying also for us, that God would open unto us a door of utterance, to speak the mystery of Christ, for which I am also in bonds: that I may make it manifest, as I ought to speak.*   *(Col. 4:3–4)*

To the Thessalonians he said sharply and strongly, *"Brethren, pray for us"* (1 Thess. 5:25).

Paul called on the Corinthian church to help him: *"Ye also helping together by prayer for us"* (2 Cor. 1:11). This was to be part of their work. They were to apply themselves vigorously to the helping hand of prayer.

Paul, in an additional and closing charge to the Thessalonian church about the importance and necessity of their prayers, said,

> *Finally, brethren, pray for us, that the word of the Lord may have free course, and be glorified, even as it is with you: and that we may be delivered from unreasonable and wicked men.*   *(2 Thess. 3:1–2)*

He impressed upon the Philippians that all his trials and opposition could be made subservient to the spread of the Gospel by the efficiency of their prayers for him. Philemon was to prepare a lodging for him, for, through Philemon's prayer, Paul was to be his guest.

Paul's attitude about this question illustrates his humility and his deep insight into the spiritual forces that project the Gospel. More than this, it teaches a lesson for all times—that if Paul was so dependent on the prayers of God's saints to give his ministry success, how much greater the necessity that the prayers of God's saints be centered on the ministry of today!

Paul did not feel that this urgent plea for prayer lowered his dignity, lessened his influence, or depreciated his piety. What if it did? Let dignity go; let influence be destroyed; let his reputation be marred—he must have their prayers. Called, commissioned, chief of the apostles as he was, all his equipment was imperfect without the prayers of his people. He wrote letters everywhere, urging them to pray for him. Do you pray for your preacher? Do you pray for him in secret? Public prayers are of little worth unless they are founded on or followed up by private praying. The praying ones are to the preacher as Aaron and Hur were to Moses. They hold up his hands and decide the issue that is so fiercely raging around them.

The plea and purpose of the apostles were to stir the church to praying. They did not ignore the grace of cheerful giving. They were not ignorant of the place that religious activity and work occupied in the spiritual life. But, not one or all of these, in apostolic estimate or urgency, could at all compare in necessity and importance with prayer. The most sacred and urgent pleas were used—the most fervid exhortation—the most comprehensive and arousing words were uttered to enforce the all-important obligation and necessity of prayer.

"Put the saints everywhere to praying" is the burden of the apostolic effort and the keynote of apostolic success. Jesus Christ strove to do this in the days of His personal ministry. As He was moved by infinite compassion at the ripened fields of the earth perishing for lack of laborers—and pausing in His own praying—He tried to awaken the sensibilities of His disciples to the duty of prayer as He charged them, *"Pray ye therefore the Lord of the harvest, that he will send forth labourers into his harvest"* (Matt.

9:38). *"And he spake a parable unto them to this end, that men ought always to pray, and not to faint"* (Luke 18:1).

Our devotions are not measured by the clock, but time is of their essence. The ability to wait and stay and press essentially belongs to our fellowship with God. Haste, everywhere unseeming and damaging, is often, to an alarming extent, a part of the great business of communion with God. Short devotions are the bane of deep piety. Calmness, grasp, and strength are never the companions of haste. Short devotions deplete spiritual vigor, arrest spiritual progress, sap spiritual foundations, and blight the root and bloom of the spiritual life. They are the prolific source of backsliding, the sure indication of a superficial piety; they deceive, blight, rot the seed, and impoverish the soil.

It is true that Bible prayers in word and print are short, but the praying men of the Bible were with God through many sweet and holy, wrestling hours. They won by few words but long waiting. The prayers Moses recorded may be short, but Moses prayed to God with fastings and mighty cryings for forty days and nights.

The statement of Elijah's praying may be condensed to a few brief paragraphs. But doubtless, Elijah, who prayed earnestly or "in prayer," spent many hours of fiery struggle and lofty communion with God before he could, with assured boldness, say to Ahab, *"There shall not be dew nor rain these years, but according to my word"* (1 Kings 17:1). The Bible record of Paul's prayers is short, but Paul prayed night and day exceedingly. (See 1 Thessalonians 3:10.)

The Lord's Prayer is a divine epitome for infant lips, but Christ Jesus often prayed all night before His work was done. And His all-night and long-sustained devotions gave His work its finish and perfection, and His character the fullness and glory of its divinity.

Spiritual work is taxing work, and men are loath to do it. Praying, true praying, costs an outlay of serious attention and time, a payment that flesh and blood does not relish. Few people are made of such strong fiber that they will make a costly outlay when inferior work will pass just as well in the market. We can habituate ourselves to our beggarly praying until it looks good to us. At least it presents a decent front and quiets the conscience— the deadliest of opiates! We can become lax in our praying, and not realize the peril until the damage has been done. Hasty devotions make weak faith, feeble convictions, and questionable piety. To be little *with* God is to be little *for* God. To cut the praying short makes the whole Christian character short, miserly, and slovenly.

It takes much time for the fullness of God to flow into the spirit. Short devotions cut the pipe of God's full flow. It takes time spent in the secret places to receive the full revelation of God. Little time and much hurrying will mar the picture.

Henry Martyn, the English missionary, lamented that "lack of private devotional reading and shortness of prayer through incessant sermon making has produced much strangeness between God and my soul." He judged that he had dedicated too much time to public ministrations and too little to private communion with God. He was very impressed with the need to set apart and devote time for fasting and solemn prayer. Resulting from this, he recorded: "I was assisted this morning to pray for two hours."

Said William Wilberforce, the peer of kings,

> I must secure more time for private devotions. I have been living far too public for me. The shortening of private devotions starves the soul; it grows lean and faint. I have been keeping too late hours.

Of a failure in Parliament he said, "Let me record my grief and shame, and all, probably, from private devotions having been contracted, and so God let me stumble." More solitude and earlier hours were his remedy.

More time and early hours devoted to prayer would revive and invigorate many a decayed spiritual life. More time and early hours for prayer would be manifest in holy living. A holy life would not be so rare or so difficult a thing if our devotions were not so short and hurried. A Christly temper, in its sweet and passionless fragrance, would not be so alien and hopeless a heritage if our stay in the prayer closet were lengthened and intensified.

We live shabbily because we pray meagerly. Plenty of time to feast in our prayer closets will bring marrow and fatness to our lives. (See Psalm 63:5.) Our ability to stay with God in our prayer chamber directly relates to our ability to stay with God out of the prayer chamber. Hasty closet visits are deceptive and defaulting. We are not only deluded by them, but we are losers by them in many ways and in many rich legacies. Tarrying in the closet instructs and wins. We are taught by it, and the greatest victories are often the results of great waiting—waiting until words and plans are exhausted. Silent and patient waiting gains the crown. Jesus Christ asks with an affronted emphasis, *"Shall not God avenge his own elect, which cry day and night unto him?"* (Luke 18:7).

To pray is the greatest thing we can do; and to do it well, there must be calmness, time, and deliberation. Otherwise, it is degraded into the smallest and meanest of things. True praying has the largest results for good; and poor praying, the least. We cannot do too much real praying; we cannot do too little of the imitation. We must learn anew the worth of prayer—enter anew the school of prayer. There is nothing that takes more time to learn. And, if we want to learn the wondrous art, we must not offer a fragment here and there—"A little talk with Jesus," as the tiny saintlets sing. But, we must demand and hold with an iron grasp the best hours of the day for God and prayer, or there will be no praying worth the name.

This, however, is not a day of prayer. Few men pray. Prayer is defamed by preacher and priest. In these days of hustle and bustle, of electricity and steam, men will not take time to pray. There are preachers who "say prayers" as a part of their program, on regular or state occasions. But, who *"stirreth up himself to take hold"* (Isa. 64:7) of God? Who prays as Jacob prayed—until he is crowned as a prevailing, princely intercessor? Who prays as Elijah prayed—until all the locked-up forces of nature were unsealed and a famine-stricken land bloomed as the garden of God? Who prays as Jesus Christ prayed, as out upon the mountain He *"continued all night in prayer to God"* (Luke 6:12)? The apostles gave themselves *"continually to prayer"* (Acts 6:4)—the most difficult thing to get men or even the preachers to do.

There are laymen who will give their money—some of them in rich abundance—but they will not give themselves to prayer, without which their money is only a curse. There are plenty of preachers who will preach and deliver great and eloquent addresses on the need of revival and the spread of the kingdom of God. But, there are many who will do that without prayer, and prayerlessness makes all preaching and organizing worse than vain. Prayer is out-of-date, almost a lost art. The greatest benefactor this age could have is the man who will bring the preachers and the church back to prayer.

519

The apostles could only glimpse the great importance of prayer before Pentecost. But the Spirit coming and filling at Pentecost elevated prayer to its vital and all-commanding position in the Gospel of Christ. Now, the call of prayer to every saint is the Spirit's loudest and most urgent call. Sainthood's piety is made, refined, and perfected by prayer. The Gospel moves with slow and timid pace when the saints are not at their prayers early and late and long.

Where are the Christlike leaders who can teach the modern saints how to pray and can put them at it? Do we know that we are raising up a prayerless set of saints? Where are the apostolic leaders who can put God's people to praying? Let them come to the front and do the work, and it will be the greatest work that can be done. An increase in educational facilities and a great increase in money will be a curse to Christianity if they are not sanctified by more and better praying than we are doing.

More praying will not come as a matter of course. The campaign for the twentieth or thirtieth century fund will hinder our praying if we are not careful. Nothing but a specific effort from a praying leadership will avail. The chief ones must lead in the apostolic effort to root, or plant deeply, the vital importance and fact of prayer in the heart and life of the church. Only praying leaders can have praying followers. Praying apostles will beget praying saints. A praying pulpit will beget praying pews. We greatly need somebody who can set the saints to this business of praying. We are not a generation of praying saints. Non-praying saints are a beggarly gang of saints who have neither the zeal nor the beauty nor the power of saints. Who will restore this breach? He who can set the church to praying will be the greatest of reformers and apostles.

We put it as our most sober judgment that the great need of the church in this and all ages is men of commanding faith, unsullied holiness, marked spiritual vigor, and consuming zeal. Their prayers, faith, lives, and ministry will be of such a radical and aggressive form as to work spiritual revolutions that will form eras in individual and church life.

We do not need men who arouse sensational stirs by novel devices, nor do we need those who attract by a pleasing entertainment. Rather, we need men who can stir things, work revolutions by the preaching of God's Word, and, by the power of the Holy

Spirit, cause revolutions that change the whole current of events. Natural ability and educational advantages do not figure as factors in this matter. However, capacity for faith, the ability to pray, the power of thorough consecration, and the ability of self-denial are all important factors. Also required are an absolute losing of oneself in God's glory and an ever present and insatiable yearning and seeking after all the fullness of God. We need men who can set the church ablaze for God, not in a noisy, showy way, but with an intense and quiet heat that melts and moves everything for God.

God can work wonders if He has a suitable man. Men can work wonders if they let God lead them. The full endowment of the Spirit that turned the world upside down would be eminently useful in these latter days. Men who can stir things mightily for God, whose spiritual revolutions change the whole aspect of things, are the universal need of the church.

The church has never been without these men. They adorn its history. They are the standing miracles of the divinity of the church. Their example and history are an unfailing inspiration and blessing. An increase in their number and power should be our desire.

That which has been done in spiritual matters can be done again, and be better done. This was Christ's view. He said,

> *Verily, verily, I say unto you, He that believeth on me, the works that I do shall he do also; and greater works than these shall he do; because I go unto my Father.* (John 14:12)

The past has not exhausted the possibilities nor the demands for doing great things for God. The church that is dependent on its past history for its miracles of power and grace is a fallen church.

God wants elect men, men of whom self and the world have been severely crucified. Their bankruptcy has so totally ruined self and the world that there is neither hope nor desire of recovery. God wants men who by this insolvency and crucifixion have turned toward Him with perfect hearts.

Let us pray ardently that God's promise to prayer may be more than realized.

Book
Seven

The Weapon of
Prayer

1

Why Prayer Is Important to God

Then shalt thou call, and the LORD shall answer; thou shalt cry, and he shall say, Here I am....Then shalt thou delight thyself in the LORD; and I will cause thee to ride upon the high places of the earth, and feed thee with the heritage of Jacob thy father: for the mouth of the LORD hath spoken it.
—Isaiah 58:9, 14

IT must never be forgotten that Almighty God rules this world. He is not an absentee God. His hand is always on the controls of human affairs. He is present everywhere in the concerns of time. *"His eyes behold, his eyelids try, the children of men"* (Ps. 11:4). He rules the world just as He rules the church—through prayer. This lesson needs to be taught and taught again to men and women. Then this lesson will affect the consciences of those whose eyes have no vision for eternal things, whose ears are deaf toward God.

In dealing with mankind, nothing is more important to God than prayer. Prayer is likewise of great importance to people. Failure to pray is failure in all of life. It is failure of duty, service, and spiritual progress. It is only by prayer that God can help people. He who does not pray, therefore, robs himself of God's help and places God where He cannot help people.

We must pray to God if love for God is to exist. Faith and hope and patience and all the strong, beautiful, vital forces of piety are withered and dead in a prayerless life. An individual believer's life, his personal salvation, and his personal Christian graces have their being, bloom, and fruit in prayer.

All this and much more can be said about how prayer is necessary to the life and piety of the individual. But prayer has a larger sphere, a loftier inspiration, a higher duty. Prayer concerns God, whose purposes and plans are conditioned on prayer. His will and His glory are bound up in praying. The days of God's splendor and renown have always been the great days of prayer. God's great movements in this world have been conditioned on, continued by, and fashioned by prayer. God has put Himself in these great movements just as men and women have prayed. Present, prevailing, conspicuous, and overcoming prayer has always brought God's presence. The real and obvious test of a genuine work of God is the prevalence of the spirit of prayer. God's mightiest forces fill and permeate a movement when prayer's mightiest forces are there.

God's movement to bring Israel from Egyptian bondage had its inception in prayer. (See Exodus 2:23–25; 3:9.) Thus, it was early in history when God made prayer one of the granite forces upon which His world movements would be based.

Hannah's petition for a son (see 1 Samuel 1:11) began a great prayer movement for God in Israel. Praying women, like Hannah, whose prayers can give men like Samuel to the cause of God, do more for the church and the world than all the politicians on earth. People born of prayer are the saviors of the state, and people saturated with prayer give life and impetus to the church. Under God they are saviors and helpers of both church and state.

We must believe that the divine record about prayer and God is given in order that we might be constantly reminded of Him. And we are ever refreshed by the knowledge that God holds His church and that God's purpose will be fulfilled. His plans concerning the church will most assuredly and inevitably be carried out. That record of God has been given without doubt; therefore, we may be deeply impressed that the prayers of God's saints are a great factor, a supreme factor, in carrying forward God's work with ease and in time. When the church is in the condition of prayer, God's cause always flourishes, and His kingdom on earth always triumphs. When the church fails to pray, God's cause decays, and evil of every kind prevails.

In other words, God works through the prayers of His people, and when they fail Him at this point, decline and deadness follow. It is according to the divine plan that spiritual prosperity comes through the prayer channel. Praying saints are God's agents for carrying on His saving and providential work on earth. If His agents fail

Him, neglecting to pray, then His work fails. Praying agents of the Most High are always forerunners of spiritual prosperity.

In all ages, those who have led the church of God have had a full and rich ministry of prayer. In the Bible, the rulers of the church had preeminence in prayer. They may have been eminent in culture, intellect, and all human abilities, or they may have been lowly in physical attainments and natural gifts. Yet, in each case prayer was the all-powerful force in the leadership of the church. This was so because God was with them in what they did, for prayer always carries us back to God. It recognizes God and brings God into the world to work and to save and to bless. The most effective agents in spreading the knowledge of God, in performing His work on the earth, and in standing as a barrier against the billows of evil, have been praying church leaders. God depends on them, employs them, and blesses them.

Prayer cannot be retired as a secondary force in this world. To do so is to retire God from moving in our lives. It is to make God secondary. The prayer ministry is an all-engaging force; it must be all-engaging to be a force at all. Prayer is the sense of a need for God and the call for God's help to supply that need. How we estimate and place prayer is how we estimate and place God. To give prayer a secondary place is to make God secondary in life's affairs. To substitute other forces for prayer excludes God and materializes the whole movement.

Prayer is absolutely necessary if we want to carry on God's work properly. God has intended it to be so. The Twelve in the early church knew the importance of prayer. In fact, when they heard the complaint that certain widows had been neglected in the daily distribution, they did not handle it all by themselves. (See Acts 6:1–2.) The Twelve called all the disciples together and told them to select seven men, *"full of the Holy Ghost and wisdom"* (Acts 6:3), whom they would appoint over that benevolent work. They added this important statement: *"But we will give ourselves continually to prayer, and to the ministry of the word"* (Acts 6:4). They surely realized that the success of the Word and the progress of the church were dependent in a preeminent sense on their giving themselves to prayer. God could effectively work through them in proportion to how much they gave themselves to prayer.

The apostles were as dependent on prayer as everyone else. Sacred work or church activities may make us so busy that they hinder praying; and when this is the case, evil always results. It is

527

better to let the work go by default than to let the praying go by neglect. Whatever affects the intensity of our praying affects the value of our work. "Too busy to pray" is not only the keynote to backsliding, but it mars even the work that is done.

Nothing is done well without prayer for the simple reason that it leaves God out of the work. It is so easy to be seduced by the good to the neglect of the best, until both the good and the best perish. How easily believers, even leaders of the church, are led by the deceptive wiles of Satan to cut short their praying in the interests of the work! How easy it is to neglect prayer or abbreviate our praying simply by the excuse that we have church work on our hands. When he can keep us too busy to stop and pray, Satan has effectively disarmed us.

"We will give ourselves continually to prayer, and to the ministry of the word" (Acts 6:4). The Revised Version states, *"We will continue stedfastly in prayer."* The implication of the word *continue* is to be strong, steadfast, to be devoted to, to keep at it with constant care, to make a business out of it. We find the same word in Colossians 4:2, which reads, *"Continue in prayer, and watch in the same with thanksgiving."* We also find it in Romans 12:12, which is translated, *"Continuing instant in prayer."*

The apostles were under the law of prayer. This law recognizes God as God and depends on Him to do what He would not do without prayer. They were under the necessity of prayer, just as all believers are, in every age and in every place. They had to be devoted to prayer in order to make their ministry of the Word effective. The business of preaching is worth very little unless it is in direct partnership with the business of praying. Apostolic preaching cannot be carried on unless there is apostolic praying.

Alas, this plain truth has been easily forgotten by those who minister in holy things! Without in any way passing a criticism on the ministry, I feel it is high time that somebody declared to ministers that effective preaching cannot take place without effective praying. The preaching that is most successful comes from a ministry that prays much. Perhaps one might go so far as to say that such a ministry is the only kind that is successful. God can mightily use the preacher who prays. He is God's chosen messenger for good, and the Holy Spirit delights to honor him. A praying preacher is God's effective agent in saving sinners and in edifying saints.

In Acts 6:1–8 we have the record of how, long ago, the apostles felt that they were losing—indeed, had lost—apostolic power because they were involved in certain duties that prevented them from praying more. So they called everything to a halt. They had discovered, to their regret, that they were too deficient in praying. Doubtless, they had kept up the form of praying, but it was seriously lacking in intensity and in the amount of time given to it. Their minds were too preoccupied with the finances of the church.

Likewise, even in the church today, we find both laymen and ministers so busily engaged in "serving" that they are glaringly deficient in praying. In fact, in present-day church affairs, people are considered religious if they give largely of their money to the church; and people are chosen for official positions, not because they are people of prayer, but because they have the ability to run church finances and to get money for the church.

Now, when these apostles looked into this matter, they determined to put aside these hindrances resulting from church finances, and they resolved to give themselves to prayer. Not that these finances were to be ignored or set aside, but ordinary laymen, *"full of faith and of the Holy Ghost"* (Acts 6:5), could work with the finances. These men were to be truly religious men who could easily attend to these financial matters without it affecting their piety or their praying in the least. They would thus have something to do in the church, and at the same time they could take the burden off of the apostles. In turn, the apostles would be able to pray more. Praying more, they themselves would be blessed in soul, and they would be more effective in the work to which they had been called.

The apostles realized, too, as they had not realized before, that they were being so pressured by attention to material things, things right in themselves, that they could not pray fully. They could not give to prayer that strength, zeal, and time that its nature and importance demand.

Likewise, we will discover, under close scrutiny of ourselves sometimes, that legitimate and commendable things may so engross our attention that prayer is omitted, or at least very little time is given to it.

How easy to slip away from the prayer closet! Even the apostles had to guard themselves at that point. How closely we need to watch ourselves at the same place! Things legitimate and right may become wrong when they take the place of prayer. Things right in themselves may become wrong things when they are allowed to fasten themselves excessively upon our hearts. It is not only the sinful things that hurt prayer. It is not only questionable things that are to be guarded against, but it is also things that are right in their places but that are allowed to sidetrack prayer and shut the door of the prayer closet, often with the self-comforting plea that "we are too busy to pray."

Possibly, busyness has had as much to do with the breaking down of family prayer in this age as any other cause. Busyness has caused family religion to decay, and busyness is one cause of the decline of the prayer meeting. Men and women are too busy with legitimate things to give themselves to prayer. Other things are given the right-of-way. Prayer is set aside. Business comes first. And this does not always mean that prayer is second, but oftentimes prayer is left out entirely.

The apostles tackled this problem, and they determined that not even church business would affect their praying habits. Prayer had to come first; then they would be God's real agents in His world, in deed and truth. God could work effectively through them because they prayed and thereby put themselves directly in line with His plans and purposes. And His plan and purpose is to work through people who pray.

When the complaint about the daily distribution came to the apostles' ears, they discovered that their work had not been accomplishing fully the divine ends of peace, gratitude, and unity. On the contrary, discontent, complaining, and division were the result of their work, which had far too little prayer in it. So they promptly restored prayer to its rightful prominence.

Praying men and women are a necessity in carrying out God's plan for saving sinners. God has made it so. God established prayer as a divine ordinance, and therefore we are to pray. The fact that God has so often employed men and women of prayer to accomplish His plans clearly proves we are to pray. It is unnecessary to name all the instances in which God used the prayers of righteous men and women to carry out His gracious designs. Time and space are too limited for the list. However, I will name one or two cases.

In the case of the golden calf, God purposed to destroy the Israelites because of their great sin of idolatry. (See Deuteronomy 9:12–21.) While Moses was receiving the law at God's hands, Aaron was swept away by the strong, popular tide of unbelief and sin. The very being of Israel was imperiled. All seemed lost except Moses and prayer, and prayer became more effective and wonder-working on behalf of Israel than Aaron's rod. God determined to destroy Israel and Aaron, for His anger grew hot. It was a fearful and critical hour. But prayer was the levee that held back heaven's desolating fury. God's hand was held fast by the prayers of Moses, the mighty intercessor.

Moses was set on delivering Israel. He prayed for forty days and forty nights; it was a long and exhaustive struggle. Not for one moment did he relax his hold on God. Not for one moment did he leave his place at the feet of God, even for food. Not for one moment did he moderate his demand or ease his cry. Israel's existence was in the balance. The wrath of Almighty God had to be stayed. Israel had to be saved at all cost. And Israel *was* saved. Moses would not let God alone. And so, today, we can look back and give the credit for the present race of the Jews to the praying of Moses centuries ago.

Persevering prayer always wins; God yields to persistence and fidelity. He has no heart to say no to praying such as Moses did. God's purpose to destroy Israel was actually changed by the praying of this man of God. This illustrates how much just one praying person is worth in this world, and how much depends on him.

Daniel, in Babylon, refused to obey the decree of the king. (See Daniel 6:1–23.) The king had decreed that no one could ask any petition of any god or man for thirty days. But Daniel shut his eyes to the decree that would shut him off from his prayer room; he refused to allow fear of consequences to deter him from calling on God. So, he *"kneeled upon his knees three times a day"* (Dan. 6:10) and prayed as he had done before, putting in God's hands all the consequences of disobeying the king.

There was nothing impersonal about Daniel's praying. It always had an objective, and it was an appeal to a great God who could do all things. Daniel did not pamper himself or look for a feeling to urge him to pray. In the face of the dreadful decree that could hurl him from his high position into the lion's den, *"he kneeled upon his knees three times a day... and gave thanks before his God, as he did aforetime"* (Dan. 6:10). The gracious result was that prayer laid its hands upon an almighty arm, which intervened in that den of vicious lions. God closed their mouths and preserved His servant Daniel, who had been true to Him and who had called on Him for protection.

Daniel's praying was an essential factor in defeating the king's decree and in defeating the wicked, envious rulers who had tried to trap him. They wanted to destroy him and remove him from his powerful position in the kingdom, but Daniel's prayers prevailed!

2

Putting God to Work

From of old no one has heard or perceived by the ear, no eye has seen a God besides thee, who works for those who wait for him.   *—Isaiah 64:4 (RSV)*

WHEN I use the expression, "putting God to work," I mean that God has placed Himself under the law of prayer and has obligated Himself to answer prayer. God has ordained prayer, and He will do things through people as they pray that He would not do otherwise. Prayer is a specific, divine appointment, an ordinance of heaven. By prayer, God purposes to carry out His gracious designs on earth and to execute and make effective the plan of salvation.

When I say that prayer puts God to work, I am simply saying that we have it in our power to move God to work by prayer. Prayer moves God to do works among people—in His own way, of course—that He would not do if the prayers were not made. Thus, while prayer moves God to work, at the same time God puts prayer to work. Since God has ordained prayer, and since prayer involves people and has no existence apart from people, then logically people's prayers are the one force that puts God to work in human affairs.

As we allude to prayer and read about prayer in the Scriptures, let us keep in mind these fundamental truths.

If prayer puts God to work on earth, then, by the same token, prayerlessness excludes God from the world's affairs and prevents Him from working. If prayer moves God to work in this world's affairs, then prayerlessness excludes God from everything concerning people. Prayerlessness leaves man as the mere creature of circumstances, at the mercy of blind fate, and without help of any kind from God. It leaves man with the tremendous responsibilities and difficult problems of the world, with all of its sorrows and burdens and afflictions, without any God at all. In reality, the denial of prayer is the denial of God Himself, for God and prayer are so inseparable that they can never be divorced.

Prayer affects three different spheres of existence: the divine, the angelic, and the human. It puts God to work, it puts angels to work, and it puts people to work. It lays its hands upon God, angels, and people. What a wonderful reach there is in prayer! It brings into play the forces of heaven and earth. God, angels, and people are subjects of this wonderful law of prayer, and all three deal with the possibilities and the results of prayer.

God has placed Himself under the law of prayer to such an extent that He is induced to work among people in a way in which He does not work if they do not pray. Prayer takes hold of God and influences Him to work. This is the meaning of prayer as it concerns God. This is the doctrine of prayer, or else there is no value whatsoever in prayer.

Prayer puts God to work in all things prayed for. While man in his weakness and poverty waits, trusts, and prays, God undertakes the work. *"From of old no one has heard or perceived by the ear, no eye has seen a God besides thee, who works for those who wait for him"* (Isa. 64:4 RSV).

Jesus Christ commits Himself to the force of prayer. *"Whatsoever ye shall ask in my name,"* He says, *"that will I do, that the Father may be glorified in the Son. If ye shall ask any thing in my name, I will do it"* (John 14:13–14). And, again, *"If ye abide in me, and my words abide in you, ye shall ask what ye will, and it shall be done unto you"* (John 15:7).

The promise of God is committed to nothing as strongly as it is to prayer. The purposes of God are not dependent on any other force as much as this force of prayer. The Word of God expounds on the necessity and results of prayer. The work of God halts or advances according to the strength of prayer. Prophets and apostles have urged the utility, force, and necessity of prayer. For example, Isaiah 62:6–7 says,

> *I have set watchmen upon thy walls, O Jerusalem, which shall never hold their peace day nor night: ye that make mention of the LORD, keep not silence. And give him no rest, till he establish, and till he make Jerusalem a praise in the earth.*

Prayer, with its antecedents and attendants, is the one and only condition of the final triumph of the Gospel. The fact that it is the one and only condition honors the Father and glorifies the Son. Little praying and poor praying have weakened Christ's power on earth, postponed the glorious results of His reign, and retired God from His sovereignty.

Prayer puts God's work in His hands and keeps it there. It looks to Him constantly and depends on Him implicitly to further His own cause. Prayer is simply faith resting in, acting with, leaning on, and obeying God. This is why God loves it so well, why He puts all power into its hands, and why He so highly esteems people of prayer.

Every movement for the advancement of the Gospel must be created by and inspired by prayer. Prayer precedes and accompanies all the movements of God as an invariable and necessary condition.

In this sense, God makes prayer identical in force and power with Himself, and He says to those on earth who pray, "You are on the earth to carry on My cause. I am in heaven, the Lord of all, the Maker of all, the Holy One of all. Now, whatever you need for My cause, ask Me, and I will do it. Shape the future by your prayers, and concerning all that you need for present supplies, command Me (Isa. 45:11). I made heaven and earth and all things in them (Acts 14:15). Ask for great things. *'Open thy mouth wide, and I will fill it'* (Ps. 81:10). It is My work that you are doing. It concerns My cause. Be prompt and full in praying. Do not abate your asking, and I will not wince or abate My giving."

Everywhere in His Word, God bases His actions on prayer. Everywhere in His Word, His actions and attitude are shaped by prayer. To quote all the scriptural passages that prove the direct relationship of prayer to God, would be to transfer whole pages of the Bible to this study. Man has personal relations with God, and prayer is the divinely appointed means by which man comes into direct connection with God. By His own ordinance, God binds Himself to hear our prayers. God bestows His great blessings on His children when they seek them along the avenue of prayer.

When Solomon closed his great prayer that he offered at the dedication of the temple, God appeared to him, approved him, and laid down the universal principles of His actions. In 2 Chronicles 7:12-15 we read as follows:

And the LORD appeared to Solomon by night, and said unto him, I have heard thy prayer, and have chosen this place to myself for an house of sacrifice. If I shut up heaven that there be no rain, or if I command the locusts to devour the land, or if I send pestilence among my people; if my people, which are called by my name, shall humble themselves, and pray, and seek my face, and turn from their wicked ways; then will I hear from heaven, and will forgive their sin, and will heal their land. Now mine eyes shall be open, and mine ears attent unto the prayer that is made in this place.

In His purposes concerning the Jews in the Babylonian captivity, God asserts His unfailing principles:

For thus saith the LORD, That after seventy years be accomplished at Babylon I will visit you, and perform my good word toward you, in causing you to return to this place. For I know the thoughts that I think toward you, saith the LORD, thoughts of peace, and not of evil, to give you an expected end. Then shall ye call upon me, and ye shall go and pray unto me, and I will hearken unto you. And ye shall seek me, and find me, when ye shall search for me with all your heart.
(Jer. 29:10–13)

In Bible terminology, prayer means calling on God for things we desire, asking God for things. Thus, we read: *"Call unto me, and I will answer thee, and show thee great and mighty things, which thou knowest not"* (Jer. 33:3). *"Call upon me in the day of trouble: I will deliver thee"* (Ps. 50:15). *"Then shalt thou call, and the LORD shall answer; thou shalt cry, and he shall say, Here I am"* (Isa. 58:9).

Prayer is revealed as a direct application to God for some temporal or spiritual good. It is an appeal to God to intervene in life's affairs for the good of those for whom we pray. God is recognized as the source and fountain of all good, and prayer implies that all His good is held in His keeping for those who call on Him in truth.

The fact that prayer is an appeal to God, communication with God, and communion with God, comes out strongly and simply in the praying of Old Testament saints. Abraham's intercession for Sodom is a striking illustration of the nature of prayer. (See Genesis 18:20–33; 19:24–25.) It is an example of communication with

God and intercession for man. Abraham encountered God's plan to destroy Sodom, and his soul within him was greatly moved because of his great interest in that fated city. His nephew and family resided there. God's purpose to destroy the city had to be changed; God's decree to destroy its evil inhabitants had to be revoked.

It was no small undertaking that faced Abraham when he decided to beseech God to spare Sodom. Abraham set about to change God's purpose and to save Sodom along with the other cities of the plain. It was certainly a most difficult and delicate work for him— to undertake using his influence with God to save those doomed cities.

He used the plea that there may be righteous people in Sodom, and he appealed to the infinite uprightness of God not to destroy the righteous with the wicked: *"That be far from thee to do after this manner, to slay the righteous with the wicked....Shall not the Judge of all the earth do right?"* (Gen. 18:25). With what deep self-abasement and reverence did Abraham begin his high and divine work! He stood before God in solemn awe and meditation, and then he drew near to God and spoke. He asked God to spare Sodom if there were fifty righteous people in the city, and he kept reducing the number until it was down to ten. He advanced step by step in faith, in demand, and in urgency, and God granted every request that he made.

It has been well said that Abraham stopped asking before God stopped granting. It seems that Abraham had a kind of optimistic view of the piety of Sodom. He scarcely expected when he undertook this matter to have it end in failure. He was very much in earnest, and he had every encouragement to press his case. When he made his final request, he thought that surely with Lot, his wife, his daughters, his sons, and his sons-in-law, he had his ten righteous people for whose sake God would spare the city. But, alas! The count failed when the final test came. There were not ten righteous people in that large population.

In his goodness of heart, Abraham overestimated the number of pious people in that city. Otherwise, God might possibly have saved it if he had reduced his figures still further. But this much is true: even if he did not save Sodom by his persistent praying, the purposes of God were postponed for a season.

This is a representative case of Old Testament praying, and it discloses God's mode of working through prayer. It further shows how God is moved to work in this world in answer to prayer, even when it comes to changing His purposes concerning a sinful community. This praying of Abraham was no mere performance—no dull, lifeless ceremony—but an earnest plea, a strong entreaty, one person with another Person. Its purpose was to have an influence, to secure a desired end.

How full of meaning is this remarkable series of intercessions made by Abraham! Here we have arguments designed to convince God; here we have pleas to persuade God to change His purpose. We see deep humility, but we see holy boldness and perseverance as well. We see how Abraham kept advancing in his requests because God kept granting each petition. Here we have large requests encouraged by large answers. God stays and answers as long as Abraham stays and asks. To Abraham, God is existent, approachable, and all-powerful; furthermore, He defers to people, acts favorably on their desires, and grants them favors asked for. Not to pray is to deny God—to deny His existence, His nature, and His purposes toward mankind.

God has given us specific prayer promises and has outlined their breadth, certainty, and limitations. Jesus Christ urges us into the presence of God with these prayer promises by the assurance not only that God will answer, but that no other being but God can answer. He urges us toward God because only by prayer can we move God to take a hand in earth's affairs and induce Him to intervene on our behalf.

Jesus said, *"All things, whatsoever ye shall ask in prayer, believing, ye shall receive"* (Matt. 21:22). This all-inclusive condition not only urges us to pray for all things, everything great and small, but it points us to and limits us to God. Who but God can cover the whole range of universal things? Who but God gives us the whole thesaurus of earthly and heavenly good from which to ask? Who but God can assure us with certainty that we will receive the very thing for which we ask?

It is Jesus Christ, the Son of God, who commands us to pray, and it is He who puts Himself and all He has so fully in the answer. It is He who puts Himself at our service and answers our demands when we pray. Jesus puts Himself and the Father at our command in prayer; He promises to come directly into our lives and to work for our good. Also, He promises to answer the demands of two or more believers who agree in prayer about any one thing. *"If two of you shall agree on earth as touching any thing that they shall ask, it shall be done for them of my Father which is in heaven"* (Matt. 18:19). None but God could put Himself in a covenant so binding as that, for only God could fulfill such a promise and reach to its exacting and all-controlling demands. Only God can keep these promises.

God needs prayer, and people need prayer, too. It is indispensable to God's work in this world, and it is essential to getting God to work in earth's affairs. So, God binds people to pray by the most solemn obligations. God commands people to pray; therefore, not to pray is plain disobedience to an imperative command of Almighty God. Prayer is such a prerequisite that the graces, the salvation, and the good of God are not bestowed on us unless we pray. Prayer is a high privilege, a royal prerogative. Manifold and eternal are the losses if we fail to exercise it. Prayer is the great, universal force that advances God's cause, the reverence that hallows God's name, and the establishment of God's kingdom in human hearts. These are created and affected by prayer.

One of the essential fortifiers of the Gospel is prayer. Without prayer, the Gospel can neither be preached effectively, proclaimed faithfully, experienced in the heart, nor practiced in the life. The reason is very simple: by leaving prayer out of the catalog of religious duties, we leave God out, too, and His work cannot progress without Him.

The things God purposed to do under King Cyrus of Persia, prophesied by Isaiah many years before Cyrus was born, were conditioned on prayer. God declares His purpose, power, independence, and defiance of obstacles, but His people still must pray. His omnipotent and absolutely infinite power encourages prayer. He has been ordering all events, directing all conditions, and creating all things so that He might answer prayer, and then He turns Himself over to His praying ones to be commanded. Then all the results and power He holds in His hands will be bestowed in lavish and unmeasured generosity to answer prayers and to make prayer the mightiest energy in the world.

The passage concerning Cyrus in Isaiah 45 is too lengthy to be quoted in its entirety, but it is well worth reading. It closes with strong words about prayer, words that are the climax of all that God says concerning His purposes in connection with Cyrus:

> *Thus saith the LORD, the Holy One of Israel, and his Maker,*
> *Ask me of things to come concerning my sons, and concerning*

the work of my hands command ye me. I have made the earth,
and created man upon it: I, even my hands, have stretched out
the heavens, and all their host have I commanded.

(Isa. 45:11–12)

The book of Job also tells of the importance of prayer. In the conclusion of the story of Job, we see how God intervenes on behalf of Job and tells his friends to present themselves before Job so that he may pray for them. *"My wrath is kindled against thee* [Eliphaz], *and against thy two friends"* (Job 42:7) is God's statement, with the further words added, *"My servant Job shall pray for you: for him will I accept"* (Job 42:8). It is a striking illustration of God intervening to deliver Job's friends in answer to Job's prayer.

I have heretofore spoken of prayer affecting God, angels, and people. Christ wrote no books while living. Memoranda, notes, sermon writing, and sermon making were alien to Him. Autobiography was not to His taste. The revelation to John was His last utterance. In the book of Revelation, we have a depiction of the great importance, the priceless value, and the high position that prayer has in the progress of God's church in the world. This depiction reveals the angels' interest in the prayers of the saints and in accomplishing the answers to those prayers:

And another angel came and stood at the altar, having a
golden censer; and there was given unto him much incense,
that he should offer it with the prayers of all saints upon the
golden altar which was before the throne. And the smoke of
the incense, which came with the prayers of the saints, as-
cended up before God out of the angel's hand. And the angel
took the censer, and filled it with fire of the altar, and cast it
into the earth: and there were voices, and thunderings, and
lightnings, and an earthquake.   *(Rev. 8:3–5)*

Translated into the prose of everyday life, these words show how the business of salvation is carried on by and made up of the prayers of God's saints on earth. The passage discloses how these prayers come back to earth in flaming power and produce mighty commotions, influences, and revolutions.

Praying men and women are essential to Almighty God in all His plans and purposes. God's plans, secrets, and cause have never been committed to prayerless people. Neglect of prayer has always brought loss of faith and loss of love. Failure to pray has been the destructive, inevitable cause of backsliding and estrangement from God. Prayerless people have stood in the way of God's fulfilling His Word and doing His will on earth. They tie the divine hands and interfere with God in His gracious designs. As praying people are a help to God, so prayerless people are a hindrance to Him.

I stress the scriptural view of the necessity of prayer even at the cost of repeating myself. The subject is too important for repetition to weaken or tire, too vital to be trite or tame. We must feel it anew. The fires of prayer have burned low. Ashes, not flames, are on its altars.

No insistence in the Scriptures is more pressing than that we must pray. No exhortation is more often reiterated, none is more hearty, none is more solemn and stirring, than to pray. No principle is more strongly and broadly declared than that which urges us to pray. There is no duty to which we are more strongly obliged than that of praying. There is no command more imperative and insistent than that of praying. Are you praying in everything without ceasing (1 Thess. 5:17)? Are you praying in your prayer closet, hidden from the eyes of others? Are you praying always and everywhere? These are personal, pertinent, and all-important questions for every soul.

God's Word shows us, through many examples, that God intervenes in this world in answer to prayer. How clear it is, when the Bible is consulted, that the almighty God is brought directly into the things of this world by the prayers of His people. Jonah fled from duty and took ship for a distant port, but God followed him. By a strange providence this disobedient prophet was cast out of the ship, and the God who sent him to Nineveh prepared a fish to swallow him. In the fish's belly he cried out to the God against whom he had sinned, and God intervened and caused the fish to vomit Jonah out onto dry land. Even the fishes of the great deep are subject to the law of prayer.

Likewise, the birds of the air are subject to this same law. Elijah had foretold to Ahab the coming of a prolonged drought, and food and water became scarce. God sent him to the brook Cherith and said to him,

> *It shall be, that thou shalt drink of the brook; and I have commanded the ravens to feed thee there. And the ravens*

> *brought him bread and flesh in the morning, and bread and*
> *flesh in the evening; and he drank of the brook.*
> *(1 Kings 17:4, 6)*

This is a man who later shut and opened the rain clouds by prayer. Can anyone doubt that this man of God was praying at this time, when so much was at stake? God intervened through the birds of the air this time, and He strangely moved them to take care of His servant so that he would not lack food and water.

David, in an evil hour, instead of listening to the advice of Joab, his prime minister, yielded to the suggestion of Satan. (See 1 Chronicles 21:1–14.) He took a census, thus displeasing God. So, God told him to choose one of three evils as a retribution for his folly and sin. He chose pestilence. Pestilence came among the people in violent form, and David went to prayer.

> *And David said unto God, Is it not I that commanded the*
> *people to be numbered? even I it is that have sinned and done*
> *evil indeed; but as for these sheep, what have they done? let*
> *thine hand, I pray thee, O LORD my God, be on me, and on my*
> *father's house; but not on thy people, that they should be*
> *plagued.* *(1 Chron. 21:17)*

Although God had been greatly grieved by David's sin, He could not resist this appeal from a penitent and prayerful spirit. God was moved by prayer to put His hand on the springs of disease and stop the fearful plague. God was put to work by David's prayer.

Numbers of other cases could be named, but these are sufficient. God seems to have taken great pains in His Word to show how He interferes in human affairs in answer to the prayers of His saints.

At this point a question might arise in some overcritical minds about the so-called "laws of nature." Those who raise this question are not strong believers in prayer; they think there is a conflict between what they call the laws of nature and the law of prayer. These people make nature a sort of imaginary god entirely separate from the almighty God. What is nature anyway? It is but the creation of God, the Maker of all things. And what are the laws of nature but the laws of God, through which He governs the material world? Since the law of prayer is also the law of God, there cannot possibly be any conflict between the two sets of laws, but prayer and nature must work in perfect harmony.

Prayer does not violate any natural law. God may set aside one law for the higher working of another law, and this He may do when He answers prayer. Or, God may answer prayer by working through the course of natural law. But, whether we understand it or not, God is over and above all nature. He can and will answer prayer in a wise, intelligent, and just manner, even though man may not comprehend it. So, in no sense is there any conflict between God's different laws when God intervenes in human affairs in answer to prayer.

Along this line of thought, another word might be said. I wrote something to which there can be no objection: prayer accomplishes things. However, it is not prayer itself that accomplishes things, but it is God working through it. Prayer is the instrument; God is the active agent. Prayer itself does not interfere in earth's affairs, but prayer moves God to intervene and do things. Prayer moves God to do things that He would not otherwise do.

It is like saying, *"faith hath saved thee"* (Luke 7:50). This simply means that God, through the faith of the sinner, saves him, faith being only the instrument that brings salvation to him.

3

The Necessity for Praying People

Praying always with all prayer and supplication in the Spirit, and watching thereunto with all perseverance and supplication for all saints. —Ephesians 6:18

Withal praying also for us, that God would open unto us a door of utterance, to speak the mystery of Christ, for which I am also in bonds: that I may make it manifest, as I ought to speak. —Colossians 4:3–4

ONE of the most pressing needs in our day is for people whose faith, prayers, and study of the Word of God have been vitalized. We need people whose hearts have written on them a transcript of the Word. We need people who will give forth the Word as the incorruptible seed that lives and abides forever. (See 1 Peter 1:23.)

A critical unbelief has eclipsed the Word of God. Nothing more is needed to clear up this haze than for the pulpit to pledge unwavering allegiance to the Bible and to fearlessly proclaim its truth. Without this the preacher fails, and his congregation becomes confused and unstable. The pulpit has done its mightiest work in the days of its unswerving loyalty to the Word of God.

In close connection with this, we must have preachers of prayer, preachers in high and low places who hold to and practice scriptural praying. While the pulpit must hold to its unswerving loyalty to the Word of God, it must, at the same time, be loyal to the doctrine of prayer, which that same Word illustrates and enforces upon mankind.

Christian schools, colleges, and education, considered simply as such, cannot be regarded as leaders in carrying forward the work of God's kingdom in the world. They have neither the right, the will, nor the power to do the work. This is to be accomplished by the preached Word, delivered in the power of the Holy Spirit sent down from heaven, sown with prayerful hands, and watered with the tears of praying hearts. This is the divine law, and we must follow it. We will follow the Lord.

Men and women are needed for the great work of soul-saving, and they are commanded to go. (See Mark 16:15.) It is no angelic or impersonal force that is needed. Human hearts baptized with the spirit of prayer must bear the burden of this message. Human tongues on fire as the result of earnest, persistent prayer must declare the Word of God to dying people.

The church today needs praying people to meet the fearful crisis that is facing her. The crying need of the times is for people in increased numbers—God-fearing people, praying people, Holy Spirit people, people who can endure hardship. We need people who will not count their lives dear unto themselves (see Acts 20:24) but count all things as loss for the excellency of the knowledge of Jesus Christ, the Savior. (See Philippians 3:8.) The people who are so greatly needed in this age of the church are those who have learned the business of praying—learned it on their knees, learned it in the need and agony of their own hearts.

Praying people are the one commanding need of this day, as of all other days, if God is to intervene in the world. People who pray are, in reality, the only religious people. People of prayer are the only people who can, and do, represent God in this world. No cold, irreligious, prayerless person can claim the right. He misrepresents God in all His work and all His plans.

Praying people are the only people who have influence with God, the only people to whom God commits Himself and His Gospel. Praying people are the only people in whom the Holy Spirit dwells, for the Holy Spirit and prayer go hand in hand. The Holy Spirit never descends upon prayerless people. He never fills them. He never empowers them. There is nothing whatsoever in common between the Spirit of God and people who do not pray. The Spirit dwells only in an atmosphere of prayer.

In doing God's work there is no substitute for praying. People of prayer cannot be replaced with other kinds of people. People of financial skill, people of education, people of worldly influence—none of these can possibly substitute for people of prayer. The life, the vigor, and the motive power of God's work is formed by praying people. A diseased heart is not a more fearful symptom of approaching death than non-praying people are of spiritual atrophy.

The people to whom Jesus Christ committed the fortunes and destiny of His church were people of prayer. To no other kind of people has God ever committed Himself. The apostles were pre-eminently men of prayer. They gave themselves to prayer. They made praying their chief business. It was first in importance and first in results. God never has, and He never will, commit the weighty interests of His kingdom to people who do not make prayer a conspicuous and controlling factor in their lives.

People who do not pray never rise to any eminence of piety. People of piety are always people of prayer. People are never noted for the simplicity and strength of their faith unless they are pre-eminently people of prayer. Piety flourishes nowhere so rapidly and so profusely as in the prayer closet. The prayer closet is the garden of faith.

The apostles allowed no duty, however sacred, to so busy them that it infringed on their time and prevented them from making prayer the main thing. The Word of God was ministered with apostolic fidelity and zeal. It was spoken by people with apostolic commissions, people who had been baptized by the fiery tongues of Pentecost. The Word was pointless and powerless unless people were freshly clothed with power by continuous and mighty prayer. The seed of God's Word must be saturated in prayer to make it germinate. It grows more readily and anchors more deeply when it is soaked with prayer.

The apostles were praying people themselves. They were also teachers of prayer, and they trained their disciples in the school of prayer. They urged their disciples to pray, not only that they might attain to the loftiest eminence of faith, but that they might be the most powerful factors in advancing God's kingdom.

Jesus Christ is the divinely appointed leader of God's people, and no single thing in His life proves His eminent fitness for that office as much as His habit of prayer. Nothing is more food for thought than Christ's continual praying, and nothing is more conspicuous about Him than prayer. His campaigns were arranged, His victories gained, in the struggles and communion of His all-night praying. His praying rent the heavens. Moses and Elijah and the Transfiguration glory waited on His praying. His miracles and His teaching had their force from the same source. Gethsemane's praying crimsoned Calvary with serenity and glory. His prayer made the history and hastens the triumphs of His church. What an inspiration and command to pray is Christ's life! What a comment on its worth! How He shames our lives by His praying!

Like all those who have drawn God nearer to the world and lifted the world nearer to God, Jesus was a man of prayer. God made Him a leader and commander of His people. His leadership was one of prayer. A great leader He was, because He was great in prayer.

All great leaders for God have fashioned their leadership in the wrestlings of their prayer closets. Many great people have led and molded the church without being great in prayer, but they were great only in their plans, great for their opinions, great for their organization, great by natural gifts, great by genius or character. However, they were not great for God.

But Jesus Christ was a great leader for God. His was the great leadership of great praying. God was greatly in His leadership because prayer was greatly in it. We would do well to be taught by Him to pray, and to pray more and more.

Herein has been the secret of the people of prayer in the past history of the church: their hearts were after God, their desires were on Him, and their prayers were addressed to Him. They communed with Him, sought nothing of the world, sought great things of God, wrestled with Him, conquered all opposing forces, and opened up the channel of faith deep and wide between themselves and heaven. And all this was done by the use of prayer. Holy meditations, spiritual desires, heavenly longings—these swayed their intellects, enriched their emotions, and filled and enlarged their hearts. And all this was so because they were, first of all, people of prayer.

The people who have thus communed with God and have sought after Him with their whole hearts have always risen to consecrated eminence. In fact, no person has ever risen to this eminence without his flames of holy desire all dying to the world and all glowing for God and heaven. Nor have they ever risen to the heights of higher spiritual experiences unless prayer and the spirit of prayer have been conspicuous and controlling factors in their lives.

The entire consecration of many of God's children stands out distinctly like towering mountain peaks. Why is this? How did they ascend to these heights? What brought them so near to God? What made them so Christlike? The answer is easy—prayer. They prayed much, prayed long, and drank deeper and deeper still. They asked, they sought, and they knocked, until heaven opened its richest inner treasures of grace to them. Prayer was the Jacob's Ladder by which they scaled those holy and blessed heights and by which the angels of God came down and ministered to them.

The men and women of spiritual character and strength always valued prayer. They took time to be alone with God. Their praying was no hurried performance. They had many serious needs to be relieved and many weighty pleas to offer. They had to secure many great answers to prayer. They had to do much silent waiting before God, and much patient asking and asking over again. Prayer was the only channel through which the supply of their needs came, and it was the only way to utter pleas.

The only acceptable waiting before God of which they knew anything was prayer. They valued praying. It was more precious to them than all jewels, more excellent than any good, and more valued than the greatest good of earth. They esteemed it, valued it, and prized it. They pressed it to its farthest limits, tested its greatest results, and secured its most glorious heritage. To them prayer was the one great thing to be appreciated and used.

The apostles, above everything else, were praying people, and they left the stamp of their prayer example and teaching upon the early church. But the apostles are dead, and times and people have changed. They have no successors by official assignment or heirship. And we do not have a commission, in our times, to make other apostles. No, the apostles' successors are those who pray.

Unfortunately, the times are not prayerful times. God's cause just now is in dire need of praying leaders. Other things may be needed, but this is the crying demand of these times and the urgent, first need of the church.

This is the day of great wealth and wonderful material resources in the church. But, unfortunately, the abundance of material resources is a great enemy and a severe hindrance to strong spiritual forces. It is an invariable law that the presence of attractive and influential material resources creates a trust in them and, by the same inevitable law, creates distrust in the spiritual forces of the Gospel. They are two masters that cannot be served at the same time. (See Matthew 6:24.) For the degree to which the mind is fixed on one, it will be drawn away from the other. The days of great financial prosperity in the church have not been days of great religious prosperity. Wealthy people and praying people are not synonymous terms.

Paul, in the second chapter of his first epistle to Timothy, emphasized the need for people who pray. In his estimation, church leaders are to be conspicuous for their praying. Of necessity, prayer must shape their characters, and prayer must be one of their distinguishing characteristics. Prayer ought to be one of their most powerful elements, so much so that it cannot be hidden. Prayer ought to make church leaders notable. Character, official duty, reputation, and life—all should be shaped by prayer. The mighty forces of prayer lie in its praying leaders in a marked way. The standing obligation to pray rests in a special sense on church leaders. The church would be wise to discover this important truth and give prominence to it.

It can be written as a rule that God needs, first of all, leaders in the church who will put prayer first, people with whom prayer is habitual and characteristic, people who know the primacy of prayer. But, even more than having a habit of prayer, church leaders are to be filled to overflowing with prayer. Their lives should be made and molded by prayer; their hearts should be made up of prayer. These are the people—the only people—God can use in the furtherance of His kingdom and in the implanting of His message in the hearts of men.

4

God's Need
for People Who Pray

We do what He commands. We go where He wants us to go. We speak what He wants us to speak. His will is our law. His pleasure our joy. He is, today, seeking the lost, and He would have us seek with Him. He is shepherding the lambs, and He wants our cooperation. He is opening doors in heathen lands, and He wants our money and our prayers.

—Anonymous

AS we proceed on the subject of prayer, we now declare that it demands prayer leadership to hold the church to God's aims and to prepare it for God's uses. Prayer leadership preserves the spirituality of the church, just as prayerless leaders make for unspiritual conditions. The church is not necessarily spiritual by the mere fact of its existence, nor by its vocation. It is not held to its sacred vocation by generation, nor by succession. Like the new birth, it is *"not of blood, nor of the will of the flesh, nor of the will of man, but of God"* (John 1:13).

The church is not necessarily spiritual because it is concerned with and deals in spiritual values. It may hold its confirmations by the thousand, it may multiply its baptisms, and it may administer its sacraments innumerable times, and yet be as far from fulfilling its true mission as human conditions can make it.

This present world's general attitude retires prayer to insignificance and obscurity. By this attitude, salvation and eternal life are put in the background. It cannot be too often affirmed, therefore, that the principal need of the church is neither people of money nor people of intelligence, but people of prayer. Leaders in the realm of religious activity are to be judged by their praying habits, not by their money or social position. Those who are placed in the forefront of the church's business must be, first of all, people who know how to pray.

God does not conduct His work solely with people of education or wealth or business capacity. Neither can He carry on His work through people of large intellects or great culture, nor yet through people of great social eminence and influence. All these qualities can be useful in God's work, provided they are not regarded as being primary. People possessing only these qualities cannot lead in God's work nor control His cause. People of prayer, before anything else, are indispensable to the furtherance of the kingdom of God on earth. No other sort will fit in the scheme or do the deed. People, great and influential in other things but small in prayer, cannot do the work that God has set out for His church to do in this world.

People who represent God and who stand here in His stead, people who are to build up His kingdom in this world, must be, in an eminent sense, people of prayer. Whatever else they may have, whatever else they may lack, they must be people of prayer. Having everything else and lacking prayer, they will fail. Having prayer and lacking all else, they can succeed. Prayer must be the most conspicuous and the most potent factor in the character and conduct of people who undertake divine commission. God's business requires people who are versed in the business of praying.

It must be kept in mind that the praying to which the disciples of Christ are called by scriptural authority, is a valiant calling. The people God wants and on whom He depends, must work at prayer just as they work at their worldly callings. They must follow through in this business of praying, just as they do in their secular pursuits. Diligence, perseverance, heartiness, and courage must all be in it if it is to succeed.

Everything secured by gospel promise, defined by gospel measure, and represented by gospel treasure is in prayer. All heights are scaled by it, all doors are opened to it, all victories are gained through it, and all grace is obtained through it. Heaven has all its good and all its help for people who pray. How marked and strong is the command of Christ that sends people from the parade of public giving and public praying to the privacy of their prayer closets, where with shut doors and in encircling silence they are alone in prayer with God!

In all ages those who have carried out the divine will on earth have been people of prayer. The days of prayer are God's prosperous days. His heart, His oath, and His glory are committed to one proclamation: that every knee should bow to Him (Phil. 2:10). The Day of the Lord, in a preeminent sense, will be a day of universal prayer.

God's cause does not suffer because of lack of divine ability, but because of lack of prayer ability in man. God's action is just as much bound up in prayer today as it was when He said to Abimelech, "[Abraham] *shall pray for thee, and thou shalt live"* (Gen. 20:7). So it was when God said to Job's friends, *"My servant Job shall pray for you: for him will I accept"* (Job 42:8).

God's great plan for the redemption of mankind depends as much on prayer now as it did when the Father first decreed the plan. Prayer makes the plan of redemption prosper and succeed, for God gives an imperative, universal, and eternal condition: *"Ask of me, and I shall give thee the heathen for thine inheritance, and the uttermost parts of the earth for thy possession"* (Ps. 2:8).

In many places an alarming state of things has come to pass, in that many church members are not praying men and women. Many of those occupying prominent positions in church life are not praying people. It is greatly to be feared that much of the work of the church is being done by those who are perfect strangers to the prayer closet. No wonder the work does not succeed.

While it may be true that many in the church say prayers, it is equally true that their praying is of the stereotyped order. Their prayers may be charged with sentiment, but they are tame, timid, and without fire or force. This sort of praying is even done by some of the few people who attend prayer meetings. Those whose names are found looming large in our great churches are not people noted for their praying habits. Yet, the entire fabric of the work in which they are engaged has to, inevitably, depend on the adequacy of prayer. This lack of praying creates a crisis like that of a country admitting to an invading enemy that it cannot fight and knows nothing about weapons of war.

In all God's plans for human redemption, He purposes that people pray. We are to pray in every place—in the church, in the prayer closet, in the home. We are to pray on sacred days and on secular days. All things are dependent on the measure of people's praying.

Prayer is the mainspring of life. We pray as we live; we live as we pray. Life will never be finer than the quality of the prayer closet. The mercury of life will rise only by the warmth of the prayer closet. Persistent non-praying will eventually depress the temperature of life below zero.

If you were to measure and weigh the conditions of prayer, you would readily discover why more people do not pray. The conditions are so perfect, so blessed, that it is a rare character who can meet them. A heart full of love, a heart that holds even its enemies in loving contemplation and prayerful concern, a heart from which all bitterness, revenge, and envy are purged—how rare! Yet, this is the only condition of mind and heart in which a man can expect to be powerful in prayer.

There are certain conditions laid down for authentic praying. People are to pray, *"lifting up holy hands"* (1 Tim. 2:8), hands here being the symbol of life. Hands unsoiled by stains of evildoing are the emblem of a life unsoiled by sin. With a clean life, people are to come into the presence of God; thus they are to approach the throne of the Highest, where they can *"obtain mercy, and find grace to help in time of need"* (Heb. 4:16).

Here, then, is one reason why people do not pray. They are too worldly in heart and too secular in life to enter the prayer closet; and even though they enter there, they cannot offer the *"effectual fervent prayer of a righteous man* [which] *availeth much"* (James 5:16).

Again, hands are the symbols of supplication. Outstretched hands stand for an appeal for help. It is the silent yet eloquent attitude of a helpless soul standing before God, appealing for mercy and grace. Hands, too, are symbols of activity, power, and conduct. Hands outstretched to God in prayer must be *"holy hands"* (1 Tim. 2:8), unstained hands. The word *holy* here means undefiled, unspotted, untainted, and religiously observing every obligation.

How remote is all this from the character of sin-loving, worldly-minded, fleshly-disposed people, soiled by fleshly lusts, spotted by worldly indulgence, unholy in heart and conduct! "He who seeks equity must do equity" is the maxim of earthly courts. Even so, he who seeks God's good gifts must practice God's good deeds. This is the maxim of heavenly courts.

Prayer is sensitive, and it is always affected by the character and conduct of the one who prays. Water cannot rise above its own level, and a spotless prayer cannot flow from a spotted heart. Straight praying is never born of crooked conduct. The character of a person gives character to his supplication. The cowardly heart cannot do brave praying. Soiled people cannot make clean, pure supplications.

It is neither words, nor thoughts, nor ideas, nor feelings that shape praying, but it is character and conduct. People must walk in an upright fashion in order to be able to pray well. Bad character and unrighteous living break down praying until it becomes meaningless. Praying takes its tone and vigor from the life of the man or woman exercising it. When character and conduct are at a low ebb, praying can barely live, much less thrive.

The man of prayer, whether layman or preacher, is God's right-hand man. In the realm of spiritual affairs, he creates conditions, begins movements, and brings things to pass.

By the fact and condition of their creation and redemption, all people are under obligation to pray. Every person *can* pray, and every person *should* pray. But when it comes to the affairs of the kingdom, let it be said at once that a prayerless person in the church of God is like a paralyzed organ in the physical body. He is out of place in the communion of saints, out of harmony with God, and out of accord with His purposes for mankind. A prayerless person handicaps the vigor and life of the whole system, just as a demoralized soldier is a menace to his army in the day of battle. The absence of prayer lessens the life-giving current of the soul, cripples faith, sets aside holy living, and shuts out heaven.

The Holy Scriptures draw a sharp line between praying saints and non-praying people. The following was written about John Fletcher of Madeley—one of the praying saints:

> He was far more abundant in his public labors than the greater part of his companions in the holy ministry. Yet these bore but little proportion to those internal exercises of prayer and supplication to which he was wholly given up in private, which were almost uninterruptedly maintained from hour to hour. He lived in the spirit of prayer, and whatever employment in which he was engaged, this spirit of prayer was constantly manifested through them all.
>
> Without this he neither formed any design, nor entered upon any duty. Without this he neither read nor conversed. Without this he neither visited nor received a visitor. There

have been seasons of supplications in which he appeared to be carried out far beyond the ordinary limits of devotion, when, like his Lord upon the Mount of Transfiguration, while he continued to pour out his mighty prayer, the fashion of his countenance has been changed, and his face has appeared as the face of an angel.

O God, raise up more people of prayer like John Fletcher! How we need, in these times, people through whom God can work!

5

Prayerless Christians

If there was ever a time when Peter, James, and John needed to remain awake, it was in Gethsemane. If James had persisted in keeping awake, it might have saved him from being decapitated a few years later. If Peter had stirred himself to really intercede for himself and others, he would not have denied his Christ that night in the palace of Caiaphas.

—Homer W. Hodge

THERE is great need in this day for Christians in the business world to infuse their mundane affairs with the spirit of prayer. There is a great army of successful businesspeople in Christ's church, and it is high time they attended to this matter. We need to put God into business. In other words, we need to put the realization and restraint of His presence and His fear into all the secularities of life.

We need the atmosphere of the prayer closet to pervade our places of business. The sanctity of prayer is needed to fill our workplaces. We need the spirit of Sunday carried over to Monday and continued until Saturday. But this cannot be done by prayerless people; we need people of prayer. We need businesspeople to go about their concerns with the same reverence and responsibility with which they enter the prayer closet. We need people who are devoid of greed and who carry God with them, with all their hearts, into the secular affairs of life.

Worldlings imagine prayer to be too impotent a thing to battle with business methods and worldly practices. Against such a misleading doctrine Paul sets the whole commands of God, the loyalty to Jesus Christ, the claims of pious character, and the demands of the salvation of the world. We must pray, and we must put strength and heart into our praying. Prayer is part of the primary business of life, and God has called His people to it first of all.

Praying people are God's agents on earth, the representatives of the government of heaven, called to a specific task on the earth. While it is true that the Holy Spirit and the angels are agents of God in carrying forward the redemption of the human race, yet among them there must be praying people. For such people God has great use. He can make much of them, and in the past He has done wonderful things through them. These are God's instruments in carrying out His great purposes on the earth. They are God's messengers, watchmen, shepherds, and workmen, who need not be ashamed. Fully equipped for the great work to which they are appointed, they honor God and bless the world.

Above all things, Christian men and women must, primarily, be leaders in prayer. No matter how conspicuous they may be in other activities, they fail if they are not conspicuous in prayer. They must give their brains and hearts to prayer. People who shape the program of Christ's church, who map out its line of activity, should, themselves, be shaped by prayer. People controlling the finances, thought, and action of the church should all be people of prayer.

In order for God's work to progress to completion, there are two basic principles: God's ability to give and people's ability to ask. Failure in either one would be fatal to the success of God's work on earth. God's inability to do or to give would put an end to redemption. People's failure to pray would, just as surely, set a limit on the plan. But, God's ability to do and to give has never failed and *cannot* fail, but people's ability to ask can fail and often does.

Therefore, the slow progress that is being made toward the realization of a world won for Christ lies entirely with people's limited asking. There is need for the entire church of God to get busy praying. The church upon its knees would bring heaven upon the earth.

The wonderful ability of God to do for us was expressed by Paul in one of his most comprehensive statements: *"And God is able to make all grace abound toward you; that ye, always having all sufficiency in all things, may abound to every good work"* (2 Cor. 9:8).

Study that remarkable statement—*"God is able to make all grace abound."* That is, He is able to give such sufficiency that we may abound—overflow—to every good work. Why are we not more fully overflowing? The answer is lack of prayer ability. "[We] *have not, because* [we] *ask not"* (James 4:2). We are feeble, weak, and impoverished because of our failure to pray. God is restrained in doing because we are restrained by our failure to pray. All failures in securing heaven are traceable to lack of prayer or misdirected prayer.

Prayer must be broad in its scope; it must plead for others. Intercession for others is the hallmark of all true prayer. When prayer is confined to self and to the sphere of one's personal needs, it dies by reason of its littleness, narrowness, and selfishness. Prayer must be broad and unselfish, or it will perish. Prayer is the soul of a person stirred to plead with God for others. In addition to being interested in the eternal interests of one's own soul, it must, in its very nature, be concerned for the spiritual and eternal welfare of others. A man is most able to pray for himself when he has compassion and concern for others.

In the second chapter of 1 Timothy, the apostle Paul spoke to those who occupied positions of influence and places of authority. He urged them with singular and specific emphasis to give themselves to prayer. *"I will therefore that men pray every where"* (1 Tim. 2:8). This is the high calling of the men of the church, and no other calling is so engaging, so engrossing, and so valuable that we can afford to relieve Christian men from the all-important vocation of secret prayer. Nothing whatsoever can take the place of prayer. Nothing whatsoever can atone for the neglect of praying. This is of supreme importance, and it should be given first priority.

No person is so high in position or in grace to be exempt from the obligation to pray. No person is too big to pray, no matter who he is or what office he holds. The king on his throne is as much obligated to pray as the peasant in his cottage. No one is so high and exalted in this world, or so lowly and obscure, that he is excused from praying. Everyone's help is needed in doing the work of God, and the prayer of each praying person helps to swell the whole. Those who are leaders in place, in gifts, and in authority are to be chiefs in prayer.

Civil and church leaders shape the affairs of this world. Therefore, civil and church leaders themselves need to be shaped personally in spirit, in heart, in conduct, in truth, and in righteousness, by the prayers of God's people. This is in direct line with Paul's words:

I exhort therefore, that, first of all, supplications, prayers, intercessions, and giving of thanks, be made for all men; for kings, and for all that are in authority. *(1 Tim. 2:1–2)*

It is a sad day for righteousness when church politics, instead of holy praying, shapes the administration of the church and elevates people to place and power.

Why must we pray for all people? Because God wills the salvation of all people. God's children on earth must link their prayers to God's will. Prayer is meant to carry out the will of God. God's will is that all people would be saved. His heart is set on this one thing. Our prayers must be the creation and exponent of God's will. We are to grasp humanity in our praying as God grasps humanity in His love, His interest, and His plans to redeem them. Our sympathies, prayers, wrestlings, and ardent desires must run parallel with the will of God and be broad, generous, worldwide, and godlike. A Christian must in all things, first of all, be conformed to the will of God, but nowhere should this royal devotion be more evident than in the salvation of the human race. This high partnership with God, as His agents on earth, is to have its fullest, richest, and most effective exercise in prayer for all people.

Believers are to pray for all people, especially for rulers in church and state, *"that we may lead a quiet and peaceable life in all godliness and honesty"* (1 Tim. 2:2). Peace on the outside and peace on the inside. Praying calms disturbing forces, allays tormenting fears, and brings conflict to an end. Prayer tends to do away with turmoil. Even if there are external conflicts, it is well to have deep peace within the citadel of the soul. *"That we may lead a quiet and peaceable life."* Prayer brings inner calm and furnishes outward tranquility. If there were praying rulers and praying subjects worldwide, they would allay turbulent forces, make wars to cease, and cause peace to reign.

Believers must pray for all people so that we may lead lives *"in all godliness and honesty,"* that is, with godliness and seriousness. Godliness means to be like God. It means to be godly, to have godlikeness, to have the image of God stamped on the inner nature, and to show the same likeness in our conduct and character. Almighty God is the very highest model, and to be like Him is to possess the highest character. Prayer molds us into the image of God. At the same time it tends to mold others into the same image in proportion to our praying for them.

Prayer means to be like God. To be godlike is to love Christ and love God, to be one with the Father and the Son in spirit, character, and conduct. Prayer means to stay with God until you are like Him. Prayer makes a person godly, and it puts within him *"the mind of Christ"* (1 Cor. 2:16), the mind of humility, self-surrender, service, pity, and prayer. If we really pray, we will become more like God, or else we will quit praying.

"Men [are to] *pray every where"*—in the prayer closet, in the prayer meeting, around the family altar—and they are to do it, *"lifting up holy hands, without wrath and doubting"* (1 Tim. 2:8). Here is not only the obligation laid upon people to pray, but instructions on how they should pray. People must pray *"without wrath."* In other words, people must pray without bitterness against their neighbors or fellow believers, without the stubbornness of a strong will, without hard feelings, without an evil desire or emotion kindled by fires in the carnal nature. Praying is not to be done by these questionable things or in company with such evil feelings, but *"without"* them, aloof and entirely separate from them.

This is the sort of praying we are called upon to do. It is the sort that God hears and the kind that prevails with God and accomplishes things. Such prayers in Christians' hands become divine agencies in God's hands for carrying on God's gracious purposes and executing His designs in redemption.

Prayer has a higher origin than man's nature. This is true whether we mean man's nature as separate from the angelic nature, or man's carnal nature unrenewed and unchanged. Prayer does not originate in the realm of the carnal mind. Such a nature is entirely foreign to prayer simply because *"the carnal mind is enmity against God"* (Rom. 8:7).

It is by the new spirit that we pray, the new spirit sweetened by the sugar of heaven, perfumed with the fragrance of the upper world, and invigorated by a breath from the crystal sea. The new spirit is native to the skies, panting after the heavenly things, and inspired by the breath of God. The new spirit produces praying from which all the old juices of the carnal, unregenerate nature have been expelled. It is praying in which the fire of God has created the flame that has consumed worldly lusts. At the same time, the juices of the Spirit have been injected into the soul. Praying that is by the new spirit is entirely divorced from wrath.

People are also to pray *"without...doubting"* (1 Tim. 2:8). The Revised Version puts it, *"without...disputing."* Praying people must have faith in God and belief in God's Word without question. There must be no doubting or disputing in the mind. There must be no opinions, no hesitancy, no questioning, no reasoning, no intellectual quibbling, no rebellion, but a strict, steadfast loyalty of spirit to God, a life of loyalty in heart and intellect to God's Word.

God is closely related to people who have a living, transforming faith in Jesus Christ. These are God's children. A father loves his children, supplies their needs, hears their cries, and answers their requests. A child believes his father, loves him, trusts in him, and asks him for what he needs, believing without doubting that his father will hear his requests. God answers the prayers of His children. Their troubles concern Him, and their prayers awaken Him. Their voices are sweet to Him. He loves to hear them pray, and He is never happier than to answer their prayers.

Prayer is intended for God's ear. It is not people but God who hears and answers prayer. Prayer covers the whole range of human need. Hence, *"in every thing by prayer and supplication with thanksgiving let your requests be made known unto God"* (Phil. 4:6). Prayer includes the entire range of God's ability. *"Is any thing too hard for the LORD?"* (Gen. 18:14). Prayer does not apply to one favored segment of man's need, but it reaches to and embraces the entire circle of his needs, simply because God is the God of the whole man. God has pledged Himself to supply the needs of the whole man: physical, intellectual, and spiritual. *"But my God shall supply all your need according to his riches in glory by Christ Jesus"* (Phil. 4:19). Prayer is the child of grace, and grace is for the whole man and for every one of the children of men.

6

Praying for Others

Our Redeemer was in the Garden of Gethsemane. His hour was come. He felt as if He would be strengthened somewhat, if He had two or three disciples near Him. His three chosen disciples were within a stone's throw of the scene of His agony; but they were all asleep that the Scripture might be fulfilled—"I have trodden the winepress alone; and of the people there was none with me." The eight, in the distance, were good and true disciples; but they were only ordinary men, or men with a commonplace call. —Alexander Whyte

No insistence in the Bible is more pressing than the command it lays upon people to pray. No exhortation contained therein is more hearty, more solemn, or more stirring. No principle is more strongly stressed than *"men ought always to pray, and not to faint"* (Luke 18:1).

In view of this command, it is pertinent to ask if the majority of Christians are praying men and women. Is prayer a fixed course in the churches? In the Sunday school, the home, and the colleges, do we have any graduates in the school of prayer? Is the church producing those who have diplomas from the great university of prayer? This is what God requires, what He commands. It is those who possess such qualifications that He must have to accomplish His purposes and to carry out the work of His kingdom on earth.

And it is earnest praying that needs to be done. Languid praying, without heart or strength, with neither fire nor tenacity, defeats its own avowed purpose. The prophet of past times lamented that in a day that needed strenuous praying, there was no one who stirred up himself to take hold of God (Isa. 64:7). Christ charges us *"not to faint"* (Luke 18:1) in our praying. Laxity and indifference are great hindrances to prayer, both to the practice of praying and the process of receiving. It requires a brave, strong, fearless, and insistent spirit to engage in successful prayer.

Trying to pray for too many things also interferes with effectiveness. Offering too many petitions breaks unity and breeds neglect. Prayers should be specific and urgent. Too many words, like too much width, causes shallowness and sandbars. A single objective that absorbs the whole being and inflames the entire person is the properly constraining force in prayer.

It is easy to see how prayer was a decreed factor in the dispensations before the coming of Jesus, how their leaders had to be men of prayer, and how God's mightiest revelations of Himself were revelations made through prayer. It is also easy to see how Jesus Christ, in His personal ministry and in His relationship to God, was great and constant in prayer. His labors and dispensation overflowed with fullness in proportion to His prayers. The possibilities of His praying were unlimited, as were the possibilities of His ministry. The necessity of His praying was equaled only by the constancy with which He practiced it during His earthly life.

The dispensation of the Holy Spirit is a dispensation of prayer in a preeminent sense. Here prayer has an essential and vital role. Without depreciating the possibilities and necessities of prayer in all the preceding dispensations of God in the world, it must be declared that it is in this latter dispensation that the exercises and demands of prayer are given their greatest authority. Furthermore, prayer's possibilities are rendered unlimited, and its necessity unavoidable.

In these days we have sore need of a generation of praying people, a band of men and women through whom God can bring His greatest movements more fully into the world. The Lord our God is not restricted within Himself, but He is restricted in us by reason of our little faith and weak praying. A breed of Christians is greatly needed who will seek tirelessly after God, who will give Him no rest, day and night, until He hearkens to their cries. The times demand people who are all athirst for God's glory, who are unselfish in their desires, who are quenchless for God, who seek Him late and early, and who will give themselves no rest until *"the whole earth be filled with his glory"* (Ps. 72:19).

Men and women are needed whose prayers will give to the world the utmost power of God, whose prayers will make His promises blossom with rich and full results. God is waiting to hear us, and He challenges us to pray that He might work. He is asking us today, as He asked His ancient Israel, to *"prove [Him] now herewith"* (Mal. 3:10). Behind God's Word is God Himself. We read in Isaiah 45:11:

> *Thus saith the LORD, the Holy One of Israel, and his Maker,*
> *Ask me of things to come concerning my sons, and concerning*
> *the work of my hands command ye me.*

It is as though God places Himself in the hands and at the disposal of His people who pray, and indeed He does.

The dominant element of all praying is faith that is conspicuous, cardinal, and emphatic. Without such faith it is impossible to please God (Heb. 11:6) and equally impossible to pray.

There is a current perception of spiritual duties that tends to separate the pulpit and the pew. The perception is that the pulpit should bear the entire burden of spiritual concerns, while the pew should be concerned only with secular and worldly duties. Such a view needs drastic correction. God's cause, obligations, efforts, and successes lie with equal pressure on pulpit and pew.

The person in the pew is not taxed with the burden of prayer as he ought to be, and as he must be, before any new visitation of power can come to the church. The church will never be wholly for God until the pews are filled with praying people. The church cannot be what God wants it to be until the members that are leaders in business, politics, law, and society are also leaders in prayer.

God began His early movements in the world with people of prayer. Abraham, a leader of God's cause, was preeminently a praying man. God chose Abraham to be the father of the race that became His chosen people in the world for hundreds of years. This was the race to whom God committed His oracles and from whom sprang the promised Messiah.

When we consider Abraham's conduct and character, we readily see how prayer ruled and swayed this great leader of God's people. *"Abraham planted a grove in Beersheba, and called there on the name of the LORD, the everlasting God"* (Gen. 21:33). It is an outstanding fact that wherever he pitched his tent and camped for a season with his household, there he erected an altar of sacrifice and of prayer. His was a personal and a family religion, in which prayer was a prominent and abiding factor.

Prayer is the medium of divine revelation. It is through prayer that God reveals Himself to the spiritual soul today, just as in the Old Testament days He made His revelations to the people who prayed. God shows Himself to the person who prays.

"God is with thee in all that thou doest" (Gen. 21:22). This was the clear conviction of Abraham's peers, and they gladly would have made a covenant with him. It was the commonly held belief that Abraham was not only a man of prayer, but a man whose prayers God would answer. This is the summary and secret of divine rule in the church. In all ages God has ruled the church by prayerful people. When prayer fails, the divine rulership fails.

As we have seen, Abraham, the father of the faithful, was a prince and a priest in prayer. He had remarkable influence with God. God held back His vengeance while Abraham prayed. His mercy was suspended and conditioned on Abraham's praying. His visitations of wrath were removed by the praying of this ruler in Israel. The movements of God were influenced by the prayers of Abraham, the friend of God. Abraham's righteous prayerfulness permitted him to share in the secrets of God's counsels, while the knowledge of these secrets lengthened and intensified his praying. With Abraham the altar of sacrifice was close to the altar of prayer. With him the altar of prayer sanctified the altar of sacrifice. To Abimelech God said, "[Abraham] *is a prophet, and he shall pray for thee, and thou shalt live"* (Gen. 20:7).

Christian people must pray for others. On one occasion Samuel said to the people, *"Moreover as for me, God forbid that I should sin against the LORD in ceasing to pray for you"* (1 Sam. 12:23). Fortunately, these sinful Israelites, who had rejected God and desired a human king, had a man of prayer.

One way to increase personal grace is to pray for others. Intercessory prayer is a means of grace to those who exercise it. It is in the paths of intercessory prayer that we enter the richest fields of spiritual growth and gather priceless riches. To pray for others is of divine appointment, and it represents the highest form of Christian service.

People must pray, and people must be prayed for. The Christian must pray for all things, of course, but prayers for people are infinitely more important, just as people are infinitely more important than things. Also, prayers for people are far more important than prayers for things because people more deeply involve God's will and the work of Jesus Christ. People are to be cared for, sympathized with, and prayed for, because sympathy, pity, compassion, and care accompany and precede prayer for people.

All this makes praying a real business, not child's play, not a secondary affair, not a trivial matter, but a serious business. The people who have made a success of praying have made a business of praying. It is a process demanding the time, thought, energy, and hearts of mankind. Prayer is business for time, business for eternity. It is our business to pray, transcending all other business and taking precedence over all other vocations, professions, or occupations. Our praying concerns not only ourselves, but all people and their greatest interests, and even the salvation of their immortal souls. Praying is a business that takes hold of eternity and the things beyond the grave. It is a business that involves earth and heaven. All worlds are touched by prayer, and all worlds are influenced by prayer. It has to do with God and people, angels and devils.

Jesus was preeminently a leader in prayer, and His praying is an incentive to pray. How prominently prayer stands out in His life! The leading events of His earthly career are distinctly marked by prayer. The wonderful experience and glory of the Transfiguration was preceded by prayer, and it was the result of the praying of our Lord. (See Luke 9:28–35.) We do not know what words He used as He prayed, nor do we know what He prayed for. But I believe it was night, and long into its hours the Master prayed. It was while He prayed that the darkness fled and His form was lit with unearthly splendor. Moses and Elijah came to yield to Him not only the palm of law and prophecy, but the palm of praying.

None other prayed as Jesus did, nor did any have such a glorious manifestation of the divine presence. None other heard so clearly the revealing voice of the Father: *"This is my beloved Son: hear him"* (Luke 9:35). Oh, to be with Christ in the school of prayer; then we would be happy disciples indeed!

How many of us have failed to come to this glorious Mount of Transfiguration because we were unacquainted with the transfiguring power of prayer! It is the going apart to pray and the long, intense seasons of prayer that make the face shine, transfigure the character, and make even dull, earthly garments glisten with heavenly splendor. But more than this: it is real praying that makes eternal things real, close, and tangible, and real praying brings the glorified visitors and the heavenly visions. Transfigured lives would not be so rare if there were more of this transfigured praying, and these heavenly visits would not be so few.

How difficult it seems to be for the church to understand that the whole scheme of redemption depends on people of prayer. The work of our Lord, while here on the earth, as well as the work of the apostle Paul, was to develop, by teaching and example, people of prayer, to whom the future of the church would be committed. How strange that instead of learning this simple and all-important lesson, the modern church has largely overlooked it. We need to turn afresh to that wondrous leader of spiritual Israel, our Lord Jesus Christ, who by example and precept instructs us to pray. And we need to turn to the apostle Paul, who, by virtue of his praying habits and prayer lessons, is a model to God's people in every age and place.

7

Preachers and Prayer

Of course, the preacher is above all others distinguished as a man of prayer. He prays as an ordinary Christian, else he were a hypocrite. He prays more than ordinary Christians, else he were disqualified for the office he has undertaken. If you as ministers are not very prayerful, you are to be pitied. If you become lax in sacred devotion, not only will you need to be pitied but your people also, and the day cometh in which you will be ashamed and confounded. Our seasons of fastings and prayer at the Tabernacle have been high days indeed; never has heaven's gate stood wider; never have our hearts been nearer the central glory. —Charles Spurgeon

PREACHERS are God's leaders. They are divinely called to their holy office and high purpose and, primarily, are responsible for the condition of the church. Just as Moses was called of God to lead Israel out of Egypt through the wilderness into the Promised Land, so also God calls His ministers to lead His spiritual Israel through this world to the heavenly land. They are divinely commissioned to leadership, and they are, by precept and example, to teach God's people what God would have them be. Paul's counsel to the young preacher Timothy was this: *"Let no man despise thy youth; but be thou an example of the believers, in word, in conversation, in charity, in spirit, in faith, in purity"* (1 Tim. 4:12).

God's ministers shape the church's character and give tone and direction to its life. In Revelation chapters two and three, the prefacing sentence in the letters to each of the seven churches in Asia reads, *"Unto the angel of the church."* This seems to indicate that the angel—the minister—was in the same state of mind and condition of life as the membership, and, moreover, the minister was largely responsible for the spiritual condition of the church. The angel in each case was the preacher, teacher, or leader.

The first Christians knew this full well and felt this responsibility. In their helplessness, which they consciously felt, they cried out, *"And who is sufficient for these things?"* (2 Cor. 2:16), for the tremendous responsibility pressed upon their hearts and heads. The only reply to such a question was, *"God only"* (Mark 2:7). So, they were compelled by necessity to look beyond themselves for help and to throw themselves on prayer to secure God. More and more, as they prayed, they felt their responsibility; and more and more, by prayer they got God's help. They realized that their sufficiency was in God.

Prayer belongs in a very high and important sense to the ministry. It takes vigor and elevation of character to administer the prayer office. Praying prophets have frequently been at a premium in the history of God's people. In every age the demand has been for leaders in Israel who pray. God's watchmen must always and everywhere be people of prayer.

It ought to be no surprise for ministers to be often found on their knees seeking divine help for the responsibilities of their call. These are the true prophets of the Lord, and they stand as mouthpieces of God to a generation of wicked and worldly-minded men and women. Praying preachers are the boldest, the truest, and the swiftest ministers of God. They mount up highest and are nearest to Him who has called them. They advance more rapidly, and in Christian living they are most like God.

In reading the Gospels, we cannot help being impressed by the supreme effort made by our Lord to rightly instruct the twelve apostles. He instructed them in all the things that would prepare them for the tremendous tasks ahead of them. His consideration was for the church, that it would have people, holy in life and in heart, who would know full well the origin of their strength and power in the work of the ministry. A large part of Christ's teaching was addressed to these chosen apostles, and the training of the Twelve occupied much of His thought and time. In all that training, prayer was laid down as a basic principle.

We find the same thing to be true in the life and work of the apostle Paul. Though he edified the churches to whom he ministered and wrote, it was his purpose to instruct and prepare ministers to whom the interests of God's people would be committed. Paul wrote two epistles to Timothy, who was a young preacher, and one to Titus, who was also a young minister. It appears that Paul's design was to give each of them needed instruction to rightly do the work of the ministry to which they had been called by the Spirit of God. Underlying these instructions was the foundation stone of prayer. Unless they were men of prayer, by no means would they be able to *"show* [themselves] *approved unto God,* [workmen] *that need*[ed] *not to be ashamed, rightly dividing the word of truth"* (2 Tim. 2:15).

The highest welfare of the church of God on earth depends largely on the ministry, and so God has always been jealous of His watchmen—His preachers. His concern has been for the character of the people who minister at His altars in holy things. They must be people who lean on Him, who look to Him, and who continually seek Him for wisdom, help, and power to effectively do the work of the ministry. So, He has designed people of prayer for the holy office, and He has relied on them successively to perform the tasks He has assigned them.

God's great works are to be done as Christ did them; they are to be done, indeed, with increased power received from the ascended and exalted Christ. These works are to be done by prayer. People must do God's work in God's way and to God's glory, and prayer is necessary for its successful accomplishment.

The thing far above all other things in the equipment of the preacher is prayer. Before everything else he must be a person who makes a specialty of prayer. A prayerless preacher is a misnomer. He has either missed his calling, or he has grievously failed God, who called him into the ministry.

God wants people who are not dullards, who *"study to show* [themselves] *approved"* (2 Tim. 2:15). Preaching the Word is essential, social qualities are not to be underestimated, and education is good. But under and above all else, prayer must be the main plank in the platform of the one who goes forth to preach the unsearchable riches of Christ to a lost and hungry world.

The one weak spot in our church institutions lies just here. Prayer is not regarded as being the primary factor in church life and activity; and other things, good in their places, are made primary. This should not be. First things need to be put first, and the first thing in the equipment of a minister is prayer.

Our Lord is the pattern for all preachers, and with Him prayer was the law of life. By it He lived. It was the inspiration of His toil, the source of His strength, and the spring of His joy. With our Lord prayer was no sentimental episode, nor a pleasing prelude, nor an interlude, nor an afterthought, nor a form. For Jesus, prayer was exacting, all-absorbing, and paramount. To Him it was the call of a sweet duty, the satisfying of a restless yearning, the preparation for heavy responsibilities, and the meeting of a vigorous need.

This being so, the disciple must be as his Lord, the servant as his Master. As the Lord Himself was, so also His disciples must be. Our Lord Jesus Christ chose His twelve apostles only after He had spent a night in praying, and we may rest assured that He sets the same high value on those He calls into His ministry today.

No feeble or secondary place was given to prayer in the ministry of Jesus. It comes first—emphatic, conspicuous, and controlling. Having prayerful habits, having a prayerful spirit, given to long, solitary communion with God, Jesus was above all else a man of prayer. The crux of His earthly history, in New Testament terminology, is condensed to a single statement, found in Hebrews 5:7:

Who in the days of his flesh, when he had offered up prayers and supplications with strong crying and tears unto him that was able to save him from death, and was heard in that he feared.

Let Jesus' ministers be like their Lord and Master, whose they are and whom they serve (Acts 27:23). Let Him be their pattern, their example, their leader, and their teacher. In some places much reference is made to "following Christ," but it is confined to the following of Him in modes and ordinances, as if salvation were wrapped up in the specific way of doing a thing. "The path of prayer Thyself hath trod" is the path along which we are to follow Him; no other path will do.

Jesus was given as a leader to the people of God, and never has any leader more exemplified the worth and necessity of prayer. Even though he was equal in glory with the Father, and anointed and sent on His special mission by the Holy Spirit, Jesus still prayed. His incarnate birth, His high commission, His royal anointing—all these were His, but they did not relieve Him from the exacting claims of prayer. Rather, they tended to impose these claims upon Him with greater authority. He did not ask to be excused from the burden of prayer; He gladly accepted it, acknowledged its claims, and voluntarily subjected Himself to its demands.

Not only was His leadership preeminent, but His praying was preeminent. Had it not been, His leadership would have been neither preeminent nor divine. If, in true leadership, prayer had been dispensable, then certainly Jesus could have dispensed with it. But He did not, nor can any of His followers who desire effectiveness in Christian activity do other than follow their Lord.

While Jesus Christ was personally under the law of prayer and while His parables and miracles were exponents of prayer, He focused on teaching His disciples the specific art of praying. He said little or nothing about how to preach or what to preach. But He spent both His strength and His time in teaching people how to speak to God, how to commune with Him, and how to be with Him. He knew very well that he who has learned the craft of talking to God will be well versed in talking to people.

Turning aside for a moment, we observe that prayer was the secret of the wonderful success of the early Methodist preachers, who were far from being learned people. But with all their limitations, they were people of prayer, and they did great things for God.

The ability to talk to people is measured by the ability with which a preacher can talk to God for people. He who does not plow in his prayer closet will never reap in his pulpit.

We must always emphasize that Jesus Christ trained His disciples to pray. This is the real meaning of the saying, "the training of the Twelve." We must remember that Christ taught the world's preachers more about praying than He did about preaching. Prayer was the great factor in the spreading of His Gospel. Prayer preserved and made effective all other factors. He did not discount preaching when He stressed praying, but rather He taught that preaching is utterly dependent on prayer.

"The Christian's trade is praying," declared Martin Luther. Every Jewish boy had to learn a trade. Jesus Christ learned two: the trade of a carpenter and the trade of praying. The one trade served earthly uses; the other served His divine and higher purposes. Jewish custom committed Jesus as a boy to the trade of a carpenter; the law of God bound Him to praying from His earliest years and remained with Him to the end.

Christ is the Christian's example, and every Christian must imitate Him. Every preacher must be like his Lord and Master and must learn the trade of praying. He who learns well the trade of praying, masters the secret of the Christian art; and he becomes a skilled workman in God's workshop, one who does not need to be ashamed, a worker together with his Lord and Master.

"Pray without ceasing" (1 Thess. 5:17) is the trumpet call to the preachers of our time. If the preachers will clothe their thoughts with the atmosphere of prayer, if they will prepare their sermons on their knees, a gracious outpouring of God's Spirit will come upon the earth.

The one indispensable qualification for preaching is the gift of the Holy Spirit, and it was for the bestowal of this indispensable gift that the disciples were charged to stay in Jerusalem. Receiving this gift is absolutely necessary if ministry is to be successful. This is why the first disciples were commanded to stay in Jerusalem until they received it. This is why they sought the gift with urgent and earnest prayerfulness. They obeyed their Lord's command to stay in that city until they were clothed with *"power from on high"* (Luke 24:49). Immediately after He had left them for heaven, they sought to secure it by continued and earnest prayer. *"These all with one accord continued stedfastly in prayer, with the women, and Mary the Mother of Jesus, and with his brethren"* (Acts 1:14 RV).

John refers to this same thing in his first epistle. He says, *"Ye have an unction from the Holy One"* (1 John 2:20). It is this divine unction that preachers of the present day should sincerely desire and pray for, remaining unsatisfied until the blessed gift is richly bestowed.

Another allusion to this same important procedure was made by our Lord shortly after His resurrection, when He said to His disciples, *"But ye shall receive power, after that the Holy Ghost is come upon you"* (Acts 1:8). At the same time Jesus directed the attention of His disciples to the statement of John the Baptist concerning the Spirit. John had said, *"I indeed baptize you with water; but...he shall baptize you with the Holy Ghost and with fire"* (Luke 3:16). This is identical to the *"power from on high"* (Luke 24:49) for which Jesus had commanded them to stay in the city of Jerusalem. Alluding to John the Baptist's words, Jesus said, *"For John truly baptized with water; but ye shall be baptized with the Holy Ghost not many days hence"* (Acts 1:5). Peter at a later date said of our Lord, *"God anointed* [Him] *with the Holy Ghost and with power"* (Acts 10:38).

These are the divine statements to preachers of that day about the mission and ministry of the Holy Spirit, and the same divine statements apply with equal force to the preachers of today. God's ideal minister is a God-called, divinely anointed, Spirit-touched man. He is separated unto God's work; set apart from secularities and questionable affairs; baptized from above; marked, sealed, and owned by the Spirit; and devoted to his Master and His ministry. These are the divinely appointed requisites for a preacher of the Word; without them he is inadequate and inevitably unfruitful.

Today, there is no scarcity of preachers who deliver eloquent sermons on the need and nature of revival, who advance elaborate plans for the spread of the kingdom of God. But the praying preachers are rare. The greatest benefactor this age can have is a person who will bring the preachers, the church, and the people back to the practice of real praying. The reformer needed just now is the praying reformer. The leader Israel requires is one who, with clarion voice, will call the ministry back to their knees.

There is considerable talk in the air about revival. However, we need the vision to see that the revival we need, and the only one worth having, is the one that is born of the Holy Spirit. This kind of revival brings deep conviction for sin and regeneration for those who seek God's face. Such a revival comes at the end of a season of real praying. It is utter folly to discuss or expect a revival without the Holy Spirit operating in His distinctive office, and this is conditioned on much earnest praying. Such a revival will begin in pulpit and pew alike; it will be promoted by both preacher and layman working in harmony with God.

The heart is the vocabulary of prayer, the life is the best commentary on prayer, and the outward conduct is the fullest expression of prayer. Prayer builds the character; prayer perfects the life. And this the ministry needs to learn as thoroughly as the laymen. There is but one rule for both.

The general body of Christ's disciples was averse to prayer, having little taste for it and having little harmony with Him in the deep things of prayer and its mightier struggles. Therefore, the Master had to select a circle of three more apt scholars—Peter, James, and John—who had more relish for this divine work. He took them aside that they might learn the lesson of prayer. These men were nearer to Jesus, more like Him, and more helpful to Him because they were more prayerful.

Blessed, indeed, are those disciples whom Jesus Christ, in this day, calls into a more intimate fellowship with Himself, and who, readily responding to the call, are found much on their knees before Him. Distressing, indeed, is the condition of the Christians who, in their hearts, are averse to exercising the ministry of prayer.

All the great eras of our Lord, historical and spiritual, were made or fashioned by His praying. So, also, His plans and great achievements were born in prayer and filled with the spirit thereof. As was the Master, so also must His servant be; as his Lord did in the great eras of His life, so should the disciple do when faced by important crises. "To your knees, O Israel!" should be the clarion call to the ministry of this generation.

The highest form of religious life is attained by prayer. The richest revelations of God—Father, Son, and Spirit—are made, not to the learned, the great, or the noble of earth, but to people of prayer. *"For ye see your calling, brethren, how that not many wise men after the flesh, not many mighty, not many noble, are called"* (1 Cor. 1:26). God makes known His deep things and reveals the higher things of His character to the lowly, inquiring, praying ones. And, again, it must be said that this is as true of preachers as of laymen. It is the spiritual person who prays, and to praying ones God makes His revelations through the Holy Spirit.

Praying preachers have always brought the greater glory to God and have moved His Gospel onward with its greatest, speediest rate and power. A non-praying preacher and a non-praying church might flourish outwardly and advance in many aspects. Both preacher and church might even become synonyms for success. But unless success rests on a foundation of prayer, it will eventually crumble into death and decay.

"Ye have not, because ye ask not" (James 4:2) is the solution of all spiritual weakness both in the personal life and in the pulpit. Either that or it is, *"Ye ask, and receive not, because ye ask amiss"* (v. 3). Real praying lies at the foundation of all the real success that the ministry has in the things of God. The stability, readiness, and energy with which God's kingdom is established in this world are dependent on prayer. God has made it so, and therefore God is eager for people to pray. He is especially concerned that His chosen ministers should be people of prayer, and so He gives this wonderful statement in order to encourage His ministers to pray:

And I say unto you, Ask, and it shall be given you; seek, and ye shall find; knock, and it shall be opened unto you. For every one that asketh receiveth; and he that seeketh findeth; and to him that knocketh it shall be opened. (Luke 11:9–10)

Thus, both command and direct promise give accent to His concern that they should pray. Pause and think on these familiar words: *"Ask, and it shall be given you."* That verse itself would seem to be enough to set us all, laymen and preachers, to praying. These words are so direct, simple, and unlimited. They open all the treasures of heaven to us, simply by asking for them.

We should study the prayers of Paul, who was primarily a preacher to the Gentiles; otherwise, we can have only a feeble view of the great necessity for prayer and of how much it is worth in the life and work of a minister. Furthermore, we will have only a very limited view of the possibilities of the Gospel to enrich, strengthen, and perfect Christian character, as well as equip preachers for their high and holy task. Oh, when will we learn the simple yet all-important lesson that the one great thing needed in the life of a preacher to help him in his personal life, to keep his soul alive to God, and to give efficacy to the Word he preaches, is real, constant prayer!

Paul, with prayer uppermost in his mind, assured the Colossians that *"Epaphras...[is] always labouring fervently for you in prayers, that ye may stand perfect and complete in all the will of God"* (Col. 4:12). He prayed that they may come to this high state of grace, *"complete in all the will of God."* So, prayer was the force that was to bring them to that elevated, vigorous, and stable state of heart.

This is in line with Paul's teaching to the Ephesians: *"And he gave some...pastors and teachers; for the perfecting of the saints, for the work of the ministry, for the edifying of the body of Christ"* (Eph. 4:11–12). These verses evidently affirm that the whole work of the ministry is not merely to induce sinners to repent, but it is also the *"perfecting of the saints."* So, Epaphras labored fervently in prayers for this thing. Certainly, he was himself a praying man, for he earnestly prayed for these early Christians.

The apostles put forth their efforts in order that Christians should honor God by the purity and consistency of their outward lives. Christians were to reproduce the character of Jesus Christ.

They were to perfect His image in themselves, incorporate His character, and reflect His behavior in all their attitudes and conduct. They were to be *"imitators of God, as beloved children"* (Eph. 5:1 RV), to be holy as He was holy (1 Pet. 1:16). Thus, even laymen were to preach by their conduct and character, just as the ministry preached with their mouths.

To elevate the followers of Christ to these exalted heights of Christian experience, the apostles were in every way true in the ministry of God's Word—in the ministry of prayer, in holy zeal, in burning exhortation, in rebuke and reproof. Added to all these, sanctifying all these, invigorating all these, and making all these beneficial, they centered on and exercised constantly the force of mightiest praying. *"Night and day praying exceedingly"* means praying superabundantly, beyond measure, and with intense earnestness.

> *Night and day praying exceedingly that we might see your face, and might perfect that which is lacking in your faith. Now God himself and our Father, and our Lord Jesus Christ, direct our way unto you. And the Lord make you to increase and abound in love one toward another, and toward all men, even as we do toward you: to the end he may stablish your hearts unblameable in holiness before God, even our Father, at the coming of our Lord Jesus Christ with all his saints.*
>
> *(1 Thess. 3:10–13)*

It was after this fashion that these apostles, the first preachers in the early church, labored in prayer. And only those who labor after the same fashion are the true successors of these apostles. This is the true, scriptural "apostolical succession": the succession of simple faith, earnest desire for holiness of heart and life, and zealous praying. These are the things today that make the ministry strong, faithful, and effective and make *"a workman that needeth not to be ashamed, rightly dividing the word of truth"* (2 Tim. 2:15).

Jesus Christ, God's leader and commander of His people, lived and suffered under this law of prayer. All His personal conquests in His life on earth were won by obedience to this law. And the conquests won by His representatives since He ascended to heaven, were gained only when this condition of prayer was heartily and fully met. Christ was under this one prayer condition. His apostles were under the same prayer condition. His saints are under it, and even His angels are under it. By every token, therefore, preachers are under the same prayer law. Not for one moment are they relieved or excused from obedience to the law of prayer. It is their very life, the source of their power, the secret of their religious experience and communion with God.

Christ could do nothing without prayer. Christ could do all things by prayer. The apostles were helpless without prayer. They were absolutely dependent on it for success in defeating their spiritual foes. Like Christ, they could do all things by prayer.

8

Prayerlessness in the Pulpit

Henry Martyn laments that "want of private devotional reading and shortness of prayer through incessant sermon-making had produced much strangeness between God and his soul." He judges that he had dedicated too much time to public ministrations and too little to private communion with God. He was much impressed with the need of setting apart times for fasting and devoting times to solemn prayer. Resulting from this he records, "Was assisted this morning to pray for two hours."   —E. M. Bounds

ALL God's saints came to their sainthood by the way of prayer. The saints could do nothing without prayer. We can go further and say that the angels in heaven can do nothing without prayer but can do all things by praying. These messengers of the Highest are largely dependent on the prayers of the saints for the sphere and power of their usefulness. Prayer opens avenues for angelic usefulness and creates missions for them on the earth. And as it is with all the apostles, saints, and angels in heaven, so it is with preachers. The preachers, also called the angels of the churches, can do nothing without prayer, which opens doors of usefulness and gives power and point to their words.

How can a preacher preach effectively, make impressions on hearts and minds, and have fruits in his ministry, if he does not get his message firsthand from God? How can he deliver a fitting message without having his faith quickened, his vision cleared, and his heart warmed by his communion with God?

It would be well for all of us, in connection with this thought, to read again Isaiah's vision. As he waited and confessed and prayed before the throne, the angel touched his lips with a live coal from God's altar.

Then flew one of the seraphims unto me, having a live coal in his hand, which he had taken with the tongs from off the altar: and he laid it upon my mouth, and said, Lo, this hath touched thy lips; and thine iniquity is taken away, and thy sin purged. (Isa. 6:6–7)

Oh, the need there is for present-day preachers to have their lips touched with a live coal from the altar of God! This fire is brought to the mouths of those prophets who are of a prayerful spirit and who wait in the secret place for the appointed angel to bring the living flame. Preachers of Isaiah's character received visits from an angel who brought live coals to touch their lips. Prayer always brings the living flame in order to unloose tongues, to open *"door*[s] *of utterance"* (Col. 4:3), and to open great and effective doors of doing good. This, above all else, is the great need of the prophets of God.

As far as the abiding interests of religion are concerned, a pulpit without a prayer closet will always be a barren thing. Blessed is the preacher whose pulpit and prayer closet are close to each other, and who goes from the one into the other.

To consecrate no place to prayer is to make a beggarly showing, not only in praying, but in holy living; for secret prayer and holy living are so closely joined that they can never be separated. A preacher or a Christian may live a decent, religious life without secret prayer, but decency and holiness are two widely different things. And holiness is attained only by secret prayer.

A preacher may preach in an official, entertaining, and learned way without prayer, but there is a great distance between this kind of preaching and the sowing of God's precious seed.

We cannot declare too often or too strongly that prayer, involving all of its elements, is the one prime condition of the success of Christ's kingdom and that all else is secondary and incidental. Only prayerful preachers, prayerful men, and prayerful women can advance this Gospel with aggressive power. Only they can put conquering forces into it. Preachers may be sent out by the thousand, and their equipment may be ever so complete; but unless they are skilled in the trade of prayer, trained to its martial and exhaustive exercise, their going will be lacking in power and effectiveness. Moreover, unless the men and women who are behind these preachers, who furnish their equipment, are men and women whose prayers are serious labor, their efforts will be vain and fruitless.

Prayer should be the inseparable accompaniment of all missionary effort, and prayer must be the one piece of equipment of the missionaries as they go out to their fields of labor and begin their delicate and responsible tasks. Prayer and missions go hand in hand. A prayerless missionary is a failure before he goes out, while he is out, and when he returns to his native land. A prayerless board of missions, too, needs to learn the necessity of prayer.

Added to all the missionary speeches, the money raised for missions, and the dozens being sent out to needy fields, is prayer. Missions has its root in prayer, and missions must have prayer in all of its plans. Prayer must precede, go with, and follow all of its missionaries and laborers.

Prayer enthrones God as sovereign and elevates Jesus Christ to sit with Him. If Christian preachers had used the power of prayer to its fullest, long before this *"the kingdoms of this world* [would have] *become the kingdoms of our Lord, and of his Christ"* (Rev. 11:15).

Huge difficulties face the church in its great work on earth, and almost superhuman and complex obstacles stand in the way of evangelizing the world. In the face of all this, God encourages us by His strongest promises: *"Call unto me, and I will answer thee, and show thee great and mighty things, which thou knowest not"* (Jer. 33:3). God commits Himself to answer the specific prayer, but He does not stop there. The revelations of God to him who is of a prayerful spirit go far beyond the limits of the actual praying.

He says, *"Ask me of things to come concerning my sons, and concerning the work of my hands command ye me"* (Isa. 45:11). Think over that remarkable pledge of God to those who pray: *"Command ye me."* He actually places Himself at the command of praying preachers and a praying church. This is a sufficient answer to all doubts, fears, and unbelief. This is a wonderful inspiration to do God's work in God's way—by prayer.

Furthermore, as if to fortify even more the faith of His ministry and of His church, to protect against any temptation to doubt or be discouraged, He declares by the mouth of the great Apostle to the Gentiles, "[He] *is able to do exceeding abundantly above all that we ask or think"* (Eph. 3:20).

It is unquestionably taught that, in going forward with their God-appointed tasks, preachers can command God in their prayers. To pray is to command His ability, His presence, and His power. *"Certainly I will be with thee"* (Exod. 3:12) is the reply to every sincere, inquiring minister of God. All of God's called workers in the ministry are privileged to stretch their prayers into regions where neither words nor thoughts can go. They are permitted to expect from Him beyond their praying. For their praying, they can expect God Himself and then, in addition, *"great and mighty things, which thou knowest not"* (Jer. 33:3).

Real, live, heart praying by the power of the Spirit—praying that is direct, specific, ardent, and simple—is the kind of praying that legitimately belongs to the pulpit. This is the kind demanded just now of the preachers who stand in the pulpit. There is no school in which to learn to pray in public except the prayer closet. Preachers who have learned to pray in the prayer closet have mastered the secret of pulpit praying. It is but a short step from secret praying to effective, live, pulpit praying. Good pulpit praying follows good secret praying. An empty prayer closet makes for cold, spiritless, formal praying in the pulpit.

Oh, preacher, study how to pray, not by studying the forms of prayer, but by attending the school of prayer on your knees before God. Here is where we learn not only how to pray before God, but also how to pray in the presence of people. He who has learned the way to the prayer closet has discovered the way to pray in the pulpit.

How easily we become businesslike and mechanical in the most sacred undertakings! Henry Martyn learned the lesson so hard to learn, that the cultivation and perfection of personal righteousness is the prime factor in the preacher's success. Likewise, he that learns another lesson so hard to learn—that live, spiritual, effective pulpit praying is the outgrowth of regular secret praying—has learned his lesson well. Moreover, his work as a preacher will depend on his praying.

The great need of the hour is for good pray-ers in the pulpit as well as good preachers. Just as live, spiritual preaching is the kind that impresses and moves men, so live, spiritual praying in the pulpit moves and impresses God. The preacher is called not only to preach well, but also to pray well. Not that he is called to pray after the fashion of the Pharisees, who love to stand in public and pray so that they may be seen and heard of men (Matt. 6:5). The right sort of pulpit praying is far removed from pharisaical praying, as far as light is from darkness, as far as heat is from cold, as far as life is from death.

Preaching is the very loftiest work possible for a person to do. And praying goes hand in hand with preaching. It is a mighty, lofty work. Preaching is a life-giving work, sowing the seeds of eternal life. Oh, may we do it well, do it after God's order, and do it successfully! May we do it divinely well, so that when the end comes, the solemn close of earthly probation, we may hear from the Great Judge of all the earth, *"Well done, good and faithful servant...enter thou into the joy of thy lord"* (Matt. 25:23).

When we consider this great question of preaching, we are led to exclaim, "With what reverence, simplicity, and sincerity it ought to be done!" What truth in the inward parts is demanded in order that it be done acceptably to God and with profit to men! How real, true, and loyal those who practice it must be! How great the need to pray as Christ prayed, with strong cryings, tears, and godly fear!

Oh, may preachers do the real thing of preaching, with no sham, with no mere form of words, with no dull, cold, professional discourses. May they give themselves to prayerful preaching and prayerful praying! Preaching that gives life is born of praying that gives life. Preaching and praying always go together, like Siamese twins, and can never be separated without death to one or the other, or death to both.

This is not the time for kid-glove methods or sugar-coated preaching. This is no time for playing the gentleman as a preacher, nor for putting on the garb of the scholar in the pulpit. We want to disciple all nations, destroy idolatry, crush the defiant forces of Islam, and destroy the tremendous forces of evil now opposing the kingdom of God. Brave people, true people, praying people—afraid of nothing but God—are the kind needed just now. There will be no smiting the forces of evil that now hold the world in bondage, no lifting of the degraded hordes of paganism to light and eternal life, by any but praying people. All others are merely playing at religion, make-believe soldiers with no armor or ammunition, who are absolutely helpless in the face of a wicked and opposing world. None but soldiers and bond servants of Jesus Christ can possibly do this tremendous work.

"Endure hardness, as a good soldier of Jesus Christ" (2 Tim. 2:3), cries the great apostle. This is no time to think of self, to consult with dignity, to confer with flesh and blood (Gal. 1:16), to think of ease, or to shrink from hardship, grief, and loss. This is the time for toil, suffering, and self-denial. We must lose all for Christ in order to gain all for Christ. (See Philippians 3:8.) People are needed in the pulpit, as well as in the pew, who are bold enough to take up and firm enough to sustain the consecrated cross. Here is the sort of preachers God wants, and this sort is born of much praying. For no prayerless preacher is sufficient for these things. Only praying preachers can meet the demand and be equal to the emergency.

The Gospel of Jesus has neither relish nor life in it when spoken by prayerless lips or handled by prayerless hands. Without prayer the doctrines of Christ degenerate into dead orthodoxy. Preaching them without the aid of the Spirit of God, who comes into the preacher's messages only by prayer, is nothing more than mere lecturing with no life, no grip, and no force. It amounts to nothing more than pure rationalism or sickly sentimentalism. *"But we will give ourselves continually to prayer, and to the ministry of the word"* (Acts 6:4) was the settled and declared purpose of the apostolic ministry. The kingdom of God waits on prayer, and prayer puts wings on and power into the Gospel. By prayer it moves forward with conquering force and rapid advance.

If prayer is left out, the preacher rises to no higher level than the lecturer, the politician, or the secular teacher. That which distinguishes him from all other public speakers is the fact of prayer. Because prayer deals with God, the preacher has God with him, while other speakers do not need God with them to make their public messages effective. The preacher above everything else is a spiritual person, a person of the Spirit, and he deals with spiritual things. And this implies that he has to do with God in his pulpit work in a high and holy sense. This can be said of no other public speaker. So, prayer must of necessity go with the preacher and his preaching. Pure intellectuality is the only qualification for other public speakers. Spirituality, which is born of prayer, belongs to the preacher.

In the Sermon on the Mount, Jesus Christ often speaks of prayer. It stands out prominently in His words on that occasion. The lesson of prayer that He taught was one of hallowing God's name, of advancing God's kingdom. We are to long for the coming of the kingdom of God. It is to be longed for, and it must be first in our communication with God. God's will must have its royal way in the hearts and wills of those who pray. The point of urgency is made by our Lord that people are to pray in earnest—by asking, seeking, knocking—in order to hallow God's name, bring His will to pass, and forward His kingdom.

And let it be kept in mind that while this prayer lesson has to do with all people, it has a special application to the ministry; for it was the twelve would-be preachers who made the request, *"Lord, teach us to pray, as John also taught his disciples"* (Luke 11:1). So, primarily, Jesus' reply was spoken first to twelve men just starting their work as ministers. Jesus was talking, as Luke records it, to preachers. He also speaks to the preachers of this day. How He pressed these twelve men into the ministry of prayer! Present-day ministers need the same lesson to be taught to them, and they need the same urgency pressing them to make prayer their habit of life.

Regardless of all a preacher may claim for himself, or how many good things may be put down to his credit, a prayerless preacher will never master God's truth, which he is called upon to declare with all fidelity and plainness of speech. Blind and blinding will he be if he lives a prayerless life. A prayerless ministry cannot know God's truth and, not knowing it, cannot teach it to ignorant people. He who teaches us the path of prayer must first of all walk in the same path. A preacher cannot teach what he does not know. The preacher who is a stranger to prayer will be a blind leader of the blind. Prayer opens the preacher's eyes, and prayer keeps them open to the evil of sin, the peril of sin, and the penalty of sin. A blind leader leading the blind will be the vocation of the one who is prayerless in his own life.

The best and the greatest offering that the church and the ministry can make to God is an offering of prayer. If the preachers of the twentieth century will learn well the lesson of prayer and use it fully in all its exhaustless effectiveness, the millennium will come to its noon before the century closes.

The Bible preacher prays. He is filled with the Holy Spirit, filled with God's Word, and filled with faith. He has faith in God; he has faith in God's only begotten Son, his personal Savior; and he has implicit faith in God's Word. He cannot do otherwise than pray. He cannot be other than a person of prayer. The breath of his life and the throb of his heart are prayer. The Bible preacher lives by prayer, loves by prayer, and preaches by prayer. His bended knees in the place of secret prayer advertise what kind of a preacher he is.

Preachers may lose faith in God, lose faith in Jesus Christ as their personal and present Savior, become devoid of the peace of God, and let the joy of salvation go out of their hearts, yet be unconscious of it. How needful for the preacher to be continually examining himself and to be checking his religious state and his personal relationship with God!

The preachers, like the philosophers of old, may defer to a system and then earnestly contend for it even after they have lost all faith in its great facts. Preachers may preach in the pulpit with hearts of unbelief; they may minister at the altars of the church while being alien to the most sacred and vital principles of the Gospel.

It is a comparatively easy task for preachers to become so absorbed in the material and external affairs of the church that they lose sight of their own souls, forget the necessity of life-giving prayer, and lose the inward sweetness of the Christian experience.

Prayer makes much of preaching, and we must make much of prayer. The character of our praying will determine the character of our preaching. Serious praying will give serious weight to preaching. Prayer makes preaching strong, gives it unction, and makes it stick. In every beneficial ministry, prayer has been a serious business.

It cannot be said with too much emphasis: the preacher must be preeminently a person of prayer. He must learn to pray. He must have such an estimate of prayer and its great worth that he feels he cannot afford to omit it from his list of private duties. His heart must be attuned to prayer, while he himself touches the highest note of prayer. Only in the school of prayer can the heart learn to preach. No gifts, no learning, no brainpower can atone for the failure to pray. No earnestness, no diligence, no study, no amount of social service will supply its lack. Talking to people for God may be a great thing, and it may be very commendable. But talking to God for people is far more valuable and commendable.

The power of Bible preaching does not lie solely in superlative devotion to God's Word and jealous passion for God's truth. Both of these are essential, valuable, and helpful. But, above these things, a preacher must have a sense of the divine presence. He must be conscious of the divine power of God's Spirit on him and in him. For the great work of preaching, he must have an anointing, an empowering, a sealing of the Holy Spirit, making him speak God's words and giving him the energy of God's right hand. Such a preacher can say,

> *Thy words were found, and I did eat them; and thy word was unto me the joy and rejoicing of mine heart: for I am called by thy name, O LORD God of hosts.*   *(Jer. 15:16)*

9

Equipped by Prayer

Go back! Back to that upper room; back to your knees; back to searching of heart and habit, thought and life; back to pleading, praying, waiting, till the Spirit of the Lord floods the soul with light, and you are "endued with power from on high." Then go forth in the power of Pentecost, and the Christ-life shall be lived, and the works of Christ shall be done. You shall open blind eyes, cleanse foul hearts, break men's fetters, and save men's souls. In the power of the indwelling Spirit, miracles become the commonplace of daily living. —Samuel Chadwick

ALMOST the last words uttered by our Lord before His ascension were those addressed to the eleven disciples. They were words which really were spoken to, and directly had to do with, preachers. These words indicated very clearly the power these people needed in order to preach the Gospel, beginning at Jerusalem. These vital words of Jesus are recorded in Luke 24:49: *"And, behold, I send the promise of my Father upon you: but tarry ye in the city of Jerusalem, until ye be endued with power from on high."*

Two things are very clearly set forth in these urgent directions. The first thing is the power of the Holy Spirit for which they must wait. This was to be received after their conversion. This power was an indispensable requisite, equipping them for the great task set before them.

The second thing is the truth that the *"promise of my Father,"* this *"power from on high,"* would come to them after they had waited in earnest, continuous prayer. A reference to Acts 1:14 will reveal that these same men, with the women, *"continued with one accord in prayer and supplication,"* and so continued until the Day of Pentecost when the power from on high descended upon them.

This power from on high is as important to those early preachers as it is to present-day preachers. This power was not the force of a mighty intellect, holding in its grasp great truths, flooding them with light, and forming them into verbal shapeliness and beauty. Nor was it the acquisition of great learning. Nor was it the result of a speech, faultless and complete by the rules of rhetoric. It was none of these things. This spiritual power was not held then, nor is it held now, in the keeping of any earthly sources of power. Human forces are essentially different in source and character; they are not a result of this power from on high. On the contrary, the transmission of such power is directly from God.

Power from on high is a bestowal, in rich measure, of the force and energy that pertains only to God. The Master transmits this power to His messenger only in answer to the longing, wrestling attitude of his soul. The messenger is conscious of his own impotency and seeks the omnipotence of the Lord he serves. He seeks God's power in order that he may more fully understand the given Word and preach it to his fellowmen.

The power from on high may be found in combination with all sources of human power, but it is not to be confused with them, is not dependent on them, and must never be superseded by them. Whatever human gift, talent, or force a preacher may possess, it is not to be made paramount, or even conspicuous. It must be hidden, lost, and overshadowed by this power from on high. The forces of intellect and culture may all be present, but without this inward, heaven-given power, all spiritual effort is vain and unsuccessful.

Even when lacking the other equipment but having this power from on high, a preacher cannot help but succeed. It is the one essential, all-important, vital force that a messenger of God must possess to give wings to his message, to put life into his preaching, and to enable him to speak the Word with power and acceptance.

I need to clarify something here. Distinctions need to be kept in mind. We must think clearly about the meaning of our terms. Power from on high means the *"unction from the Holy One"* (1 John 2:20) resting on and abiding in the preacher. This is not so much a power that bears witness to a person being the child of God as it is a preparation for delivering the Word to others. Also, unction must be distinguished from pathos. (Pathos causes an emotional response in the hearer; unction causes a spiritual response.) Pathos may exist in a sermon in which unction is entirely absent. So also unction may be present and pathos absent. Both may exist together, but they are not to be confused, nor should they be made to appear to be the same thing. Pathos promotes emotion, tender feeling, sometimes tears. Quite often it results when a sad story is told or when the tender side is appealed to. But pathos is neither the direct nor the indirect result of the Holy Spirit resting upon the preacher as he preaches.

However, unction is. Here we are given the evidence of the workings of an indefinable agency in the preacher; these workings result directly from the presence of this power from on high. Unction is deep, conscious, life-giving, and carrying. It gives power and point to the preached Word. It is the element in a sermon that arouses, stirs, convicts, and moves the souls of sinners and saints. This is what the preacher requires, the great equipment for which he should wait and pray. This *"unction from the Holy One"* (1 John 2:20) delivers from dryness, saves from superficiality, and gives authority to preaching. It is the one quality that distinguishes the preacher of the Gospel from other people who speak in public; it is that which makes a sermon unique, unlike any other public address.

Prayer is the language of a person burdened with a sense of need. It is the voice of the beggar, conscious of his poverty, asking of another the things he needs. It is not only the language of lack, but of *felt* lack, of lack consciously realized. *"Blessed are the poor in spirit"* (Matt. 5:3) means not only that poverty of spirit brings the blessing, but also that poverty of spirit is realized, known, and acknowledged. Prayer is the language of those who need something—something which they, themselves, cannot supply but which God has promised them—and so they ask.

In the end, poor praying and prayerlessness amount to the same thing; for poor praying proceeds from a lack of the sense of need, while prayerlessness has its origin in the same soil. Not to pray is to declare there is nothing needed and to admit there is no realization of a need. This is what magnifies the sin of prayerlessness. It represents an attempt at instituting an independence of God, a self-sufficient ruling of God out of the life. It is a declaration made to God that we do not need Him and hence do not pray to Him.

This is the state in which the Holy Spirit, in His messages to the seven churches in Asia, found the Laodicean church. The "Laodicean state" has come to stand for one in which God is ruled out, expelled from the life, put out of the pulpit. The entire condemnation of this church is summed up in one expression: *"Because thou sayest, I...have need of nothing"* (Rev. 3:17). This is the most alarming state into which a person, a church, or a preacher can come. Trusting in its riches, in its social position, in its outward and material things, the church at Laodicea omitted God, leaving Him out of their church plans and church work. They declared, by their acts and by their omission of prayer, *"I...have need of nothing."*

No wonder the self-satisfied declaration brought forth its sentence of punishment: *"Because thou art lukewarm, and neither cold nor hot, I will spue thee out of my mouth"* (Rev. 3:16). The idea conveyed is that such a backslidden state of heart is as repulsive to God as spoiled food is to the human stomach. As the stomach expels that which is objectionable, so Almighty God threatened to vomit out of His mouth these people who were in a religious condition so repulsive to Him.

All of it was traceable to a prayerless state of heart, for no one can read this word of the Spirit to the Laodicean church and not see that the very core of their sin was prayerlessness. How could a church given to prayer openly and arrogantly declare, *"I...have need of nothing,"* in the face of the Spirit's assertion that it needed everything: *"Thou...knowest not that thou art wretched, and miserable, and poor, and blind, and naked"* (Rev. 3:17)?

In addition to their sins of self-sufficiency and independence of God, the Laodiceans were spiritually blind. Oh, what dullness of sight, what blindness of soul! These people were prayerless, and they did not know the import of such prayerlessness. They lacked everything that makes up spiritual life and force and self-denying piety, and they vainly supposed themselves to need nothing but material wealth. Thus, they tried to make temporal possessions a substitute for spiritual wealth. They left God entirely out of their activities. They relied on human and material resources to do the work that is possible only to divine and supernatural intervention through prayer.

Nor let it be forgotten that this letter (in common with the other six letters) was primarily addressed to the preacher in charge of the church. All this strengthens the impression that the *"angel of the church"* (Rev. 3:14) himself was in this lukewarm state. He himself was living a prayerless life, relying on things other than

God, practically saying, *"I...have need of nothing"* (Rev. 3:17). For these words are the natural expression of the spirit of him who does not pray, who does not care for God, and who does not feel the need of Him in his life and work and preaching. Furthermore, the words of the Spirit seem to indicate that the *"angel of the church"* at Laodicea was indirectly responsible for this sad condition into which the Laodicean church had fallen.

May not this sort of a church be found in modern times? Could we not discover some preachers who fall under a condemnation similar to that of the *"angel of the church"* at Laodicea?

Preachers of the present age excel those of the past in many, possibly in all, human elements of success. They are well abreast of the age in learning, research, and intellectual vigor. But these things neither ensure power from on high nor guarantee a righteous life or a thriving religious experience. These purely human gifts do not bring with them an insight into the deep things of God, a strong faith in the Scriptures, or an intense loyalty to God's divine revelation.

The presence of these earthly talents, even in the most commanding and impressive form and richest measure, do not in the least abate the necessity for the added endowment of the Holy Spirit. Herein lies the great danger menacing the pulpit of today. All around us we see a tendency to substitute human gifts and worldly attainments for that supernatural, inward power that comes from heaven in answer to earnest prayer.

In many instances modern preaching seems to fail in the very thing that should distinguish true preaching, that is essential to its being, and that alone can make it a powerfully aggressive agency. It lacks, in short, power from on high, which alone can make it a living thing. It fails to become the channel through which God's saving power can appeal to people's consciences and hearts.

Quite often, modern preaching fails to reach people because it does not have a potent influence that disturbs people in their sleep of security and awakens them to a sense of need and of peril. There is a growing need of an appeal that will quicken and arouse the conscience from its ignoble stupor, an appeal that will give the conscience a sense of wrongdoing and a corresponding sense of repentance. There is need of a message that searches into the secret places of a man's being, dividing, as it were, the joints and the marrow and laying bare the mysterious depths before himself and his God (Heb. 4:12).

Much of our present-day preaching lacks power to infuse new blood into the heart and veins of faith, to arm with courage and skill for the battle against the powers of darkness, and to get a victory over the forces of the world. Such high and noble ends can never be accomplished by human qualifications. Nor can these great results be secured by a pulpit clothed only with the human elements of power, however gracious, comfortable, and helpful they may be.

The Holy Spirit is needed. He alone can equip the ministry for its difficult and responsible work in and out of the pulpit. Oh, that the present-day ministry may come to see that its one great need is an outpouring of power from on high. May they see that this one need can be secured only by the use of God's appointed means of grace—the ministry of prayer.

Prayer is needed by the preacher in order that his personal relationship with God may be maintained, for there is no difference between him and any other person as far as his personal salvation is concerned. This he must work out *"with fear and trembling"* (Phil. 2:12) just as all other people must do. Thus, prayer is of vast importance to the preacher in order that he may possess a growing religious experience. Prayer enables him to live such a life that his character and conduct will back up his preaching and give force to his message.

A person must have prayer in preparing to preach, for no minister can preach effectively without prayer. He also has use for prayer in praying for others. Paul was a notable example of a preacher who constantly prayed for those to whom he ministered.

But we come, now, to another sphere of prayer: people praying for the preacher. *"Brethren, pray for us"* (1 Thess. 5:25). This is the cry that Paul set in motion, and this has been the cry of spiritually-minded preachers—those who know God and who know the value of prayer—in all succeeding ages. No amount of success or failure must abate the cry. No amount of refinement and no abundance of talents must cause that cry to cease. The learned preacher, as well as the unlearned, has equal need to call out to the people he serves, *"Withal praying also for us"* (Col. 4:3).

Such a cry voices the felt need of a preacher's heart, a preacher who feels the need for his people to be in harmony with him. Such a cry is the expression of the inner soul of a preacher who feels his insufficiency for the tremendous responsibilities of the pulpit. He realizes his weakness and his need of the divine unction, and therefore he throws himself upon the prayers of his congregation and calls out to them: *"Praying always with all prayer and supplication in the Spirit...and for me, that utterance may be given unto me"* (Eph. 6:18–19). It is the cry of the preacher who deeply feels in his heart that he must have this prayer made specifically for him so that he may do his work in God's own way.

When this request to a people to pray for the preacher is cold, formal, and official, it freezes instead of bearing fruit. To be ignorant of the necessity for the cry, is to be ignorant of the sources of spiritual success. To fail to stress the cry, and to fail to have responses to it, is to sap the sources of spiritual life. Preachers must sound out the cry to the church of God. Saints everywhere and of every kind and of every faith speedily respond and pray for the preacher. The imperative need of the work demands it. *"Pray for us"* (1 Thess. 5:25) is the natural cry of the hearts of God's called ministers, the faithful preachers of the Word.

Saintly praying in the early church helped apostolic preaching mightily, and it rescued apostolic believers from many severe troubles. It can do the same thing today. It can open doors for apostolic labors; it can open doors for apostolic lips to utter bravely and truly the gospel message. Apostolic movements wait their ordering from prayer, and avenues long closed are opened to apostolic entrance by and through the power of prayer. The messenger receives his message and is schooled as to how to carry and deliver the message by prayer. The forerunner of the Gospel, and that which prepares the way, is prayer, not only by the praying of the messenger himself, but by the praying of the church of God.

Writing along this line in his second epistle to the Thessalonians, Paul was general at first in his request and said, *"Brethren, pray for us."* Then he became more minute and particular:

> *Finally, brethren, pray for us, that the word of the Lord may have free course, and be glorified, even as it is with you: and that we may be delivered from unreasonable and wicked men: for all men have not faith.*   *(2 Thess. 3:1–2)*

In the Revised Version, *"have free course"* is replaced by the word *"run."* *"The word"* means doctrine, and the idea conveyed is that this doctrine of the Gospel is running a race. In other words, it is being rapidly propagated. This verse is an exhortation to exert oneself, to strive hard, to expend strength. Thus, the prayer for the spread of the Gospel gives the same energy to the Word of the Lord as the greatest output of strength gives success to the racer. Prayer in the pew gives the preached Word energy, attainment, and success. Preaching without the backing of mighty praying is as limp and worthless as can be imagined. Prayerlessness in the pew is a serious hindrance to the running of the Word of the Lord.

The preaching of God's Word fails to run and be glorified from many causes. The difficulty may lie with the preacher himself, if his outward conduct is out of harmony with the rule of the Scriptures and his own profession. He must live the Word and not just preach the Word; his life must be in harmony with his sermon. The preacher's spirit and behavior out of the pulpit must run parallel with the Word of the Lord spoken in the pulpit. Otherwise, a man is an obstacle to the success of his own message.

Again, the Word of the Lord may fail to run, may be seriously encumbered and crippled, by the inconsistent lives of those who are the hearers of it. Bad living in the pew will seriously cripple the Word of the Lord as it attempts to run on its appointed course. Unrighteous lives among the laity heavily weigh down the Word of the Lord and hamper the work of the ministry.

Yet, prayer will remove this unrighteous living that seriously handicaps the preached Word. It will tend to do this in a direct way or in an indirect way. For just as you set laymen to praying, for the preacher or even for themselves, it awakens conscience, stirs the heart, and tends to correct evil ways and promote good living. No one will pray for long and continue in sin. Prayer breaks up bad living, and bad living breaks down prayer. Praying goes into bankruptcy when a person goes into sin. Obeying the cry of the preacher, *"Brethren, pray for us"* (2 Thess. 3:1), gets people to do that which will induce right living in them; it tends to break them away from sin.

For these reasons it is worth a great deal to get the laity to pray for the ministry. Prayer helps the preacher, is an aid to the sermon, assists the hearer, and promotes right living in the pew. Prayer also moves the one who prays for the preacher and for the Word of the Lord. It moves him to use all his influence to remove any hindrance to the Word which he may see and which lies in his power to remove.

But prayer reaches the preacher directly. God hears the praying of a church for its minister. Prayer for the preached Word is a direct aid to it. Prayer for the preacher gives wings, as well as feet, to the Gospel. Prayer makes the Word of the Lord go forward strongly and rapidly. It takes the shackles off of the message and gives it a chance to run straight to the hearts of sinners and saints alike. It opens the way, clears the track, and furnishes a free course.

The failure of many a preacher may be found just here. He is hampered, hindered, and even crippled by a prayerless church. Non-praying church workers stand in the way of the Word preached; they become veritable stumbling blocks in the way of the Word, definitely preventing its reaching the hearts of the unsaved.

Unbelief and prayerlessness go together. It is written of our Lord in Matthew's gospel that when He entered into His own country, *"he did not many mighty works there because of their unbelief"* (Matt. 13:58). Mark puts it a little differently but gives the same idea:

And he could there do no mighty work, save that he laid his hands upon a few sick folk, and healed them. And he marvelled because of their unbelief. (Mark 6:5–6)

Unquestionably, the unbelief of that people hindered our Lord in His gracious work and tied His hands. And, if that is true, we would not be stretching the Scriptures to say that the unbelief and prayerlessness of a church can tie the hands of its preacher and prevent him from doing many great works in the salvation of souls and in edifying saints.

Prayerlessness, therefore, as it concerns the preacher, is a very serious matter. If it exists in the preacher himself, then he ties his own hands and makes his own preaching of the Word ineffective and void. If prayerless people are found in the pew, then they hurt the preacher, rob him of an invaluable help, and interfere seriously with the success of his work.

How great the need of a praying church to help move forward the preaching of the Word of the Lord! Both pew and pulpit are jointly concerned in this preaching business. It is a copartnership. The two go hand in hand. One must help the other; one can hinder the other. Both must work in perfect accord. Otherwise, serious damage will result, and God's plan concerning the preacher and the preached Word will be defeated.

10

The Preacher's Cry:
"Pray for Us!"

That the true apostolic preacher must have the prayers of others—good people—to give to his ministry its full quota of success, Paul is a preeminent example. He asked, he coveted, he pleaded in an impassioned way for the help of all God's saints. He knew that in the spiritual realm as elsewhere, in union there is strength; that the consecration and aggregation of faith, desire, and prayer increased the volume of spiritual force until it became overwhelming and irresistible in its power. Units of prayer combined, like drops of water, make an ocean that defies resistance. —E. M. Bounds

To what extent does praying for the preacher help preaching? It helps him personally and officially. It helps him to maintain a righteous life; it helps him in preparing his message; and it helps the Word he preaches to run to its appointed goal, unhindered and unhampered.

A praying church creates a spiritual atmosphere most favorable to preaching. What preacher who knows anything about the real work of preaching doubts the veracity of this statement? The spirit of prayer in a congregation produces an atmosphere supercharged with the Spirit of the Highest, removes obstacles, and gives the Word of the Lord the right-of-way. The very attitude of such a congregation constitutes an environment most encouraging and favorable to preaching. It renders preaching an easy task; it enables the Word to run quickly and without friction, propelled by the warmth of souls engaged in prayer.

People in the pew given to praying for the preacher, are like the poles that hold up the wires along which the electric current runs. They are not the power, nor are they the specific agents in making the Word of the Lord effective. But they hold up the wires along which the divine power runs to the hearts of men. They give liberty to the preacher and keep him from being hampered. They make conditions favorable for the preaching of the Gospel.

Many preachers have had much experience and know the truth of these statements. Yet, how hard they have found it to preach in some places! This was because they had no *"door of utterance"* (Col. 4:3) and were hampered in their delivery, there appearing no response whatsoever to their appeals. On the other hand, at other times thought flowed easily, words came freely, and there was no failure in speaking. The preacher "had liberty," as the old men say.

The preaching of the Word to a prayerless congregation falls at the very feet of the preacher. It has no traveling force; it stops because the atmosphere is cold, unsympathetic, and unfavorable to its running to the hearts of men and women. There is nothing to help it along. Just as some prayers never rise above the head of the one who prays, so the preaching of some preachers goes no farther than the front of the pulpit from which it is delivered. It takes prayer in the pulpit and prayer in the pew to make preaching arresting, life-giving, and soul-saving.

The Word of God is inseparably linked with prayer. The two are joined together, twins from birth and twins through life. The apostles found themselves absorbed by the sacred and pressing duty of distributing the alms of the church, until time was not left for them to pray. They directed that other men be appointed to do this task so that they would be better able to give themselves continually to prayer and to the ministry of the Word.

Likewise, the church's prayer for the preacher is also inseparably joined to preaching. A praying church is an invaluable help to the faithful preacher. The Word of the Lord runs in such a church, and it is glorified by the saving of sinners, by the reclaiming of backsliders, and by the sanctifying of believers. Paul connected the Word of God closely to prayer in writing to Timothy:

> *For every creature of God is good, and nothing to be refused, if it be received with thanksgiving: for it is sanctified by the word of God and prayer.* (1 Tim. 4:4–5)

And so the Word of the Lord depends on prayer for its rapid spread and for its full, glorious success.

Paul indicated that prayer transforms the ills that come to the preacher: *"For I know that this shall turn to my salvation through your prayer, and the supply of the Spirit of Jesus Christ"* (Phil. 1:19). It was through their prayers that these benefits would come to him. So, it is through the prayers of a church that the pastor will be the beneficiary of large spiritual things.

In the epistle to the Hebrews, Paul asked the Hebrew Christians to pray for him. He based his request on the grave and eternal responsibilities of the office of a preacher:

> *Obey them that have the rule over you, and submit yourselves: for they watch for your souls, as they that must give account, that they may do it with joy, and not with grief: for that is unprofitable for you. Pray for us: for we trust we have a good conscience, in all things willing to live honestly.*
>
> *(Heb. 13:17–18)*

How little the church understands the fearful responsibility attached to the office and work of the ministry! *"For they watch for your souls, as they that must give account."* Preachers are God's watchmen, appointed to warn when danger is near. They are God's messengers, sent to rebuke, reprove, and exhort with all long-suffering. They are ordained as shepherds to protect the sheep against devouring wolves. How responsible is their position! They are to give account to God for their work; they are to face a day of reckoning. How they need the prayers of those to whom they minister! And who should be more ready to do this praying than God's people, His own church, those who are presumably in harmony with the minister and his all-important work, divine in its origin?

Among the last messages of Jesus to His disciples are those found in the fourteenth, fifteenth, and sixteenth chapters of John's gospel. In the fourteenth, as well as in the others, are some very specific teachings about prayer, designed for the disciples' help and encouragement in their future work. We must never forget that these last discourses of Jesus Christ were given to disciples alone, away from the busy crowds, and seem primarily intended for them in their public ministry. In reality, they were words spoken to preachers, for these eleven men were to be the first preachers of the new dispensation.

With this thought in mind, we are able to see the tremendous importance given to prayer by our Lord. We can see the high place He gave it in the lifework of preachers, not only preachers in His day, but also preachers in future generations.

First, our Lord proposes that He will pray for these disciples that the Father might send them another Comforter, *"even the Spirit of truth, whom the world cannot receive"* (John 14:17). He preceded this statement by a direct command to them to pray, to pray for anything, with the assurance that they would receive what they asked for. (See John 14:13–14.)

If, therefore, there was value in their own praying and in our Lord's interceding for them, then, of course, it would be worthwhile in the future for their people to pray for them. It is no wonder, then, that the apostle Paul took the key from our Lord; several times he broke out with the urgent exhortation, *"Pray for us"* (1 Thess. 5:25; 2 Thess. 3:1).

True praying done by the laymen helps in many ways, but in one particular way. It very much helps the preacher to be brave and true. Read Paul's request to the Ephesians:

> *Praying always with all prayer and supplication in the Spirit, and watching thereunto with all perseverance and supplication for all saints; and for me, that utterance may be given unto me, that I may open my mouth boldly, to make known the mystery of the gospel, for which I am an ambassador in bonds: that therein I may speak boldly, as I ought to speak.*
> *(Eph. 6:18–20)*

We do not know the extent to which the prayers of the church helped Paul be bold and true. But, it is unquestionable that through the prayers of the Christians at Ephesus, Colossae, and Thessalonica, he received much aid in preaching the Word. He would have been deprived of this aid had these churches not prayed for him. Likewise, in modern times the gift of ready and effective preaching has been bestowed upon a preacher through the prayers of the church.

The apostle Paul did not desire to fall short of that most important quality in a preacher of the Gospel, namely, boldness. He was no coward or chameleon or man-pleaser, but still he needed prayer. Prayer would give him courage to declare the whole truth of God. Prayer would keep him from fearing men and declaring the truth in an apologetic, hesitating way. He desired to remove himself as far as possible from an attitude of fear. His constant desire and effort was to declare the Gospel with freedom and consecrated boldness. *"That I may open my mouth boldly, to make known the mystery of the gospel...that therein I may speak boldly, as I ought to speak"* (Eph. 6:19–20). It would appear that, at times, he was really afraid that he might exhibit cowardice or be affected by the fear of man. But to speak boldly was his great desire.

This is a day that has urgent need for people from the mold of the great apostle—people of courage, brave and true. We need people who are not swayed by the fear of man. We need people who are not reduced to silence or apology by the dread of consequences. One way to secure these people is for the pew to engage in earnest prayer for the preachers.

In Paul's word to the Ephesian elders, given when on his way to Jerusalem, Paul cleared himself from the charge of bloodguiltiness, in that he had not failed to declare the whole counsel of God to them. (See Acts 20:26–27.) To the Philippian believers, also, he said that through their prayers he would prove to be neither ashamed nor afraid. (See Philippians 1:19–20.)

Nothing, perhaps, can be more detrimental to the advancement of the kingdom of God than a timid or doubtful statement of revealed truth. The man who states only half of what he believes is the same as the man who states all but only half believes. No coward can preach the Gospel and declare the whole counsel of God. To do that, a man must be ready to do battle, not from passion, but from deep conviction, strong conscience, and complete courage. Faith is in the custody of a gallant heart; timidity always surrenders to a brave spirit.

Paul prayed, and prevailed on others to pray, that he might be a man of resolute courage, brave enough to do everything but sin. The result of this mutual praying is that history has no finer example of courage in a minister of Jesus Christ than that displayed in the life of the apostle Paul. He stands in the premier position as a fearless, uncompromising, God-fearing preacher of the Gospel.

God seems to have taken great pains with His prophets of old to save them from fear while they were delivering His messages to mankind. He sought in every way to safeguard His spokesmen from the fear of man. By means of command, reasoning, and encouragement, He sought to render them fearless and true to their high calling.

One of the besetting temptations of a preacher is the fear of man. Unfortunately, not a few surrender to this fear. Either they remain silent at times when they should be boldly eloquent, or they deliver a stern mandate softened with smooth words. *"The fear of man bringeth a snare"* (Prov. 29:25). With this sore temptation, Satan often assails the preacher of the Word, and there are few who have not felt the force of this temptation. It is the duty of ministers of the Gospel to face this temptation with resolute courage, to steel themselves against it, and, if need be, to trample it underfoot. To this important end, the preacher should be prayed for by his church. He needs deliverance from fear, and prayer can drive fear away and free his soul from its bondage.

In the seventeenth chapter of the book of Exodus, we have a striking picture of the preacher's need for prayer and for what a people's prayers can do for him. Israel and Amalek were in battle, and the contest was severe and close. Moses stood on top of the hill and held up his rod, the symbol of power and victory. As long as Moses held up the rod, Israel prevailed, but when he let down the rod, Amalek prevailed. The outcome of the battle was at stake. Aaron and Hur came to the rescue, and when Moses' hands were heavy, these two men *"stayed up his hands...until the going down of the sun. And Joshua discomfited Amalek and his people"* (Exod. 17:12–13).

This incident is a striking illustration of how a people may sustain their preacher by prayer. It further illustrates how victory comes when the people pray for their preacher.

Some of the Lord's very best men in Old Testament times had to be encouraged by Almighty God not to be afraid. Moses himself was not free from the fear that harasses and compromises a leader. God told him, in these words, to go to Pharaoh: *"Come now therefore, and I will send thee unto Pharaoh, that thou mayest bring forth my people the children of Israel out of Egypt"* (Exod. 3:10). But Moses, largely through fear, began to offer objections and excuses for not going. Finally, God became angry with him and said that He would send Aaron along to do the talking, for Moses had insisted that he was *"slow of speech, and of a slow tongue"* (Exod. 4:10). But the fact was, Moses was afraid of the face of Pharaoh. It took God some time to circumvent his fears and nerve him to face the Egyptian monarch and deliver God's message to him.

Joshua, too, the successor of Moses and a man seemingly courageous, needed to be fortified by God against fear, lest he should shrink from duty and be reduced to discouragement and timidity. God said to him,

> *Have not I commanded thee? Be strong and of a good courage; be not afraid, neither be thou dismayed: for the LORD thy God is with thee whithersoever thou goest.* (Josh. 1:9)

Jeremiah, a good and true man, was sorely tempted to fear. He had to be warned and strengthened, lest he should prove false to his charge. When God ordained him to be a prophet to the nations, Jeremiah began to excuse himself on the ground that he could not speak, saying, *"I am a child"* (Jer. 1:6). Therefore, the Lord had to safeguard him from the temptation of fear so that he might not prove faithless. God said to His servant,

> *Thou therefore gird up thy loins, and arise, and speak unto them all that I command thee: be not dismayed at their faces, lest I confound thee before them.* (Jer. 1:17)

Since these great men of old were so beset with this temptation and disposed to shrink from duty, we need not be surprised that preachers of our own day are found in a similar case. The Devil is the same in all ages, and human nature has not undergone any change. How needful, then, that we pray for the leaders of our Israel, especially that they may receive the gift of boldness and speak the Word of God with courage.

No wonder Paul insisted so vigorously that the believers pray for him. Prayer would give him an open door to preach, deliverance from the fear of man, and holy boldness in preaching the Word.

The challenge and demand of the world in our own day is that Christianity be made practical. The demand is for precepts to be expressed in practice, for principles to be brought down from the realm of the ideal to the levels of everyday life. This can be done only by praying men who, being much in harmony with their ministers, will not cease to bear them up in their prayers before God.

All alone, a preacher cannot meet the demands made upon him, any more than the vine can bear grapes without branches. The men who sit in the pews are to be the fruit-bearing ones. They are to translate the "ideal" of the pulpit into the "real" of daily life and action. But they will not do it, they cannot do it, if they are not devoted to God and given to much prayer. Devotion to God and devotion to prayer are one and the same thing.

11

Modern Examples of Praying Men

When the dragon-fly rends his husk and harnesses himself in a clean plate of sapphire mail, his is a pilgrimage of one or two sunny days over the fields and pastures wet with dew, yet nothing can exceed the marvelous beauty in which he is decked. No flowers on earth have a richer blue than the pure color of his cuirass. So is it in the high spiritual sphere. The most complete spiritual loveliness may be obtained in the shortest time, and the stripling may die a hundred years old, in character and grace. —The Life of David Brainerd

GOD has not confined Himself to Bible days in showing what can be done through prayer. In modern times, also, He is seen to be the same prayer-hearing God as before. Even in these latter days He has not left Himself without witness. Religious biographies and church history alike furnish us with many noble examples and striking illustrations of prayer. These examples show us prayer's necessity, its worth, and its fruits.

All these examples also encourage the faith of God's saints and urge them on to more and better praying. God has not confined Himself to Bible times in using praying people to further His cause on earth. He has placed Himself under obligation to answer our prayers just as much as He did the saints of old. A selection from these praying saints of modern times will show us how they valued prayer, what it meant to them, and what it meant to God.

Take, for example, Samuel Rutherford, a Scottish preacher, exiled to the north of Scotland, forbidden to preach, and banished from his home and pastoral charge. Rutherford lived between 1600 and 1661. He was a member of the Westminster Assembly, principal of New College, and rector of St. Andrew's University. He is said to have been one of the most moving and affectionate preachers of his time, or, perhaps, of any age of the church. Men said of him, "He is always praying." Concerning his and his wife's praying, one wrote,

> He who had heard them either pray or speak, might have learned to bemoan his ignorance. Oh, how many times have I been convinced by observing them of the evil of insincerity before God and unsavoriness in discourse! He so prayed for his people that he himself says, "There I wrestled with the Angel and prevailed." (See Genesis 32:24–28.)

Rutherford was ordered to appear before Parliament to answer the charge of high treason, even though he was a man of scholarly attainments and rare genius. At times he was depressed and gloomy, especially when he was first silenced and banished from preaching, for there were many murmurings and charges against him. But his losses and crosses were so sanctified that Christ became more and more to him. Marvelous are his statements of his estimation of Christ. This devoted man of prayer wrote many letters during his exile to preachers, to state officers, to lords temporal and spiritual, to honorable and holy men, to honorable and holy women. These were precious letters, all breathing an intense devotion to Christ and all born of great devotion to prayer.

Ardor and panting after God have been characteristics of great souls in all ages of the church, and Samuel Rutherford was a striking example of this fact. He showed that he who always prays will be enveloped in devotion and will be joined to Christ in bonds of holy union.

Then there was Henry Martyn—scholar, saint, missionary, and apostle to India. Martyn was born on February 18, 1781 and sailed for India on August 31, 1805. He died at Tokai, Persia, October 16, 1812. Here is part of what he said about himself while a missionary:

> What a knowledge of man and acquaintance with the Scriptures, and what communion with God and study of my own heart ought to prepare me for the awful work of a messenger from God on business of the soul.

Someone said of this consecrated missionary,

> Oh, to be able to emulate his excellencies, his elevation of piety, his diligence, his superiority to the world, his love for souls, his anxiety to improve on all occasions to do souls good, his insight into the mystery of Christ, and his heavenly temper! These are the secrets of the wonderful impression he made in India.

It is interesting and profitable to note some of the things that Martyn records in his diary. Here is an example:

> The ways of wisdom appear more sweet and reasonable than ever, and the world more insipid and vexatious. The chief thing I mourn over is my want of power, and lack of fervor in secret prayer, especially when attempting to plead for the heathen. Warmth does not increase within me in proportion to my light.

If Henry Martyn, so devoted, ardent, and prayerful, lamented his lack of power and fervor in prayer, how our cold and feeble praying ought to lower us into the very dust! Alas, how rare are such praying men in the church of our own day!

Again, I quote an entry from his diary. He had been quite ill, but he had recovered, and he was filled with thankfulness because it had pleased God to restore him to life and health again.

> Not that I have yet recovered my former strength, but I consider myself sufficiently restored to prosecute my journey. My daily prayer is that my late chastisement may have its intended effect and make me, all the rest of my days, more humble and less self-confident.
>
> Self-confidence has often led me down fearful lengths and would, without God's gracious interference, prove my endless perdition. I seem to be made to feel this evil of my heart more than any other at this time. In prayer, or when I write or converse on the subject, Christ appears to me my life and my strength; but at other times I am thoughtless and bold, as if I had all life and strength in myself. Such neglects on our part are a diminution of our joys.

Among the last entries in this consecrated missionary's journal we find the following:

In solitude, I sat in the orchard and thought, with sweet comfort and peace, of my God—my Company, my Friend, my Comforter. Oh, when shall time give place to eternity!

Note the words "in solitude." Away from the busy haunts of men, in a lonely place, like his Lord, he went out to meditate and pray.

Brief as this summary is, it suffices to show how fully and faithfully Henry Martyn exercised his ministry of prayer. The following may well serve to end our portrayal of him:

By daily weighing the Scriptures, with prayer, he waxed riper and riper in his ministry. Prayer and the Holy Scriptures were those wells of salvation out of which he drew daily the living water for his thirsty immortal soul. Truly may it be said of him, he prayed *"always with all prayer and supplication in the Spirit, and watch*[ed] *thereunto with all perseverance"* (Eph. 6:18).

David Brainerd, the missionary to the Indians, is a remarkable example of a praying man of God. Robert Hale said this about him,

Such invincible patience and self-denial; such profound humility, exquisite prudence, indefatigable industry; such devotedness to God, or rather such absorption of the whole soul in zeal for the divine glory and the salvation of men, is scarcely to be paralleled since the age of the Apostles. Such was the intense ardor of his mind that it seems to have diffused the spirit of a martyr over the common incidents of his life.

Dr. A. J. Gordon spoke thus of Brainerd:

In passing through Northampton, Massachusetts, I went into the old cemetery, swept off the snow that lay on the top of the slab, and I read these simple words:

"Sacred to the memory of David Brainerd, the faithful and devoted missionary to the Susquehanna, Delaware and Stockbridge Indians of America, who died in this town, October 8th, 1747."

That was all there was on the slab. Now that great man did his greatest work by prayer. He was in the depths of those forests alone, unable to speak the language of the Indians, but he spent whole days literally in prayer.

What was he praying for? He knew he could not reach these savages, for he did not understand their language. If he wanted to speak at all, he must find somebody who could vaguely interpret his thought. Therefore he knew that anything he could do must be absolutely dependent upon God. So he spent whole days in praying, simply that the power of the Holy Ghost might come upon him so unmistakably that these people would not be able to stand before him.

What was his answer? Once he preached through a drunken interpreter, a man so intoxicated that he could hardly stand up. This was the best he could do. Yet scores were converted through that sermon. We can account for it only that it was the tremendous power of God behind him.

Now this man prayed in secret in the forest. A little while afterward, William Carey read about his life, and by its impulse he went to India. Payson read it as a young man, over twenty years old, and he said that he had never been so impressed by anything in his life as by the story of Brainerd. Murray McCheyne read it, and he likewise was impressed by it.

But all I want is simply to enforce this thought, that the hidden life, a life whose days are spent in communion with God, in trying to reach the source of power, is the life that moves the world. Those living such lives may be soon forgotten. There may be no one to speak a eulogy over them when they are dead. The great world may take no account of them. But by and by, the great moving current of their lives will begin to tell, as in the case of this young man, who died at about thirty years of age. The missionary spirit of this nineteenth century is more due to the prayers and consecration of this one man than to any other one.

So I say. And yet the most remarkable thing is that Jonathan Edwards, who watched over him all those months while he was slowly dying of consumption, should also say: "I praise God that it was in His Providence that he should die in my house, that I might hear his prayers, and that I might witness his consecration, and that I might be inspired by his example."

When Jonathan Edwards wrote that great appeal to Christendom to unite in prayer for the conversion of the world, which has been the trumpet call of modern missions, undoubtedly it was inspired by this dying missionary.

John Wesley bore this testimony about David Brainerd's spirit:

> I preached and afterward made a collection for the Indian schools in America. A large sum of money is now collected. But will money convert heathens? Find preachers of David Brainerd's spirit, and nothing can stand before them. But without this, what will gold or silver do? No more than lead or iron.

Some selections from Brainerd's diary will be of value to show what manner of man he was:

> My soul felt a pleasing yet painful concern, lest I should spend some moments without God. Oh, may I always live to God! In the evening I was visited by some friends, and we spent the time in prayer, and such conversation as tended to edification. It was a comfortable season to my soul. I felt an ardent desire to spend every moment with God.
>
> God is unspeakably gracious to me continually. In time past, He has given me inexpressible sweetness in the performance of duty. Frequently my soul has enjoyed much of God, but has been ready to say, "Lord, it is good to be here," and so indulge sloth while I have lived on the sweetness of my feelings. But of late God has been pleased to keep my soul hungry almost continually, so that I have been filled with a kind of pleasing pain. When I really enjoy God, I feel my desires of Him the more insatiable, and my thirstings after holiness the more unquenchable.
>
> Oh, that I may feel this continual hunger, and not be retarded, but rather animated, by every cluster from Canaan, to reach forward in the narrow way, for the full enjoyment and possession of the heavenly inheritance! Oh, may I never loiter in my heavenly journey!
>
> It seems as if such an unholy wretch as I never could arrive at that blessedness, to be holy as God is holy. At noon I longed for sanctification and conformity to God. Oh, that is the one thing, the all!
>
> Toward night I enjoyed much sweetness in secret prayer, so that my soul longed for an arrival in the heavenly country, the blessed paradise of God.

If someone should ask about the secret of David Brainerd's heavenly spirit, his deep consecration, and his exalted spiritual state, the answer can be found in the last sentence of the preceding quote. He was given to "much...secret prayer," and he was so close to God in his life and spirit that prayer brought much sweetness to his inner soul.

We have cited the foregoing cases to illustrate the fundamental fact that God's great servants are devoted to the ministry of prayer. They are God's agents on earth who serve Him in this way, and they carry on His work by this holy means.

Louis Harms was born in Hanover in 1809. There came a time when he was powerfully convicted of sin. He said, "I have never known what fear was. But when I came to the knowledge of my sins, I quaked before the wrath of God, so that my limbs trembled." He was mightily converted to God by reading the Bible.

Rationalism, a dead orthodoxy, and worldliness blinded the multitudes in Hermansburgh, the town where he lived. His father, a Lutheran minister, died, and Harms became his successor. He began with all the energy of his soul to work for Christ and to develop a church of a pure, strong type. The fruit was soon evident. There was a quickening on every hand. Attendance at public services increased; reverence for the Bible grew; conversation about sacred things revived. Meanwhile, unbelief, worldliness, and dead orthodoxy vanished like a passing cloud.

Harms proclaimed a conscious and present Christ, the Comforter, in the full energy of His mission, which is the revival of apostolic piety and power. The entire neighborhood began to attend church regularly; the Sabbath was restored to its sanctity and hallowed with strict devotion; homes began to have family devotions; and when the noon bell sounded, every head was bowed in prayer. In a very short time the whole aspect of the town was entirely changed.

The revival in Hermansburgh was essentially a prayer revival. It was brought about by prayer and yielded fruits of prayer in a rich and abundant harvest.

William Carvosso, an old-time Methodist leader, was one of the best examples in modern times of what the religious life of Christians was probably like in the apostolic age. He was a prayer leader, a class leader, a steward, and a trustee, but he never aspired to be a preacher. Yet, a preacher he was of the very first quality, and he was a master in the art and science of soul-saving. He was a singular example of a man learning the simplest rudiments late in life.

Up until the age of sixty-five, he had never written a single sentence. Yet, he later wrote letters that would make volumes, and he wrote a book that was regarded as a spiritual classic in the great worldwide Methodist church.

Not a page nor a letter, it is believed, was ever written by him on any other subject but religion. Here are some of his brief statements, which give us an insight into his religious character. "I want to be more like Jesus." "My soul thirsteth for Thee, O God." "I see nothing will do, O God, but being continually filled with Thy presence and glory."

This was the continual cry of his inner soul, and this was the strong inward impulse that moved the outward man. One time he exclaimed, "Glory to God! This is a morning without a cloud." Cloudless days were native to his sunny religion and his joyful spirit. Continual prayer and turning all conversation toward Christ in all company and in every home, was the law he always followed.

On the anniversary of his spiritual birth, he remembered his salvation experience with great joyousness of spirit, and he broke forth:

> Blessed be Thy name, O God! The last has been the best of the whole. I may say with Bunyan, "I have got into that land where the sun shines night and day." I thank Thee, O my God, for this heaven, this element of love and joy, in which my soul now lives.

Here is a sample of Carvosso's spiritual experiences, of which he had many:

> I have sometimes had seasons of remarkable visitation from the presence of the Lord. I well remember one night when in bed being so filled, so overpowered with the glory of God, that had there been a thousand suns shining at noonday, the brightness of that divine glory would have eclipsed the whole. I was constrained to shout aloud for joy. It was the overwhelming power of saving grace. Now it was that I again received the impress of the seal and the earnest of the Spirit in my heart. Beholding as in a glass the glory of the Lord, I was changed into the same image from glory to glory by the Spirit of the Lord (2 Cor. 3:18). Language fails in giving but a faint description of what I there experienced. I can never forget it in time nor to all eternity.

Many years before I was sealed by the Spirit in a somewhat similar manner. While walking out one day, I was drawn to turn aside on the public road, and under the canopy of the skies, I was moved to kneel down to pray. I had not long been praying with God before I was so visited from Him that I was overpowered by the divine glory, and I shouted till I could be heard at a distance. It was a weight of glory that I seemed incapable of bearing in the body, and therefore I cried out, perhaps unwisely, "Lord, stay Thy hand." In this glorious baptism these words came to my heart with indescribable power: "I have sealed thee unto the day of redemption." (See Ephesians 4:30.)

Oh, I long to be filled more with God! Lord, stir me up more in earnest. I want to be more like Jesus. I see that nothing will do but being continually filled with the divine presence and glory. I know all that Thou hast is mine, but I want to feel a close union. Lord, increase my faith.

Such was William Carvosso—a man whose life was saturated with the spirit of prayer, who lived on his knees, so to speak, and who belonged to that company of praying saints that has blessed the earth.

Jonathan Edwards must be placed among the praying saints— one whom God mightily used through the instrumentality of prayer. As in the instance of this great New Englander, purity of heart should be ingrained in the very foundation of every person who is a minister of the Gospel. A sample of the statements of this mighty man of God is here given in the form of a resolution he wrote down:

> Resolved to exercise myself in this all my life long, viz., with the greatest openness to declare my ways to God, and to lay my soul open to God—all my sins, temptations, difficulties, sorrows, fears, hopes, desires, and everything and every circumstance.

We are not surprised, therefore, that the result of such fervid and honest praying was to lead him to record in his diary,

> It was my continual strife day and night, and my constant inquiry, how I should be more holy, and live more holily. The heaven I desired was a heaven of holiness. I went

611

on with my eager pursuit after more holiness and conformity to Christ.

The character and work of Jonathan Edwards exemplified a great truth: prayer is the activating agency in every truly God-ordered work and life. He himself gives some particulars about his life as a boy. He might well be called the "Isaiah of the Christian Dispensation." There were united in him great mental powers, ardent piety, and devotion to study; these were unequaled except by his devotion to God. Here is what he said about himself:

> When a boy I used to pray five times a day in secret, and to spend much time in religious conversation with other boys. I used to meet with them to pray together. So it is God's will through His wonderful grace, that the prayers of His saints should be one great and principal means of carrying on the designs of Christ's kingdom in the world. Pray much for the ministers and the church of God.

Edwards used the great powers of his mind and heart to get God's people everywhere to unite in extraordinary prayer. His life, efforts, and character are an exemplification of his statement. He said,

> The heaven I desire is a heaven spent with God: an eternity spent in the presence of divine love, and in holy communion with Christ.

At another time he said,

> The soul of a true Christian appears like a little white flower in the spring of the year, low and humble on the ground, opening its bosom to receive the pleasant beams of the sun's glory, rejoicing as it were in a calm rapture, diffusing around a sweet fragrance, standing peacefully and lovingly in the midst of other flowers.

Again, he wrote,

> Once, having ridden out into the woods for my health, I alighted from my horse in a retired place, for my manner has been to walk for divine contemplation and prayer. I had a

view, that for me was extraordinary, of the glory of the Son of God as Mediator between God and man, and of His wonderful, great, full, pure, and sweet grace and love, and His meek and gentle condescension. This grace that seemed so calm and sweet, appeared also great above the heavens. The person of Christ appeared ineffably excellent with an excellency great enough to swallow up all thought and conception, which continued, as near as I can judge, about an hour. It kept me the greater part of the time in a flood of tears and weeping aloud. I felt an ardency of soul to be, what I know not otherwise how to express, emptied and annihilated, to lie in the dust; to be full of Christ alone, to love Him with my whole heart.

As it was with Jonathan Edwards, so it is with all great intercessors. They come into that holy, elect condition of mind and heart by a thorough self-dedication to God, and by periods of God's revelation to them, which make distinct, marked eras in their spiritual history. These eras are never to be forgotten. During these eras faith *"mount*[s] *up with wings as eagles"* (Isa. 40:31). The intercessor has a new and fuller vision of God; a stronger grasp of faith; a sweeter, clearer vision of all things heavenly and eternal; and a blessed intimacy with, and access to, God.

12

More Modern Examples
of Praying Men

Edward Bounds did not merely pray well that he might write well about prayer. He prayed for long years upon subjects to which easy-going Christians rarely give a thought. He prayed for objects which men of less faith are ready to call impossible. Yet from these continued, solitary prayer-vigils, year by year there arose a gift of prayer-teaching equaled by few men. He wrote transcendently about prayer because he was transcendent in its practice. —*Claudius L. Chilton, Jr.*

LADY Maxwell was a contemporary of John Wesley, and she was a fruit of Methodism in its earlier phases. She was a woman of refinement, of culture, and of deep piety. Separating herself entirely from the world, she sought and found the deepest religious experience, and she was a woman fully set apart to God.

Her life was one of prayer, of complete consecration to God, of living to bless others. She was noted for her systematic habits of life, which entered into and controlled her religion. Her time was economized and ordered for God. She arose at four o'clock in the morning and attended preaching at five o'clock. After breakfast she held a family service. Then, from eleven to twelve o'clock she observed a season of intercessory prayer. The rest of the day was given to reading, visiting, and acts of benevolence. Her evenings were spent in reading. At night, before retiring, religious services were held for the family, which sometimes were spent in praising God for His mercies.

Rarely has God been served with more intelligence or out of a richer experience, a nobler zeal, or a greater nobility of soul.

Strongly, spiritually, and ardently attached to Wesley's doctrine of entire dedication, she sought it with persistency and a never-flagging zeal. She obtained it by faith and prayer, and she illustrated it in a life as holy and as perfect as is given to mortals to reach. If Wesley's teaching of entire dedication had, today, models and teachers like Lady Maxwell of Edinburgh and John Fletcher of Madeley, it would not be so misunderstood. No, it would commend itself to the good and pure everywhere by holy lives, if not by its phraseology.

Lady Maxwell's diary yields some rich counsel for secret prayer, holy experience, and consecrated living. One of the entries reads as follows:

> Of late I feel painfully convinced that I do not pray enough. Lord, give me the spirit of prayer and of supplication. Oh, what a cause of thankfulness it is that we have a gracious God to whom to go on all occasions! Use and enjoy this privilege and you can never be miserable. Who gives thanks for this royal privilege? It puts God in everything, His wisdom, power, control, and safety. Oh, what an unspeakable privilege is prayer! Let us give thanks for it. I do not prove all the power of prayer that I wish.

Thus, we see that the remedy for non-praying is *praying*. The cure for little praying is more praying. Praying can procure all things necessary for our good.

For this excellent woman, praying embraced everything and included everything. To one of her most intimate friends she wrote,

> I wish I could provide you with a proper maid, but it is a difficult matter. You have my prayers for it, and if I hear of one I will let you know.

So small a matter as a friend's need for a maid was not too small for her to take to God in prayer.

In the same letter she tells her friend that she wants "more faith. Cry mightily for it, and stir up the gift of God that is in you." (See 2 Timothy 1:6.)

Whether the need was a small, secular thing like a servant, or a great spiritual grace, prayer was the means to attain that end and supply that need. She wrote to a dear correspondent:

There is nothing so hurtful to the nervous system as anxiety. It preys upon the vitals and weakens the whole frame, and what is more than all, it grieves the Holy Spirit.

Her remedy, again, for a common evil, was prayer.

How prayer lifts the burden of care by bringing in God to relieve and possess and hold!

The apostle said,

> *Be careful for nothing; but in every thing by prayer and supplication with thanksgiving let your requests be made known unto God. And the peace of God, which passeth all understanding, shall keep your hearts and minds through Christ Jesus.* (Phil. 4:6–7)

These verses tell us that God keeps and protects us. Picture a besieged and distressed garrison, unable to protect the fort from attacking enemies, when suddenly strong reinforcements come pouring in. Into the heart oppressed, distracted, and discouraged, true prayer brings God, who holds it in perfect peace and perfect safety. Lady Maxwell fully understood this truth, not only theoretically, but, even better, experientially.

Christ Jesus is the only cure for needless care and overanxiety of soul, and we secure God, His presence, and His peace by prayer. Care is so natural and so strong that no one but God can drive it out. It takes the presence and personality of God Himself to expel the care and to enthrone quietness and peace. When Christ comes in with His peace, all tormenting fears leave. Trepidation and vexing anxieties surrender to Christ's reign of peace, and all disturbing elements depart.

Anxious thought and care assault the soul, and feebleness, faintness, and cowardice are within. Prayer reinforces with God's peace, and the heart is kept by Him. *"Thou wilt keep him in perfect peace, whose mind is stayed on thee"* (Isa. 26:3). All now is safety, quietness, and assurance. *"The work of righteousness shall be peace; and the effect of righteousness quietness and assurance for ever"* (Isa. 32:17).

But to ensure this great peace, prayer must pass into strenuous, insistent, personal supplication, and thanksgiving must bloom into full flower. Our exposed condition of heart must be brought to the knowledge of God *"by prayer and supplication with thanksgiving"*

(Phil. 4:6). The peace of God will keep the heart and thoughts fixed and fearless. Peace—deep, exhaustless, wide, flowing like a river—will come in.

Referring again to Lady Maxwell, we remember her words:

> God is daily teaching me more simplicity of spirit, and He makes me willing to receive all as His unmerited gift. He is teaching me to call on Him for everything I need, as I need it, and He supplies my wants according to existing needs. But I have certainly felt more of it this last eighteen months than in former periods. I wish to *"pray without ceasing"* (1 Thess. 5:17). I see the necessity of praying always, and not fainting (Luke 18:1).

Again, we recall her words: "I wish to be much in prayer. I greatly need it. The prayer of faith shuts or opens heaven. Come, Lord, and turn my captivity." If we felt the need of prayer as this saintly woman did, we could be like her in her saintly ascension. Prayer truly shuts or opens heaven. Oh, for a quality of faith that would test to the uttermost the power of prayer!

Lady Maxwell uttered a great truth when she said,

> When God is at work, either among a people or in the heart of an individual, the adversary of souls is peculiarly at work also. A belief of the former should prevent discouragement, and a fear of the latter should stir us up to much prayer. Oh, the power of faithful prayer! I live by prayer! May you prove its sovereign efficacy in every difficult case.

A record among Lady Maxwell's writings shows us that in prayer and meditation she obtained enlarged views of the full salvation of God. What is thus discovered in prayer, faith goes out after, and according to faith's strength are its returns.

> I daily feel the need of the precious blood of sprinkling [she said] and dwell continually under its influence, and most sensibly feel its sovereign efficacy. It is by momentary faith in this blood alone that I am saved from sin. Prayer is my chief employ.

If this last statement, "Prayer is my chief employ," had ever been true of all of God's people, this world would have been by this time quite another world; and God's glory, instead of being dim, shadowy, and only in spots, would now shine with universal and unrivaled brilliance and power.

Here is another record of her fervent and faithful praying: "Lately, I have been favored with a more ardent spirit of praying than almost ever formerly."

We need to study the words "favored with a more ardent spirit of praying," for they are pregnant words. The spirit of prayer, the ardent spirit of prayer, and the more ardent spirit of prayer—all these are of God. They are given in answer to prayer. The spirit of prayer and the more ardent spirit are the result of fervent, persistent, secret prayer.

At another time Lady Maxwell declared that secret prayer was the means whereby she derived the greatest spiritual benefit.

> I do indeed prove it to be an especial privilege. I could not live without it, though I do not always find comfort in it. I still ardently desire an enlarged sphere of usefulness, and find it comfortable to embrace the opportunities afforded me.

An "enlarged sphere of usefulness" is certainly a proper theme of intense prayer, but that prayer must always be accompanied by an embracing of the opportunities one already has.

Many pages could be filled with extracts from Lady Maxwell's diary about the vital importance and the nature of prayer, but we must conclude. For many years she was in fervent supplication for a larger sphere of usefulness, but all these years of ardent praying may be condensed into one paragraph:

> My whole soul has been thirsting after a larger sphere of action [she said] agreeably to the promises of a faithful God. For these few last weeks I have been led to plead earnestly for more holiness. Lord, give me both, that I may praise Thee.

These two things—more work and more holiness—must go together. They are one, and they are not to be separated. The desire for a larger field of work without the accompanying desire for more consecration is perilous, and it may be supremely selfish, the offspring of spiritual pride.

John Fletcher, also a contemporary of John Wesley, was intimately associated with this founder of Methodism. Fletcher was a scholar of courtesy and refinement; a strong, original thinker; a speaker of simple eloquence and truth. What qualified him as a spiritual leader was his exceedingly great faith in God, his nearness to God, and his perfect assurance of a dear, unquestioned relationship with his Lord. Fletcher had profound convictions about the truth of God, possessed a perpetual communion with his Savior, and was humble in his knowledge of God. He was a man of deep spiritual insight into the things of God, and his thorough earnestness, his truth, and his consecration marked him as a man of God. He was well equipped to be a leader in the church.

Unceasing prayer was the sign and secret of Fletcher's sainthood, as well as its power and influence. His whole life was one of prayer. So intently was his mind fixed on God that he sometimes said, "I would not rise from my seat without lifting up my heart to God." A friend related the fact that whenever they met, Fletcher's first greeting was, "Do I meet you praying?" If they were talking about theology, in the midst of it he would stop abruptly and say, "Where are our hearts now?" If the misconduct of any person who was absent was mentioned, he would say, "Let us pray for him."

The very walls of his room, so it was said, were stained by the breath of his prayers. Spiritually, Madeley was a dreary, desolate desert when he went to live there, but it was so revolutionized by his prayers that it bloomed and blossomed like the garden of the Lord. A friend of his thus wrote of Fletcher:

> Many of us have at times gone with him aside, and there we would continue for two or three hours, wrestling like Jacob for the blessing, praying one after another. And I have seen him on these occasions so filled with the love of God that he could contain no more, but would cry out, "O my God, withhold Thy hand or the vessel will burst!" His whole life was a life of prayer.

John Foster, a man of exalted piety and deep devotion to God, said this about prayer while on his deathbed:

> *"Pray without ceasing"* (1 Thess. 5:17) has been the sentence repeating itself in my silent thoughts, and I am sure that it will be, it must be, my practice till the last conscious hour of my life. Oh, why was it not my practice throughout that long, indolent, inanimate half century past! I often think

mournfully of the difference it would have made in me. Now there remains so little time for a genuine, effective spiritual life.

The Reformation of the fifteenth century owes its origin to prayer. In all of Martin Luther's lifework—its beginning, continuance, and ending—he was devoted to prayer. The secret of his extraordinary activity is found in this statement: "I have so much work to do that I cannot get along without giving three hours daily of my best time to prayer." Another one of his sayings was, "It takes meditation and prayer to make a clergyman." His everyday motto was, "He that has prayed well, has studied well."

Another time he confessed his lack by saying, "I was short and superficial in prayer this morning." How often is this the case with us! Remember that the source of decline in religion and the proof of decline in a Christian life is found right here, in "short and superficial" praying. Such praying foretells and causes coldness between us and God.

William Wilberforce once said of himself,

> I have been keeping too late hours, and hence have had but a hurried half hour to myself. I am lean and cold and hard. I had better allow more time, say two hours, or an hour-and-a-half, daily to religious exercises.

A person must be very skillful and regular in long praying for his short prayers not to be superficial. Short prayers make shallow lives. Longer praying would work like magic in many a decayed spiritual life. A holy life would not be so difficult and rare if our praying were not so brief, cold, and superficial.

George Müller, that remarkable man of such simple yet strong faith in God, was a man of prayer and Bible reading. He was the founder and promoter of the noted orphanage in England, which cared for hundreds of orphan children. He conducted the institution solely by faith and prayer. He never asked a man for anything, but he simply trusted in the providence of God, and it is a well-known fact that the orphans at the home never lacked any good thing. From his newsletter he always excluded money matters, and financial difficulties found no place in it. Nor would he mention the sums that had been given him, nor the names of those who had made contributions. He never spoke of his needs to others or asked for a donation.

The story of his life and of this orphanage read like a chapter from the Scriptures. The secret of his success is found in this simple statement made by him: "I went to my God and prayed diligently, and I received what I needed." That was the simple course that he pursued. There was nothing he insisted on with more earnestness than that, no matter what the expenses were or how suddenly they increased, he must not beg for anything. There was nothing that he told more excitedly than that he had prayed for every need he had ever had in his great work. His was a work of continuous and persevering praying, and he always confidently claimed that God had guided him through it all. His work was proof of the power of simple faith, divine providence, answered prayer. A stronger proof cannot be found in church history or religious biography.

John Wesley, in writing to a friend one time, helped, urged, and prayed. Here are John Wesley's own words:

> Have you received a gleam of light from above, a spark of faith? If you have, let it not go! Hold fast by His grace that earnest of your inheritance. Come just as you are, and come boldly to the throne of grace. You need not delay. Even now the bowels of Jesus yearn over you. What have you to do with tomorrow? I love you today. And how much more does He love you! "He pities still His wandering sheep, and longs to bring you to His fold." Today hear His voice, the voice of Him that speaks as never man spake.

The seekings of Madame Guyon after God were sincere, and her yearnings were strong and earnest. She went to a devout Franciscan friar for advice and comfort. She stated her convictions and told him of her long and fruitless seeking. After she had finished speaking to him, the friar remained silent for some time, in inward meditation and prayer. Then he said to her,

> Your efforts have been unsuccessful, because you have *sought without* what you can only *find within.* Accustom yourself to seek God in your heart, and you will not fail to find Him.

Charley Finney said this about prayer:

> When God has specially promised the thing, we are bound to believe we shall receive it when we pray for it. You

have no right to put in an "if," and say, "Lord, *if* it be Thy will, give me Thy Holy Spirit." This is to insult God. To put an "if" in God's promise when God has put none there, is tantamount to charging God with being insincere. It is like saying, "O God, if Thou art in earnest in making these promises, grant us the blessing we pray for."

We may fittingly conclude this book by quoting a word of Adoniram Judson's, the noted missionary to Burma. Speaking of the prevailing power of prayer, he said,

"Nothing is impossible," said one of the seven sages of Greece, "to industry." Let us change the word, "industry," to "persevering prayer," and the motto will be more Christian and more worthy of universal adoption....God loves importunate prayer so much that He will not give us much blessing without it. God says, *"Behold, I will do a new thing; now it shall spring forth; shall ye not know it? I will even make a way in the wilderness, and rivers in the desert....This people have I formed for myself; they shall show forth my praise"* (Isa. 43:19, 21).